District Gazetteers of India Series 148

MADRAS DISTRICT GAZETTEERS

SALEM

District Gazetteers of India Series 148

MADRAS DISTRICT GAZETTEERS

SALEM

F. J. RICHARDS

23 VOLUMES (IN 25 BINDINGS)

(16th, Vol. 1, Part I)

GYAN

Published by

Gyan Publishing House
5, Ansari Road
Daryaganj, New Delhi-110002
Phone: 011-47034999, 9811692060
E-mail: books@gyanbooks.com

Distribution Network
gyanbooks.com
India, USA, Canada, UK, Australia, France

ISBN: 978-93-6208-562-7 (Set) 23 Volumes (In 25 Bindings)
978-81-212-5849-4 (PB)

First Published, 1916

2nd Impression 2024

Printed at: Gyan Press, Delhi.

MADRAS DISTRICT GAZETTEERS (16th, Vol. 1, Part I)
Author: F. J. RICHARDS

LIST OF VOLUMES

S. NO.	ISBN NO.	VOLUME	TITLE	AUTHOR	PRICE	PAGES
			ASSAM DISTRICT GAZETTEERS			
1	9788121285926	1st	Cachar	B. C. Allen	600	300
2	9788121285919	2nd	Sylhet	B. C. Allen	750	378
3	9788121285902	3rd	Goalpara	B. C. Allen	400	203
4	9788121285896	4th	Kamrup	B. C. Allen	675	344
5	9788121285889	5th	Darrang	B. C. Allen	725	364
6	9788121285872	6th	Nowgong	B. C. Allen	560	280
7	9788121285865	7th	Sibsagar	B. C. Allen	675	343
8	9788121285858	8th	Lakhimpur	B. C. Allen	690	347
9	9788121285841	9th	Naga Hills and Manipur	B. C. Allen	580	294
10	9788121285834	10th	The Khasi And Jaintia Hills, The Garo Hills And The Lushai Hills	B. C. Allen	675	363
11	9788121285827	11th	The Sadiya and Balipara Frontier Tract	B. C. Allen	375	190
			BENGAL DISTRICT GAZETTEERS			
12	9788121218672	1st	Angul	L. S. S. O'Malley	340	168
13	9788121259637	2nd	Bakarganj	J. C. JACK	970	194
14	9788121218696	3rd	Balasore	L. S. S. O'Malley	450	228
15	9788121259590	4th	Bankura	L. S. S. O'Malley	1000	199
16	9788121218375	5th	Bhagalpur	J. Byrne	390	194
17	9788121218290	6th	Birbhum	L. S. S. O'Malley	300	150
18	9788121259651	7th	Eastern Bengal and Assam - Bogra	J. N. Gupta	940	188
19	9788121218351	8th	Burdwan	J. C. K. Peterson	450	227
20	9788121259538	9th	Calcutta District Gazetteer - Statistics, 1901 - 02		340	68
21	9788121218313	10th	Champaran	L. S. S. O'Malley	410	205
22	9788121259613	11th	Eastern Bengal District Gazetters - Chittagong	L. S. S. O'Malley	1080	216
23	9788121259552	12th	Chota Nagpur Tributary		130	26
24	9788121259415	13th	The Cooch Behar Gazette: Statistics		1460	292
25	9788121218412	14th	Cuttack	L. S. S. O'Malley	490	248
26	9788121261357	15th	Eastern Bengal District Gazetteers Dacca	B. C. Allen	400	207
27	9788121218436	16th	Darbhanga	L. S. S. O'Malley	360	180
28	9789362089335	17th	Darjeeling	L. S. S. O'Malley	500	248
29	9788121259453	18th	Eastern Bengal District Gazetteers - Dinajpur	F. W. Strong	890	178
30	9788121259392	19th	Faridpur	L. S. S. O'Malley	700	140
31	9788121218474	20th	Gaya	L. S. S. O'Malley	540	270
32	9788121214032	21st	Bihar and Orissa District Gazetteer: Hazaribagh	E. Lister	715	234
33	9788121218337	22nd	Hooghly	L. S. S. O'Malley	680	340
34	9788121218191	23rd	Bengal District Gazetteer Howrah	L. S. S. O'Malley	390	199
35	9788121259293	24th	Eastern Bengal and Assam - Jalpaiguri	John F. Gruning	890	178
36	9788121259279	25th	Jessore	L. S. S. O'Malley	960	192
37	9788121259231	26th	Khulna	L. S. S. O'Malley	1100	220
38	9788121259217	27th	Malda	G. E. Lambourn	670	134
39	9788121267854	28th	Manbhum	H. Coupland	600	313
40	9788121218498	29th	Midnapore	L. S. S. O'Malley	500	252
41	9788121218597	30th	Monghyr	L. S. S. O'Malley	560	280
42	9788121259156	31st	Murshidabad	L. S. S. O'Malley	1250	250
43	9788121259576	32nd	Bengal District Gazetteers - Muzaffarpur	L. S. S. O'Malley	940	188
44	9788121259132	33rd	Mymensingh	F. A. Sachse	960	192
45	9788121259118	34th	Nadia	J. H. E. Garrett	1070	214
46	9788121259095	35th	Eastern Bengal and Assam - Noakhali	J. E. Webster	580	115
47	9788121218450	36th	Feudatory States of Orissa	L. E. B. Cobdenramsay	790	395
48	9788121259071	37th	Pabna	L. S. S. O'Malley	710	142
49	9788121218511	38th	Palamau	L. S. S. O'Malley	380	190
50	9788121218634	39th	Patna	L. S. S. O'Malley	500	250
51	9788121218535	40th	Puri	L. S. S. O'Malley	650	328
52	9788121218757	41st	Purnea	L. S. S. O'Malley	440	220
53	9788121258937	42nd	Rajshahi	L. S. S. O'Malley	1080	216
54	9788121256681	43rd	Bihar and Orissa District Gazetteers: Ranchi	M. G. Hallett	1350	278
55	9788121258913	44th	Eastern Bengal and assam - Rangpur	J. A. Vas	890	178
56	9788121218559	45th	Sambalpur	L. S. S. O'Malley	480	242
57	9788121214056	46th	Santal Parganas	L. S. S. O'Malley	940	308
58	9788121218610	47th	Saran	L. S. S. O'Malley	380	190
59	9788121218658	48th	Shahabad	L. S. S. O'Malley	380	190
60	9788121256704	49th	The Gazetteer of Sikhim	H. H. Risley	960	481
61	9788121218573	50th	Singhbhum, Saraikela And Kharsawan	L. S. S. O'Malley	560	280
62	9788121259439	51st	Eastern Bengal District Gazetteers - Tippera	J. E. Webster	730	146
63	9788121259033	52nd	24 Parganas	L. S. S. O'Malley	1420	284

S. NO.	ISBN NO.	VOLUME	TITLE	AUTHOR	PRICE	PAGES
			CENTRAL PROVINCES DISTRICT GAZETTEERS			
64	9789362081728	1st, Vol. A	Akola (Descriptive)	A. E. Nelson, C. Brown	870	436
65	9789362085481	2nd, Vol. A	Amraoti (Descriptive)	S. V. Fitzgerald, A. E. Nelson	1050	524
66	9789362089267	3rd,Vol. A	Balaghat (Descriptive)	R. V. RUSSELL	430	216
67	9789362083494	4th, Vol. A	Betul (Descriptive)	R. V. RUSSELL	610	306
68	9789362085146	5th, Vol. A	Bhandara (Descriptive)	R. V. RUSSELL	580	292
69	9789362088390	6th, Vol. A	Bilaspur (Descriptive)	R. V. RUSSELL	870	434
70	9789362086044	7th, Vol. A	Buldana (Descriptive)	A. E. Nelson	1090	543
71	9789362089014	8th, Vol. B	Chanda (Descriptive)	R. V. RUSSELL	470	234
72	9789362086938	9th	Chhattisgarch Feudatory State	E. A. De Brett	880	440
73	9789362082961	10th	Chhindwara (Descriptive)	R. V. RUSSELL	550	274
74	9789362089342	11th, Vol. A & B	Damoh (Descriptive and Statistical Tables 1891-1901)	R. V. RUSSELL	830	414
75	9789362081230	12th, Vol. A	Durg (Descriptive)	A. E. Nelson	460	232
76	9789362086037	13th, Vol. A	Hoshangabad (Descriptive)	R. V. RUSSELL	860	430
77	9789362086792	14th, Vol. A	Jubbulpore (Descriptive)	A. E. Nelson	950	474
78	9789362089663	15th, Vol. A & B	Mandla (Descriptive and Statistical Tables 1891-1901)	R. V. RUSSELL	370	186
79	9789362086419	16th, Vol. A	Nagpur (Descriptive)	R. V. RUSSELL	790	394
80	9789362080646	17th, Vol. A	Narsinghpur (Descriptive)	R. V. RUSSELL	510	257
81	9789362084835	18th, Vol. A	Nimar (Descriptive)	R. V. RUSSELL	600	299
82	9789362087737	19th, Vol. A	Raipur (Descriptive)	A. E. Nelson	790	396
83	9789362080264	20th, Vol. A	Saugor (Descriptive)	R. V. RUSSELL	570	285
84	9789362081117	21st, Vol. A	Seoni (Descriptive)	R. V. RUSSELL	460	232
85	9789362084965	22nd, Vol. A	Wardha (Descriptive)	R. V. RUSSELL	600	302
86	9789362083401	23rd, Vol. A	Yeotmal (Descriptive)	R. V. RUSSELL	550	277
87	9789362080325	24th, Vol. I, Pt. I	Gwalior (Text and Tables)	R. V. RUSSELL	980	489
88	9789362087133	24th, Vol. I, Pt. II	Gwalior (Maps)	R. V. RUSSELL	400	198
89	9789362086341	24th, Vol. I, Pt. III	Gwalior (Village List)	R. V. RUSSELL	810	406
90	9789362085467	24th, Vol. I, Pt. IV	Gwalior (Photos)	R. V. RUSSELL	1400	698
91	9789362087393	25th, Vol. II	Indore (Text and Tables)	C. E. Luard	1050	524
92	9789362084422	26th, Vol. III	Bhopal (Text and Tables)	C. E. Luard	540	272
93	9789362086815	27th, Vol. IV	Rewah (Text and Tables)	C. E. Luard	500	250
94	9789362087584	28th, Vol. V, Pt. A	Western States - Malwa (Text)	C. E. Luard	1520	762
95	9789362087300	29th, Vol. VI, Pt. A	Eastern States - Bundelkhand (Text)	C. E. Luard	930	463
96	9789362082169	30th, Vol. VI, Pt. B	Eastern States - Bundelkhand (Tables)	C. E. Luard	830	417
			GAZETTEER OF THE BOMBAY PRESIDENCY:			
97	9788121283441	1st, Part I	History of Gujarat	Ed.: James M. Campbell	3220	644
98	9788121285582	1st, Part II	History of the Konkan Dakhan and Southern Maratha Country	Ed.: James M. Campbell	4200	840
99	9788121285568	2nd	Gujarat, Surat and Broach	Ed.: James M. Campbell	2990	598
100	9788121285544	3rd	Kaira and Panch Mahals	Ed.: James M. Campbell	1690	339
101	9788121285520	4th	Ahmedabad	Ed.: James M. Campbell	1860	372
102	9788121285506	5th	Cutch, Palanpur, and Mahi Kantha	Ed.: James M. Campbell	2390	478
103	9788121285483	6th	Rewa Kantha, Narukot, Cambay, and Surat States	Ed.: James M. Campbell	1450	290
104	9788121285469	7th	Baroda	Ed.: James M. Campbell	3260	652
105	9788121285445	8th	Kathiawar	Ed.: James M. Campbell	3790	758
106	9788121285421	9th, Part I	Gujarat Population - Hindus	Ed.: James M. Campbell	3170	636
107	9788121285407	9th, Part II	Gujarat Population - Musalmans and Parsis	Ed.: James M. Campbell	1520	304
108	9788121285384	10th	Ratnagiri and Savantvadi	Ed.: James M. Campbell	2500	501
109	9788121285360	11th	Kolaba and Janjira	Ed.: James M. Campbell	2550	513
110	9788121285346	12th	Khandesh	Ed.: James M. Campbell	3190	638
111	9788121285322	13th Part I	Thana	Ed.: James M. Campbell	2050	413
112	9788121285308	13th Part II	Thana	Ed.: James M. Campbell	1770	357
113	9788121285285	14th	Thana - Places of Interest	Ed.: James M. Campbell	3290	659
114	9788121285261	15th Part I	Kanara	Ed.: James M. Campbell	2340	348
115	9788121285247	15th Part II	Kanara	Ed.: James M. Campbell	1740	348
116	9788121285223	16th	Nasik	Ed.: James M. Campbell	3490	698
117	9788121285209	17th	Ahmadnagar	Ed.: James M. Campbell	3860	772
118	9788121285186	18th Part I	Poona	Ed.: James M. Campbell	2930	586
119	9788121285162	18th Part II	Poona	Ed.: James M. Campbell	2680	537
120	9788121285148	18th Part III	Poona	Ed.: James M. Campbell	2500	503
121	9788121285124	19th	Satara	Ed.: James M. Campbell	3450	692
122	9788121285100	20th	Sholapur	Ed.: James M. Campbell	2730	547
123	9788121285087	21st	Gazetteer of the Bomaby Presidency: Belgaum	Ed.: James M. Campbell	2570	514
124	9788121285063	22nd	Dharwar	Ed.: James M. Campbell	4200	841
125	9788121285049	23rd	Gazetteer of the Bombay Presidency:Bijapur	Ed.: James M. Campbell	3550	712
126	9788121285025	24th	Kolhapur	Ed.: James M. Campbell	2250	450

S. NO.	ISBN NO.	VOLUME	TITLE	AUTHOR	PRICE	PAGES
127	9788121285001	25th	Botany	Ed.: James M. Campbell	2040	408
128	9788121284981	26th, Part I	Materials Towards a Statistical Account of the Town and Island of Bombay - History	Ed.: James M. Campbell	2500	504
129	9788121284967	26th, Part II	Materials Towards a Statistical Account of the Town and Island of Bombay - Trade and Fortifications	Ed.: James M. Campbell	2690	538
130	9788121284943	26th, Part III	Materials Towards a Statistical Account of the Town And Island of Bombay - Administration	Ed.: James M. Campbell	2450	702
131	9788121284929	27th	General Index	Ed.:R. E. Enthoven	2190	428
			MADRAS DISTRICT GAZETTEERS			
132	9788121258814	1st	Anantapur	W. Francis	1140	227
133	9788121258555	2nd	Malabar	C. A Innes & F. B Evans	3010	602
134	9788121258791	3rd	Bellary	W. Francis	1890	377
135	9788121258777	4th	Statistical Appendix For Chingleput		280	56
136	9788121258753	5th	Coimbatore	K. N. Krishnaswami Ayyar	3420	628
137	9788121232814	6th	Madras District Gazetteers District Gazetteer Cuddapah	C. F. Brackenbury	1120	285
138	9788121258715	7th	Statistical Appendix For Ganjam		370	73
139	9788121256766	8th, Vol. 1st	Godavari District Gazetteer	F. R. Hemingway	650	320
140	9788121256803	8th, Vol. 2nd	Godavari District Gazetteer	F. R. Hemingway	160	83
141	9788121258678	9th	Statistical Appendix For Kistna		640	127
142	9788121258654	10th	Statistical Appendix For Kurnool		270	54
143	9788121258616	11th	Madura	W. Francis	1900	379
144	9788121258579	12th	Statistical Appendix For Madura		740	148
145	9788121258630	13th	The Nilgiris	W. Francis	2190	437
146	9788121234276	14th	Madras District Gazetteers Gazetteer Of The Nellore District Brought Upto 1938		1150	386
147	9788121258517	15th	North Arcot		590	118
148	9788121258494	16th, Vol. 1, Part I	Salem	F. J. Richards	1710	343
149	9788121258593	16th, Vol. 1, Part II	Salem	F. J. Richards	1800	360
150	9788121258456	17th	South Arcot	W. Francis	2400	480
151	9788121258470	18th	Statistical Appendix For South Canara		400	80
152	9788121258432	19th, Vol. 1st & 2nd	Tanjore: Main Volume and Statistical Appendix		2070	401
153	9788121258395	20th	Tinnevelly	H. R. Pate	2740	547
154	9788121258418	21st	Statistical Appendix For Tinnevelly		320	64
155	9788121258371	22nd, 1st & 2nd	Trichinopoly: Main Volume and Statistical Appendix	F. R. Hemingway	2440	487
156	9788121241953	23rd	Vizagapatam District Gazetteer	W. Francis	760	385
			PUNJAB DISTRICT GAZETTEERS			
157	9788121255943	1st	Ambala District 1883-84		620	124
158	9788121255967	2nd	Amritsar		1180	236
159	9788121255981	3rd	Delhi		1300	260
160	9788121256001	4th	Ferozepore		950	188
161	9788121256025	5th	Faridkot		350	70
162	9788121256049	6th	Gujranwala 1893-94		1270	254
163	9788121256063	7th	Gujrat	C. E. Luard	1140	228
164	9788121256087	8th	Gurdaspur 1891-92		1260	252
165	9788121256100	9th	Gurgaon 1883-4		1020	203
166	9788121256124	10th	Hazara	H. D. Watson	2290	458
167	9788121256148	11th	Hissar district and Lohar State		1840	367
168	9788121256162	12th	Hoshiarpur		1420	283
169	9788121256186	13th	Jhang		1070	213
170	9788121256209	14th	Jhelam		1010	202
171	9788121256223	15th	Jalandhar District 1883-84		540	108
172	9788121256247	16th, Vol. XIV-A	Jullundur District, with maps and Kapurthala		1990	398
173	9788121256261	17th, Pt. I	Kangra (Proper)		1450	290
174	9788121256285	17th, Pt. II	Kangra (Kulu, Lahual, Spiti)		1800	357
175	9788121256308	18th	Karnal		1930	386
176	9788121256322	19th	Kohat		1540	307
177	9788121256346	20th	The Lahore District 1883-84		1220	244
178	9788121256384	21st	Ludhiana and Maler Kotla		1680	335
179	9788121256407	22nd	Lyallpur		735	147
180	9788121256421	23rd	Mianwali		1170	234
181	9788121256445	24th	Montgomery	P. J. Fagan	1590	318
182	9788121258364	25th	Multan (1901-02)	E. D. Maclagan	2400	480
183	9788121258708	26th	The Rohtak District 1883-84		980	196
184	9788121258746	27th, Vol. III A	Dujana State 1904		500	16
185	9788121256483	28th	Shahpur District		1780	356
186	9788121256506	29th	Simla District		800	159

S. NO.	ISBN NO.	VOLUME	TITLE	AUTHOR	PRICE	PAGES
187	9788121256520	30th	The Chamba State		2040	408
188	9788121256544	31st	The Chenab Colony 1904		1550	310
189	9788121256568	32nd	Kalsia State		270	53
190	9788121256582	33rd	Suket and Mandi		770	154
191	9788121256605	34th	Phulkian States, Patiala Jind And Nabha 1904		2070	414
192	9788121256643	35th	Simla Hill States		2220	443
193	9788121256667	36th	Sirmur		920	183
			RAJPUTANA DISTRICT GAZETTEERS			
194	9789362088994	1st, Vol. I-A & B	Ajmer-merwara (Text and Statistics Tables)	C. C. Watson	1230	246
195	9789362080882	2nd. Vol. II-A & B	Mewar Residency (Text and Statistics Tables)	K.D. Erskine	1700	339
196	9789362088444	3rd, Vol. III-A & B	The Western Rajputana States Residency And The Bikaner Agency	K.D. Erskine	3590	718
			UNITED PROVINCES OF AGRA AND OUDH DISTRICT GAZETTEERS			
197	9789362087560	Vol. I	Agra	H. R. Nevill	2260	452
198	9789362082466	Vol. II	Aligarh	H. R. Nevill	1300	260
199	9789362089779	Vol. III	Allahabad	H. R. Nevill	2050	409
200	9789362081346	Vol. IV	Almora	H. G. Walton	1670	333
201	9789362085658	Vol. V	Azamgarh	D. L. Drake Brockman	1750	349
202	9789362080547	Vol. VI	Bahraich	H. R. Nevill	1410	281
203	9789362085214	Vol. VII	Ballia	H. R. Nevill	1750	350
204	9789362084668	Vol. VIII	Banda	D. L. Drake Brockman	1750	349
205	9789362086518	Vol. IX	Bara Banki	H. R. Nevill	1720	344
206	9789362084101	Vol. X	Bareilly	H. R. Nevill	1640	327
207	9789362086631	Vol. XI	Basti	H. R. Nevill	1610	321
208	9789362083814	Vol. XII	Benares	H. R. Nevill	2290	458
209	9789362086105	Vol. XIII	Bijnor	H. R. Nevill	1820	363
210	9789362081674	Vol. XIV	Budaun	H. R. Nevill	1890	378
211	9789362086891	Vol. XV	Bulandshahr	H. R. Nevill	2100	419
212	9789362081520	Vol. XVI	Cawnpore	H. R. Nevill	2210	442
213	9789362088031	Vol. XVII	Dehra Dun	H. G. Walton	1710	342
214	9789362088710	Vol. XVIII	Etah	E. R. Neave	1600	320
215	9789362082992	Vol. XIX	Etawah	D. L. Drake Brockman	1390	277
216	9789362082220	Vol. XX	Farrukhabad	E. R. Neave	1620	324
217	9789362083869	Vol. XXI	Fatehpur	H. R. Nevill	1890	377
218	9789362085962	Vol. XXII	Fyzabad	H. R. Nevill	1700	339
219	9789362087997	Vol. XXIII	Garhwal	H. G. Walton	1270	254
220	9789362089892	Vol. XXIV	Ghazipur	H. R. Nevill	1600	320
221	9789362085436	Vol. XXV	Gonda	H. R. Nevill	1650	330
222	9789362080271	Vol. XXVI	Gorakhpur	H. R. Nevill	1890	378
223	9789362086129	Vol. XXVII	Hamirpur	D. L. Drake Brockman	1390	277
224	9789362087638	Vol. XXVIII	Hardoi	H. R. Nevill	1680	336
225	9789362081636	Vol. XXIX	Jalaun	D. L. Drake Brockman	1180	236
226	9789362084309	Vol. XXX	Jaunpur	H. R. Nevill	1750	350
227	9789362084187	Vol. XXXI	Jhansi	D. L. Drake Brockman	1960	391
228	9789362089168	Vol. XXXII	Kheri	H. R. Nevill	1650	330
229	9789362086778	Vol. XXXIII	Lucknow	H. R. Nevill	1760	352
230	9789362088635	Vol. XXXIV	Mainpuri	H. R. Nevill	1740	348
231	9789362080424	Vol. XXXV	Meerut	H. R. Nevill	2170	434
232	9789362081087	Vol. XXXVI	Mirzapur	D. L. Drake Brockman	2430	486
233	9789362085443	Vol. XXXVII	Moradabad	H. R. Nevill	1900	380
234	9789362082763	Vol. XXXVIII	Muttra	D. L. Drake Brockman	2140	428
235	9789362089915	Vol. XXXIX	Muzaffarnagar	H. R. Nevill	2260	451
236	9789362086143	Vol. XL	Naini Tal	H. R. Nevill	1890	377
237	9789362086761	Vol. XLI	Partabgarh	H. R. Nevill	1560	312
238	9789362081124	Vol. XLII	Pilibhit	H. R. Nevill	1570	314
239	9789362084453	Vol. XLIII	Rai Bareli	H. R. Nevill	1610	322
240	9789362088284	Vol. XLIV	Rampur	H. R. Nevill	1170	234
241	9789362083654	Vol. XLV	Saharanpur	H. R. Nevill	2190	438
242	9789362083142	Vol. XLVI	Shahjahanpur	H. R. Nevill	1510	302
243	9789362083623	Vol. XLVII	Sitapur	H. R. Nevill	1590	317
244	9789362089939	Vol. XLVIII	Sultanpur	H. R. Nevill	1330	266
245	9789362080851	Vol. XLIX	Unnao	H. R. Nevill	1530	305

AGENTS FOR THE SALE OF MADRAS GOVERNMENT PUBLICATIONS.

IN INDIA.

BUTTERWORTH & Co. (Ltd.,) 6, Hastings Street, Calcutta.
R. CAMBRAY & Co., Calcutta.
E. M. GOPALAKRISHNA KONE, Pudumantapam, Madura.
HARTLEYS, Mount Road, Madras.
HIGGINBOTHAMS (Ltd)., Mount Road, Madras.
V. KALYANARAMA Iyer & Co., Esplanade, Madras.
G. C. LOGANADHAM BROTHERS, Madras.
S. MURTHY & Co., Madras.
G. A. NATESAN & Co., Madras.
THE SUPERINTENDENT, NAZAIR KANUN HIND PRESS, Allahabad.
P. R. RAMA IYER & Co., Madras.
RAMAKRISHNA & SONS, Lahore.
D. B. TARAPOREVALA SONS & Co., Bombay.
THACKER & Co. (Ltd.), Bombay.
THACKER, SPINK & Co., 3, Esplanade East, Calcutta.
S. VAS & Co., Madras.
S.P.C.K. PRESS, Vepery, Madras.

IN THE UNITED KINGDOM.

B. H. BLACKWELL, 50 & 51, Broad Street, Oxford.
CONSTABLE & Co., 10, Orange Street, Leicester Square, London, W.C.
DEIGHTON, BELL & Co. (Ltd.), Cambridge.
T. FISHER UNWIN (Ltd.), 1, Adelphi Terrace, London, W.C.
GRINDLAY & Co., 54, Parliament Street, London, S.W.
KEGAN PAUL, TRENCH, TRÜBNER & Co. (Ltd.), 68-74, Carter Lane, London, E.C., and 25, Museum Street, London, W.C.
HENRY S. KING & Co., 65, Cornhill, London, E.C.
P. S. KING & SON, 2 and 4, Great Smith Street, Westminster, London, S.W.
LUZAC & Co., 46, Great Russell Street, London, W.C.
B. QUARITCH, 11, Grafton Sreet, New Bond Street, London, W.
W. THACKER & Co., 2, Creed Lane, London, E.C.
OLIVER and BOYD, Tweeddale Court, Edinburgh.
E. PONSONBY (Ltd.), 116, Grafton Street, Dublin.
W. WESLEY & SON., 28, Essex Street, Strand, London.

ON THE CONTINENT.

ERNEST LEROUX, 28, Rue Bonaparte, Paris.
MARTINUS NIJHOFF, The Hague, Holland.

MADRAS DISTRICT GAZETTEERS.

SALEM.

VOLUME I—PART I.

MADRAS DISTRICT GAZETTEERS.

SALEM.

BY

F. J. RICHARDS,

INDIAN CIVIL SERVICE.

VOLUME I—PART I.

MADRAS:

PRINTED BY THE SUPERINTENDENT, GOVERNMENT PRESS.

1918.

NOTICE.

SINCE this Gazetteer was written, the taluk of Namakkal has been retransferred to the Salem district under G.O. No. 641, Revenue, dated 14th February 1918. A full description of Namakkal taluk is given in Mr. Hemingway's Gazetteer of Trichinopoly District, 1907.

PREFACE

MR. LEFANU'S " Salem Manual " is a classic, and its revision is a work of vandalism. In preparing the revised volumes, as much as possible of the original matter is retained, but a plethora of new material and the exigencies of space necessitate ruthless condensation. Perhaps before long Mr. LeFanu's volumes will be reprinted.

My thanks are due to those whose assistance is acknowledged in the foot-notes to the text, and especially to the District Officers of all departments for the unfailing courtesy of their co-operation. Chapter II (History) is based on a memorandum specially drawn up by the late M.R Ry. Rai Bahadur V. Venkayya, and owes much to M.R.Ry. Rao Sahib H. Krishna Sastri and Professor S. Krishnaswami Ayyangar. Invaluable help has been rendered by Lieut.-Col. R. K. Mitter (on Public Health), by Messrs. F. L. C. Cowley-Brown and H. A. Latham (on Forests), Messrs. J. Inglis and A. R. deChazal (on Irrigation), Mr. Alfred Chatterton, C.I.E (on Textiles), Mr. S F. Chetham (on Crime) and M.R.Ry P. S. Abbāyi Nāyudu, M.R.Ry. Rao Sahib K. D. Subrahmanya Ayyar and others (in collecting ethnographic data).

For convenience of reference a list of the principal books consulted is printed on page ix.

The spelling of vernacular names presents serious difficulties, owing partly to the circumstance that the District is triglott, and names crop up in Tamil, Telugu, Kanarese and Sanskrit forms, and partly to the ineradicable carelessness, in this respect, of official correspondence. The language locally prevailing has been ordinarily preferred; thus *Kōta* is used in a Telugu tract *Kōttai* in a Tamil taluk and *Kōte* in the Kanarese country. I have adopted the forms "*Kāvēri*" and "*Pennaiyār*" in preference to the cacophonous anglicized corruptions "*Cauvery*" and "*Penner*," and have taken the liberty of splitting up some sesquipedalian place-names by hyphens into their component parts, because, to English readers, a word like "*Anantakrishnarayasamudram*" is even more uncouth than "*Fortsaintgeorge*" or "*Burtonontrent.*" In such cases the duplicate consonants are usually dropped, e.g., "*Palli-patti*," instead of *Palli-ppatti*; and the doubled ச்ச I have transliterated as *ch*, instead of *cch*, *c'ch*, *chch*, or *chchh*, which are unnecessarily "frightful." The names of those who have kindly lent a hand to the Sisyphean task of proof-reading are too numerous for insertion, yet I fear that perfect consistency in the spelling of South Indian proper names is humanly unattainable.

Nāmakkal Taluk was transferred to Trichinopoly in 1910, and Tiruppattūr Taluk to North Arcot in 1911. Hence statistics later than 1910 cannot adequately illustrate the growth and progress of the District in comparison with former years, and have been, for the most part, omitted. The revised volumes were completed early in 1913, and the task of incorporating changes subsequent to that date has been carried out in the office of the Board of Revenue.

VELLORE, *7th March 1916.* F. J. RICHARDS

BOOKS OF REFERENCE.

ALLAN, CAPT. A. *Views in the Mysore Country*, 1794.

ANON. *Memoirs of the Late War in Asia*, by an Officer of Col. Baillie's Detachment, 1788.

BEATSON, LT.-COL. ALEXANDER. *A View of the Origin and Conduct of the War with Tippoo Sultaun*, 1800.

BERTRAND, FATHER J. *La Mission du Maduré*, 1847–50.

BETHAM, MAJOR R. M. *Marathas and Dekhani Musalmans* (Hand-books for the Indian Army), 1908.

BEVAN, MAJOR H. *Thirty Years in India*, 1839.

BLAGDON, F. W. *A Brief History of Ancient and Modern India*, 1805.

BOWRING, L. B. *Haidar Ali and Tipu Sultan* (Rulers of India), 1899.

BRADSHAW, JOHN. *Sir Thomas Munro* (Rulers of India), 1894.

BRANDIS, SIR DIETRICH. *Indian Trees*, 1906.

BUCHANAN, FRANCIS. *Journey from Madras through Mysore, Canara and Malabar*, 1807.

CLARKE, RICHARD. *Regulations of the Government of Fort St. George in force at the end of* 1847.

COTTON, J. J. *List of Inscriptions on Tombs and Monuments in Madras possessing historical or archæological interest*, 1905.

COX, A. F., and STUART, H. A. *Manual of North Arcot District*, 1894 and 1895.

DANIELL, THOMAS. *Oriental Scenery*, 1795–1807.

DUBOIS, THE ABBÉ J. A. *Hindu Manners, Customs and Ceremonies* (ed. H. K. Beauchamp, 1897).

DUFF, JAMES GRANT. *History of the Mahrattas*, 1826.

DYKES, J. W. B. *Salem, an Indian Collectorate*, 1853.

ELLIOT, SIR WALTER. *Coins of Southern India* (Part 2 of Vol. III of Marsden's *Numismata Orientalia*), 1885.

FERGUSSON, JAMES. *History of Indian and Eastern Architecture*, 1897.

FRANCIS, W. *Bellary Gazetteer*, 1904. *South Arcot Gazetteer*, 1906. *Madura Gazetteer*, 1906.

FULLARTON, WILLIAM. *A View of the English Interests in India and an Account of the Military Operations in the Southern Parts of the Peninsula*, 1782–84, 1787.

GLEIG, REV. G. R. *The Life of Major-General Sir Thomas Munro, Bart.*, 1830.

HEMINGWAY, F. R. *Tanjore Gazetteer* 1906. *Trichinopoly Gazetteer*, 1907.

HERKLOTS, G. A. *Qanoon-e-Islam*, 1833.

HUNTER, LIEUT. JAMES. *Picturesque Scenery in the Kingdom of Mysore*, 1805.

INNES, C. A. *Malabar Gazetteer*, 1908.

KANAKASABHAI, V. *The Tamils Eighteen Hundred Years Ago*, 1904.

KEARNS, REV. J. F. *Kalyana Shataku, or the Marriage Ceremonies of the Hindus of South India*, 1868.

KRISHNASWAMI AYYANGAR, S. *Ancient India*, 1911.

LAUNAY, ADRIEN. *Histoire des Missions de l'Inde*, 1898.

LEFANU, H. *Salem District Manual*, 1883. (Referred to as S.D.M.)

MACQUOID, CAPT. C. E. K. *Strategy Illustrated by British Campaigns*, 1904.

MILES, COL. W. *History of Hydur Naik, etc.*, 1842.

NANJUNDAYYA, H. V. *The Ethnographical Survey of Mysore*, 1907–12. (Referred to as E.S.M.)

NATESA SASTRI, PANDIT S. M. *Hindu Feasts, Fasts and Ceremonies*, 1903.

NELSON, J. H. *The Madura Country*, 1868.

NICHOLSON, F. A. *Manual of the Coimbatore District*, 1887 and 1898.

OMAN, J. C. *Brahmans, Theists and Muslims of India*, 1907.

OPPERT, GUSTAV. *On the Original Inhabitants of Bharatavarsa or India*, 1893.

PHILLIPS, DR. MAURICE. *Evolution of Hinduism*, 1903.

RICE, B. L. *Mysore* (referred to as *Mysore Gazetteer*), 1897. *Epigraphia Carnatica*, Vols. I to XII, 1886–1905. *Mysore and Coorg from the Inscriptions*, 1909.

RISLEY, SIR H. H. *The People of India*, 1908.

SALT, HENRY. *Views taken in St. Helena, the Cape, India*, etc., 1809.

SCURRY, JAMES. *The Captivity and Escape of James Scurry*, 1824.

SEWELL, R. *A Forgotten Empire* (*Vijayanagar*), 1900. *The Indian Calendar*, 1896.

SHORTT, DR. JOHN. *Hill Ranges*. 1870.

SMITH, V. A. *The Early History of India*, 1904.

THOMPSON, REV. E. W. *A History of India*, 1909.

THURSTON, DR. E. *Ethnographic Notes in Southern India*, 1906. *Castes and Tribes of Southern India*, Vols. I to VII, 1909.

VALENTIA, GEORGE, VISCOUNT. *Voyages and Travels to India, Ceylon*, etc., 1811.

WATT, SIR GEORGE. *The Commercial Products of India*, 1908.

WELSH, COL. JAMES. *Military Reminiscences*, 1830.

WILKS, COL. MARK. *Historical Sketches of the South of India, in an attempt to trace the History of Mysore*. (The references quoted relate to the second edition, 1869.)

WILSON, W. J. *History of the Madras Army*, 1882–1889.

YULE, SIR HENRY. *Ser Marco Polo*, 1903.

ZIEGENBALG, B. *Genealogy of the South Indian Gods*, 1869.

Reference has also been made to the *Imperial Gazetteer of India*, the *Census Reports* of Madras and Mysore, the *Annual Progress Reports* of the Archæological Survey of Madras and Coorg, the *Annual Reports* of the Government Epigraphist, 1888–1912 (referred to as G.E.), to *Epigraphia Indica* (Ep. Ind.), to the *Madras Museum Bulletins*, to Dr. Hultzsch's *South Indian Inscriptions* (S.I.I.), to the *Bombay Gazetteer*, to *Baramahal Records*, Sections I Management and III Inhabitants (published by the Madras Government, 1907), to the *Press List of Ancient Records in the Salem District*, 1906, to *A Concise History of the Jagheers and Poliems in the District of North Arcot* (North Arcot Collectorate Press, 1864–65), to the *Madras Catholic Directory*, to the *Indian Antiquary* (Ind. Ant.), to the *Asiatic Quarterly Review*, and to the Journals of the Royal Asiatic Society (J.R.A.S.), the Folk-Lore Society and the Mythic Society (Bangalore). Proceedings of the Board of Revenue and Orders of Government, Madras, are referred to as B.P. and G.O., respectively.

PLAN OF CONTENTS.

PART I.

GAZETTEER

OF THE

SALEM DISTRICT.

VOLUME I—PART I.

CHAPTER I.

PHYSICAL DESCRIPTION.

General Description.—Position and Boundaries— Taluks—Natural divisions—(A) Bālāghāt—(B) Bāramahāl—(C) Talaghāt. Hydrography. River Systems.—(A) Kāvēri system—(1) Sanat-kumāra-nadi—(2) Toppūr River—(3) Sarabhanga-nadi—(4) Tiru-mani-muttār—(B) Vellār system—(1) Vasishta-nadi—(2) Swēta-nadi—(C) Pennaiyār system—(1) Mārkanda-nadi—(2) Kambaya-nallūr River—(3) Pāmbār—(4) Vaniyār. Hills. I. Bālāghāt. II. Upper Ghats—Mēlagiris—Pikkili—Guttirāyan—Anchetti Valley—Natarā-pālaiyam—Urigam—Rāya-kōta Group—Ankusagiri Group—Mahā-rāja-gadai—Bāramahāl Durgams. III. Lower Ghats—Perumbālai Hills—Manu-konda and Vattala-malai—Shevaroys—Kavara-malai Group—Tenāndē-malai — Tirta-malai—Chittēri — Aranūttu-malai— Kōttai-patti—Tumbal Pass—Kalrāyans. IV. Talaghāt Hills.—Kolli-malai—Pachai-malai—Bōda-malai—Jerugu-malai and Tēn-malai—Sitā-malai—Sankagiri Group—Kanja-malai—Gōdu-malai. Climate. Rainfall—Shevaroys. Hail. Temperature—Shevaroys. Wind. Geology—(A) Archæan Rocks—The Kōlār Schist Band—(B) Intrusive Rocks—(1) The Charnockite Series—(2) Younger Igneous Intrusions—(a) Basic Dykes—(b) Magnesite Series—(c) "White Elephant" Rocks—Subaerial Rocks—Soils.—Mineral Products—Ores of Iron—Magnetic Iron Beds—Magnesite—Chromite—Corundum—Gold—Mica—Steatite—Kankar—Clays and Earths—Building Stone—Fuller's Earth. Flora—Ferns. Fauna—(A) Domestic Animals—Cattle—Horses—(B) Big Game—Elephants—Tigers—Other *Felidæ*—Rewards—Other Big Game—(C) Minor Fauna—Mammals—Small Game—Snakes—Fish. Appendix.—List of References on Geology.

Salem District lies between North Latitude 11° 14′ 46″ and 12° 53′ 30″, and between East Longitude 77° 30′ 52″ and 78° 53′ 05″.[1]

---

[1] These values are based on the preliminary charts of the Survey of India, according to the practice of the Madras Survey Department. If brought into accord with the Synoptical Volumes of the Survey of India, the values would read "between 11° 14′ 43·30″ and 12° 53′ 27·30″ in latitude, and between 77° 30′ 51·25′ and 78° 53′ 04·26″ in longitude."

CHAP. I. GENERAL DESCRIPTION.

Position and boundaries.

It comprises an area of 6,300 square miles, the size of Wales, less Anglesey and Glamorgan.[1] On the north it is bounded by the Bangalore and Kōlār Districts of Mysore; on the west it is separated by the Kāvēri from Coimbatore; on the south it touches the District of Trichinopoly; on the east those of North and South Arcot. Its extreme length from north to south is 112 miles, its greatest breadth is 105 miles.[2]

Taluks.

The District as at present constituted, contains eight Taluks; in the south, Salem, Ōmalūr, Tiruchengōdu, Āttūr; in the north, Dharmapuri, Ūttankarai, Krishnagiri, Hosūr. The Taluk of Nāmakkal in the south was in 1910 transferred to Trichinopoly, that of Tiruppattūr in the north in 1911 to the newly formed District of North Arcot.

Natural divisions.

The present boundaries of the District are the outcome of political chance and administrative convenience. It is divided by Nature into three tracts, which have little connection with each other, physical, ethnic, or historical. These three divisions are commonly known as the Bālāghāt, the Bāramahāl, and the Talaghāt.

I. Bālāghāt.

(1) The Bālāghāt[3] is part of the Mysore table-land, and resembles Mysore in its general features; to the north and east an undulating plateau, studded with rocky "kopjes," and poorly wooded; to the south and west densely jungle-clad. The average elevation is about 3,000′ above sea level, dipping to the south-west towards the Kāvēri. At the time of the cession of this portion of the District in 1799, the term Bālāghāt was applied to what is now the Taluk of Hosūr. This is not strictly correct, for the Bālāghāt proper, i.e., the plateau country, extends over a large portion of Krishnagiri Taluk, while nearly half of Hosūr Taluk is below Ghats.[4]

II. Bāramahāl.

(2) The Bāramahāl is an extensive basin, intermediate between the Mysore table-land and the plains. Its general elevation is about 1,300′ above sea level. Roughly speaking, it comprises the Taluks of Dharmapuri, Ūttankarai, the greater part of Krishnagiri, and portions of Hosūr. It is bounded on the north and west by the Mysore plateau; on the south and east by a second line of

---

[1] Inclusive of Nāmakkal and Tiruppattūr Taluks, the area of the District was 7,530 square miles, i.e., 160 square miles larger than Wales with Anglesey.

[2] I.e., from the tri-junction of Tiruchengōdu, Erode and Nāmakkal Taluks to the Mysore border of Hosūr Taluk, and from the tri-junction of Hosūr and Kollegal Taluks with Mysore territory to the tri-junction of Āttūr, Perambalūr and Vriddhāchalam Taluks.

[3] The word Bālāghāt means "the tract above the ghats".

[4] In the east, the country round Vēppana-palli; in the west, the valleys adjoining the Kavēri.

CHAP. I. GENERAL DESCRIPTION.

Ghats,[1] the most conspicuous members of which are the hill ranges of the Javādis, Tīrta-malai, the Chittēris, the Shevaroys, and the Manukonda-malai. On the south-west this barrier is represented by the broken country between Pennāgaram and Ōmalūr, which is skirted on the District frontier by the Kāvēri. The word Bāramahāl is variously interpreted as "Twelve Palaces" and "Twelve Districts." The latter is the more probable meaning, for by popular tradition Jagadēva Rāya had twelve sons, to whom he assigned twelve administrative divisions, and Colonel Miles, in his *History of Hydur Naik*, speaks of the Bāramahāl as the "Twelve Purgunas." The Rāya's sons may be mythical, but the tradition of the division of the country into twelve administrative charges seems correct. No two lists, however, of the twelve "Mahāls" agree.[2]

III Talaghāt.

(3) The Talaghāt, as its name implies, is the country below the ghats, and differs little in general aspect from the adjacent districts of Trichinopoly, South Arcot and Coimbatore. The watershed between the Kāvēri and the Vellār river systems divides the Talaghāt into two portions, the eastern of which coincides with the taluk of Āttūr, the western with Salem, Ōmalūr and Tiruchengōdu. Salem Taluk, with Ōmalūr, slopes gradually from a maximum elevation of about 1,200′ in the plains, Salem Town being 900′ above sea level; Āttūr Taluk is somewhat lower; Tiruchengōdu Taluk is lower than Āttūr, and near Erode is not more than 550′ above sea level.

HYDROGRAPHY.

On a glance at the map it will be observed that Salem District is intersected by numerous ridges and valleys more or less

---

[1] Called hereafter the "Lower Ghats" to distinguish them from the "Upper Ghats" which fringe the Bālaghāt plateau.

[2] The names of the "Twelve Purgunas" as given by Buchanan are—

(1) Krishnagiri.	(7) Katorgarh.
(2) Jagadevagarh (Jagadēvi-durgam).	(8) Tripaturu.
(3) Varanagarh (Vírabhadra-durgam).	(9) Vaniambadi.
(4) Kāvalgarh.	(10) Ganganagarh.
(5) Maharajgarh (Mahārāja-gadai).	(11) Sudarsanagarh.
(6) Bajangagarh.	(12) Thattakallu.

It is by no means certain that the term Bāramahāl dates back to the time of Jagadēva Rāya, and if it does, it does not follow that the above list is as old, or even that it is correct. With the vicissitudes through which the District passed, administrative divisions must have undergone changes. For instance, up to 1808, Kangundi was part of the Bāramahāl, while Mallappādi in Buchanan's time belonged to the Nawab of Arcot. Rāya-kōta was newly included in the Bāramahāl by Lord Cornwallis' Treaty of 1792. From this it would appear that, strictly speaking, the Bāramahāl is confined to the Taluks of Krishnagiri and northern Tiruppattūr. The historic Bāramahāl, i.e., the eastern portion of the geographical Bāramahāl, has a history somewhat distinct from that of the western or Dharmapuri-Ūttankarai portion.

parallel to one another, the general trend of which is N.N.E. and S.S.W. On the other hand, the general direction of the main rivers is at right angles to this. The explanation of this phenomenon is to be sought in the geological structure of the area concerned.

The surface drainage of the Mysore table-land would naturally take the shortest course to the sea. Hence the general direction of the plateau drainage through the District, as represented by the Pennaiyār and Pālār and the upper reaches of the Kāvēri, is from W.N.W. to E.S.E. But the direction of these "master streams" is modified, and that of their tributaries determined, by the relative hardness or softness of the rocks over which they flow.

The Archæan rocks, which compose the greater part of the District, were crushed and folded in very early geological times by forces acting apparently in a S.E.-N.W. direction. The axes of the folds so formed necessarily run at right angles to this, i.e., N.E. and S.W. Throughout the whole of the geological time during which the tremendous thickness of sedimentary rocks known in England and elsewhere was being deposited, the Archæan rocks of Salem District were subjected to continuous denudation. The amount of rock removed by denudation must have been vast, a thickness possibly of five or six miles. Denudation, as it advanced, would expose the edges of the folded rock-beds, and the general direction of the outcrop of bedding, or "strike",[1] as it is technically called, would be the same as that of the axes of the folds, viz., N.E. and

[1] A cursory examination of the geological map shows that the general direction of strike from Dharmapuri, across the country north of the Shevaroys, and across the Tenāndē-malai, to the main mass of the Kalrāyans, is north-east and south-west. Towards Tirta-malai the strike tends to become north and south. As the hills approach the Salem-Āttūr valley, however, the strike approximates to east-and-west, parallel to the course of the Vasishta-nadi, and this holds good in the hilly tract between Salem and Rāsipuram. On the other hand, west of the Salem-Nāmakkal road the general strike is almost north-and-south, i.e., parallel to the course of the Tiru-mani-muttar. In the neighbourhood of the Chalk Hills, and of Paittūr, both dip and strike vary in a bewildering way. The regularity with which valleys and ridges follow the direction of strike, in the portions of the District which have been surveyed, make it tolerably certain that the same principles will be found to hold good in the unsurveyed area too. The Āttūr valley may, or may not, represent the course once taken by a main line of drainage; in any case, the east-and-west trend of the Vasishta-nadi and Swēta-nadi, and of the Jerugu and Tēn-malai hills, appears to follow the line of strike, and these exceptions only go to prove the rule. In the extreme south of the District the rocks form a vast horse-shoe curve. This huge curve, which includes the whole mass of the Kolli-malais and the Talai-malai in Nāmakkal Taluk, has its apex to the west, outside of the limits of the area surveyed by the Geological Surveyors; but the curve of many of the inner (upper) beds was traced with perfect ease, demonstrating the reality of the flexure.

CHAP. I. HYDROGRAPHY.

S.W. Soft rocks are denuded more rapidly than hard rocks. Hard rocks stand out as ridges, soft rocks are hollowed out to form river valleys. Both ridges and valleys run in a direction parallel to the direction of strike. Such "strike valleys" are well represented in the Passes of Kōttai-patti, Manjavādi and Mallāpuram, while the ridges of the Javādis, Chittēris, Tenāndē-malais and Vattala-malais mark the outcrop of harder rocks.

Two causes tend to modify the general principles above laid down: (1) the local variations in the direction of strike, (2) the occurrence in some places of the extremely hard and compact rocks of the Charnockite Series, which appear to have been formed either by the melting down of crushed rocks, or by the injection of a molten magma at great depths. Owing to their great resistance to denudation, these masses of charnockite are left as hills, of which the Shevaroys are a typical example, while the surrounding country is worn down to a lower level.

It would seem that the Kāvēri and the Pennaiyār are not able to cut through the harder rocks athwart their course so rapidly as their tributaries erode the strike valleys through which they flow. The result is that, wherever one of these streams is joined by an important tributary, it abruptly changes the direction of its course at the point of junction, and follows for some distance the direction of its tributary.[1]

River systems.

The river systems are three in number:—(A) The Kāvēri system, within the watershed of which lie the southern portion of Hosūr and Dharmapuri drained by the Sanat-kumāra-nadi and the Toppūr River, and the taluks of Salem, Ōmalūr and Tiruchen-gōdu, drained by the Sarabhanga-nadi and the Tiru-mani-muttār. (B) The Vellār system, comprising the Vasishta-nadi and Swēta-nadi of Āttūr Taluk, twin rivers which unite east of the District boundary, forming the Vellār of South Arcot, which flows into the sea at Porto Novo. (C) The Pennaiyār, which drains the northern portion of the Bālāghāt, and the Bāramahāl, the south-western corner of Dharmapuri excepted. The chief tributaries to this are the Mārkanda-nadi, the Kambaya-nallūr River, the Pāmbār and the Vāniyār.

A. The Kāvēri.

The Kāvēri skirts the District on the west. Four times in its course along the District border it turns sharply at right angles, namely, at the points where it is joined by (1) the Sanat-kumāra-nadi, below the celebrated falls of Hogēna-kal, (2) the Kollegāl

[1] A characteristic of many rivers, especially in India. Familiar examples of such change of course are (1) Kistna and Ṭungabhadra, (2) Rhône and Saone, (3) Missouri and Mississippi.

Pālār, some 14 miles below the falls, (3) the Toppūr River at Sōlappādi, and (4) the Bhavāni River at Bhavāni. At each turn it adopts the direction pursued by its tributary in preference to its own. The Kāvēri is usually fordable, within the District limits, in March and early April, and again late in May and throughout June. For the rest of the year it is unfordable. When in fresh the river rises 10, 15 or even 20 feet. At intervals in its upper course, generally at points where it cuts through hard rocks, it forms deep natural pools, locally known as *maduvus*, which, even in the driest season, retain water to a depth of 30 or even 60 feet. The position of these *maduvus* is permanent, and does not shift from year to year, and they occur at points where the river course bends, narrows or drops, or where it is obstructed by rocky barriers. The bed of the Kāvēri, in its course along the District border, is too deep and too rocky to allow of its water being used for irrigation.

Of its tributaries (1) the Sanat-kumāra-nadi, otherwise called the Chinnār,[1] rises in the hill of Dēvara-betta (3,368′) near Tali, in a *jonai*, or sacred well, said to have been constructed by a sage named Sanatkumāra. After flowing through Tali, it takes an eastward course to within a mile of Kela-mangalam, where its career is checked by the rock mass of Hudē-durgam. Thence it flows south to the Pikkili Hills, where it is again deflected, this time to the west. It joins the Kāvēri just below the Hogēna-kal Falls.

(2) The Toppūr River, otherwise known as the Vēppādiyār, rises near Muluvi, on the Shevaroys, whence it flows north-east through the ravine along which the Mallāpuram Ghāt road is traced. In this ravine is the small village of Vēppādi, from which the river takes one of its names. Near Mallāpuram it turns due west, passes Toppūr, and joins the Kāvēri at Sōlappādi.

(3) The Sarabhanga-nadi takes its name from a Rishi who is believed to have done penance at one of its sources. It is formed by two streams which unite at Ōmalūr, where they are locally known as the East and West Rivers. The first of these, usually called the Periyār, rises in Yercaud. Shortly after leaving the

[1] There are many "Chinnārs" or "Little Rivers" in the District. The nomenclature of rivers is perplexing. An ordinary villager knows only the river of his own village, which he calls simply "the River." If there are two, he distinguishes them as "Big River" and "Little River." To distinguish the river which flows through his own village from that which flows through another village, he calls each river by the name of the village through which it flows. Hence, in practice, a river tends to change its name whenever it passes a village boundary. Sometimes a river is called after the largest town or village through which it passes, e.g., Salem River or Mattūr River. More rarely it earns a descriptive title, such as White River or Milk River.

Yercaud lake, it plunges down the Kiliyūr falls, and then turns westward, towards Ōmalūr. The second feeder, called variously the Patti-pādi River, the Pariankuli River, the Kūttār, or the "Ghāt River" in various parts of its course, rises on the western slopes of the Shevarāyan, and flows down the Kādaiyāmpatti Ghāt ravine. After crossing the railway line it turns south, and continues in that direction till it joins the Periyār. The combined stream fills several large tanks near Edappādi in Tiruchengōdu, and joins the Kāvēri near Kāvēri-patti.

(4) The Tiru-mani-muttār (Tamil = "river of the sacred pearl") is so called from the fact that the freshwater mussels, which abound in its lower reaches, sometimes produce pearls. It is commonly called the Salem River. It is formed by two streams, which take their rise near the Manjavādi Pass, and unite about three miles above Salem. From Salem it flows due south and joins the Kāvēri in Nāmakkal Taluk. Its chief tributary is the Ēlūr River, which drains the southern slopes of the Bōda-malais and the basin in which Rāsipuram lies. A small stream from the Kanja-malai, called the Ponnār or "Gold River," fills the Malla-samudram Tank, and joins the Salem River four miles below.[1]

B. The Vellār system.

The country between the Kalrāyans and the Kolli-malai-Pachai-malai range is drained by two rivers, the Vasishta-nadi and the Swēta-nadi. The watershed between these two rivers is formed by the Paittūr Hills. The word Swēta-nadi in Sanskrit means "White River," and the Tamil for "White River" is "Vellār." The term Vellār is applied to both these twin streams indifferently by some people, though why the term is used is not clear, for both rivers, when in fresh, flow with ruddier waters than any other river in the District. There is a legend that Arjuna, the Pāndava, when on a pilgrimage, came to the spot where the river rises, and, when he wished to perform *pūja*, he could not find water; so he drove a hole in the rock with his arrow, and the water welled up and formed a river. As Arjuna is called Swēta-vāhana, the river was called Vellār. The Vasishta-nadi is said to derive its name from the Rishi, Vasishta, who performed a *yāgam*, or sacrifice, near Bēlūr; some white rock to be found north of that village is supposed to be the ashes of the sacrifice, and is used by Saivite worshippers as *vibhūti*, for making the sacred marks upon their foreheads.

---

[1] A jewel of the Goddess in the Siva temple, Mettu Street, Salem, is set with a pearl said to have come from the Tiru-mani-muttār. It is in the shape of a grain of wheat, and six times as large. It is said that, when it was first discovered, it was as large as the top of the little finger of a man's left hand. A much smaller pearl from this river is preserved as an heirloom in the family of Mr. Sundram Chettiyār of Shevāpet.

CHAP. I. RIVERS.

The Vasishta-nadi, which is the northern of the sister streams, and is sometimes called the Perār, rises in the Aranūttu-malai and flows north for about seven miles. It then turns abruptly south, through the Kīri-patti valley, entering the plains near Bēlūr. Two miles below Bēlūr it receives the waters of the Kariya-kōvil River, which drains the Kalrāyans and is itself reinforced by the Ammā-pālaiyam River, flowing from the head of the Kōttai-patti Pass. As it approaches the Salem-Āttūr road, the Vasishta-nadi bends eastwards, and, close to Krishnāpuram, receives another tributary, the Singāpuram river, this time from the south. The main stream keeps close to, and almost in sight of, the Cuddalore road, as far as Talaivāsal, where it is crossed by a bridge. Just west of Āttūr, a third tributary, known as the Mekka-palli River, flowing from Malli-karai, joins the main stream. The Vasishta-nadi fertilises some of the richest land in the District and is crowded with anaikats. Its freshes rarely fail.

The Swēta-nadi, which is the southern of the sister streams, receives almost the entire drainage of the Kolli-malai and Pachai-malai Hills. In the fertility and constancy of its freshes it resembles the Vasishta-nadi. It is joined by no tributaries of importance.

C. The Pennaiyār.

The Pennaiyār takes its rise near Nandidrūg in Mysore, where it is known as the Southern Pinākini. The name is said to be derived from *pināka*, the bow of Siva. The Tamil name is difficult to account for. The forms "Pennaiyār" and "Ponnaiyār" are used indifferently. It is believed that, during a great drought, Siva bade Pārvati go forth from Nandidrūg in the form of rivers, that the goddess obeyed and flowed in two directions, forming the rivers known as the Northern and the Southern Pinākini, and that the rivers were so named from the figure traced out by their courses, which faintly resembles the outline of a bow. The Pennaiyār is thus a manifestation of Pārvati, and so sacred are its waters, that even the Ganges comes and bathes in them for five days every year, to cleanse itself of the sins it has washed from sinners.

The Pennaiyār enters Hosūr Taluk in a south-easterly direction at a spot three miles north-west of Bāgalūr. After crossing the Mālūr road, its waters make their way southwards in a very irregular course, till the Sūlagiri road is crossed. Its course is then more uniform to within a mile of the Rāya-kōta road, when it turns due east and passes to the Bāramahāl, where it is joined by the four tributaries already named. At the points of junction with each of these tributaries the Pennaiyār alters the direction of its course. The first two bends, where it meets the Mārkanda-nadi and the

Kambaya-nallūr River, are obtuse; the last two, where it unites with the Pāmbār and Vāniyar, are remarkably acute. After crossing the Bāramahāl it quits the District through the Chengam gap, between Tīrta-malai and the Javādis, south of Singārapet, and pursues its course to Cuddalore. The bed of the Pennaiyār, till it reaches the Bāramahāl, is too deep and rugged to admit of irrigation. In the Bāramahāl it is still, when in fresh, a violent and rapid stream, but its waters supply the Bārūr Project, and in the vicinity of Kāvēri-patnam it feeds many spring channels which afford abundant direct irrigation and terminate in tanks.

Of its tributaries, (1) the Mārkanda-nadi, otherwise called the Chinnār, flows due south from the Mysore Plateau through the valleys of Tīrtam and Vēppana-palli and joins the Pennaiyār soon after the latter emerges on the low country of the Bāramahāl.

(2) The Kambaya-nallūr River drains the major portion of Dharmapuri Taluk; by the Pula-halli River it receives the run-off of the Pikkili Hills and the country round Pālakōdu, and by the Dharmapuri River that of the northern slopes of the Vattala-malai.

(3) The Pāmbār rises on the Javādis and Yēlagiris of Tiruppattūr Taluk, and from Tiruppattūr southwards it follows a course of remarkable straightness through Ūttankarai to the Pennaiyār, which receives its waters shortly before quitting the District. *En route* it is joined by the Bargūr River, the Mattūr River and the Sandūr River.

(4) The Vāniyār rises in the Shevaroys near Yercaud. The gorge down which it flows is the grandest in the District. The river reaches the plains at Venkata-samudram; thence, crossing the road, it passes Harūr and joins the Pennaiyār just below its confluence with the Pāmbār.

HILLS.
I. THE BĀLĀGHĀT.

The Hills of Salem District afford perhaps its greatest charm. The Bālāghāt plateau itself is rather monotonous, the only conspicuous heights being Dēvara-betta (3,364′) where the Sanatkumāra-nadi takes its rise, and the Pagoda Hill at Hosūr (3,116′). To the south and east, however, the plateau breaks into the upper line of Ghāts which fringe the Bāramahāl on the north and west. From the plateau side the approach to Ghāts is marked by a scattered chain of hill forts, which constituted the last line of defence against an invading army from the plains. The chief of these are Sūlagiri, Tiyārana-durgam (2,930′), Anchetti-durgam, (3,192′), Munēsvara-konda (south of Jakkēri, 2,982′), Nīlagiri (3,054′), the group of hills of which Hudē-durgam (3,182′) and Ratnagiri (2,805′) are the best known, and lastly, near the head of the Anchetti Ghāt, Mallikārjuna-durgam (2,996′) and Kundukōta-konda (3,319′).

CHAP. I. HILLS.

The upper line of Ghāts is divided into four sections by the valleys of the Sanat-kumāra-nadi, the Pennaiyār and the Mārkanda-nadi.

II. THE UPPER GHATS. A. Mēlagiris.

The broken country between the Sanat-kumāra-nadi and the Kāvēri is commonly called the Mēlagiri Hills. The former river, in its course from near Tali to Hogēna-kal, describes a crescent the horns of which point west. A chord to this arc is formed by a massive ridge of mountains running north-east by north, and south-west by south, which culminates in the Guttirāyan (4,579′). This ridge determines the course of the Āne-bidda-halla, which drains its west flank. Between the Āne-bidda-halla and the Kāvēri lie five valleys, each trending north and south, the third and largest of which opens out into the Anchetti basin, drained by the Dodda-halla. The Urigam basin lies to the west of the Anchetti valley, the basin of Nātarāpālaiyam to the east. The other two valleys are of minor importance.

(a) Anchetti.

The Anchetti Valley is formed by the confluence of two streams, one of which drains the Sūlivāram plateau and descends by the Kundu-kōta Ghāt, and the other rises near Javulagiri and flows via Pāni and Mariyālam. Their united waters are reinforced further south by streams from the valleys of Miladikki and Tagatti, and by the Ebhalla from the Manchi plateau, forming the Dodda-halla River, which flows for six miles through a deep ravine, and discharges into the Kāvēri. The Anchetti basin is closed on the north-east by the Mariyālam hill (3,449′), on the south by Chikkā-bētta, (3,356′), and on the east by the Manchi plateau, but it gives easy access to Urigam via Tagatti on the west, to Biligundlu (870′) via Nātarāpālaiyam on the south, and to Pennāgaram via Geratti and the Āne-bidda-halla valley on the south-east.

(b) Nātarāpālaiyam.

The Nātarāpālaiyam basin is much smaller than that of Anchetti. Its general level is little over 1,700′. It is closed in on the west by Chikka-betta, on the south by Chellappan-betta (3,145′) and on the east by a ridge rising to 2,900′. On the north-east, however, it opens towards the Geratti flat, and a good view is obtained of the Guttirāyan.

(c) Urigam.

The Urigam basin is a flat valley, about six miles long and three miles wide. The village Urigam, at the head of the valley, is 1,960′ above sea level. At Kottevūr, two miles further south, the elevation is 1,870 . The valley is accessible from Anchetti via Tagatti (1,900′). The valley is bounded on the east by the lofty ridge on which lies Attinattam village (3,164′) and "Hundred-and-one Swāmi" Hill. On the west is a similar ridge running from Pillikallu village (3,070′) to Tadagane (or Tatakani, 2,910′). Beyond this ridge is a series of hills and valleys, dominated by the lofty peak of Chokka-betta (3,718′) the westernmost corner of the District.

II. UPPER GHATS. The Guttirāyan.

The Guttirāyan (4,579′) is accessible without much difficulty from the village of Ayyūr, where there is a good forest rest-house. The distance due south is about 11 miles. The path runs through some of the finest bamboo jungle in the District, skirts the western flank of the Bētta-mugalālam plateau, and overlooks the Āne-bidda-halla ravine. After passing the jungle-choked sites of several deserted villages, the path leads to the head of the great east-and-west Tirumalavādi ravine, and emerges from the forest at the village of Kōdiyūr, perched on a level terrace on the north flank of the Guttirāyan. Kōdiyūr is inhabited by Sivāchārs, who still remember the wholesale abandonment of the country at the time of the Great Famine. The innumerable *rāgi* pits in the vicinity of the village prove that its cultivation was once far more extensive than it is now. From Kōdiyūr a steady climb of some three miles leads across grassy glades, alternating with dense evergreen forests[1], to the summit of the Guttirāyan. The summit is bare of tree growth, and carpeted with springy turf spattered with gray lichen-clad rocks. The view is one of the finest in the District. To the west is a wilderness of mountain and jungle, with here and there a tiny patch of cultivation. The Kāvēri can be seen winding its way through the maze of hills, and beyond it tower the Ponnāchi Mountains of Kollegāl. To the east is a bird's eye view of the Morappūr amphitheatre and the plains beyond, to the south the vale of Pennāgaram, breaking away to meet the Kāvēri at Hogēna-kal, and far beyond to the south-east is the mountain mass of the Shevaroys.

The western side of the Āne-bidda-halla ravine is bounded by the cultivated plateau of Toluvu-betta and Manchi. The Toluvu-betta plateau rises to a height of nearly 4,000′[2]. The general level of the Manchi plateau is about 3,000′; it rises to 4,612′ on the Āne-bidda-halla side, and tails off towards the south in a long ridge.

The arc between the Āne-bidda-halla and the Sanat-kumāra-nadi is bisected by a ravine running from west to east in the direction of Pālakōdu. This ravine, at the head of which stands the hamlet of Kēsaraguli, forms part of the Tirumalavādi Mitta. North of the ravine is the plateau of Bētta-mugalālam, on which are the Glenshaw estate and Mēlagiri Fort. The highest points in the coronet of hills that surrounds this plateau are Jenkal-betta (4,150′) and Ijalhatti-kal (4,089′). South of the ravine is a

---

[1] The chief species are *Terminalia arjuna* and *Eugenia jambolana.*

[2] Adkal 3,820′, Gubi-kal 3,969′, Vadar-guddai 3,877′.

CHAP. I. HILLS. II. UPPER GHATS.

huge amphitheatre of hills opening to the south, which was once cultivated, but is now (except for a few scattered hamlets) a lonely jungle. In the heart of the valley is the deserted site of Morappūr village (1,690′). The west of the valley is guarded by the mountain mass of the Guttirāyan, with its offshoot Kavilai-drūg or Kāgal-malai (3,538′); to the north are Uchikal (3,904′) and Ērimalai (3,510′), and to the east the hamlet of Kōttaiyūr (c. 3,000′).

Pikkili Hills.

To the south-west of this Morappūr valley the course of the Sanat-kumāra-nadi is deflected westward by a remarkable ridge known as the Pikkili Hills. But for the obstruction offered by this ridge, the Sanat-kumāra-nadi would flow into the Pennaiyār and not into the Kāvēri. Between the ridge and the river there is now a level plateau or shelf, on which the once prosperous village of Pikkili, with its hamlets, is situated. The south of the ridge rises into three peaks, Tambirāyan (3,367′), Kukli-malai (3,183′) and Adda-malai (3,107′).

B. Rāya-kōta Group.

The Ghāt line between the Sanat-kumāra-nadi and the Pennaiyār is occupied by a wedge of chaotic mountains jutting southwards into the plains, of which Rāya-kōta-durgam (3,239′), Vīrabhadra-durgam (3,038′) and Bole-Timmarāya-durgam (3,389′) are the most conspicuous members.

C. Ankusagiri Group.

The Bāramahāl is bounded on the north by the portions of the Mysore plateau comprised in the Kōlār District and Kangundi Zamindāri. Here the plateau thrusts long southward-trending buttresses into the plains below, intersected by narrow valleys formed by the head waters of the Mārkanda-nadi, the Mattūr River and the Bargūr River. The Mārkanda-nadi valley has two branches, separated by a long low ridge known as the Ada-konda or Adara-konda. The western branch forms the Tīrtam basin, and the eastern branch the Vēppana-palli valley. The western wall of the Mārkanda-nadi valley is formed by the mountain mass which rises sharply north of the Pennaiyār, and culminates in Bālakonda-rāya-durgam (3,046′), Ankusagiri and Kundāni-malai. The Tīrtam basin lies north of this, and opens on the north in the Pass of Būdi-kōta, the old *Dandu Oni* or "Army Road", which gave access to the Mysore plateau in the days of Colonel Joseph Smith. To the west, the basin is hemmed in by the fringe of hills, of no great altitude, which marks the termination of the Bālā-ghāt portion of Bērikai Pālaiyam, and on the north by a long low ridge known as the Pāl-māl-konda, between which and the Adara-konda is another pass leading to Kāma-samudram. The east of the Mārkanda-nadi valley is bounded by a long serrated ridge which, starting from Malappa-konda Hill (3,600′), the trijunction of Chittoor and Salem Districts with Mysore State, rises to a height of 2,700′, ending in a group of hills of which Geddi-konda (2,424′), Malakonda (2,310′) and Boggulu-konda (2,501′) are the highest.

II. UPPER GHATS. D. Mahārāja-gadai.

East of this ridge we enter the watershed of the Mattūr River, backed by the mountain mass of Mahārāja-gadai Hill (3,383′), a landmark for many miles around. The village of Mahārāja-gadai lies at the mouth of a ravine which separates this hill from the ridge east of Vēppana-palli. Up this ravine runs a path which leads to Kuppam.

The Bargūr River takes its rise in three valleys east of Mahārāja-gadai Hill, opening respectively on to the villages of Pungūrutti, Medugam-patti and Oppattu-vādi. They are of little importance, the hills which encircle them rarely exceeding 2,100′ in altitude.

The Bāramahāl Durgams.

Outliers of the Mysore plateau are scattered over the Bāramahāl, the chief being Gaganagiri, otherwise called Periya-malai (3,436′), Tattakkal (2,629′), Jagadēvi-durgam (2,647′), Nāga-malai, Pū-malai (North of Mallappādi 2,599′), Mallappādi Hill (2,364′) and Krishnagiri Fort Rock (2,409′).

III. THE LOWER GHATS

The second line of Ghāts, to the south and east of the Bāramahāl, is divided into six sections by the Passes of Toppūr, Mallāpuram, Manjavādi, Kōttai-patti and Chengam. The section north of the Chengam Pass, comprising the Javādi Hills, has been transferred to the new North Arcot District.

1. Perumbālai area.

(1) The country between the Kāvēri and the Toppūr Pass is in general level intermediate between Pennāgaram Division and Ōmalūr Taluk. It is intersected by two valleys, that of the Maddala-pallam and that of the Pālār, Pāmbār, or Perumbālai River.

Between the Maddala-pallam and the Kāvēri the country rises to a lofty ridge, overlooking, and parallel to, the course of the Kāvēri. The chief peaks of this ridge are Biyanūr-malai (2,788′)[1], Koppu-malai (2,627′), Kadriappan-malai (2,936′) and Sēgala-malai (2,168′). These eminences are distant some 3 or 4 miles from the Kāvēri bank. In the intervening space is a second ridge, less regular and less lofty, the highest points being Karala-malai (1,609′) and Karungal (1,524′).

The Maddala-pallam averages 1,000′ in elevation, towards the north it rises to 1,200′ or even 1,300′, and towards the south it sinks to 800′. The chief villages in this depression are Sigarala-palli, Ajjam-patti (1,120′) and Neruppūr (900′).

---

[1] The Kāvēri above Hogēna-kal flows straight towards Biyanūr-malai and it is at the very foot of this hill that the river is deflected at a right angle.

CHAP. I. HILLS. III. LOWER GHATS.

Between the Maddala-pallam and the Perumbālai River is an extensive plateau of rocky undulating ground, covered with low jungle, the ordinary elevation of which is from 1,400′ to 1,500′, though occasionally rising to 1,800′ or 1,900′. This plateau is cut in all directions by small streams, the valleys of which lie about 200′ below the plateau level. The highest portion of this plateau is round the village of Donnakutta-halli, which itself is situated on a high table-land. East of this village is Bonthal-betta (1,826′), west is Janda-Karunkal (1,633′), and south-west Garadi-gutta (1,981′). The Perumbālai valley runs from Indūr in a south-westerly direction to join the Toppūr River. The bed of the Pāmbār is low, relatively to the surrounding hills. The levels are Rāskōl-patti 1,070′, Rānihalli 1,030′, Perumbālai 970′. On nearing the latter village the valley opens out. Between the Pāmbār and the Toppūr Ghāt Road is a plateau, ranging in elevation from 1,400′, the general level, to 1,500′, and sometimes even 1,600′. Towards the south, this plateau falls away to the Toppūr River, the level of which at Toppūr is little more than 1,100′ above sea level. South of the river are outliers of this plateau in the Gundakal ridge (1,502′), the Rāmaswāmi-malai (1,094′) and the Ēlattūr Reserve (1,539′).

2. Manukonda and Vattala-malai.

(2) The Hills between the Toppūr Pass and the Mallāpuram Ghāt are intersected by the Toppūr River. The southern portion rises to a height of 3,164′ in the Manukonda-malai, round the western base of which the Ghāt Road curves. The hills eastward of the Manukonda-malai do not exceed 2,400′ [1]. North of the Toppūr River the ground rises rapidly [2] (save for the Reddi-halli gap, which gives access from Laligam to Mallāpuram) towards the Vattala-malai, an abrupt narrow ridge 11 miles in length, culminating in the conspicuous Mūkkanūr Peak (4,201′) which overhangs the Morappūr-Dharmapuri Railway. On the summit of the Vattala-malai there are several hamlets.

3. The Shevaroys.

(3) Through the Mallāpuram Ghāt runs the Madras-Calicut Railway; the highest point in the line being 1,508′ above sea level. Through the Manjavādi Pass runs the Trunk Road from Madras to Salem. The highest point in the road is 1,800′ above sea level.

Between the Mallāpuram Ghāt and the Manjavādi Pass are the Shevaroy Hills, the noblest mountain mass in the District.

---

[1] In Lokūr Reserve, Pula-malai (2,252′), Pamala-malai (2,251′) and Bōda-malai (2,391′).

[2] Close to Toppūr are Tamarai-malai (2,920′), Gundal-Guddai (2,360′), Ethu-malai (2,640′) and Kuchu-karadu (2,303′).

MAP OF SHEVAROY HILLS

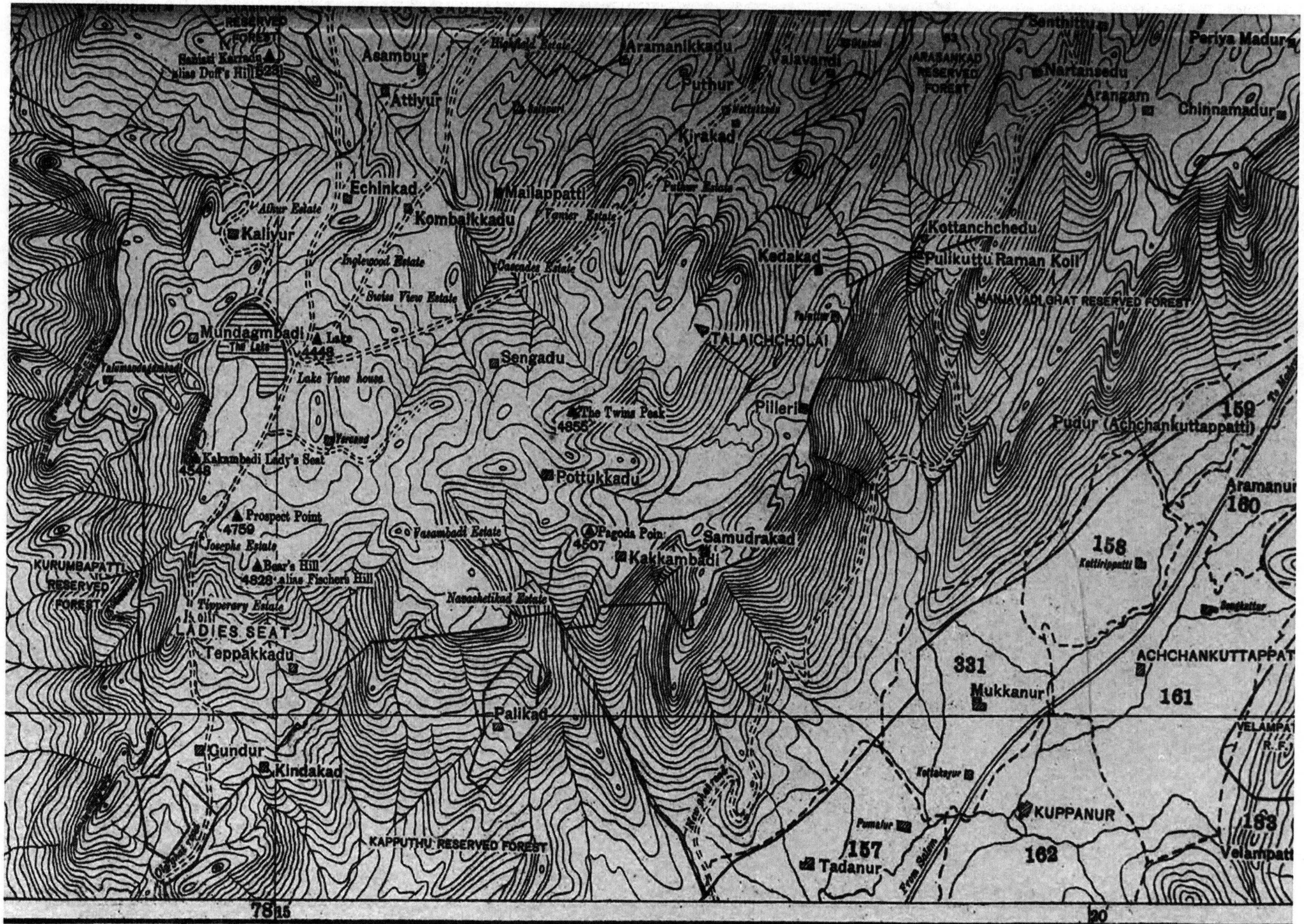

g No. 549

Scale 1 Inch = 1 Mile

Helio-Zinco., Survey Office, Madr

CHAP. I. HILLS. III. LOWER GHATS.

The greatest length of the Hills is 17 miles, the greatest width is 12. They cover about 100 square miles. The southern slopes rise abruptly from the plains to a height of from 4,000′ to 4,800′ above sea level, except for the spur on which the villages of Gundūr and Tappa-kādu are situated and up which the Old Ghāt ascends. This abruptness determines the watershed, and most of the drainage of the Hills flows towards the north. Hence the northern slopes of the Shevaroys, like those of the Kolli-malais, are broken with deep ravines.

The range is severed into two portions by the Vāniyār valley, which rises in the south near Sengādu, and flows in a north-easterly direction, almost exactly parallel to the Manjavādi Pass.

The two sections into which the plateau is thus divided are dissimilar. That to the east is cut into ridges and ravines running in the same direction as the Vāniyār, that to the west is comparatively massive and attains a loftier elevation.

The eastern section comprises the mountain mass on which lies Talaisōlai and the Māra-mangalam plateau. Between the two is the saddle on which the village of Kottan-chēdu is situated.

The western section of the Shevaroys is divided into two portions at Taylor's Saddle, which marks the watershed between the Vāniyār and the Kādaiyām-patti River, a stream which flows west-north-west, at right angles to the Vāniyār, and whose valley gives access to Kādaiyām-patti Railway Station by the Āttūr Ghāt.

The southern half of the western section is the irregular plateau on which Yercaud is situated. Yercaud itself is cut off from a view of the plains by a circlet of hills, varying in height from 4,500′ to 4,800′[1]. This plateau terminates to the north in Duff's Hill (5,231′), otherwise known as Sanyāsi-malai. West of this, a massive buttress juts out from the hill, forming a plateau of from 2,800′ to 2,900′ above sea level, on which is situated the Malaiyāli villages of Kondayanūr and Sōnappādi.

The northern half of the western section consists of a central backbone, of high peaks with a plateau on either side, that of Nāgalūr to the west, and that of the Green Hills to the east. The central ridge follows a line drawn from Duff's Hill parallel to the Vāniyār valley, and includes the Shevarāyan (5,342′), Blanfill (5,410′), Balamadies (5,370′) and Cauvery Peak (5,086′). At Cauvery Peak the ridge forks, the left branch running due north to Pulivarai (4,567′) and the right branch following the Vāniyār valley.

---

[1] Lady's Seat	..	4,548′.	Pagoda Point	... ...	4,507′.
Fischer's Hill	..	4,828′.	The Twins Peak	... ...	4,855′.
Church Hill	...	4,813′.	Prospect Point	... ...	4,759′.

CHAP. I. HILLS. III. LOWER GHATS.

The Nāgalūr plateau is for the most part under 4,000′ in height. It overlooks the Vēppādi valley (also parallel to the Vāniyār valley), up the eastern side of which climbs the trace of the abandoned Mallāpuram Ghat. West of the Vēppādi valley is the Yērimalai ridge (3,200′), and beyond this another valley and another ridge, all trending in the same direction.

The Green Hills plateau overlooks the Vāniyār valley, towards which it presents some bold cliffs, the most striking being Hawthorne (4,899′) and Honey Rocks (4,533′). Opposite the latter, the Vāniyār flows at a level of 2,490′, though only a mile distant.

Kavara-malai Group.

The Kavara-malai is an irregular group of hills, 9 miles long by 3 miles broad, lying between Mallāpuram and Tenkarai-kōttai, and separated from the Shevaroys, of which it forms an outlier, by the Bairanattam valley. There are more than half a dozen separate peaks exceeding 2,500′ in height, the highest being Kavara-malai itself, 2,994′.

South-west of the Shevaroys is another outlier, the Nagara-malai, a small group of hills very bare of vegetation, and covering some two square miles of country. The highest point is towards the west (2,030′).

4. Tenāndē-malai.

Tenāndē-malai [1] is a term somewhat loosely applied to the hills between the Manjavādi Pass and the Kōttai-patti-Tumbal valley. The total length of these hills, measured from north-east to south-south-west, is over 30 miles, the greatest width is about 12 miles. This area may be divided into three natural divisions: (*a*) to the north, the Tīrta-malai Hills; (*b*) central, the Chittēri plateau, and (*c*) the Āranūttu-malais to the south.

(*a*) The Tīrta-malai Hills of Ūttankarai Taluk are divided from the Chittēri plateau in the latitude of Kōttai-patti by the east-and-west valleys of Kambutūkki and Velimadurai, and rise to a height of 3,220′ in Tīrta-malai Hill, which lies almost on the banks of Pennaiyār. The Tīrta-malai ridge is drained on the east by the Kōttai-patti valley, on the west by the Vāniyār. On the north it is cut off from the Javādis by the Pennaiyār and the Chengam Pass [2]. Except Tīrta-malai itself, the peaks of this ridge rarely rise above 2,500′.

North of Tīrta-malai are two groups of low outliers, covered by the Pūvam-patti Forest Reserve and its Extension. The northern of these attains a height of 1,994,′ and is in the form

---

[1] The chief Guru for all the Malaiyālis resides at Chittēri and is called Tenāndē Kavundan.

[2] Perumāl-malai, north-west of Singārapet, is 2,273′; Singārapet itself is about 1,100′.

CHAP. I. HILLS. III. LOWER GHATS.

of a ridge running exactly parallel to the Vāniyār. This ridge affords an interesting object lesson in the effect of hard rock on the course of rivers. After crossing the railway, the Pennaiyār flows due east; within two miles of its junction with the Pāmbār it inclines to the north-east; at its junction with the Pāmbār it makes an acute bend and follows the direction of the Pāmbār almost due south, pointing to the southern end of the Pūvam-patti ridge; at its junction with the Vāniyār it bends abruptly to the north-east again, following the direction of the Vāniyār and running parallel with the ridge, which is clearly the cause of the deflection. A similar deflection occurs further east, where the Pennaiyār meets the stream that flows from the Kōttai-patti valley.

(*b*) The Chittēri plateau is a tangled mass of highland and ravine, which it would be tedious to describe in detail. On the west, where it overhangs Palli-patti, it rises into lofty peaks, the western slopes of which are very abrupt. Most of these peaks are nearer 4,000′ than 3,000′ in height, one due north of the little village of Tongalūttu rises to 3,957′ and 2 miles south-west of this is Sāmi-malai (3,993′). The plateau is scattered with numbers of small Malaiyāli villages, the chief of which, Chittēri, is over 3,000′ above sea level. To the east the slopes are gentle and the elevation less, often not more than 2,000′. The villages vary in altitude between 2,500′ and 3,000′. The general course of ridges and valleys is, as elsewhere, north-east and south-west. The southern slopes of this plateau rise to well over 3,000′ where it adjoins Neyya-malai in Sekkadi-patti Mitta (Koppu-malai, 3,131′). Neyya-malai is bounded on the west by the feeders of the Vasishta-nadi, on the east it overhangs Tumbal.

(*c*) Aranūttu-malai or "Siva's Spring Hill," is a term applied to the hills in Salem Taluk immediately east of the Manjavādi Pass. In them the Vasishta-nadi takes its rise. The eastern side of the Manjavādi Pass is bounded by a sharply defined ridge, with steep slopes, rising to nearly 4,000′. About a mile and a half east of this, and parallel to it, runs another ridge, exactly similar in appearance and general configuration. Between the two runs a straight valley, which is quite one of the most beautiful in the District. Down this valley flows the Vasishta-nadi in a direction north-north-east for nearly 7 miles. Then it suddenly takes an acute bend, and flows due south, down the Kīri-patti valley towards Bēlūr. In the angle so formed is a large block of lofty mountains rising to 3,822′, on which lies the small village of Pilāppādi (over 3,000′).

The Kōttai-patti-Tumbal Pass.

The Kōttai-patti valley lies between the Tīrta-malai ridge and the Kaḷḷāyans of Kalla-kurchi Taluk, South Arcot. It is reached

CHAP. I. HILLS. — III. LOWER GHATS.

from Tīrta-malai by a road which passes through the Tīrta-malai Reserve, and runs as far south as Kōttai-patti. The northern part of the valley is about 4 miles wide. South of the village of Baira-nāyakkam-patti the valley branches in two, the westward branch forming the Kambutūkki valley, which severs the Tīrta-malai ridge from the Chittēri plateau, and the eastern branch continuing through to Kōttai-patti. South of Kōttai-patti this valley branches again, the eastward branch running into the Kalrāyans at Avalūr, and the main valley continuing to Chittilingi. Beyond Chittilingi there is a third fork, the minor valley running westward into the Chittēri plateau at Tādam-patti. The main valley continues via Vēlanūr, Ammāpālaiyam and Māmanji to Tumbal, and thence to Bēlūr. The Pass is practicable with difficulty for double bullock carts. The watershed is crossed between Vēlanūr and Ammā-pālaiyam, the highest point being 1,486′ above sea level. The distances from Kōttai-patti (1,135′) are ; Vēlanur, 12 miles ; Ammā-pālaiyam (1,344′), 17 miles ; Māmanji, 21 miles ; Tumbal, 23 miles ; Bēlūr, 31 miles ; Vālappādi, 36 miles.

5. The Kalrāyans.

The Kalrāyans of Āttūr Taluk measure 16 miles from north to south, and present to the Vellār valley a continuous front of 23 miles from east to west. For half the latter distance, however, only the southern slopes are in Salem District, the main body of the plateau behind them being the Jadaya-Kavundan-Nād of South Arcot. The same remark applies to the unbroken wall of 11 miles which overlooks the Kōttai-patti valley on the east, and forms the western boundary of the Ariya-Kavundan-Nād ; the slopes only are in Salem District. Even then, however, the Āttūr Kalrāyans cover more superficial area than any other block of hills in the District, excepting only the doab of the Kāvēri and Sanat-kumāra-nadi in Hosūr.

The Āttūr Kalrāyans are divided in two by the valley running eastward from Tumbal to Pāpi-Nāyakkam-patti. The northern portion is called the Chinna Kalrāyans, the southern portion the Periya Kalrāyans.

(*a*) The Chinna Kalrāyans form a plateau about 2,700′ in height, the surface of which is much broken by mountains and ravines. On the north and east this plateau is continuous with the Ariya-Kavundan and Kurumba-Kavundan Nāds of the Kalla-kurchi Kalrāyans. To the west it overhangs the Kōttai-patti-Tumbal valley.

(*b*) The Periya Kalrāyans form a similar plateau, which is cut in two by a lofty ridge. The north-west portion is called Mēl-Nād, the south-east portion Kīl-Nād. Both these platforms are continuous with the South Arcot Kalrāyans.

CHAP. I. HILLS.

(i) The Mēl-Nād averages also about 2,700′ in height. Its chief village is Kōvil-Pudūr. It is most easily accessible from the north, where the slopes towards the Tumbal valley are comparatively gentle. Towards the south-west the ground rises rapidly to the small plateau of Perandūr (3,200′) which is joined by a very narrow saddle (2,600′) to the block of hills on which the Mannūr Reserve is situated. The Mannūr ridge rises to nearly 3,475′ in Mannūrmalai. South-west of this again is another ridge, rising to 2,556′, and joined to the Mannūr ridge by a similar narrow saddle.

(ii) The Kīl-Nād presents a bold front to the south. The loftiest part of the whole range overhangs the town of Āttūr. The loftiest peaks are Avvaiyār-malai (4,124′)[1], Sengal-malai, 2 miles to the north-east (4,124′), Kōvil-malai, ¾ mile from this (4,256′), Nāgalūr-malai and Kallūr-malai (4,229′). The chief village of this portion of the plateau is Nāgalūr. The most popular route from Āttūr lies via the small Government village of Kīl-Avarai.

The southern slopes of the Jadaya-Kavundan-Nād of South Arcot decline in height from 3,395′ on the west, to 1,190′ on the extreme east of the District, the average height being well over 2,000′.

IV. TALAGHĀT HILLS.

The Hills of the Talaghāt include (A) the Kolli-malai Group, with which are associated the Pachai-malais in the west and the Bōda-malais, Jerugu-malais and Tēn-malais on the east, and (B) a few isolated hills and ridges scattered over the four southern taluks.

A. Kolli-malai Group. 1. Kolli-malais.

(A) The Kolli-malais, which lie partly in Trichinopoly District, are separated from the Pachai-malais by the Turaiyūr valley and the pass leading thence to Tammam-patti, and from the Bōda-malais by the Ayil-patti Ghat. They form a fine hill mass, measuring some 18 miles from north to south by 12 miles from east to west, and situated half in Nāmakkal and half in Āttūr. On the south, east and west they rise abruptly from the plains to a height of about 4,000′. The northern slopes are broken by ravines running *en échelon* in a north-east-by-east direction, the chief of which are (1) Varagūr-kombai, (2) Mūlai-kurichi, (3) Periya-kombai and (4) Vāla-kombai. The Nāmakkal portion of the hills comprises a high level plateau made up of basin-shaped depressions covered with terraced cultivation, and resembling vast verdure-clad amphitheatres. The Āttūr Kolli-malais are rather different in structure. To the south-west is the massive and lofty

---

[1] Apparently this name commemorates the famous Tamil poetess Avvaiyār (see Vol. II, p. 249).

CHAP. I. HILLS.

IV. TALAGHĀT HILLS.

dome of Bayil-Nād, from which the valleys already referred to appear to radiate. The paths which cross the heads of these ravines command splendid views of the plains and of the hills (Shevaroys, Tenāndē-malai and Kalrāyans) that bound them to the north. The edge of the plateau to the west towers above the plains to a height of over 4,000′ above sea level. The north-west heights are about 400′ lower. The ridges which separate the northern valleys are at their top 3,000′. The highest peak on the Āttūr Kolli-malais is Vētakkāra-malai (4,663′).[1]

2. Pachai-malais.

The main mass of the Pachai-malais lies in Trichinopoly District. The Salem portion consists of a series of valleys and ridges radiating to the north and east from a plateau in the south-west, which is continuous with the Trichinopoly hills. The plateau consists of three areas, grouped in a triangle round the loftiest peaks of the range (3,380′ to 3,513′). South of this ridge lies the Pakkalam flat, north of it that of Māyambādi, each about 2,800′ above sea level. Between the two, and south of the peaks referred to, is the Kōtankal river, which flows due east across the third flat, that of Mangalam (about 2,300′) and then plunges to the plains, following the line of boundary between Trichinopoly and Salem Districts, and almost cutting the range in two. It is on account of this valley that the plan of the Pachai-malais has been compared to an hour glass. North of this valley, and parallel to it, is the valley in which Vēppadi is situated, and north of this is the low plateau of the Gangavalli Reserve. The highest point is Ammaya-mēdu (2,167′) situated to the north. The general elevation is less than 2,000′. The northern front of the Pachai-malais is penetrated by the valleys of (*a*) Vēppantattai and (*b*) Vēlūr. Between the two is a small plateau, on which is situated the little village of Vedambīyam. The Vēlūr or western valley is narrow, and about 4 miles long. It penetrates as far as Nallamati, rising within this distance from 900′ to 1,200′. It is flanked on the west by the imposing spur of the Man-malai, the summit of which is crowned with fertile fields. The slopes of the Pachai-malai ravines are clothed with thick bamboo forests. The cultivated flats are rocky and the soil is poor. The length of the range within Salem limits is about 12 miles from east to west, and its width from north to south not more than 8 miles.

3. Bōda-malai.

The Bōda-malai is a lofty ridge running east and west, at a distance of about 9 miles south of Salem, and separating the

---

[1] The general level of the plains on the west and north is between 800′ and 900′.

Panamarattu-patti valley from Rāsipuram. Its length is 12 miles. The main ridge is divided into two masses, at a spot five miles from its western extremity, by streams flowing north and south. The saddle between these two blocks is about 2,664′ above sea level. Each block is crowned by a small plateau.

CHAP. I. HILLS. IV. TALA-GHĀT HILLS

(*a*) The western plateau is guarded on all sides by imposing precipices. Access is usually gained by a spur on the north-west, which descends to within two miles of Mallūr. A stiff climb leads to the village of Mēlūr (3,653′), tenanted by Malaiyālis from the Kolli-malais. The highest point on this plateau is east of the village (3,855′). South of this, and about 700′ lower, is a second village (Kīlūr).

(*b*) The eastern plateau also contains two villages, Kedda-malai (2,963′) and Jambūttu (2,139′). At its western extremity is the highest point on the range, Jandakatti-mēdu, 4,015′. The precipice to the north of this is one of the finest in the District. On the south-east the ridge resolves itself into an irregular group of hills, the highest of which (Periya-malai, 3,124′) overhangs the Ayil-patti ghāt leading from Rāsipuram to Āttūr. The range terminates on the north-east in a fine spur, the highest point of which is Tēn-kal (2,661′).

4. Jerugu-Tēnmalai.

North of the Bōda-malais are three sets of hills "*en échelon*". The westernmost of these, blocking Salem City on the south, is called the Jerugu-malai. There is no regular name for the other two, but they are often called the Tēn-malai, from the highest peak in the range. At the back of the whole range runs the Panamarattu-patti valley, and its continuation on the Āttūr side. The valley of Jallūttu is hemmed in by a circle of heights between 2,000′ and 2,700′ high, and its drainage runs through a narrow valley, three miles long, to the north-east. The mouth of this valley is guarded by the Tēn-malai (2,709′) on the north, and the Sakkiliyan-kal (2,172′) on the south. There is a comparatively low col (about 1,400′) leading into the Panamarattu-patti valley on the south and to Periya-Kavundā-puram on the north.

B. Isolated Hills. 1. The Sītā-malai.

The line of the Kāvēri to the west of the taluks of Tiruchengōdu and Ōmalūr is marked by the barren ridge of the Sītā-malai, which runs roughly parallel to the Kāvēri for a distance of some 12 miles and rises to a height of 2,479′ on the south, and 2,751′ on the north. The ridge is covered by the Pakkanād and Vanavāsi Reserves, and is continued to the north by the low ridges of the Gōnūr and Sōlappādi Reserves. The southern end of the ridge approaches very close to the Kāvēri bank, and almost opposite to it, on the Coimbatore side, is the Pāla-malai (4,922′). Between the two it is proposed to construct a dam which will create a lake many

CHAP. I. HILLS. IV. TALAGHAT HILLS.

square miles in extent, reaching back to Sōlappādi. The bank of the Kāvēri west of the ridge is little over 600′ above sea level, and as the country east of the ridge is much higher (the eastern edge of the Pakkanād Reserve is 1,100′ above sea level), the contours are peculiarly favourable for the scheme.

Further south, and running roughly parallel to the course of the Kāvēri after it passes Kumāra-pālaiyam, are the Sūriya-malai (2,070′), Sankagiri (2,345′), Mōrūr Hill (1,643′) and Tiruchengōdu (1,901′).

2. Kanja-malai

Some five miles south-west of Salem is the Kanja-malai, one of the most interesting hills in the District. It is a rough ridge running east and west, 4½ miles long and 2 miles broad. Its highest peak is 3,236′. The Madras Railway runs within half a mile of the southern base. The geological structure is interesting, as the rocks dip at sharp angles towards the axis of the mountain, which is thus a synclinal. The result of this structure, and of the unevenness of the rocks, is that the slopes of the hill are scarred by ridges, which, at a distance, look like the ruined battlements of an ancient fort. From the top of the Shevaroys the hill, with its long serrated summit, looks like a gigantic saurian. Its rocks are full of magnetic iron.

3. Gōdu-malai

Between the Aranūttu-malai and Tēn-malai, and just south of the Salem-Āttūr road is the Gōdu-malai, a very fine bold mass, rising to upwards of 1,500′ above the centre of the great Salem-Āttūr valley, and forming part of the watershed between the basins of the Kāvēri on the west, and the Vellār on the east of the Pass. The Gōdu-malai is about four miles long from west to east, which is very nearly the direction of the axial ridge of the mass; its extreme width at the eastern end, where broadest, is about three miles, including the north and south spurs of the hill.

Many hills of minor importance are scattered over the Talaghāt, such as the Paittūr Hills, south-west of Āttūr, which mark the watershed between the Vasishta-nadi and Swēta-nadi; the Mallikarai Peak on the road from Āttūr to Tammam-patti; and the Alavai-malai, west of Andagalūr on the Salem-Nāmakkal road.

CLIMATE. Rainfall.

Rainfall is registered officially at the head-quarters of all Tahsildars and Deputy Tahsildars, and also by the Medical Officers at Tali, Rāya-kōta, Tammam-patti, and by the Sub-Registrar at Valappādi. Details of the rainfall are given in the Separate Appendix. The mountainous character of the District causes sharp variations in the rainfall of different localities. So capricious are the showers round Salem, that an inch may fall at the Collector's office and not a drop at the Club. CHAP. I. CLIMATE

The annual average from 1870 to 1904 for Salem Town was 39·65"[1]. This is higher than at any other recording station except Yercaud. The lowest average for the same period is at Tiruchengōdu (27·06") and Sankaridrug (29·98"). Āttūr registers 36·06", Tammam-patti a little more, Tali a little less. The rest of the District (except Yercaud) ranges between 31" and 33". Āttūr is the wettest taluk and Tiruchengōdu the driest[2].

The distribution of rainfall throughout the year is uneven. Rain usually sets in towards the end of April, and there is, normally, a heavy fall in May. During June and July, rain is irregular. Between August and October occurs most of the fall of both monsoons. November is a very uncertain month. December comparatively dry.

Shevaroys

At Yercaud the annual rainfall exceeds that of Salem City by an amount varying from 20" in a dry year to nearly 40" in a year of heavy rainfall. The annual fall in the north of the Shevaroys is about 10" or 12" less than that at Yercaud, and naturally, the south-west monsoon falls more heavily on the southern slopes, the north-east monsoon on the northern portion of the hills[3].

Hail

In the hottest of the hot weather in the hottest part of the day, Salem is occasionally visited by hail storms. This phenomenon was observed by Munro on May 17, 1795. The stones were "perfectly smooth and round and about the size of small pistol balls"[4].

---

[1] The highest recorded rainfall for a whole year for Salem was 60·12" in 1882, the lowest 20·76" in 1891.

[2] For detailed statistics, see Separate Appendix pp. 8–10.

[3] The annual average for the ten years ending 1906 is as follows:—

Salem	38·61"
Scotforth	50·40"
The Grange	57·01"

Scotforth is north of Muluvi, and has a northern aspect. "The Grange" is to the east of Yercaud. The heaviest fall recorded at "The Grange" in a single day was 8" in December 18, 1884; the highest annual fall occurred in 1890 (88·02"), the lowest in 1899 (48·23").

For "The Grange" statistics I am indebted to Mr. R. W. B. Gompertz, for those of the Scotforth to the late Mr. H. W. Leeming.

[4] Gleig's "Life", Vol. I, p. 174. In the *Madras Mail*, April 9, 1904, an observer writes: "The maximum shade temperature in Salem has averaged 99° for some weeks past and the minimum about 75°. This afternoon (8th instant) at 2–30 the heat was suddenly reduced by a violent hail storm accompanied by thunder and lightning. The hail stones were large and numerous, many of them were half an inch in diameter. The storm is now over, but the thermometer registers over 80°".

CHAP. I.

TEMPERATURE.

The average temperature for a series of years, as recorded in Salem Town[1] and reported by the Meteorological office, Madras, is shown in the margin. The hot weather begins early in March, reaches its worst in April and May, and from June onwards steadily declines. The highest recorded temperature for the 16 years ending 1905 was 108° (May 9, 1900), the lowest 55·2° (January 30, 1902).

Month.		Average Maximum.	Average Minimum.	Mean.
January	...	88·3	63·7	76·0
February	...	93·6	65·5	79·6
March	...	98·6	70·8	84·7
April	...	100·7	75·8	88·2
May	...	99·2	75·9	87·6
June	...	95·2	74·2	84·7
July	...	93·1	73·0	83·1
August	...	92·2	72·5	82·3
September	...	91·3	71·9	81·1
October	...	89·6	71·1	80·3
November	...	87·3	68·5	77·9
December	...	86·4	65·3	75·9
Annual	...	93·0	70·7	81·9

The average maximum is higher in February than in July, but the nights are much cooler. The difference between maximum and minimum in February is over 28°,[2] in October and November it is less than 19°. Owing to the stillness of the atmosphere in September and October, the temperature is more trying then than in February or early March, though the maximum is higher in the latter months.

The dryness of the atmosphere, the comparatively cool nights, and the drop in temperature from June onwards when the south-west monsoon bursts on the West Coast, render the climate of Salem pleasanter than that of the eastern and southern districts.

Shevaroys.

No official record is kept of the Meteorology of the Shevaroys. The temperature is most equable. A series of thermometer readings registered in a first-floor room at "The Grange" at 6 A.M., noon, 4 P.M. and 11 P.M. and extending over a period of 24 years, shows a maximum of 82° (on May 23, 1906) and a minimum of 60½°; thus the difference, in doors, between the hottest part of the hottest day and the coldest part of the coldest night, over a period of nearly a quarter of a century, is only 21½°. In any one year the variation between the highest and lowest recorded temperature has never exceeded 17°. It is very rare that the temperature rises above 80°. In fact, the hot weather midday temperature does not often exceed 77° (April and May), and in December the

---

[1] Temperature is recorded in the compound of the Collector's Office. The anemometer is fixed on the roof of that building.

[2] In Cuddalore the difference in February between maximum and minimum is 16·5 and in Tanjore it is only 12·3. The contrast is striking.

TEMPERATURE.

usual reading is 67°, occasionally sinking to 64°. It frequently happens that the four readings on a single day show no variation at all. Of course in the open air the maximum is greater[1], and on the grass in the valleys, frost is not unknown, the thermometer sinking to 31° or even 30° [2].

WIND.

The connection between wind and rainfall is striking. The averages for Salem Town are shown side by side in the margin. The heaviest falls of rain occur in the months when the wind is weakest. The rain stops as soon as the wind freshens. From October to March a north-easterly wind prevails. In April the wind veers towards the south and from May to September the general direction is south-east or south-west. The windiest months are February and March. In April the wind is a little less strong. There is a marked drop in velocity in May, and a sharp rise in June. From July it slackens, month by month, till October, which is the calmest month of the year. It then once more begins to freshen.

Month.		Velocity of wind in miles.	Average rainfall.
January	...	115	0·19
February	...	127	0·30
March	...	127	0·60
April	...	110	1·86
May	...	98	5·28
June	...	120	2·99
July	...	113	3·83
August	...	96	6·67
September	...	82	6·87
October	...	60	6·07
November	...	74	3·44
December	...	94	1·15
The year	...	101	39·65

GEOLOGY.

The geological structure of Salem District is (so far as it is known [3]) very simple :—

(*a*) By far the larger part is made up of rocks belonging to the great metamorphic or gneissic series of Southern India, the Archæan Series.

(*b*) Intrusive in these are (1) the older Charnockite Series and (2) younger igneous intrusions, of which the Basic Trap Dykes

---

[1] Dr. Shortt (Hill Ranges, part II, page 16) says, "The hottest months are March, April and May, when the thermometer attains 87° in the shade during the day."

[2] For the above information I am indebted to R. W. B. Gompertz, Esq.

[3] The only portion of the District which has been surveyed in detail by the Geological Survey of India is the area included in sheet 79 of the Indian Atlas, the results of the survey being embodied in volume IV of the Memoirs. The immediate environs of Salem have been treated by Sir T. Holland in Memoirs G.S.I., XXX, pp. 103–168 and the corundum deposits by Mr. C. S. Middlemiss in Records G.S.I., XXX, pp. 118–122 and XXIX, part 2, pp. 39–50. Mr. Middlemiss has also contributed notes on the Chalk Hills in pp. 32–33 of the same volume. Lastly, the extension of the Kōlār Gold Fields schist belt into the western part of Krishnagiri Taluk has been described by Mr. Bosworth Smith.

CHAP. I. GEOLOGY.

and the Magnesian Series of the Chalk Hills are the most conspicuous features.

The remaining part is occupied by a few unimportant subaerial deposits and the alluvia of the different rivers which are also very little noteworthy; simple though the geological features of the District are, they are of much greater interest than is generally the case in mainly metamorphic regions.

A.—The Archæan Series.

The Archæan Rocks, so called from their petrological resemblance to the oldest gneisses and schists of Europe and America, may be roughly classed as (1) granites, (2) gneisses and (3) schists. But the relation between the several members of the series has yet to be determined.

The older theory, that of Captain Newbold, regards the schists as the oldest rocks of the series, the schistose rocks being at a later age broken up by granitic intrusions.

The later theory, that of Mr. R. Bruce Foote, regards the granites and gneisses as fundamental, the schists being deposited over them and included in the Dharwar System, a transitional system, younger than the gneisses, and older than the Cuddapah System, which represents the older palæozoic age.

Captain Newbold, who passed through the District in 1841, regarded the greater portion of Southern India as occupied by two great series of rocks, viz. :—(1) a metamorphic series, which he termed hypogene schists, (2) and a series of plutonic granites, which he regarded as having penetrated and broken up the hypogene schists. This view is strongly combated by Mr. Bruce Foote, who writes,[1] "There can be no doubt that such eruptive action of granite never took place on a large scale, and that the vast area of granitoidal rock now seen was really the old foundation on which the gneisses, and after them the Dharwar rocks, were quietly deposited."

Mr. Bruce Foote has accordingly divided the Archæan Series into—

(*a*) Granitoids, which he regards as being the oldest rocks, and correlates with the Bandelkhand Gneiss of Central India.

(*b*) Gneisses, which he regards as metamorphosed sedimentary rocks, younger than the granitoids, and older than the Dharwar Schists. Newbold's "hypogene schists" thus include both the gneisses of Mr. Bruce Foote's Division (*b*), and the Dharwar Schists.

Mr. Bruce Foote's opinion can hardly be accepted as final, as more recent work in Mysore points clearly to a return to the older

---

[1] Page 28 (Bellary Memoir), Mem. G.S.I., XXV.

views of Newbold, viz., that large irruptive masses of granite do exist, which have broken up and penetrated the older gneisses and schists. A good deal of evidence has been adduced by the Mysore Geological Department to show that the Dharwar Series of schists is largely of igneous origin, and is the oldest formation; that these schists have been intruded and broken up by a very extensive series of granitic gneisses, corresponding to the fundamental granitoid gneiss of Mr. Bruce Foote, and that both have been intruded by large masses of granite and by the rocks of the Charnockite Series.[1]

Space forbids any detailed technical description of the Archæan Rocks of the District. A list of references dealing with the District is given in the Appendix to this Chapter.

The Kōlār Schist Band.

A band of the gold-bearing rocks of the Kōlār Gold Fields has been traced by Mr. P. Bosworth Smith as far as Malappa-konda Hill, the trijunction of Salem and Chittoor Districts with Mysore State. Here it splits into two. "The easterly branch may be seen keeping about three-quarters of a mile broad and running straight down south. It rises in the hills that fringe the Mahārāja-gadai valley on the western side, and runs south to a point opposite the village of Mahārāja-gadai, and there it seems to die out."[2]

The westerly branch starts out to the west of Malappa-konda and, "standing out conspicuously in a small line of hills, turns round south again through Ada-konda, thus forming the main portion of the hills that border the western side of the Vēppana-palli valley. The band seems to end with the line of hills which drop away by Tattattarai."

Several thin bands of schist have been traced east of Krishnagiri, but their relation to the main bands has not yet been made out.

(1) The Charnockite Series.

Much of the District is covered by a very interesting series of igneous rocks which are now recognised as the "Charnockite Series."[3] For instance, the whole mass of the Shevaroy Hills belongs to this series. The Charnockite Rocks are apparently

---

[1] For the above I am indebted to Dr. W. F. Smeeth, State Geologist, Mysore. Further information in this interesting controversy is to be found in—

(1) *Report of the Chief Inspector of Mines* for the year 1899, appendix, pages i to xii (Mysore Geological Department), Madras, 1901.

(2) *Records*, Volume III, Mysore Geological Department.

(3) *Bulletin* No. 3, Mysore Geological Department.

The Occurrence of Secondary Augite in the Kolar Schists, by W. F. Smeeth, M.A., D.Sc., Bangalore, 1905.

[2] *Report on Kolar Gold Fields*, 1889, p. 11, sq.

[3] For a general description of the whole group see *Memoir Geological Survey of India*, Vol. XXVIII, part 2, p. 119 sq. The term used for this group of rocks in Germany is "pyroxene granulites", in France "pyroxene gneisses"; Messrs. King and Bruce Foote refer to them as "syenitoid gneisses."

CHAP. I. GEOLOGY.

intrusive in relation to both the schists and biotite gneisses already referred to, and are therefore considered to be of younger age.[1]

The rocks exposed in the neighbourhood of Salem include a fairly complete list of the known varieties of the Charnockite Series, garnetiferous and non-garnetiferous. Those whose composition is intermediate between the acid and basic extremes are by far the most abundant, and are typically represented in the Shevaroy masses, where they are as a rule non-garnetiferous. Basic varieties, however, occur as small autoliths in the more prevalent type of the Series, and also form separate and comparatively large masses of roughly lenticular shape in the old biotite gneisses.

(2) Younger Igneous Intrusions.

The distinctly igneous intrusions of Salem District form three groups :—

(a) Basic Dykes.

(b) The Magnesian Series of the "Chalk Hills."

(c) The "White Elephant Rocks" of the Shevaroy Hills.

(a) Basic Dykes.

(a) Although not very numerous, several of these are of sufficient size and importance to form outstanding features of the parts of the District where they occur. "The intrusions are of very ancient date, and probably connected with the volcanic outbursts of the Cuddapah System," long subsequent, of course, to the crushing of the gneiss.

The largest exposures of these intrusive dykes are met with in the Bāramahāl and in Āttūr Taluk.

(b) The Magnesite Series.

(b) The name "Chalk Hills" is given to a barren tract of slightly hilly ground, north and north-west of Salem Town. Over a great part of this tract the surface is whitened by small veins of magnesite, the white colour of which explains the name.[2] The tract covers some twelve square miles; in two areas, stretching from a little west of the Railway, a couple of miles north-west of Sūra-mangalam Station, north-eastward to the western foot of the Shevaroys. The northern area is roughly leg-of-mutton-shaped in plan, with the broad end abutting on the spurs of the Shevaroys, and much obscured by low jungle. The southern and smaller area is composed of a series of low hills, the highest of which are about 50′ above the plains.

---

[1] Sir Thomas Holland, who has devoted much time to the observation of these rocks, considers that the Charnockite Series in the vicinity of Salem, though younger than the biotite gneisses of the same area, is not necessarily younger than other biotite gneisses in the District. A long junction line which exists between the pyroxene-granulites and the biotite gneisses of the Bāramahāl, will probably afford valuable evidence of the general relations of the two series of rocks, when opportunity for investigation presents itself.

[2] According to Hindu tradition, these deposits are the bones of Jatāyu, the eagle king, which attempted to rescue Sita when she was carried off by Rāvana, but was slain by the latter.

"Associated with the magnesite are minute veins of baltimorite or fibrous serpentine, generally of pale green colour, but, here and there, the largest of these veins (never exceeding 6" in thickness) show pieces of a rich bluish green.[1] Weathered and waterworn pieces often show rich tints of yellow, brown, red and purple, but on the outside only. Of compact serpentine only very small fragments were found in one or two nullahs as pebbles." A yellow wax-like variety of serpentine known as retinalite has also been found. "Thin coatings of chalcedony not unfrequently cover the surface of the magnesite, or penetrate the mass of it; the chalcedony itself is frequently covered with a layer of minute crystals of quartz."

Magnesite also occurs in smaller masses, but under very similar conditions, at Īsvara-malai and Singāpuram in Āttūr Taluk, and near the Kanja-malai.

The magnesite of the "Chalk Hills" was probably formed by the action of carbonic acid at high temperatures on eruptive peridotites.[2] The predominant type of peridotite is olivine-rock containing, like the similar dunite of New Zealand, quantities of magnetite and chromite, with sometimes enstatite. Secondary alteration of the peridotites has resulted in the formation of magnesite, chalcedony, serpentine and talc. The action of carbonic acid gas in large quantities and at high pressure on the unstable silicate of magnesia (olivine) would produce carbonate of magnesia and free silica. Most, if not all, of the peridotite eruptions of South India are accompanied by masses and veins of pure white quartz containing considerable quantities of carbonic acid gas, and the constancy of this association suggests a genetic relationship. The picrolite is probably the result of hydration of the olivine by subterranean water accompanying the carbonic acid and included in the original magma. The serpentine is due to the hydration, possibly by subaerial agencies, of portions of the olivine which escaped the action of the carbonic acid. The formation of these three minerals is due to entirely different processes; the magnesite came first, the serpentine last.

(c) The White Elephant Rock.

Two masses of white quartz are exposed, one on either side of the Gundūr spur of the Shevaroys. This quartz is presumably of

[1] Mr. Comber writes, "I have found weathered and waterworn pieces of baltimorite ranging from almost white to dark blue. Fracture shows the same colour. Pieces of apparently massive serpentine are found in the northern area, but many show traces of an apparently fibrous structure."

[2] Messrs. King and Bruce Foote inferred that the original rock of the Chalk Hills were metamorphic. Sir T. Holland, however, in 1892 proved that the primary rocks were periodtites (XXIV) (cf. *Records, Geological Survey of India*, XXIX, p. 36).

CHAP. I. GEOLOGY.

plutonic origin; there are no signs of the clastic structure distinctive of a quartzite, and no regular arrangement of crystals characteristic of infiltrated vein quartz. The quartz is sometimes colourless and transparent, but usually white, owing to innumerable cavities containing liquid carbonic acid. At the base of the quartz mass which lies east of the spur, large masses of crystalline calcite occur in close association with the quartz.

Subaerial Rocks.

Two forms of subaerial rocks are developed commonly, though not extensively, in the District, viz., the calcareous tufa popularly known as "kankar" (or "kunkur"), and (2) the pseudo-laterite found on the summit of the Shevarāyan and other mountains. The former is formed by the decomposition of lime-holding rocks by rain-water, which deposits the lime, when evaporating, at or very near the surface. The latter is a ferruginous clay incrustation formed on the surface of ferruginous rocks weathering in a damp atmosphere. In the same category should be placed the local aggregations, loose or compacted, of clayey hæmatite pellets often found in, or underlying, highly ferruginous rocks.

Peat.

True peat forms largely on the Shevaroy Hills at elevations of over 4,000 feet.[1]

Soils.

The soils of the District depend on its geology. The classification of soils by the Settlement Department is not a satisfactory guide to their nature, first because the system of classification is unscientific, secondly because it leaves out of account all except ryotwari areas. Only two[2] classes of soil were recognised at the original Settlement, namely, "red" and "black." White sands and saline and calcareous soils were classed as "red" or "black" according to the classifier's caprice[3]. The percentages under each series recognised at the original Settlement for the seven old taluks comprised in the District as now re-organized are as follows:—

—	Dry.		Wet.	
	Red.	Black.	Red.	Black.
Hosūr	100	...	70	24
Dharmapuri	83	17	24	76
Krishnagiri	92	8	41	59
Uttankarai	95	5	54	46
Salem	96	4	49	51
Tiruchengōdu	99	1	35	65
Āttūr	80	20	44	56

[1] *Mem., G.S.I.*, XII, p. 252.

[2] Except for a small area classed as "Permanently Improved."

[3] These inconsistencies do not by any means involve anomalies in assessment. Settlement classification is invariably adjusted to the merits of the soil, and sterile sands or saline tracts are usually treated as "worst sort" and assessed at the lowest rates prevailing in the village in which they occur.

CHAP. I
GEOLOGY.

A few remarkable deposits of true black soil occur in the south of the Bāramahāl, and in the Bālāghāt. The best known are (1) near Dharmapuri and Adaman-kōttai in Dharmapuri Taluk, (2) east of the Vattala-malai, round Kadattūr, (3) in the Vāniyār valley, (4) in the Kōttai-patti valley, Ūttankarai Taluk. The geological origin of these black soils is still a moot point.

MINERAL PRODUCTS.

Ores of Iron.

The iron ores[1] of Salem District are well nigh inexhaustible. By far the most abundant ore is magnetite. This mineral occurs in well-defined octahedral crystals, embedded in chlorite schist, in comparatively small quantities, but magnetite also occurs, associated with quartz, and forming a schist, in which the crystals of magnetite are crushed out in the direction of foliation to a roughly almond-shape. All gradations in size are found, down to an almost aphanitic rock, in which the constituent minerals are, to the naked eye, indistinguishable as individual crystals—a type common to all the groups of iron beds. "The incipient expansion of the mass, accompanying the oxidation and hydration of the magnetite, has, in many places, been sufficient to produce a rock that crumbles under the slightest blow, or even between the fingers. These are the pieces exclusively used by the native smelters on account of their friable nature. They are invariably found in the talus at the foot of the hills, and probably are simply the more weathered representatives of the compact specimens occurring in the beds above. A further form in which magnetite occurs in the District is that of segregation from the main mass of the rock into cavities and pockets, as innumerable small crystals. Magnetite occurs also, together with small crystallised fragments of quartz, hornblende, garnets and other minerals, as sand in river-beds, being derived from the disintegration of the numerous crystalline rocks within the area. In the trappean rocks, in granites, and in the more basic gneisses, magnetite occurs in disseminated grains, but not in quantities sufficient for economic use. In almost any locality in the south of Salem District a magnet dipped into a bed of river sand becomes coated with large quantities of magnetic grains."

Hæmatite is seldom found in large crystals in Salem District. In the hills to the south of Nāmagiripet, small crystals of specular iron occur in larger masses of crypto-crystalline hæmatite, forming, with quartz, a schist bedded in conformity to the adjacent magnetite-bearing seams. Frequently both magnetite and hæmatite are found intermixed with quartz, and in some cases magnetite cores have been noticed, surrounded by hæmatite to varying degrees—

[1] The account of iron ores which follow is taken almost entirely from Sir Thomas Holland's Preliminary Report on the Iron-ores and Iron-industries of the Salem District, *Records of Geological Survey*, Vol. XXV, p. 135 sq.

CHAP. I. MINERAL PRODUCTS.

producing, in fact, minute crystals of martite, which is probably, in most cases, pseudomorphous after the magnetic oxide. Hæmatite is quite subordinate in importance to magnetite in Salem District.

Under the action of atmospheric influences, hæmatite takes up water and passes into turgite, and ultimately into göthite and limonite, or brown hæmatite. These may be carbonated to produce the various forms of clay-ironstone and chalybite. Various stages of these processes are represented amongst the Salem iron-ores, especially the production of small quantities of yellow ochre by oxidation and hydration of the magnetite. But none of these ores occur in sufficient quantities to be of value for metallurgical purposes in comparison to the magnetite and hæmatite.

Pyrites is conspicuously rare in the rocks of the District. Finely disseminated grains occur scattered through some of the intrusive igneous rocks, but not in large quantities.

Small crystals of titaniferous iron-ore have been found in some of the eruptive rocks of Salem, but never in large quantities. Pyrrhotine, or magnetic pyrites, occurs in small quantities, as minute hexagonal prisms; it is of no metallurgical value.

Ferruginous clays, limonitic pellets, ferruginous sands, and laterite frequently occur in different parts of the District; but these iron-bearing deposits, although in some places valuable as sources of the metal, and for building and other purposes, are developed on a small scale in Salem District, when compared with the enormous deposits of richer iron oxide.

The Magnetic Iron beds.

"The magnetic iron beds," writes Mr. R. Bruce Foote, "are the most remarkable and interesting of all the gneissic rocks in Salem District, on account of their economic value, and forming, as they do, in many places very striking natural features of the country, and affording the geologist who is endeavouring to unravel the structure of the metamorphic region greater assistance than do the members of any of the other groups." The iron ore occurs not in lodes, but in regular bedded masses of banded iron ore and quartz, associated with the gneiss. [1]

The five principal groups of magnetic iron beds are those of (1) Kanja-malai, (2) Gōdu-malai, (3) Singāpuram, (4) Kolli-malai, (5) Tīrta-malai. Rich beds occur also at Malli-karai, and on the south flank of the Paittūr Hills in Āttūr Taluk, and close to the southern base of Kedda-malai in Salem Taluk.

---

[1] The ore, even that of the highest quality, appears extremely siliceous, but as the crystals of magnetic iron and of silica are distinct components of the ore mass, it would lend itself to magnetic concentration, which would be necessary if iron working on a large scale were attempted.

CHAP. I. MINERAL PRODUCTS

Magnesite.

For some years a London Syndicate has been opening up the deposits of magnesite at the Chalk Hills, and there is every prospect of a paying industry being in time established. The magnesite is of very high grade, and its products compare favourably with those of other localities. Lightly calcined, the magnesite can be used for plaster, tiles, artificial stone, boiler coverings, etc. "Dead burnt," i.e., submitted to a much higher temperature, it is one of the most refractory materials known, and is useful for fire-bricks, the lining of steel furnaces and other purposes.

Chromite.

Chromite is to be found in the northern area of the Chalk Hills, and also on the Kanja-malai. In the former locality it was worked by the Porto Novo Company till about 1860.

Corundum.

Corundum occurs at Kuttampundi, south-east of Tiruchengōdu Taluk, and in four areas in Dharmapuri Taluk, viz., (1) Pāppāra-patti, (2) Rangāpuram, (3) near Rāya-kōta, (4) on the Dharma-puri-Morappūr road.[1]

Gold.

Gold was at one time worked near Vēppana-palli, and it is not known when the working ceased.[2]

Mica.

Mica was worked about 1897 near Edappādi and Arasirāmani in Tiruchengōdu Taluk, but the stuff was poor in quality, and of no commercial value, and the digging was soon abandoned.

Steatite.

Steatite, an impure hard talc, occurs in the gneissic rocks in several localities in the District, notably on the Īsvara-malai, south of the Ayilpatti-Mallikarai road in Āttūr Taluk, and in Ōmalūr Taluk, north-east of the Tāra-mangalam-Nangavalli road. It is used for the manufacture of culinary vessels, for which the material is specially suitable, owing to its power of resisting the action of fire.

Kankar, etc.

Kankar supplies most of the lime used in the District. The quality of the lime produced from it is excellent, and kankar lime is exported in considerable quantities to the Kōlār Gold Fields. Stone suitable for building purposes is abundant all over the District. Fuller's earth is an item of importance in Tiruchengōdu Taluk, whence it is exported to Calicut.

FLORA.

No systematic survey has yet been made of the Flora of Salem District, and it is therefore impossible to describe its distinctive features.[3] A few words, however, on the ferns of the Shevaroys may be of interest.

Ferns.

Near Yercaud every wall is clothed with the Geranium Fern (*Pellæa geraniæfolia*), the heart-shaped *Hemionitis cordata*, the

---

[1] These have been described in detail by Mr. C. S. Middlemiss, in *Records G.S.I.*, XXXIX and XXX.

[2] See note on the Kōlār Schist Band, p. 27 *supra*, and the reference quoted in the footnote.

[3] An account of the chief Forest products is given in Chapter V.

CHAP. I. FLORA.

Flannel Fern (*Niphobolus fissum*) and *Asplenium furcatum*; the undergrowth of copses is brightened with the pale green fronds of *Nephrolepis cordifolia*, and open spaces are covered with the common Bracken (*Pteris aquilina*). Other common species are the Lace Fern (*Stenoloma chinensis*), *Davallia tenuifolia*, the Silver Fern (*Cheilanthes farinosa*), the Royal Fern (*Osmunda regalis*), the Oak Fern (*Drynaria quercifolia*), the Edible Fern (*Lastrea aristata*), *Pteris quadri aurito* and *Gymnopteris Feei*. In shady ravines, where running water flows, Tree Ferns (*Alsophila latebrosa*) are not uncommon, and, on the lower slopes, the Maiden-hair Fern (*Adiantum caudatum*) and Palm Fern (*Actiniopteris dichotoma*) are abundant. The Golden Fern (*Gymnogramme sulphurea*), a Himalayan species, has become naturalised on the Shevaroys. Among the rarer forms, *Angiopteris evecta*, *Lygodium microphyllum*, and *Microlepia platyphylla* are to be met with, and, on the slopes of the Shevarāyan, *Lindsaya heterophylla* has been found, a species occurring elsewhere only on the Tinnevelly Hills. A very pretty fern, *Cheilanthes mysorensis*, is to be found all over the District at comparatively low elevations, such as the Paittūr Hills, the Bāramahāl Durgams, at Bārūr and throughout Hosūr Taluk [1].

FAUNA. Domestic Animals. Cattle.

Salem is one of the chief cattle-breeding districts in the Presidency. The chief breeds are three, namely, the Mysore, the Ālambādi and the Tiruchengōdu. The first is bred in the forests bordering on the Kāvēri in the Denkani-kōta Division, the second in those round Pennāgaram. The Mysore breed is of larger frame than that of Ālambādi, but shorter in the leg. The males of both these breeds are in much demand for draught, and command good prices in the great cattle fairs of the southern districts, never less than Rs. 100 a pair, a good pair of trotters selling for as much as Rs. 400. The Tiruchengōdu breed is of diminutive size, the cows are excellent milkers. The use of cows for ploughing and for baling water is not uncommon in the Talaghāt.

Horses.

In the northern portion of the District the breeding of country ponies is of great antiquity, and dealers from Madura still resort to Denkani-kōta and Pennāgaram for their purchase. A full grown "tat" of four years or so will fetch from Rs. 25 to 30.

Pony-breeding.

Efforts have been made by Government from time to time to improve the quality of the breed, but without much success. Attempts to encourage mule-breeding have also failed.

---

[1] For the list of Ferns I am indebted to Miss H. Lechler of Yercaud.

CHAP. I. FAUNA.

Sheep and Goats.

The breeding of sheep and goats appears to be on the increase in spite of Forest Reservation.[1]

Big Game[3] Elephants.

Elephants are no longer found in the District, except [2] in the jungles along the Kāvēri, and on the Mēlagiri hills. A small herd not uncommonly crosses the river from the Coimbatore side in March or April, and remains for about a month. In 1901 a herd of five penetrated to within 4 miles from Denkani-kōta. The Kalrāyans were once called the "Elephant Hills," and in 1882 a pair of elephants with a calf found their way from the Kallakurchi Taluk of South Arcot, penetrated the Javādis as far as Mōttūr, and thence crossed the valley and ascended the Yēla-giris. They then returned *viâ* Singārapet. Shortly afterwards the bull was shot by two European officers.

Tigers.

At the beginning of the nineteenth century, tigers infested nearly all the forests of the District. They are now very rare and occur only in the jungles round Denkani-kōta, straying occasionally into the limits of Dharmapuri Taluk. On the Javādis the last tiger is said to have been shot in 1892.

Other *Felidæ*.

Panthers, leopards, jungle-cat, civet-cat and other *Felidæ* are found all over the District. In villages such as Rāya-kōta, Uddanapalli, Sūlagiri, situated at the foot of rocky kopjes, a panther may occasionally be seen in the day time, basking in the sun. One bold beast took up his abode in the bath-room of the D.P.W. bungalow at Bārūr. It is not unusual for panthers to enter the compounds of houses at Yercaud, and in 1907 a pet watch-dog was carried off by one.

Rewards.

Rewards to the extent of Rs. 7,830 were disbursed by Government during the ten years ending 1905 for the destruction of wild animals. About 45 panther skins are brought in annually for reward. A tiger-skin was presented for reward at Hosūr in 1896, another in 1906, and another in 1909. It is said that only about one in every fifty kills is reported to the authorities. Most of the tigers and panthers killed are shot in reserved forests, and the shikaris that shoot them are generally reluctant to claim a reward for fear of being taxed with the offence of shooting in a reserve without a license.

---

[1] F. 1281 (1871–2) 44,225; F. 1286 (1876–7) 577,373; F. 1291 (1881–2) 666,171; F. 1309 (1889–1900) 1,225,423; F. 1319 (1909–10) 1,210,732: the last figure excludes statistics for Nāmakkal and Tiruppattūr.

[2] Major H. Bevan, writing in the early part of the nineteenth century, speaks of elephants committing great havoc among the gardens round Rāya-kōta. *Thirty Years in India*, Vol. I, p. 65.

[3] For the note on Game I am indebted to the Hon. Mr. Justice C. G. Spencer, I.C.S.

CHAP. I.
FAUNA.

Other Big Game.

The common Indian sloth bear occurs throughout the District in hilly tracts. Among the best known localities are the Kolli-malais, the Javādis, the Shevaroys, the Chittēris, the jungles near Vēppana-palli and the Kundu-kōta hills. Native shikaris will never shoot bears, believing them to descend from Jāmbavān, the Bear King, who helped Rāma in his invasion of Ceylon. Bison or gaur were formerly common, but were almost exterminated at the time of the Great Famine. Small herds of three or four are still to be found in the deepest recesses of the Denkani-kōta, Dharmapuri and Ūttankarai jungles. Nilgai or blue bull is very occasionally met within the jungles of Dharmapuri and Denkani-kōta which adjoin the Kāvēri. Sāmbur occur in the jungles of Hosūr, Dharmapuri, Ūttankarai and at the foot of the Shevaroys, but not in large numbers. The best place to find them is on the banks of the Kāvēri near Hogēna-kal and Biligundlu, especially in the months of March and April, when all jungle streams and pools are dry, and animals are driven by thirst to the Kāvēri. The covert is too thick for successful stalking, and the only way to secure a bag is to beat the jungle. Black buck can be found all over the District. They frequent the open country and are never found in thick jungle. In the Talaghāt they may be had at the foot of the Kolli-malais. But their principal habitats are round Hosūr, Denkani-kōta, Matagonda-palli, Tali, Bērikai and Atti-mugam, all in Hosūr Taluk.[1] Within a radius of six miles of Hosūr there are a dozen herds. They are very shy and cautious; once disturbed, they never stop within five miles. Spotted deer (chetal) and barking deer are met with throughout the Bārama-hāl. The best localities for the former are near Javulagiri, Hogēna-kal, and in the reserved forests of Kōttai-patti, Mallāpuram and Harūr. Mouse deer, known in the vernacular as the "goat footed hare," is not unknown, especially in the Javādis. It is caught in nets and easily tamed.

Big game is fast disappearing in the District. Sāmbur, bison and spotted deer in particular are in danger of extirpation. What with native shikaris and wild dogs killing everything, whether stag, hind or young, the wonder is that any are found. A good deal of illicit shooting goes on in the jungles between

---

[1] Mr. J. D. Ramasubbier writes, "at Onnalavādi, 4 miles from Hosūr on the Uddana-palli road; on the high ground, near Pārānda-palli on the Hosūr-Sūlagiri road; near Nallūr on the Hosūr-Mālūr road; at about the 4th mile on the Bangalore road; on the high ground near Aggonda-halli on the Kela-mangalam road, they are always found; as also near Binna-mangalam, 3 miles from Matta-gonda-palli, near Tali on the Maru-palli high ground, and at Jūghir Karu-palli, 4 miles from Denkani-kōta."

Pennāgaram and Denkani-kōta. "Hogēna-kal especially is the resort of a number of shikaris from Dharmapuri and Pennāgaram. The banks of the Kāvēri at this spot are generally lined with *machāns* from which deer that come to drink in the river are shot at night. On a moonlight night each of these *machāns* will have its tenant." For the European big game is not easy to bag, for want of efficient beaters. Moreover, covert is unlimited and uninterrupted, and hence the game is difficult to locate.

Other Mammals.

Wild pigs abound wherever there are jungles, and are very destructive to crops. They are shot in large numbers by villagers. Good sport can be had by camping at Mallūr and working the jungles round the foot of the Bōda-malais.

The common monkey is a regular pest, especially round Salem and Hosūr. Fruit growers are put to much trouble in warding off their depredations. The Madras Langūr (*Presbytis priamus*) is found in the jungles near Anchetti, and in Dharmapuri Taluk, and is much sought after, its flesh being eaten by natives on account of its supposed medicinal virtues. It is especially common on Manukonda-malai near Toppūr. The nocturnal *Loris lydekkerianus* is also not uncommon.

Madras Langūr. (*Presbytis priamus*).

Hyenas, wolves, red dog, jackals and foxes are found everywhere. It is commonly believed that, if a goat or sheep is pulled down by a wolf, the flock will thrive. Another belief is that a man who kills a wild dog will soon die. Hence wolves and wild dogs are never killed by native shikaris. In the days when Mr. (now Sir Frederick) Price was Sub-Collector, a pack of hounds was kept up at Hosūr, and foxes and jackals afforded good hunting.

Otters are common in the Kāvēri, especially above Hogēna-kal Falls, and may often be seen swimming down-stream, 30 or 40 in a pack. During flood-time they infest the creeks and inlets along the Kāvēri banks. Hares, hedgehogs, porcupines, the mongoose and the pangolin may be met with all over the District.

Small Game.

Though not a famous shooting District, Salem at least provides what is dear to the heart of every true sportsman,—a "mixed bag." The number of small tanks in the District, especially in the northern taluks, is legion. These tanks are visited in the cold season by numbers of teal and duck, and the latter, owing to the coolness of the Mysore plateau and the Bāramahāl, seem to defer their migration till later than is the case in other plain districts. Most of these tanks are not so big as to render the duck inaccessible. Besides duck and teal of all varieties in the tanks, the wet lands irrigated by the tanks and on the foreshore frequently

CHAP. I. FAUNA.

contain a fair sprinkling of snipe. In the dry fields that must be crossed to reach the tank, a quail is seen, now and again, to bustle out of a field of gram, or from a tuft of grass on the field margin. On the stretches of uncultivated, and often rocky, uplands lying between the villages, partridges, sand-grouse, plover, occasionally a hare or two, and sometimes florican are to be found. The bushes lying along dry water-courses afford a shelter to which they betake themselves at the first alarm. Bustards may be seen in pairs along the Kāvēri banks when the water is low. Woodcock visit the higher hill ranges in small numbers in the cold weather. Green and blue pigeon, pea-fowl, spur-fowl and jungle-fowl may be added to the list. In short, most of the feathered species characteristic of South India are met with in the District.

Snakes.

Snakes are represented by no less than 48 species.[1] None of these are peculiar to the District, but *Lachesis macrolepis* has hitherto been recorded only from the Āna-malais, Palnis and Shevaroys; possibly it occurs on the Kolli-malais and other hills of the District. Only three species of poisonous snakes are common, namely, the cobra, Russell's viper and the common green viper. The krait (*Bungarus candidus*) is less common than elsewhere; the other poisonous species are rare. Some of the harmless species bear an extraordinarily close resemblance to some of the deadliest, for example, the young python or "rock snake" and *Eryx conicus* to the Russell's viper; the rat snake (*Zamenis mucosus*) to the cobra; and some of the *Lycodons* to the dreaded krait; the harmless species in each case being much more numerous than the poisonous ones. The reported human death-roll from snake-bite in Salem District between 1885 and 1906 was 3,499, an average of about 160 annually. The average number of reported deaths among cattle is 50 per annum.

---

[1] The following list has been compiled by Mr. Robert Foulkes; *Typhlops braminus; T. beddomii; T. acutus; Python molurus; Eryx conicus; Eryx johnii; Silybura ocellata; S. ellioti; S. urevis; S. nigra; S. nitida; S. rubrolineata; S. arcticeps; Plectrurus perroteti; Xylophis perroteti; Lycodon striatus; L. travancoricus; L. aulicus; Hydrophobus nympha; H. gracilis; Ablabes calamaria; Simotes arnensis; Oligodon venustus; O. brevicauda; O. affinis; Polycdontophis subpunctatus; Zamenis mucosus; Z. fasciolatus; Tropidonotus beddomii; T. stolatus; T. piscator; T. plumbicolor; Helicops schistosus; Dipsas trigonata; Dryophis dispar; D. mycterizans; D. pulverulentus; Hypsirhina enhydris; Callophis trimaculatus; Hemibungarus nigrescens* (coral snake); *Bungarus* † *candidus; Naia tripudians* †; *Naia bungarus* †; *Echis carinata; Vipera russellii* †; Russell's viper or "duboia" †; *Lachesis macrolepis* †; *L. strigatus* †; *L. gramineus.*

Note.—Those marked with a † are "poisonous."

CHAP. I. FAUNA. Fish.

Mahseer[1] frequent the waters of the Kāvēri below the Hogēna-kal Falls, but they are very shy. Carnatic Carp (*Barbus carnaticus*, Tam. sel-kendai) and Red Carp (*Labeo fimbriatus*, Tam. ven-kendai) abound in the Kāvēri and prawns are common. The chief fishing centres on the Kāvēri are at Sōlappādi and near Erode. In the rainy season, when the tanks are full, Kāvēri fish find their way up the tributary streams and are to be found in tanks fed by these streams, many miles from the Kāvēri itself.

In the larger tanks, especially in the big tank at Bārūr, the fresh-water shark (*Wallago attu*, Tam. vālai) attains considerable size. In minor streams and tanks several species of carp are to be found, e.g., *Labeo kontius* (Tam. karumani or karumuli-kendai), "Chilwa" (Tam. velicchai, three or four species), *L. ariza* (Tam. kolarinjan), *L. calbasu*, *L. boga*, *Barbus melanostigma*, *B. vittatus*, *B. dorsalis*, *B. micropogon*, *B. pinnauratus*, *B. dubius*, *B. bovanicus*. Murral (*Ophiocephalus marulius*, Tam. viral), Black Murral (*O. striatus*, Tam. kuravai), Loach (*Lepidocephalichthys thermalis*, Tam. asarai), "scorpion fish" (*Saccobranchus fossilis*, Tam. kelutti) and *Silundia gangetica* (Tam. ponatti), are all of local commercial importance. During the breach in the Grand and Lower Anaikats in 1909–10, "Hilsa" (*Clupea ilisha*) were traced as far up as Hogēna-kal. *Catla buchanani* were introduced into the Bārūr Tank in 1910–11 by the Fishery Department. Eel (*Anguilla bengalensis*, Tam. vilangu) and the sand-eel or spine-eel (*Mastacembelus armatus*, Tam. aral) are sometimes caught in the anaikat pools of Āttūr Taluk.

---

[1] For the note which follows I am indebted to Sir Frederick Nicholson, K.C.I.E.

APPENDIX TO CHAPTER I.

References.

1. Memoirs of the Geological Survey of India, Vol. IV, Part 2. "On the geological structure of portions of the districts of Trichinopoly, Salem and South Arcot, Madras, included in sheet No. 79 of the Indian Atlas; by William King, Junior, and R. Bruce Foote."

2. Memoirs of the Geological Survey of India, Vol. XII—The Geological Features of the Southern Mahratta Country and adjacent Districts; by R. B. Foote.

3. Memoirs of the Geological Survey of India, Vol. XXVIII, Part 2, pages 119 to 249.
"The Charnockite Series."

4. Memoirs of the Geological Survey of India, Vol. XXX, pp. 103 to 168, with map facing page 168.
Geology of the neighbourhood of Salem, with special reference to Leschenault de la Tour's observations; by T. H. Holland.

5. Records of the Geological Survey of India, Vol. XXIV, pp. 157 to 200.
Lacroix; "Gneissose rocks of Salem and Ceylon."

6. Records; Geological Survey of India, Vol. XXV, pp. 135 to 159.
Preliminary Report on the Iron Ores and Iron-Industries of the Salem District, by Thomas H. Holland.

7. Records; Geological Survey of India, Vol. XXIX, Part 2, 1896.
(*a*) Preliminary notes on some Corundum localities in the Salem and Coimbatore districts, Madras; by C. S. Middlemiss, pp. 39 to 50.
(*b*) Notes on the Ultra-basic Rocks and derived minerals of the Chalk (magnesite) hills and other localities near Salem, by C. S. Middlemiss, pp. 32 to 38.

8. (*a*) Records; Geological Survey of India, Vol. XXX, pp. 16 to 42.
On some Norite and associated Basic Dykes and Lava-flows in Southern India; by T. H. Holland.
(*b*) Records; Geological Survey of India, Vol. XXX, pp. 118 to 122.
Report on some trial excavations for Corundum near Palakod, Salem District; by C. S. Middlemiss.

9. Report on the Kolar Gold Field, and its Southern Extension; by P. Bosworth Smith, Esq., F.G.S., Government Press, Madras, 1889.

10. Manual of the Geology of India; R. H. Oldham (ed. 1893).

CHAPTER II.

HISTORY.

A. PREHISTORIC. — Neoliths — Neolithic Factory — Iron Age. B. HISTORY.— General character of Salem History. I. ANCIENT HISTORY.— (1) Mauryas, (2) Romans. II. PALLAVA PERIOD.—The Pallavas—Nandivarman Pallavamalla. — Disruption—(1) Ganga-Pallavas—(2) Nolamba-Pallavas—(3) Bānas —(4) Western Gangas. III. FEUDAL PERIOD.—Character of the Period— Govinda III., 783—814 A.D.—Amōghavarsha I., 814—877 A.D.—Rāshtrakūta Decline—Tiru-Parambiyan—The Chōla Expansion, Āditya I.— Parāntaka I.—Nolamba Aggression—Fall of Bānas.—Revolution in Talakād —Krishna III., 940—956 A.D.—Takkōlam, c. 950 A.D.—Rāshtrakūta Collapse. IV. CHOLA ASCENDENCY.—Rājarāja I.—Chōla-Chālukyan Duel— Chōla Administration in the 11th Century. V. THE HOYSALA EMPIRE.— The 12th Century—Hoysala Conquest of Gangavādi—War of Pāndyan Succession—Adigaimāns of Dharmapuri—Collapse of Kalyāni Chālukyas— Ballāla II.—Hoysala-Pāndyan Duel—Vira Rāmanātha—The Muhammadan Cataclysm. VI. VIJAYANAGAR.—Founding of Vijayanagar—First Dynasty— Revolution—Third Dynasty—Talikōta, 1565 A.D. VII. 1565—1761.—After Talikōta—Dissolution—(1) Rise of Mysore—(2) Rise of Madura—Tirumala Nāyaka—Poligārs of the Marches—Madura-Mysore Duel—Bijāpur and Golconda intervene—Kantirava Narasa Rāja—Ascendency of Mysore— Chikka Dēva Rāja—The Marāthas— Reconquest—The Mughals— Break up of Mughal Empire—The Cuddapah Nawābs—Rise of Haidar Ali and the British. VIII. THE MYSORE WARS.—First Mysore War, 1767-9—Marātha Advance—English Occupation of Bāramahāl—Haidar's Invasion of the Bāramahāl—Āmbūr—Haidar's Retirement from the Bāramahāl—January to August 1768—Col. Joseph Smith's Invasion of the Bālāghāt—Col. Wood's Campaign—Junction of Smith and Wood—Wood's Disasters, November 1768—Haidar's Invasion of the Carnatic—Second Mysore War, 1780-84— Third Mysore War, 1790-92—General Medow's Campaign, 1790—Maxwell's Advance—Campaign of Cornwallis, 1791—Pennāgaram—Krishnagiri—Close of the War—Interlude, 1792-99—Fourth Mysore War—1799. IX. DISTRICT GARRISONS.

A. PREHISTORIC.

NEITHER eoliths nor palæoliths have hitherto been found in Salem District. Implements of the later Stone Age are on the other hand abundant, and their workmanship shows a higher finish than do the neoliths of the Deccan.[1]

Neolithic implements have been found on the Shevaroys, the Kalrāyans, the Kolli-malais, Vattala-malais, Mēlagiris and on the Guttirāyan. They do not occur in the plains. The commonest implements are celts and hammer-axes, the former with sharp cutting edges, the latter blunt. Mr. Bruce Foote's collection in the Madras Museum includes no less than 70 celts from Salem District, 5 hammer-axes, 3 "slick-stones"[2], one pestle and a

[1] For the information on neoliths, I am mainly indebted to the late Mr. R. Bruce Foote.

[2] Or "slacking stones," for putting a gloss on cloth.

CHAP. II. A. PREHISTORIC.

biconical stone perhaps representing a phallus. No scrapers or spindles have yet been discovered, and there is nothing to show what neolithic man ate, and how he was clothed; the "slickstones", however, indicate that the art of weaving was not unknown. The favourite materials for implements are hypersthene-granite, diorite and diabase. Except at the Bargūr "Factory" no neoliths have been found *in situ*, and no ancient habitation site has yet been traced. The implements are turned up by the plough of the modern Malaiyāli, gathered into shrines, and worshipped as gods. A few bits of neolithic pottery have been found on the Shevaroys; some of these fragments have been ground into circular discs about two inches in diameter, and these were probably used as pawns in some game.

Neolithic Factory.

Near Bargūr in Krishnagiri Taluk an interesting discovery has been made by Messrs. R. Bruce Foote and P. Bosworth Smith. "To the east of Varatana-palli, about two miles north of the 149th milestone on the Madras-Bangalore Trunk Road, there is a large doleritic dyke which seems to be a continuation of the 'Mysore mine trap-dyke'. Under the temple hill here it will be seen that the dyke branches into two veins of about equal size. The rock, which forms the two small branches, is a fairly coarse-grained dolerite, giving a hackly fracture, but at the junction of these two, where the dyke rises in a small hillock, the vein, although more than three times the width, is composed of an exceedingly fine-grained stone, having a highly conchoidal fracture, so much so that the stone has been used largely for hatchets, etc., by the old palæolithic men, and specimens that have evidently come from this vein can be found on many of the durgams round about. From the number of flakes and "wasters" found on the hillock, it can be readily seen that this has been an old chipping ground."[1]

The workmanship of these Bargūr celts is very crude; they are merely chipped, and neither ground nor polished. Mr. Bruce Foote concludes that they were probably rejecta, left behind because too bad in form to be worth advancing to a second, third and fourth stage.

Iron Age.

Relics of the Iron Age are abundant, but they have not been systematically investigated. A monograph by the Rev. Maurice Phillips, published in 1872, is the most recent work on the subject. Dr. Phillips classes the tumuli as (1) cromlechs[2], or tumuli lined

---

[1] P. Bosworth Smith's *Report on the Kolar Gold Field and its Southern Extension*; Government Press, Madras, 1889, pp. 20-21.

[2] The use of the word "cromlech" is not here strictly accurate, the term being properly confined to circles of upright stones.

with four perpendicular stone slabs, in the shape of a cist or box, and (2) cairns, or tumuli which have no internal lining of stone. Some cairns contain large earthen urns, others have none. In outward appearance cairns and cromlechs are alike. "They present themselves to the eye as mounds of earth and small stones of various sizes; circular in shape, and often surrounded with circles of large stones. They measure from 3′ to 20′ in diameter, and from 1′ to 4′ in height. Very often in the stone circles, four large stones opposite the four points are seen towering above the others; and in the case of cromlechs the entrance is from the east.

"After clearing away the mound and stones, it is found generally, but not invariably, that the mouth of the tumulus is covered with a stone slab varying in size from 2′ long by 2′ broad and 4″ thick, to 9′ long by 6′ broad and 14″ thick."

"Cromlechs" generally contain small urns and iron implements but no bones except very small pieces which appear charred. The chambers vary much in size. Some of them are as small as 3′ long, 2′ wide, and 2′ deep; and others are as large as 5′ long, 3½′ wide, and 4′ deep. The large urns found in the cairns invariably contain human bones and small vessels; and very often some iron implements and ornaments. They are hardly large enough to contain the body of a full-grown man, though placed in a sitting posture, with the legs and thighs drawn up, and the head bent downwards between the knees, as is sometimes found in tumuli in Europe. If, therefore, full-grown men were buried in them, the body must have been either cut up, or partly burnt, before interment. The position of the bones in layers, one upon the other, seems to indicate the same conclusion. The cairns which contain no urns are the most barren in results. In some of them nothing is found; and in others only small urns with small bits of iron, the crumblings of some instruments; and small pieces of bones which look like the remnants of cremation.

The large urns are so brittle that they invariably fall to pieces by their own weight as soon as the surrounding earth is moved. They very much resemble the large chatties or *sāls* now used by the Hindus to hold water or grain in their houses. Some vessels are red and some black; some are red inside and black outside and *vice versâ*. The surface of some has been polished by rubbing it with the mucilaginous juice of *Abutilon indicum*, a process still in vogue in India. The ornaments found are round and oval beads of different sizes and colour, which must have been worn by women as necklaces and bracelets. According to Dr. Hunter they are made of carnelian ornamented with a pure white enamel of considerable thickness, which has been let into the stone by

CHAP. II. A. PREHISTORIC.

grinding the pattern, filling in probably with oxide of tin and exposing the stone to heat. The enamel is very hard, cannot be touched with a knife, and is not acted upon by strong nitric acid. The iron implements most commonly found are knives or short swords, from 12″ to 22″ in length, but they occur in such a crumbling state, that it is difficult to procure one unbroken.

These tumuli are, as elsewhere in South India, popularly associated with the Pāndava brothers, and are known as Pāndava-Kuli or Pāndava-Kōvil; terms as valueless historically as the epithet "Cyclopæan" in Greece, or as the "Nimrod" legends in Babylonia. With the usual inconsistency of legend, the cairns are also said to have been built by dwarfs, a span or cubit in height, who were endowed with the strength of giants. Pāndava "pits" and "shrines" are found all over the District, notably on either side of the Morappūr-Harūr road, in the vicinity of Kundāni, and on a hill near Gummalāpuram. Some urns were discovered at Mundagambādi when the Yercaud Ghat road was constructed, and a bill-hook about 2½′ long was found with them.

B. HISTORY. General character of Salem History.

The History of South India is the record of a never-ending struggle between the peoples of the Deccan plateau and the peoples of the south, an unceasing ebb and flow of nations. The border-line between these contending forces is formed by the Eastern Ghāts, which run in an irregular line from east to west, from Kālahasti and the Tirupati Hills of Chittoor District to the Nilgiris and the Pālghāt Gap. It is on this border-line that Salem District is situated, and the history of the District is essentially the history of a march land. Moreover, the physical barrier of the Kalrāyan-Shevaroy mountain ranges has been in the past of vast political importance, and the history of the Bāramahāl is for the most part a thing apart from that of the Talaghāt. Geographically the Talaghāt belongs to the ancient Kongu country, which comprised most of what is now Coimbatore District, together with the taluks of Karūr, Nāmakkal, Salem, Tiruchengōdu and Ōmalūr. Its history is dependent on that of the Chōla country (Trichinopoly and Tanjore), and in a less degree on that of the western districts of the present state of Mysore. The history of the Bāramahāl, on the other hand, is dependent on that of the ancient Tondai-mandalam[1] (the present South Arcot, Chingleput, and North Arcot Districts) and, almost as intimately, on that of the eastern districts of Mysore, and the hinterland to the north of them (Cuddapah, Anantapur, and even Bellary). Hence it is that Salem District has never formed a political entity, and therefore

---

[1] See below, p. 46 for an explanation of the name Tondai-mandalam.

claims no separate history of its own. Wedged between the Deccan and the plains, it has owned allegiance in turn to Pallava, Chōla, and Pāndya, to Manyakheta[1], Dorasamudra and Vijayanagar. Ruled at one time by the Viceroy of a distant Emperor, at another by his feudatory vassals; placed on the highway of conquering and vanquished armies; plundered again and again by Pathān and Marātha freebooters, and by local adventurers ever ready to profit by the weakness of a suzerain, fought over by Madura Nāyak and Mysore Odeyār, by Haidar Ali and "John Company"; too poor to support a capital, a dynasty or an army of its own, and too important strategically to be left in peace by a powerful neighbour, Salem District has had a troubled past.

I. ANCIENT HISTORY. (1) Mauryas.

The Edicts of the Mauryan Emperor Asōka (272-231 B.C.) depict the three historic kingdoms of South India, Chōla, Chēra and Pāndya, as friendly independent states. The southernmost Mauryan inscription is at Siddapūr, in the Chitaldrug District of Mysore, and between the Mauryan Empire and the Dravidian Kingdoms a broad belt of forest intervened. It is possible, therefore, that in the Mauryan period Salem District was covered with primeval jungle. If it were worth claiming, it must have belonged to Chēra or Chōla.

(2) Romans.

On the death of Asōka (231 B.C.) his empire crumbled. The three kingdoms of the south did not share in the Mauryan decay. Their mutual wars, no doubt, kept them virile. In 47 B.C., Julius Cæsar was master of Alexandria, and the Romans at once began to develop the Red Sea trade[2]. It is certain that, by the beginning of the first century of the Christian era, a vigorous trade was established between the South Indian Kingdoms and the ports of Egypt. In 47 A.D. a further impetus was given to commerce by the discovery that, taking advantage of the monsoon winds, a shorter and safer course could be steered to the Malabar Coast. The most noteworthy articles of commerce were the pepper of Malabar, the pearls of Ceylon, and beryl. Beryl of the colour approved by Roman society under the Julian Emperors was available at only one spot in the then known world, viz., at Padiyūr in Coimbatore District[2]. Large hoards of Roman coins have been found at Madura, the old Pāndyan capital, at Karūr, the old Chēra capital, and at Pollāchi, Sāvadi-pālaiyam and Vellalūr in Coimbatore. Most of these coins belong to the reigns

---

[1] In G.E. Report for 1902, page 3, Dr. Hultzsch questions the correctness of the generally accepted identification of the Rāshtrakūta capital with Malkhed, in the Nizam's Dominions.

[2] Vide Mr. R. Sewell in J.R.A.S., XXIII, pp. 591-637.

CHAP. II. I. ANCIENT HISTORY.

of Augustus and Tiberius, a few to Claudius and Caligula. It is clear that a regular trade route existed from Madura to Coimbatore via the Kāvēri valley. Hoards of Roman coins have also been found in the neighbourhood of Bangalore.[1] It is not known what trade the Romans had with the Deccan at this period, or whether the traffic thither passed via Coimbatore. In any case, it is certain that, in the first century A.D., Salem was touched on the south, the west and the north by peaceful, prosperous states, and though it is unlikely that the trade routes actually passed through Salem District, the country must at least have profited indirectly.

It is in this period that some scholars have placed the golden age of Tamil literature, the age of the Tamil Sangam or Academy, when Paranar, Kapilar, Tiruvalluvar (the author of the Kural) and a host of other literary luminaries flourished. Not the least among them was the poetess Avvaiyār, who flourished under the patronage of Adiyamān Nedumān Anji of Tagadūr.[2] It was then that the Chēra King Senguttuvan ruled from his capital at Vanji, on the West Coast at the mouth of the Periyār, his dominion extending into the Kongu country, and the Kolli-malais were the seat of Government of the Chēra prince Māntharam Sōral Irumporai. It is true that the existence of a matured Tamil civilization in the first century A.D. is not supported by epigraphic records, but it is difficult to assign the zenith of Tamil literature to any other period, and it is hardly conceivable that the coins of the Julian Emperors of Rome would be distributed so freely over a country not well advanced in culture.[3]

II. THE PALLAVAS.

On the death of Nero a change came over Roman society. Luxury waned, manners became simpler, and the eastern trade declined. The History of South India remains a blank till the 4th century A.D., when the Pallavas are found firmly established in the east coast country, known for centuries after as Tondaimandalam.[4] The Pallavas appear to have ruled from several

---

[1] *Coimbatore Manual*, II, p. 363, *Indian Antiquary* V, p. 237. [2] Dharmapuri.

[3] See *Ancient India*, p. 336 sq. and *The Tamils Eighteen Hundred Years Ago*, pp. 100 and 107.

[4] The modern districts of North and South Arcot and Chingleput. Tondaman (=Tonda king). "Tonda" may have been a country or a people. The tradition ascribing the origin of the word to the administration of the Pallava country by a Chōla prince Adondai, born to king Kokkilli by a Nāga princess, is a late invention to account for the origin of the Pallavas. "At the time when this story was invented, the Pallavas were probably looked upon as the outcome of a mixture of Chōla and Nāga blood."—Mr. V. Venkayya in G.O. No. 1070 Rev. of 1904. Cf. a note by Mr. S. Krishnaswami Ayyangar in "Celebrities in Tamil Literature"—*Ind. Ant.* Vol. XXXVII, p. 235.

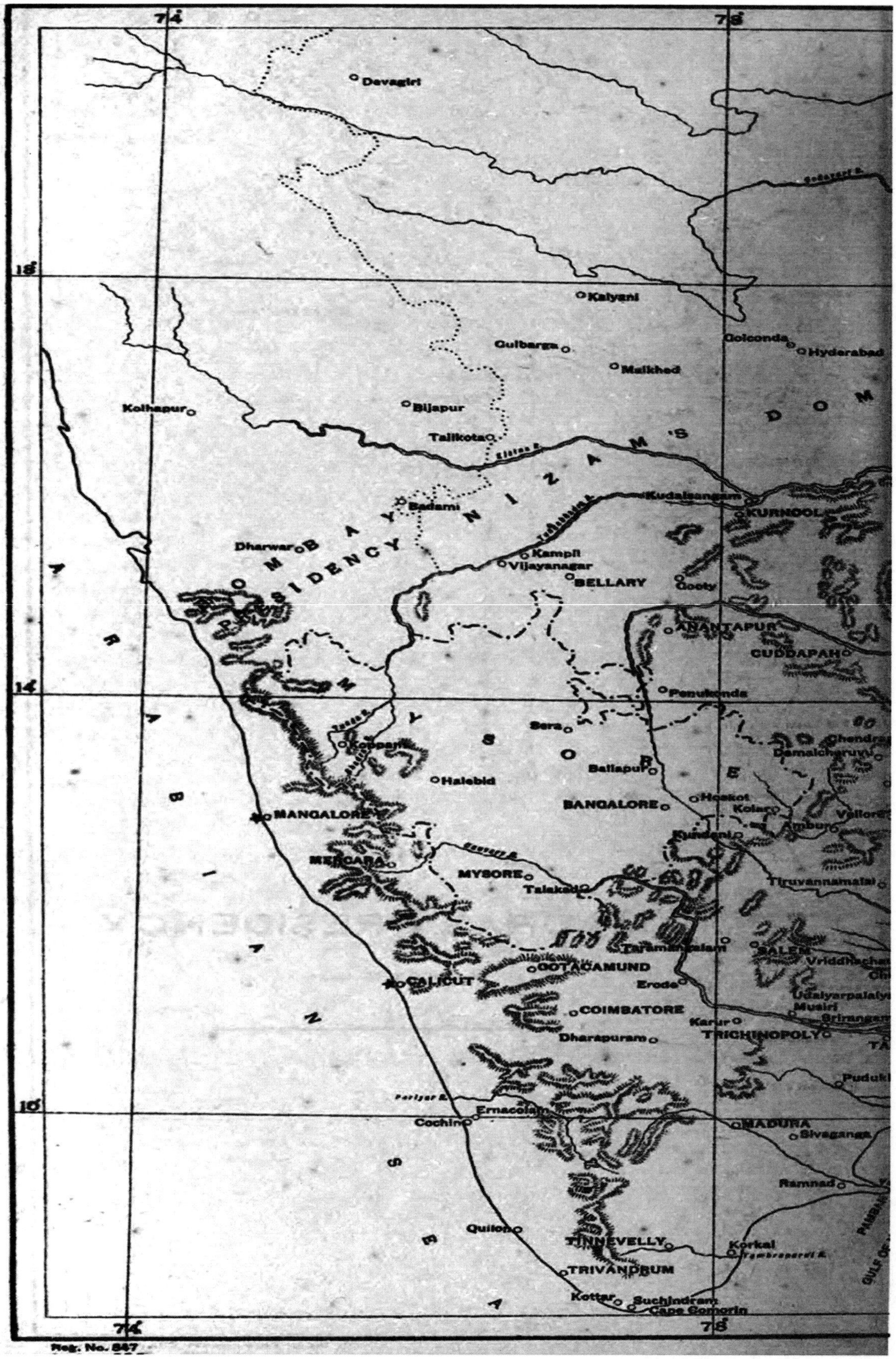

74
78
18
14
10
Devagiri
Godavari R.
Kalyani
Golconda
Hyderabad
Gulbarga
Malkhed
Kolhapur
Bijapur
Talikota
Krishna R.
NIZAM'S DOM
Kudalsangam
KURNOOL
Badami
BOMBAY PRESIDENCY
Dharwar
Kampli
Vijayanagar
BELLARY
Gooty
ANANTAPUR
CUDDAPAH
Penukonda
MYSORE
Sera
Halebid
Ballapur
BANGALORE
Hoskot
Kolar
Chendra
Vellore
Tiruvannamalai
MANGALORE
MERCARA
Kaveri R.
MYSORE
Talakad
Taramangalam
SALEM
OOTACAMUND
CALICUT
Erode
COIMBATORE
Udaiyarpalaiya
Musiri
Srirangam
Karur
TRICHINOPOLY
Dharapuram
Pudukk
Periyar R.
Ernaculam
Cochin
MADURA
Sivaganga
Ramnad
Quilon
TINNEVELLY
Korkai
Tambraparni R.
TRIVANDRUM
Kottar
Suchindram
Cape Comorin
ARABIAN SEA
GULF OF

Reg. No. 847

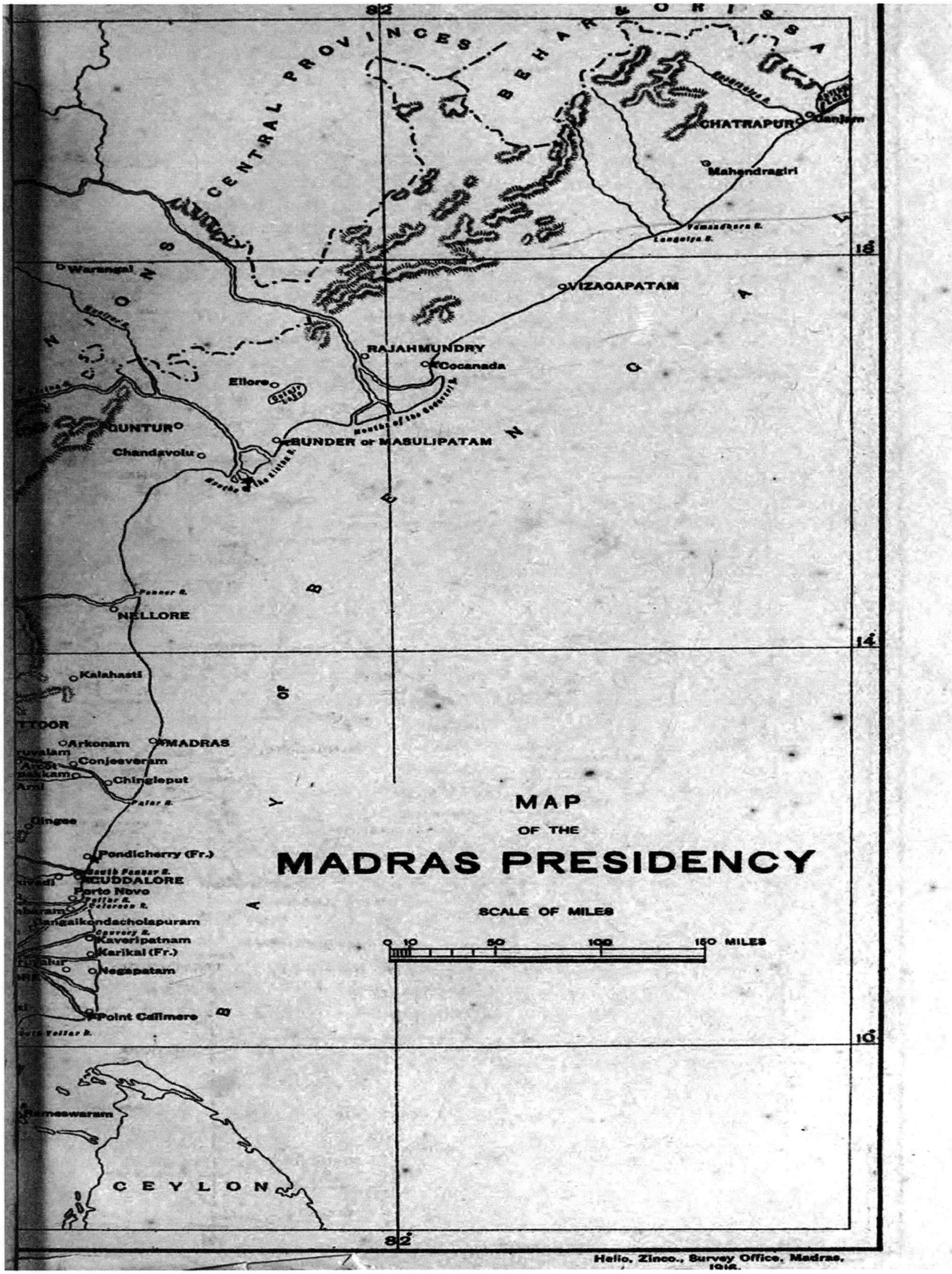

Helio. Zinco., Survey Office, Madras, 1916.

different capitals, among them Kānchi, Vēngi[1] on the Godavari, and Palakkada. Apparently the two latter were independent of each other, and the king of Kānchi exercised some sort of overlordship over both. It has been surmised with some probability that "the Pallava power was superimposed upon the ancient territorial states much in the same way as the Marātha power was in later times" and "was confined ordinarily to the levying of tribute and blackmail." Some such hold the Pallavas may have exercised over Salem District, though there is no evidence of Pallava rule till the eighth century A.D., when the legitimate monarchs of Kānchi, discredited by their expulsion from the Deccan at the hands of the Bādāmi Chālukyas, were ousted from the succession by Nandi-varman Pallava-malla, the scion of a collateral branch of the royal family. "Chosen by his subjects," he had to fight for the sovereignty, and owed his ultimate success to the devotion of his general Udayachandra, who rescued him when beset by the "Dramila Princes," adherents no doubt, of the legitimate line, whose leader Chitramāya was slain by Udayachandra's own hand. This soldier won victories for his master's armies from Tinnevelly to Nellore. His name is peculiarly interesting from its connection with the village of Udayēndiram on the Pālār, on the border of Tiruppattūr Taluk, just within the limits of North Arcot District. The "Udayēndiram Plates"[2] may be claimed as the earliest historical record of Salem District, and they prove that, early in the eighth century, part, at least, of the District was within the pale of civilization.

Nandivarman Pallava-malla.

Nandi-varman Pallava-malla lived to see at least the 50th year of his reign. For 22 years he preserved his Empire intact; but soon after 733 A.D. his kingdom was invaded by Vikramāditya II, grandson of the monarch of the same name, who restored the Chālukya Empire and expelled the Pallavas from the Deccan. The invader entered Kānchi, but did not sack the city; instead he contented himself with setting up a pillar of victory "near the ocean," and, after granting heaps of gold to the principal Siva temple in the place, he withdrew.

Disruption.

The Bādāmi Chālukyas did not long survive their victory, for in 757 A.D. their Empire was completely overthrown by the Rāshtrakūtas of Mālkhed. The defeat of Nandi-varman Pallava-malla also marks the end of Pallava greatness, and after his death all that remained of the Pallava Empire was divided between the dynasty known as the Ganga-Pallavas, apparently the direct

[1] Afterwards the capital of the Eastern Chālukyas.

[2] See *S.I.I.*, Vol. II, pt. II, p. 361.

CHAP. II.
II. THE PALLAVAS.

descendants [1] of Pallava-malla, and the "Later Pallavas," who may represent either the successors of Chitramāya, who led the "Dramila Princes" and was slain by Nandi-varman Pallava-malla's general Udayachandra, or the descendants of Paramēsvara-varman II, whose throne Pallava-malla had usurped.[2]

(1) Ganga-Pallavas.

The kings of the so-called Ganga-Pallava Dynasty are distinguished by the prefix "Kō" (=King) and "Vijaya", as part of their proper names, and, as in the case of the Pallava kings, their names terminate in "varman [3]". Though the area over which they ruled was large, their civilization must have been inferior to that of their predecessors, most of the records being set up to commemorate the death of heroes in cattle raids. Their records are found in the districts of Tanjore, Trichinopoly, Chingleput, the two Arcots, as far north as Gudimallam, and in the north-west of Salem District.[4] The Chōlas seem to have acknowledged their overlordship. There are several names, however, of rulers bearing the titles of this dynasty whom it is not easy to locate. At Hanumanta-puram, near Pennāgaram, in Dharmapuri Taluk, there are two inscriptions of the 17th year of one Vijaya Īsvara-varman, whose name is also mentioned in an inscription at Hebbani near Mulbāgal.[5] The "Rāya-kōta Plates[6]" are dated in the 14th year of one Kō-Vijaya-Skandasishya-Vikrama-varman and record a grant made at the request of "Mahāvali-Vānarāja", i.e., the Bāna king. There is yet another name, that of Kō-Vijaya-Narasimha-varman[7], whose inscriptions have been found at Kīl-Muttugūr, in

---

[1] According to the unpublished Vēlūr-pālaiyam Plates, "Danti-varman" (see below note 3) was a son of Pallava-malla. J.R.A.S., 1911, p. 522.

[2] The inscriptions of the "Later Pallavas" occur in the districts of Tanjore, Chingleput and the two Arcots. The political relationship between the Ganga-Pallavas and the "Later Pallavas" cannot be satisfactorily made out, and it is possible, though at present evidence is wanting, that the two lines may be identical. No date can be fixed for the "Later Pallavas," and there is no evidence to show that their rule extended into Salem District. See J.R.A.S., 1911, p. 522, and G.E. Report, 1910–11.

[3] (i) Danti-varman reigned at least 51 years.
(ii) Nandi-varman " 62 "
(iii) Nripatunga-varman " 26 "
(iv) Aparājita " 18 "

There was also a Kampa-varman whose reign lasted at least 23 years. He appears to have been a son of Nandi-varman and brother of Nripatunga-varman. He may have been a co-regent with or independent of his brother. It is certain that the reigns of some of these rulers overlapped.

[4] G E. 1904, p. 7, paragraph 13.

[5] *Ep. Ind.* VII, p. 24; cf. *Ep. Carn.* Vol. X, Kolar, No. 211 of Mulbāgal Taluk.

[6] *Ep. Ind.* V, p. 49.

[7] *Ep. Ind.* IV, p. 360 and VII, p. 22.

North Arcot, and also in Mulbāgal Taluk[1]; one of these mentions the chief of Tagadūr-Nād, the modern Dharmapuri.[2]

(2) Nolamba-Pallavas.

Another relic of the Pallava Empire survived in the territory north and east of the Talakād Gangas, namely the Nolamba-Pallavas, descendants, perhaps, of Pallavas who settled in the Deccan after the sack of Bādāmi by Narasimha-varman I (642–655 A.D.) The territory occupied by these settlers became known as the "Nolamba-vādi 32,000," the nominal number of villages comprised within it.

(3) Bānas.

Another principality which attained a precarious independence with the fall of Kānchi and Bādāmi was that of the Bānas, whose territory is described as being Vadugavaliyin-merku, a term which may mean either "the country to the west of the Āndhra Road," or "the Western portion of the Āndhra Road."[3] Vadugu-vali was the name of the district over which the Bānas ruled. Their territory certainly extended over part of Mysore and part of Salem and North Arcot and their inscriptions are found as far north as Nellore. Their capital was probably at Tiruvalam in Gudiyāttam Taluk of North Arcot, anciently called Vānapuram. They were essentially guardians of the Ghāts. A rock inscription of one of their kings occurs at Rāya-kōta,[4] and, from the "Rāya-kōta Plates" above referred to, it would appear that the Bārama-hāl was ruled, in the ninth century by Bāna kings under the suzerainty of some collateral branch of the Ganga-Pallava family.

(4) Western Gangas.

Advantage had been taken of the confusion into which South India was plunged on the fall of the Bādāmi Empire by a prince

---

[1] Ep. Carn. Vol. X, (Kolar) No. 227 of Mulbāgal Taluk.

[2] Mr. Krishna Sastri suggests (p. 63 of G.E. Report for 1910–11) that "the major portion of the North Arcot district, with the bordering portions of Salem and Kolār were, even in the earlier Pallava times, under the sway of local chiefs who claimed, in a way, some distant relationship with the ruling dynasty of the Pallavas," that in the confusion that followed the usurpation of Nandi-varman Pallava-malla, they tried to assert their independence, with Rāshtrakūta aid, and that under Nripatunga, or perhaps in his father's time, they succeeded in establishing themselves as a dominant dynasty.

[3] The strategic importance of the Bāna territory can be abundantly illustrated from history, e.g., the defeat of the Nawab Dost Ali Khan at Dāmal-cheruvu in 1740, the defeat of Anwar-ud-din in 1754, and most of the campaigns of Haidar Ali and Tipu against the British.

[4] The Bānas traced their descent from the demon Mahābali, but their connection with the Seven Pagodas (Mahābali-puram) is "due to nothing but fancy, because there is no evidence whatever to show that their territories extended so far." The Seven Pagodas, Māmalla-puram, or Mahāmalla-puram, were evidently called after the Pallava Narasimha-varman, one of whose titles was "Mahāmalla" the "Great Wrestler"—See G.E. 1904, para. 26 and Rice, *Mysore Gazetteer* I 300 sq.

CHAP. II. II. THE PALLAVAS. (4) Westren Gangas.

of Ganga race by name Sivamāra. He was the hereditary ruler of what was known as the "Kongal Nād Eight Thousand." There are records in Mysore which may be assigned to him, one of which mentions him solely by name, without any regal title of any kind, but uses a technical expression which stamps him as holding a rank and authority considerably greater than those of any mere local Governor, and others which speak of him as the "Konguni King," a term applied to all his successors. His date has been tentatively fixed as 755–765 A.D. He was succeeded by his son (or grandson) Srīpurusha Muttarasa.[1] His title at first was the same as his father's, but there is evidence on his inscriptions that he gradually felt his way to independence. He is known later by the title "Mahārāja" and finally he adopts the full titles of a paramount king "Mahārājādhirāja" and "Paramēsvarā." The territory he ruled over coincided more or less with the south-eastern portion of what is now Mysore State; it was technically known as the "Gangavādi 96,000" i.e., a province of 96,000 villages; his capital was Talakād, a sand-buried city on the banks of the Kāvēri near Kollegāl. His reign was a long one of at least 42 years, and his date may be tentatively fixed as 764–805 A.D.

III. FEUDAL PERIOD.

The period extending from the middle of the eighth century to the end of the tenth may be called the Feudal period. It opens with the subversion of the Bādāmi Chālukyas by the Rāshtrakūtas, and closes with the subversion of the Rāshtrakūtas by the Chālukyas of Kalyāni. The Ganga-Pallavas struggle for existence for a century and a half, and finally fall before the Chōlas. Chōla expansion is checked for a time by the Rāshtrakūtas and their feudatories, but the fall of the Rāshtrakūtas is followed by the conquests of Rājarāja the Great, and by the end of the tenth century the political forces of South India are once more concentrated in the hands of two hostile Emperors.

Character of the period.

The Feudal period may be conveniently divided into three phases, each phase dependent on the tone of Rāshtrakūta rule:—

(1) A phase of war and consolidation coincident with the rule of Gōvinda III, 783–814.

(2) A peace phase, answering to the long reign of Amōghavarsha I, 815–878 A.D.

---

[1] Two Vatteluttu inscriptions (G.E. Nos. 211 and 212 of 1910) have recently been discovered at Odda-patti, near Bommidi Railway Station, dated in the 27th and 7th year respectively of Sripurusha. As Odda-patti is situated almost in the extreme south-east corner of the Bāramahāl, it would follow that Sripurusha's sway extended over the greater part, if not the whole, of the northern taluks.

(3) A phase of anarchy answering to the period of Rāshtrakūta decline (878–973 A.D.), with a short period of revival under Krishna III (940–968).

Gōvinda III.

By the beginning of the ninth century the Rāshtrakūta Gōvinda III was master of the Deccan. By establishing his suzerainty over the Western Gangas of Talakād, Gōvinda III indirectly influenced the history of Salem District for the next two centuries. Srīpurusha Muttarasa was not permitted to enjoy his paramount title for long. It is known from Rāshtrakūta records that king Dhruva imprisoned a Ganga prince, and that Gōvinda III "released him from a long captivity and sent him back to his own country." This prince abused his captor's generosity, and Gōvinda III was "compelled to reconquer the Ganga, who through excess of pride stood in opposition to him, and to put him in fetters again." This would be about 810 A.D.

The name of this adventurous prince is not given. It appears that Muttarasa had two sons, the elder Sivamāra II and the younger Rana-vikrama. It is claimed, in the spurious Mannē Grant, that one Sivamāra won a name for himself by victories over the armies of the Rāshtrakūtas, Chālukyas and others, and that he "defeated the countless cavalry of Dhruva which had overrun the whole earth." It is possible that Sivamāra II was entrusted with the command of his father's armies, and during the campaign was defeated and captured by Dhruva, that, on his father's death, he was liberated by Gōvinda III, "to take up the leadership of the Gangas," and was crowned by him as his vassal, (about A.D. 805). It is possible that Sivamāra II, on regaining his throne, rebelled, and that his second captivity let in his younger brother to the Western Ganga succession. If the imprisoned Ganga prince was not Sivamāra II, he must have been Srīpurusha Muttarasa himself, and his assumption of imperial titles would be the immediate cause of his downfall. It is certain that Muttarasa's son, Rana-vikrama, began to reign about 810, and that he was a loyal vassal to the Rāshtrakūta kings. It is also certain that about this time the Western Ganga dominions were divided and that the eastern portion became a separate State under Sivamāra II and his descendants, with their capital at Kōlār.[1]

Amōghavarsha 814-877.

Govinda III was (c. 815-A.D.) succeeded by his son, Amōghavarsha I, whose reign extended to the phenomenal length of 62 years. He was religiously minded, a devout supporter of the

[1] The Kolar Gangas were:—(1) Sivamāra II, (2) Prithivīpati I, (3) Mārasimha, (4) Prithivīpati II Hastimalla.

CHAP. II. III. FEUDAL PERIOD.

Jain faith and a great patron of literature. He enjoyed to the full the fruits of the great wars of Gōvinda III, kept at bay the Eastern Chālukyas, and resigned the sovereignty in extreme old age to his son, the Yuvarāja Krishna II.

The march land enjoyed comparative peace during this reign; it is a period of political marriages, suggestive of the palmy days of mediæval chivalry. An alliance was made between the Ganga-Pallavas and the Rāshtrakūtas, and the Ganga-Pallava king, Nandi-vikrama-varman, whose reign lasted at least 62 years, took to wife the daughter of Amōghavarsha.[1] The Bāna king, Vikramāditya I, acquiesced in the overlordship of the Ganga-Pallavas. The relations between the two branches of the Western Gangas appear amicable. The Kōlār Ganga Sivamāra II was succeeded by his son Prithivīpati I, who seems, like Amōghavarsha and Nandi-vikrama-varman, to have enjoyed a very long reign. His daughter married the Bāna Vikramāditya I, and he was in close alliance with the Ganga-Pallavas. The Talakād-Gangas appear to have enjoyed a period of peace and prosperity under Rana-vikrama (son of Srīpurusha-Muttarasa) and his son Rājamalla (c. 840—871). The latter cemented an alliance with the Nolambas by giving his daughter Jayabbe to the Nolamba king Nolambādhirāja,[1] son of Pallavādhirāja.

Rāshtrakūta Decline.

The death of Amōghavarsha in 877 A.D. marks the beginning of Rāshtrakūta decline, and the weakness of his successors was the signal for unrest in the South.

Tiru-Parambiyam.

The Ganga-Pallava Nandi-vikrama-varman was succeeded by his son Nripatunga, who appears to have been the most successful monarch of his line. It is significant that, during his reign, the Ganga-Pallavas abandoned the Ganga emblems of elephant and swan, and reverted to the bull crest of the ancient Pallavas. He directed his energies towards extending his dominions to the south in the direction of Trichinopoly and Tanjore.

The advance of the Ganga-Pallavas was, however, checked by a counter-movement of the part of the Pāndyans under Varaguna-varman, who ascended the Pāndyan throne in 862–3 A.D.[2] The struggle culminated in a pitched battle, fought at Tiru-Parambiyam near Kumbakōnam, in which Varaguna was confronted by the united forces of the Ganga-Pallavas, under Aparājita, and the Kōlār-Gangas, under Prithivīpathi I; Prithivīpathi I was slain, but Varaguna was routed and the Ganga-Pallavas were saved for a while.

---

[1] *Ep. Ind.* VI, p. 60, cf. *Mysore Gazetteer*, Vol. I, p. 307.

[2] G.E. 1907, p. 67.

The battle of Tiru-Parambiyam was pregnant with results. The ruin of Varaguna paved the way for the Chōla Empire. In about 880 A.D., a prince named Āditya I, ascended the Chōla throne. According to the *Kongu-dēsa-rājākkal*, he conquered Kongu in 894 A.D. The statement is consistent with certain inscriptions [1] copied at Salem and Tiruchengōdu. But his greatest achievement was the invasion of Tondai-mandalam, the defeat of Aparājita and the complete subversion of the Ganga-Pallavas.

Chōla Expansion Āditya I.

In 906-7 Āditya I was succeeded by his son Parāntaka I, a clever statesman and an able soldier. His reign extended to 948 A.D. His inscriptions have been found from Cape Comorin to Kālahasti in Chittoor. His capture of Madura led him to adopt the title "Madirai-Konda," [2] and his records at Salem and Tiruchengōdu, the latest of which is dated in his 37th year, prove that under him the southern portion of Salem District was a settled and orderly province of the Chōla dominions.

Parāntaka I.

Meanwhile the Bāramahāl became the field for Nolamba aggrandisement. Rāja-malla, it will be remembered, had given his daughter Jayabbe in marriage to the Nolamba king, Nolambādhirāja. Their son Mahēndra, a nephew through his mother of Butuga I, succeeded to the Nolamba throne in or before 878-9 A.D. He seems to have been of a turbulent disposition. He waged war on the Bānas, and claims to have destroyed them. He certainly ousted them from the Bāramahāl, for an inscription of his has been found at Dharmapuri, dated 892-3 A.D. and Nolamba rule continued at Dharmapuri till 930-1 A.D., the date of an inscription of Mahēndra's great-grandson Irula.[3]

Nolamba Aggression.

---

[1] The Chōla kings called themselves alternately Rājakēsari-varman and Parakēsari-varman. The latter title was adopted by Parāntaka I, and therefore the former was applicable to Āditya I. The early Chōlas of this dynasty give no other name. The records of the later members of the family usually give a distinctive name. Inscriptions of Rājakēsari-varman are found at Salem (e.g., G.E. Nos. 47 and 49 of 1888) and at Tiruchengōdu (e.g., Nos. 625, 627 and 629 of 1905, dated respectively in the 16th, 14th and 13th regnal years). These are all gifts of gold for feeding Brahmans. It is not unlikely that the Tiruchengōdu inscriptions are of Āditya I.

[2] G.E. Nos. 632, 633, 640 of 1905 give the epithet "Madirai Konda," and are dated respectively in his 37th, 20th and 27th year. They record gifts of gold for temple lamps. There are several other inscriptions of Parakēsari-varman at Tiruchengōdu which may or may not be his. The inscription of "Ko-Parakēsari-varman" in the Sukavanēsvara temple of Salem, dated in the 5th and 6th regnal years, probably belong to him (See G.E. 1888).

[3] G.E., No. 198 of 1910. Mahēndra was succeeded by his son, Ayyappa, two of whose inscriptions occur at Dharmapuri, viz., G.E. Nos. 304 and 305 of 1901, which have been edited by Mr. Krishna Sastri in *Ep. Ind.*, Vol X, pp. 44 sq. Ayyappa was succeeded in turn by his son Anniga, and Anniga by his son Irula. The last of the line was Dilīparasa. See G.E. Report for 1910-11, p. 65.

Fall of the Bānas.

The overthrow of the Ganga-Pallavas by Āditya I deprived the Bānas of their hereditary allies, and the attacks of Mahēndra robbed them of half their territory. Vikramāditya I, the loyal vassal of the Ganga-Pallava Nandi-vikramavarman, was succeeded by his son, Vijayāditya II, whose inscriptions, dated in 897 and 904 A.D. acknowledge no suzerain. His successor, Vikramāditya II, threw in his lot with the Rāshtrakūtas and allied himself with Krishna II. The Kōlār-Gangas were wiser. Prithivīpati I, the hero of Tiru-Parambiyam, was succeeded by his son Mārasimha, of whom little is known. His son, however, Prithivīpati II, otherwise called Hastimalla, boldly threw in his lot with Parāntaka I. Some time prior to 914 A.D. Parāntaka attacked and wiped out the Bāna kingdom, and set up the Kōlār-Ganga Hastimalla as lord over it.[1] The choice was a wise one, for Hastimalla's father's sister had married the Bāna Vikramāditya I. Hastimalla adopted the Bāna black-buck banner and bull crest, and ruled as a faithful Chōla vassal so long as the Chōlas remained paramount.[2] Parāntaka, in his endorsements on the two Udayēndiram Plates of Nandi-varman Pallava-malla, confirmed those ancient Pallava grants, and indicated thereby his ambition that the Chōlas should rebuild the Empire which the Pallavas had lost.

Revolution in Talakād.

There is reason to believe that the policy of Mahēndra was inspired by a revolutionary movement among the Western Gangas in Talakād. Rājamalla was succeeded in about 870 A.D., by his son Butuga I. Butuga I was followed in about 908 A.D. by his son Ereyappa, a prince who is nowhere shown in the inscriptions as Yuvarāja. Perhaps an explanation is found in the fact that in 891–2 a Ganga prince, Rāchēya Ganga by name, was slain in battle by the Nolambas. All the available evidence goes to show that Ereyappa was a close ally of the Nolambas,[3] and hostile to the Rāshtrakūtas, and it is possible that Rāchēya Ganga was an elder son of Butuga I, and that Ereyappa, after the Nolambas had slain his elder brother, took advantage of the temporary weakness of the Rāshtrakūtas to form an alliance with the Nolambas and throw off his allegiance to the paramount power.[4]

---

[1] See Udayēndiram Plates of Nandi-varman Pallava-malla and Hastimalla, *Ep. Ind.* III, p. 142 sq., and S.I.I., Vol. II. pp. 361 and 387.

[2] See also the Sholinghur inscription, *Ep. Ind.* IV, No. 32, p. 221, where Hastimalla is called also Vira-Chōla.

[3] It is interesting to note that Mahēndra himself, his son Ayyapa and his grandson Anniga, all married Ganga princesses.

[4] Butuga I, 870–908

Rāchēya Ganga slain 891–2 ?	Ereyappa, 908–938
Butuga II, 940–953.	Rācha-malla—slain 938–9 by Butuga II.

Krishna III

The above explanation is suggested by what followed on Ereyappa's death, in about 938 A.D. Ereyappa was succeeded by his son Rācha-malla shortly after Krishna III succeeded to the throne. Krishna III at once formed an alliance with one Butuga, who married his elder sister Rēvakka. Within a year of Ereyappa's death, this Butuga had, with Krishna's help, slain his son Rācha-malla, and reigned in his stead. In the language of the inscriptions, Rācha-malla was a poisonous tree which was uprooted, and Butuga II was a pure tree which Krishna III had planted in his place.[1] It is a probable conjecture that this Butuga II was a son of the Rāchēya Ganga slain by the Nolambas in 891-2 A.D., and that the revolution effected by Krishna III was merely the restoration to the Ganga throne of the rightful line which Ereyappa had supplanted.

Takkōlam.

The installation of Butuga II was a skilful stroke of diplomacy on the part of Krishna III. Partly as dowry from his wife and partly in return for the slaying of Rācha-malla, the new Ganga king was entrusted with a large extent of territory.[2] Krishna's confidence in Butuga was not misplaced. With his western flank protected, Krishna III was free to advance southward, and curb the rising ambitions of the Chōlas. The Chōla dominions were invaded, and, within a year (949-950 A.D.), a pitched battle was fought at Takkōlam (near Arkonam), the Chōla forces were routed, and, with Butuga's assistance, the Chōla prince Rājāditya was slain.[3] Hastimalla the Kōlār-Ganga made a virtue of necessity, and became the vassal of the victor.

Rāshtrakūta Collapse.

Krishna III ruled for about 20 years after his great victory at Takkōlam. Butuga II died about 953 A.D. Of his grandson, Rācha Ganga, who appears to have succeeded him, little is known.[4]

About 963 A.D. Mārasimha acceded to the Western Ganga throne, and proved himself the mainstay of the Rāshtrakūta power. One of his first exploits was to crush the turbulent Nolambas; for this service he was rewarded by his suzerain with the Nolambavādi province of 32,000 villages, and he adopted the title Nolamba-kulāntaka, "Death to the Nolamba race." He also acquired the "Santalige 1,000." These acquisitions, together with

[1] *Ep. Ind.* VI, p. 70.

[2] Rēvakka's dowry consisted of the Purigere 38, the Belvola 300, the Kisukād 70 and the Bāginād 70. For killing Rācha-malla Butuga II was awarded the Gangavādi 96,000, in other words he took over *in toto* the Ganga dominions.

[3] For this service Butuga II was rewarded with the Banavase 12,000. See *Ep. Ind.* Vol. VI, p. 57.

[4] Banavase, granted by Krishna III to Butuga II, had to be reconquered from the viceroys to whom Butuga had entrusted it.

CHAP. II. III. FEUDAL PERIOD.

his hereditary dominions, made him one of the most powerful monarchs of South India,[1] and he was able to assist Krishna III substantially in his campaign against Gujarat. But the days of the Rāshtrakūta Empire were numbered. Within a few years of Krishna III's death, the Rāshtrakūta Empire was subverted, in spite of the loyal assistance of Mārasimha, by Taila II, the founder of the Later or Kalyāni Chālukyas. The Western Gangas did not long survive. In 974 Mārasimha abdicated in favour of his son Pānchāla-dēva and "died in the practice of religion at the feet of a Jain teacher named Ajitasēna at Bankapur, starving himself to death by a three days' fast." Pānchāla-dēva attempted to recover independence, but was shortly afterwards defeated and slain by Taila II. A son of Pānchāla-dēva named Rācha-malla succeeded, and an inscription of his shows that he was reigning in 978 A.D. He aimed at independence, and the events that led to his downfall are not known. He was the last of his line. After his death the Ganga dominions seem to have been absorbed in the Chālukya Empire, as it was from the Chālukyas that the Chōlas took Gangavādi.

IV. CHŌLA PERIOD.

Chōla Ascendency. Rājarāja I.

It took nearly fifty years for the Chōlas to recover from the blow dealt them at Takkōlam in 949–950 A.D. In 985, after thirty-five years of prostration and dynastic dissensions, Rājarāja I, the Great,[2] acceded to the Chōla throne. In A.D. 997 the Chālukya Taila died. This event afforded Rājarāja his opportunity, and in the following year he launched on one of the most remarkable campaigns known to history. He overran Gangavādi, Nolambavādi, (Bellary),[3] Coorg, and Vēngi, the capital of the Eastern Chālukyas. By his conquest of Vēngi he put an end to a thirty years' period of anarchy, set up a king of the old Eastern Chālukya line, and shortly afterwards gave his daughter in marriage to the Vēngi Prince Vimalāditya, who afterwards became king. In 1002–3 A.D., he had subdued Ceylon, Quilon and Kalinga. In 1004 his army invaded the Deccan a second time, and his son Rājēndra, the Crown Prince, captured the Western Ganga capital of Talakād. His last recorded exploit was in 1013–4 A.D., and this is probably the year of his death.

The Chōla-Chālukyan Duel.

The history of the eleventh century is mainly a history of the duel between the Chōlas and Western Chālukyas, the details of which do not concern Salem District Though Gangavādi

---

[1] An inscription at Lakshmeswar, in Dharwar District, gives him the paramount title Paramēsvara.

[2] Mummudi Chōla Dēva, King of Three Crowns, i.e., Three Kingdoms. Cf. *Ind. Ant.*, XXII, p. 65.

[3] He could not keep it. It was feudatory to Vikramāditya V. 1009–11. A.D.

changed hands several times, Chōla sovereignty in the District probably remained undisturbed. At the end of the century honours were even between the two contending powers.

CHAP. II. IV. CHŌLA PERIOD.

Chōla administration in the Eleventh Century.

For administrative purposes the Chōla dominions [1] were divided into six provinces called *mandalams*, each of which comprised what was, prior to the conquest, an independent kingdom. Each *mandalam* appears to have been named after an Emperor who conquered it, or Viceroy whose rule over the province was specially distinguished [2]; but the foreign names did not always displace the familiar traditional [3] names. The six *mandalams* were;

(1) Tondai-mandalam otherwise called Jayamgonda-Chōla-mandalam, after Rājādhirājā I. It comprised roughly the Pallava country, i.e., the East Coast plains from the Southern Pennaiyār to its northern namesake;
(2) Chōla-mandalam, the Chōla country proper (Tanjore and Trichinopoly);
(3) Rājarāja-mandalam, the Pāndya and part of the Kērala country (Madura, Tinnevelly, and Travancore);
(4) The Kongu country, otherwise called Adhirājarāja-mandalam or Chōla-Kērala-mandalam;
(5) Gangai-konda-Chōla-mandalam, including the Western portion of the Ganga country;
(6) Nigarili-Chōla-mandalam, embracing the Eastern part of the Ganga country, together with the Bāna kingdom.

The Northern part of Salem fell within Nigarili-Chōla-mandalam, as is proved by inscriptions at Mallāpuram [4] (near Pālakōdu), Tīrta-malai [5] and Tiruppattūr. [6] The Southern part of Salem District was included in Kongu. Kongu comprised the whole of Coimbatore District, as well as the Salem Talaghāt, and was divided into three portions, North, West and South Kongu. The southern limit of Northern Kongu was probably the Kāvēri, the present District of Coimbatore falling within West and South Kongu. In the time of Rājēndra I and Vīra-Rājēndra I, Kongu was known officially as Adhirājarājā-mandalam [7]; under Kulōttunga III it was known as Chōla-Kērala-mandalam, under Vikrama Chōla as Vīra-Chōla-mandalam, a term which was

---

[1] Exclusive of the Vengi country, which remained throughout a dependent ally.

[2] See Mr. S. Krishnaswami Ayyangar's *Ancient India*, p. 174. Cf., however, *Mysore and Coorg from the Inscriptions*, p. 86, and *Mysore Gazetteer*, Vol. I, p. 333. The terms used were frequently changed.

[3] The Chōlas also changed the names of towns they conquered, e.g., Talakād became Rājarājapuram, but the new names did not acquire permanence.

[4] G.E. No. 18 of 1900. [5] G.E. No. 670 of 1905.

[6] G.E. No. 248 of 1909. [7] *S.I.I.*, Vol. III, page 31.

CHAP. II. IV. CHŌLA PERIOD.

continued under the Pāndyan[1] regime, and even into the time of Achyuta Rāya and Sadāsiva.[2]

Some *mandalams* were in turn divided into *kōttams*, and the *kōttams* into *nāds*, but in Salem District it would seem the word *kōttam* was rarely used, and the general term *nād* was applied to both the larger and the smaller divisions. Thus in an inscription at Kambaya-nallūr,[3] Puramalai-Nād is spoken of as a sub-division of Tagadai-Nād; and in the Mallāpuram inscription[4] Tagadai-Nād is a sub-division of Ganga-Nād, which in turn is a sub-division of Nigarili-Chōla-mandalam. The Ādaiyūr-Nād is mentioned in an inscription of Tīrta-malai[5] and an Eyyil-Nād in one of Tiruppattūr.[6]

In the Talaghāt the inscriptions speak of the Kīlkarai Pūndurai-Nād,[7] the Vada-Pūvāniya-Nād,[8] the Ēlukarai-Nād,[9] and the Ēlūr-Nād.[10]

V. HOYSALA PERIOD. The Twelfth Century.

The twelfth century witnessed the decline of the Chōla Empire and the final ruin of that of Kalyāni. In about 1116 A.D., an event had taken place which was fraught with peril to both Chōlas and Chālukyas.

Conquest of Gangavādi by the Hoysalas.

The Hoysala Ballālas were originally feudatories of the Western Chālukyas, and their first capital was Bēlūr, in Hassan District of Mysore.

In 1104 A.D. Bitti-Dēva, better known as Vishnu-vardhana, succeeded to the chieftaincy.[11] Himself an able soldier and statesman, he was ably supported by a general of Ganga stock called Ganga Rāja. There is a significance in the prominence of Ganga Rāja's claim to Ganga descent and his distinction as one of the three chief supporters of the Jain religion.[12] It shows that the movement he led was a patriotic and religious revolt. He established his capital at Halebīd (Dorasamudra), and reduced Nolambavādi to obedience. But a richer prey awaited him.

At the opening of the twelfth century, Gangavādi was Chōla territory, in charge of the Adigaimān of Dharmapuri. The Chōla

---

[1] See Tiruchengōdu inscription of Jatā-varman Sundara-Pāndya—G.E. No. 682 of 1905.

[2] The term is found in unpublished translations of G.E. Nos. 19, 21 and 22 of 1900 kindly supplied me by Mr. V. Venkayya.

[3] G.E. No. 9 of 1900. [4] G.E. No. 18 of 1900.

[5] G.E. No. 662 of 1905. Cf. G.E. No. 204 of 1909, and Report for 1910, p. 88. Cf. also J.R.A.S., 1911, p. 811.

[6] G.E. No. 246 of 1909. [7] G.E. No. 646 of 1905 (Tiruchengōdu).

[8] G.E. Nos. 19, 22, and 27 of 1900 (Tāra-mangalam).

[9] G.E. No. 21 of 1900 (Tāra-mangalam). [10] G.E. No 13 of 1900 (Nāmakkal).

[11] Rice, page 337, Dr. Fleet gives as his earliest date 1117, his latest 1137 A.D.

[12] Chāmundarāya, minister of Mārasimha the Talakād Ganga, and Hulla, the minister of the Hoysala Narasimha I.

CHAP. II. V. HOYSALA PERIOD.

rule was not popular. The Chōlas were foreigners, and out of sympathy with the people. They had ruthlessly destroyed the Jain temples and trampled upon the local religion. The fruit was ripe for picking. Vishnu-vardhana invaded Gangavādi, routed the Chōla Governor at Talakād, and captured the ancient Ganga capital.

Ostensibly the Hoysala conquest of Gangavādi was undertaken on behalf of Vishnu-vardhana's Chālukya suzerain. But Vishnu-vardhana proved himself a formidable vassal, and the precedent he set was dangerous. He claims to have captured Kōlār, sacked Koyatūr [1] and overrun Kongu. There is no reason to discredit these claims, though in other respects the language of his inscriptions indulges in hyperbole. There is, however, no evidence that he effected a foothold in the Bāramahāl or Talaghāt. He does not claim to have descended the Salem or North Arcot Ghāts, and probably his operations were confined to Western Kongu. The Chōla authority in Northern Kongu and the Bāramahāl apparently remained undisturbed for another century.

War of Pāndyan Succession.

The immediate successors [2] of Kulōttunga I are better known as patrons of literature than as warriors. Vikrama-Chōla, Kulōttunga's son, whose name appears in an inscription at Kambaya-nallūr, appears to have maintained the prestige of Chōla rule. In the reign of Rājādhirājā II (1171–86), however, the Chōlas became involved in a war between rival claimants to the ancient Pāndyan throne which lasted two generations, and at one time threatened the very existence of the Chōla power.[3] Rājēndra Chōla I had set up a member of his own house as ruler of the Pāndyas, and this line became known as "Chōla-Pāndyas." By the middle of the twelfth century these Chōla-Pāndyas had died out, and the throne was claimed by rivals of the old Pāndya stock. The Chōla dominions were invaded by the Singhalese, and though in the end Kulōttunga III was able to expel the invaders, and set his nominee, Vikrama-Pāndya, on the Pāndyan throne, the re-establishment of the Pāndyan kingdom was fatal to the Chōla power.

---

[1] Koyatūr has been identified with Coimbatore, but more probably it should be identified with a place known as Laddigam in the Punganūr Zamindari, which is called Koyatūr in ancient inscriptions.

[2] Vikrama Chōla (1118–1135), Kulōttunga II (1123–1146), Rājarāja II (1146–1163), Rājādhirāja II (1163–1181), Kulōttunga III (1178–1217), Rājarāja III (1216–1248), Rājēndra III (1246–1268). The initial dates of each ruler are those astronomically verified by Prof. Kielhorn; the terminal dates are based on the last regnal years as yet available from epigraphic records. See *Ep. Ind. IX*, p. 209 seq.

[3] See G.E. 1899. paras. 23, sq.

CHAP. II. V. HOYSALA PERIOD.

Adigaimāns of Dharmapuri.

That the decline was appreciated by the Chōla feudatories is evident from contemporary history of the Adigaimāns of Tagadūr, the modern Dharmapuri. The princes of Tagadūr were known for many generations by the title of Adiyama or Adigaimān.[1] Who the early Adigaimāns were is not known. In the Tamil Periya-Purānam an Adigan is said to have fought against the Chōla King—Pugal Chōla.[2] In the Pāndya grant of Jatilavarman Nedunjadaiyan, one Adiyan fought against the Pāndiyan king at Āyiravēli, Ayirūr and Pugaliyūr, and both Pallavas and Kēralas are said to have been his allies. A Chera king, known from Tamil literature, claimed to have conquered his capital Tagadūr.

When Vishnu-vardhana drove the Chōlas from Talakād,[3] it would appear that the Adigaimān of Tagadūr was Governor both of Gangavādi and of Nigarili-Chōla-mandalam. In the twentieth year of Kulōttunga III (c. 1198 A.D.) the "Lord of Takatā" (Tagadūr) was one Vidukādalagiya-Perumāl, son of Rājarāja-Adhika (Adigaimān), *alias* Vāgan. Vidukādalagiya-Perumāl claims to have been descended from one Elini, a scion of the family of the kings of Chēra.[4] An inscription of his at Kambaya-nallūr,[5] dated 1199-1200 A.D., describes him as ruling over the three rivers—Pāli, Pennai and Ponni (Pālār, Pennaiyār and Kāvēri). But the most significant records connected with him are two political compacts discovered at Chengam. One of these,[6] dated in the 20th year of Kulōttunga III, is an agreement between two chiefs[7] in which one Sambuvarāyan undertakes that (1) as long as he and the other party to the compact lives, they shall be faithful to each other: (2) in case alliance or hostility has to be declared by either with Piranda-Perumāl, son of Rājarāja Adigan, it shall be done with the approval of the other; (3) he (Sambuvarāyan) will not join the enemies of the other party, neither will he enter into transactions hostile to the interests of the other party. The second compact[8] appears to be a sequel to the first, and Vidukādalagiya-Perumāl is a party to it along with the two chiefs mentioned in the first. In it he declares that (1) as long as the other two chiefs continue faithful to him he will be true to them; (2) their enemies shall be his

---

[1] In *Ep. Ind.*, VI, p. 331, it is stated that Adigai = Tiruvadi near Cuddalore and that Adigaimān = "Lord of Adigai."

[2] *Ind. Ant.*, XXII, pp. 66 and 73.

[3] *Supra* p. 59.

[4] See Inscription of Tirumalai near Pōlūr, edited in *Ep. Ind.*, VI, p. 331; cf. *S.I.I.*, Vol. I, p. 106.

[5] See G.E. No. 8 of 1900; *cf. Ep. Ind.*, VI, p. 332.

[6] G.E. No. 115 of 1900; G.E. 1900, p. 13.

[7] Their names are Karikāla-Sōla-Ādaiyūr-Nadālvān and Sengēni-Ammaiyappan-Attimallan *alias* Vikrama-Sōla-Sambuvarāyan.

[8] G.E. No. 107 of 1900.

enemies; (3) his enemies shall be their enemies; (4) he will form no alliance with certain other chiefs. It is clear from these records that the Lord of Takatā was virtually an independent prince, though owing a nominal allegiance to Kulōttunga III, and they indicate an atmosphere of political lawlessness and treachery consistent only with the growing rottenness of the Chōla power.

Collapse of the Kalyāni Chalukyas.

Meanwhile disaster had overtaken the Chālukyas of Kalyāni. The history of the short-lived Kalachurya Dynasty (1155–83 A.D.), and the persecution of the Lingāyat sect, the brief revival of the Chālukyas and the final partition of their territory between the Yādavas of Dēvagiri under Bhillama, and the Hoysalas of Dorasamudra under Ballāla II, a grandson of Vishnu-vardhana, do not immediately concern Salem District. In 1191 Ballāla II assumed the titles of a paramount sovereign, and by 1196 A.D. the Hoysala Empire was firmly established.

Ballāla II.

Hoysala-Pāndyan Duel.

The history of the thirteenth century resolves itself into a duel between Hoysalas and Pāndyas. Kulōttunga III died about 1215 A.D., and was succeeded by his son Rājarāja III (1216–1248). In 1216 Māravarman Sundara-Pāndya I[1] ascended the Pāndyan throne. In about 1220 the Hoysala Ballāla II gave place to his son Narasimha II.[2] Already by 1213 A.D., the Hoysalas had been driven from their northern territories by the warlike Yādava Singhana. Taking the line of least resistance, Narasimha II extended his dominions southwards, and adopted the policy of propping up the tottering Chōla power. It is known that Vīra-Sōmēsvara, son of the reigning Hoysala Narasimha II, was in Coimbatore by 1224, and that a year later Narasimha II recognised Rājarāja III as overlord. By 1224[3] the Hoysalas had established a capital at Kannanūr, within five miles of Srīrangam. This was a strategic move. Māravarman Sundara-Pāndya I claims to have burnt Tanjore and Uraiyūr and "presented the Chōla country." Narasimha II claims that "like a thunderbolt he cleft open the rock that was the Pāndya King.[4]" This suggests that the Hoysalas interfered in a civil war among the Chōlas, and reinstated Rājarāja III after he had been temporarily ousted by a rival claimant who owed his elevation to the Pāndyas.[5]

---

[1] See G.E. 1906, para. 27.

[2] An inscription of Narasimha II has been found at Adaman-kōttai, dated 1234 A.D. (G.E. No. 201 of 1910).

[3] G.E. Report for 1910–1911, p. 81. Cf. *Ep. Ind.*, VII, p. 162.

[4] This is in an inscription at Harihar in Mysore dated 1224.

[5] G.E., 1900, paragraphs 29 and 30. It is inferred that one Tikka, a Telugu Chōla, from the North, and the Ganapati of Orissa took part in the war. It is also conjectured that Rājendra Chōla III may have been a rival claimant, but the history of the period is obscure.

CHAP. II. V. HOYSALA PERIOD.

But Rājarāja III was to suffer another unpleasant experience. A Chōla feudatory, Perunjinga by name, who claimed Pallava descent, and adopted the title "Lord of all the earth," rose suddenly against his overlord, and, with the help of the Singhalese, seized his person. Narasimha, who was in his capital Dorasamudra at the time, marched to the rescue, defeated and captured the rebel, reinstated the imprisoned Chōla and adopted the title "Establisher of the Chōla Kingdom."[1] These events took place prior to the year 1231–2 A.D.

In 1233–4 A.D., Narasimha II died, and was succeeded by Vīra-Sōmēsvara. This monarch maintained his ground, and lived on peaceful terms with the reigning Pāndya, Māravarman Sundara-Pāndya II (1238–51), acknowledging him as overlord.[2] On the death of Māravarman came a change. His successor Jatāvarman-Sundara-Pāndya I (1251–1261), who claims to have "conquered all countries," drove Vīra-Sōmēsvara out of the Chōla territory.[3] It is doubtful, however, whether he made himself master of the Salem Talaghât.[4]

Vīra-Rāmanātha.

Vīra-Sōmēsvara appears to have died about 1254 A.D., and shortly after, the Hoysala Empire was divided between his two sons;[5] Narasimha III received as his portion the greater part of what is now Mysore, Vīra-Rāmanātha succeeded to the remainder, and fixed his capital apparently at Kundāni to protect the "Army Road" from the Bāramahāl to Kōlār.[6] Records of Narasimha have been found dated 1293 A.D., and the latest record of Vīra-Rāmanātha is dated in his forty-first year (1295 A.D.).[7] The

---

[1] This title was also adopted by Vīra-Sōmēsvara. An inscription of Rājarāja III (G.E. No. 208 of 1910) has been found at Adaman-kōttai dated 1241 A.D., six years later than that of Narasimha II above referred to (G.E. No. 1 of 1910); and at the same place is an inscription of Sōmēsvara dated 1247 A.D.

[2] G.E., 1900, paragraph 13 of G.E., 1907, p. 69, where Sōmēsvara is spoken of as uncle (or father in-law) of Māravarman II. Cf. also G.E. Nos. 138 and 156 of 1894.

[3] In 1264–5 it is certain that Kannanūr was in Pāndyan possession. See G.E. 1905, p. 55.

[4] See G.E., 1906, paragraph 27, where some of the inscriptions of Jatāvarman-Sundara-Pāndya discovered at Tiruchengōdu are tentatively assigned to the first king of that name. If this assumption is correct, it follows that Kongu was reconquered by the Hoysalas under Vīra-Rāmanātha, and that a second Pāndyan conquest took place under Jatāvarman-Sundara-Pāndya II. The point is not yet clear from the records, but in view of *Ep. Ind.*, VI, p. 310 seq., the Tiruchengōdu inscriptions should more probably be attributed to Jatāvarman Sundara-Pāndya II, along with those of Tāra-mangalam.

[5] G.E. Report for 1910 "Vīra-Rāmanātha succeeded to the throne in Saka 1177 (= A.D. 1255) apparently during the lifetime of his father."

[6] *Infra*, s. v. Kundāni and cf. *Ep. Carn.*, Vol. x, Kōlār. p. XXXII.

[7] *Ep. Carn.*, Vol. x, Kōlār, p. XXXII, (Bowringpet) No. 25 (*a*).

territories of the latter were extensive, for his records have been found from Trichinopoly District (1262 A.D.)[1] to Bellary (1275–7),[2] and the whole of Salem District seems to have come under his rule, as his inscriptions are found in Tāra-mangalam (1268 and 1274 A.D.), Rāya-kōta[3] and Adaman-kōttai[4] (1260 A.D.), while those of his son and successor Vīra-Visvanātha, who reigned for about four or five years only, have been found at Kambaya-nallūr,[5] Kundāni and Tiruppattūr (1288).[6] The history of this period is obscure. There is reason to believe that, towards the close of Rāmanātha's reign, an effort was made to extend his authority over the portion of the Hoysala territories that did not belong to him. But the attempt was not successful, for by the end of the century the whole Hoysala Empire was re-united under Ballāla III, son of Rāmanātha's rival brother Narasimha III.

Meanwhile, in the south, the Pāndyas had been steadily encroaching on the Hoysala possessions. The fiction of Chōla rule was for a time preserved under Rājēndra III (1246–67), and then it vanished. In 1268 Māravarman Kulasēkhara I succeeded to the Pāndyan throne, and he continued to reign till 1308. He has been identified with the "Kales Devar" of Muhammadan writers. In 1275 Jatāvarman-Sundara Pāndya II was ruling, apparently as a coregent,[7] and he continued till at least 1290. There is every probability that he was the "Sender Bandi" of Marco Polo, who touched on the Coromandel Coast in 1292, and that he was the real conqueror of the Salem Talaghāt, who left his inscriptions at Tāra-mangalam and Tiruchengōdu.[8]

---

[1] G.E. No. 597 of 1902 (Anbil) and 542 of 1905 (Tiruvellarai).

[2] G.E. Nos. 33 and 34 of 1904, from Kogali in Bellary District.

[3] G.E. Nos. 20, 26 and 29 of 1900.

[4] G.E. No. 202 of 1910.

[5] Nos. 9 and 10 of 1900.

[6] No. 250 of 1909. Cf. *Ep. Carn* x, p. XXXII, inscription of Visvanātha at Kurubūr in Chitamani Taluk (Ct 45).

[7] Marco Polo describes the province of Malabar as divided between five kings, all brothers, who were constantly at war with each other. His account is strongly corroborated by Muhammadan writers. See Yule's *Marco Polo*, II, p. 331 sq. (ed. 1903).

[8] See *Ep. Ind.*, v, p. 310 sq. G.E. Nos. 23, 24, 25, 30 of 1900, 622, 642 and 644 of 1905 and No. 5 of 1906. The boundary between Hoysala and Pandya during the latter half of the Thirteenth Century fluctuated in a most perplexing manner. The Pāndyan Kings of this period are thus dated by Professor Kielhorn in *Ep. Ind.*, Vol. IX, pp. 226–229 :—

1. Jatāvarman Kulasēkhara	1190–1216.
2. Māravarman Sundara-Pāndya I ...	1216–1235.
3. Māravarman Sundara-Pāndya II ...	1238–9 to 1251.
4. Jatāvarman Sundara-Pāndya I	1251–1261.
5. Vīra-Pāndya	1252–3 to 1267.
6. Māravarman Kulasēkhara I	1268–1308.
7. Jatāvarman Sundara-Pāndya II ...	1275–6 to 1286.
8. Māravarman Kulasēkhara II	1314–1325.

CHAP. II. V. HOYSALA PERIOD.

The Muhammadan Cataclysm.

At the opening of the fourteenth century South India was divided among four states, all about equally powerful. To the north-west the Yādavas of Dēvagiri guarded the line of the Nermada, to the north-east the Kākatīyas of Warangal barred invasion from Bengal or the Central Provinces. In a second line of defence lay the Hoysalas of Dorasamudra. South of them lay the Pāndyas.

Till 1293 A.D., no Muhammadan ruler had ventured across the Vindhya mountains. In that year began the series of raids that carried the Muhammadan armies to Rāmēsvaram, and by 1310 A.D., every one of the four South Indian Empires was ruined beyond retrieve. Every flicker of independence was ruthlessly stamped out by the armies of Malik Kāfūr, Mubārak, and the Tughlaks Giyās-ud-dīn and Muhammad. But the Moslem conquest was not permanent.[1] Under Muhammad Tughlak the terrors of Islam began to wane. The Hindus at last learned the folly of discord. Out of the ashes of the southern kingdoms rose the Empire of Vijayanagar,[2] and for nearly two centuries and a half the Hindus were able to present a united front against Muhammadan aggression.

VI. VIJAYANAGAR. First or Sangama Dynasty.

The early years of the First or Sangama Dynasty of Vijayanagar were years of war with Muhammad Tughlak, and, after 1347 A.D., with the Bahmani Sultāns of Gulbarga. In 1365-66, however, Bukka I turned his attention to the south, and sent his son, Kampanna Udaiyār, or Kampa II, to overthrow the Muhammadan Sultānate of Madura. Sometime prior to 1384, Harihara II sent his son Virūpāksha on an expedition to the south, and this prince claims victories over the kings of Tondai-mandalam, the Chōlas, the Pāndyas and Ceylon. One or other of these campaigns must have brought Salem District under the sway of Vijayanagar.

The earliest inscriptions of this dynasty yet discovered in the District are those of Immadi-Bukka,[3] son of Harihara II, who eventually succeeded his father as Bukka II. They are dated 1386-7 A.D. Two inscriptions of Vijaya Bhūpathi [4] and one of Dēva-Rāya II [5] have been found at Tīrta-malai.

---

[1] Ballāla III, however, appears to have maintained a shadow of sovereignty first at Tondanūr, or Tonnūr, near French Rocks in Mysore District, and afterwards, till 1342, at Tiruvannāmalai.

[2] The City of Vijayanagar was founded in 1336.

[3] G.E. No. 11 of 1900, (Kambaya-nallūr), and G.E. No. 664 of 1905 (Tīrta-malai).

[4] Nos. 658 and 659 of 1905, dated respectively 1409 and 1411 A.D. In the latter Vijaya Bhūpathi is called Udaiyār. As he was not reigning at the time, he must have been a provincial Governor under his father Dēva-Rāya I.

[5] No. 666 of 1905 dated 1428-9. Dēva-Rāya is called Udaiyār; as he was reigning at the time, the reason for the use of this title is not clear.

CHAP. II. VI. VIJAYA-NAGAR. Revolution

Dēva-Rāya II died some time after 1450–1 A.D.[1] The events of the next half century are not easy to unravel. The latest known date of the First Dynasty is 1486–7 A.D. Between the death of Dēva-Rāya and this date at least four names occur. It is not certain whether these names refer to two persons or four or more.[2] The one certain fact of this period is that the ruling Kings were men of poor capacity, and that under them the Empire deteriorated. But there was at least one capable ruler in the State, of the Sāluva family, which traced its descent from Yadu, and claimed relationship with the royal family of Vijayanagar. One of the family, Sāluva Mangu, had done yeoman service for Kampa II in his expedition against the Sultan of Madura. Mangu's great-grandson Narasimha rose to great power during the latter half of the fifteenth century. His dominions comprised the whole of North Arcot, Chingleput and Nellore, with parts of South Arcot, Cuddapah, Kistna and Mysore. Further, the war against the Bahmani Sultān, Muhammad Shah II (1463–82), who penetrated at this period to Mālūr in Mysore, and to Conjeeveram, was conducted on behalf of the Emperor by this powerful Sāluva chief. Sāluva Narasimha was well served during this period by his General, Īsvara "of the Tulu family." The reigning Monarch became so hopelessly imbecile, that Narasimha decided that nothing but a change of rulers could prevent the Empire falling a prey to its hereditary foes, the Sultāns of Gulbarga. With the consent of the chief ministers and generals of the state, he accordingly seized the throne himself, and allowed the king to escape. The date of this usurpation cannot, at present, be fixed. It must have taken place between 1486–7 and 1495–6 A.D. Sāluva Narasimha had not enjoyed the royal power long before he died. He left two young sons, and appointed as regent the son of his old officer Īsvara, by name Narasa Nāyak. The eldest son was murdered by an enemy of Narasa Nāyak, to bring odium on the regent.[3] This act forced Narasa Nāyak about 1501–2 A.D. to assume the supreme authority. The Sāluva's son, Immadi Narasimha, was deposed from the throne and allowed to reign, as a petty Rāja, at Penukonda;[4] the regent Narasa Nāyak founded the

[1] G.E., 1904, para. 22.

[2] The names given by Mr. Sewell are, (1) Mallikārjuna, (2) Rājasēkhara, (3) Virūpāksha, (4) Praudha Dēva Rāya.

Of these, Mallikārjuna and Virūpāksha are the most prominent. The first has dates ranging from 1449–50 to 1462–3 A.D. (vide G.E., 1906, para. 47) Virūpāksha's inscriptions range between 1469 and 1478. The name Rājasēkhara occurs in 1468–9 and 1486–7. In the present state of epigraphy it is hardly possible to solve the riddle.

[3] G.E., 1906, para. 58. [4] See *Ep. Ind.*, VII, p. 74.

CHAP. II, VI. VIJAYANAGAR.

Third or Tuluva Dynasty of Vijayanagar. He was succeeded by his eldest son Vīra Narasimha, who, after a short reign gave place to his younger brother, Krishna-Dēva-Rāya, the greatest of all the Vijayanagar Emperors. This double revolution did not seriously disturb the civil administration of the Empire. An interesting inscription at Buddi-Reddi-patti[1] appears to refer to the infant son of Sāluva Narasimha, under the name of Tammaya Dēva-Mahārāja, and speaks of Narasa Nāyaka as his agent.

While these events were in progress in the Hindu State, the Bahmini Empire was subverted, and its place was taken by the five kingdoms of the Deccan, which played an important rôle in the sixteenth century.[2]

The Third or Tuluva Dynasty.

Under the Third Dynasty the history of Salem was as uneventful as under the First. An inscription of Krishna-Dēva-Rāya the Great has been found at Indūr,[3] west of Dharmapuri, and another at Tiruchengōdu.[4] The latter records an assignment of market-tolls for the upkeep of certain festivals. Two inscriptions of Achyuta-Rāya have been found at Tāra-mangalam. Of these,[5] one records a grant of the proceeds of certain taxes for the upkeep of a *matam*, the other[6] a private grant of a village for the maintenance of a temple. His successor Sadāsiva was a mere puppet in the hands of his minister Rāma-rāja. An inscription of his reign has been found at Kāri-mangalam[7] and another at Tāra-mangalam[8].

Talikōta.

In 1565 A.D., the glory of Vijayanagar was laid in the dust by the combined armies of the Deccan Sultāns,[9] on the field of Talikōta. The capital was given over to pillage for five months and ceased to exist. The catastrophe was sudden and unexpected. It plunged South India into the most terrible anarchy known to

---

[1] G.E., 155 of 1905, vide G.E., 1905, para. 44.

[2] Imad Shahs of Birār ... ... 1484–1572.
Ādil Shahs of Bijāpur ... ... 1489–1686.
Nizām Shahs of Ahmadnagar ... ... 1490–1626.
Barid Shahs of Bidar ... ... 1492–1609.
Qutb Shahs of Golconda ... ... 1512–1688.

[3] G.E. No. 13 of 1900.

[4] G.E. No. 651 of 1905.

[5] G.E. No. 21 of 1900 (No. 3 of Mr. Sewell's Lists, Vol. I, p. 200), dated 1541–2 A.D.

[6] G.E. No. 28 of 1900, dated 1539–40 A.D.

[7] G.E. No. 5 of 1900.

[8] G.E. No. 27 of 1900 (No. 5 of Mr. Sewell's Lists, Vol. I, page 201). Gift of a village by one of the Mudalis of Tāra-mangalam to a temple called Rāma Kūdal.

[9] Hussain Nizam Shah of Ahmadnagar, Ali Ādil Shah of Bijāpur, Ibrahim Qutb Shah of Golconda and Kāsim Barid Shah II of Bidar,

history, an anarchy only terminated by the storm of Seringapatam in 1799 A.D.

After Talikōta.

The immediate effect of Talikōta was the razing of the Imperial City, and the flight of Tirumala, with the puppet king Sadāsiva, to Penukonda. A *roi fainéant* at such a time was grave danger, and if any relics of imperial power were to be saved, the removal of Sadāsiva was a political necessity. Hence after 1569–70 A.D. Sadāsiva disappears, and Tirumala becomes Emperor.

The truncated Empire about this time was divided into six viceroyalties—

(1) Āndhra.	(3) Madura.	(5) Gingee.
(2) Karnāta.	(4) Chandragiri.	(6) Tanjore.

The Āndhra or Telugu districts round Penukonda were ruled directly by the Emperor. In 1575 A.D. Tirumala died. His eldest (?) son, Ranga II, succeeded him at Penukonda; another son, Rama III, was entrusted with the Viceroyalty of Karnāta with head-quarters at Seringapatam, and a third son, Venkata I, ruled in Madura. As a matter of form, the ruler at Penukonda was regarded as Emperor, but his authority over the other two viceroyalties varied according as his personality was strong or weak. This quasi-partition of the Empire marks the lines of political cleavage during the seventeenth century, which is in the main a record of the struggle between Mysore and Madura, with a shadowy Rāya flitting from place to place in spasmodic efforts at piecing together the shattered Empire of his ancestors.

Dissolution.

The time was ripe for military adventurers. The members of the imperial house quarrelled among themselves. Viceroys and local chieftains carved out principalities on their own behalf. Bāgalūr and Ankusagiri, Hosūr and Denkani-kōta, Salem and Amara-kundi became the capitals of princelings, while the Jagadēva Rāyas of Chennapatna ruled the Bāramahāl and a large strip of the Mysore plateau stretching to the Western Ghāts. These lesser principalities, however, were soon eclipsed by the rising states of Mysore and Madura.

(1) Rise of Mysore.

The rule of Rāma III at Seringapatam was weak, and the local chieftains rebelled. On Rāma's death, his young son Tirumala II was sent to Madura, to the care of his uncle Venkata I, and Seringapatam was left in charge of a vice-regent. In 1586 A.D. Ranga II of Penukonda died, and the whole Empire passed to Venkata I. The young nephew Tirumala II thereupon proceeded to Seringapatam, and assumed an attitude of hostility to his imperial uncle. This coolness led directly to the taking of Seringapatam by Rāja Odeyar of Mysore, whose act was countenanced by Venkata I, and whose actual possession was confirmed by the Rāya in 1612 A.D.

CHAP. II. VII. 1565-1761.

Rāja Odeyār next began systematically to absorb the territories of the Poligārs to the south and east, and encroached extensively on the possessions of Jagadēva Rāya, which lay to the north. His grandson Chāma Rāja (1617–37 A.D.), by the conquest of Chennapatna after a series of Bijāpur invasions, completed the expulsion of Jagadēva Rāya's house from what is now Mysore territory.

(2) Rise of Madura.

The rise of the Madura Nāyakas began in 1559 A.D. with Visvanātha's victory over his rebel father on behalf of the Vijayanagar Emperor. Visvanātha's[1] viceroyalty lasted till 1563, and under the guidance of his able minister Āryanātha, passed to his descendants. Āryanātha died in 1600 A.D. The infant Rāj grew steadily in strength, and reached its zenith under the Great Tirumala Nāyaka, who acceded in 1623 A.D.

Tirumala Nāyaka.

Tirumala Nāyaka had a difficult game to play, and he played it ably and unscrupulously. The empty fiction of imperial suzerainty was no longer consistent with a strong centralised government. The Madura frontier was already in hostile contact with the growing kingdom of Mysore. Chāma Rāja was chafing to revenge a reverse his arms had recently suffered. In the north loomed the cloud of Mughal invasion. So long as the energies of the Deccan Sultāns were absorbed in the Mughal war, the Hindu kingdoms were safe from their inroads. Immediately the pressure was relaxed, the fighting Sultāns must inevitably seek compensation for their losses by the invasion and pillage of South India. Tirumala adopted and perfected the policy of his predecessors for the defence of his northern frontier.

Poligārs of the Marches.

The power of the Nāyakas was established in a frankly feudal basis. "There were 72 bastions to the fort of Madura, and each of them was now formally placed in charge of a particular chief, who was bound for himself and his heirs to keep his post at all times and under all circumstances. He was also bound to pay a fixed annual tribute, to supply and keep in readiness a quota of troops for the Governor's armies, and to keep the Governor's peace over a particular tract of country; and in consideration of his promise to perform these and other services, a grant was made to him of a tract of country." Among the seventy-two chief Poligārs of the Madura feudal system were Rāmachandra Nāyaka and Gatti Mudaliyār of Kongu.

Each of these names is that of a line of Poligārs, rather than of an individual. For instance, Robert de' Nobili found a Rāmachandra Nāyaka established at Sēndā-mangalam in 1623. The horoscope of another of these Rāmachandra Nāyakas came into

---

[1] Mr. Nelson's *Madura Manual*, p. 98.

the hands of Colonel Mackenzie, from which it appears he was born in October 1652 and died in 1718[1]. The name is associated with Talai-malai, a hill overlooking the Kāvēri in the south of Nāmakkal Taluk, and the Nāmakkal fort is said to have been built by a prince of the line.

The Gatti Mudaliyārs ruled in power and splendour the most dangerously exposed province of the kingdom. Kāvēri-puram, on the right bank of the Kāvēri, was their strategic capital, commanding, as it does, one of the principal passes to the Mysore Plateau. The centre of their power seems, however, to have been Tāra-mangalam, where they built a costly temple. It is said that their dominions extended as far as Talai-vāsal to the east, Dhārāpuram in the west, and Karūr in the south[2]. The forts of greatest strategic importance held by them in Salem District were Ōmalūr and Āttūr. A glance at the map will show that the disposition of these forts guarded against an invasion from Mysore. Kāvēri-puram guarded the foot of the only ghāt at which the Madura dominions touched Mysore[3]. Ōmalūr served as a *pointe d'appui* against any force proceeding by the routes through Toppūr or Perumbālai. In this quarter the petty Poligārs of Denkani-kōta, Ratnagiri, Ālambādi, etc., intervened between the two great rivals. Āttūr commanded the shortest route to the coast, and guarded against any flank move on Trichinopoly by way of the Vellār valley. The Gatti Mudaliyārs are also associated with Amara-kundi, Sankaridrug, Tiruchengōdu, Mēchēri, Idanga-sālai, and Pūlāmpatti.[4] Salem itself appears, at least during part of the seventeenth century, to have been ruled by an independent Poligār, Chennappa Nāyaka, whose name tradition also connects with Tenkarai-kōttai[5].

The Madura-Mysore duel.

The opening of hostilities between Mysore and Madura is obscure for want of accurate dates and synchronisms. It would appear that early in Tirumala Nāyaka's reign, Coimbatore was invaded by Chāma Rāja, who penetrated as far as Dindigul, and was there checked by Tirumala's able general Rāmappayya. The

---

[1] Mackenzie Manuscripts, I, 79.

[2] Another account gives Eraya-mangalam (in Kokkarāyanpet Mitta, 9 miles S.W. of Tiruchengōdu, on the Kāvēri), as the southern limit of their dominions and Andiyūr, in Bhavāni Taluk, as the western boundary.

[3] Buchanan, Vol. I, p. 422, speaks of Kāvēri-puram as an important outpost, with two outlying forts, Nadu-kāval and Chikka-kāval which protected it from the aggressions of the Hill Poligārs.

[4] For further details regarding the Gatti Mudaliyārs, see below, Vol. II, pp. 259 and 264, *s.v.* Amara-kundi, and Tāra-mangalam. Cf. p. 95, *s.v.* Robert de'Nobili.

[5] Cf. Vol. II, pp. 228 and 250, and the suggested identification of the Mora-mangalam of Robert de'Nobili with Māra-mangalam, p. 95, n. 2.

CHAP. II. VII. 1565–1781.

Madura army then took the offensive, and drove the Mysore troops up the Ghāts, storming one of their principal fortresses. The quarrel then assumed a new aspect, with the sudden intervention of the Sultāns of Bijāpur and Golconda.

Bijāpur and Golconda intervene.

In 1634 A.D. the Mughals (under Shāh Jahān) captured Ahmadnagar and ended the dynasty of the Nizam Shahs. The Sultān of Bijāpur made his peace with the Mughals, and then arranged with the Sultān of Golconda to conquer the Carnatic. They had been invited south by several Hindu princes, who solicited their aid in finally throwing off the yoke of Vijayanagar.[1] About 1635 A.D., a new Rāya, Ranga, ascended the throne and determined to revive the authority of his house. Tirumala Nāyaka formed a league against him, which the Nāyakas of Tanjore and Ginjee joined. The only State which remained loyal to the Rāya was Mysore. When the Rāya marched against him, Tirumala invited the Sultān of Golconda to attack the Chandragiri territory from the north. The Rāya countermarched to meet his new enemy, was routed, and took refuge with the Nāyaka of Ikkēri (North Mysore). The Golconda army then marched south to reduce the rebels who had so rashly invoked its aid, and laid siege to Ginjee. Tirumala then asked the Bijāpur Sultān to help him. When the Bijāpur troops arrived at Ginjee, they at once joined with their fellow Muhammadans. Ginjee fell; Tirumala lost heart, and purchased peace by becoming their humble feudatory. The date of these events is uncertain. The war was apparently over by 1644 A.D.

Bijāpur conquers Bāramahāl.

Meanwhile the main army of Bijāpur had been otherwise employed. In 1636 an expedition started under Randhula Khan, with Shāhji (Sivāji's father) as second in command. After raiding the country near Bednūr, the invaders appeared in 1638 before Seringapatam, where, after a political revolution, Kantīrava Narasa Rāja had been placed on the throne by the Dalavāy, (Commander-in-Chief). The new king was no puppet; he beat off the assaults delivered by the Muhammadans, and the siege was raised. The invaders then turned east, took Bangalore from the Poligār, Kempe Gauda, and reduced the north and east of what is now Mysore State. In the course of this campaign the Bāramahāl was made subject to Bijāpur, and, by 1644 A.D., the new conquests were formed into two Provinces (Carnatic-Bālāghāt

---

[1] Wilks, i, p. 65. It is "stated in Hindu Manuscripts that they were invited by several of the usurpers who, under the title of Naiks, Rājās, Udayārs, Poligārs and even Gouds of single villages, had erected separate principalities and foolishly hoped to preserve or extend them by the aid of foreign force."

and Carnatic-Payīnghāt) and bestowed as a *jāghir* on Shābji, who fixed his head-quarters at Bangalore.[1]

Later on (the date again is uncertain) the Rāya, aided by Mysore, made one last attempt to recover his authority. Tirumala threw open to the Muhammadans the passes into Mysore which he commanded, and the last flicker of the great Hindu Empire was extinguished.

Kantīrava Narasa Rāja.

Kantīrava Narasa Rāja adopted the policy of appropriating territory whenever he could do so with impunity. According to Wilks, he took several places in Coimbatore from Gatti Mudaliyār in 1641 A.D. Six years later, he seized Ratnagiri from one Itibal Rao, and in 1652 he was strong enough to take from Bijāpur the Western Bāramahāl, including Vīrabhadradrug, Pennāgaram, and Dharmapuri. In the same year he took Denkani-kōta from the Itibal Rao, from whom he had wrested Ratnagiri. In 1653 he again raided Coimbatore, and took several important fortresses from the Madura feudatory. In the next year, Hosūr was taken from one Chandra Sankar.

The reigns of Kantīrava Narasa Rāja and Tirumala Nāyaka closed in 1659 A.D. with one of the most vindictive wars on record. The offensive was taken by the Mysoreans, who threatened Madura itself. The invaders were then driven back, and the Madura historians claim that Mysore was invaded, its king captured and his nose cut off in revenge for the cruelty of the Mysoreans, who had cut off the noses of all their captives.[2]

Ascendency of Mysore.

From 1659 Madura declined and Mysore grew powerful. The latter State was ruled in turn by two capable men, Dodda Dēva Rāja (1659–1672) and Chikka Dēva Rāja (1672–1704). In the reign of the first named, the latter repulsed a desperate attack made on Erode by Tirumala's successor, Chokkanātha Nāyaka of Madura, in combination with the Nāyaka of Ginjee and Venkōji of Tanjore in 1667. The raid ended in total failure, and Dodda Dēva Rāja wrested Erode and Dhārāpuram from the Nāyaka, and Ōmalūr from Gatti Mudaliyār.

Chikka Dēva Rāja.

Chikka Dēva Rāja was the ablest statesman of his time, except Sivāji himself. The keynote of his policy was friendship with the Mughal Aurangzīb. His financial reforms, his strenuous home administration, gave stability to his authority. Whenever he could do so without affront to Aurangzīb, he extended his

---

[1] His summer residence was at Nandi and his winter residence at Kōlār.

[2] There is no reference in Mysore history to this cutting off of the noses, although there are abundant allusions to insults of this character in literature and inscriptions. There is mention for instance of Rāja Odeyār having whipped "across the body, like the holy thread" the Odeyār of Karugahalli for some insult.

CHAP. II. VII. 1565–1761.

dominions by conquest. Between 1675 and 1678 A.D. he brought his frontier in contact with that of Bijāpur.

The Marāthas.

The aggressions of the Marāthas, however, checked his enterprise. In 1664 Shāhji had died, and Venkōji entered on his inheritance. By 1674 Venkōji had established himself in Tanjore. In 1677 Sivāji advanced on Gingee, through the Dāmalchēri Pass, to claim his inheritance from his half-brother, and in July of the same year the two brothers came to terms. It would appear that, for a few years, the Bāramahāl, and perhaps also the Talaghāt, passed under Marātha rule.

Reconquest.

Chikka Dēva Rāja studiously refrained from interfering with the Marāthas, who came to loot and not to rule. With the death of Sivāji in 1680, and the fall of Bijāpur and Golconda, he came in closer contact with the Mughals, and made fast friends with the Mughal general Qāsim Khān. In 1689 he assisted in the final ruin of Madura. In 1685 he had been negotiating with Venkōji for the purchase of Bangalore. Before the bargain was completed, Qāsim Khān seized the place, and sold it to Mysore for the stipulated price, three lakhs of rupees. In 1688–9 Chikka Dēva Rāja felt strong enough once again to invade the Bāramahāl, which had apparently thrown off its allegiance. Dharmapuri, Manukonda, Ōmalūr and Paramati were taken from "the people of Aura;" Kāvēri-patnam and Anantagiri (i.e., Āttūr) "by the treaty concluded by Lingurājayah with the Aurachee."[1] By 1704, when Chikka Dēva Rāja died, almost the whole of Salem District was within his dominions.

The Mughals.

Bijāpur fell to the Mughals in 1687 A.D., and Golconda in 1688. In 1690 Aurangzīb placed Qāsim Khān in command of the Carnatic provinces lately dependent on the two Sultānates. These provinces comprised three well-marked territorial divisions; (A) Carnatic Haidarābād Bālāghāt, composed of the five Circars of (1) Sidhout, (2) Gandi-kōta, (3) Gooty, (4) Gurramkonda, and (5) Kambam; (B) Carnatic Haidarābād Payīnghāt, extending from Guntūr to the Coleroon, and including almost all the Coromandel Coast, with Tanjore, Gingee, and Trichinopoly; (C) Carnatic Bijāpur, situated west of Carnatic Haidarābād, and comprising the plateau country round Sīra and Bangalore. In 1691 the Carnatic Payīnghāt appears to have been made a separate command under Zulfikār Khān, who was entrusted with the reduction of Gingee, a task which occupied him till 1698. In that year Qāsim Khān was defeated by the Marāthas, and died, either by his own hand or by the dagger of an assassin. He was

[1] Wilks I, p. 132.

succeeded by Zulfikār Khān, who ruled the Carnatic provinces for nearly 19 years, "a period of incessant and destructive warfare"[1].

CHAP. II. VII. 1565-1761.

Break up of Mughal Empire.

On the death of Aurangzīb, in 1707 A.D., rapid disintegration set in throughout the Mughal dominions. Zulfikār Khān went north, to watch the struggle for the succession that ensued. Daud Khān, who was left in command of the Carnatic provinces, followed northwards shortly after, nominating as his deputy Sādat-ulla Khān. The territory directly under Sādat-ulla Khān comprised Carnatic Haidarābād Payīnghāt and Carnatic Bijāpur, which by this time came to be known as the provinces of Arcot and Sīra respectively. Meanwhile, in Mysore, Chikka Dēva Rāja had been succeeded by his son, a deaf-mute, and henceforward that State was ruled by its ministers, in the names of puppet Rājas. Sādat-ulla Khān at first enjoyed, under the suzerainty of the Nizām, the undivided control of the two Carnatics, but, after four years, his jurisdiction was restricted to the province of Arcot, and a new Nawāb, Amīn Khān, was appointed for Sīra. Sādat-ulla Khān resented the removal of the rich State of Mysore from his jurisdiction, and formed a conspiracy with the Nawābs of Cuddapah, Kurnool, Savanūr and the Marātha chief Morāri Rao Ghorpade of Gooty to seize it. The new Nawāb, Amīn Khān, compromised by suggesting joint action against the Rāja of Mysore. Accordingly the confederates levied blackmail to the extent of a crore of rupees. Henceforward the funds of the unfortunate State of Mysore were looked on as the lawful property of any one who was strong enough to demand their surrender.

The Cuddapah Nawābs.

Meanwhile, four of the five Circars of the Carnatic Haidarābād Bālāghāt had been absorbed by Abdul Nabi Khān, the Pathān[2] Nawāb of Cuddapah; the fifth, Gooty, falling to the Ghorpade Marāthas. Abdul Nabi Khān was theoretically a subordinate[3] of the officer holding the joint command of the Carnatics, but he sometimes dealt directly with the Subēdar of the Deccan. Before, however, Nizām-ul-mulk had consolidated his power, Abdul Nabi Khān had become practically independent. He

---

[1] According to the Bāramahāl tradition, (*S.D.M.*, Vol. I, p. 89), Zulfikār Khān took northern Salem from the Marāthas on behalf of the Mughals, and ruled it for 8 years.

[2] In the early years of the eighteenth century, the Pathān families of Savanūr, Kurnool, and Cuddapah, began "to rally around them the remains of the genuine Pathāns, or ferocious bands of the same tribe, who were perpetually descending from the Indian Caucasus to improve their fortunes in the south". Wilks, Vol. I, p. 136.

[3] According to the Bāramahāl tradition, (*S.D.M.*, Vol. I, p. 89), the Bāramahāl was granted by Zulfikār Khān as a Jāghīr to Abdul Nabi Khān.

CHAP. II. VII. 1565–1761.

extended his possessions southward along the back of the Eastern Ghâts nearly to the Kāvēri, and, by 1714 A.D., he had made himself master of the Bāramahāl.[1]

Rise of Haidar Ali and the British—1748–1761 A.D.

The Nizām-ul-mulk died in 1748. A war of succession followed, in which the French and English took sides, and for the first time came into political prominence. The field of war was outside Salem District, which at the time was divided between Cuddapah and Mysore. Nanja Rāj, chief minister of the latter State, played a double game; he tried to get the cession of Trichinopoly from Muhammad Ali, and then intrigued with the French. His share in the war cost him money, but brought him no gain. It was in this war that an obscure adventurer, Haidar Ali, became the most powerful subject in the service of Mysore.

Conquest of the Bāramahāl by Haidar.

In 1758 Cuddapah was invaded by the Marāthas, who stripped the Nawāb of half of his territory. One Asad Khān, at the time Governor of Bāramahāl on behalf of Cuddapah, had recently been superseded by another officer. He promptly went over to Haidar, and advised him to essay the conquest of the Bāramahāl. Haidar deputed his brother-in-law, Makhdum Ali, for the purpose. This officer, as a preliminary step, first reduced the Poligār of Ānekal, whose territory intervened between that of Haidar and the Bāramahāl. This object was effected in 1760. Meanwhile the French had been vanquished at Wandiwash (January 22, 1760), and Lally, as a last resort, applied to Haidar for help. Haidar thereon sent Makhdum Ali to Pondicherry to negotiate. The treaty was to stipulate the cession to Mysore of Tiyāga, a fort which commanded the Āttūr Pass. At the conclusion of the war, Trichinopoly, Madura, and Tinnevelly were to be ceded to Haidar. Makhdum Ali proceeded to Pondicherry before the end of June, and ratified the treaty, when he was recalled with all his forces by the urgent necessity of Haidar. The conspiracy of Khande Rao with the puppet Rāja and the Marāthas had all but terminated his career. Makhdum Ali, after hard fighting, got as far as

---

[1] The names, dates, and order of succession of the Cuddapah Nawābs, present a hopeless puzzle. Mr. Gribble, in the Cuddapah Manual, p. 91, gives the following order: (1) Abdul Nabi Khān, (2) his son, Mahazid Khān, (inscription dated 1732 A.D.), (3) Mabasim Khān, brother of (2), (4) Alim Khān. The tradition preserved in the Bāramahāl, quoted by Mr. Le Fanu, *S.D.M.*, Vol. I, p. 89, gives the following order: (1) Abdul Nabi Khān, (2) Abdul Muhammad Khān, (ruled 10 years), (3) Abdul Musum Khān, (11 years), (4) Abdul Muzzad Khān, (8 years), (5) Abdul Musum Khān again, for another 5 years. According to Grant Duff, it was Mohammad Khān who murdered Nāzir Jang in 1750. According to the Punganūr tradition, (*North Arcot Manual*, Vol. II, p. 408), Abdul Mahsim was slain in the disastrous battle with the Marāthas near Cuddapah in 1757. According to Wilks, Vol. I, p. 402, Alim Khān joined Nizām Ali on the eve of the Chitaldrug campaign of 1777.

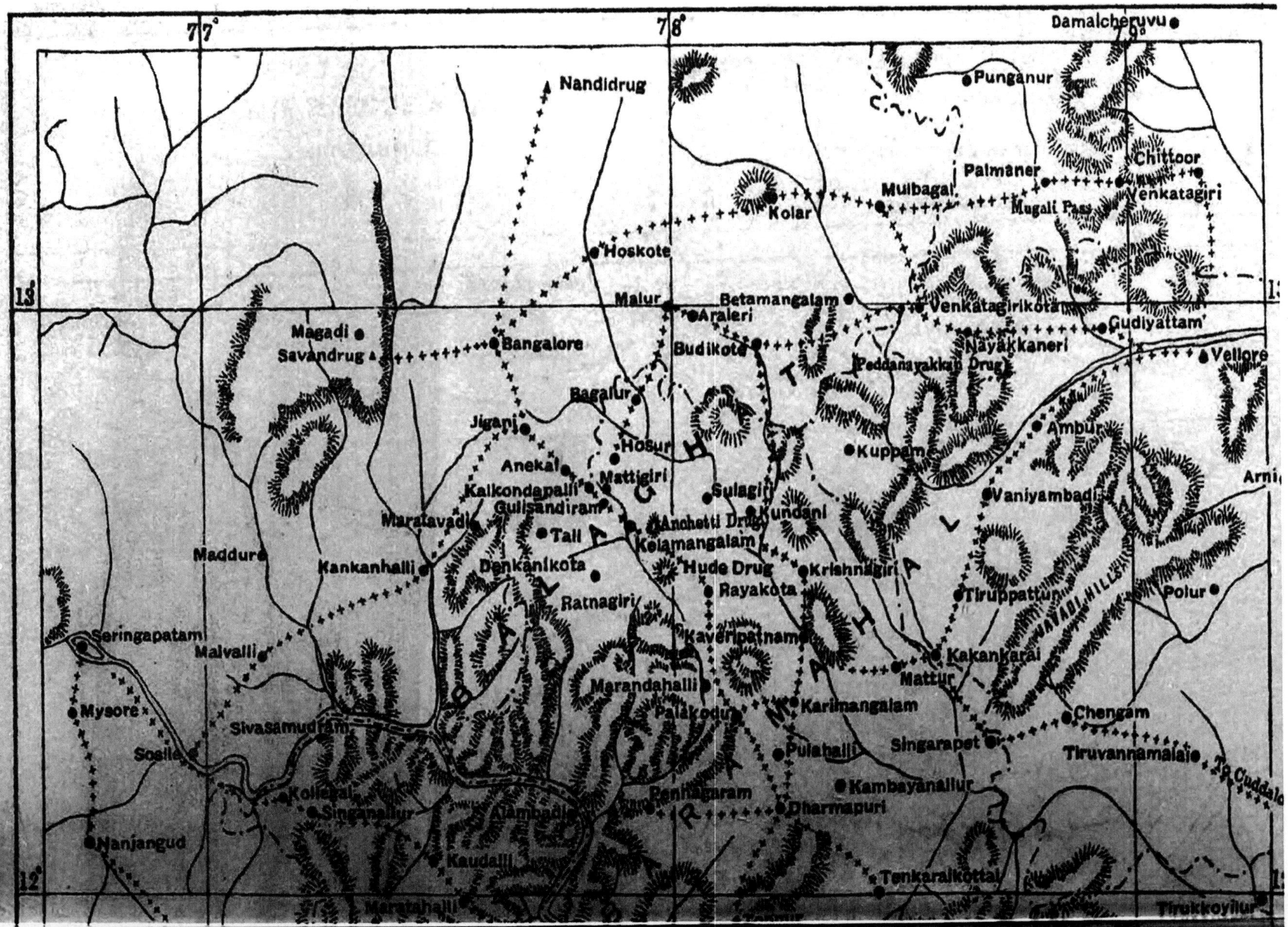

77°
78°
79°
13°
12°
Damalcheruvu
Punganur
Nandidrug
Chittoor
Palmaner
Mulbagal
Venkatagiri
Mugali Pass
Kolar
Hoskote
Malur
Betamangalam
Araleri
Venkatagirikota
Gudiyattam
Vellore
Magadi
Savandrug
Bangalore
Budikota
Nayakkaneri
Peddanayakkan Drug
Bagalur
Jigani
Hosur
Kuppam
Ambur
Anekal
Mattigiri
Kalkondapalli
Gulisandiram
Sulagiri
Kundani
Vaniyambadi
Arni
Maratavadi
Tali
Anchetti Drug
Kelamangalam
Maddur
Kankanhalli
Denkanikota
Hude Drug
Krishnagiri
Rayakota
Tiruppattur
Javadi Hills
Polur
Ratnagiri
Seringapatam
Malvalli
Kaveripatnam
Kakankarai
Mattur
Marandahalli
Mysore
Sivasamudram
Palakodu
Karimangalam
Chengam
Singarapet
Tiruvannamalai
To Cuddalore
Sosile
Pulahalli
Kambayanallur
Kollegal
Singanallur
Alambadi
Pennagaram
Dharmapuri
Nanjangud
Kaudalli
Tenkaraikottai
Maratahalli
Tirukkoyilur

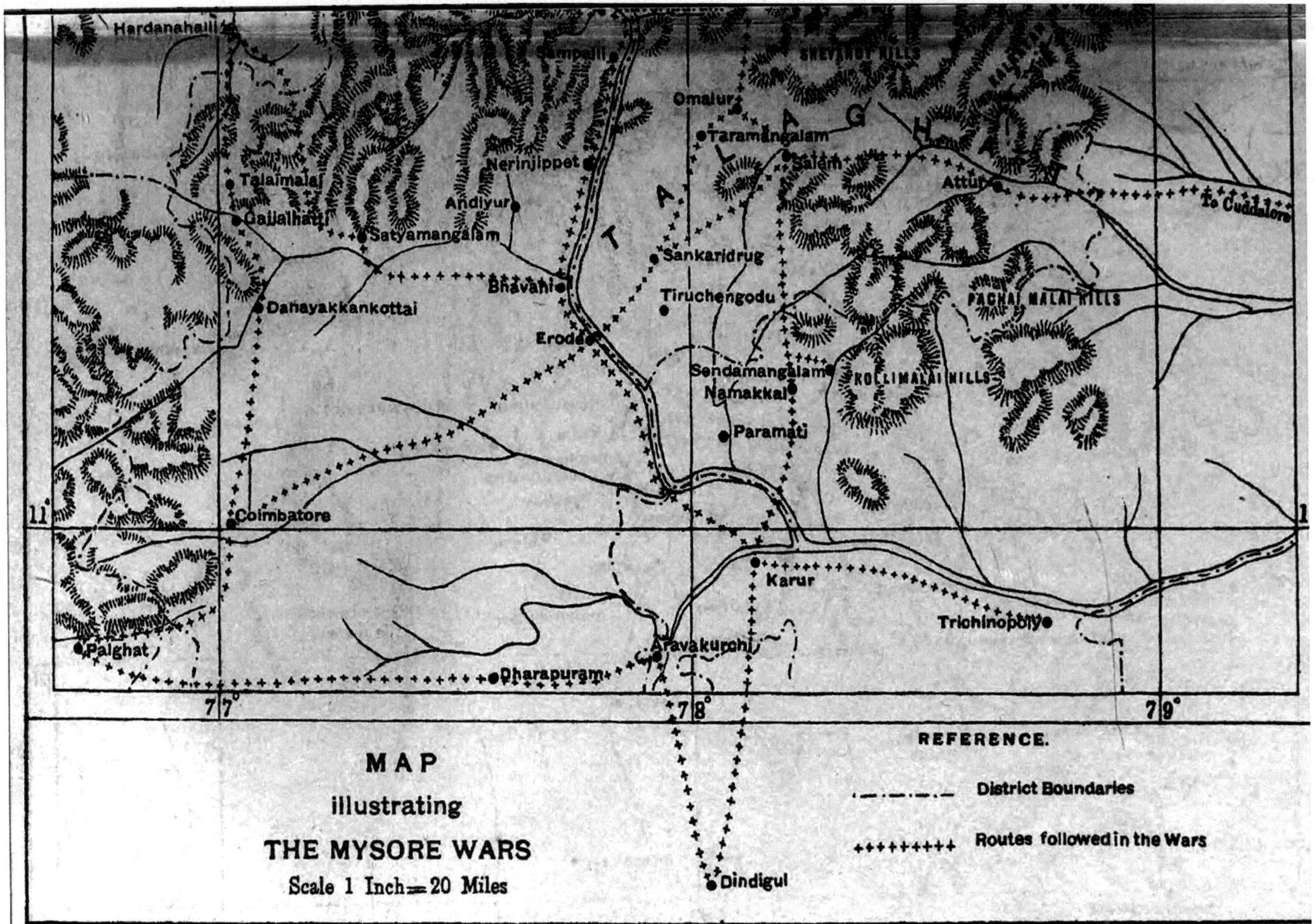

Reg: No. 548
Copies 620

Helio-Zinco., Survey Office, Madras.
1916

CHAP. II. VII. 1565–1761.

Kela-mangalam and occupied Anchetti-durgam. Here he was closely blockaded, and every attempt of Haidar's force at Ānekal to effect a junction failed. Haidar then resorted to the expedient of bribing the Marāthas to desert Khande Rao. The bribe, as usual, succeeded. Three lakhs were paid, the Bāramahāl was ceded. Haidar joined his brother-in-law, defeated Khande Rao, and assumed the supreme control of Mysore affairs.

VIII. THE MYSORE WARS. Prelude, 1761–66.

The year 1761 was eventful in Indian history. On January 15th, Pondicherry surrendered to the English, and French dominion in India ceased to exist. Eight days previously (January 7th) two hundred thousand Marāthas perished at Pānipat in battle against the Afghan Abdāli, and in the massacre which ensued. In the same year Haidar Ali, emboldened by the catastrophe at Pānipat, usurped the government of Mysore. By these events the political aspect was completely changed.

Haidar overrated the effect of Pānipat. Before the year 1761 had expired, he had, in alliance with the Nizām's brother Basālat Jang, driven the Marāthas out of Sīra, and on the payment of three lakhs, he was created Nawāb of Sīra, a title which Basālat Jang had not the faintest authority to bestow. The seizure of Sīra by Haidar was an insult to the Marāthas which brought speedy retribution. In 1764 the Peshwa himself invaded Mysore; by June, Haidar had sustained a crushing defeat, and in February of the following year he bought off the Marāthas with an indemnity of 32 lakhs. In 1766, the pageant Rāja died. His son, a youth of 18 years, was set on the throne by Haidar. The young prince chafed against Haidar's authority. Haidar confiscated all his property, and placed him in confinement. This act determined the Marāthas and Nizām Ali on Haidar's deposition, and precipitated the First Mysore War.

First Mysore War, 1767–9 A.D.

The War of 1767–9 is of peculiar interest in the history of Salem District, within the limits of which its chief operations were conducted. The war was a sequel to the treaty of November 12, 1766, between the Company and Nizām Ali. Under this, the Company accepted in fief from the Nizām the Northern Circars, already granted them by a firman of the Delhi Emperor, and engaged "to have a body of their troops ready to settle the affairs of His Highness' (the Nizām's) Government, in everything that is right and proper whenever required." In pursuance of this undertaking, plans for a joint invasion of Haidar's territory were agreed to by the Marāthas, the Nizam and the English.

CHAP. II. VIII. THE MYSORE WARS.

Marātha invasion.

The Marāthas moved first, and early in March, 1767, before their allies could join them, they had overrun the Mysore dominions as far as the Bāramahal, brought Haidar to his knees, and agreed to withdraw from the war on the payment of 17½ lakhs cash down, and the pledge of Kōlār District as security for the payment of a like sum in addition. The balance was paid early in May, and on the 11th of that month the Marāthas finally moved northwards.

Meanwhile the army of the Nizām had, by March 9th, reached the Tungabhadra, and was joined by Colonel Joseph Smith, with six battalions of infantry and some guns. On March 24th the allies learned that the Marāthas had been bribed to withdraw. Colonel Smith soon discovered that Haidar was making overtures to the Nizām also, which the latter was prepared to accept. He accordingly withdrew part of his force, but the Madras Government insisted on three battalions remaining in the Nizām's camp, as proof of confidence. This force was soon afterwards reduced to five companies, and the latter were suffered by the Nizām to depart within a few days of the actual outbreak of hostilities between Haidar and the British.

The English occupy the Bāramahāl.

While the Nizām's army was approaching Bangalore from the north, a respectable force of 3,000 foot, 500 of whom were British, was despatched from Madras with the object of seizing the Bāramahāl. The mud forts of Vāniyambādi, Tiruppattūr and Kāvēri-patnam fell without serious opposition, and on June 3rd an unsuccessful attempt was made to storm Krishnagiri. The siege was then converted into a blockade, the prosecution of which absorbed the energies of the whole force, and precluded further active operations.

Haidar invades the Bāramahāl.

On his return from the Nizām's camp near Bangalore, Colonel Smith was directed to assume general command of the British troops in the Bāramahāl. In the latter part of August the combined armies of Haidar and Nizām Ali[1] descended the Krishnagiri

[1] Smith estimated the relative strength of the armies as follows :—

	Cavalry.	Infantry.	Guns.
Nizām Ali	30,000	10,000	60
Haidar	12,860	18,000	49
Total ...	42,860	28,000	109
BRITISH—			
European	30	800	...
Native	...	5,000	16
Muhammad Ali	1,000	...	...
Total ...	1,030	5,800	16

Passes, and on the 25th, the transport cattle which were grazing in the vicinity of the British camp near Kakankarai,[1] were surprised and driven off. Smith's cavalry hastily moved out for their recovery, and were unexpectedly assailed by very superior numbers under Makhdum Ali, who charged them into the very lines of the encampment after destroying about one-third of their number, and carried off the greater part of the cattle.[2]

The same evening Haidar appeared before Kāveri-patnam, which was held by Captain McKain, with three companies of the 3rd Battalion of Coast Sepoys. Two assaults were delivered and repulsed; but Captain McKain, finding the place untenable, capitulated on August 27th.

By this time Colonel Wood was advancing with reinforcements from Trichinopoly towards Tiruvannāmalai,[3] and it became a matter of vital moment that Colonel Smith should join him. Smith, crippled by the loss of cattle on the 25th, was unable to move till the 28th. He fell back eastward, reaching Singārapet on the 30th, Palli-patti on the 31st, and Chengam on September 1st. Haidar followed close on his heels.

It was lucky for the British that he did not forestall them and seize the Chengam Pass. On September 2nd [*] Smith turned to bay at Chengam and won a victory. In this action he lost 48 Europeans and 67 sepoys killed and wounded; the enemy lost 4,000 men, 64 guns and a vast quantity of stores.[4] Smith then proceeded to Tiruvannāmalai. Finding no provision there, he was compelled to move further eastward in search of supplies. On September 8th he was joined by Colonel Wood, and on the 14th he retraced his steps to Tiruvannāmalai. There on the 26th he brought on a pitched battle with Haidar and won a decisive victory.[5] The Nizām and his army bolted, 55 field pieces were taken, and Haidar was compelled to retire into the Bāramahāl. Colonel Smith, unable for want of supplies to follow up his victory, dispersed his

---

[1] Now a railway station between Tiruppattūr and Sāmalpatti.

[2] Wilks i, 311.

[3] Commonly but wrongly called "Trinomalee," "Trinomally" etc., etc.

[4] Wilks estimates the loss of the confederates at 4,000 men and 64 guns with tumbrils. The loss to the British was 170 men killed and wounded.

[5] His total force amounted to 10,430 effective men with 1,500 bad horse.

European Infantry	1,400
Native Infantry	9.000
European Cavalry	30
Native Cavalry	1,500
Field Pieces	34

[*] According to Wilks, Vibert and Fortescue the battle of Chengam was fought on September 3rd.

CHAP. II. VIII. THE MYSORE WARS.

army into cantonments at Vellore, Conjeeveram, Wandiwash and Trichinopoly for the rainy season, and himself proceeded to Madras in the hope of effecting some improvement in the departments of Supply.

Āmbūr.

For a month the discomforted confederates remained at Mattūr[1] each blaming the other for the disaster at Tiruvannāmalai. Early in November Haidar, led by the continued inactivity of the British to believe himself safe from molestation, resumed the offensive, recaptured Tiruppattūr on the 5th, and Vāniyambādi on the 7th, and appeared before Āmbūr on the 10th. Vāniyambādi was surrendered by Captain Robinson, on parole not to serve again during the war, a promise which (apparently under Government orders) he subsequently broke.[2]

Captain Calvert's spirited defence of Āmbūr was ended on December 7th by the appearance of Colonel Smith with a detachment from Vellore. On the following day Smith came in touch with Haidar at Vāniyambādi. Haidar fought a rear-guard action, retiring as soon as his retreat was secured, and abandoning Vāniyambādi. In this action Haidar's corps of European horse, under Monsieur Aumont, moved off in a body and joined the English army.[3] The main body of the latter had to halt at Vāniyambādi to await provisions from Āmbūr, but Colonel Tod with the advance guard occupied Tiruppattūr on the 9th. The allies retreated towards Kāvēri-patnam, the defences of which had been so strengthened by Haidar since its capture, that Colonel Smith, meanwhile reinforced by Colonel Wood, who had advanced from Trichinopoly by the Singārapet Pass, declined to attack it.

Haidar quits the Bāramahāl.

At this juncture the allies learned of demonstrations by the Bombay Government against Mysore from the West Coast, and by Bengal troops from the Northern Circars against Haidarābād, and of a revolt of the Nāyars of Malabar. In consequence of this, Haidar, on December 14th, despatched his heavy guns and baggage with Tipu to the West, and four days later Nizām Ali hurriedly

---

[1] Wilks gives the name "Calaimuttoor." It is known that Haidar on one of his marches crossed the river at Kambaya-nallūr, which is only 4 miles from Irumattūr. As Mattūr, however, is easier to reach from Singārapet, and strategically covers Krishnagiri and Kāvēri-patnam, the probabilities favour Mattūr as the place of Haidar's halt.

[2] In December this Captain Robinson was second in command at Erode, when it was surrendered to Haidar under disgraceful circumstances. Haidar, after promising that the garrison should be allowed to proceed on parole to Trichinopoly, sent them all to the dungeons of Seringapatam. His plea was that Robinson's broken word of honour absolved him from his own promise.

[3] Wilks I, p. 326. This troop of foreign hussars numbered about 60 men, cf. Wilson *Madras Army*, I, p. 280.

re-ascended the Ghāts. Haidar, before following his main army, made one vigorous attempt in person to cut off a convoy, composed of the 1st Battalion[1] of Sepoys in charge of provisions, advancing under Captain R. V. Fitzgerald from Tiruvannāmalai. Smith anticipated the move, and despatched Major Thomas Fitzgerald, with two companies of Grenadiers, the 5th Battalion[2] of Sepoys, and two field-pieces to reinforce the convoy before Haidar could attack it. Haidar attacked the united forces in person on December 29th, with a force of 4,000 horse, 2,000 foot and 5 guns, and was badly beaten. Immediately after this, Haidar followed his main army up the Ghāts, leaving Makhdum Sahib with a strong force, mainly cavalry, to watch the British, and act on their supplies. At the same moment the British army was compelled to fall back eastward on its communications, to save itself from starvation.

January to August, 1768.

For seven months Haidar was fully occupied with affairs in the north and west, and the field was clear for the British forces. Divided counsels paralysed efficient action. The Government wished to invade the Bālāghāt, and strike directly at Bangalore and Seringapatam. Colonel Smith realised that his force was quite inadequate for the campaign without any proper commissariat, and proposed to occupy the whole of the country contiguous to the frontier, from Vāniyambādi through the Bāramahāl and Talaghāt down to Dindigul and Pālghāt, with a view to establishing depots as a base for subsequent operations. The result was an attempt to carry out both plans with a force inadequate for either.

Colonel Smith's Column.

The army was formed into two columns. Colonel Smith with 1,500 Europeans and 7,500 sepoys was to invade the Bālāghāt, Colonel Wood with 600 Europeans and 4,400 sepoys to reduce the lowland forts in detail.[3] On February 23rd the former appeared before Kāvēri-patnam, which was promptly abandoned. He then received orders to proceed to the camp of the Nizām at Punganūr. The Nizām had made overtures of peace to Colonel Smith as early as December 1767. A treaty was concluded between the Nizām and the Nawāb on February 23rd, which was signed by the members of Council on the 26th idem. Shortly afterwards Smith returned to

---

[1] Now the 61st Pioneers.

[2] Now the 64th Pioneers.

[3] Colonel Smith's column was composed of the 1st and 2nd European Regiments, a detachment of artillery, the Foreign Legion, Capt. Achmuty's Bengal Battalion, and the 1st, 3rd, 5th, 6th, 13th, 14th and 16th Madras Battalions. Colonel Wood's detachment consisted of the 3rd European Regiment, a party of artillery, the 4th, 7th, 8th and 11th Battalions, and 5 companies of the 10th.

CHAP. II.
VIII. THE MYSORE WARS.

the Bāramahāl, and undertook the blockade of Krishnagiri, which did not surrender till May 2nd.

Smith invades Bālāghāt.

On June 8th an advanced detachment of the British army, under Colonel Donald Campbell,[1] moved from Krishnagiri and ascended the Pass of Būdi-kōta[2]; on the 16th Venkatagiri-kōta was occupied, and the direct road to Vellore via Peddanāyakan-durgam secured. On the 23rd, Mulbāgal was taken, on the 28th, Kōlār. Meanwhile Colonel Smith, with the main army, had ascended the Būdi-kōta Ghāt, and arrived at Aralēri, where he directed Colonel Campbell to rejoin him. On July 3rd the united forces moved via Bāgalūr for the siege of Hosūr, which fell on the 11th. The Bāgalūr Poligār, a feudatory of Haidar, prudently abstained from hostilities with the English, "at the same time representing to Haidar his inability to resist, and the necessity of temporizing until he had a better opportunity of evincing his allegiance."[3] Shortly after the fall of Hosūr, a detachment under Captain Cosby seized Ānekal and Denkani-kōta. Several days were then wasted by the attempt of a detachment under Colonel Lang to occupy a number of villages surrounded by almost impenetrable jungles between Denkani-kōta and the Kāvēri, a move which Muhammad Ali thought might increase his revenues, but which could not be of any conceivable strategical importance.

At Hosūr, Smith was joined by the advance guard of Morāri Rao, the Marātha ruler of Gooty, whose services had been bargained for by the British and secured. Smith then moved to Hoskōte, where, on August 4th, he was joined by Morāri Rao in person. On that very day Haidar re-entered Bangalore. Haidar's first move was a night attack on the camp of Morāri Rao at Hoskōte; the attack was repulsed (August 22nd). Both armies now turned their attention to the advance of Colonel Wood.

Colonel Wood's Detachment.

This officer had begun his task of reducing the lowland forts with the siege of Tenkarai-kōttai, which capitulated, on the eve of assault, on February 12th. Dharmapuri was carried by assault. The slaughter of the defenders was so severe that only one other garrison (that of Erode) dare face Wood's storming party. The forts of Salem, Āttūr, Sēnda-mangalam and Nāmakkal surrendered without a blow. Wood then crossed the Kāvēri, secured the passes from Coimbatore to the plateau, and penetrated to Pālghāt. Doubling back through the south of Coimbatore District, by August 3rd he was master of Dindigul. He then received orders

[1] Colonel Campbell's force comprised detachments of the 1st and 2nd European Regiments, and of the 3rd, 5th, 14th and 16th Battalions.

[2] For the Būdi-kōta Ghāt vide Vol. II, p. 108.

[3] Wilks, I, p. 340.

CHAP. II. VIII. THE MYSORE WARS.

to join Smith in Mysore. Marching via the Toppūr Pass, he reached Krishnagiri on September 1st.

Junction of Smith and Wood.

Colonel Wood was expected to reach Būdi-kōta on September 5th, and move thence to Mālūr on the 6th. Colonel Smith, however, having lost touch with Haidar on the 3rd, thought it wise to advance and meet Wood's force. He threw his baggage into Mālūr on the 5th, and on the 6th morning advanced towards Būdi-kōta. The move was a fortunate one, and might have led to Haidar's destruction, but for the fool-hardiness of Colonel Wood.[1] Haidar, carefully concealing his movements, had taken up such a position at a bend of the defile up which Wood must march, that he could enfilade the advancing troops from chosen positions, and, taking advantage of the ensuing confusion, annihilate the British force. As Smith advanced, he received early intelligence of the movements of Wood and Haidar, and realised that the latter could be trapped. He sent messengers to apprise Colonel Wood of his intentions. He shortly afterwards reached the corner of the defile where he hoped to attack Haidar, when both he and Haidar were startled by "a regular salute which Colonel Wood thought proper to fire in honour of Colonel Smith on receiving the message of his approach." The warning was enough, Haidar withdrew and Smith and Wood joined their forces without opposition, but the chance of dealing the enemy a severe blow was lost. Haidar now offered the cession of the Bāramahāl, and an indemnity of ten lakhs, as the price of peace. The terms were rejected. The Government were soon to repent their rashness in rejecting these proposals.

The British army next moved on Kōlār. Meanwhile Haidar recovered Mulbāgal. On October 3rd Wood[2] retook the Pēta and failed at the Fort. On the following day Wood was attacked in force by Haidar, and barely escaped defeat.

Towards the end of October, Smith was summoned by the Government to Madras, and on November 14th he set out from Kōlār towards Venkatagiri-kōta with Muhammad Ali and the two Deputies, with whom Government had thought fit to hamper the discretion of their Commander-in-Chief. Smith's column moved

---

[1] Smith's force comprised the 1st and 2nd European Regiments, the 1st, 3rd and 5th Battalions and Achmuty's Bengal Battalion. Wood had with him the 3rd Regiment of Europeans, the 8th and 11th Battalions of Sepoys and 4 companies of the 7th Battalion.

[2] In consequence of the displeasure expressed by Colonel Smith at Colonel Wood's incomprehensible salute of September 6th, the latter desired permission to resign his command, and Colonel Lang took his place. Colonel Wood, however resumed his command by the end of September. (Wilks, i, p. 345–346).

CHAP. II. VIII. THE MYSORE WARS.

eastward to cover their march, Wood remaining in command at Kōlār. On the first day's march of the Nawāb's party, news was received that Haidar was attacking Hosūr. Smith accordingly detached the 2nd European Regiment and Captain Cosby's Battalion of Sepoys to reinforce Wood. The remainder of Smith's force, under Major Fitzgerald, occupied Venkatagiri-kōta, to cover the retreat of the Nawāb and the Deputies.

On November 16th Wood marched to the relief of Hosūr.[1] On the 17th he reached Bāgalūr and deposited there his baggage, camp equipage and surplus stores, with two brass 18-pounders, as a preliminary to a night attack on Haidar's camp. From Bāgalūr to Hosūr is 7½ miles. Wood started from Bāgalūr at 10 P.M., and reached Hosūr at 7 A.M. on the morning of the 18th. Haidar allowed him to enter the fort unmolested. His cavalry kept Wood's force amused with demonstrations in all directions, while his infantry by a flank march proceeded to Bāgalūr. It was not till 2 P.M. that the sound of firing to the north convinced Colonel Wood of the situation. He hastily retraced his steps to Bāgalūr, but arrived too late. Haidar, without attempting an attack on the Fort, had entered the Pēta, packed nearly the whole of the stores and baggage of the British army on his carts, tumbrils and gun-carriages, and marched them off to Bangalore with the two 18-pounders. By the time Wood reached Bāgalūr, nearly the whole of Haidar's army was out of sight. An awful panic in the Pēta had resulted in the loss of over 2,000 human lives and as many bullocks.

On November 20th, Wood returned to Hosūr, and gave the garrison what ammunition and stores he could spare. On the 21st he marched via Bāgalūr to Aralēri, where there was a small supply of provisions. There he was attacked in force by Haidar on the 22nd and 23rd, and was only saved from annihilation by the arrival of Major Fitzgerald from Venkatagiri-kōta, with every man he could muster. On Fitzgerald's approach, Haidar, thinking he had the dreaded Smith to deal with, drew off to a respectful distance, and permitted the united forces of the British to proceed to Venkatagiri-kōta. Wood was sent under arrest to Madras and Colonel Lang took command.

Haidar invades the Carnatic and ends the War.

As soon as Haidar discovered that Smith was no longer in the field against him, he threw to the winds all anxiety for the safety of Bangalore. Early in November Fazl-ulla-Khān had been organizing a force at Seringapatam, and towards the end of the

[1] His force consisted of the 2nd and 3rd Eeropean Regiments (about 700 men) and 5 Battalions of Sepoys, among them the 6th, 11th and 16th.

month, he swooped down on Coimbatore District through the Passes of Gajalhatti and Kāvēri-puram.[1] On December 6th Haider himself marched into the Bāramahāl viâ Pālakōdu, and debouched on the Talaghāt through the Toppūr Pass. Four days later, Major Fitzgerald started in pursuit with a select force of 5,000 men[2], but he could not come up with Haidar. Colonel Wood's short-lived conquests in the Bāramahāl and Salem were garrisoned mostly by the troops of the Nawāb, without any mixture of English sepoys. Capture after capture was reported to Fitzgerald, Dharmapuri on December 6th, Tenkarai-kōttai on the 7th, Ōmalūr 12th, Salem 15th, Nāmakkal 17th, Karūr 19th, Erode 25th, Dindigul 31st. Fitzgerald pushed straight for Trichinopoly. Lang fell back from Kōlār on Vellore. Within six weeks Haider had won back every post that had been taken from him except Krishnagiri, Venkatagiri-kōta and Kōlār, the first of little strategic value, the other two untenable. Haider's final move is famous in history. When 140 miles south of Madras, he suddenly despatched his whole army, guns and baggage, through the Bāramahāl, reserving for his purpose only 6,000 horse and 200 chosen foot. With these he marched 130 miles in three days and a half, and on March 29th he appeared with his cavalry before Madras. He dictated peace on his own terms. A treaty was signed on April 3, 1769, stipulating the mutual restitution of prisoners and places, and a mutual defensive alliance.[3]

Haidar invades the Carnatic and ends the War.

Second Mysore War (1780–84).

The Second Mysore War is a tedious record of disaster from the British point of view. Throughout the War, Salem District was Haidar's own, and its soil was never violated by the tread of hostile troops. The Treaty of Mangalore was signed on March 11, 1784 and under it the *status quo ante* was restored. The Company was not in position to claim a foot of Salem soil.

Third Mysore War.

At the end of December 1789 Tipu attacked the Travancore Lines and was beaten off. In April 1790 he carried them by storm.

---

[1] An interesting account of the Kāvēri-puram Ghāt is given by Buchanan, Vol. I, pp. 406–422. His itinerary was Siva-samudram, Sattēgalam, "Pailia" Singānallūr, Hannūr, Kandhalli, Maratahalli, Nadukkāval, Chikka-Kaval, Kāvēri-puram. Cf. Bevan, *Thirty Years in India*, I, p. 53, sq.

[2]

European and Native Cavalry	500
3rd Regiment European Infantry	350
Grenadier Companies 1st and 2nd Regiments ...	150
Five Battalions of Sepoys	4,000

8 six-pounders, 6 three-pounders and a detail of artillery men. The Sepoy Battalions were the 3rd, 5th, 6th, 13th and 16th.

[3] "In case either of the contracting parties shall be attacked, they shall, from their respective countries, mutually assist each other to drive them out." Aitchison's Treaties, Vol. V, p. 253).

CHAP. II. VIII. THE MYSORE WARS.

This began the Third Mysore War. The English formed an alliance with the Marāthas and Nizām to curb Tipu's aggressiveness.

Medows' Campaign, 1790.

The first stage of the War was mostly confined to operations in Coimbatore and Salem. General Medows left Trichinopoly on May 26th,[1] seized Karūr on June 15th, and proceeded to reduce the fortresses scattered over Coimbatore in detail. Coimbatore itself was occupied without resistance on July 21st. Erode fell on August 6th, and Dindigul on August 23rd. A force was sent against Pālghāt, and another against a body of 4,000 horse which Tipu had posted in the country for observation. This force was driven up the Gajalhatti Pass, and Satya-mangalam was surprised and taken. But these operations, while leaving Medows master of Coimbatore, had split his army into three divisions between Pālghāt, Coimbatore and Satya-mangalam. Tipu, hitherto inactive, now began to move. On the 2nd September, at the head of 40,000 men, he left Seringapatam, passed south through the Gajalhatti Pass (September 11th) and crossed the Bhavāni river (September 12th). The moves and counter-moves of the next few days compelled Medows to return from the line of the Bhavāni to Coimbatore, where he concentrated his scattered forces between September 18th and 26th. Meanwhile Tipu marched on Erode, which at his approach was evacuated (September 25th). By this move he recovered several of the places taken, and inflicted several minor reverses on the British arms.

Maxwell's Advance.

Meanwhile a second English field force, 9,500 strong, had concentrated at Ārni under Colonel Kelly.[2] On September 24th that officer died, and the command devolved on Colonel Maxwell. Exactly a month later (October 24th) Maxwell entered Tipu's territory near Vāniyambādi; on November 1st he approached Krishnagiri, but, instead of attacking, drew off and fixed his head-quarters at Kāvēri-patnam (November 3rd).

As soon as Tipu heard of Maxwell's advance, he started post-haste for the Bāramahāl. By November 9th Tipu's light cavalry reached Kāvēri-patnam. On the 12th Tipu appeared in full force, and attempted, by a variety of evolutions, to find the means of attacking Maxwell with advantage; but the strong position assumed by that officer, his admirable dispositions and his promptitude in anticipating every design, frustrated these intentions, and the Sultān drew off. The same manœuvres were repeated on the

---

[1] His force amounted to about 15,000 men. For details see Wilson, *Madras Army*, ii, p. 191.

[2] For details see Wilson, II, p. 193.

13th and 14th. Meanwhile Medows had started in pursuit of Tipu. He crossed the Kāvēri on November 8th; on the 14th he encamped at the south extremity of the Pass of Toppūr. On the following day he cleared the Pass, and reached a camping ground at the northern extremity, situated about 29 miles from Kāvēri-patnam. Here a camp was espied, six miles away. Thinking it was Maxwell's, the English fired three signal guns. In five minutes every tent in the supposed English camp was struck, and heavy columns were seen in full march to the west. Medows now realised that he was in sight of Tipu's army. He did not give pursuit, his junction with Maxwell was more important. This was effected on the 17th at Pula-halli, 12 miles south of Kāvēri-patnam.[1] Tipu now decided to double back through the Toppūr Pass, and try his fortune in the Carnatic. On the 18th both armies were in motion, both pointing to the Pass of Toppūr, and both intending to clear it in two easy marches. The two armies were actually preparing to encamp within four miles of each other, before they discovered each other's presence. Tipu's columns had entered the Pass by the time the main body of the English army arrived on the camping ground. It was a golden opportunity for cutting off a portion of the enemy's infantry, and attacking the remainder while entangled in the Pass. Medows let the chance slip. Tipu's army cleared the Pass, with the exception of three infantry battalions in the rear of the main column, which were intercepted and compelled to retreat in the opposite direction, and the majority of the cavalry, which disappeared towards Pennā-garam, and rejoined the main body by a circuitous route some days later. Tipu held on without halting for Trichinopoly, and Medows' campaign was rendered abortive.

Campaign of Cornwallis, 1791.

Shortly after, Medows was called to Madras to confer with Lord Cornwallis, who arrived there on December 12th. His arrival marks the second stage in the War. The English now had a definite objective, namely, Seringapatam. The Governor-General concentrated at Vellore on February 10th. To meet his advance, Tipu doubled back from the Carnatic viâ Chengam and Pālakōdu. Cornwallis had feigned the invasion of the Bāramahāl. His real intention was to advance on Kōlār by the Mogili Pass, west of Chittoor. This plan he carried out on February 17th, and on the 28th Kōlār fell.[2] Bangalore was stormed on March 21st; on May 4th Cornwallis started for Seringapatam; but the rains set in, his commissariat broke down, and he had to return to Bangalore. By July he began a series of operations for the reduction of Tipu's

[1] For details of the brigading of the combined forces, see Wilson, II, p. 201.

[2] He marched via Chittoor, Palmanēr, Mulbāgal, Kōlār, Hoskōte, Bangalore.

CHAP. II. VIII. THE MYSORE WARS.

outlying forts. Hosūr, Anchetti-durgam, Nīlagiri, Ratnagiri, were taken without resistance. Some sharp fighting under Major Gowdie was seen at Rāya-kōta, when the lower fort was stormed on July 20th; the upper fort surrendered two days later. About the same time Hudē-durgam and other small hill forts capitulated.[1] Garrisons were placed in Rāya-kōta, Anchetti-durgam and Hudō-durgam. The other places were dismantled. In September the British directed their efforts to reducing the country north of Bangalore.

Pennāgaram.

In October 1791 a diversion was caused in the Bāramahāl by a force under Bakir Sahib, an active young officer, son of the venerable Killedar of Dhārwar. He descended into Coimbatore and entered the Bāramahāl by the Toppūr Pass. His object was threefold; (1) to throw reinforcements into Krishnagiri, (2) to harass the English communications, (3) to sweep off in a southern direction the population and cattle of the whole District. Colonel Maxwell was despatched against him. The plunderers had ensconced themselves and their captives in the fort of Pennāgaram. Colonel Maxwell appeared before the fort on October 31st, and called on the garrison to surrender. In reply, the flag of truce was fired upon. The fort was instantly assaulted and carried by escalade with little loss to the assailants; but of the garrison two hundred men were killed before the indignation of the troops could be restrained. Bakir Sahib soon found the Bāramahāl untenable, thanks to Maxwell's activity, and retired via Chengam to the Coromandel.

Krishnagiri.

Maxwell now proceeded to Krishnagiri, and seized the Pēta by surprise on November 7th. His attempts on the Rock itself were repulsed.

Close of the War.

Soon afterwards Maxwell rejoined the main army, which was again preparing for the march on Seringapatam. What followed does not concern this narrative. Tipu was brought to his knees before the end of February, and a peace was ratified on March 19th, which stripped Tipu of half his dominions, and crippled him with a fine of over thirty million rupees. By this treaty the whole of the present Salem District, except Hosūr Taluk, came under the Company's rule.

Interlude, 1792-99.

The interval between the Third and Fourth Mysore Wars contains little of interest, except from an administrative point of view. This is dealt with in its proper place. The military forces were placed under the charge of Captain Alexander Read, the first Collector, whose head-quarters were at Krishnagiri with the 15th

---

[1] Including Chendrāya-durgam, see note on p. 87.

Battalion.[1] The 4th Battalion[2] was at Pennāgaram, under Captain Turing, who died there in 1793. The 22nd Battalion was quartered under Captain Oram at Sankaridrug, with a detachment under Lieutenant Macdonald at Salem. The quarters of the 23rd Battalion were fixed at Āttūr under Captain Campbell, and a detachment under Lieutenant Lang was posted to Nāmakkal.[3]

Fourth Mysore War, 1799.

The last Mysore War possesses little of interest so far as it concerns Salem District. Tipu never had a chance. His whole force did not exceed 33,000 foot and 15,000 horse. His territory was invaded from Coorg by General Stuart with 6,400 men, from the Bāramahāl by General Harris with a well equipped army of nearly 30,000. Colonel Read (the first Collector of Salem) secured abundant supplies for the advancing troops. General Harris left Vellore on February 11, 1799, and marched through the vale of Āmbūr. On the 18th he was joined by the Nizām's contingent "consisting of above 6,000 of the Company's troops subsidised by His Highness; about the same number of his own infantry, including a proportion of Peron's, the late French corps, now commanded by British officers, and a large body of cavalry."[5] On the 28th, this army encamped at Kāri-mangalam. Thence it proceeded via Pālakōdu and "Suntamarinelly" to Rāya-kōta, where it encamped on March 4th. Hostilities began on the 5th, when

---

[1] Davis-ki-paltan, now the 75th Carnatic Infantry.

[2] Baillie-ki-paltan, now the 64th Pioneers. The following additional information has been furnished by the courtesy of Captain H. F. Murland from the regimental records of the 64th Pioneers (Baillie-ki-paltan). At the close of hostilities in 1792 a detachment of the 4th Battalion of about 50 strong, was posted at Vírabhadra-durgam, and another about 130 strong, at Tiruppattūr. In 1794 there were detachments at Vírabhadra-durgam (Lt. MacRae), Tiruppattūr, Chendrāya-durgam and Sōlappadi. In 1795 the regiment was stationed at Rāya-kōta under Captain Gabriel Doveton, with detachments at Vírabhadra-durgam (Lt. MacRae) Chendrāya-durgam (Lt. MacGregor) and Kangundi (Lt. Grant). In 1797 and 1798 there were detachments at Salem (300 strong under Captain Innes), Virabhadra-durgam (Lt. Brown), Chendrāya-durgam (Lt. Cormick) and Kangundi (Lt. Symons). Chendrāya-durgam lies about one mile from Nam-mānda-halli, in the extreme west of Krishnagiri Taluk. Ruins of fortifications and other buildings are still to be seen on the hill-top, and on the plain to the north is a plot of land traditionally known as the "drill-ground." The village site at the foot of the hill is no longer inhabited. Chendrāya-durgam is referred to in Allan's *Views* as a small but strong hill fort which fell to Maxwell on July 23rd, 1791, the day after the capitulation of Rāya-kōta to Major Gowdie (p. 86 above). It is also mentioned as an important strategic stronghold in *Supplementary Despatches of the Duke of Wellington*, edited by his son (1858) Vol. I, pp. 55-67.

[3] See Wilson, II, p. 239.

[4] Main Army, 20,802; Nizam's detachment, 6,536; Nizam's Infantry, formerly French Corps, 2,621—Total, 29,959.

[5] Beatson, p. 53.

CHAP. II. VIII. THE MYSORE WARS.

a detachment under Major John Cuppage occupied without resistance the small hill forts of Nīlagiri and Anchetti-durgam. Hudē-durgam surrendered to Lieut.-Col. Oliver on the 7th, and Ratnagiri was occupied after slight resistance on the 8th. Meanwhile, on the 7th, General Harris had established his head-quarters at Kela-mangalam, and by the 9th his whole army was collected there.

At this moment Tipu was at Maddūr. A party of 1,500 horse had been detached to Hosūr, to watch the movements of the army, and to burn forage. It was the policy of General Harris to keep him in the dark, as long as possible, as to the route by which he would advance on Seringapatam. Three alternatives offered themselves. (1) The shortest route from Kela-mangalam was via Tali, Maralavādi and Kankanhalli; but "the Pass of Tali had never been examined, and it appeared that, besides the uncertainty of finding it passable for heavy guns, the probable time it would require to explore and to repair it would more than counterbalance the advantage which might be gained on the distance". The routes (2) via Ānekal and Kankanhalli, and (3) via Ānekal and Chennapatna, had already been surveyed, the former having been traversed by Lord Cornwallis in May 1791. The Ānekal-Kankanhalli route was determined on by General Harris after careful deliberation, the idea being to deceive Tipu into a belief that Bangalore was his first objective.

Lord Harris moved from Kela-mangalam on March 10th. The Sultan's horse harassed the advancing columns at first and succeeded, near the village of Gulisandiram, in cutting up a light company of the rear-guard of the Nizam's contingent. The army camped at Kalugondapalli (on the present Hosūr-Tali road) for the night, and owing to delay in the transport, was compelled to halt there during the 11th. The march was resumed on the 12th. On the 27th Tipu was defeated at Malavalli, and on May 4th Seringapatam was stormed and the Sultān slain.

DISTRICT GARRISONS

In the division of territory which followed the capture of Seringapatam, the Bālāghāt taluks of Hosūr, Denkani-kōta, Kela-mangalam, Venkatagiri-kōta, and Ālambādi, with the Pālaiyams of Bāgalūr, Bērikai and Sūlagiri were added to Salem District.[1] On November 5, 1799, a general redistribution of garrisons and detachments throughout the Presidency was effected, under the orders of Lord Clive, then Governor of Fort St. George. Under these arrangements, Krishnagiri was selected as the headquarters for the Bāramahāl, and Sankaridrug for the Talaghāt while a garrison at Rāya-kōta guarded the Bālāghāt. One

[1] Aitchison's Treaties, V. p. 183.

Battalion of Native Infantry was allotted to Krishnagiri and Rāya-kōta; one Battalion to Sankaridrug, and five companies were detached from the latter to garrison Salem, Nāmakkal and Āttūr; Krishnagiri, Rāya-kōta and Sankaridrug were made Government Commands in the Centre Division of the Madras Army, while Salem, Nāmakkal and Āttūr were classed among "other posts or stations which were occasionally occupied by troops furnished by detachments from the principal stations." Krishnagiri, Rāya-kōta, Sankaridrug and Āttūr were made ordnance stations. The garrison at Pennāgaram was apparently withdrawn.

In 1814 four Native Veteran Battalions[1] were formed for garrison duties, and shortly afterwards the garrisons of the District seem to have been reduced, for, between 1816 and 1851, the only troops, with few exceptions, which figure in the lists were detachments from Native Veteran Battalions.

In 1823 Salem seems to have taken precedence of Sankaridrug as the chief military station in the Balāghāt. By 1824 Āttūr had ceased to be a military station, by 1832 Nāmakkal had shared the same fate, and soon after 1832 Sankaridrug and Krishnagiri disappear from the list.

In 1850 Salem was transferred from the Centre or Presidency Division, to the South or Trichinopoly Division of the Madras Army, and was allotted two companies of the first Native Veteran Battalion, and in the following year Rāya-kōta was attached to the Bangalore Command, and garrisoned by a company detached from Regiments stationed at Bangalore. This arrangement continued till 1857, when a general redistribution of the army was brought into force, resulting in the withdrawal of detachments from out-posts, and the concentration of troops as far as possible in the head-quarters of Divisions and Brigades. Rāya-kōta was handed over to a half company of the 2nd or Ārni Native Veteran Battalion, who were finally relieved by the Police in 1860.

---

[1] 1st (in Madras) Native Veteran Battalion, Head-quarters, Fort St. George.
2nd (in Ārni) Native Veteran Battalion, Head-quarters, Chingleput.
3rd (in Ganjām) Native Veteran Battalion, Head-quarters, Chicacole.
4th (in Dindigul) Native Veteran Battalion, Head-quarters, Dindigul.

CHAPTER III.

THE PEOPLE.

POPULATION—Growth—Density—LANGUAGE—RELIGIONS—CHRISTIANS—Roman Catholic Missions—London Mission—Lutheran Missions. MUHAMMADANS—Moharram. HINDUS—Villages—Houses—Dress—Tattooing—Food—Games. RELIGION—I. Brahmanic—(A) Siva—(B) Vishnu. II. Pāndava Cult III. Manmatha Cult. IV. Vira-Saivas. V. Grāma Dēvatās, comprising (A). Ayyanār Cult—(B) Sakti Cults—(C) Demon Cults—Hook-swinging. SOCIAL ORGANISATION—Caste—Right and Left Hand Factions—Polity—Ordeals—Oaths. CUSTOMS—Pollution—Childbirth—Customs of Childhood—Marriage Customs—Funeral Customs. SURVEY OF CASTES—(A) Brahmans—(B) Non-Brahmans—(1) Agricultural—(i) Tamil—Vellālars—Pallis—Nāttāns—Agamudaiyans—Udaiyāns—Vettuvans—Malaiyālis—(ii) Telugu—Kāpus—Kammas—(iii) Kanarese—Vakkiligas. (2) Pastoral—Idaiyans—Kurubas—Gollas. (3) Fishermen—Sembadavans. (4) Hunters—Vēdars and Bōdars. (5) Traders—Chettis—Balijas. (6) Industrial—(i) Weavers—Kaikōlars—Dēvāngas—(ii) Oil-pressers—Vāniyars—(iii) Toddy-drawers—Shānārs—(iv) Potters—(v) Salt-workers—Uppiliyans—(vi) Mat-makers—Vēdakkārans—(vii) Artizans—Kammālars. (7) Labourers—Oddars—Pallans. (8) Menials—Barbers—Dhobies. (9) Military Castes—Marāthas. (10) Sectarian—Lingāyats. (11) Mendicants. (12) Miscellaneous—Kanakkans—Sātānis—Koravas—Dommaras—Lambādis—Irulas. (13) Panchamas—Pariahs.

POPULATION. THOUGH Census Statistics can claim no scientific accuracy prior to 1871, yet the estimates of population made at earlier periods since the British occupation are not without their interest. The marginal statement gives such figures as are available. It will be observed that, during a century of British Rule, the population has nearly quadrupled, an eloquent testimony to the *Pax Britannica*. The total for 1901 was over half a million greater than the total population of Wales in that year; after the excision of

Year.	Population.
1797 ..	594,252 [1]
1800	612,871 [2]
1835	905,190
1838	898,233
1850	1,195,365
1861	1,493,221
1866	1,619,233
1871	1,966,995
1878	1,559,896 [3]
1881	1,598,640
1891	1,962,591
1901	2,204,974
1911	1,766,680 [4]

[1] Read's estimate of 594,252 excludes, of course, the Bālāghāt. The estimate for 1850 exclusive of the Bālāghāt is 1,054,958.

[2] The figures apply to South Salem and Coimbatore—vide part II, p. 58.

[3] Famine Census. Drop due to Famine of 1876–77.

[4] Drop due to exclusion of Nāmakkal and Tiruppattūr Taluks.

Nāmakkal and Tiruppattūr, the total for 1911 is about double that of Wales less Glamorganshire.

Growth of population.

The fluctuations in population since 1871 is a matter of great interest, in view of the devastations caused by the Great Famine of 1876-77. From columns 2, 6, 7 and 8 of the subjoined statement it will be seen that the Bāramahāl suffered far more than the Talaghāt, and recovered much more slowly; that the Bālāghāt fared worse even than the Bāramahāl, failing to recover itself for three decades; and that, of the Talaghāt taluks, Āttūr possesses by far the greatest power of resistance, being virtually famine-proof. It will also be noted that the rate of increase in the decade 1881-91 immediately following the Famine was, except in Hosūr, nearly double that of the next decade (1891-1901); and that in the latter decade the increase varies inversely with the decrease in 1881. By 1891 the southern taluks had recovered their equilibrium between population and food supply, and the northern taluks had not.

—	Decade, 1871-1881.	Decade, 1881-1891.	Decade, 1891-1901.	Decade, 1901-1911.	Twenty years from 1871-1891.	Thirty years from 1871-1901.	Forty years from 1871-1911.
1	2	3	4	5	6	7	8
	PER CENT.	PER CENT.	PER CENT.	PER CENT.	PER CENT.	PER CENT.	PER CENT.
Hosūr	— 30	+ 18½	+ 18¾	+ 5¾	— 21⅜	— 2¼	+ 3½
Krishnagiri	— 29	+ 26	+ 15¼	+ 8⅛	— 12	+ 3	+ 6¼
Dharmapuri	— 27	+ 31	+ 15½	+ 9⅛	— 5	+ 10	+ 20
Ūttankarai	— 27	+ 26	+ 15½	— 1⅞	— 9	+ 6	+ 4
Salem	— 19	+ 27½	+ 12¾	*	+ 3⅜	+ 16½	*
Tiruchengōdu ...	— 22¼	+ 30	+ 16½	*	+ ¼	+ 17½	*
Āttūr	— 2½	+ 15½	+ 9	+ 4	+ 12⅝	+ 22⅞	+ 27¾
Salem District ...	— 18¾	+ 23¼	+ 12½	*	— ¼	+ 12½	*

* Not known, as the Taluk boundaries were modified before the Census of 1911 was taken.

Density.

The number of persons per square mile in 1911 was 280, against 230 for Wales in the same year. The density in the Bālāghāt is 161, in the Bāramahāl 224, in the Talaghāt 392. Salem and Tiruchengōdu are the most thickly populated taluks, and Ōmalūr stands third. Next to Hosūr, the most sparsely peopled area is Ūttankarai.[1]

[1] The following statement shows the number of persons per square mile in each taluk in 1911 :—

Hosūr	161	Salem	487
Krishnagiri	276	Ōmalūr	377
Dharmapuri ...	238	Tiruchengōdu ...	489
Ūttankarai	172	Āttūr	247

CHAP. III. POPULATION.

With the sole exception of Salem City,[1] the population shows no very marked tendency to gravitate to towns, of which only seven are recognised in the Census Lists.[2]

LANGUAGE.

Out of every 1,000 of the population, 747 speak Tamil as their house language, 148 Telugu, 76 Kanarese, 22 Hindustāni, 4 Patnūli and 3 Marāthi. In other words, about three-fourths of the total population are Tamil, a little over one-eighth Telugu, and a little over one-sixteenth Kanarese.

The percentage of Tamil-speakers is 81 in the Talaghāt and 74 in the Bāramahāl; in the Bālāghāt it falls to 43. Telugu is fairly evenly distributed throughout the District, owing to the number of Telugu ryots who settled in the Talaghāt in the wake of Vijayanagar conquests. Kanarese on the other hand is most in evidence in the Bālāghāt, where it exceeds 30 per cent., and in the Northern Bāramahāl Taluks of Krishnagiri and Dharmapuri, where it is just under 10 per cent. In the remaining taluks of the District the Kanarese speakers are under 5 per cent., falling in Āttūr to 2 per cent. Hindustāni, and also Marāthi, are more frequently met with in the Bālāghāt and Bāramahāl than in the Talaghāt; the proportion is highest in Hosūr, Krishnagiri coming second. This is clearly due to the circumstance that Hosūr and Krishnagiri have had a more martial past than the rest of the District. Patnūli (a dialect of Gujarati, sometimes written in Telugu characters) is confined to the silk-weavers of Salem. The Lambādi dialect is spoken by 855 persons, mostly in Hosūr, Dharmapuri and Ūttankarai, and 202 persons (mostly in Ūttankarai) are returned as speaking the Yerukala or Korava dialect.

Tamil is understood throughout the District, except in certain parts of the Bālāghāt where Kanarese predominates. The quality of the Tamil spoken is not pure, but a detailed account of the local dialect is beyond the scope of this book. Ryots are very apt to substitute *l* for *r*, and *vice versa*, especially with foreign words;

[1] Salem City increased from 10,000 in 1801 to 70,000 odd in 1901—*vide infra*, Vol. II, p. 247.

[2] ——	1891.	1901.	1911.
Rāsipuram	10,539	11,512	15,238
Āttūr	9,295	9,673	10,992
Krishnagiri	9,726	10,446	10,887
Dharmapuri	6,989	8,102	6,458
Hosūr	5,756	6,695	5,913
Kāvēripatnam	4,457	4,954	5,171
Tiruchengōdu	7,511	8,196	4,645

LANGUAGE.

e.g., "lubber" instead of "rubber," or "rantern" instead of "lantern". Not infrequently *v* (வ்) is substituted for *p* or *b* (ப்) (*e.g.*, வைத்தூர் instead of பைத்தூர்), and sometimes *y* (ய்) takes the place of *s* (ச்) (*e.g.*, Srīnivāyan instead of Srīnivāsan). Another local peculiarity is the occasional substitution of *k* (க்) for *b* (ப்), *e.g.*, the familiar name Subramaniyam is often corrupted to Sukkramani or Sukku, a change which suggests the familiar philological equation *equus* = *hippos*. The letter ழ is usually pronounced like ள.

Though most Muhammadans profess to speak Hindustāni, the house language of the Labbais is ordinarily Tamil, and of the Pinjāris Telugu (p. 104). The majority of the Muhammadans in the northern taluks are returned as speaking Hindustāni, but, in the ultra-Tamil Taluks of Tiruchengōdu and Āttūr, only two-thirds and one-half, respectively, of the Muhammadans appear to know of the language.

The polyglot character of the District must have presented serious difficulties to Read and his Assistants. The *paimaish* records of Salem, Āttūr and Tiruchengōdu are written in Tamil. One-fifth of those at Ūttankarai are in Tamil, two-fifths in Kanarese, two-fifths in Marāthi. The Marāthi is corrupted with a number of Hindustāni words. Nine-tenths of the Dharmapuri records are in Kanarese, the rest being in Marāthi, Tamil and Hindi. In Krishnagiri, two-thirds are in Kanarese, one-third in Marāthi. In Tiruppattūr, half are in Tamil, half in Telugu. Lastly in Hosūr three-fourths of the accounts are in Kanarese and one-fourth in Marāthi. Marāthi was the official language of the District till 1851, when Mr. Phillips procured the Board's sanction for its abolition in revenue correspondence. In October 1854 the Board ordered that the practice of submitting *jamābandi* accounts to their office in Marāthi should be discontinued; thenceforward the Marāthi language ceased to have any official existence in the District.

RELIGIONS.

Of every thousand inhabitants, 967 are Hindus, 25 Muhammadans and 8 Christians. The Muhammadans are above the District average in Hosūr (55 per mille), Krishnagiri (45), and Ūttankarai (32); the Christians only in Salem and Āttūr (each 13 per mille). The proportion of Muhammadans for the District is less than half that for the Presidency.

CHRISTIANS.

Christians in 1911 numbered 15,002 or less than one per cent. of the total population. Of these, 584 were Europeans or Eurasians, and 14,418 were Indians. Of the Indian Christians, 13,301, or 92 per cent. were Roman Catholics, the remaining 8 per cent. being divided among the various Protestant denominations; 652 (rather

CHAP. III. CHRISTIANS.

less than 5 per cent.) belonged to the London Mission,[1] 177 to the various Lutheran Missions, 124 were Anglicans, and the remainder were attached to minor sects, or were unspecified.[2]

Roman Catholics.

St. Francis Xavier, the Apostle of India, came from Portugal to Goa in 1540, and made innumerable converts during the ten years of his ministration in the country. The work begun by him was taken up by the Jesuit Fathers towards the end of the sixteenth century. In 1606 the celebrated Robert de'Nobili, a relation of Pope Julius III, arrived in Madura, and entered on a career of preaching which lasted 40 years. His early work was in Madura. Deeply versed in all the languages and customs of the country, he made himself "all things to all men" to win the people to the faith. He adopted the habit of life of the Brahmans, was attended by Brahman servants only, and observed in the minutest particulars the customs of those in whose midst he sojourned.

In June 1623, after he had set the Christian Church at Madura on a firm basis, Robert de'Nobili left Madura for the north. Tirumala Nāyaka had but lately acceded to the throne, and had made Trichinopoly his residence. There were a few Christians at his Court, but de'Nobili could do little work among them, as every one was in a turmoil of warlike preparations. De'Nobili, therefore, pursued his journey to Sōnda-mangalam (in Nāmakkal Taluk), where he was well received by the reigning prince, Rāmachandra Nāyaka, a vassal of Madura, who offered him a handsome site on which to build a church. Robert de'Nobili, however, intent on further conquests, was forced for the moment to decline the generous offer, and pushed on to Salem, then ruled by Salapatti Nāyaka, another feudatory of Madura. At the outset, the populace of Salem adopted an attitude of hostility to the efforts of the "great Sanyāsi." Every gate was shut against him, and he had to content himself with the shelter of a wretched *chāvadi*, exposed on all sides to wind and rain. Here he remained forty days, during which he fell seriously ill. At length one of the townsfolk, moved with pity, offered him the shelter of his house; the offer was accepted, and everything at once assumed a new

---

1 The mission returns give a total of 1,108, which includes, no doubt, most of those who are "unspecified" in the Census returns.

2 Mission work seems rather stagnant, if the marginal figures are correct. The totals exclude figures for Nāmakkal and Tiruppattūr. Even then the total for 1911 is lower than that for 1901 by 12 per cent., and has even fallen below that of 1891; while the increase between 1881 and 1901 is only 13 per cent. against 51 per cent. for the total population of the same taluks.

Year.				Number of Christians.
1881	...	...	...	13,950
1891	...	...	...	15,576
1901	...	...	...	16,634
1911	...	...	...	15,003

aspect. The preacher recovered his health; the feelings of the people changed; these who had hitherto rejected the Apostle became eager to hear him. The Rājā of Salem expressed a desire to see him, and offered to grant him whatever favour he desired. De'Nobili replied that he desired nothing but his friendship. The prince assured him he would always remain his friend, and allotted him a house in the Brahman quarter to live in.[1] People flocked to him for instruction, and a number of miracles won their conversion. Among his most earnest listeners was Tirumangala Nāyaka, elder brother of Rāmachandra Nāyaka, the Rāja of Sēnda-mangalam, who had driven him from his kingdom. About the end of 1624, Robert de'Nobili left Salem for Cochin to visit his Provincial. The Salem Mission seemed firmly established, and there was every prospect of Tirumangala Nāyaka and his sons, the eldest of whom was heir-apparent of the Sēnda-mangalam chieftaincy, embracing Christianity. Political intrigues, however, made havoc of his plans, and Tirumangala Nāyaka had to flee for safety from Salem to the Rājā of "Moramangalam."[2] There he wrote to Robert de'Nobili to come and baptise him with his family. Robert responded to his call, but, thanks again to political intrigues, he met with a very cool reception at the hands of the Rājā, who granted him no place of residence. De'Nobili had to content himself with a wretched hovel. However, before long, Tirumangala brought him his four sons to be baptised, and after some hesitation he himself received baptism on Christmas Day, 1625. Numerous conversions followed, a church was built and the mission prospered. "Moramangalam" was placed in charge of Father Emmanuel Martinz,[3] who had come with Robert de'Nobili from Cochin in the previous year, and Robert returned to Madura (1626 A.D.).

The subsequent history of the "Moramangalam" mission is lost.[4] The zeal of the Jesuit Missionaries, however, did not flag.

---

[1] Launay, *Histoire des Missions de l'Inde*, Vol. I, p. xiv, cf. Bertrand *La Mission du Maduré*, Vol. II, p. 225 to 251.

[2] Possibly one of the Gatti Mudaliyārs of Amarakundi, adjoining the modern village of Māra-mangalam; vide p. 69. In Bertrand, Vol. II, p. 242, "Moramangalam" is said to be "eight leagues from Salem". Māra-mangalam is about 5 miles north-west of Ōmalūr. The Mudalis of Māra-mangalam are mentioned in an inscription of the 14th year of Jatāvarman Sundara-Pāndya II, 1290 A.D., vide G.E. No. 23 of 1900.

[3] See Bertrand, Vol. II, pp. 251 and 271. According to Launay, p. xiv, Ant. Vico was in charge.

[4] Father Martinz was in charge in 1626 (Bertrand, Vol. II, p. 271); in December 1628 Father Laerzio wrote "The Fathers are building houses and churches at Moramangalam and in a place near Salem," but after 1628 the letters are silent.

CHAP. III. CHRISTIANS.

It is possible that in 1648 Robert de'Nobili revisited the Christian settlements he had founded on his way to Mylapore where he spent the last eight years of his life.[1] In about 1650 the Mysore Mission was founded from Goa, and their centre of operations appears to have been Seringapatam. In 1675 Father Jean de Britto visited Dharmapuri, where he found a flourishing mission in charge of two European priests, Fathers Antoine Ribeira and Moucciarelli[2], whom he describes as "Missionaries of Mysore."[3] In 1678 Ōmalūr and Salem are spoken of as Missionary "provinces" attached to the Madura Mission.[4] Between 1678 and 1685 no fewer than six Fathers in the Madura Mission died, and, owing to the paucity of workers, the Madura Mission handed over a large tract of country, including most of Coimbatore District and part of Salem, to the Mysore Mission.[5] It is also recorded that Father de Britto, after his return from Europe, made his way from Gingee through the wild forests of the Javādis to Dharmapuri whence he proceeded to the Marava country, the scene of his martyrdom in 1693.

Meanwhile, in 1663, the Capuchins landed in Pondicherry and assumed charge of the European congregations. In 1689 the Jesuit Fathers, who had been expelled from Siam, took over mission work among the Indians. Another wave of missionary enthusiasm brought Father Beschi,[6] with a body of priests from Goa, to evangelise the Tamils. Early in the eighteenth century there were mission stations at "Capinagati" and "Caguti" in Hosūr Taluk, and a letter from Father San Iago to Father Manoel Savay, dated "Capinagati,[7] August 8, 1711" relates how Father Dacunha was ill-treated and wounded at Caguti, and died of his wounds at Capinagati. It was perhaps in the early part

---

[1] Robert de'Nobili died on January 16, 1656, at the age of 80.

[2] Bertrand, Vol. III, p. 255.

[3] According to the account prepared for Mr. LeFanu by Father Thirion they were called Susia-pere-Swāmiār and Antoniār. "Tradition has it that, in the outset a European priest was appointed exclusively to minister to the higher castes and was called the 'Priest of Brahmans', while another, called 'Pandāram-Swāmi' ministered to the Pariahs, so that caste prejudices should not stay the progress of conversions."

[4] Bertrand, Vol. III, p. 296.

[5] These particulars have been kindly supplied by the Rev. Father L. Besse of Trichinopoly.

[6] Father Beschi served the Madura Mission from 1711 to 1740, when he retired to the Malabar Coast. He died there on February 4, 1747.

[7] See *Missions de l' Inde*, Vol. I, p. lxiv. Capinagati is probably to be identified with Kappiganatti, half a mile north of Kela-mangalam, and Caguti might be Kadūdi, 7 miles south-east of Kela-mangalam. If these identifications are correct, M. Launay should have written "south-east" instead of "south-west" but the distances given by him are approximately accurate.

of the eighteenth century that the Christian settlement of Tigalara-halli (1½ miles north of Tali), was colonised from Dharmapuri and Ganjām (Seringapatam), under Goanese influence. From Tigalara-halli the community migrated[1] to Matagonda-palli, where land was granted them, it is said, by the villagers, in gratitude for rains which fell in a season of drought in answer to the prayers of the new settlers.

By the middle of the eighteenth century it was estimated that the number of converts amounted to three millions. But misfortune was at hand. In 1773 the Society of Jesus was suppressed, "a misfortune felt as irreparable to the present day, for the missions of India, founded at the price of so many privations, being deprived of their missionaries, many of the Christian communities were lost, and it was not till the beginning of the nineteenth century that the work could be seriously taken on hand."[2] As a temporary measure, on the destruction of the Order, the care of their congregations was made over to the Bishop of Verapoly. In 1776 the Mission of the Karnatic was entrusted to the priests of the Paris Society of Foreign Missions, in whose charge Salem District still remains. But before the work of reconstruction could be got under way, a still more serious blow to the Christian cause in Salem District was inflicted by the persecutions of Tipu.

The history of Tipu's persecution concerns more directly the history of Mysore. It began in 1784, and continued till 1787, when Tipu received the envoys of Louis XVI, and negotiations were opened for its cessation. Meanwhile missionaries were expelled, churches destroyed, and Indian Christians given the choice between the "Honour of Islam and death." The Christian communities at "Capinagati" and "Caguti" vanished. The churches at Tigalara-halli, Chikkana-halli (near Ānekal) and Selve-kuppam (near Matagonda-palli) were swept away, and all that remains is a tamarind tree in Tigalara-halli, and a stone cross in each of the other two hamlets, which mark the traditional site of the buildings which perished. Orders were given for the destruction of Kōvilūr (near Adaman-kōttai) and Kadagattūr, but these two settlements, as well as Edappādi and Kalkāvēri, appear to have survived the storm.

On the defeat of Tipu after the Third Mysore War, the work of reconstruction began in earnest, under the auspices of the famous Abbé Dubois,[3] who "fled from the horrors of the French

[1] The reason for this migration and its date are not known, vide Launay, loc. cit.

[2] Pére Thirion, loc. cit.

[3] Vide letter of the Abbé Dubois to Colonel Read, dated September 13, 1797.

CHAP.. III. CHRISTIANS.

Revolution" in 1792, and was attached to the Pondicherry Mission. The Abbé was the fourth of the Missionaries sent for the work of reorganisation by Mgr. Nicholas Champenois, Bishop of Doliche, and Vicar Apostolic of Pondicherry.[1] "We took profit," wrote the Abbé in 1793, "of the tolerance and protection accorded by the British to every religion to penetrate into the provinces acquired by them, and took care of the Christians dispersed by the persecution of Tipu Sultan. We gathered together three or four thousand souls in four or five of the principal churches, and I took charge of the congregation."

The Abbé's work lay more particularly in the territory ceded by Tipu, and he seems to have had a special fondness for Salem District. The ruined churches were rebuilt, partly at the Abbé's expense, and partly by the congregation. In 1797 the Abbé had occasion to complain to Colonel Read that efforts were being made by certain Goanese Missionaries to subvert his spiritual authority, and oust him from his churches.

"Black Priests," he wrote, "have arrived from the Malabar Coast in this country, and lodged, without my permission, without even preventing me, in my several churches. Amazed by the boldness and impoliteness of such a conduct, I asked the cause of it, when I was answered that they came to take this mission from me, and to take possession of all the Christian churches in Bāramahāl and Salem's country; saying that I was nothing else but an usurper, and that if I should oppose any difficulty to their undertakings, they were bearers of orders from the Right Honourable the Governor of Madras to compel me to leave without delay this country, and that the orders of which they are bearers are of so compelling a nature that they leave no choice or alternative. Their bold and determined discourses filled me with surprise and care . . . The calumnies they have spread everywhere against me among those ignorant and credulous people, by saying that I am a French priest, and that all the Frenchmen have, since their revolution, fallen into heresy, and have been, without exception, excommunicated by the Pope, that the doctrine I am announcing is not the true doctrine of the Roman Catholic Church, that the English Government, sensible of all these motives, has entrusted them with the charge of all the missions in this country, these and a thousand other absurd discourses, and above all their likeness, by colour, manners and morals, with the people of this country, have won them the affection and confidence of all; and they are received and triumphing in all my churches, while despised of all, I am obliged to fly from a cottage to another, and I hardly meet with persons compassionate enough to give me shelter in their thatched houses.[2]"

---

[1] The Abbé was born in 1765, and ordained in the Diocese of Viviers in 1792, the year of his departure for India. He returned to France in 1823, and at once became Director of the Missions Etrangéres in Paris. He died in 1848 at the age of 83. See *Hindu Manners, Customs and Ceremonies* (ed. H. K. Beauchamp), Clarendon Press, 1897.

[2] Letter of Abbé Dubois to Colonel Read, dated September 13, 1797. See *Correspondence between Abbé Dubois and Col. Alexander Read on the subject of the Disputes between Abbé Dubois and the Black Priests*, Government Press Madras, 1905.

Col. Read replied that he could not interfere in matters of spiritual jurisdiction, and advised the Abbé to compound with his persecutors. The Abbé then waived the question of spiritual right, but claimed compensation for the cost incurred by him in building "Churches and Lodgings" in the District. The correspondence[1] does not state exactly how the matter was settled, but the Abbé's work by no means suffered. The British authorities allowed him an annual grant of Rs. 42 for the church at Dharmapuri-Kōvilūr, and similar grants for those at Kalkāvēri and Tiruppattūr.[2] After the fall of Seringapatam, he was invited[3] to proceed thither to reorganise the Mysore Mission, and he worked there till 1823. He did not, however, lose interest in Salem District, and used periodically to visit Rāya-kōta and Krishnagiri. Major Bevan gives the following account of him :—

> "He presided over the whole of the Catholics in the Salem and Bāramahāl districts. A residence of thirty years in India, and a life spent among the natives on a most friendly and intimate footing, whose dress and habits he in some measure adopted, combined with his talents and other acquirements, enabled him to form a just estimate of the characteristic traits of the Indians. His flock looked up to him with the esteem and reverence that he merited. His views, with reference to the conversion of the heathen, were rather against his success. He warmly advocated the rights and privileges of the Hindus, especially the female part, declaring that they possessed those moral and correct feelings which form the bond of social intercourse and the basis of domestic happiness.[4]"

The history of the nineteenth century is one of steady progress. In 1838 Gregory XVI established the Vicariate Apostolic of the Coast of Coromandel. In 1850 Pius IX divided the field into the three Apostolic Vicariates of Pondicherry, Mysore and Coimbatore. In 1886 Leo XIII constructed the Vicariate Apostolic of Pondicherry into an Archbishopric and Mysore became a Diocese. A year later Pondicherry was made the Metropolitan See of an Ecclesiastical Province. In 1899 Leo XIII erected the Diocese of Kumbakōnam, by dismemberment from the Archdiocese of Pondicherry.

Salem District at present is divided between the Archdiocese of Pondicherry, the Diocese of Kumbakōnam, and that of Mysore. The major portion of the District falls within the

---

[1] "For building Kalkāvēri's Church and lodging 150 rupees, for Edappādi's lodging 54 rupees, for Dharmapuri's lodging 47 rupees, for getting a statue of St. Peter for Tiruppattūr's church 18 rupees—Total 269 rupees" (Letter of October 8, 1797).

[2] Launay, Vol. I, p. 191.

[3] According to the *Mysore Gazetteer*, Vol. I, p. 483, the invitation came from the Catholic congregation. Mr. Beauchamp refers to a statement that the invitation was given by Col. Wellesley himself (*Hindu Manners and Customs*, p. xii).

[4] *Thirty Years in India*, Vol. I, p. 77.

CHAP. III.
CHRISTIANS.

jurisdiction of the Pondicherry See, and contains nine stations. In the Talaghāt there are stations at Salem, Āttūr and Akkaravaram[1], half way between the two; a fourth at Setti-patti, a hamlet of Kamalāpuram, near Ōmalūr; and a fifth at Edappādi. On the Shevaroys, Yercaud and Balmadies are treated as one station. Dharmapuri Taluk is served by Kōvilūr near Adamankōttai, and Kadagattūr. The jurisdiction of the former extends over the southern part of Ūttankarai Taluk. Krishnagiri Taluk is served by the mission at Elattagiri, and the northern portion of Ūttankarai from Kōvilūr, three miles from Tiruppattūr town. In 1907 eight French and two Indian priests were working in the portion of the District included within the limits of the Archdiocese. The Diocese of Kumbakōnam is bounded on the north by the Vellār, or rather that branch of it which in Salem District is called the Swēta-nadi. It contains two stations, viz., Kōnēri-patti in the south of Āttūr Taluk, and Kalkāvēri (Kākkāvēri) near Rāsipuram. There is only one Salem station within the Diocese of Mysore, namely Mattigiri.

The congregation of the European and Native Sisters of St. Joseph of Cluny have a branch at Yercaud, where a boarding school is maintained. At Yercaud there are also Convents belonging to the Presentation Nuns of St. Joseph's, Vepery, and St. Mary's, Madras. The Congregation of the Native Nuns of the Sacred Heart of Mary, established in 1844 under the rules of the Third Regular Order of St. Francis of Assisi for the instruction of native girls, maintain schools at Akkaravaram, Kōvilūr, Salem, Setti-patti and Elattagiri.

The London Mission.[2]

In June 1827 Messrs. Tyerman and Bennet, on behalf of the London Missionary Society, selected Salem as a field for missionary effort, and in October of the same year the first Missionary, the Rev. Henry Crisp, began his task. He took over from the Collector, Mr. M. D. Cockburn, five small schools, which were at the time under the Collector's management. Mr. Crisp met with a good deal of opposition, and in Ammāpet he was mobbed and stoned. In 1829 he was deprived by death of the devoted assistance of his wife; his own health gave way shortly after, and in 1832 an attack of malaria proved fatal. In that year the first church was built, and two converts were baptised.

Mr. Crisp's successor was the Rev. George Walton, an East Indian, whose work, lasting over eight years, was crippled by ill-health. Mr. Walton got involved in serious loss by litigation for

---

[1] Hamlet of Kūri-patti.

[2] The information on the London Mission has been furnished by the Rev. W. Robinson.

which he was in no way responsible; the Famine of 1833 added to his troubles; in 1839 Mrs. Walton died, and two years later he himself succumbed.

Shortly before Mr. Walton's death, he was joined by the Rev. J. M. Lechler, a distinguished Tamil scholar, who had been associated with the great missionary Rhenius. Mr. Lechler vigorously revived the Mission work in outlying stations, specially in Āttūr Taluk. Ably helped by his wife, he opened homes in Salem for training the children of converts, and taught them weaving, carpentry, blacksmiths' work, mat-making and other industries. Artizan missionaries from Germany were employed, and, thanks to the efforts of Mr. C. Rahm, who for ten years developed the work with ungrudging effort, the Industrial School prospered.

In June 1861, Mr. Lechler died. What followed was "a series of blunders worse than crimes." "Two elderly Missionaries of the old regime," writes the Rev. J. P. Ashton, "had seen fit to smash up, in one day, the two boarding schools and the industrial school. I could never understand the reason of this step, unless it was they were much too successful and financially prosperous institutions to be tolerated in a mofussal station. We juniors could only helplessly look on at the destruction."

In 1862 the Rev. G. Mabbs and his wife came to Salem, and had to inherit the blunders of their immediate predecessor. Papers and documents were in a terrible state of confusion, and the Mission is indebted to the careful patience of Mr. Mabbs for reducing the chaos of the Mission records to order. Mr. Mabbs was succeeded by the Rev. W. E. Morris, who had laboured already in Coimbatore, and had a unique mastery over the dialectical vagaries of the Tamil language. His career was prematurely cut short by an attack of sun-stroke, and early in 1870 he was relieved by the Rev. Henry Toller, who died of cholera within a few days of his arrival, leaving his young widow to return home in the ship which brought her to India as a bride.

In 1862 the Rev. Mr. Phillips was appointed to Tiruppattūr, and took up his residence in that station. Mr. Phillips laboured earnestly as a vernacular preacher, and gave a great impetus to work in the northern half of the District. When Mr. Toller died, the Directors of the Society decided to give up Salem. In 42 years four Missionaries and three of the ladies of the Mission had died, and two men had been compelled to retire because of broken health. It was therefore declared advisable to ask the Arcot Mission to take charge of Salem. This proposal was set aside, however, and the Rev. Mr. Phillips was directed to take over the

CHAP. III. CHRISTIANS.

work at Salem. He did so, retaining Tiruppattūr. Henceforward the work of the Mission steadily progressed. In 1891 the Australian Auxiliary Society sent Miss Cox as a Zenana Missionary. After 11 months of work she was compelled to retire owing to ill-health, and was succeeded by Miss Crouch and Miss Lodge. In 1908 the Rev. Geo. Wilkins started mission work in Hosūr, in connection with the Bangalore Kanarese Mission.

In 1907 an interesting work was started among the Koravas of the Salem-Āttūr valley, a number of whom had expressed a desire to become Christians and lead a settled and honest life. As many of them were on the "K.D." register, and had no permanent abode, it became necessary to bring them together into one settlement. Mr. Robinson accordingly darkhasted for a piece of waste land near Sukkampatti, about half way between Salem and the Manjavādi Ghāt, and settled ten families upon it. The people built their own houses, and pay kist for their land through the Mission. The Mission assumed responsibility for the good conduct of the settlers. A code of rules was drawn up and strictly enforced; the catechist in charge has to see that each member of the community is in his house at night, and enters his name in a register, and a Police constable visits the place every night and checks the register. Crime has not been entirely banished, but it has decreased to a surprising extent, and on several occasions the villagers themselves have reported cases of theft, and given the offenders over to the authorities. The settlement is now known as Elizabethpet, and in 1912 numbered 56 souls. A similar settlement was established in 1909 at Muttampatti by Mr. Robertson, and in 1912 it numbered 84 members.

In 1912, in addition to the Mission work in Salem Town, there are congregations in Yercaud, Āttūr, Vīraganūr, Kōnēri-patti, Sendāra-patti, Sankaridrug, Kīra-patti, Elizabethpet, Muttampatti, Tōppa-patti (near Rāsipuram), all attached to the Salem Mission, and at Dharmapuri, Harūr, Elattagiri in the Tiruppattūr Mission.[1] In addition to the three churches in Salem, there are churches in Yercaud, Sankaridrug, Narasingapuram (Āttūr), Kōnēri-patti, Sendāra-patti, Dharmapuri, Pālakōdu and Elattagiri.

Lutheran Missions.

The Missouri Evangelical Lutheran Mission started work[2] in the District in 1895 under the Rev. Theodor Naether, who, after travelling throughout the District, selected Krishnagiri as

---

[1] These congregations are estimated to number in all 1,108 souls.

[2] Under the auspices of the German Evangelical Lutheran Synod of Missouri, Ohio and other States, one of the largest Lutheran bodies in North America, working chiefly among immigrants from Germany and Scandinavia.

CHRISTIANS.

an unworked field. In the following year a second station was opened at Āmbūr by the Rev. F. Mohn. In the latter part of 1897 work was taken up in Vāniyambādi by the Rev. R. Freche, and in the following year the Rev. G. O. Kellerbauer completed the chain by establishing a station at Bargūr.[1] The four stations of Āmbūr, Vāniyambādi, Bargūr and Krishnagiri form a compact little district for concentrated effort.

The Leipzig Evangelical Lutheran Mission began work on the Shevaroys in 1862, and the first chapel was built on the hill on which Mr. Rahm's bungalow now stands. A new chapel was begun in December 1875, and consecrated in the following June. It stands in the quarter of Yercaud known as Lutherpet.

Other Missions.

A branch of the Danish Missionary Society was opened on the Shevaroy Hills in 1883 by the Rev. Kofoed, who had to visit Yercaud on account of ill-health. The mission station is located on the flank of the Shevarāyan, about 3 miles from Yercaud. Most of the missionary's work is among the Malaiyālis.

The Society for the Propagation of the Gospel maintains an Indian Priest at Salem.

MUHAMMADANS.

The Muhammadans number in all 43,421. Though they represent only 2½ per cent of the total population of the District, their local settlements are of no small importance. This is especially the case with the chief centres of trade, and with places which in former days were garrisoned with troops. In such localities they sometimes exceed one-fourth of the total population.[2]

Muhammadans are commonly spoken of as divided into two classes, Dakhanis and Labbais; the former, as their name indicates, being regarded as immigrants from the Deccan, the latter as descendants of indigenous races.

Dakhanis.

The Dakhanis class themselves as Sheikhs (24,387), Saiyads[3] (6,800), Pathāns (7,115) and Mughals (693), but, thanks to the fact that they are untrammelled by endogamous laws, these divisions have little or no ethnic significance. Their house language is Hindustāni.

Labbais.

The Labbais, who are returned as 3,851, are supposed to be of almost pure Dravidian descent. Their house language is Tamil

---

[1] Each of these pioneers had previous experience in Indian Mission work under the Leipzig Mission, which they left owing to their strict adherence to the doctrine of scriptural inspiration.

[2] E.g. Denkani-kōta, Hosūr, Krishnagiri, Kela-mangalam, etc.

[3] Strictly speaking a Saiyad is a direct descendant of the Prophet, a Sheikh a direct descendant of one of the first three Khalifas, a Sharif is the son of a Sheikh father by a Saiyad mother.

CHAP. III. MUHAMMADANS.

and many of them do not understand Hindustāni. In most respects they are orthodox Sunnis. It is said[1] that they observe a number of Hindu customs, but no evidence of this is forthcoming so far as the Labbais of Salem District are concerned. They are a frugal and industrious community, and persevering traders.

Pinjāris.

In addition to the Dakhanis and Labbais, there is a section of Muhammadans who speak a corrupt form of Telugu, and are variously known as Pinjāris, Panjāris, Panju-vettis, Achu-kattis or Dūdē-kulas.[2] As their name implies, their distinctive means of livelihood is cotton-cleaning; they are also weavers and mat-makers. There are several settlements of them[3] in Āttūr Taluk, and they are to be found in Ammāpet, Tāra-mangalam, Rāsipuram, Hosūr, Mattigiri and Bērikai. It is said that their customs approximate closely to those of the Hindus, that both men and women dress like Hindus, that the women wear a *pottu* of red *kunkumam* on their forehead, and that the men sometimes shave the beard and wear a *kudumi*; *tāli* is tied at marriages; they adopt Hindu terminations (Appa, Amma, etc.) to their names; *gosha* is not observed; they sometimes worship in Hindu Temples, and at Bakrīd do *pūja* to the implements with which they earn their livelihood, on the analogy of the Hindu Āyudha-pūja. Such practices are, however, by no means universal among them, and the modern tendency is towards assimilation with orthodox Muhammadan observances.

In social and religious matters the Muhammadans of the larger towns are strongly organised into separate communities, each under its own committee (*jamāyat*). Many of the customs in vogue among the ruder classes are anathema to the orthodox, but the efforts at reform that are from time to time made by zealous puritan preachers excite a great deal of opposition, and meet with little success. Among the chief items of controversy are the use of green pandals, and of tom-toms and music on religious occasions, the employment of dancing girls at marriages, the tying of *nādā* (tape) round the wrist at Muharram, and the processions, masques and general procedure which characterise the celebration of the Muharram. Worship at the graves of Pīrs (Saints), which is very

---

[1] See, *Castes and Tribes*, s. v.—The customs of the Labbais have never been systematically worked out, and the available information on the subject is scanty and vague.

[2] Dūdē-kula means in Telugu "cotton-cleaners"; Panju-vetti is Tamil for the same; Achu-katti means "loom-making." See *Castes and Tribes*, II, p. 195, s.v. Dūdē-kula.

[3] At Āttūr, Olaippādi, Nadavalūr, Gangavalli, Vīraganūr, Tidūvūr and Tāndavarāyapuram.

prevalent in the District, is also discountenanced by the strict Musalmān. The bodies of Pīrs are popularly supposed to be incorruptible; miracles are performed at their tombs, and oblations (*urs*) are offered on the anniversary of their death. It is a curious feature of these tomb-cults that Hindus frequently take part in them.[1]

Festivals.

The three chief Muhammadan festivals are, as elsewhere, (1) Ramzān, (2) Bakrīd and (3) Muharram. The Ramzān *Kutbā* celebrates the close of the Lenten Fast, which is observed throughout the month of Ramzān. The Bakrīd commemorates Abraham's intended sacrifice of Ishmael (who in Muhammadan tradition takes the place assigned to Isaac in the Hebrew version), and is celebrated on the ninth day of the month Zillhaj. On both the Ramzān and Bakrīd *Kutbās* all male Muhammadans shave themselves and bathe, and, dressed in new clothes of the purest white, with shawls, turbans and vests of the gayest colours, flock *en masse* to the *Idgas*, or praying walls, situated on the outskirts of their town or village, and offer prayers. The Bakrīd is also celebrated in each household that can afford it by the sacrifice of a sheep. To die on either of these festal days is held to be most fortunate, and the bodies of those who so die are carried to the *Idga*, and special prayers are recited over the biers at the conclusion of the *Kutbā* service.

Muharram.

As already stated, the thirteen days' festival of Muharram, which commemorates the defeat and martyrdom of Hussain at Kerbelā (680 A.D.), is accompanied by many ceremonies which violate the principles of Islam. The centre of operations is a *Makhān* called *Ashūr-khāna* or *Allāswāmi Kōvil*, an unpretentious building where the *panjās* are kept and where the *tābūts* are constructed. The *panjā* is a metal device, mounted on a pole, which is supposed to represent the standard of Hussain; its shape varies; sometimes it is in the form of a hand, sometimes of a *fleur-de-lis*.[2] The *tābūt* is a model of a mausoleum, constructed of paper, tinsel, mica, etc., mounted on a platform, which is carried on the shoulders of men in the manner of a Hindu wheel-less car.

Among the most pleasing features of the Muharram celebrations are the *Giros*, or troupes of brightly-clad boys, who enliven the towns and villages with songs and dances. Of the different guises there is infinite variety. In Salem City, these *Giros* are organised on an unusually elaborate scale, each quarter of the

---

[1] The first Indian Pīr was Abdul Kādir, who was born at Bagdad, A.H., 471 (1078-79 A.D.) and died A.H., 571 (1175 A.D.). See *Qanoon-e-Islam*, p. 432.

[2] Vide the illustrations in *Qanoon-e-Islam*.

CHAP. III. MUHAMMADANS.

town having its own particular masque.[1] Roughly speaking the Salem *Giros* are of two types, the *Nānak*[2] type and the *Pākkand* or *Sanyāsi* type.

In addition to the *Giros*, the Muharram is made the occasion for a great display of individual *vēshams*, of which the familiar *puli-vēsham* or tiger-masque is the most popular. The variety of guises is, however, too great for detailed description, and the processions are swelled by athletes (*pailwāns*) from the local gymnasia (*tālims*) who give elaborate exhibitions of sword-play, wrestling, fencing with sticks and clubs, and the innumerable feats of skill and dexterity in which athletic Musalmāns delight.

The opening days of the festival are spent in preliminary rites and ceremonies. The *panjās* are taken out daily from the 6th to the 10th days. On the evenings of the 5th, 6th, 7th and 8th days, it is usual for the *Giros* to visit one another at some selected rendezvous (*chauk*), and the night is passed in songs, and dances, and ribald repartee which sometimes leads to blows. The favourite meeting places are in Shevāpet, Salem, Pension Lines, and the Fort. The Fort *chauk* attracts a specially large concourse, on account of its side-shows and tableaux.[3]

On the ninth night all the *tābūts* and *panjās* are carried in torchlight procession through the main bazaar street, accompanied by the *giros* and their supporters, the *tālīmdars*, and a vast crowd of Hindus and Muhammadans of both sexes. The order in which the *giros* march is prescribed by custom, and should one *giro* dash forward to get in front of another which claims precedence, a free fight is likely to ensue. On the afternoon of the tenth day (the *Shahādat-ka-rōz* or Day of Martyrdom) *tābūts*, *panjās*, *giros*, etc., are assembled on the left bank of the river above the bridge, and conducted in procession through the two Agrahārams to the river bank, beside the *anaikat* near Fischer's compound. The lads who carry the *panjās*, some of whom are mounted on ponies, not infrequently display the most extraordinary symptoms of religious hysteria, swaying to and fro like drunken men, oblivious to their surroundings, and apparently endowed with preternatural strength. When the procession arrives at the *anaikat*, the *panjās* are taken out of the *tābūts*, and the domes of the *tābūts* are taken off and placed inside. All the

---

[1] A list of 47, by no means exhaustive, is given in *Qanoon-e-Islam*, pp. 189 to 216.

[2] Apparently connected with Nānak, the founder of the Sikhs. See *Qanoon-e-Islam*, pp. 212 and 435.

[3] See *Qanoon-e-Islam*, p. 208. Several of tahe tbleaux therein described are to be seen at the Fort *chauk*.

panjās are sprinkled with water, and *fatiha*[1] is offered. The *tābūts* are covered with cloths and carried back to the *Ashūrkhāna*, kept there for three days, and then dismantled. The *panjās* are carefully stored, and the festival is at an end.

Fire-walking.

One of the most distinctive features of the Muharram in the larger towns is the fire-walking ceremony, which usually takes place on the eighth or ninth night of the festival. One or more circular pits (*alāv*) are dug in the public street, or in an open space fronting one of the *Allāswāmi Kōvils*. The pits are from 4′ to 6′ deep, and from 8′ to 10′ in diameter. In the afternoon a bonfire is lighted in each pit, and is kept burning till about midnight. The flames are then allowed to die down for half an hour or so, and sometimes some salt is sprinkled on the embers to prevent the flames from flickering. A few steps are then cut in the earth of the pit's edge, and the devotees are led up to the brink, one at a time. The devotees are usually in a frantic state of religious excitement and shout "Ali, Ali." Then one by one they run down the steps, on to the glowing embers, walk across, climb up the other side, turn to the right, rush along the pit's brink back to their starting place, and repeat the performance twice. Their friends then douse them with water, the *afflatus* leaves then, and in a few seconds they become ordinary mortals once more. What connection these sensational performances have with Islam is not clear, and it is not at all uncommon to find Hindus among the devotees.

HINDUS.
Villages.

In the Talaghāt and in the southern and eastern Bāramahāl the village-site (*grāma-nattam*) is usually open, but in the Bālāghāt and in the portions of the Bāramahāl that adjoin the Bālāghāt, villages were formerly protected by defensive walls and a fort, which in many cases are still in a fair state of preservation.[2] Some villages are surrounded with a hedge of the milk-hedge plant (*Euphorbia tirucalli*), and on the hills a stout palisade of split bamboo fencing is not uncommon. The houses are usually built in fairly regular streets and are not scattered. Sometimes the houses occupied by the several households of a joint family are grouped in a fenced compound. Brahmans, Muhammadans, and some of the larger Non-Brahman castes, usually live in separate streets or quarters; Pariahs and Chucklers are relegated to hamlets (*Paracheris, Sakkili-nattams*) of their own, situated as a rule at some distance from the main village, and they do not intermingle with one another. Most villages are provided with a platform (*jagili*) of earth, rivetted with stone, about 3′ in

---

[1] Prayers, accompanied sometimes by oblations of food.

[2] Vide Vol. II, p. 112.

CHAP. III HINDUS.

height, shaded by a banyan or some other tree, where the village elders foregather for gossip or for the settlement of disputes. An open *maidān* or green, where the villagers congregate on festival occasions, is usually to be found in the centre of the village, with the principal village temples adjoining it. The commonest suffixes for rural place names are-*patti*,-*doddi*, and-*halli*, which are respectively the Tamil, Telugu and Kanarese equivalents for "cattle-pen."

Houses.

Most of the rural population lives in tiled or thatched houses, a terraced house being regarded as the mark of a wealthy man. Houses of more than one story are rare. Thatched houses predominate in the Talaghāt and on the hills, and tiled houses elsewhere. The favourite thatching material is kambu straw; paddy straw, chōlam stalks, palmyra leaves, and coco-nut *kīths* are also used when available, and, in the vicinity of the hills, coarse jungle grasses. The poorest classes have to content themselves with an one-room hut, about 10′ square, but most people of the ryot class have at least two rooms; a sleeping-room opening into the street, and a cook-room opening into the sleeping-room, and also a front verandah. In Hosūr villages the cattle are often accommodated in the sleeping apartment, and in the cook-room are kept three or four huge earthenware jars of grain.[1] An improvement on this arrangement is to have the cow-house opposite to, and equal in length to, the dwelling house, with a narrow yard, fenced at either end, intervening. Town houses are more elaborate. A new house is usually "warmed" by giving a feast to friends and relatives before it is occupied, and some castes observe the sacrifice of a fowl or goat, or perform some other rite, or call in a Brahman *purōhit* to cleanse the building with the *punyāha-vāchanam* rite, before they venture to live in it.

The picturesque little "bee-hive" villages of the Malaiyālis, that nestle on the plateaus and slopes of the Shevaroys, differ from anything found in the plains. The huts are circular, the walls are made of split bamboo, daubed with clay, and the conical roof is thickly thatched with grass. The eaves extend about 2½′ from the inner wall, which is encircled by a second wall of the same material, the intervening space being partitioned into two or three compartments, to accommodate calves, kids, poultry, etc. At the level of the inner walling is a loft, which answers the purpose of a store-room. The only entrance is a door, about 3½′ high and 2½′ wide, and there are no windows.[2] The hut of the

---

[1] Vide *infra*, pp. 210–11.

[2] Shortt's *Hill Ranges*, Vol. II, p. 44, from which the above description is taken.

Pachai-malais and Kolli-malais is of similar material, but rectangular in plan, and with a raised pial in front, beneath which is a small compartment closed with a door, where fowls are penned.[1]

Dress.

Except in the case of the Malaiyālis (q.v. pp. 156–57), the Hindus of Salem District follow the practice of adjacent districts in matters of dress. Boys usually go naked till they are 3 or 4 years of age, when they don a small *kōmanam*, 3″ or 4″ wide, supported by a waist-cord. The flap of the *kōmanam* hangs outwards, and is not, as in more southern districts, tucked in. Sometimes boys wear the waist-cord without the *kōmanam*, and sometimes they are protected against the cold by a little shirt or jacket of inadequate length. After they lose their first milk-teeth, they are clad, if their parents can afford it, in a small white waist cloth, about 7½′ long and 3′ wide. For the ordinary man the waist-cloth (*vēshti*) and turban suffice, and in cool or wet weather, especially on the hills and in the Bālāghāt, he carries about with him a blanket (*kambli*) or a sheet of coarse thick cotton (*duppatti*). Those who can afford it wear also a body-cloth (*anga-vastiram*) loosely laid across the shoulders, and sometimes the turban is worn thus. In towns, sleeved jackets of European pattern are in vogue, and the well-to-do wear a lace bordered *anga-vastiram*, neatly folded and passed across the left shoulder and under the right arm. The waist-cloth is ordinarily white, but modern depravity of taste affects a cloth dyed partially of an execrable magenta-crimson hue, which has the advantage of economising the dhoby's charges. In the Bālāghāt short drawers, of the type common in Mysore, are often worn in lieu of the *vēshti*, and caps are often to be seen. Leather sandals are in general use.

Little girls, up to the age of about 3, wear nothing but the little heart-shaped piece of silver suspended by a waist-cord (*arai-mūdi*) "which calls attention to what it purports to conceal." They are then promoted to a miniature "female" cloth known as *sittādai*; or, in the case of Christians and of well-to-do Hindus, to a jacket (*sokkāy*) and skirt (*pāvādai*). The usual colour of the ordinary *pudavai* is the familiar red that harmonises so perfectly with an Indian environment. Rich orange-yellows are sometimes seen in the Talaghāt, and in the Bālāghāt green or indigo (popularly called "black") are much in vogue. Some castes eschew the black *pudavai* altogether, and others prohibit it at marriages. White is confined to the Malaiyālis of the Kolli-malais, and the widows of Brahmans, Reddis, and a few other castes. The bodice (*ravikkai*) is in very general use, especially in towns and in the Bālāghāt, but it is not usually worn by girls under ten years of age.

[1] *Trichinopoly Gazetteer*, p. 126.

CHAP. III. HINDUS.

Tattooing.

Tattooing is tolerated by almost every caste, the most notable exception being that of the Malaiyālis of the Kolli-malais, whose abhorrence of the practice is so strong that they will not permit a tattooed person to enter their houses. Most of the higher castes,[1] however, discountenance the tattooing of males, and nowhere is the practice carried to extremes. The art of tattooing is almost confined to itinerant women of a Koravar sub-caste popularly known as Pachai-kutti Koravars, whose work is skilful and correct. Kuruba women sometimes take to the profession.[2]

Food.

The staple food among the higher castes is rice, and among the masses rāgi and kambu. Brahmans and the higher castes favour *pacharisi* (*i.e.*, rice husked without boiling), but the poorer people content themselves with *pulungarisi* (rice husked after boiling). Ragi is prepared as food in three ways, (1) *kūshu* (or *kanji*), gruel, (2) *kali*, porridge, the ragi balls of jail diet, (3) *rotti*, bread or biscuit. It is usually eaten with dhall or avarai. Kambu is generally eaten in the form of *kanji* or *kali*. Horse-gram is an article of diet in the Bāramahāl. The majority of the population are flesh-eaters, the chief abstainers being the Brahmans, Kōmatis and Lingāyats. The flesh of sheep or goats is a general article of diet throughout the District, much more so than in the districts adjoining on the south and east. The eating of fish (both fresh and salted),[3] fowls, and most birds that pick up their food with their bills, is generally permitted. Pork is eaten by a very large proportion of the community, including Arasa-Pallis, Vakkiligas, Malaiyālis, Kongu-Vellālars, Udaiyāns, Shānārs, Koravars, Oddas, and all Panchamas. The flesh of the Hanumān or black-faced monkey (*Semnopithecus entellus*) is highly valued as a medicine, and Dr. Shortt notes that the Malaiyālis cut the carcase into small pieces, 2" square, and sell these pieces at 2 annas each or even more, a whole carcase being valued at Rs. 7 to Rs. 10.[4] The flying-fox is relished as food by Pallis, Pallars, and several other castes. Field rats are eaten by most of the lower castes, who drive them out of their holes with smoke. The practice of eating frogs gives a certain section of

---

[1] Notably the Lingāyats, Kūpus, Vōdars, Gollas and Vēttuvans.

[2] Some interesting information on tattooing, with copious illustrations, is given in the Mysore *Census Report* for 1901, Part I, pp. 556–62.

[3] Fresh fish is brought every Tuesday to Shevāpet Shandy, from the Kāveri near Erode, from Ōmalūr and from villages within a radius of 10 miles or so of Salem. Murrel and some of the smaller fish are sold alive. There is a large import trade in dried and salted fish from the West Coast. Up to the end of April the fish imported are of small size, sardines (*Matti* and *Velluri*), anchovy (*Nettali*), "mango fish" (*Kāla*) and horse mackerel (*Kora*). When the south-west monsoon bursts, larger fish are brought in, such as seer, cat-fish, tunny, etc.

[4] *Hill Ranges*, Vol. II, p. 45.

Pariahs the distinctive appellation of *Tavalai-tinni* (see p. 202), and Arasa-Pallis are distinguished from their Panda-muttu Palli cousins by eating crabs. A few castes (including certain Pallis) are said to eat the iguana (*udumbu*). White ants are considered a delicacy by many of the agricultural and labouring castes. The universal condiments are salt, chillies, and tamarind, the last named being so valued that even the fallen blossoms that strew the roads are carefully swept up by the frugal housewife and stored for use. The flowers of āvāram (*Cassia auriculata*) are used to brew tea. In times of famine the fruit of prickly-pear is freely eaten by the poorer classes, who are sometimes driven to digging out ant-hills to get the grain (*pill-arisi* or "grass-rice" as it is called) that the ants have stored.

Games.

It would be tedious to give a detailed account of the many games played by children and adults. *Kummi* and *kōlāttam*[1] are of course familiar everywhere. Boys amuse themselves with endless varieties of hop-scotch (*jillu* or *pāndi*), tip-cat (*kitti*), prisoner's-base (*bāri-kōdu*), marbles (*gōli*), and kite-flying (*pattam*). *Uchi-āttam* is a favourite four-a-side game in some parts. *Ainthām-kal* is a forfeit game which consists in throwing up five stones into the air and catching them in various ways. *Pallān-kuzhi* is a rather complicated game for two, played with a board with two rows of little pits (or the pits are made in the ground) into which a certain number of seeds are dropped in succession. *Dāyam* is the name for several games akin to backgammon, played on diagrams of various patterns. The best known of these is the game called in Hindustani *pachīs*. Another set of games, played on various diagrams, and bearing various names, resemble the European game of Fox-and-Geese. One of the best known of these is called *pathinainthām-puli* ("fifteenth tiger") or *puli-kattam*, and is played with 3 "tigers" and 15 "sheep." Of card games, *kēlvi-koduvē* is a curious adaptation of Nap, and "*out*"-*āttam* of Bezique. Cock-fighting is occasionally met with in Salem City, in Rāsipuram, and in parts of Ōmalūr Taluk. In Āttūr Taluk it is very popular, especially in the villages round Bēlūr and Tāndavarāyapuram, where regular tournaments are held, each competing village being represented by several champions. Several formidable varieties of spurs are used, straight and curved, broad-bladed and narrow, some of them 4″, or even 6″, in length.

Religion.

No scientific survey has yet been made of the religious cults of Salem District, and only a cursory notice is possible. The

[1] Dance-songs, the former accompanied by clapping the hands, and the latter by striking sticks together.

CHAP. III. HINDUS. — RELIGION.

Religion of South Indian Hindus, like their social organisation, is a blend of two cultures, the Aryan and the Dravidian, the former represented by immigrant Brahmanism, the latter by indigenous cults. The various cults may be roughly classified as follows:—

I. Brahmanic Cults proper, comprising the cults associated with (A) Siva and (B) Vishnu. II. The Pāndava Cult. III. The Manmatha-Rati Cult. IV. The Vīra-Saiva Cult. V. The Cults of the Grāma-Dēvatās or village deities, comprising (A) the Ayyanār Cult, (B) the Sakti Cults, (C) Demon Cults.

I. Brahmanic. (A) Siva Cults.

The worship of Siva and Pārvati, and their sons, Vignēsvara and Subrahmanya, is universal throughout the District. Most of the large temples of the District are dedicated to Siva, and there are few villages without this shrine. The worship of Vignēsvara is an essential element in most of the more important Hindu ceremonies, and there are several temples of no small affluence dedicated to Subrahmanya.

A Siva temple of the correct pattern should have seven *prākārams* or ambulatories, one within the other, but this arrangement is not found in any temple in Salem District. The precincts of most of the large temples of the District are surrounded by a wall, varying in height and length with the importance and wealth of the temple. In the centre of this enclosure is the main block of buildings, which consists of three parts, (1) the *mahā-mantapam*, (2) the *ardha-mantapam*, and (3) the *garbha-griham*, corresponding to the 5th, 6th and 7th *prākārams* of an ideal temple. The *garbha-griham*, or Holy of Holies, is a perfect cube, and contains the god in the form of a *lingam*.[1] On the northern side of the *garbha-griham* is a small drain, terminating outside the shrine in a spout (*gōmukham* or *sōma-sūtram*), which carries off the water used in the god's ablutions (*abhishēkham*). The worshippers drink this water, which is held very sacred.[2] The *garbha-griham* is usually topped by a superstructure (*vimāna*), ornamented with more or less elaboration, and surmounted with a brass ornament (*kalasam*), which is sometimes covered with gold. The *garbha-griham* usually opens on its eastern side[3] into the *ardha-mantapam*, a small ante-room, rather narrower than the *garbha-griham*, and connecting it

---

[1] The *mūla-vigraha*, as the representation of the deity fixed in the Holy of Holies is called, in contrast to the *utsava-vigraha* used for processional purposes.

[2] In temples where the god is installed according to the Saiva *Āgama*, Smārta Brahmans decline to take *tīrtam* from the Archakar, and where the god is installed according to Smārta *Āgama*, Saiva Brahmans decline to take *tīrtam* from a Smārta Archakar.

[3] In some temples, *e.g.*, the Kailāsanātha Temples at Tāra-mangalam and Rāsipuram, the *garbha-griham* faces west.

with the *mahā-matapam* or main *mantapam*, a pillared hall or portico where most of the best of the ornamental work of the temple is concentrated.

South-west of the main shrine should be a temple to Vignēsvara, and north-west of the same another to Subrahmanya, both facing east. Pārvati's temple is usually in the north-east of the temple compound, and faces south. The position of these three shrines varies, however, in different temples. In front of the main mantapam, in order from west to east are (1) a *nandi* (bull, Siva's *vāhanam*), facing the *garbha-griham* and usually surmounted by a stone canopy, (2) a *dhwaja-stambham* or flag-post, a tall mast, sometimes of wood, sometimes of copper, with a flag-shaped device on top, decorated sometimes with bells, (3) a *bali-pītam*, or altar of sacrifice, a pedestal topped by a stone in the form of a lotus, the eight petals of which are supposed to represent the guardians of the Eight Carbinal Points (Ashta-dik-Pālakas). On this *bali-pītam* offerings of flowers and fruits are laid by worshippers.

Siva is credited with 1,008 theophanies in as many different localities, and he is known by at least as many names [1].

He is most commonly known as Sōmēsvara in the Northern Taluks (*e.g.*, Adaman-kōttai, Rāya-kōta, Indūr, Krishnagiri, also Sankaridrug and Nangavalli) and Kailāsanātha in the Talaghāt (*e.g.*, Rāsipuram, Tiruchengōdu and Tāra-mangalam). The Chōlas and Pāndyas [2] have claimed him for their Lord and the Sōlēsvara (*e.g.*, Āragalūr, Malla-samudram, Kadagattūr) and Pāndīsvara (*e.g.*, Kumāra-mangalam, and Tiruchengōdu) Temples scattered over the District are relics of their rule. Other popular designations are Mallik-Arjunēsvara (*e.g.*, Dharmapuri, Vellār and Mallik-Arjuna-Durgam), Chokkanāthēsvara (Amarakundi), Paramēsvara (Pālakōdu), and Sāmba-mūrti (Ēttāppūr). Rarer forms associated with particular localities are Chūdanāthēsvara (Hosūr, Bāgalūr), Sukavanēsvara (Salem), Sūkāya-nir-malēsvara (Āttūr), Jalakantēsvara (Kāvēri-patnam), Dēsināthēsvara (Kambaya-nallūr), Dēsēsvara (Hogēna-kal), Tīrtigirīsvara (Tīrta-malai), Arunēsvara (Kāri-mangalam), Pennēsvara (near Nedungal) and Sri-Kāmanāthēsvara (Āragalūr). The most important shrines are those at Salem, Rāsipuram, Tāra-mangalam, Tiruchengōdu, Tīrta-malai, Hosūr, and Ēttāppūr.

Siva's consort Pārvati has no temples of her own apart from the shrine allotted her in the temples of Siva, except as Kāmākshi,

---

[1] A list of 87 names is given in Ziegenbalg (p. 44 sq.).

[2] Sōmēsvara was a favourite name among the Hoysalas, and possibly the frequent recurrence of this name in Salem District is a survival of Hoysala rule.

CHAP. III. HINDUS. — RELIGION. Vignēsvara.

patroness of the Kammālars (p. 187), and as Kanyakā-Paramēsvari, the goddess of the Kōmatis (p. 175).[1]

To the masses Vignēsvara, or Pillaiyār as he is popularly called, as the God of Hindrance, is the most important deity of the Hindu Pantheon.[2] "If the mild Hindu would go a journey, or plough the field that is to support him and his family for the coming year, 'Pillāri dēvadu' must be first invoked to help the work in hand; incense must burn, and the milky coco-nut must be broken before the aldermanic god."

Subrahmanya.

Subrahmanya, whose *vāhanam* is a peacock, is worshipped under the name of Kandaswāmi (see below Vol. II, p. 275, s.v. Kāli-patti) or Muttu-Kumāra-swāmi. Except as adjuncts to the larger Siva temples, his shrines are not numerous. He is the patron deity of the Kaikōlars, and Tuesdays are considered sacred to his worship.

(B). Vishnu Cults.

Vaishnavism is represented by the Vishnu Temples, to be found in most villages of any importance, and the Hanumān shrines, which are still more numerous. Vishnu, like Siva, enjoys a multitude of names, those most commonly used in Salem being Venkataramana (Āttūr, Indūr, Chappadi, Kāvēri-patnam), Narasimha, the Man-Lion (Nangavalli, Gummalāpuram, Halē-Dharmapuri, Krishnagiri), Varadarāja (Tārā-mangalam, Pāppāra-patti), Vēnugōpāl (Bēlūr, Tali), Chendarāya (Adaman-kōttai, Vīrabhadra-Durgam) and Lakshmi-Nārāyana (Kāri-mangalam, Rāya-kōta). The names Bētrāya (Denkani-kōta) and Alagiri (Salem) are less common. Vishnu temples are less well endowed than those of Siva; the richest is that of Bētrāya-swāmi at Denkani-kōta with an annual *tasdik* of over Rs. 1,800. Vishnu under his popular name of Perumāl appears to have a predilection for the summits of the rocky eminences so common in the District, and to him are usually dedicated the plain little masonry shrines with which such kopjes are often crowned.[3]

Vishnu's consort Lakshmi has no temples of her own, and is only worshipped conjointly with Vishnu. Among the masses, Hanumān, as Rāma's *fac-totum*, seems at one time to have enjoyed a popularity second only to that of Vignēsvara. In addition to his association with all Vishnu temples, huge bas-reliefs of the monkey god are to be found throughout the District, especially in the Bāramahāl and Bālāghāt. Many of these bas-reliefs, gaudy with scarlet paint, are carved on the enormous boulders with

---

[1] And also, perhaps, as one of the village goddesses, if their lineage as Saktis be correctly traced to Pārvati.

[2] He is also called Ganesh, Vināyaka and Ganapati.

[3] See Ziegenbalg, p. 83.

which the country side is littered, some of them protected by a mantapam, and some not. Such carvings are usually to be found in the vicinity of the gateways of ruined forts, for Hanumān seems to have been generally revered as the guardian of the gates.[1]

II. Pāndava Cult.

The worship of the five Pāndavas and their joint wife Draupadi is, curiously enough, confined to non-Brahmans, in spite of the reverence in which the *Mahābhārata* is held by orthodox Brahmans. The most ardent votaries of this cult are the Pallis, from whom most of the *pūjāris* are drawn. The temples are popularly called after Draupadi-amman, sometimes after Dharmarāja; they are plain, unpretentious buildings, of simple design.

The annual festival, which is held in spring-time and lasts about 18 days, is usually signalised by recitations of the *Mahābhārata*, and sometimes by dramatic representations of scenes from that Epic; a colossal prostrate figure of Duryōdhana, the king who persecuted the five brethren, is formed in mud in the vicinity of the temple, and the sacrifice of Aravān, son of Arjuna by a Nāga Princess, is commemorated by the slaughter of a goat, the entrails of which are afterwards entwined on a pole surmounted with a hideous red mask which represents the head of the heroic youth.

With the Pāndava Cult a fire-walking ceremony is usually associated. For instance at Edappādi the annual festival takes place about the middle of Panguni (February-March) and lasts for 18 days. The *pūjāri* of the temple, who is a Golla by caste, for the first 15 days takes food only once a day in the temple, and for the last 3 days he subsists solely on a diet of fruit. In front of the temple a shallow pit is dug, about 25′ long, 20′ broad, and 2′ deep. At one end of this pit is a ditch, about 3′ broad, which is filled with water. On the last day of the festival a fire is kindled in this pit at about 10 A.M. and continues till about 5 P.M., when the embers are beaten down with bamboo poles and spread evenly over the area. The fuel is mostly supplied by devotees who have taken a vow to do so. Meanwhile, those who have taken a vow to pass through the fire, smear themselves and their clothes with saffron, and worship the *karagam*, a brass vessel filled with water and decked with a pyramid of flowers, which is consecrated for the occasion. When the embers of the fire have been levelled, the crowd of fire-walkers approaches the fire-pit (*agni-gundam*) and led by the *pūjāri* with the *karagam*, the devotees call on their gods and rush round the pit in the direction of the sun, then across it, and into the ditch

[1] Vide the gigantic bas-relief at Mahārāja-gadai, Vol. II, p. 179 below.

CHAP. III. HINDUS. RELIGION.

of water. Some of the more enthusiastic cross the fire twice or thrice. At Edappādi women as well as men are said to go through the ordeal, and even infants in arms are carried across. The crowd of fire-walkers numbers about 200. It is said that if the *pūjāri* is a married man, a few embers are taken from the pit before the walking begins and tied in the new saffron-dyed cloth that his wife dons for the occasion, and she then walks round a small "milk-post" planted near the fire-pit[1].

III. Manmatha.

The legend[2] of Manmatha, he god of love, and his incineration by a glance from the third eye of Siva is commemorated among most of the inferior castes in the *Kāman-Pandikai* ("Festival of *Kāman*" = Desire, a synonym for Manmatha) which takes place about the time of the full moon of the solar month Māsi, coinciding with that of the lunar month Phālguna. The festival is essentially a feast of spring-time, and it synchronises with the *Hōli* Festival of Northern India.[3] The commemorative rite is the burning of Kāman on the night of the full moon, Kāman being represented by a stalk of the castor-oil plant with some wisps of *nānal* grass attached to it, which is set up at the meeting points of the principal thoroughfares in towns and villages, 4 or 5 days before full-moon day. In some places a human effigy of straw and paper is also burnt. Kāman has no temple or *pūjāri*, nor are offerings made to him, but in Salem two lads are dressed up to represent Manmatha and his wife Rati, and are taken in procession thorugh the town, with a cortege of masqueraders and gymnasts, very much in the style of the Muharram celebrations, but on nothing like such an elaborate scale. The festival is marked by a certain amount of rough and *risqué* fun as elsewhere in India, and the youngsters amuse themselves by dousing each other with green or crimson dye. Sometimes the lower castes dramatise the Manmatha cycle of stories in a series of *nātakās*, which take place on the nights preceding the festival.

IV. Vira-Saivas.

The religion of the Vīra-Saivas or Lingāyats is a reformed aspect of Siva worship. As a sect the Vīra-Saivas sprang into political prominence in the middle of the twelfth century, shortly after the collapse of the Kalyāni Chālukyas and during the reign of the

---

[1] Cf. a description of a similar ceremony in Bangalore, published in the *Quarterly Journal of the Mythic Society*, Vol. II, p. 29.

[2] For the legend see Ziegenbalg, p. 92.

[3] The direct connection between the *Hōli* and *Kāman* Festivals is obscure. The former is observed in Salem District by Marātha Brahmans and Mārwāris. Both are vernal festivals. For the story of the female demon Holika, see the late Pandit S. M. Natesa Sastri's *Hindu Feasts, Fasts and Ceremonies*, p. 42 and Mr. J. C. Oman's *Brahmans, Theists and Muslims of India*, p. 250. The former writer says that the five days before the full moon are known as *Hōli-Pandikai* and the next three days as the *Kāman Pandikai*.

Kalachūrya Bijjala. The rise of the Lingāyats under the leadership of Basava was essentially [1] anti-Brahmanic and anti-Jain. The salient feature of their worship is their reverence for the *lingam*, which is always worn on their persons. Their temples are not infrequent in the Bālāghāt and in Dharmapuri Taluk. They are usually plain rectangular structures, surmounted with a large masonry bull, [2] with miniature bulls at the corners. Each temple contains a *lingam*, a Nandi, or a stone figure of Siva in his form of Vīrabhadra.[3] These Lingāyat temples are popularly called "Bull Temples" or temples of "Basavēsvara-swāmi." Basava means "bull" and Basava, the Moses of Vīra-Saivism, is revered as an incarnation of the bull Nandi, the *vāhanam* (vehicle) of Siva. Vīra-Saivas are strict vegetarians, and their ritual prohibits blood-sacrifice.

V. Grāma-Dēvatas. (A) Ayyanār.

The Cult of Ayyanār, the son of Siva and Mōhini (the female form of Vishnu) is fairly common in Āttūr Taluk, and is also to be met with in the other Talaghāt Taluks, but it is comparatively rare elsewhere. It is in all respects identical with the Ayyanār Cult of the adjoining Tamil Districts.[4]

(B) The Saktis.

It is unnecessary here to discuss the philosophic explanation of the Saktis as manifestations of the "female energy" of the supreme deity as represented by Pārvati, the consort of Siva in the form of Kāli. To the simple villager the Saktis are goddesses who rule over evil spirits, and who must be propitiated by bloody sacrifices of fowls, sheep, goats, pigs and even buffaloes, to induce them to protect the fields and villages from malignant demons, from pestilence, famine, war, flood and fire. The cult of these deities has very little in common with the cult of Siva as observed by Brahmans and Lingāyats. The worship of such goddesses was almost universal at the dawn of civilisation in Europe and Africa, as well as in Asia, and the syncretism which explains all these local cults in South India as various aspects of Siva's consort, presents an interesting analogy with the absorption of the goddesses of Egypt, Babylonia, Persia, Greece and Rome in the cult of the Great Mother of the Gods in the early centuries of the Christian era. With its love of sacred numbers, orthodox Hinduism enumerates nine Saktis, *viz.*, (1) Māri-amman, (2) Ellamma, (3) Ankāl-amma, (4) Pidāri, (5) Chāmundi, (6) Bhadra-Kāli,

---

[1] Vide *Castes and Tribes*, Vol. IV, s.v. Lingāyat, p. 237 sq.

[2] The Lingāyat fashion of adorning their temples with large masonry bulls seems to have influenced the architecture of certain Hindu temples, *e.g.*, the Siva and Vignēsvara temples at Kela-mangalam, the Siva temple at Sōlappādi, etc.

[3] Kurubas as well as Lingāyats often worship in these Vīrabhudra temples.

[4] Vide *South Arcot D.G.*, p. 99, and Ziegenbalg, pp. 133-5.

CHAP. III. HINDUS. — RELIGION.

(7) Durga, (8) Pūranai, (9) Pudkalai. In addition to these there are several other female deities of similar type, foremost among them being Pattāl-amman, Selli-amman, Nāchi-amman, Gang-amma, Padavattamman, Ponnamma, Pongal-amma and Muttiyāl-amma. Pūranai and Pudkalai, the wives of Ayyanar have no separate cult of their own, and the worship of Durga is rare.[1] The ritual observed in the worship of these deities differs greatly in different localities, and space permits only a passing reference to a few salient characteristics.[2]

Māri-amman.

By far the most important deity in the District is Māri-amman, and there is scarcely a village without her shrine. She is *par excellence* the Grāma-Dēvata of the Talaghāt Tamils, and her cult exists all over the Bāramahāl and Bālāghāt.[3] She is worshipped by practically all castes except Brahmans, Kōmatis and Lingāyats. She is especially associated with small-pox and kindred contagious diseases, but there are few cures she cannot effect, and few boons she cannot confer.

The votaries of Māri-amman torture themselves in honour of their deity. For instance at the Reddiyūr festival near Salem, men and boys were observed with a number of skewers, sharpened to a very fine point, thrust through their skin, some 4″ below each armpit. The skewers are about 18″ long, and most of those in use were the ribs of defunct umbrellas. Some devotees were content with one skewer under each arm; one man had fourteen. When more than one were inserted, the punctures were very close together. The points protruded about ½″. When all were thrust in, the devotee clapped his elbow to his side, and held the blunt ends of the skewers lightly between his fingers, which he clasped. The operation must be painful, as several of the adults winced, and little lads of 4 or 5 cried bitterly when they were trussed. Other of the male devotees stitched a thread through parts of the body, the favourite place being just above the hip. In one place were two men yoked by stout cords to a model wooden car, about 5′ high, drawn on clumsy solid wheels. The ends of the cords were fastened to iron hooks, two of which were driven into the muscles of each man's back, 4″ below each scapula and 4″ apart A friend stood between the traces, and gave a helping tug to the car when it had to be moved. One man, who was evidently regarded as the most devout of all, balanced on his head a chatty of blazing fire.

---

[1] For a description of Durga—see Ziegenbalg, p. 145.

[2] For a detailed description of the seven principal *Saktis*—see Ziegenbalg, pp. 136–145.

[3] For further descriptive details—see Ziegenbalg, p. 138.

Female devotees were treated differently. Their tongues were pierced with silver needles about 5″ long, the blunt ends of which were neatly fashioned as spear-blades or tridents. The puncture was made on the right side of the tongue, about 1½″ from the tip. The women seemed to find the operation painful, and clasped a corner of their cloth to their face to conceal any expression of pain.

Ellamman

Ellamman, whose name is explained as "Mother of All," or "Lady of the Boundary," is especially popular among the Telugus. A curious legend attaches her to the Vishnu cycle. Rēnuka, the royal wife of the sage Jamadagni, fell from perfection and fled for refuge from her husband's wrath to a settlement of Mādigas (see p. 204). At his father's behest her son Parasurāma struck off the heads of all the Mādiga women, as well as that of his mother. The father, delighted with his son's dutiful obedience, offered to grant him anything he wished. The pious son asked that his mother should be restored to life. The boon was granted, but the son was unable to identify his mother's body, and by mistake stuck her head on the body of one of the Mādiga girls. Ellamman is conventionally represented by a wooden image in a sitting posture with fiery face, four arms and hands, and a crown of serpents. But "her principal image to which offerings are made is of stone, representing but her head, in the earth, to indicate that only her head was made alive and put on the body of another woman."[1] Local tradition is, however, rather vague as to the exact significance of this head, and it is often spoken of as the head of the *Sakkili Pen*, or Mādiga girl, who was an attendant of Rēnuka, and is identified with the famous Mātangi, the goddess of the Mādigas, whose body is Rēnuka's though her head is that of a Mādiga girl.

Bhadra-kāli.

The chief temple of Bhadra-Kāli is at Mōchēri (Vol. II, p. 260); her shrine at Tāra-mangalam is also worthy of note (p. 266). She is more popular in the Talaghāt than in the Bāramahāl Her worship is frequently associated with buffalo sacrifice.

Ankāl-amman.

Ankāl-amman, the patron goddess of the Sembadavans (see p. 173), is worshipped by most Non-Brahman castes in the Talaghāt. Her *pūjāri* is usually a Sembadavan, but Pallis, Kaikōlars and members of other castes sometimes officiate. She is honoured with sacrifices of sheep, goats, fowls, pigs and arrack. Her annual festival begins on *Mahā-Siva-Rātri* and during its course is celebrated the grim *Mayāna-pūja*, or ceremony of the

---

[1] Ziegenbalg, p. 136. There are many alternative versions of the story—vide *Castes and Tribes*, IV, p. 297, sq. s.v. Mādiga, esp. p. 306; cf. *E.S.M.* XVII, p. 24.

burning ground (see p. 173). In Āttūr her festival lasts ten days the car procession taking place on the ninth day.

On the seventh day the *pūjāri* is garlanded with the entrails of a freshly-slaughtered sheep, and accompanies the goddess in procession round the town; devotees place money on this gruesome necklace and pour milk over it. Similar practices are connected with her worship elsewhere.

Chamundi.

Chāmundi, the patron goddess of the Dēvānga weavers and destroyer of the buffalo-headed demon Mahisha, enjoys an annual festival beginning in *Vijaya-dasami*. Her shrines, and those of Pidāri, are less frequently met with than those of the other Saktis.

Of the other "mother" goddesses the most popular are Selli-amman, Pattāl-amman and Gangamma. Selli-(or Sellāndi)-amman, who appears indistinguishable from Kāli, is a favourite deity among the ryots, especially among Pallis. She is propitiated with the blood of fowls, goats and buffaloes but not of pigs. Pattāl-amman is an important deity at Kela-mangalam, where the chief tank is named after her (see Vol. II, p. 140). At Pālakōdu and Kāri-mangalam the *pūjāri* who serves her is a Janappan. Her shrines are found mostly in the Bāramahāl and Bālāghāt, and she appears to be more favoured by the Telugus and Kanarese than by the Tamils. Her worship sometimes includes a fire-walking ceremony. Gangamma too is more at home in the northern taluks than in the Talaghāt.

A detailed account, however, of the "mother goddesses" in the District would fill volumes. Sometimes they bear quaint local names, sometimes they are vaguely called "Great Mother" (Periya-thāyi or Doddamma), sometimes their names are merely descriptive of the spot where she presides, such as Vella-pārai-amman, "Lady of the White Rock." On the bund of Pālaiyam Tank at Kōdihalli, near Pennāgaram, is a shrine to Oddammāl, the spirit of an Odda girl who was sacrificed when the bund was built.[1] In southern Ūttankarai and in Tiruchengōdu the tank bunds are under the protection of the Ākāsa-Kannigal or Heavenly Maidens.[2]

[1] It is a curious circumstance that the bund of this tank has no stone revetment.

[2] E.g. the tanks of Venkata-samudram, Ālāpuram and Tenkraai-kōttai. What connection these deities have with the Seven Kannimār of a Siva Temple or of a Muni cult (see below page 121) is not quite clear and the traditions connected with them are conflicting. Mr. S. G. Roberts writes that the Āāsa-Kannigal are female centaurs who guard tanks and make them break by stamping on the bund when quarrelling. This version of the Kannimār is, however, unknown in Salem District. They are worshipped by the Vettuvans on the festival of the 18th Ādi.

CHAP. III. HINDUS. — RELIGION.

Bikkana-halli, not far from Denkani-kōta, is noted for a curious custom connected with the worship of two sister deities known as Doddamma and Chikkamma, to whom the Halē Kurubas of the Bāramahāl and of Mysore State are specially devoted. At the annual festival, women of all ages, who have bound themselves by a vow, foregather at night at a sacred tank, divest themselves of all clothing, bathe in the cold water, and, on ascending the steps, put on loose jackets made of *pungam* or *margosa* leaves. They then arrange themselves in order of precedence, the Mysore Kurubas taking the lead, and with lighted lamps of rice flour on their dishevelled locks, march in procession to the accompaniment of music thrice round the temple. Their nearest relatives move with them, forming a sort of bodyguard to protect them from the vulgar gaze. The third circuit accomplished, they make obeisance to the deity, doff their leafy attire and resume their proper dress. The above procedure is believed to ensure offspring.[1]

(C) Demons.

Demon worship is a grade lower in the theological scale than the cults of the mother goddesses. The simple villager is never free from the fear of the malignant beings, *Pēys* and *Bhūtams*, with which the darkness is peopled. On lonely village roads, or in his own back-yard, he is liable to be seized with "panic terror,"[2] and sometimes actually dies of fright. These evil spirits must be propitiated, and not unnaturally their cult is ubiquitous. To guard his children, the Brahman offers *pongal*, and the Non-Brahman sacrifices a fowl or goat, to the spirit that haunts his back-yard.[3] Trees in particular are favourite abodes of these unpleasant beings, and hence the worship of a demon is very commonly located under the tree he haunts. These demons are usually worshipped under the name of Muni, Muni-appan, Muni-swāmi, and local epithets such as Kōttai (fort), Ellai (boundary), Kāsi (Benares), etc., are prefixed to their names. A demon popular in Āttūr and Salem Taluks is Madurai-Vīran,[4] the hero of Madura, who is worshipped on Fridays with offerings of blood

---

[1] The above is the account of an eye-witness in 1906. The account given by Mr. LeFanu, Vol. II, page 165, differs in several points; either it has been embellished by his informants or else the Kurubas have grown more modest.

[2] The Greek cult of Pan offers many points of analogy to the Muni cults of South India, especially with regard to the "panic" which he inspires.

[3] Mr. S. G. Roberts writes that in Conjeevaram Municipality there is a constant demand for private licenses for the slaughter of sheep to propitiate Purakadai Īsvaran (Lord of the Back-yard).

[4] For the tradition of Madurai Vīran see *South Arcot District Gazetteer*, page 191, where he is described as a servant of Ayyanār. The Rev. Thomas Foulkes identified him with Ayyanār himself. He is sometimes called by metathesis Maruda Vīran, or sometimes simply Vīrakkāran. In Salem he is honoured with festivals in Tai, Māsi and Panguni, which take place on any specially chosen lucky day, shortly before the full moon of those months.

CHAP. III. HINDUS. — RELIGION.

and spirituous liquors, and ganja. Other names in common use are Karuppan (or Karuppannan) and Vēdi-appan. In parts of Salem and Āttūr, cross-roads are believed to be haunted by a demon known as Santhi-appan, but his vogue is limited, and he is not held in high esteem. Of minor demons the name is legion, but all alike have the same taste for blood and alcohol, and, if appropriately honoured, will guard their votaries from pestilence and famine, and relieve them of demoniacal possession or the curse of barrenness.

Hook-swinging.

Hook-swinging is an ancient religious custom general throughout Southern India,[1] and there are still many men in Salem District who have undergone the ordeal, and bear on their backs the scars of their wounds. Hook-swinging is practically obsolete, so far as human beings are concerned, but throughout the District the upright posts of wood or stone (*Siddhi-kal*) are still to be seen in front of the temples of the village goddess, and the ceremony is still performed in effigy.[2]

SOCIAL ORGANISATION. The Village community.

The population of a typical village or small town is made up somewhat as follows:—

(1) A large agricultural community, with a few fishermen, hunters and herdsmen.

(2) An industrial community composed of oil-pressers, weavers, artizans, potters, toddy-drawers, etc.

(3) A community of traders and money-lenders.

(4) Brahmans.

(5) Menials, such as washermen and barbers.

(6) Out-caste coolies such as Pariahs and Chucklers.

(7) A few Muhammadans and perhaps Christians.

(8) A few alien immigrants, such as Marāthas, who have preserved their nationality in their new environment.

The Agricultural and Industrial Classes vary inversely with each other, according as the character of the settlement is rural or urban. Brahmans, Muhammadans and Christians gravitate to towns, and Muhammadans are particularly numerous in places which were formerly of military importance.

Each of the communities above specified is composite. The Brahmans are divided into a number of smaller communities by differences in religion or language. The agriculturists may include Tamil Pallis and Vellālars, Telugu Kāpus and Kanarese Vakkiligas, and each of these again is subdivided into smaller

---

[1] Vide *Ethnographic Notes*, page 487.

[2] For "pseudo-hook-swinging," see *Ethnographic Notes*, page 500.

groups. The Weavers may include Tamil Kaikōlars, Telugu Togatas and Kanarese Dēvāngas, the Fishermen, Tamil Sembadavans and Telugu Bestas, and so with all the other communities.

SOCIAL ORGANISATION. The *Jus Connubii.*

It is an essential feature of the Hindu social organisation that intermarriage between these petty subdivisions of each community is prohibited. In other words, the unit of Hindu Society is the endogamous group, or SUB-CASTE, as it may conveniently be called, the members of which may, except within the prohibited degrees of relationship, freely intermarry; and the limits of each sub-caste are rigidly[1] fixed by its *jus connubii.* Not infrequently all the members of the sub-caste trace their origin to a common ancestor, who may be eponymous. The sub-caste is itself divided into a number of smaller groups, which are governed by the law of exogamy, and which may conveniently be called CLANS.[2] The members of a clan are theoretically descendants in the male line of a common ancestor, and are regarded as "dāyādis"; thus a marriage between two members of one clan would be looked on as within the prohibited degrees of relationship, and therefore as incestuous. Hence a Hindu must choose his bride from any clan within the sub-caste save his own, the bride becoming a member of the clan into which she marries. In some castes there is strong evidence that their clans are totemistic in origin, *i.e.*, the members are all theoretically descended from some animal or plant, which gives its name to the clan, and which is regarded by the clan with peculiar reverence. It can hardly be said that totemism is a characteristic of South Indian caste, but it is quite possible that the apparent traces of totemism in the clan are survivals of an earlier social phase. It sometimes happens that two clans regard themselves as "cousin-brothers" and may not intermarry.[3]

---

[1] The blending of two endogamous groups is technically known as *fusion*, and the splitting of an endogamous group into smaller endogamous units as *fission*. Fusion, except between a few advanced sections of Brahmans, is unknown in Salem District, and the modern tendency is jealously to restrict the *jus connubii*, in other words it is a tendency towards fission.

[2] The Brahmanic *Gōtra* is strictly an exogamous group, but it implies descent from a patron saint or Rishi, and the term is not commonly in vogue among non-Brahman castes. The Tamils use the term *Vaguppu*, "group," to describe the exogamous group, but the term is too vague for general application. The same objection applies to the word *Inti-pērlu* (= house names) used for the exogamous group by the Telugus. The term *Kula* or *Kulam* (family) is in general use among Tamils, Telugus and Kanarese, but the word is also often used with a larger and more general meaning, and its adoption in a restricted meaning would lead to confusion. The term *Kilai* (branch), used by a few Tamil castes, is too local for general use.

[3] They are spoken of as *Dāyādi Vaguppus.*

CHAP. III. HINDUS. — SOCIAL ORGANISATION.

A CASTE is usually composed of several sub-castes, between which interdining is allowed, but not intermarriage. Roughly speaking, it may be said that the SUB-CASTE is defined by the *jus connubii*, and the CASTE by the *jus convivii*. It is usually the case that the ancestors of the sub-castes are supposed to be brothers or half-brothers. Several castes are sometimes lumped together under a common name, based usually on community of occupation, and such combinations may conveniently be termed "caste groups," though the term "caste" is often loosely applied to the whole.

Four Barriers.

The ramifications of the *jus connubii* are determined by a variety of factors, foremost among which are (1) linguistic differences, (2) differences in occupation, (3) territorial differences and (4) differences in religious or philosophic tenets. It is by no means the case that these factors are of uniform importance in all classes of the community. In some castes it is primarily a difference of dogma that has led to social segregation, in others a difference of language, in others of vocation, in others of residence. All four factors may have contributed to the creation of a sub-caste; all four are influenced by and react upon pride of birth or status, and the resultant complex is crystallized by custom and fiction.[1] The causes of caste are multitudinous, though their expression in the limitation of the *jus connubii* is universally uniform.

1. Language.

A difference of language is almost universally a bar to intermarriage. For instance, Kanarese Dēvāngas may not marry with Telugu Dēvāngas, or Kanarese Kurubas with Telugu Kurubas, or Tamil Barbers, Dhobies or Potters with Telugu or Kanarese Barbers, Dhobies or Potters. Unfortunately this distinction has not been observed in tabulating the Census Statistics of Caste. Thus Kurubas are officially supposed to speak Kanarese and Dēvāngas Telugu, and it is obvious that large numbers of Mālās and Holeyas have been returned as Paraiyans, of Mangalas and Kelasis as Ambattans, of Tsākalas and Agasas as Vannāns, of Kummaras and Kumbāras as Kusavans, etc. Hence in the Census of 1901, though over 153,000 persons are shown as speaking Kanarese, the Kanarese speaking castes totalled just over 89,000, while in 1911 the proportion is about 134,000 Kanarese speakers to 50,000 persons of Kanarese castes, and in the latter Census many of the Kanarese castes have vanished altogether.

2. Occupation.

Difference in occupation is the dominant formative principle in the Industrial Castes, which may be described as endogamous guilds based on hereditary apprenticeship.

---

[1] For the influence of Fiction see Risley, *People of India*, page 265.

SOCIAL ORGANISATION. 3. Location.

A difference in the place of origin or of residence is naturally of importance among the Agricultural Castes, whose prosperity is rooted in the soil. Hence arise the distinctions between the Vellālars of Tonda-mandalam, of Kongu, of the Chōla or Pāndya country; between the Malaiyālis of the Kolli-malais, the Pachai-malais and the Periya-malais. Of analogous origin is the Gangadikara (Gangavādi) division of the Vakkiligas and the Morasu division of the Kāpus.

4. Sect.

Sectarian differences are of paramount importance among the numerous sub-castes of Brahmans. A Saivite may not marry a Vaishnavite, a Mādhva may not marry a Smārta. The great Lingāyat caste is essentially sectarian in origin. Among other castes, however, sectarian distinctions are usually disregarded.

Right and Left Hand Factions.

The well-known division of South Indian Castes into the Right and Left Hand Factions (Valangai and Idangai) is recognised throughout the District, except in the Taluk of Attūr. The origin of this distinction is unknown, and no satisfactory explanation of it has yet been advanced.[1] The factions could not have sprung out of purely racial antipathies, for Tamils, Telugus and Kanarese are alike divided by it. Probably it sprang, like the factions of the Guelfs and Ghibellines in Mediæval Italy, from disputes that were in nature partly religious, partly political, partly economic and partly social, but when or how the dispute arose is an unsolved mystery, buried in remote antiquity.[2] The salient distinction between the two factions is that at festivals and marriages the Right Hand Castes employ Pariah musicians with pipes and horns, while the Left Hand Castes employ only Chuckler musicians, with drums and tom-toms of various kinds. There are also

[1] Dr. Oppert (*Original Inhabitants of India*, p. 61) traces the feud to the struggle between Jainism and Brahmanism. "The influence of the Jainas was perhaps strongest in towns, where the artisan classes form an important and powerful portion of the population, while the Brahmans appealed to the land-owning and agricultural classes, whom they won over by entreaties or by threats. The Brahmans have not joined and strictly speaking do not belong to either side, but their interests lie mainly with the right side. As in various localities the same castes have embraced different sides, it is difficult to assign to all a permanent position." Dr. Oppert quotes a civil suit, tried in Salem in 1843 before a Brahman, in which it was held that the Kammālars "had no right to study the Vēda or to undertake any Prāyascitta or any other religious ceremony whose performance is a privilege of the Brahmans."

[2] The Right and Left Hand factions are mentioned in an inscription of the reign of Dēva Rāya II of Vijayanagar, dated A.D. 1446–47 (G.E. No. 23 of 1905 see Report for 1905, p. 58), and the privileges of the Left Hand faction are dealt with in inscriptions, dated in the 48th year of Kulōttunga I (1117 A.D., see G.E. No. 479 of 1908 and Report for 1909, p. 95), and in the 15th year of Kōnerinmaikondān (G.E. No. 186 of 1910, see Report for 1911, p. 78, and G.E. No. 151 of 1905, see Report for 1905, p. 62, and South Indian Inscriptions, Vol. III, p. 46 sq.), the latter being on palæographical grounds assigned to the thirteenth century.

CHAP. III. HINDUS. — SOCIAL ORGANISATION.

certain exclusive privileges to which each faction lays claim, "but as these alleged privileges are nowhere defined and recognised, they result in confusion and uncertainty and are with difficulty capable of settlement."[1] Yet in the days of Abbé Dubois a trespass by one faction on the so-called rights of the other would lead to riot and bloodshed throughout the countryside, and the worthy Abbé records how he had seen the rioters "stand up against several discharges of artillery without exhibiting any sign of submission." The danger of friction has under British Rule abated, but it has by no means disappeared. The Right Hand Faction claims precedence over the Left Hand in the distribution of *pān-supāri*, sandal, etc., at marriages and other social and religious gatherings. At the annual festival to Māri-amman the Right Hand Faction worships first, and it is often necessary, in the interests of peace, that the worship of each faction should take place on a different day.

Popularly the Right Hand Faction is spoken of as the Eighteen Panams, the Left Hand Faction as the Nine Panams. The word *Panam* is said to be a corruption of the Sanscrit *Varnam* "Colour," i.e., "Caste." Bu tthe Castes returned as Right Hand number many more than eighteen, and those returned as Left Hand number many more than nine, and no two lists agree.[2] Brahmans and many non-Brahman Castes are neutral in the quarrel.

The life and soul of the Left Hand Faction is the Artizan Caste of Kammālars, who are actuated with the bitterest animosity against Brahmans. Another Caste which always figures in the Left Hand section is that of the Bēri Chettis, a community bitterly opposed to the Kōmatis, who are Right Hand. Similarly Pallans are at feud with Pariahs.

Among the Castes returned in Salem District as Left Hand are the Kammālars, Bēri Chettis, Nagarattu Chettis, Vēdars, Gollas, "Two-Bull" Oil-pressers, Rāzus, Kaikōlars, Pallans and Irulans. It may be noted that most of these castes either repudiate the authority of Brahmans altogether, or rarely employ them as *purōhits*. The chief of the Right Hand Castes are the Kōmatis, Vellālars, Reddis, Balijas, with Barbers, Dhobies and Potters. Other Right Hand Castes reported are Agamudaiyans, Bestas, Bōyas, Darzis, Idaiyans, Janappans, Koravas, Kurubas, Lambādis, Malaiyālis, Patnūlkārans, Shānāns, Togatas, Vakkiligas and Vēdakkārans.

---

[1] Abbé Dubois, 1897, p. 25-6.

[2] See the lists quoted by Dr. Oppert in *Original Inhabitants of India*, p. 63, taken from a Chingleput judgment of 1809.

SOCIAL ORGANISATION. Polity.

In matters of social administration each caste is an autonomous unit. In almost every village each sub-caste has its headman, who is variously known as *Ūr-Kavundan*, *Periya-Tanakkāran*, *Mūppan*, *Kutti-maniyam*, *Kāriyastan*, etc. He is usually assisted by a peon (*Kōlkāran*), and sometimes by a sort of vice-headman (*Kāriyastan*, *Kāriyakāran*). In some castes the *Ūr-Kavundan* gives his decisions on his own responsibility, in others in consultation with his assistant, and in others again in consultation with a *panchāyat* of the leading householders of his village.[1] The *Ūr-Kavundan's* jurisdiction is usually confined to petty matters of social discipline. Appeals against his decision and disputes of a grave character are referred to a higher tribunal, consisting usually of a council of *Ūr-Kavundans*, presided over by an officer variously entitled *Nāttān*, *Dorai*, *Ejaman*,[2] *Reddi*, *Chetti*, etc. This tribunal exercises authority over a number of villages, the number varying with the strength and distribution of the communities concerned. The territorial jurisdiction of such a tribunal is variously known as a *Nādu*, *Palli* or *Hōbali*. In most castes the decisions of this second court are subject to a third, or even a fourth, tribunal, the constitution of which varies with almost every caste. Among the castes which acknowledge Brahmanic authority the supreme decision usually vests in a Brahman *Guru*. In other castes several Nāds are grouped together under the jurisdiction of an officer called *Pattakkāran*, *Periya-Nāttān*, *Periya Dorai*, *Pedda Ejamān*, *Rāja*, *Gadi Nāttān*, etc., who is usually assisted by a *Mandiri* (Prime Minister) and presides over a bench of subordinate *Nāttāns*. Sometimes the decisions of Pattakkārs are referred to a board of *Pattakkārs*, and sometimes to a *Guru*. The Left Hand Castes own the authority of the *Dēsāyi Chetti*, who is by caste a Balija.[3]

The offices above referred to are usually hereditary, or at least confined to one family; sometimes, however, they are elective. The higher offices are usually regarded as sacred in character, and in some castes, *e.g.*, among the Lingāyats, the whole caste administration is of a strictly hierarchical nature. The efficiency of the control exercised by these courts varies

---

[1] In some castes the *panchāyat* is composed entirely of men belonging to the caste or sub-caste concerned; in others, especially among the Left Hand Castes and the Telugus and Kanarese, the *panchāyat* is drawn partly from the caste concerned (*kulastar*) and partly from other castes (*panastar*).

[2] Spelt also *Yejamānan*, or *Yejamān*.

[3] The usual Kanarese system is the Katte-mane, the Nād, and the Dēsa, the latter being governed by a Dēsāyi Gauda. Among the Kanarese it is common for the *Shānbhōg* and *Patēl* (Karnam and Munsif) to sit on the ordinary caste *panchāyat*.

CHAP III. HINDUS. — SOCIAL ORGANISATION.

greatly with different communities; with the scattered immigrant community of the Balijas, for instance, caste control is loosely knit and vaguely defined; with the compactly grouped Malaiyālis, on the other hand, the jurisdiction of the several courts is sharply defined, and their control fairly rigorous. British Rule, by ignoring caste politics, has tended to disintegrate caste solidarity, and the Civil Courts of Judicature have done much to undermine the authority of caste tribunals, to the financial detriment of the communities concerned.

The position of the *Guru* is quite different from that of a *Purōhit*. The *Guru*, who in some castes is not a Brahman, is the supreme authority in matters of caste discipline; he can excommunicate, and without him re-admission to caste is impossible. The *Purōhit* on the other hand would be more correctly described as the family priest and astrologer, who determines what dates are propitious or inauspicious for family undertakings, and whose services are requisitioned at all births, marriages and funerals, at the consecration of tanks, wells, houses and temples, and whenever ceremonial pollution has to be removed (see s.v. *punyāha-vāchanam*, p. 130). The higher castes employ Brahmans as *Purōhits*, and many castes of inferior status seek to enhance their social dignity by discarding their ancestral *Purōhits* in favour of Brahmans.

For the ordinary purposes of caste discipline fines and sometimes corporal chastisement suffice. In some castes the offender is subjected to some loathsome and degrading ceremony (*e.g.*, p. 199), and he usually has to provide a banquet for all his fellow-caste-men of his own or adjoining villages. Serious breaches of caste law or defiance of caste authority are met by excommunication, which prohibits the offender and the members of his family from taking meals with any of his fellow-caste-men, or from receiving fire or water at their hands, or even speaking to them or entering their houses, deprives him of the services of the barber and washerman, and forbids all members of the caste from entering his house, even on occasions of marriage or death. Before the ban can be removed, the *Guru* must be called in to perform *punyāha-vāchanam* (p. 130), and perhaps brand the offender on the tongue with a needle of gold; and among the higher castes the unhappy sinner must drink the *pancha-gavya* (p. 131). The *Guru* must be heavily feed for his services, and the caste-men fed.

Ordeals.

The ordeal is still resorted to as a means of deciding caste disputes. The usual form of ordeal requires the litigant parties, after performing their ablutions, to proceed in public to the local temple, where, after *pūjā* has been performed, they prostrate

CHAP. III. HINDUS — SOCIAL ORGANISATION.

before the idol and are garlanded by the *pūjāri*; each party then dips his right hand in boiling ghee, and the suitor whose hand is uninjured wins his suit. Sometimes a piece of red-hot iron takes the place of the boiling ghee. Another test is for an accused person to throw fresh *tumbai* flowers into boiling oil or ghee; if they fade, he is guilty; if they do not, he is innocent.

Oaths and Pledges

A more usual way, however, of pressing a suit is by taking oath. It is against the principles of a Brahman to take an oath, but there are many ways open to Non-Brahman Hindus for emphasising good faith. The usual course among the higher castes is for both parties, after bathing, to resort to a temple, where the oath-taker extinguishes burning camphor, or a ghee-fed lamp lit by the other party, in the presence of a deity.

A favourite oath in the Bāramahāl, as well as in the Talaghāt, is to swear by the "sixtieth step" (*Aruvathām-padi*) at Tiruchengōdu[1], and it is not necessary to go to Tiruchengōdu to swear this oath. A man may swear by his wife or child (*penjāthi-pillai-uthavarāppalē*), placing his hand on their heads; or by his family or village deity, especially by Māri-amman or Selli-amman; or he will touch the ground and point to the sky, and swear by earth and heaven (*bhūmi-sātchi-āgāsa-sātchi-yāga-sollugirēn*). If it is not convenient to go to the temple, the oath-taker may stand within a circle drawn on the ground and so repeat his oath, or he may throw a cloth on the ground and step over it, or cross over seven parallel straight lines drawn on the ground within the space of a foot or two.

Betel and salt are alike sacred; betel represents Lakshmi, the goddess of wealth, and salt is a necessity of life; and hence a man may swear by touching 3 pieces of salt placed on a betel-leaf, or with a piece of betel or salt on his head. An oath may be taken by touching the foot of a Brahman, or a man may swear by the Rāmāyana. If a document is in dispute, the plaintiff may challenge the defendant to draw his pen across the paper, and a creditor may challenge his debtor to tear up his bond. Custom prohibits the taking of an oath by a minor under fifteen years of age, by a woman (except against a woman), by a man who is blind or deaf, by a man of bad character, by a drunkard or by an idiot.[2] In Pennāgaram a man will give a piece of cow-dung to the purchaser of his cattle, and the latter dare not then recede from his bargain. In Denkani-kōta, when selling cattle, the owner of a beast will hand a piece of straw and a little cow-dung

---

[1] Vide *infra* Vol. II, p. 286.

[2] *Baramahal Records*, III, p. 56.

CHAP. III. HINDUS. — SOCIAL ORGANISATION.

to the purchaser when he hands over the cattle. It is common in the presence of a *Panchāyat* to break a straw in two and throw the pieces over one's head as a token of veracity. Among the lower castes a straw is broken at dissolution of marriage. A low caste illiterate man, when called on to sign a document, will break a straw and place it on the ground, in token that he acknowledges the mark affixed in lieu of signature.

CUSTOMS.

The social customs of Sonth India are a blend of two cultures, the Aryan and Dravidian. The terms Kshatriya, Vaisya and Sudra have no ethnographic significance in South India; the term Brahman has, for it represents Aryanism.

For the sake of scientific convenience, Hindus in Salem District may be classed as Brahman and non-Brahman[1]; and the non-Brahman castes may be graded *inter se* by the degree to which they have assimilated their customs to Brahmanic practice. The cardinal features of the Aryan culture are (1) infant marriage, (2) taboo on the re-marriage of widows, (3) taboo on animal food, (4) the worship of Siva or Vishnu, (5) prohibition of animal sacrifice, and (6) the performance of *srāddhas*, i.e., the annual ceremony in honour of dead ancestors.

Pollution.

Pollution is incurred by breaches of the *jus connubii* or *jus convivii* or by excommunication (see above p. 128); by the touch of a low caste man or even by his presence,[2] by menstruation, childbirth or death. Pollution usually extends to the near relatives and to all who come in contact with the person polluted.

The most usual purificatory ceremony is *punyāha-vāchanam*,[3] a ceremony observed by almost all castes. As a preliminary, the house is prepared by rubbing the floor with cow-dung and water and whitewashing the walls, and sometimes a pandal is erected in front of the doorway. All the members of the family should bathe, anoint their head with oil, and don clean clothes. A measure of rice on a plantain leaf is placed before the persons who are to be purified, and on this is placed a brass vessel of water, the mouth of which is covered with mango leaves. The *purōhit* or family priest then recites *mantras* (spells) over the vessel, and

---

1 As the claim of certain castes to be classed as Kshatriyas or Vaisyas is not generally recognised, the use of the more general term Non-Brahman is necessary to avoid confusion.

2 See *Malabar District Gazetteer*, p. 102 sq., for the distinction between "contact" and "distance" or "atmospheric" pollution, and *Census Report, Madras*, 1901, p. 137 sq. for lists of castes who pollute by touch and by proximity. The graded "scale of distances" observed in Malabar is, however, unknown in Salem.

3 Called also *Stala-suddhi*.

then sprinkles the water so consecrated (*tirtam*) over all the members of the family who are present and over the house. Several subsidiary ceremonies are performed, but they are not all essential. The most potent and efficacious of all purificatory rites, however, is the drinking of the *pancha-gavya*, or the five products of the cow, viz., milk, curds, ghee, cow-dung and cow-urine; a ceremony in vogue only among the higher castes, and reserved for special occasions.

On attainment of maturity a girl must be segregated for a prescribed period in a separate room of the house, or in a temporary shed erected (usually by her maternal uncle) outside the village. Custom sometimes requires that a new hut should be constructed every three days or so, the old hut being burned. Every precaution is taken to guard the girl from the Evil-Eye or molestation by evil spirits. She must undergo numerous ceremonial ablutions, and custom rigidly lays down how often and when she should change her clothes. Sometimes she is given special diet. In some castes, after a few days' isolation outside the village, the girl is admitted into the house, and she and her relatives remain under "minor" pollution till the end of the pollution period. The pollution period varies greatly even within the same caste.[1] Brahmans observe pollution for ten days, Malaiyālis sometimes for a full month, Lingāyats none at all. Pollution terminates with final ablutionary ceremonies, formal presentation of new cloths and other gifts, the inevitable *punyāha-vāchanam* and a family feast. At subsequent menstruations segregation for three, four or five days suffices, and pollution ends with a bath. After childbirth similar precautions and ceremonies are observed, but the mother is permitted to remain in the house.

Childhood.

Between birth and maturity a Brahman has to undergo five important ceremonies, (1) *nāmakaranam* or naming ceremony, (2) *chevulu-kuttēdi* or ear-boring ceremony, (3) *anna-prāsanam* or weaning ceremony, (4) *chaulam* or tonsure ceremony and (5) *upanayanam* or investiture with the *pūnūl* or sacred thread. Most of the castes which claim to be *Dvija* or "twice born" observe these ceremonies, but many of the other Non-Brahman castes ignore them. For ear-boring no particular month is specified, and any convenient day is chosen by the parents provided it is auspicious. The weaning ceremony among Brahmans takes place when the boy is six months old, the tonsure[2] at the

[1] Little or no consistency as to the duration of pollution can be traced between the accounts given in *Castes and Tribes*, *E.S.M.*, etc., and information derived locally.

[2] Dubois, loc. cit., p. 160.

CHAP. III. HINDUS. — CUSTOMS.

end of the third year, and the *upanayanam*[1] between the fifth and ninth year, and usually between the months of March and June.

Kōmatis and Nagarattus follow Brahman practice, but other castes that adopt the *pūnūl* are usually invested with it on the eve of marriage. The *nāmakaranam* is generally performed at the time of purification after childbirth, sometimes it is reserved till the fifth, seventh or ninth month and sometimes it is deferred till even the third year. The ceremonies observed differ greatly in different castes, and it is a general practice to seek the advice and blessings of a family or village deity. The names usually selected are those of ancestors, of local deities, or of deities who are believed to be the special guardians of the family, e.g., Ardhanāri is a popular name round Tiruchengōdu, Bētrāyan round Denkani-kōta, and Muni-appan or Muniswāmi near Vēppana-palli. The eldest son is usually named after his parental grandfather, but, as his mother may never utter the name of her husband, her father-in-law or her mother-in-law, be they alive or dead, her child must necessarily have a nickname for domestic use. Personal names are common, such as Mūkkan (*anglice* "Beak"), Karuppan (Black-fellow), Mīn-vāyan (Fish-mouth), etc. If the first and second children die in infancy, the third child is called Kuppu-swāmi, or Kuppan, or if a girl, Kuppammāl, and is rolled thrice on a muck heap, its nostril is bored and a ring inserted, and the infant is nominally sold away to a third person for a sum of not more than half an anna.

The practice of branding infants as a prophylactic against fits, swellings or jaundice is largely resorted to, sometimes immediately after birth. The parts branded are the forehead, the joints of the limbs, and the abdomen, and the branding is done with a red-hot needle, or a piece of thread dipped in boiling oil. A circle branded on the knee joint is a specific against rheumatism.

Betrothal.

The betrothal ceremonies are usually simple. The proposal is made by the parents (or guardians) of the bridegroom elect, who visit the girl's house, taking with them money, *pān-supāri*, and sometimes a new cloth, rice, coco-nuts, plantains, jaggery, flowers, dust of sandal-wood, saffron, turmeric and other auspicious articles. If any evil omen is observed on their way, they of course turn back. When they arrive at the girl's house they are received by the girl's parents, take their seats and make known the object of their visit. Both parties then wait in silence for an

[1] Dubois, loc. cit., p. 162.

omen, usually the chirping of a lizard.[1] If the omen is favourable, the parents of the girl formally accept the offer. The girl is anointed and bathed by her mother. She dons new clothes and returns to the company. The boy's mother then ties some of the gifts above referred to in the girl's cloth, and places the money, etc., before her. The fathers of the contracting parties then exchange *pān-supāri*, an act which clinches the bargain. A general distribution of *pān-supāri* among the assembled guests follows, and the ceremony closes with a feast. It is usually necessary that the local head of the caste and the principal housheolders, as well as the maternal uncles of both boy and girl and other relatives, should be present throughout the proceedings.

The Pariyam.

The payment of a bride-price (Tamil *pariyam*, Telugu *tera*, Kanarese *ōli*) by the parents of the bridegroom to the parents of a bride is a custom almost universal among non-Brahman castes. Among Brahmans, on the other hand, the payment of a bride price is prohibited and this prohibition is a distinctive mark of Brahmanic culture.

Mēnarikam.

The most suitable match for a boy is considered to be his maternal uncle's daughter.[2] His paternal aunt's daughter is next in favour, and in some castes he has a preferential right to marry the daughter of his sister. So strong is this custom that in some castes, if the parents of the girl whose hand can thus be claimed marry her to a man other than the relative who has this right of first refusal, they will be excommunicated from caste. A girl who is thus married by virtue of her relationship to her husband is called an "*urimai* girl," while one chosen to enhance her husband's position or wealth is called a "*perumai* (dignity) girl"[3]. The rule, which is common among both Tamils and Telugus, is known to the latter as *mēnarikam*. It is curious that the Kōmati Vaisyas are subject to it. The Kōmati custom is thus described[4]:—

"If a sister has a son and her brother has a daughter, it is an invariable rule for the brother to give his daughter in marriage to his sister's son, and let the girl be handsome or ugly, the sister's son

---

[1] In *Baramahal Records*, section III, three omens are especially referred to as favourable: (1) A crow flying from left to right, (2) a Brahmani kite from right to left, (3) a lizard chirping in the south. A crow or kite flying in the reverse direction or a lizard chirping in the north are evil omens. Many Telugu castes light a lamp as soon as the visitors arrive, and if the lamp goes out during the proceedings, the proposal is dropped.

[2] The rule is observed among the Veddas of Ceylon: see *Folk-Lore*, 1911, p. 523.

[3] Vide *Trichinopoly District Gazetteer*, p. 94.

[4] *Baramahal Records*, section III, p. 88.

CHAP. III
HINDUS.
—
CUSTOMS.

must marry her. If a brother have two sisters, and the sisters have each a son, and he himself should have two daughters, he is obliged to give one of the daughters in marriage to each of his sister's sons. However, if the brother should have three or more daughters and his sisters should have a plurality of sons, the brother is only obliged to give one of his daughters to each of the eldest of his sister's sons, and he may dispose of the rest of his daughters as he pleases, and so in like monner may the sisters dispose of their younger sons. If the brother's daughter be blind, lame or deformed, his sister's son must take her in marriage, but on the contrary, if the sister's son should happen to be blind, lame or in any other shape deformed, the brother is not obliged to give his daughter in marriage to him. But if the sister should have a daughter and a brother a son, the sister is not obliged to give her daughter to her nephew, but may give her to whom she pleases."

Possibly the custom is a sort of compromise between matrilineal succession and Brahmanic law. There is reason to believe that "mother-right" prevailed in early Dravidian Society. Under a system of inheritance through females, a man had no interest whatever in finding out who his father might be. When, however, the idea of paternity began to take shape, as it certainly must have done under Aryan influences, fathers would begin to take a paternal interest in their sons. But under "*mother-right*" a man cannot transmit what he inherits to his own children, for his sister and his sister's children are his heirs. The only way he can secure the family property in the enjoyment of his own children is to marry them to the children of his sister. The same advantages would accrue to a marriage between himself and his sister's daughter, the family property being saved from disruption. A marriage between his own daughter and his sister's son would be still better, for it would unite the properties of his wife and his mother.

The degree of rigour with which this rule of *mēnarīkam* is enforced varies in different castes. In some castes it is a mere matter of form to offer the fortunate uncle or cousin the first refusal.[1] In other castes (*e.g*, Malaiyālis) it is said to be carried to such an extreme that sometimes an immature boy is married to a woman old enough to be his mother, the boy's father or father's brother performing the functions of a husband to the bride, and

---

[1] It is significant that in Tamil one word (*māman*) does duty for (1) wife's father, (2) maternal uncle, (3) paternal aunt's husband, and one word (*machinan*) for (1) brother-in-law, (2) maternal uncle's son, (3) paternal aunt's son, while the feminine form of the latter word (*machini*) stands for (1) sister-in-law, (2) wife's younger sister, (3) younger brother's wife, (4) maternal uncle's daughter and (5) paternal aunt's daughter.

raising up progeny for his son. The existence of this practice is emphatically denied by most of the castes of whom it is recorded, and it is probable that it will yield before long (if it has not already done so) to the pressure of a more enlightened public opinion, and vanish.

Illatam.

Another practice not uncommon among the Telugus and Kanarese[1] is that of affiliating a son-in-law, commonly known as *illatam*. Failing male issue, a father is at liberty to marry his daughter to a man who agrees to become a member of the family, and who thereafter resides in the father-in-law's house and inherits the estate.

The practice of dedicating the eldest daughter as a *Basavi* (dancing girl), about which so much has been written, is probably intended to serve a similar purpose, for a *Basavi* is entitled to inherit her father's property as a son, and to transmit it to her offspring.

Marriage Customs.

Marriage customs are of too great variety to be dealt with in the detail they deserve, and it is unsafe to attempt to describe the wedding ceremonies of Hindus as a whole or those of any specific caste group, because each sub-caste has its own peculiarities, and even within the sub-caste there are deviations from standard, and practice varies in different localities.

Weddings usually take place in Chittrai or Vaiyāsi (April and May) when agricultural work is suspended, and in some communities the marriage season extends to Āni or Āvani (June, July, August). In most castes the chief ceremonies take place at the house of the bride's parents; less commonly [2] the bridegroom's people are the hosts, and in a few communities the ceremonies are performed in the houses of both the contracting parties.[3]

Consummation.

In the case of infant marriage, consummation follows the girl's attainment of puberty, as soon as the pollution period is over. In the case of adult marriage, consummation is usually postponed for at least three months after the wedding, as it is considered unlucky for a child to be born within the first year of wedlock. Consummation is not usually accompanied by any public ceremony.

Re-marriage.

The re-marriage of widows is altogether prohibited among the higher castes, and even among such castes as tolerate the practice it is regarded as a sort of legalised concubinage (*kattuppādu*). The marriage ceremony is of the simplest description, the widow

---

[1] E.g., Bēdas, Kammas, Kāpus, Vakkiligas, Gollas.

[2] E.g., among Malaiyālis, Udaiyāns. [3] E.g., among the Panta Reddis.

CHAP. III. HINDUS. — CUSTOMS.

puts on a new cloth presented her by her lover, and the latter ties the *tāli*[1] in the presence of the headman. No married woman should be present, and the bridegroom has usually to pay a reduced bride-price to the family of the widow's deceased husband, and sometimes a fine to the caste *Guru*, and he also has to provide a feast for his fellow castemen. Where divorce is allowed, *divorcées* are usually permitted to remarry, the wedding ceremony being similarly truncated.

Funerals

The Aryan custom is to burn the dead, the Dravidian to bury. Brahman, Kshatriya and Vaisya ritual requires cremation. Some of the higher castes of the so-called Śudras also cremate, and in many others cremation is adopted by the well-to-do, while the poorer families have to be content with the less costly sepulture. There is a tendency for the Vaishnavite members of a caste to prefer cremation, and for the Saivites to bury. Infants are usually buried,[2] and so also are those who die of small-pox or cholera.[3] Burial is also adopted in the case of men who have acquired a great reputation as *Sanyāsis*, even among Brahmans, and with those who wear the *lingam*.

The Brahmanic monthly ceremonies in honour of the deceased are observed with variations by the Kōmatis and Nagarattars, but rarely by other castes. Annual ceremonies (*srāddhas*) in a very mutilated form are observed by a few of the higher castes,[4] but for Hindus generally the *Mahālaya Amāvāsai* or Hindu All Souls' Day (the new moon of Purattāsi) suffices for the propitiation of ancestors.

SURVEY OF CASTES. (A) BRAHMANS.

The **Brahmans** number 23,371, of whom about one-half (11,905) are Tamils and nearly one-third (6,900) Telugus. Kanarese Brahmans (3,883) number rather more than half the Telugus. The remaining 683 are mostly Marāthas.

The number of Brahmans per mille is 13, a lower figure than can be found in any other district in the Presidency except the Nilgiris. But in a district like Salem, where over 96 per cent of the population is illiterate, Brahmans naturally acquire an

---

[1] Such marriages are called *Kudike* (concubinage) among the Kanarese, also *Udike* or *Sirudike* (" putting on clothes ").

[2] Infants under six months of age among Brahmans, under three years among Vaisyas (Kōmatis and Nagarattus), and children who have not shed their milk teeth among castes which are not classed as the twice-born.

[3] But not among the twice-born.

[4] The essential item is usually the feeding and feeing of a few needy Brahmans, the performance of ablutions and the putting on of new clothes. Sometimes the ceremonies are more elaborate (*vide* *Baramahal Records*, Section III, p. 150).

CHAP. III. SURVEY OF CASTES. (A) BRAHMANS.

influence altogether out of proportion to their number. In general ability they have no rivals. In the remoter villages of the northern taluks the Brahman Karnam is, not unfrequently, the only literate person accessible to the villagers. He keeps the Village Munsif's accounts, writes his reports for him, communicates and explains the Sirkar's orders, settles petty disputes between the villagers, writes petitions for them and acts as a general fac-totum in all business that requires the use of brains.

The Brahman's position in Salem District is, as elsewhere, primarily political in origin. Epigraphic records point clearly to the privileged position enjoyed by Brahmans from the time of Pallavas to the British Rāj. Without the Brahman, no Hindu Rāj ever prospered. The Brahman followed in the wake of armies, and on him fell the work of settlement and administration. Many of the village offices are still practically, though not theoretically, hereditary in Brahman families, and the origin of the office is proudly traced to the grant of some Rājā whose name is long since forgotten. Brahman officers are, from time immemorial, the links that connect the village administration with the centre of political power, and any attempt to disturb this connection, like that of Tipu who tried to administer the District by illiterate Muhammadan Tahsildars, was sure to meet with disaster. The ebb and flow of conquest are marked by Brahman settlements founded for the prosperity of the reigning dynasty.[1]

There are few sections of South Indian Brahmans unrepresented in Salem District, but space forbids any detailed account of them.[2] The ritual of Saivite temples is for the most part in the hands of Gurukkals[3], (commonly called " bell ringers "), who form an important section of the community, though they are rather looked down upon by other Brahmans. The Golconda Viyāpāris of Krishnagiri Taluk are an interesting community. They migrated from the Deccan to the Bāramahāl with Jagadēva Rāya,

---

[1] E.g., the Kanarese Mādhvas in Ettāppūr, Pedda-Nāyakkan-pālaiyam and Āttūr (Vol. II, pp. 298, 303, and 297) and the Tamil Vaishnavas at Denkani-kōta, (Vol. II, p. 130); see also the Sankaridrug grant, Vol. II, p. 281.

An interesting and elaborate account will be found in *Castes and Tribes*, Vol. I, pp. 267 to 393, *Tanjore District Gazetteer*, p. 78 sq. Brahmanic customs are described in minute detail in Dubois " *Hindu Manners, etc.*"

[3] See *Castes and Tribes*, Vol. I, p. 347.

CHAP. III. SURVEY OF CASTES.

(A) BRAHMANS.

and made themselves useful to each succeeding sovereign power, receiving as reward for their labour grants of land and administrative appointments. They are said to be an off-shoot of the Telugu Niyōgis, and closely connected with the Āruvēlu and Nandavarīki groups. Their name[1] (Viyāpāri = merchant) they account for by a legend that when migrating southward to escape the Muhammadan cataclysm, they transported the royal treasure in the disguise of merchants.[2] They call themselves Ayyar, but they are all Vaishnavites, and wear the *nāmam*. Another community worthy of note is that of the Mārka Brahmans settled in Tali. Most of the Mārkas are Kanarese Mādhvas, but some are Smārtas. They are a wealthy and ambitious community, but their Brahmanic status is not admitted by other Brahmans, and they are compelled to keep aloof.[3]

(B) NON-BRAHMANS.

In the absence of any satisfactory scientific classification of castes, a rough and ready provisional arrangement is adopted, based mainly on the primary formative principle of the several castes concerned. Castes are grouped as (1) Agricultural, (2) Pastoral, (3) Fishermen, (4) Hunters, (5) Traders, (6) Industrial, (7) Labourers, (8) Menials, (9) Military, (10) Sectarian, (11) Mendicants, (12) Miscellaneous Castes which cannot conveniently be brought under other heads, and (13) Panchamas.

(1) Agricultural Castes.

The backbone of the population is of course the great agricultural caste groups of Pallis, Vellālars and Kāpus or Reddis. Dykes' remarks on these three great divisions are worth quoting.[4]

"The Vellālar is frugal and saving to the extreme[5]; his hard working wife knows no finery, and the Vellālichi willingly wears for the whole year the one blue cloth which is all that the domestic economy of the house allows her. If she gets wet, it must dry on her; and if she would wash her sole garment, half is unwrapped to be operated upon, which in its turn relieves the other half, that is then and there similarly hammered against some stone by the side of the village tank or on the banks of the neighbouring stream. Their food is the cheapest of the 'dry' grains which they happen to cultivate that year; and not even the village feasts can draw the money out of a Vellālar's clutches: it is all expended on his land, if the policy of

---

[1] The Nandavariki Brahmans take their name from Nandavaram in Cuddapah District.

[2] See Vol. II, p. 168, for further details.

[3] In spite of papal bulls issued by the Sringēri Matam on behalf of the Smārtas and by the Parakāl Matam at Mysore on behalf of the Vaishnavas; *Castes and Tribes*, Vol. I, p. 368.

[4] Dykes, pp. 131—3.

[5] It is said that Vellālars eat their evening meal by the light of the fire by which it was cooked to save the cost of lamp-oil.

the revenue administration of the country be liberal, and the acts of Government such as to give confidence to the ryots or husbandman; otherwise their hoarded grains are buried. The new moon or some high holiday may perhaps see the head of the house enjoy a platter of rice and a little meat, but such extravagance is rare.

"The Pallis and Pallars are the very reverse; they have no heed for the morrow, but spend their money as fast as they get it. Their women wear the gayest-coloured cloths to be found in the bazaar; ornaments are eagerly sought for; and their diet is the best rice they can afford, with meat so often as it is to be had or can be eaten by the Hindu without injury to his health.

"The Reddis, both Kanarese and Gentu, are as provident as the rice growers are improvident. They spend their money on the land, like the Vellālars, but they are not parsimonious; they are always well dressed if they can afford it; the gold ornaments worn by the women or the men are of the finest kind of gold; their houses are always neat and well built; and (if fairly dealt with) they invariably give the idea of good substantial ryots. They chiefly live on ragi, and are a fine powerful race."

(2) Tamil Cultivators. Vellālars.

The **Vellālars** number 268,649. They are strongest in the Talaghāt, especially in the Taluks of Tiruchengōdu and Salem (about 96,000 and 65,000 respectively). In Āttūr there are about 29,000 and in Ūttankarai about 31,000.

The principal sub-castes returned for Salem District are (1) Kongu, (2) Velli-kai, (3) Pavalam-katti, (4) Tondai-mandalam, (5) Tuluva, (6) Nīrpūsi, (7) Nāyanār, (8) Pūsaikkāra, (9) Kārai-kāttu, (10) Sōliya. Unfortunately the Census Returns give no idea of the relative strength of these divisions, but local enquiries indicate that the Konga Vellālars, as might be expected, are by far the most numerous.

The traditional boundaries of the ancient Kongu country are on the west the Aliyār River of Pollāchi Taluk, on the north the Pāla-malai, on the east the Kolli-malais, on the south the Palni Hills. The Konga Vellālars are divided into the following territorial groups: (1) Ten-talai (corrupted into Sentalai; located in Tiruchengōdu Taluk and in part of Coimbatore), (2) Vada-talai (Salem, Āttūr, and Ūttankarai), (3) Pālai (Coimbatore), (4) Padai-talai (Coimbatore), (5) Narambu-katti (residing round Pūlām-patti), and (6) Pavalam-katti. To these must be added the Velli-kai Vellālars of the Bāramahāl and the Nāttāns (see p.144), who are said to have sprung from the Ten-talai section. The Narambu-kattis ("entrail-tying") are said to be so named because they wear entrails round the neck.[1]

[1] Possibly this is an uncharitable variant on Arumbu-katti, "those who tie flower buds"—vide *Castes and Tribes*, Vol. VII, p. 377.

CHAP. III. SURVEY OF CASTES.

Vellālars.

The chief settlements of the Konga Vellālars are in Tiruchengōdu and Uttankarai. Salem Taluk contains many settlements of them, and they are known in Dharmapuri and Āttūr. The Pavalam-katti Vellālars are so-called on account of the circlets of coral beads worn by their women on the left arm. They are to be found fairly commonly in the Taluks of Tiruchengōdu, Salem and Ōmalūr, and in Dharmapuri, especially in the Pāgalpatti Firka. The Velli-kai ("silver arm") or Velli-kāppu Vellālars are so called on account of the silver bangles which their women wear on the upper arm. They are common in Dharmapuri, and in Hosūr in the Sanat-kumāra-nadi valley and on the adjoining hills[1]. They are also found in Krishnagiri and at Kanavāy Pudūr in Ōmalūr, but they are not found in Āttūr, Salem or Tiruchengōdu. They are organised for caste administration into three *Gadi-vārams* or Districts, each under a *Periya* or *Gadi-Nāttān*, namely (1) Rāya-kōta *Gadi*, under Sakkai Kavundan of Dodda-Timmana-halli (Krishnagiri Taluk), (2) Krishnagiri *Gadi* under Venkatapati Kavundan of Mora-madugu and (3) Vīrabhadra-Durgam *Gadi* under Muniswāmi Kavundan of Golla-halli. Each *Gadi-vāram* is divided into a number of *Hōbalis*[2] or groups of villages, each *Hōbali* being under a *Chinna* or *Hōbali-Nāttān*. Each village has its *Ūr-Kavundan*. Appeals in caste matters lie from the Ūr-Kavundan to the *Hōbali-Nāttān*, and second appeals to the *Gadi-Nāttān*, and if the parties are still dissatisfied, they can appeal to a full bench of the three *Gadi-Nāttāns* sitting together.

True Tondai-mandalam Vellālars, who are strict vegetarians, are very rare in the Salem District. They occur sporadically in the Talaghāt, and also in Dharmapuri and Ūttankarai[3]. Tuluva Vellālars occur in the Talaghāt taluks, and are also found in Dharmapuri and Ūttankarai[4]. Some authorities class them as a section of the Tondai-mandalam Vellālars, but this classification is not generally accepted in Salem District, as they are flesh-eaters, while the true Tondai-mandalam Vellālan is said to be a strict vegetarian. In Āttūr they are called Vettilai-kārar or Kodi-kāl Vellālars, and are said to be experts in the cultivation of the

---

[1] Their chief settlements are at Pālakōdu, Pennāgaram and Kāri-mangalam in Dharmapuri, and at Pancha-palli and Betta-mugalālam in Hosūr.

[2] E.g., the *Hōbalis* of Ratnagiri, Chenrāya-Durgam, Baratāngi, Attiyambatlu and Sugana-halli belong to the Rāya-kōta-*Gadi-vāram*, those of Togara palli, Kundāra-palli and Mahārāja-gadai to the Krishnagiri-*Gadi-vāram*, etc.

[3] They are met with in Gangavalli and Kondayampalli in Āttūr, at Karuppur and Enādi in Ōmalūr, and also in Salem and Sūra-mangalam.

[4] There are large settlements of them in Salem, in Āttūr Town and in Mangōdu near Pennāgaram.

Vellālars.

betel-vine.[1] The so-called Maniyakkārars of the Bāramahāl are said to be Tuluva Vellālars, organised under a Pattakkāran at Harūr who appoints Nāttārs for Kambaya-nallūr, Ānandūr Kāvēri-patnam, Jagadēvi, and Pennāgaram.

Most of the Vellālars of Krishnagiri Taluk call themselves Nāyanār[2] and they acknowledge the Dharma-Sivāchār Guru of Nerinjipet. Nāyanārs are also found in Salem and Ōmalūr.[3] In the latter taluk, as well as in Dharmapuri, they are said to be identical with Nīrpūsi and Pūsaikkāra Vellālars, but in Krishnagiri these three sections are reported to be distinct. The term Nīrpūsi is derived from the sacred ashes (*nīru*) which they apply to their foreheads, and all Nīrpūsis are Saivites. There are a few families of Nīrpūsis at Mallāpuram and Kadagattūr, both in Dharmapuri Taluk, and a settlement of Pūsaikkāra Vellālars at Vadakumarai in Āttūr, whose Guru lives at Vriddhāchalam in South Arcot.[4]

Kārai-kāttu Vellālars are to be found in several villages in the Taluks of Ōmalūr (near the Kāvēri) and Āttūr (near the Trichinopoly border [5]). In Salem and Tiruchengōdu they are rather rare. In Dharmapuri there are a few settled near Sōlappadi.

Sōliya (or Chōla) Vellālars are not common, but they are said to occur in all the Talaghāt Taluks,[6] and also rarely, in Dharmapuri and Ūttankarai, as well as in the villages of Angondapalli and Mattigiri in Hosūr Taluk.

No systematic attempt has yet been made to differentiate the customs of the numerous sub-castes of Vellālars, except in the case of the Kongu group. Generally speaking their customs are of the ordinary Tamil type, with a strong tendency towards Brahmanic ritual. The customs of the Konga Vellālars are

[1] According to Mr. Francis, however (*Census Report*, 1901), the Kodikāls are a section of Sōliya Vellālars.

[2] Their chief settlement is in Kudimēnahalli Taraf.

[3] E.g., Nallūr, Rāsipuram, Setti-appanūr, Muttu-Nāyakkan-patti and Ōmalūr.

[4] Reports received of these three groups of Vellālars are full of maddening contradictions. The Pūsaikkāra Vellālars of Āttūr are said to be a section of Tondai-mandalam Vellālars. Mr. Francis (Census Report of 1901) classes Nīrpūsis as Pāndya Vellālars and Nāyanārs as Tōndaimandalam Vellālars. Others class them with Kārai-kāttu Vellālars, and others again with Kongu Vellālars.

[5] Their chief settlements are Nāvalūr, Dalavāy-patti and Pedda-Nāyakkan-pālaiyam in Āttūr, and Tāra-mangalam, Kūkkuttai-patti, Pottanēri, Enādi and Vellār in Ōmalūr.

[6] E.g., Singalāndapuram in Salem, Pottunēri in Ōmalūr, and Eranāpuram in Tiruchengōdu.

CHAP. III. SURVEY OF CASTES.

practically the same as those of the Nāttāns, who are dealt with in detail below (pp. 144-8).[1]

Pallis.

The **Pallis** number 482,631, forming by far the largest caste in the District. They dominate the Bāramahāl even more conspicuously than they do the Talaghāt. There are about 125,000 in Dharmapuri, 75,000 in Krishnagiri, 32,000 in Ūttankarai; in Salem there are some 75,000, in Tiruchengōdu 60,000, and in Āttūr 24,000. The name Palli is connected by savants with Pallan, Kallan, Paraiyan, etc., but the Pallis themselves indignantly disown such associations, and claim to be Kshatriyas of the Fire Race (Agni-kula Kshatriyas), and connect the name Palli with the ancient Pallava dynasties; this claim Hindu Society is by no means inclined to admit, though in some places the Pallis have taken to wearing the sacred thread of the twice-born. The term Palli, however, is considered opprobrious, in spite of the royal pedigree which the word connotes, and Pallis prefer to be called Vanniyars, from the *vanni*[2] tree (*Prosopis spicigera*) which is held sacred by the caste, or Padaiyāchis.

Their most important sub-castes are (1) Arasa Vanniyars and (2) Panda-mutta Vanniyars. The former are the more numerous, but the latter consider themselves superior. Both sub-castes are common throughout the District, except in Hosūr and Krishnagiri Taluks. Other well-recognised sub-castes are the (3) Ōlai Vanniyars and (4) Nāgavadam Vanniyars, both of which are said to be off-shoots of the Arasa-Vanniyars. Other sections reported are the Kongu, Vengāya[3] (Onion), Nīla-kanta, Sugambu, Gangapāla, Sāmba, Pāsupatha, Vanniyars all of Salem Taluk; the Kūda-katti Vanniyars of Toppūr side, and the Kal or Lingam-katti Vanniyars of Baira-Nāyakkam-patti in Ūttankarai Taluk. It is doubtful whether any of these sections are true sub-castes.

---

[1] For Konga Vellālars see also *Trichinopoly District Gazetteer*, pp. 102-5. Much miscellaneous information is given in *Castes and Tribes*, Vol. VII, p. 361 sq. In *Baramahal Records* an account is given of "*Karakava*" Vellālars and Tonda-mandalam Vellālars, and under the head of "Vellālas" a long list of agricultural castes is given, which includes several sections of Kāpus and Vakkiligas.

[2] The word *vanni* is also said to denote king—see *Castes and Tribes*, Vol. VI, p. 9 sq.

[3] The Kanarese-speaking Tigalas of Mysore are called Ulli Tigalas or "Onion Tigalas", and correspond apparently to the Vengāya Pallis. They are said to be called Onion Tigalas on account of the following incident; "A troupe of Dombars gave an acrobatic performance in a village of which all except Tigalas were invited to witness the show. The latter felt insulted, and, in order to out-do the Dombars in their own profession, they constructed a pole by lashing together onion stalks, and made ropes by twisting together the filaments of the same frail material, and surpassed the Dombars' feats of skill." (E.S.M. IX, p. 2.)

The Panda-muttu Vanniyars derive their name from their curious custom of piling up two columns of *kalasams* in their marriage pandals. The number of pots in each column must be odd, and there may be as many as 11, 13 or 15, and they reach to the roof. The pots, which must be new, are coated with chunam, and empty. Each column is based on a curious four-cornered earthenware stand, the corners being fashioned to represent an elephant, a horse, a sheep and a peacock respectively; above this stand is placed a crude earthenware figure of a peacock, on the top of which the column rests.[1] The roof of the pandal is adorned with earthenware coco-nuts, plantains and mangoes.

The Arasa Vanniyars are more numerous than the Panda-muttu sub-caste, but they are somewhat less Brahmanised. They differ from the Panda-muttu Vanniyars in the following particulars, (1) they tolerate the re-marriage of widows, (2) they use a smaller *tāli* than that of the Arasa sub-caste, (3) they use only one *kalasam* at weddings, (4) they use cotton thread instead of the gold *kārai* for tying the *tāli*, (5) they use bamboo baskets instead of copper trays for carrying the bride's *pariyam* and other presents, (6) they may not tie a knot in the necklaces of black beads (*karumani*) that they wear. In other respects the customs of the Arasa Vanniyars resemble closely those of their Pandu-muttu cousins.[2]

Ōlai Pallis are numerous in the Taluks of Hosūr,[3] Dharmapuri, Krishnagiri and Ūttankarai, and are also found in Salem Taluk. They derive their name from the fact that their women wear in their ears rolls of palm leaf (*ōlai*) instead of *kammals*.

Nāgavadam Pallis are common in Hosūr,[4] Krishnagiri and Dharmapuri. Their name refers to a curious shoe-shaped ear ornament, bearing a serpent's head in gold, which is worn by their womenfolk. The Nāgavadam Pallis claim superiority to all other Pallis, and have substituted the distinctive title Vanni for Nāgavadam.[5]

---

[1] See the illustration facing p. 19 of *Castes and Tribes*, Vol. VI.

[2] In one or two points accounts differ. On attainment of maturity it is said a girl is segregated for 12 or 15 days in a temporary hut of cholam or kambu straw decorated with margosa leaves. After childbirth *punyāha-vāchanam* is performed on the 10th day, and sometimes the infant is named on the same day. The bride price is Rs. 11, in addition to food. The milk-post must have leaves of the *arasa* tree (*Ficus religiosa*) tied to it.

[3] Chief settlement at Aliyālam, Hosūr Taluk.

[4] Chief settlement at Sāntapuram, Hosūr Taluk.

[5] An immigrant section of Pallis (Tigalas) at Bangalore, who speak a hybrid patois of Tamil and Kanarese, are known as Dharmarāja Okkalu, and they are ardent votaries of the Dharmarāja cult.

CHAP. III. SURVEY OF CASTES.

Wherever Pallis occur, their settlements are rather large, and each village has its headman, who is variously known as *Ūr-Kavundan*, *Nāttān*, *Nāttānmai-kāran*, *Panniya-kāran* or *Periya-tanakkāran*. The *panchāyat* usually consists of ten members.

Nattans.

The **Nāttāns** are treated in the Census Reports as a distinctive caste, though, strictly speaking, they are a sub-caste of Konga Vellālars,[1] sprung from the Ten-talai section of that caste group. According to the Census of 1911 they number nearly 12,000, of whom over 7,000 reside in Salem Taluk, and over 4,000 in Tiruchengōdu. They are said to have migrated in the first instance from Tondai-mandalam and the Chōla country, and to have fixed their head-quarters at Kāngayam in Coimbatore District. East of the Kāvēri they distributed themselves into three Nāds, (1) Kīl-Karai Pundurai-Nād, now known as Morūr, which is the chief of their Nāds in Salem District, (2) Pūvāni Nād, the capital of which is Tāra-mangalam, and (3) Rāsipuram Nād. These three Nāds have since split into seven, viz., (1) Morūr, (2) Molasi (an off-shoot of Morūr Nād[2]), (3) Parutti-palli, (4) Malla-samudram (an off-shoot of Parutti-palli), (5) Rāsipuram, (6) Salem (an off-shoot of Rāsipuram) and (7) Elūr. An eighth Nād is said to have existed, with its centre at Kalyāni, but it became extinct. The Nāds are *exogamous*, i.e., a member of one Nād must not choose a bride from his own Nād, and even the two Nāds of Morūr and Molasi are regarded as agnate divisions (*dāyādi-vaguppus*), and intermarriage between them is prohibited. Morūr and Molasi belong to one and the same *Kulam* or *Gōtram*, called Kanna-Kulam; Rāsipuram belongs to Vijaya-Kulam and Parutti-patti to Sella-Kulam.

The Nāttāns are distinguished from the Konga Vellālars in the following customs :—

(1) The Nāttāns are called Nāttār Kavundar, while the Konga Vellālars are called Kudiyāna Kavundar. The Nāttāns of Morūr Nād also have the titles Immudi and Kāngayam.

(2) The *pariyam* of the former is Rs. 4 and 32 *vallams* of rice, that of the latter Rs. 25 and 18 *vallams* of rice.

(3) The *tāli* of the former is simple unspun yarn ; the *tāli* of the latter is spun yarn of 7, 9 or 11 strands.

---

1 See above, pp. 139 and 141–2.

2 Local tradition explains the term Elu-karai Nād as signifying the seven Nāds here referred to. The identification appears doubtful, however, for Elu-karai Nād referred to in an inscription of 1540 A.D. (No. 21 of 1900) existed in the 16th century as a territorial division quite distinct from Kīl-karai-Pundurai Nād (G.E. 646 of 1905, dated 1599 A.D.), and Pūvāni Nād (G.E. 19 of 1900, dated 1568 A.D., G.E. 27 of 1900, dated 1544 A.D., and G.E. 22 of 1900). See below, p. 189.

(4) When the Nāttān bridegroom goes to the bride's house for the wedding, he is heralded by a Pulavan who sings a panegyric on the caste (கட்டியம்). No such practice is observed among the Konga Vellālars.

(5) Nāttān girls are tattooed with dots on each cheek, the Konga Vellālars tattoo one dot on the right cheek only.

(6) The Nāttān bride rides to the bridegroom's house, but no such custom exists among the Konga Vellālars.

(7) The former tie an amulet (குளிசம்) to the necklace (சிந்தாக்கு), the latter tie it to the *tāli* proper.

(8) Nāttān females salute both men and women with their hands put together and raised above their heads, the Konga Vellālars do not do so.

Their caste administration is conducted by elective *panchāyats*, which can levy fines up to Rs. 2, the proceeds being devoted to temple funds. The *panchāyat* is not, however, a strong body, and its authority is said to be decaying.

Each Nād has its Brahman Guru. The Guru of Morūr and Molasi Nāds is by caste a Gurukkal, and he lives in Natta-Kādayūr [1], in Kāngayam Nād of Coimbatore. The Gurus of Malla-samudram and Parutti-palli Nāds are also Gurukkal Brahmans, the Guru of the former living at Ayyam-pālaiyam, in Paramati Division, his title being Immudi Sitambala Nāyinār, and the Guru of the latter Nād residing at Kallan-kulam in Salem Taluk. The Guru of Rāsipuram Nād is a Dīkshitar and lives at Pāsūr in Erode Taluk.

Nāttāns ordinarily employ Brahmans as *purōhits* only for *punyāha-vāchanam*. All other priestly duties are performed by barbers, whether it be at deaths, or marriages, or other ceremonies The richer classes, however, (Mittadars, etc.), have sought to raise themselves in the social scale by employing Brahmans only for all ceremonies except those connected with females, but it is said that the ceremonial services of barbers cannot even then be dispensed with.

The marriage customs of the Nāttāns are curiously complex. The chief actors in the ceremonies are the *arumaikkāran* and his wife and the barber. The *arumaikkāran* and his wife (*arumaikkāri*) are priests of the caste, who are appointed under rather peculiar conditions. To become an *arumaikkāran*, a man must be well on in years, of good character, and blessed with children, and his wife must be alive. He cannot be made an *arumaikkāran* except at the marriage of his first, third or last son. Husband and wife

---

[1] In Dhārāpuram Taluk, one mile from Palaiya-kōttai.

are " consecrated " together. The ceremony[1] is conducted by the barber (நாவிதன்) assisted by other *arumaikkārans*, and after it is over the couple go and dig cooked rice out of the pot in which rice is boiled for their son's marriage; they are then qualified to officiate in other marriages in the caste.

The prominence of the barber in the marriage rite is accounted for in the following story. A Vēttuva Rāja, out for his morning ride, saw a Konga Vellālan being shaved by the road-side. The Rāja, who wanted a shave, ordered the barber at once to attend on him, and the obedient barber complied, leaving the unfortunate Vellālan half shaved. The Vellālan, feeling shy of appearing in public, shut himself up at home, and begged his son to complete the barber's unfinished task; the son refused, however, saying that, if he complied, no parent, whether within or outside the caste, would ever accept him as son-in-law. A potter overheard this, and offered his daughter in marriage on condition that the son finished shaving his father. The son accepted the offer, and ever after the son was called " barber ", and a barber has had to conduct the marriage rite among Konga Vellālans and Nāttāns. It is said to be in consequence of this marriage between a Vellālan and a potter girl that the Potters sometimes call themselves Vellāla Chettis.

When a boy becomes eligible for marriage, his maternal uncle goes to his parent's house with a few rupees, some *tenai* (millet) and a mould used for making palmyra jaggery. The *tenai*-flour is mixed with water, and made into a big ball, and into it is put the jaggery mould. The whole is boiled, and the ball is placed on the threshold of the house where the boy's parents live; the parents, in company with their *arumaikkāran* and his wife, then break the ball in two with a pickaxe. If the jaggery mould is found to be uninjured, the marriage will be auspicious. If it be damaged, the marriage will be unlucky.

The next test is to mix some red dye in ghee; this mixture the *arumaikkāri* daubs on the pit of the throat of the bridegroom's mother, and the stream of liquid is watched as it trickles down between her breasts; if the marriage is to be auspicious the stuff must trickle down in a straight line to the navel; if its course is deflected the omen is bad. Sometimes the mixture is applied at the back of the neck, in which case it must trickle straight down the valley which marks the backbone.

If these omens are favourable the two parents proceed to the shandy, and buy salt and turmeric, and smear red *kunkumam* on

---

[1] Vide *Trichinopoly Gazetteer*, p 104.

CHAP. III. SURVEY OF CASTES. Nāttāns.

their foreheads. It is only after the ceremony above described that the bridegroom's father is permitted to erect a pandal in front of his house. The boy's father then proceeds with some elders of his village in search of a bride.

A bride is chosen usually in some village within a radius of 10 or 15 miles of the bridegroom's house. The betrothal consists, as in other castes, of exchange of courtesies between the parents, followed by a feast in the house of the bride's father. Just before the wedding, the father and mother of the bridegroom will sometimes pass through a hoop made by splitting a twig of tamarind, the object of this being to avert the Evil Eye.

The bridegroom leaves his village on the eve of his wedding, riding usually on horseback and preceded by a Pulavan, who sings songs as the procession proceeds. The party takes with it the dowry, which may be one of three kinds: the full *sīr*, the half *sīr* and the quarter *sīr*. The full *sīr* consists of 64 *vallams* of rice, 25 moulds of palmyra jaggery, 5 bundles of betel leaves, 1 Madras measure of areca-nut, 1 measure of turmeric, 4 measures of ghee, a *kūrai* or cloth for the bride, the *tāli* and a gold necklace[1].

When the party reaches the Pillaiyār Kōvil of the bride's village, a halt is called, and the bride's brother comes to meet the bridegroom, riding on a horse or ox. The bridegroom and his party are then conducted to a guest house (விடுதி வீடு) set apart for the purpose, and take their seats on a coir cot, over which the Dhoby has spread some white cloths. The bridegroom's sister is then given a new red cloth which she has to wear; she has to carry the *kūrai* in a basket (*pēzhai*) to the bride's house, and there a few rupees are tied in the corner of her cloth as her perquisite. Then follows a feast given to the bride's maternal uncles, after which they (the uncles) carry the bride, dressed in the *kūrai* but bare to the waist, and closing her eyes with her two hands, to the *nāttu-kal*[2], a stone set up in the village boundary. There the *arumaikkāri*, under the supervision of the barber, ties a piece of yarn round the stone, the bride witnessing the process and sitting on the basket. This done, the bride is carried back again by her

---

[1] The full *sīr* of the Konga Vellālars consists of Rs. 45 in cash, 10 *vallams* of rice, 25 moulds of jaggery with coco-nuts, *pān-supāri*, plantains, etc.; the three-quarter *sīr* is Rs. 9 in cash, 18 *vallams* of rice, large pots of jaggery, one pot of ghee, and one of oil, with plantains, etc.

[2] The *nāttu-kal* is said to represent the 24 Nāds into which the Konga Vellālars are distributed; theoretically no marriage should take place without the presence of the representatives of all the 24 Nāds; as this rule is impossible in practice, the *nāttu-kal* was introduced as a substitute for the absent representatives. In Trichinopoly the *nāttu-kal* is said to represent the Konga King, whose permission was essential to every marriage. (*Trichinopoly District Gazetteer*, pp. 104—5.)

CHAP. III. SURVEY OF CASTES.

Nāttāns.

uncles to her parents' house, and on her arrival there the *arumaikkāri* ties the *tāli*, in this case a mere piece of country yarn; the *tāli* ornament being attached afterwards. In former days it is said the *tāli* was tied by the barber.[1]

The bridegroom, who till now has been waiting in the guest-house, is next conducted to the bride's house and introduced to the bride. The couple clasp hands, an act which is considered the binding portion of the ceremony. The bridegroom next dips his little finger in some red dye, and smears it on the bride's shoulder, the bride returning the compliment. The couple next exchange betel, and then the barber with the *arumaikkāran* and his wife, souse the pair from head to foot with water. Then ghee is brought in a golden bowl, and the bridegroom and bride's brother eat out of it together in the presence of the bride. In poorer houses a brass bowl is used in which a golden ring is put. The bridegroom next goes to the pandal, and the Pulavars there sing a song of blessing. The bridegroom then returns to the *nāttu-kal*, and there the chuckler meets him with a new pair of sandals, which the bridegroom puts on, paying the chuckler a few annas. The bride also is presented with a new pair of sandals at the entrance of her house. This closes the first day's ceremonies, and the bridegroom and the party return to their village.

On the second day the bridegroom's female relatives proceed to the bride's village and meet the women of the bride's party at the Pillaiyār Shrine. There the two parties salute each other and then adjourn to the bride's house and presents are exchanged.

On the third day the bride pays a visit on horseback to the bridegroom's village, and meets him in his house. Here, too, the barber is master of the ceremonies.

On the fifth day bride and bridegroom together are conducted back to the bride's house, and the wedding terminates.

Other Tamil Agricultural Castes.

The Tamil agricultural castes are further represented by (4) Agamudaiyans (11,414), (5) Udaiyāns[2] (25,028), (6) Vettuvans (11,130), and (7) Malaiyālis (28,596).

Agamudaiyans.

The **Agamudaiyans** occur mostly in the Taluks of Āttūr, Ūttankarai and Krishnagiri. In the Bāramahāl they are organised into five Nāds, each under its *Nāttān*. The head-quarters of the *Nāttāns*, in order of their precedence, are (1) Ānandūr, (2)

---

1 In recent years it has been the practice to permit the bridegroom to visit the bride's house to see the *tāli* tied, and in the most advanced families the bridegroom is even asked to tie the *tāli* himself.

2 The difference between the to talfor Udaiyāns and the sum of the totals for the three sub-castes represents those Udaiyāns whose sub-caste is unspecified.

Kāvēri-patnam, (3) Jagadēvi, (4) Mahārāja-gadai, and (5) Paipālaiyam.[1] In every village there is an *Ūr-Kavundan*, who is entitled to two shares at marriages, and on other occasions. The *Ūr-Kavundans*, however, are not entitled to summon *panchāyats*, a privilege which vests exclusively in the *Nāttāns*. The Bāramahāl Agamudaiyans are said to own allegiance to a Guru who lives at Palni. The Ūttankarai Agamudaiyans are also said to recognise a Guru at Tiruvannāmalai, known as Konga-Namassivayya-swāmi. In the Southern Districts they bear some affinity to the Maravans and Kallans.[2] Their customs closely follow those of the Vellālars, and there is reason to suppose that in Salem District a large number of the caste have returned themselves as Vellālars.[3] They are said to belong to the Siruntāli section.

Agamudaiyans.

The **Udaiyāns** are divided into three well marked endogamous sub-castes, (*a*) Malaimāns 10,027, (*b*) Nattamāns 12,421 and (*c*) Sudarmāns 1,499. They trace their descent from three foster daughters of the poetess Avvaiyār, who became the wives of a king of Tiru-kōyilūr in South Arcot, where their Guru still resides. Over two-thirds of the Malaimāns are to be found in Salem and Ōmalūr Taluks, especially in the Rāsipuram Division, most of the remaining third residing in Āttūr[4]. Two-thirds of the Nattamāns, and more than half the Sudarmāns occur in Āttūr Taluk. Outside these three taluks, the Udaiyāns are rare. Their original settlements were in the western portion of South Arcot, and thence they have spread into Trichinopoly and Salem. Many of the Catholic converts round Rāsipuram are Malaimāns by caste, and it is said that "interdining", and even intermarriage, between the converted and unconverted families are tolerated.[5] Weddings are celebrated in the bridegroom's house.

Udaiyāns.

The **Vettuvans** are to be found mostly in Tiruchengōdu Taluk; in Salem Taluk they number about 1,000. The Vettuvans of the Kongu country trace their descent from the followers of an ancient Rāja of Kālahasti, by name Muttani Rāja.[6] In the 2300th year of

Vettuvans.

---

[1] Pai-pālaiyam is about 4 miles south of Kuppam, in North Arcot District.

[2] *Castes and Tribes*, Vol. I, p. 5.

[3] *Census Report*, 1901, p. 140.

[4] Malaimāns are numerous in Pudupālaiyam near Rāsipuram, and in Palli-patti and Pachudaiyān-pālaiyam, south of Nāmagiripet.

[5] For a more detailed description of the Udaiyāns, see *Trichinopoly Gazetteer*, p. 108, and *South Arcot Gazetteer*, p. 109, and *Castes and Tribes*, Vol. VII, p. 206.

[6] For this account I am indebted to Mr. O. Sītāpati Rao, Sub-Magistrate of Nāmakkal, whose information is based on a booklet in the possession of Uma Mahēsvara Pandittar, chief *Guru* of the Talaghāt Vettuvans.

CHAP. III.
SURVEY OF CASTES.
Vettuvans.

the Kali-yuga, or about 800 B.C., when South India was ruled by the Chēra, Chōla and Pāndya kings, the king of the Chēras, growing old, was seized with a desire to eschew the world, and with his consort to go to Heaven without dying. After searching long and fruitlessly for a teacher who would guide him in the right way, he at length heard of a Saint of great sanctity, residing at Tiruvārūr in Tanjore District. Him he consulted; the holy man suggested that the king, if he wanted to make a really great sacrifice, should hand over the kingdom to him. This the king consented to do; the Saint bade him enter a *pushpaka-vimānam*, (aeroplane decorated with heaven-born flowers), which had been brought to earth for his convenience, and the King and Queen proceeded to Heaven, leaving the kingdom in the holy man's charge. The latter soon shifted his regal responsibilities by handing the kingdom over to Brahman administrators. These Brahmans ruled for some four centuries, towards the end of which period the kingdom suffered severely from the depredations of certain raiders called Ottiars and Salliars, who represented, it is said, the Kallars and Maravars of to-day. The Brahmans in their trouble applied for advice to the holy man who had given them the kingdom, and who must have lived to a great age. The Saint informed them that in the 2249th year of the Kali-yuga, when the Chēra, Chōla and Pāndya kings were in like quandary, they had sought and obtained help from the then Rāja of Kālahasti (in Chittoor District), and suggested that the Brahman rulers should do likewise. Envoys were accordingly sent, and, after some difficulty, the Rāja of Kālahasti, Muttani Rājan by name, after consultation with his Guru Umāpathi Dēsikar, was prevailed on to assist. On the 10th day after the new moon in the month of Tai in the year Pramatha, 2700 years after the beginning of the Kali-yuga, the Rāja of Kālahasti set out for the south. On the Kāvēri bank he settled his Guru at Nanjai-Edaiyār.[1] The Rāja and his fighting men then crossed the Kāvēri and moved on Karūr, where he worshipped at the ancient shrine of Pasupatīsvara-swāmi. From Karūr the Rāja conducted a successful campaign against the raiders, and, after crushing them, he repaired again to Nanjai-Edaiyār. Rāja and Guru then visited the Siddha Kōvil at the

[1] The locality is described in the original as follows:—
பொன்னிநதி தெற்கு புகழ் முத்தா நதி கிழக்கு நண்ணியதோர்
சங்குமுக நன்றாய் கன்னிபதம் ஏற்றி அருள் பெரும் புகழ் குருசாமி
க்கு மிக வீற்றிருக்க நல்லவிடமே.
the gist of the text being that the site chosen was the "Doab" formed by the Kāvēri and the Tirumani-muttār.

foot of the Kanja-malai, to enjoy the society of the Rishis and Yōgis then living there. After their return to Nanjai-Edaiyār, the king was requested by the Brahman rulers to take over the kingdom as a reward for his services. The king consented, making Karūr his head-quarters, and posting a chief at Kapila-malai (15 miles south-west of Nāmakkal) and another at Siva-malai (near the boundary between Erode and Dhārāpuram Taluks).

This Muttani Rāja of Kālahasti seems to be the same as the Muttu Rāja referred to in the traditions of the Ambalakkārans, the Muttiriyans (Mutrāchas), the Urālis and the Valaiyans.[1] According to Vettuva legend, Muttani Rāja was a son of one Vijayan, born to him by a jungle girl, with whom he fell in love when hunting, and whose father he slew.[2] Vijayan's father was Kannappa Nāyanār, a hero whose name is associated with the traditions of the Vēdans, Bēdas, Ambalakkārans, and Valaiyans, and who is identified with one of the sixty-three Saivite Saints. Kannappa Nāyanār[3] was the eldest of ten brothers, sons of a Vēdar girl who contracted a *gāndharva* marriage with a descendant of Yayāthi, one of the heroes of the *Mahābhārata*.[4] No historical evidence has been adduced to corroborate the migration legends of these castes, but the community of tradition probably points to a community of origin, and the legend of a Vettuva Rāja still clings to Sankaridrug.[5]

---

[1] Vide *Castes and Tribes*, Vol. I, page 27 (Ambalakkārars, and *Muttarasankoradu*), Vol. V, p. 127 (Mutrāchas), Vol. VII, pp. 242 and 243 (Urālis), and perhaps Vol. VII, p. 279 Muttāl Ravuttan, the special caste god of the Valaiyans).

[2] Hence the name "Vettuvan," one who cuts.

[3] Vide *Castes and Tribes*, Vol. VII, p. 332 (Vēdans), Vol. I, p. 26 (Ambalakkāran), *Trichinopoly District Gazetteer*, p. 114 (Valaiyans), and *E. S. M.* No. III Bēdas, p. 9.

[4] The second of the ten brothers earned the title Kāvalan, by guarding the environment of the Rishi Uthangi while he performed a *yāgam*. The third brother rode round the earth on a horse of the Dēvas and won the title Bhūvalan. The fourth son fell in love with two girls whom he met on the banks of the Tungabhadra, and wedded them on condition that he adopted the family title of their father, Māvalar. These three brothers became the progenitors of three tribes the Kāvalans, the Bhūvalans (or Pūvalans) and the Māvalans. The Bhūvalans are said still to exist near Perūr in Coimbatore Taluk, the other two tribes have not been traced.

[5] See Vol. II, p. 281. Mr. V. Venkayya suggests that the "Vidukādan *alias* Vatturāyan" mentioned in a fragmentary inscription of the Narasimha-Perumāl temple at Nāmakkal (No. 11 of 1906) may be connected with the Vettuva Rājas. Another tradition states that the Konga kings invited Vettuvans from the Chōla and Pāndya countries to assist them against the Kēralas, and a third tradition relates how the Vettuvans assisted the Chōla king Ādityavarma to conquer the Kongu country in the latter part of the ninth century (*Castes and Tribes*, Vol. III, p. 394).

CHAP. III. SURVEY OF CASTES.

Vettuvans.

No clearly defined sub-castes appear to exist among the Vettuvans. The following exogamous clans are reported: (1) Anthi, (2) Mūlai, (3) Pattali, (4) Karadi, (5) Vanni, (6) Kattu, (7) Billai, (8) Varagu, (9) Santhappadai, (10) Pāndi. Caste disputes are decided by *panchāyats* presided over by an hereditary officer called *Kottukkāran*, and appeals lie to a *Pattakkāran*, of whom there are three; one at Irukkūr near Kapila-malai (Nāmakkal Taluk); another, entitled Kālahasti Kavundar, at Pavitram (Karūr Taluk); and a third at Siva-malai (Dhārāpuram Taluk). The full title of a *Pattakkāran* runs *Immudi-pattam-kumāra-allāla-rāma-pāthira-Idumba-Ilaiya-Nāyakkar*, the word Idumba being his personal name. Pattakkārs only are known as Nāyakkar, a title bestowed upon them, it is said, by Tirumala Nāyaka of Madura, the ordinary caste title being Kavundar. Vettuvans employ as *purōhits* a sect of Tamil speaking Smārta Brahmans known as Sivadvījas, who are rather looked down upon by other Brahmans. These *purōhits* officiate at the purifactory ceremonies after childbirth, and on the 3rd and 16th days after death, and among the more advanced classes during the performance of *srāddhas*. Their Guru, as already stated, resides at Nanjai-Edaiyār and bears the title Umāpathi-Dēsikar or Umā-Mahēsvara-Gurukkal; he claims descent from the Guru who migrated with the Vettuvans from Kālahasti. At Nanjai-Edaiyār is a *matam*, and a shrine where Siva and his consort are still worshipped as Kālahasti Īsvarar and Gnānāmbikai.

Malaiyālis.

The **Malaiyālis** are the principal inhabitants of the Talaghāt Hills, their chief settlements being on the Shevaroys, Kalrāyans, Chittēris, Kolli-malais and Pachai-malais. In Āttūr Taluk they number 12,800, in Salem Taluk 7,300 odd, in Ūttankarai just under 7,000 and there are a few returned for Ōmalūr and Ūttankarai. Thanks to their isolation and the feverish climate of their habitat, they form a far more homogeneous community than any of the castes of the plains, and afford an interesting object lesson in ethnology. They trace their origin to Conjeeveram.[1] The legend runs that three brothers, by name Periyannan, Naduvannan and Chinnannan, went a hunting in a forest accompanied by three hunting hounds, and it came on to rain so heavily for two

[1] The Pachai-kutti and Pachai-kuttātha Vellālars of the North Arcot Javādis have also a tradition of migration from Conjeeveram, but they are quite a distinct caste from the Malaiyālis of Salem, Trichinopoly and South Arcot, though, curiously enough, they own some sort of allegiance to the Vēdar Poligārs of Kangundi. Legend has it that the Kalrāyans, Pachai-malais and Kolli-malais were wrested by the three brothers from two heroes known as Vēda-Vellāla and Kāna-Koravar.

days that they were not able to quit the forest. Their hounds, however, returned home, and their wives, seeing the dogs without their masters, concluded that their husbands had died in the jungles, and accordingly, as all loyal widows should do, set fire to their houses and perished in the flames. On the third day the hunters returned to find their houses in ashes and their wives dead. The bereaved husbands thereupon consoled themselves by marrying again; Periyannan chose a Kaikōlar girl, and settled on the Kalrāyans; Naduvannan chose a Vēdachi as his bride, and the Pachai-malais as his residence; Chinnannan married a Dēvēndra Pallan, and made his home on the Kolli-malais. These three brothers thus became the progenitors of the three clearly defined sub-castes into which the Malaiyālis are divided, the Periya-Malaiyālis, the Pachai-Malaiyālis and the Kolli-Malaiyālis.

The Malaiyālis are also divided into a large number of exogamous clans which they call *vaguppus*. A curious feature in connection with these *vaguppus* is that certain groups of them (called *dāyādi vaguppus*) are *inter se* exogamous also. The members of these *dāyādi* clans call one another brothers (*annan-tambigal*), and marriage between them is, for some unknown reason, regarded as incestuous. For instance, in Sittūr Nād there are seven *vaguppus*; five of which (Pīlan, Mūkkāndi, Pūsan, Mānikkan and Tiruvichi) form one *dāyādi* group, and the remaining two (Kannan and Tillān) another; no member of the first group of clans may marry into any other clan of that group, but must go to some other clan for his bride. Similarly the Kōnān clan of the Mūnūr Malaiyālis may not intermarry with either the Māttayān, the Emaiyāndē, or Kannathan clan of Tiruppuli Nād, but may take a bride from the Alātti or Punnan clan of that Nād, though all the five clans of Tiruppuli Nād are *inter se* exogamous. Similarly among the Pachai-Malaiyālis there are about fifty clans, arranged in about eight *dāyādi* groups. Some of these *vaguppus* bear quaint and outlandish names which would afford unlimited scope for a philologist's fancy, but it cannot be said they are totemistic in origin.

Of the three sub-castes, the Kolli-Malaiyālis are the most conservative and the best organised. They are to be found on the Kolli-malais of Nāmakkal and Āttūr Taluks, on the Bōda-malais and in the valley between the Bōda-malais and Jerugu-malais.[1] On the Kolli-malais they are organised into four groups of which two, the Three-Nād and the Four-Nād Malaiyālis, are

[1] Kolli-Malaiyālis are also found on Pāla-malai, Bergūr-malai and Kāli-malai in Bhavānī Taluk.

CHAP III. SURVEY OF CASTES. — Malaiyālis.

in Nāmakkal with head-quarters respectively at Sēlūr and Valappūr; and two, the Anjūr (five-village) and Mūnūr (three-village) Malaiyālis are in Āttūr. The Anjūr Malaiyālis comprise the five Nāds of Bayilam, Tiruppuli, Edappuli, Pirakarai and Sittūr, with a population of 6,641, and the Mūnūr Malaiyālis the three Nāds of Kunduni, Alattūr and Pelāppādi, with a population of 1,501. The Anjūr Malaiyālis are under the jurisdiction of the *Periya-Pattakkāran* of Bayil-Nād, whose office is hereditary. He is not called *Rāja*, and has no *Mandiri*. Each of the five "Ūrs" has its *Ūr-Kavundan*, who is elected. Caste disputes are decided in the first instance by the *Ūr-Kavundan* in consultation with a number of *Karakkārans*, who are elected, one from each clan, in the *Ūr* concerned. An appeal from the decision of the *panchāyat* so constituted lies to the *Periya-Pattakkāran* of Bayil-Nād, who finally settles the dispute in conjunction with the *Karakkārans* of Bayil-Nād and the *Ūr-Kavundan* and *Karakkārans* of the *Ūr* in which the dispute arose. It is not, however, essential that all the *Karakkārans* should be present in this appellate court, and a quorum of five will suffice. Among the Mūnūr Malaiyālis, however, the *Ūr-Kavundans* refer disputed decisions to the Rāja of the Four Nāds at Valappūr, whose decision is final. The Kolli-Malaiyālis of the Bōda-malais and the adjoining valley are ruled by a *Nāttān* resident at Kīlūr, who exercises authority over the Kolli-Malaiyālis of Bhavāni Taluk also, and from whom an appeal may be preferred to the *Periya-Pattakkāran*[1] of Bayil-Nād.

The Pachai-Malaiyālis are organised into three Nāds, of which two (Ven-Nād and Tembara-Nād) are in Trichinopoly[2] District, and the third, Atti-Nād, covers the Pachai-malais of Āttūr. The Pachai-Malaiyālis extend, however, across Āttūr Taluk through the Paittūr Hills to the villages of the Tumbal Valley, the upper Vasishta-nadi, the Ārunūttu-malais and the Manjavādi Ghāt, and are found even as far afield as the hamlets of Kanjēri and Pālamēdu at the western foot of the Shevaroys, and at Vēppādi, near the headwaters of the Toppūr River. For the purposes of caste administration they are divided into Sub-Nāds, *Karais* or *Tumukkus*; for instance, Nallaya-Kavundan Nād, Kalatti-Kavundan Nād on the Pachai-malais, Manmalai Nād west of the

[1] During the minority of the Rāja of Valappūr, his powers were exercised by his mother who was called *Rāni*, aided by a *Mandiri* or Prime Minister. The administrative machinery in the Nāmakkal Nāds is different from that of the Āttūr Nāds; each village or *patti* having its *Ūr-Kavundan* or *Kutti-maniyam* and each Nād its *Nāttān*, from whom appeals lie to the *Pattakkāran* or *Rāja* of Valappūr or Sēlur. See *Trichinopoly District Gazetteer*, p. 125.

[2] Vide *Trichinopoly Gazetteer*, p. 124.

Pachai-malais, and Paittūr Nād. There are *Nāttāns* also at Māmanji in the Tumbal valley, at Aladi-patti on the Aranūttu-malais, at Kīri-patti in the Vasishta-nadi valley north of Bēlūr, at Karamandai with jurisdiction over the Manjavadi villages and the slopes of the Shevaroys, and at Tomba-Kallanūr a hamlet of Pattukunam-patti north of the Manjavādi Pass, with jurisdiction extending to the south-western *Kombais* of the Chittēris and the northern and western *Kombais* of the Shevaroys. The Sub-Nāds are divided into *pattis*, each under the jurisdiction of an *Ūr-Kavundan*, whose title is *Mūppan*, and who is assisted by a *Kungāni*. Each Sub-Nād is ruled by a *Nāttān*, *Nāttu-Kavundan* or *Kutti-Kavundan*, assisted by one or more *Karakkārans*, whose appointment is subject to his approval. The *Nāttāns* in turn are subject to the authority of a council of seven *Chinna-Dorais*,[1] presided over by a *Periya-Dorai*, who is sometimes called Rāja and resides at Sēthakam on the Pachai-malais. Under the *Dorais* are certain *Mandiris* or Prime Ministers, whose powers seem a little vague. There are *Mandiris* at Pakkalam, on the Pachai-malais, at Paittūr and at Kīri-patti. The Paittūr *Mandiri* is acknowledged by 12 *Karais*, the Kīri-patti *Mandiri* by six *Karais*. The Paittūr *Mandiri* lays claim to a precedence over the Pakkalam *Mandiri*, which is not admitted by some influential members of the community.

The Periya-Malaiyālis hold the Kalrāyans, the Shevaroys and the Chittēris. They call themselves Kārālans[2], a name which some authorities connect with Kērala, the ancient name for Malabar. The Kalrāyans (population in Kallakurchi Taluk a little over 20,000, in Āttūr Taluk not quite 10,000) are said to have been colonised by five Chieftains, whose descendants still govern the five Kalrāyan Jāghirs,[3] as a sort of priestly hierarchy, each Jaghir being divided into several Sub-Nāds. Intermarriage between the Malaiyālis of the Kalrāyans and those of the Shevaroys is extremely rare, owing, no doubt, to distance, a frequent cause of fission in the caste system. The Shevaroys are divided into three Nāds, (1) Sēla-Nād (Salem), (2) Moha-Nād, (3) Mutta-Nād each under its own *Pattakkāran*, and each containing nine

---

[1] The *Chinna-Dorais* live at Māyambādi, Mangalam, Manjarai (2), Pudūr, Pakkalam and Nallamati.

[2] The term appears in the inscriptions of Asōka and is supposed to be identical with Chēra, see *Malabar District Gazetteer*, p. 27. The Malaiyālis of the Pachai-malais and Kolli-malais also lay claim to the title Kārālan.

[3] (1) Periya-Kalrāyans, (2) Chinna-Kalrāyans, (3) Jadaya-Kavundan Nād, (4) Kuruba-Kavundan Nād, (5) Ariya-Kavundan Nād; see below, Vol. II, p. 299, and of *South Arcot District Gazetteer*, p. 329 sq. for the functions of these Poligārs.

CHAP. III. SURVEY OF CASTES — Malaiyālis.

pattis under *Mūppans*, who are elected as a rule, each from a *vaguppu* prescribed by custom. The *Pattakkārans* are assisted by *Maniyakkārans*, who give notice of marriages to the villages of the Nād concerned, and summon the villagers to attend; the *Mūppans* are assisted by *Kangānis*. The village of Chittēri is the residence of a *Guru*, who appears to be revered by all three sub-castes of Malaiyālis.

Brahman *purōhits*[1] are not usually employed by Malaiyālis, and the *purōhit's* duties at marriages and other domestic occurrences are performed by the caste officers above enumerated, in addition to their judicial functions. A *Pattakkāran* or *Dorai* is treated with great respect, and his dignity requires that whoever meets him should prostrate before him.

Though the traditions of the Malaiyālis trace their origin to Conjeeveram, their customs point to Malabar, and it has been conjectured that they migrated from the ancient Kingdom of Kērala.[2] Kalrāyan inscriptions (Vol. II, p. 300) throw no light on the subject. It is possible, however, that certain Malaiyāli customs are survivals of a state of civilization which at one time was common to both the east and west of the Indian Peninsula, and which is now confined to the Malabar Coast. The customs referred to are the following:—

(1) Among the Kolli-Malaiyālis, boys and girls wear the forelock (*mun-kudumi*) which is such a becoming and universal feature of the West Coast Hindus, the rest of the head being shaved. Boys retain this forelock till they are about 12 years of age, and girls till they attain puberty; boys then have this forelock shaved off, and grow a *kudumi* at the back of the head in accordance with the fashion universal[3] in the East Coast Districts, and girls allow all their hair to grow. Among the Pachai-Malaiyālis also, little girls wear the forelock, but, unlike their Kollimalai cousins, they do not wait for puberty before they shave it off.

(2) The women of the Kolli-malais wear cloths of white cotton, tied across the breast and under the armpits, never passed over the shoulder, and falling a little below the knees. The other two sub-castes, however, follow the fashion of the plains.

(3) The women of the Kolli-malais wear beneath their ordinary cloth a short loin-cloth of white cotton about a yard and

---

[1] The Kolli-Malaiyālis of Bhavāni Taluk are, however, said to acknowledge as *Guru* an Ayyangār Brahman residing at Pulaveri.

[2] A suggestive article by Mr. M. D. Subbaroyan is printed in Vol. V, p. 821 sq. of the *Indian Review* (1904). The theories therein advanced are not, however, tenable in the light of historical criticism.

[3] Except among Sōliya Brahmans and Dīkshitars, see *Castes and Tribes*, Vol. I, p. 341.

a half long and three-fourths of a yard wide, which serves no apparent useful purpose, but bears a striking resemblance to that worn by the girls of Malabar. Similar cloths are worn by the women of the other two sub-castes beneath their coloured *pudavais*.[1]

(4) Though tattooing is permitted among the Pachai-Malaiyālis and the Periya-Malaiyālis, yet the Kolli-Malaiyālis entertain such a strong prejudice against the practice, that they will not permit any tattooed person to enter one of their houses. Why their feeling on the subject should be so strong is not clear, but it is a significant fact that on the Malabar Coast, tattooing is practically unknown.[2]

(5) On attainment of maturity some Malaiyāli girls remain under pollution for 30 days, a period longer than any recognised in the plains, but by no means uncommon in Malabar. There appears, however, to be a tendency among Malaiyālis to shorten the period.

(6) The only ear-ornament worn by girls among the Kolli-Malaiyālis is a "big boss-shaped hollow cylinder of gold or gilt from an inch to an inch-and-a-half or more in diameter",[3] an ornament which requires the lobe of the ear to be largely extended in order that it may be fitted in, and which resembles the *tōda* worn by Nāyar women.

It is impossible to believe that the above customs, which differentiate the Malaiyālis from the Hindus of the plains, are innovations on their ancestral observances, and they must therefore be survivals. It is clear, too, that the Malaiyālis of the Kolli-malais have been less affected by the forces of assimilation than their cousins. Whatever be the source to which these survivals should be traced, the suggested affinity with the civilization of Malabar seems further corroborated by certain marriage customs which appear to be the reminiscences of a polyandrous civilization such as that which has made the Nāyars and kindred communities famous.

The Malaiyālis observe the rule of *mēnarīkam* (see p. 133) with unusual rigor, and with curious results. An inconvenience inherent in the *mēnarīkam* system is that sometimes the *urimai*-girl is a good deal older than the husband allotted to her by fate and custom. Hence it sometimes happens that "sons when mere

---

[1] Mr. S. Krishnaswami Ayyangar writes "Two pieces of cloth were worn by all women in early times, though I am not certain when actually the practice drops out. It seems to be quite an Aryan practice, as I have seen it referred to quite often in Sanscrit literature." As a general usage it survives on the West Coast. See *Malabar District Gazetteer*, p. 143.

[2] The practice of tattooing among the Pachai-Malaiyālis is traced traditionally to the Vēdachi bride of Naduvannan.

[3] Vide *Malabar District Gazetteer*, p. 145.

CHAP. III. SURVEY OF CASTES. Malaiyālis.

children are married to mature females and the father-in-law of the bride assumes the performance of the procreative function"—and raises up a progeny on his son's behalf. "When the putative father comes of age, and in their turn his wife's male offspring are married, he performs for them the same office that his father did for him." If the boy-husband's father is dead, or is not particularly fond of his daughter-in-law, one of his brothers or some other near male relative may be requisitioned to take charge of the girl.[1] Another curious custom reported of the Periya-Malaiyālis is that the wedding *tāli* is not tied by the bridegroom, but by a stranger known as the Kaniyān, whose function seems analogous to that of the *Manavālan* in a *tāli-kettu-kalyānam* in Malabar.[2] Yet more significant is the fact that though a woman lives openly in adultery, all the children she bears to her paramour[3] are regarded as the lawful children of her rightful husband. In fact, divorce is not permitted among the Periya-Malaiyālis, is discountenanced by the Kolli-Malaiyālis, and a husband never loses the proprietary right over his wife's children, whoever their father may be. The Pachai-Malaiyālis are said to allow divorce on payment of a fine of Rs. 25, but the practice is presumably an innovation, imitative of the customs of the plains.

On the whole the marriage customs of the Malaiyālis differ but little from those of the plains[4]. The betrothal contract is settled in the presence of the *Ūr-Kavundan*, and if the contracting parties belong to different villages, the *Ūr-Kavundans* of both villages should be present, and the *Pattakkāran's* consent should be obtained. The bride-price varies, and is often paid in kind; the Pachai-Malaiyālis of Ūttankarai give four *kandagams* of grain,

---

[1] It is a custom that the Malaiyālis are not proud of, and they are reluctant to admit its existence. That the practice was once widespread cannot be doubted. See *Trichinopoly District Gazetteer*, p. 94, cf. p. 103 (Konga Vellālars), and p. 123 (Tōttiyans).

[2] See *Malabar District Gazetteer*, pp. 101 and 173. On the Kolli-malais the *tāli* is said to be tied by the *Ūr-Kavundan*. Intercourse between the Kaniyān and the bride would be considered incestuous. Mr. Le Fanu writes that "on the day of marriage the Malaiyāli bride in the Chittēri villages is the common property of all the villagers except the person chiefly interested, but after that date she belongs to him exclusively," and adds with reference to the last sentence "in theory at least, for the village houses have generally two doors, at one of which the paramour deposits his slippers on entering; should the master of the house after seeing these persist in entering his own house, he would be held guilty of a very serious breach of village etiquette." [*Salem District Manual*, Vol. II, p. 274.] Local enquiries show that this custom is still observed.

[3] Provided of course that he is a Malaiyāli; a *liason* with a man of another caste invariably involves excommunication.

[4] For a description of a Malaiyāli wedding on the Shevaroys see *Castes and Tribes*, Vol. IV, p. 220.

4 pagodas (Rs. 14) in cash, and a cow with calf; elsewhere it ranges from Rs. 10 to Rs. 50. A fee of Rs. 10–8–0 should also be paid to the officers of the caste[1], but this may be remitted by the Pattakkāran. On the Pachai-malais the preliminary *nalangu* is performed on Sundays, the pandals erected at the houses of both bride and bridegroom[2] on Wednesday, and the *Muhūrtam* takes place at the bride's house on Thursday. At the house of each party a *kalasam* is prepared of three new vessels placed one above the other, and is taken to the Vignēsvara temple on the Wednesday night. The order in which *pān-supāri* is distributed is governed by rigid etiquette. The *Periya-Dorai* receives five shares, the other *Dorais* four each, the *Mandiris* three each, the *Kutta-Kavundan* two and the *Mūppan* one. The bridegroom then presents the bride with the *kūrai*, a white or red cloth with a black border, measuring from 12 to 17 cubits in length and from 2 to 3 cubits wide[3]. On the Kolli-malais the ceremonies take place at the bridegroom's house, whither the bride is taken between daybreak and 7 A.M. on the wedding morning. The bridegroom places the *tāli* on the girl's neck, and the *Ūr-Kavundan*, standing behind her, ties it. It is the *Ūr-Kavundan*, too, who places the hand of the boy in that of the girl, and who pours water over their clasped hands.

Widow re-marriage is permitted in all three sub-castes[4]. The Kolli-Malaiyālis do not permit a widow to marry her husband's brother; the Pachai-Malaiyālis allow such unions. At a widow marriage among Kolli-Malaiyālis the bridal couple kneel opposite each other, and a cloth is suspended between them; the bridegroom passes the *tāli* under the cloth, and places it on the bride's neck, but he is not allowed to see the face of the bride till the *tāli* is tied by the *Ūr-Kavundan*. When a widow marries, the children she bore to her first husband are taken charge of by their father's nearest male relative, and it is usual for a father to register his patta land in the name of his children to prevent it being enjoyed

---

[1] See Dr. Shortt's *Hill Ranges*, Vol. III, pp. 39 and 40. "The poor generally pay at the time only a portion, whilst the remainder of the dowry is paid by yearly instalments, and instances have come to my knowledge where the son was paying by dribs and drabs the dowry due by his father when he married his mother. Should an elderly man marry a young girl, he has to pay a much larger dowry than would be required of a young man."

[2] Marriage at the bridegroom's house appears to have been the original custom, but the *Pattakkāran* may claim the privilege of fixing the place where the wedding should be celebrated. Cf. Dr. Shortt's *Hill Ranges*, Vol. II, p. 39.

[3] The *kūrai* of the Periya-Malaiyālis is said to be only three or four cubits in length.

[4] This practice is said to be prohibited among the *Dorais* of the Pachai-Malaiyālis.

CHAP. III. SURVEY OF CASTES. Malaiyālis.

by his widow's husband. Divorce proceedings among the Pachais Malaiyālis are of the simplest description; the husband declares in the presence of the *Guru*, that he has abandoned his wife, and he tenders her a bit of straw or a splinter of wood in token of repudiation. She is not allowed, however, to marry a second husband till her first husband dies.

It is possible that a pollution period of thirty days on attainment of maturity was at one time observed throughout the caste, and that the period has subsequently been shortened in imitation of lowland practice. On the Pachai-malais, it is said, the girl is kept in a hut outside the village for five days, and on the 6th she is bathed and admitted into the house, but the house remains under minor pollution for another thirty days, and no villager may enter it. Throughout these thirty days the girl is bathed daily, water being poured over her head, and the house is cleansed once a week. The Pachai-Malaiyālis of Ūttankarai Taluk, however, observe segregation and pollution for twelve days. Some Kolli-Malaiyālis observe thirty days' pollution, some only fifteen. Among the Periya-Malaiyālis the period varies from seven to eleven days. For the purification ceremony it is the fashion for the few who can afford it to employ Brahman *purōhits*. Purification after childbirth is said to take place on the 12th, 15th or 16th day, but the Pachai-Malaiyālis observe pollution of a minor kind for thirty days. No formal child-naming ceremony is performed, and no fixed rule appears to exist as to when a child should be named. A Kolli-Malaiyāli child is named sometimes on the 10th day, sometimes in the 3rd month after birth, on the Pachai-malais at the end of a year, while on the Shevaroys the name is given on the 3rd day. It is not uncommon to consult the local *pūjāri* as to what name should be selected, the priest, after certain ceremonies, announcing the name under divine inspiration. Children are often named after popular deities, e.g., Kongan (Kongāy, if a girl), Vadaman (Vadami), Sirangan (Sirangi), Pidavan (Pidāri), Kāli, Arppali, etc.; in fact boys are more frequently named after a God than after their grandfather (p. 132). Popular nicknames are Kariyan (black), Vellaiyan (fair), Kuttaiyan (short), Sadaiyan (curly), Periya Payal (big boy), Chinna Payal (little boy), etc. It is the practice among the Kolli-Malaiyālis to bore the left nostril,[1] among the Pachai-Malaiyālis the right nostril, and among the Periya-Malaiyālis neither nostril. Malaiyāli women never wear the *ravikkai*, and, while at home or in the field, they leave bare the shoulders, arms and upper part of the body; before strangers,

[1] Dr. Shortt, *Hill Ranges*, Vol. II, p. 37.

CHAP. III. SURVEY OF CASTES. Malaiyālis.

however, and when going to market "the upper end of the cloth is loosened from over the breast or waist and carried across the left shoulder, and thrown loosely over the back, shoulders, and arms." The Pachai-Malaiyālis seem peculiarly fond of colour; their women never wear white except on their wedding day, when they don the *kūrai* (p. 159), which is never tied above the waist. They are permitted to wear either "black" or red cloths, and generally prefer a dash of yellow, orange, or green; they wear green and crimson glass in their ear-rings, and even the men affect bright colours in their only article of attire, the *kōmanam*. Their dietary is of the usual type, and includes pork. Malaiyālis of both sexes are ardent smokers. The practice of producing fire by silica and steel survives among the Pachai-Malaiyālis, only two or three men in a *patti* possessing the necessary apparatus, which, together with some charred cotton, is kept in a small leather pouch. The houses and agricultural methods of the Malaiyālis are referred to elsewhere (pp. 108 and 211). The duties of the barber, dhoby and midwife are performed by people of their own caste. They engage Pariahs, however, to play tom-toms, etc., on ceremonial occasions, and Pariahs are employed as agricultural labourers and assist them on their hunting excursions. When any of their cattle die, they will not go near or touch the carcase, but send for the nearest Pariahs to come and remove it; but should an animal get injured intentionally or accidentally, and be likely to die of the injury, they will then sell them to the coolies for a trifle. Some of the Malaiyālis are in great repute as cow-doctors, and they will set a broken leg very well. They will not touch a cow-hide or use it as ropes for their ploughs, etc., nor do they make any attempts to secure the hide of their cattle that die; it becomes the perquisite of the Pariahs who remove the carcase.[1]

Malaiyālis ordinarily bury their dead, but they burn those who die of cholera, leprosy or any other infectious or epidemic disease. When cremation is resorted to, the milk-ceremony is omitted. The rites observed are similar to those of the plains. The bier is sometimes covered by a canopy, in which case it is called a *ter*. The pollution period varies; on the Pachai-Malais it is said to last a month, among the Pachai-Malaiyālis of Ūttankarai for ten days, among the Periya-Malaiyālis for twelve or fifteen days, and on the Kolli-malais it closes on the third day. The ghosts of the dead are believed to haunt the house, and must be propitiated with sacrifices of fowls, goats, pigs, etc., as the *pūjāri* prescribes, or a peg of *Strychnos nux-vomica*, or a nail is driven into the grave over

[1] Dr. Shortt's *Hill Ranges*, Vol. II, p. 41.

CHAP. III. SURVEY OF CASTES. — Malaiyālis.

the head of the corpse. No *srāddhas* are performed, but the spirits of departed ancestors are worshipped on occasions of marriage, childbirth and puberty, during public festivals, and on Fridays, as *pattavans* or household deities. A Malaiyāli's house is held sacred, and not even a Brahman is allowed to enter it with shoes on.

The Malaiyālis worship both Siva and Vishnu impartially, and they wear both *nāmam* and *vibhūti*, the former being reserved usually for religious worship, and the latter for everyday use. They do not, however, ordinarily resort to Brahmanic temples or employ Brahman *archakars*.[1] The patron deity of the caste is Kari-Rāman, an incarnation apparently of Vishnu. His chief shrine is at Kōvil-Pudūr, in the Mēl-Nād of the Periya Kalrāyans. He has a shrine at Tammampatti, and a somewhat pretentious temple in his honour was built a few years ago at Karadiyūr on the Shevaroys. It contains idols of Siva and Pārvati, Vishnu and Lakshmi, Vignēsvara, and a dozen upright stones in two rows, decorated with white spots. The entrance is adorned with *Sanku*, *chakram* and *nāmam*, the superstructure with figures of Vishnu, Rāma, four Garudas and four Nandis. *Pūja* is performed every Saturday, and a car-festival takes place in Māsi. The *pūjāri* is prohibited from tasting flesh, and may not attend any animal sacrifice, or dine with flesh-eaters. No blood-sacrifices are made to Kari-Rāman, and it is said that any who have taken part in a blood-sacrifice are prohibited from entering his temple till after the lapse of three or four days. In pursuance of a vow Malaiyālis of both sexes dedicate their hair at the shrine.

A similar vagueness appears to exist regarding the god whose shrine is on the Shevarāyan Hill. Dr. Shortt preserves a tradition that "a Shervacaran or Commander of a body of soldiers, being a pious and holy man, visited this hill from the low country to worship Rāmaswāmi, the then presiding deity. His piety gained him much more honour and fame, and when he died, which he did on this hill, it was called after him, and images of stone were made and placed in the temple. Rāmaswāmi was forgotten and Shervacaran took his place."[2]

The cult of Vishnu survives also in a vague form in the Perumāl-kōvils to be found in many Malaiyāli villages; this

---

[1] The temple of Arappalīsvaran in Valappūr Nād is an exception. (*Trichinopoly District Gazetteer*, p. 175.) They also regard with great reverence the Vishnu temple of Srīrangam.

[2] *Hill Ranges*, Vol. II, p. 48. The shrine is said to have once contained an idol of gold, but this was stolen and a stone idol took its place. For a description of the festival, see *Castes and Tribes*, Vol. IV, p. 415 sq.

Perumāl cult is harldy recognisable as Vishnu worship,[1] and sometimes the deity is unprovided with a shrine. The cult is, however, entirely dissociated from blood-sacrifice, and the *pūjāri* (a Malaiyāli) is usually a vegetarian. The appropriate day for Perumāl worship is Saturday. The Kolli-Malaiyālis worship a god they call Arangattappan or Aranga-Sivan, whom they regard as the tribal god of the three eponymous ancestors of the caste, and who appears to be a counterpart of Kari-Rāman. In Kunduni Nād[2] he is served by a Brahman Gurukkal, and the ritual observed is hardly distinguishable from that of an ordinary Siva temple; *abhishēkham* consists of bathing the idol first with water, then with milk, and thirdly with gingelly oil; it is then dressed in a new cloth and marked with sandal and *kunkumam*; *dhūpam* is then offered; lamps are lighted, a plantain leaf full of cooked food is placed before the idol, the usual *mantras* are repeated, and camphor is burnt; blood-sacrifices are altogether avoided, and the only offerings made are boiled grain, milk, sugar, fruit and other items appropriate to Siva worship. His attendant Aranga Sēvagan receives worship as a distinct deity,[3] but his priest is a Malaiyāli and not a Brahman. The cult of Vignēsvara is as ubiquitous among the Malaiyālis as elsewhere, and he is often worshipped in the form of neolithic implements placed upright or heaped promiscuously in a little dolmen[4] or in a shrineless walled enclosure. Monday is the proper day for the worship of Vignēsvara. There is a temple of Subrahmanya under the familiar name of Kandaswāmi in Pirakarai Nād; with a three days' festival in Panguni (March—April), but otherwise his cult is rare. Kāmākshi is also honoured with a few shrines and there are a few Dharmarāja temples devoted to the Pāndava cult.

The list of minor deities worshipped by the Malaiyālis is a long one. Their favourite Saktis are Kāli, Pidāri and Māri; Ayyanār, too, is worshipped. Kāli has an annual car-festival in Edappuli Nād in Chittrai or Vaiyāsi. Saturday is in some parts her special day of worship. Pidāri has many epithets, such as Periya, Chinna, Soka, Pudu, Karum, Kārakkāttu, Malunguttu, etc. Her favourite week-day and her annual festivals vary in

---

[1] One such cult in Gundūr Nād, Nāmakkal Kolli-malais, goes by the extraordinary name of "Pēy (Demon) Perumāl."

[2] Also in Gundūr Nād of the Nāmakkal Kolli-malais.

[3] According to some accounts both Aranga-Sivan and his peon are honoured with the sacrifice of fowls and goats. Some informants, however, actually identify Aranga-Sēvagan with Arangattappan.

[4] E.g., at Mēlūr and Kākkambādi on the Shevaroys.

CHAP. III. SURVEY OF CASTES.

Malaiyālis.

different Nāds. The chief festival of Māri-amman, or Māriyāyi as she is often called, occurs in the spring months, Tai, Māsi, or Panguni, about the time of full moon. Her special week-days are Tuesdays and Fridays. Other important "mother goddesses" are Nāchi-amma, Pongalāyi, Kongalāyi and Ponnāyi. Nāchi is variously known as Mēla-Nāchi, Koda-kara-Nāchi, Ariya-Nāchi, Elaya-Nāchi, Ēlu-karai-Nāchi, etc. Her special week-day appears to be Thursday. She must be worshipped in perfect silence, and the *prasāda* is taken home by the worshippers. She is said to be a patron goddess of the Vēdans, and the existence of her cult among the Kolli-Malaiyālis is traced to their Vēdachi ancestress.[1] Pongalāyi is called by many epithets, e.g., Kosakkuli, Mayilati, Tannipāli, Vēlarayān, Mūlakādu, Panikkankādu, Pēkkādu, etc. The demons worshipped by the Malaiyālis are known by many names, such as Periya-Āndavan, Āndi-appan, Nambi-āndān, Sadayan, Vettukkāran, Māsi-Malaiyan, Urulaiyān, etc., but by far the most important cult is that of Karuppan, who is propitiated in every village by pig sacrifice, his special perquisite being the livers of the victims. With him is sometimes associated a female deity known as Kanni-amma.

Many of these minor deities have no shrines, and are worshipped in the open air or in a roofless walled enclosure, especially in the case of Karuppan. They are served by *pūjāris* of Malaiyāli caste, who are known as Tāthans or Āndis, and whose office is often hereditary. It is usual for one and the same *pūjāri* to serve several deities, and he is sometimes distinguished from his fellow Malaiyālis by his turban, by growing his hair long, and sometimes by abstaining from animal food for a period or throughout his life. The chief general festivals observed by Malaiyālis are Pongal, Dīpāvali and the 18th Ādi. The second day of Pongal (Māttu-Pongal) is celebrated by a great hunting excursion, and by bull-dances.[2]

(ii) Telugu Cultivators

The Telugu ryots are known by the general name Kāpu, a term which is loosely applied to the caste groups otherwise known as Reddis, Kammas, Telagas and Velamas, and even Balijas, and is extended to the Kanarese Vakkiligas also. The "Kāpus" number over 44,000, of whom 35,000 are returned for Hosūr Taluk, over 2,000 for Salem and about the same number for Āttūr. Most of the Hosūr Kāpus, however, are Kanarese Vakkiligas. The Kammas (4,681) are found mostly in Hosūr

[1] Cf. her cult at Anganāmalai (Mahārāja-gadai), the former centre of Vēdan (Kangundi) influence, Vol. II, p. 178.

[2] See description of a bull-dance in *Castes and Tribes*, Vol. IV, p. 417.

CHAP. III. SURVEY OF CASTES.

and the Telagas (841) in Salem. The Velamas[1] number only 91, all in Hosūr Taluk. The exact relationship between these castes has not yet been clearly determined; it is probable, however, that they, together with the Balijas (see p. 178) and the Rāzus (see p. 191), come originally of the same stock, and settled in the District in the wake of the Vijayanagar conquests. The Telagas, Balijas and Rāzus claim military antecedents, and there is evidence for classing the Kammas as Balijas. One more important class of Telugu cultivators deserves mention, viz., the Tōttiyas, who number 6,410, and who are found mostly in the Taluks of Salem, Tiruchengōdu and Ōmalūr. They are an interesting Telugu caste peculiar to the Tamil country.[2]

Telugu Cultivators.

Kāpus

The best known sub-castes of **Kāpus** in Salem District are :—

(1) the Pōkanātis, (3) the Nerati and
(2) the Pedakanti, (4) the Panta Reddis.

The Pōkanāti Reddis are commonest in Dharmapuri Taluk;[3] a few occur near Tumbal, in the north of Āttūr Taluk, but not in the Swēta-nadi Valley.

Pedakanti Reddis are found in the south-west and south of Ūttankarai Taluk, in Dharmapuri and in Hosūr.[4] In the *Baramahal Records* the name[5] is spelt "Perdagantuwaru," and is said to be derived from *peradu*, a back-door, the legend being that once on a time a Guru camped near the village where their ancestor dwelt, and sent an attendant *Dāsari* to apprise the villagers of his arrival; when the *Dāsari* came to the Reddi's house, the latter, out of meanness, bolted out of the back-door, and the Guru, on hearing of it, declared that he and his descendants should henceforth have no Guru.[6] The same authority divides the "Perdagunta" Reddis

---

[1] The Velamas (who call themselves Naidu) trace their origin to Kālahasti in Chittoor District. They bear a close affinity to the Kammas. They repudiate any connection with the Balijas, who call them Gūni Tsākalavāndlu (hunchbacked-washermen). Vide *North Arcot Manual*, Vol. I, p. 216, and *Castes and Tribes*, Vol. VII, p. 336.

[2] Tōttiyans are described in detail in *Madura District Gazetteer*, p. 106, and *Trichinopoly District Gazetteer*, p. 121; cf. Madras Census Report, 1891, paragraph 361, and Madras Census Report, 1871, p. 146; also *Castes and Tribes*, Vol. VII, p. 183.

[3] E.g., Mārānda-halli, Pālakōdu, Golla-patti.

[4] E.g., Baira-nattam and Kōtu-Reddi-patti in Ūttankarai, and Achitta-palli in Hosūr.

[5] The name is also sometimes given as "Penakanti," and they say they came from a place called Gandi-kōttai "near Penukonda." Possibly the name Pedakanti is an atrocious corruption of Penukonda. Gandi-kōta is a stronghold of historic fame, a few miles south-west of Jammalamadugu in Cuddapah District.

[6] They are reported, however, to acknowledge as *Guru* one Srī Saila Sūrya-Simhāsanam Bhiksha-pati Ayyar of Jigūr in Komārna-palli Taraf, Hosūr Taluk.

CHAP. III. SURVEY OF CASTES.

Kāpus;

into two sections, Chinna-gumpu and Pedda-gumpu, and sub-castes bearing these names occur in Ōmalūr Taluk and in the adjoining portion of Dharmapuri.[1] They have no Guru, but own the authority of a *Pattakkāran* at Vellār. They interdine with the Pōkanātis.

The Reddis of Āttūr Taluk almost all belong to the sub-caste known as Panta Kāpu, but the term Kāpu is never used among them. Their chief settlements are in the valley of the Swēta-nadi,[2] in villages bordering on Trichinopoly District; in fact, they are closely akin to the Reddis of Trichinopoly, and are probably off-shoots of the Telugu settlements formed in the lower valley of the Kāvēri, when Trichinopoly and Madura became the seats of Vijayanagar Viceroys.[3]

The Nerati Kāpus are the most numerous sub-caste of Kāpus in Hosūr, their chief settlement being at Morasūr. They also occur in Dharmapuri. Like the Pōkanātis and Pedakantis, they acknowledge the Guru at Jīgūr.

In addition to the above sections, there are communities of Koditti (or Kodatha), Sajjala, Yelochi and Simpari Kāpus reported from Hosūr Taluk. In Dharmapuri Kantha Reddis are to be found near Toppūr, and Perumba Reddis also occur. Whether any of these are true sub-castes, or whether they are to be identified with the better-known divisions is uncertain. The Kāpus employ Brahman *purōhits* and are almost all votaries of Vishnu.[4]

Kammas.

The **Kammas** are said to derive their name from the word *kamma* (Tamil, *kammal*), a large ear-ornament worn by their women. Their customs approximate closely to those of the Balijas. They are divided into two sub-castes, (1) Gōda Chātulu and (2) Gampa Chātulu,[5] the legend being that two sisters were bathing, when a king passed by, and the bashful maids hid, one behind a wall (*gōda*) and the other behind a basket (*gampa*) and these two sisters were respectively the mothers of the two castes.

---

[1] Chinna-gumpu Reddis are found at Ondi-kōta, round Toppūr in Dharmapuri, and in Rāmi-Reddi-patti and Arūr-patti, Ōmalūr Taluk; Pedda-gumpu Reddis at Nallūr, Kongu-patti and Vellār.

[2] E.g., Sendūra-patti, Tammampatti, Kondayam-galli, Vīraganūr, Kadambūr, Pidāvūr, Naduvalūr, Gangavalli, Anaiyāmpatti. They also occur at Panamarattu-patti.

[3] Vide *Trichinopoly District Gazetteer*, pp. 117 to 119. The Trichinopoly Reddis are represented by the Pōkanātis and Pantas. The Pōkanātis are extremely rare in the Bālāghāt tracts of Salem District, and their alternative name Pongala Reddis is said to be unknown.

[4] For details regarding the customs of the Kāpus and allied castes see *Trichinopoly District Gazetteer*, p. 117; *North Arcot Manual*, Vol. I, pp. 214-7; *Castes and Tribes*, Vol. III, pp. 222-47.

[5] Vide the legend recorded in *North Arcot Manual*, Vol. I, p. 215.

CHAP. III. SURVEY OF CASTES. Kammas.

Another variation is that in a desperate battle at Gandi-kōta almost all the Kammas[1] were destroyed, except a few who took refuge behind a wall or in baskets.[2] Possibly the Muttu-kamma (or Musa-Kamma) Balijas, who are found very rarely in Salem Taluk, should properly be classed as Kammas. In the *Baramahal Records* Kammas are divided into two sections, the Musuku-Kammas and the Bairu-Kammas.

(iii) Kanarese Cultivators, Vakkiligas.

The general term for Kanarese ryots is **Vakkiliga**, or, in its Tamilised form, Okkiliyan. As already stated, the words Vakkiliga and Kāpu are often interchangeable, and it is certain that many Vakkiligas have been returned as Kāpus, especially in Hosūr Taluk, where no Vakkiligas have been returned at all. The Census for 1911 shows 3,078 Vakkiligas, most of them occurring in Dharmapuri Taluk. The Vakkiligas are of immense importance in Mysore State, where they form the backbone of the population. Three well-marked divisions occur in Salem District —(1) Morasu, (2) Kunchiga and (3) Gangadikāra.

The Morasu Vakkiligas derive their name from the ancient Morasu Nād, which comprised the eastern districts of Mysore State and the adjoining taluks of Salem and Chittoor Districts. They predominate in Hosūr Taluk, and are the only division represented in Krishnagiri.[3]

The Morasu Vakkiligas apparently include several sub-castes,[4] among them the *Ichi-viralu*, or "finger giving,"[5] Vakkiligas, so-called from the custom which compelled every woman of the caste, previous to piercing the ears of her eldest daughter as a preliminary to betrothal,[6] to have the last joints of the ring and

---

[1] Vide *Castes and Tribes*, Vol. III, p. 96.

[2] Vide *North Arcot Manual*, Vol. I, p. 215. For *Gandi-kōta* see above p. 165, foot-note 5, s.v. Perdaganti Kāpus.

[3] Their chief settlements are at Pedda-Nallūr and Sūdiyālam (Achitta-palli taraf), in Hosūr and at Mādē-palli in Krishnagiri Taluk.

[4] Vide *E.S.M.*, No. XV, Morasu Okkalu, p. 5.

[5] Or *Beral-kodura* (Kan.), for the finger-giving Vakkiligas comprise both Telugu and Kanarese sub-sections, who, it is said, intermarry.

[6] According to Buchanan (quoted in *Castes and Tribes*, Vol. V, p. 75), Abbé Dubois (*Hindu Manners and Customs*, 1897, p. 18), Mr. L. Rice (*Mysore Gazetteer*, Vol. I, p. 230) and *E.S.M.*, No. XV, p. 10. Abbé Dubois, howev9r, says two joints in each finger are lopped off. Other authorities (e.g., *Madras Census Report*, 1891, S.D.M., Vol. I, p. 137) connect the finger-giving with the birth of a grandchild. Mr. Le Fanu writes "when a grandchild is born in a family, the eldest son of the grandfather, with his wife, appear at the temple for the ceremony of boring the child's ear, and there the woman has the last two joints of the third and fourth fingers of her right hand chopped off. It does not signify whether the father of the first grandchild born be the eldest son or not, as in any case it is the wife of the eldest son who has to undergo the mutilation."

CHAP. III. SURVEY OF CASTES. Vakkiligas.

little fingers of her right hand chopped off by the village blacksmith's chisel, as a sacrifice to the caste-god Bandi-Dēvaru [1] (the "Cart God"), who is by some identified with Siva. The legendary origin of this curious custom is as follows:—"When the demon Bhasmāsura had obtained the power of reducing everything he touched to ashes by severe *tapas*, he wished to test his power first on god Siva, the donor himself. The deity fled from the demon and hid himself in the fruit of a creeper, which to this day resembles a *linga* in appearance. The demon who was pursuing the god, suddenly losing sight of the latter, asked a Morasu man who was ploughing in the fields there, in which direction the fugitive had escaped. The man of the plough wished to evade the wrath of both the mighty parties and while saying he had not observed, pointed with his fingers to the creeper on the hedge which had sheltered the fleeing god. Just in the nick of time Vishnu came to the help of his brother in the shape of a lovely maiden, Mōhini. The Rākshasa became enamoured of her, and like a fool, forgetting the fatal virtue that his bare touch had been endowed with, he was lured by the damsel to place his hand on his own head, and was immediately reduced to a heap of ashes. Siva now triumphant was about to punish the treacherous rustic with the loss of his erring finger, but his wife, who had carried his food, begged hard that the deprivation would render him unfit to do his field work and offered two fingers of hers for one of her husband." [2] The practice is now obsolete, having been stopped by the Mysore Government, and the women now content themselves with "putting on a gold or silver finger-stall or thimble, which is pulled off instead of the finger itself." [3]

Kunchiga Vakkiligas occur both in Hosūr and Dharmapuri Taluks.[4]

Gangadikāra Vakkiligas derive their name from the ancient country of Gangavādi.[5] Denkani-kōta and Tagatti are the headquarters of two Nāds or *Gadis*, each under its own *Nāttu-Kavundan*, but they are most numerous in Dharmapuri Taluk, where they outnumber the other divisions of Vakkiligas. The name Gangadikāra, however, is not in general use in the taluk, most of the members of the community calling themselves Laddagiri

---

[1] The finger-giving Vakkiligas are also known as Bandi Vakkiligas. In *Baramahal Records* they are described as Bandi Vellallu.

[2] *E.S.M.*, No. XV, p. 8. Similar legends in endless variety are given in other authorities, e.g., *Baramahal Records*, III, p. 109, *Castes and Tribes*, loc. cit., etc.

[3] *Mysore Gazetteer*, Vol. I, p. 230.

[4] E.g., Gummalāpuram in Hosūr; Biliyanūr and Erappalli in Dharmapūri.

[5] They are numerous in Mysore, Hassan and Bangalore Districts of Mysore State.

Vakkiligas, and they appear to form a separate endogamous group, distinguished from the Gangadikāras proper by the fact that their womenfolk are strict vegetarians. They are to be found in the villages of Rōni-halli, Donnakutta-halli, Ajjampatti, Banijagara-halli in Pennāgaram Division. The significance of the name Laddigiri is not clear.[1]

Vakkiligas.

In addition to the above, a settlement of Musuku Vakkiligas exists in Tōra-palli Agrahāram, and a community of Dāsiri Vakkiligas at Jekkēri, both in Hosūr Taluk. Whether these are true sub-castes is uncertain. A section known as Anchakāra Vakkiligas is said to occur in Kalapambādi, Erra-palli, Ādanūr and other villages south of Pennāgaram.

(2) Pastoral Castes.

The Pastoral Castes (64,746) are represented by the Tamil Idaiyans (21,395), the Telugu Gollas (9,386) and the Kurubas (33,965), who speak both Telugu and Kanarese.[2] The Idaiyans and Gollas tend cattle, the Kurubas sheep and goats. The Idaiyans[3] are strongest in Āttūr (7,000), Ūttankarai and Krishnagiri; the Gollas in Hosūr, Dharmapuri, Ōmalūr and Āttūr; the Kurubas in Hosūr (15,000), Dharmapuri (7,300), Krishnagiri (6,800), Ūttankarai (2,700), very few indeed occurring in the Talaghāt. This distribution of the Pastoral Castes shows clearly that grazing is of far greater importance in the Bālāghāt and Bāramahāl than in the comparatively poorly-wooded Talaghāt.

Kurubas.

The **Kurubas** or Kurumbars as they are sometimes called, are classed as Ūru-Kurubas and Kādu-Kurubas, or Town Kurubas and Country Kurubas.[4] Those in Salem District belong to the former group, and most of them speak Kanarese. The Ūru-Kurubas are divided into three clearly defined sub-castes, (1) Hosa (new), also called Hālu (milk) or Hatti (cotton) Kurubas, who use a marriage *kankanam* of cotton, (2) the Halē (old), also called Kambli (blanket), Unne (wool) or Jādi Kurubas, whose *kankanam*

---

[1] The Laddigiri Vakkiligas state that Laddigiri is a village somewhere near the Tungabhadra in Bellary or Kurnool District. Mr. E. S. Lloyd, Collector of Kurnool, writes, "there is a small and rather insignificant village called Laddigiri on the Handri, a tributary of the Tungabhadra. It is about 20 miles from the Tungabhadra itself. The nearest railway station is Veldurthi, 8 or 10 miles off."

[2] The Census figures cannot be relied on, for the Idaiyans show an increase of 6,624 (nearly 50 per cent) on the figures for 1901, which is impossible, especially as the 1901 figures include Tiruppattūr and Nāmakkal, while the 1911 figures do not. Obviously many Gollas, or Kurubas, or both, must have been returned as Idaiyans by Tamil-speaking enumerators.

[3] For a description of the Idaiyans see *Madura District Gazetteer*, p. 96, *Castes and Tribes*, Vol. II, p. 352, and the authorities quoted in *Census Report*, 1901, Part I, p. 155. Among the sub-castes given in *Castes and Tribes*, both Gollas and Kurubas have been included.

[4] For the legends of their origin see *E.S.M.*, No. I, Kuruba, pp. 2–3.

CHAP. III. SURVEY OF CASTES. — Kurubas.

is of white, black and yellow wool, and (3) the Andō Kurubas, whose *kankanam* is of cotton and wool mixed. Males of these three groups may interdine. The Old Kurubas weave *kamblis*; the New Kurubas tend sheep; the Andē Kurubas consider themselves superior to both, claim to have been a warrior caste, and call themselves Andē-Ravuts. Kurubas formed an important fighting element in the armies of Haidar Ali and of the Ankusagiri Poligārs, and several fiefs of military origin still remain in the possession of Inamdars of the Andē sub-caste. Their favourite caste title is Nāyaka.

All three divisions are split into exogamous clans called *Kulas*.[1] The following *Kulas* are reported in Salem District; for the "New" Kurubas, Dēva-kulam, Ari-kulam (according to Mr. Nanjundayya, Ari = *Bauhinia racemosa*), Pīsa-kulam, Mādē-kulam, Sangini-kulam, Sanna-kulam, Rājā-kulam; for "Old" Kurubas, Pottu-kulam, Basiri-kulam, Gaudi-kulam, Hēgē-kulam, Arasu-kulam, Sangama-kulam, Āla-marattu-kulam. It would seem that some of these names are not confined to one sub-caste. A large proportion of them are names of plants, and the clan so named observe a quasi-totemistic reverence for the plants after which they are called. The Sanku-kulam clan of the Andē Kurubas is so named from the Chank shell (*Turbinella pyrum*), and it is said that the members of this clan may not use the Chanks as a feeding bottle for their babies, a use to which the shell is put throughout South India.

The "Old" Kurubas distinguish themselves as belonging to the Ballāla-Rāyan-Vamsam and the Bījjala-Rāyan-Vamsam. The "New" Kurubas are divided into three groups, named after three week days, Monday, Thursday, and Sunday Kurubas. Yet another distinction exists, which is said to be common to all three sub-castes, namely, the Maduve-Sālu or offspring of regular marriage, the Kūdike-Sālu or offspring of informal marriage, and the Basavi-Sālu or offspring of unmarried girls.[2] Exogamous clans are said to equal in number the grains in four seers of paddy.

The Guru of the Andē Kurubas is a Lingāyat, and the men of certain clans who exercise priestly functions among them wear a *lingam* round their neck and abstain from flesh and alcohol. The Lingāyat influence in the caste is, in fact, strong. At the same time the Andē and "Old" Kurubas employ Brahman *purōhits* at weddings and funerals, but the "New" Kurubas content themselves with *purōhits* of their own caste.

---

[1] Mr. H. V. Nanjundayya in *E.S.M.* gives a list of 111 *Kulas*.

[2] *E.S.M.*, No. 1, p. 5.

Kurubas.

Males are not allowed to be tattooed. Among the "New" Kurubas, women wear white cloths, and black cloths are considered inauspicious. "Old" Kuruba women, on the other hand, invariably wear a black *kambli*, any other colour being prohibited; the *kambli* is not thrown over the shoulders, but is tied tightly over the breasts and under the armpits, and secured round the waist with a girdle of coir rope, a fold being made in the *kambli* to conceal the existence of the rope. The bodice (*ravikkai*) is worn only by women of the Andē sub-caste, whose cloths may be of any colour. After marriage, Kuruba women should wear shoes and not walk abroad barefooted.

The "Old" Kurubas observe a curious custom in their annual festival to Bīra Dēvar.[1] The images are set in a row in an open space and garlanded, and flowers, milk, coco-nuts, etc., are offered to them. Such of the worshippers as have vows to perform, garlanded and covered with saffron, dance in front of the deities, and work themselves up into a state of frenzied excitement, and when the climax is reached, the devotees sink to the earth with one leg bent under and the other stretched out in front (or else simply kneel), while the *pūjāri* breaks quantities of coco-nuts on their heads. The operation looks painful, and some of the enthusiastic wince as the blow falls, but broken skulls are unheard of, and the coco-nut is certainly the weaker vessel. No anmial sacrifice is offered at this festival. The fragments of broken coco-nut belong "by right to those whose skulls have cracked them and who value the pieces as sacred morsels of food. For a month before this annual ceremony all the people have taken no meat, and for three days the *pūjāri* has lived on milk alone. At the feast therefore all indulge in rather immoderate eating, but drink no liquor, calling excitedly on their particular God to grant them a prosperous year."[2]

Gollas.

The Gollas, the great Telugu caste of cattle graziers, rank high in the social scale, though, curiously enough, they do not employ Brahman *purōhits*. They sometimes call themselves Yādavas, and claim kinship with the Yādava dynasty of Dēvagiri. One section of the caste, known as Bokkasa or Bokkusa Gollas, has given up shepherding and taken to guarding treasure as an hereditary occupation; hence the treasury servants who are entrusted with lifting, carrying and packing bullion are officially known as Gollas, though they do not necessarily belong to the Golla caste. Gollas may mess with Nāttāns, Kaikōlars, Vellān Chettis and Ravuts, but not with Pallis or Tōttiyans. The Salem

---

[1] Vide Oppert, op. cit., p. 238. [2] Madras Census Report, 1891.

CHAP. III. SURVEY OF CASTES. Gollas.

Gollas trace their origin to Gooty, and a quaint story,[1] is told to explain their migration thence. When the Gollas were settled at Gooty one of the ruling sovereigns (a Nawab, tradition calls him) fell in love with a Golla maid and sought her hand in marriage. Refusal spelt ruin, and the panic-stricken Gollas consented to the match. A time and place for the wedding was fixed, and a marriage pandal erected. But when, on the wedding day, the Nawab arrived at the bride's house, he found the pandal deserted, save for a dog dressed up in girl's clothes; the Gollas had quitted his kingdom to a man.

The caste exhibits an extraordinary variety of sub-divisions, the exact correlation of which is far from clear.[2] No less than eight endogamous groups are reported for Salem District alone, namely, (1) Gūti (Gooty), (2) Karna (Carnatic), (3) Tūmāti, (4) Manthai (sheep or cattle-pen), (5) Doddi (hut), (6) Sana, (7) Akalu, (8) Mondi. The caste is also said to be sub-divided into seven *gōtras*, most of them associated with plant totems, viz., (1) Māmanthila-vādu, who revere the *mavalinga* tree, (2) Siru-pūvalu-vādu, worshipping the *nerinji* plant, (3) Pūchanthila-vādu, a section in which black beads and black cloths are forbidden, (4) Vāninthila-vādu, (5) Āriyanthila-vādu, who honour the *atti* tree, (6) Pulavanthila-vādu, who may neither cut nor burn the *pūlām* tree, and (7) Bangāru-vādu (gold).[3] All the members of the first four of these *gōtras* are looked on as *dāyādis* and are not allowed to intermarry. The same theory holds good for the last three *gōtras*. Thus a man belonging to the first batch of *gōtras* must choose his bride from the second batch, and vice versa.

(3) Fishermen.

The fishing castes are represented by the Tamil Sembadavans (7,393) and Telugu Bestas (735). Probably a few Kanarese Toreyas should be included among one or other of these heads, as they numbered 1,852 in 1901. About half the Sembadavans occur in Tiruchengōdu Taluk, the rest being distributed evenly throughout the District. The Bestas are confined to Hosūr Taluk.[4]

Sembadavans.

The chief settlement of **Sembadavans** is at Edappādi, where they have to some extent abandoned their ancestral occupation as

---

[1] A similar story is told of the other castes, e.g., the Morasu Vakkiligas (*E.S.M.*, No. XV, p. 3), Bēri Chettis (*Castes and Tribes*, Vol. I, p. 213).

[2] According to *E.S.M.*, No. XIV, Gollas (exclusive of the Kādu-Gollas) are divided into three sub-castes (1) Uru, (2) Ketta Hatti, and (3) Maddina. In *E.S.M.*, No. XX, however, eight other sub-castes are specified. In *Baramahal Records*, III, p. 135, twelve sub-castes are named.

[3] Only the last of these clan names is given in *E.S.M.*, or *Castes and Tribes* and the lists given in those two works are also mutually exclusive.

[4] An excellent account of the Bestas is given in *E.S.M.*, No. V; cf. *Castes and Tribes*, Vol. I, p. 218.

Sembadavans.

fresh-water fishermen and boatmen in favour of trade and the manufacture of castor-oil and *pūnāk* (Vol. II, p. 273). It appears that the Sembadavans form a homogeneous community and recognise no sub-castes. They are divided into about 96 exogamous clans, called by rather outlandish names, which are said to be derived from tribal heroes.[1] Caste disputes are settled in the first instance by a *panchāyat* nominated by the assembled elders, and presided over by an hereditary *Kāriyastan*. From this *panchāyat* an appeal lies to the *Pattakkāran* and from the *Pattakkāran*, a second appeal lies to an officer known as Konga-Rāyar, who lives in Konga-Rāya-pālaiyam in Kalla-kurchi Taluk. The Sembadavans employ Brahman *purōhits* (usually Tamil or Telugu Smārtas) for the ceremonies connected with marriage, childbirth, puberty, house-warming, *srāddhas* and the 16th day death ceremony, and in the case of Vaishnavites for the *mudrādhāranam*, or sealing ceremony, when they are branded in two or three places with a metal *sanku* or *chakram*.

The spirits of the dead are propitiated with animal sacrifice. The Sembadavans are specially devoted to the cult of Ankāl-amman, who is said to have been the daughter of a Sembadava girl of whom Siva was enamoured. In connection with her worship a peculiar ceremony is observed. Once a year the worshippers assemble at dead of night in a burning ground; cooked rice, plantains and other offerings are laid on a cloth spread on the ground, and sheep, goats, and fowls are sacrificed. Ankāl-amman is then worshipped, and the cooked food is distributed among the worshippers. This ceremony, known as *Mayāna-pūja* (cemetery *pūja*) is performed to the beating of a *pambai* drum. The *pūjāri* gathers five handfuls of the ashes of the burning ground, and mixes them with the sacred ashes of Ankāl-amman's shrine, the mingled ashes being afterwards distributed to worshippers. The ashes and the cooked grain distributed on these occasions are considered a specific against barrenness.[2]

(4) Hunters. Vēdars.

The hunting castes include the Telugu Vēdans and the Kanarese Bēdas or Bōyas, as well as a few (515) Telugu Patras. The Vēdans according to the Census of 1911 number 4,402, of whom about 2,400 are in Hosūr and 1,200 in Krishnagiri Taluk. No Vēdans are returned in the Census of 1901. In 1901 there were 7,385 Bōyas and 4,570 Bēdas; in 1911 the Bōyas number

---

[1] E.g. (1) Ulaganāthar, (2) Mainā-kappiriyan, (3) Anjāppuli, (4) Tiripuramkali, (5) Vāthāyi, (6) Mallan, (7) Mazhaventhi, (8) Tikkāli, (9) Iralvān, (10) Emigirippiriyan, (11) Sūriyappiriyan, (12) Ponnāttumannan.

[2] For a description of a similar, but much more elaborate, ceremony at Malayanūr (Tindivanam Taluk, South Arcot) see *Castes and Tribes*, Vol. VI, p. 356.

CHAP. III. SURVEY OF CASTES.

8,077 and the Bēdas *nil*. Apparently there has been some confusion between the Bēdas and Vēdans, and also between the Bēda Bōyas and the Odda Bōyas (see s.v. Odde, p. 187).[1]

Vēdars and Bēdas.

Both **Vēdars** and **Bēdas** come of the same stock and trace their descent to Vālmīki, who is identified with the author of the Rāmāyana. Vālmīki, it is said, was the illegitimate son of a Brahman by a Vēdar woman and adopted the profession of highwayman. One day Rāma [2] appeared to the bandit, convinced him of the sinfulness of his life, and converted him to probity. The reformed robber had twelve sons, who were the ancestors of both Vēdars and Bēdas. Another eponymous hero, who figures prominently in Vēdar tradition and custom, is one Kannayya or Kannappa, who is identified by some with one Kannappa Nāyānar, one of the sixty-three Saivite saints, a tradition which seems to connect them with the Ambalakārans and Valaiyans of Tanjore and Trichinopoly.[3]

Both Vēdars and Bēdas were originally fighting castes, who spread southwards with the armies of Vijayanagar. On the downfall of Vijayanagar many of their chieftains established themselves as independent Poligārs; in fact the Vēdar dynasty of the Kangundi Zamindars still preserves a shadow of authority over the Vēdars of the eastern Balaghāt and Bāramahāl, as well as on the Javādi hills of Tiruppattūr. Bēdas formed the pick of Haidar Ali's army, and several families of these cousin-castes still enjoy Umbilikkai *māniyams* (see Vol. II, p. 54) granted to them by former Poligārs as guardians of the Ghāts.[4]

(5) Traders.

The most important trading castes are the Balijas, who number 47,270, and include many communities that would more correctly be described as agricultural or military; and the Chettis, who number 33,636. The word "Chetti" [5] is used as a general term for trader, and covers a multitude of castes. In a more limited sense the term is applied to a group of sub-castes which all claim to be Vaisyas. Of these the most important are the Kōmati Vaisyas and next to them is the caste group of the Nagarattu Chettis. Of the non-Vaisya merchants who call themselves Chettis the

---

[1] In 1901 Bōyas + Bēdas = 12,138; In 1911 Bōyas + Vēdans = 12,479.
The title Bōyi is used by Oddes, and Bestas, as well as by a Telugu caste of palanquin-bearers.

[2] Or the sage Vasishta (*E.S.M.*, No. III, p. 1) or the seven Rishis (*Castes and Tribes*, Vol. I, p. 189), for there is, as usual, an infinite variety in the details of the legend.

[3] See *Castes and Tribes*, Vol. VII, p. 332, and *E.S.M.*, No. III, p. 2; cf. *Trichinopoly District Gazetteer*, pp. 105 and 114.

[4] E.g., Krishnappa-Nāyani-Pōdūr and Batimadugu in Bōrikai Pālaiyam, and Ankusagiri-Kottūr in Sūlagiri.

[5] "Chetti" 12,511, "Kōmati" 11,615, "Janappan" 9,510; total 33,636.

most important a o the Janappars. The Nāttu-kōttai Chettis of Dēva-kōttai are very rare in Salem District.[1] Other castes which adopt the term "Chetti" are the Vāniyars (oil-pressers) who appear to bear some affinity to the Nagarattu Chettis (p. 183), the Shānārs (toddy drawers), the Dēvāngas (weavers), the Lingāyats, the Oddars of Āttūr (Odda-Chetti), the Potters of Pennāgaram Division (Kosa-Chetti) and the Senaikkudaiyāns. Dēsāyi Chetti is the title of the Balija who presides over the "Eighteen" Right-Hand Castes.

Traders.

Kōmatis

The **Kōmatis** trace their origin to Ayōdhya; 714 families, it is said, migrated to Penukonda, where a king called Vishnu-Vardhana fell in love with a beautiful girl of the caste named Vāsavāmba. The Kōmatis dare not refuse Vishnu-Vardhana's proffer of marriage but on the appointed day the maid, her parents and a married couple from each of 102 families immolated themselves on a funeral pyre. These 102 families are identified as the *gōtra*[2] groups into which the Kōmatis are now divided, the remaining 612 forming the Nagarattu Chettis and allied castes. Personal beauty having thus proved the bane of the caste, Providence ordained thenceforth that no Kōmati girl should be beautiful. Vāsavāmba is now worshipped as the tutelary goddess of the caste, under the name Kanyakā-paramēsvari, and is regarded as an incarnation of Pārvati.[3] The Kōmatis rank high in the social scale, and strenuously live up to their claim to be true Vaisyas. It is curious, however, that, though their right to wear the sacred thread is undisputed, very few castes will accept water at their hands or take food in their houses.[4] In some mysterious way they are connected with the Mādigas, and are sometimes called "Midday Mādigas."[5] Their caste *panchāyats* are of the Telugu type, presided over by a *Chetti* and a *Yejamān*. Appeals lie to Brahman *Gurus*, entitled Bhāskarāchāryas, of whom there are several families, each with its own territorial jurisdiction. Some Kōmatis are Saivites and some Vaishnavites, but sect is no bar to intermarriage. In their customs, though the Vedic ritual is not

---

[1] For a description of these famous sowkars, see *Madura District Gazetteer*, p. 99.

[2] One of the families is said to have become extinct at the great holocaust, the last surviving pair having perished on the pyre. A list of the 101 *gōtra* groups is given on pp. 32 to 41, *E.S.M.*, No. VI. Each group has its appropriate Rishi on the analogy of Brahmanic *gōtras*, but several of these groups contain more than one exogamous clan and each *gōtra* bears the name of a tree, plant or grain the use of which is tabooed by the members of the *gōtra*.

[3] There are several variants of the story, see *E.S.M.*, No. VI, p. 4.

[4] According to *E.S.M.*, No. VI, only Bēdas, Mādigas and Korachas will eat in a Kōmati house.

[5] See *Castes and Tribes*, Vol. III, pp. 325 sq.

CHAP. III. SURVEY OF CASTES.

Kōmatis.

employed, they closely follow the Brahmanic model, while they observe in addition a multitude of Dravidian rites. Flesh-eating, adult marriage, widow re-marriage, divorce, etc., are rigorously eschewed, and annual *srāddhas* are observed, as well as monthly ceremonies during the first year of mourning. Exchange of daughters in marriage between two families is prohibited,[1] and *mēnarīkam* is enforced with a strictness that is proverbial.[2]

Nagarattu Chettis.

The **Nagarattu Chettis,** like the Kōmatis, claim to have migrated from the ancient City of Ayōdhya (Oudh),[3] and they are said to be descended from the 612 families of Penukonda who did not join with the 102 Kōmati families in Vāsavāmba's immolation. Nagarattus are strict vegetarians and wear the sacred thread. Some of them are Saivites, and some are Vaishnavas. They are divided [4] into Tamil, Telugu and Kanarese sections, and difference of language is a bar to intermarriage.

The term " Nagarattu " is applied to most of the non-Kōmati Chettis of Hosūr and Krishnagiri Taluks ;[5] it also occurs in Salem, Ōmalūr, Tiruchengōdu and Āttūr. The Nagarattu Chettis of Hosūr are said to speak Kanarese, but elsewhere Tamil is their predominant house language. The term **Bēri Chetti,** according to the *Baramahal Records*, is applied to the Telugu section of the Nagarattu Chettis, but in Krishnagiri and Dharmapuri Taluks, where they occur, they are reported to speak Tamil.[6] A section known as Neikāra Chettis (ghee men)[7] is numerous in Tiruchengōdu, and occurs also in Salem and Ōmalūr (Aranganūr) ; they speak Tamil and are described as a division of the Nagarattu Chettis

---

[1] " There should be no turning back of the creeper " as they say ; that is, when a girl has married into a family, the latter cannot give a girl in marriage to that girl's family ever afterwards (*E.S.M.*, No. VI, p. 8).

[2] *Kōmati-Mēnarīkam* is " a proverbial expression to denote a relation that cannot be escaped or evaded " (*E.S.M.*, loc. cit.).

[3] Hence their name Nagarattu, men of the city (Ayōdhya-Nagaram).

[4] The following sub-divisions are reported : (1) Sivāchār Nagarattus, (2) Emmaladu Nagarattus, (3) Bēri Nagarattus, (4) Nāmadhāri Nagarattus, (5) Kūgūr Nagarattus. The Sivāchār and Emmaladu Nagarattus wear the *lingam*, the other three divisions are Vaishnavas.

[5] Their chief settlements are at Hosūr, Bāgalūr, Krishnagiri and Kāvēripatnam.

[6] The exact relationship between the Bēri Chettis and the Nagarattu Chettis is not clear. The Bēri Chettis are said to be distinct from the Bēri Nagarattus referred to in footnote 4, though in the Tamil districts Bēri Nagarattus are commonly called Bēri Chettis. Most Bēri Chettis profess to be vegetarians, but the rule is not everywhere observed. In Trichinopoly, Tanjore, and Pudu-kōttai they speak Tamil, in Chittoor and Arcot, Telugu. Three divisions are reported (*a*) Samayapurattār, (*b*) Molagu-muri, (*c*) Māman-tāli-katti, the last named taking their name from a custom that requires a girl's maternal (*māman*) uncle to tie a prenuptial *tāli* (cf. the *tāli-kettu-kalyānam* of Malabar, *Malabar District Gazetteer*, p. 173).

[7] Cf. the Nēti Kōmatis of Shimoga, *E.S.M.*, No. VI, p. 5.

Beri Chettis.

who trade in ghee. Certain Neikāra Chettis of Hosūr Taluk, however, speak Kanarese. Sīlakāra Chettis (cloth-men) are found in Hosūr, Dharmapuri and Āttūr.[1] In Hosūr they speak Kanarese, in Dharmapuri Telugu, in Āttūr Tamil. Nūlkāra Chettis (threadmen), otherwise called Vellān Chettis, occur in Dharmapuri and in all the Talaghāt Taluks.[2] They are described as Nagarattu Chettis who sell twist (*nūl*). In Salem they call themselves Bhū-Vaisyas. They are said to wear no *pūnūl*. Pattars are reported to be a sub-caste of the Vellān Chettis who wear a *lingam* on the neck or on the right arm. Sōliya Chettis are common in Tiruchengōdu, and also occur in the other Talaghāt Taluks,[3] and in Dharmapuri, Acharapākkam and Tovaram-katti Chettis are found in Tiruchengōdu Taluk, but are not common; the former take their name from their chief settlements at Acharapākkam in Madurāntakam Taluk, Chingleput District. Kāsukkāra Chettis (coin-men) are common in Dharmapuri, and are also found in Āttūr, Tiruchengōdu and Salem; they are described as Nagarattu Chettis who exchange coins. In Salem Taluk there are a few so-called Pannirendām (twelfth) Chettis, who devote one-twelfth of their income to the god of Ratnagiri, Kulittalai Taluk, Trichinopoly District.[4]

Most, if not all, of the communities above enumerated appear to belong to the Nagarattu caste-group, and there is reason to believe that they are true sub-castes, based on territorial or occupational distinctions. Most of them acknowledge the supremacy of a Guru entitled Dharma-Sivāchār, residing at Nerinjipet in Bhavāni Taluk, Coimbatore District, and many of them call themselves Dharma-Sivāchār Vaisyas.

Janappars.

The **Janappars** (9,510) are most numerous in the three Bāramahāl Taluks of Dharmapuri (3,489), Krishnagiri (2,529), and Ūttankarai (1,998); there are a few in Hosūr, Salem and Ōmalūr, but they do not occur in Āttūr or Tiruchengōdu. Harūr is their chief settlement. They acknowledge Ayyangār Gurus at Tōrapalli (Hosūr), Rāya-kōta and Kētānda-patti (near Vāniyambādi). Their name is said to be derived from the word *janappu* (= hemp), the cultivation of hemp and its conversion into gunny bags being the hereditary occupation of their forefathers. Some members of the caste, living near Kāri-mangalam and in Kondayana-halli near Sōlappādi, still follow the ancestral industry, but most of

[1] Kela-mangalam, Tali, Dharmapuri, Adamau-kōttai, Pudupet.

[2] E.g., Pedda-Nāyakkan-pālaiyam, Anaiyāmpatti, Kondayampalli, Naduvalūr, all in Āttūr Taluk, Kōnagapādi in Ōmalūr, and in the vicinity of Tiruchengōdu.

[3] Konganāpuram, Aranganūr and Pottanēri.

[4] *Trichinopoly District Gazetteer*, p. 282.

CHAP. III. SURVEY OF CASTES.

Janappars.

the caste have abandoned it in favour of trade and money-lending. These now call themselves Telungas, Telugu being their house language. The cattle trade of the District is almost entirely in their hands (v. p. 280). Their customs follow the Telugu type. They worship Pārvati under the name of Durga, and Ankāl-amman is regarded as a special patroness of the caste. They are divided into 24 clans.

Balijas.

The **Balijas** represent the Telugu military and trading element in the District, being evenly distributed throughout the Talaghāt and Bāramahāl, and totalling over 10,000 in Hosūr Taluk. In the Tamil country they are usually called **Kavarais** or Vadugars (Northerners). They are popularly classed as (A)[1] Kōta Balijas, who are military in origin and claim kinship with the Emperors and Viceroys of Vijayanagar and the Kandyan Dynasty, and (B) Pētā Balijas, who are traders. Their caste title is Nāyudu or, as it is more familiarly spelt, Naidu. Many of them are prosperous merchants and landowners, others attain distinction in the higher ranks of Government service; they provide the Army, the Police and the peons establishments of Government Offices with some of their best recruits. Their largest settlements occur in towns and villages such as Sankaridrug, Salem, Āttūr and Perumbālai, that were held by garrisons under the suzerainty of the Vijayanagar or Madura Dynasties.

Sub-castes among the Balijas are not easily demarcated. As befits an immigrant and widely scattered race that prides itself in the purity of the blood, the general law of endogamy is narrowed down to the condition precedent to all marriage contracts, that between the contracting families the existence of a previous matrimonial alliance must be proved, this rule being of course subject to the exogamous principle that the house-names (*inti-pērlu*) of bride and bridegroom must differ. Thus the circle within which a man may choose his bride is limited, within the sub-caste, to families that bear house names which have previously been connected by marriage with his own.

Most of the Balijas of Salem District are of the Gājulu section of the Pētā Balijas. The only other section of importance is that of the Musuku Balijas, who occur in every taluk, but are not numerous, except in Krishnagiri Taluk and Pennāgaram Division. The Ravuts, a section of Balijas descended from sowars who served under the petty Rajas of the 17th Century, are found in Shevapet, Ōmalūr, Tiruchengōdu and Sankaridrug.

---

[1] According to some authorities (e.g., Mr. Francis, *Census Report*, 1901) the word Dēsa is applied to the Kōta Balijas; according to other authorities it is applicable to Pēta Balijas only, Dēsa meaning "Mofussil."

All these three sections appear to be true sub-castes; they interdine, but may not intermarry, and all acknowledge a Vaishnavite Brahman Guru at Tirukkōyilūr [1] in South Arcot. Of the other sections known in the District the Sukamanchi Balijas are said to occur rarely in Krishnagiri, and two sections known as Eluttukkārar and Oppanakkārar are reported from Ōmalūr. All these are true Balijas, and each section is said to be endogamous. Pagadāla (coral) Balijas occur rarely in the Talaghāt; accounts vary as to whether they form a true sub-caste, or whether Pagadāla is merely a "house-name"; in Āttūr they are called Kammas. Two obscure sections in Hosūr Taluk, known as Vengāya Vadugar and Puliyambu Vadugar, are said to abstain from the flesh of goats, though they are allowed to eat sheep. The terms Rālla (gem-stones), Pūsa (beads), Perikē (salt) and Tōta (garden) sometimes applied to Balijas are reported to be mere occupational terms which do not indicate true sub-castes. The Golla Balijas are probably Gollas (q.v.) who call themselves Naidus; the Kamma Balijas are perhaps to be identified with the Kammas (q. v. p. 166), and Linga Balija or Sivāchār Kavarai appears to be a popular term for Kanarese Lingāyats. The Musuku Balijas are so called because their women cover their heads when they leave their homes (*musuku* = veil). Their customs resemble closely those of the Gājulu Balijas.

CHAP. III. SURVEY OF CASTES.

Balijas

The customs of the Balijas vary in different places. They employ Brahman *purōhits*, and formerly recognised the authority of the Dēsāyi Chetti, who was of Balija caste, but their caste polity has suffered disintegration.[2] Their marriage customs are of the Telugu type.

(6) Industrial Castes.

The Industrial castes may conveniently be grouped as (i) Weavers (89,871), (ii) Oil-pressers (15,825), (iii) Toddy-drawers (45,282), (iv) Potters (13,384), (v) Salt-Workers (4,210), (vi) Mat-makers (3,204), and (vii) Artizans (32,688).

(i) Weavers.

Of the Industrial castes, the Weavers are by far the most important. The strongest numerically are (1) the Tamil Kaikōlars (41,291). Next to them come (2) the Dēvāngas or Jēdars (32,497), who include both Telugu and Kanarese sections, though unfortunately in the Census Returns they are only shown under one head. The Telugu (3) Sālēs (6,516), and (4) Togatas, (1,144), are also represented, and lastly (5) the Patnūl-kārans (8,423),

[1] Other *matams* honoured by the Balijas are at Srīperumbūdūr, Srīvilliputtūr, Srīrangam, Pulavēri and Tiruvallūr.

[2] E.g., accounts differ widely as to the duration of pollution on attainment of puberty, childbirth, etc.

or Silk-Weavers, of Salem form an important community. Several other castes earn a living by weaving, notably the Kanarese Panchamas known as Maggas (see below, p. 203), but separate statistics for these are not available.

Kaikōlars.

Most of the **Kaikōlars** reside in the Talaghāt (Salem 15,205, Tiruchengōdu 10,981, Ōmalūr 4,682, Āttūr 3,444), but there are a few thousands in the Bāramahāl also. According to their own account they are immigrants from Conjeeveram, which city is still the head-quarters of their caste.

They claim to be descended from the Nine Heroes (*Nava-Vīra*) created by the God Siva to help Subrahmanya to purge the earth of certain demons whose leader was called Padmāsura. The legend is as follows:—"The people of the earth, being harassed by certain demons, applied to Siva for help. Siva was enraged against the giants, and sent forth six sparks of fire from his eyes. His wife, Pārvati, was frightened, and retired to her chamber, and, in so doing, dropped nine beads from her anklets. Siva converted the beads into as many females. These nine maidens fell in love with Siva, and out of mere love they became pregnant. Pārvati in jealousy cursed them that they might not be delivered. The pain-stricken maidens begged Siva to intercede, which he did, and Pārvati relieved them of the curse, and they were delivered of nine sons, each of whom was born with full grown moustaches and a dagger. These nine heroes, with Subrahmanya at their head, marched in command of a large force, and destroyed the demons. The Kaikōlars, or Sengundar, are said to be the descendants of Vīrabāhu,[1] one of these heroes. After killing the demon the warriors were told by Siva that they should become musicians, and adopt a profession, which would not involve the destruction or injury of any living creature, and, weaving being such a profession, they were trained in it.[2]"

The Kaikōlars are said to be divided into nine sub-castes, but a complete list of these sub-castes is not forthcoming. The Salem Kaikōlars belong to the Konga section. Like the Vellālars, the Kaikōlars recognise a distinction between Perun-tāli and Siru-tāli, and the Konga Kaikōlars belong to the Perun-tāli section. The Kaikōlar caste is divided into 72 Nāds, of which the Konga Kaikōlars of Salem District recognise seven, viz., (1) Kānchi, (2) Pūvāni, (3) Ēlūr, (4) Araiya, (5) Vanni, (6) Pūndurai,

---

[1] Vīrabāhu is also said to be a progenitor of the Pariahs.

[2] *Census Report*, Madras, 1891. The word "Sengundar," (men of the red dagger), is said to refer to the dagger carried by Subrahmanya, and the word *Kai-Kōl* is explained in the same way, though a more natural philology would derive it from *kai* = hand, and *kōl* = shuttle.

Kaikōlars.

(7) Salem. The administrative divisions, it will be noted, bear a close analogy to those of the Nāttāns, Pallans and Konga Vellālars [1] The premier Nād is that of Kānchi (Conjeeveram), where the *Mahānāttān* resides. The Pūvāni Nād (of which Tāra-mangalam is the head-quarters) exercises a sort of appellate jurisdiction over the other five. Caste disputes are settled by a committee composed of (1) a *Periya-tanakkāran*, (2) a *Nāttānmaikkāran*, (3) twelve *Kāriyakkārans*, and (4) a *Sangūdi*. The first two offices are hereditary, the others elective for life tenure. Meetings are convened by the *Sangūdi*. The *Periya-tanakkāran* of Mallūr is the highest authority of the Kongu Nāds in the District.[2] Kaikōlars adopt the caste title Mudali.

Kaikōlars employ Brahman *purōhits* for purification after childbirth and death, but not on attainment of puberty. Most Kaikōlars are Saivites, Subrahmanya under the name of Muttukumāra-swāmi being the particular patron of the caste, as half-brother and comrade of the caste ancestor Vīrabāhu. At Āragalūr (see Vol. II, p. 295) the cult of Ambairamman is specially associated with the caste.

Dēvāngas.

The **Dēvāngas** (commonly called Jēdars) are most numerous in Salem Taluk, where their number exceeds 17,000. In Tiruchengōdu there are 5,732, in Ōmalūr 4,523 and in Dharmapuri 2,128, but elsewhere they are comparatively rare. Their legendary [3] ancsetor is Dēvālan or Dēvāngam (" body of god "), who was created by Siva at the request of the Dēvas, and who overthrew five Asuras with the help of the Goddess Chaudēsvari (Chāmundi), the patron deity of the caste. The blood of the five Asuras was coloured respectively yellow, red, white, green and black, and Dēvālan used their blood for dyeing thread.

The Dēvāngas of Salem District say they migrated from Hampi, the capital of the Vijayanagar Empire, where the spiritual head of the caste still resides; and their first settlement was Amarakundi, the capital of the Gatti Mudaliyārs, and the present head-quarters of their headman, to whom all appeals against decisions of local *panchāyats* are referred. They are divided into two main groups, one speaking Telugu, and the other speaking a corrupt form of Kanarese. These two groups may not intermarry and appear to be true sub-castes.[4] Their clans are exceedingly

---

[1] See pp. 144 and 189.

[2] For further details regarding caste organisation, see *Castes and Tribes*, Vol. III, p. 35.

[3] For the legend see *Castes and Tribes*, Vol. II, p. 155; *Baramahal Records* Section III, p. 179.

[4] The Dēvāngas of Salem, however, will not intermarry with their fellow castemen in Ōmalūr, Bhavāni or Elampillai (west of Kanja-malai).

CHAP. III. SURVEY OF CASTES.

numerous.[1] For the settlement of caste disputes they are divided into groups known as *pangalams*, presided over by a *Chetti* (*Settikkāran*), who is assisted by one or more deputies called *Pettan*. The Dēvāngas employ Brahman *purōhits*, and have adopted many Brahmanic customs, especially in connection with marriage.

Sālēs.

Of the 6,500 odd **Sālēs**[2], nearly three-fourths occur in Salem Taluk, the rest being scattered throughout the District. Most of the Salem Sālēs are Padma-Sālēs. They trace their descent to Bhavāni Rishi, who is worshipped as their patron deity, and who was created by the Rishi Mārkanda from a ball of fire. Their customs bear a close resemblance to those of the Dēvāngas.

Patnūlkārans.

The silk-weavers popularly known as **Patnūlkārans** are immigrants from Gujarat, and call themselves Saurāshtra Brahmans. The community is virtually confined to Salem City. Their fair reddish complexion, unlike anything Dravidian, stamps them as northerners. Consistently with their Brahmanic traditions they wear the *pūnūl*, and their women-folk carry their water-vessels on the hip, and never on the head.[3]

(ii) Oil-pressers.

Tamil oil-pressers are known as Vāniyars, Telugu oil-pressers as Gāndlas, and Kanarese oil-pressers as Gānigas. The Vāniyars (13,689) are distributed throughout the District, but are markedly stronger in the Bāramahāl taluks than elsewhere. The Gāndlas (2,138) are confined mostly to Hosūr and Dharmapuri Taluks. No Gānigas have been shown in the Census figures for 1911, but it is probable that they have been included among the Vāniyars and Gāndlas, as there were 256 Gānigas returned in the previous Census.

Vāniyars.

The Tamil **Vāniyars** of Salem District belong entirely to the Irandu-māttu, or Irattai-chekkān, section, so-called because they

---

[1] According to the local account there are 700 exogamous clans. See list in *Castes and Tribes*, Vol. II, p. 161.

[2] According to *E.S.M.*, No. X, p. 2, there are three sub-castes of Sālēs—(1) Padma-Sālēs who speak Telugu, (2) Pattu-Sālēs who speak Kanarese, and use silk in weaving, (3) Sakuna-Sālēs, who are later immigrants; all three sub-castes trace their origin to the Rishi Mārkanda. According to *Castes and Tribes*, Vol. VI, p. 267, "Sukūn" and "Suka" Sālēs speak Marāthi. Dr. Thurston gives a separate account of Karna-Sālēs (*Castes and Tribes*, Vol. III, p. 252), who differ from Padma-Sālēs in not observing *upanayanam*, the mock pilgrimage to Benares, and pot-searching at weddings, and in using 12 pots (the Padma-Sālēs use 16). Two sections of Sālēs are referred to in *Baramahal Records*, Section III, pp. 174 and 185, viz., (1) Padma Sālēs and (2) Pedda-Sālēs, whose customs are almost identical.

The legend is variously given in *Castes and Tribes*, Vol. VI, p. 267, *E.S.M.*, No. X, p. I, *Baramahal Records*, Section III, p. 174, etc.

[3] For their industrial methods see p. 266; further details connected with the caste will be found in *Madura District Gazetteer*, p. 109 sq., and in *Castes and Tribes*, Vol. VI, p. 160.

yoke two bullocks to their mill. They are a leading caste of the Left Hand Faction. In common with the Bēri Chettis, with whom they appear to have some connection, they reverence as Gurus Dharma Sivāchārya of Nerinjipet in Bhavāni Taluk and Gnāna-Sivāchārya of Mullandram in Ārni Jāghīr. Unlike some Bēri Chettis, however, they do not abstain from flesh. Like the Kōmatis they are regarded with aversion by other castes, and to meet a Vāniyan is believed to bring bad luck. They claim to be Vaisyas, and wear the sacred thread. They employ Brahman *purōhits*, practise infant marriage, prohibit re-marriage of widows, and usually burn their dead. They call themselves *Jyōti-Nagarattārs* (people of the city of light) and their caste title is Chetti. They are an enterprising community, and many of them, notably in Dharmapuri, have abandoned their ancestral occupation in favour of trade and money-lending, and have achieved great success. — Vāniyars.

Gāndlas. The Telugu **Gāndlas** are almost entirely of the Onti-erudu, or Ottai-chekkān, section using only one bull to a mill. In contrast to the Tamil "two bull" Vāniyars, they are attached to the Right Hand Faction. Generally they are less wealthy and less enterprising than the Vāniyars, but in a few localities, such as Kāri-mangalam and Buddi-Reddi-patti, they have taken to trade with success. They claim to be superior to the Vāniyars,[1] and will not dine with them.

(iii) Toddy Drawers. The Toddy Drawers include (1) the Tamil Shānārs (42,695) and (2) the Telugu Īdigas[2] (2,385) and (3) Gamallas (202). The Shānārs are widely distributed throughout both the Talaghāt and the Bāramahāl, but three-fourths of their total number are to be found in the two Taluks of Tiruchengōdu (nearly 20,000) and Salem (over 10,000). Īdigas are confined to Hosūr, Krishnagiri and Dharmapuri Taluks, and Gamallas to Hosūr.

Shānārs. The Salem **Shānārs** (called also Maramēris, or Tree Climbers) are divided into two endogamous groups, the Konga-Shānārs being descended from the first wife, and the Kalyāna-Shānārs[3] from the second wife of a certain Mūppan whose name is lost.

---

[1] They also occur at Bēlūr, Ettāppūr, and Narasingapuram in Āttūr and at Kumāraswami-patti, in Salem Municipal limits.

[2] For an exhaustive account of the Īdigas, see *E.S.M.*, No. XVIII.

[3] Konga Shānārs are to be found in Pi-mara-patti, and Panangūttūr, a hamlet of Malla-samudram; Katti-pālaiyam, a hamlet of Māmundi; Kūttampālaiyam and Timmi-pālaiyam, hamlets of Karumanūr; Kalyāna Shānārs occur in Kūttampālaiyam; Sembam-pālaiyam, also a hamlet of Karumanūr; Pālamēdu, a Mitta village south of Malla-samudram; Kalyāni and Pāla-pālaiyam in Rāsipuram Firka, and Kachi-palli in Sankari Firka.

CHAP. III. SURVEY OF CASTES.

Shānārs.

Each of these groups is divided into six territorial *Karais* [1] which are mutually exogamous, like the divisions of the Nāttāns and Pallans (pp. 144 and 189). Caste disputes are settled in *panchāyat*, against whose decision there is no provision for appeal; the authority of the *panchāyat* is waning, and the maximum penalty they can inflict is said to be Rs. 2.

(iv) Potters.

Tamil Potters are known as Kusavans, Telugu Potters as Kummaras, and Kanarese Potters [2] as Kumbāras. The Kusavans number 12,775, and are distributed fairly evenly throughout the District. The Kummaras (609) are confined to Hosūr Taluk. The Kumbāras, like the Gānigas, are ignored in the Census of 1911, but are probably included in one or both of the other classes as 452 were returned for the District in 1901. Kusavans and Kumbāras do not intermarry or "interdine."

The Potters are an essential element in every village community; they are the traditional bone-setters of the village, they often officiate as priests to the village deities, and in connection with marriage ceremonies they have important duties to perform. Yet little is known of their customs and social organisation, which afford a promising field for future investigation. They belong to the Right Hand Faction and employ their own *purōhits*. It is said they put on the sacred thread on marriage occasions.

(v) Salt workers.

The Salt workers include the Tamil Uppiliyans (3,927) and the Telugu Upparas (283).[3] Most of the former are to be found in the Taluks of Tiruchengōdu and Salem, of the latter in Hosūr.

Uppiliyans.

The **Uppiliyans** of Salem District claim to be immigrants from a hill called Kappiyangiri or Kappangiri in "the north." "They were created by Siva from drops of sweat that fell from his forehead." [4] Their title is Nāyakkar. Nine clans are reported, (1) Siru-kulingiyān, (2) Pūdampalliyān, (3) Idaiyāttān, (4) Todiyattān, (5) Nangavarattān, (6) Parutti-palli Periya-vīttukkāran,

---

[1] (1) Elūr, (2) Karumanūr, a Mitta village south of Malla-samudram, (3) Marapārai, a Mitta village south of Karungal-patti, (4) Pūndurai, (5) Mūramangalam (Ōmalūr Taluk) and (6) Murungavelam. The villages of Aval-Pūndurai and Tuyyam-Pūndurai in Erode Taluk still contain large settlements of Shānārs.

[2] For Potters see *Census Report*, 1891, paras. 502, 503; *North Arcot Manual* I, p. 231; *South Canara Manual* I, p. 168; *Madura District Gazetteer*, p. 101; Buchanan's *Mysore*, I, pp. 191–312, *Castes and Tribes*, Vol. IV, sub voc. Kusavan, Kummara, Kumbāra.

[3] Uppara is the Telugu form and Uppāra the Kanarese form. Writing of the Uppiliyans of Trichinopoly District, Mr. Hemingway states that they are divided into three sub-castes by language (1) the Kongas, (2) the Kavarais, (3) the Kannadiyas. (*Trichinopoly District Gazetteer*, pp. 115-7.)

[4] For other traditions of origin, see *Castes and Tribes*, Vol. VII, p. 230.

(7) Vijayamangalam Periya-vīttukkāran, (8) Pūnduraiyān, (9) Pāla-tozhuvān.[1] The first three of these clans cannot intermarry among themselves, the fourth and fifth likewise form a *dāyādi* group, and also the sixth and seventh. The last two, however, can intermarry with any of the other groups.[2] The *panchāyat* is presided over by a *Pattakkāran*, assisted by a *Tōttiyathan*. Both offices are hereditary, and the *Pattakkarans* belong either to the Siru-kulinjiyān, Pūnduraiyān or Parutti-palli clan. An appeal lies to a *Pattanam Chetti*, who resides at Paramati, and who is not an Uppiliyan by caste.

CHAP. III. SURVEY OF CASTES. Uppiliyans.

(vi) Mat Makers, Medaras.

The mat-making **Mēdaras,** or **Vēdakkārans** as they are called among the Tamils, according to the Census of 1911 numbered only 204 and are confined to the Taluks of Hosūr and Dharmapuri. There is, however, a large mat-making community in Salem City, and it is possible that they were returned as Vēdakkārans, and that this name, in the course of tabulating, got confused with that of some other caste. Their ancestral occupation is the working of bamboo into mats, baskets, sieves, cradles, fans, boxes, umbrellas, etc.[3] They are usually returned as a Telugu-speaking caste, but some of those in Salem speak Tamil, and in the Mysore country there is an important Kanarese community. Language, as usual, is a bar to intermarriage.[4] The Salem Mēdaras call themselves "Chetti." The Telugus are mostly Vaishnavas, and the Tamils are Saivites. A large number of clans are reported,[5] those of Salem including (1) Kanikaram, (2) Tamminēna, (3) Pōtala, (4) Urē, (5) Vāsam, (6) Ēkkam, (7) Tāma, (8) Mettuku, (9) Pānthakotta, (10) Kāngayam, (11) Kanjam, (12) Kōnē. Caste disputes are settled by a *panchāyat* presided over by a *Periya-Chetti* and a *Chinna-Chetti*, whose offices are hereditary, and who should be related to each

---

[1] Cf. the list of six *pattams* given in *Trichinopoly District Gazetteer*, page 115, which includes the names Sirukkalinji, Pudambili, and Pundarai. The orthography of such traditional caste names is always rather vague.

[2] Uppiliyans are also distinguished as (1) *Mezhugu-Bottu*, who wear an ordinary *bottu* (*tāli*) and (2) *Lakshmi-Bottu*, who wear a *bottu* with a figure of Lakshmi on it. Each of these two divisions is endogamous. According to the *Trichinopoly District Gazetteer* (p. 117), the Tamils and Kanarese wear the Lakshmi *bottu* and the Telugus the ordinary *bottu*.

[3] The Koravas (see below p. 196) also work in bamboo; unlike the Mēdaras, however, they manufacture mats of date leaves. Mēdaras split the bamboo from the top, or thin end, downwards, Koravas split it from the thick end upwards (*E.S.M.*, No. XIX).

[4] Three sub-castes are recorded in *E.S.M.*, No. XIX, viz., (1) Gavarigas, (2) Palli-Mēdārs, (3) Bandikāra-Mēdars.

[5] See the list in *Castes and Tribes*, Vol. V, page 54, which is utterly different from the Salem list. Cf. also *E.S.M.*, No. XIX, p. 2.

other as *māman* and *machān*, i.e., one is the uncle of the other. The *panchāyat* is made up of a senior member from each household. They employ Brahman *purōhits*, the *purōhit* of the Salem Mēdaras being a Vadagalai Tamil Vaishnava.

(vii) Artizans.

The Artizans comprise the Tamil **Kammālars** (30,251), the Telugu **Kamsalas** (2,437) and the Kanarese **Pānchālas.** The latter, like the Gānigas and Kumbāras, are ignored in the Census of 1911, though they numbered 1,181 in the previous Census. Probably they have been enumerated among the Kammālars or Kamsalas. The Kammālars are distributed throughout the District, and are most numerous in Salem and Tiruchengōdu Taluks. The Kamsalas are confined to Hosūr.

The Artizans are leaders of the Left Hand Faction, and repudiate the superiority of Brahmans, whom they regard as inferiors and call Go-Brahmans (cow-Brahmans). They maintain that they themselves are the only true Brahmans, and are descended from Visvakarma, the architect of the Gods. Their priestly families call themselves Visva-Brahmans, a title which the whole caste now adopts. Their *gurus* and *purōhits* are drawn exclusively from their own caste. Their caste titles are Āsari and Pattar, corresponding to the Brahmanic Āchārya and Bhatta. They wear the sacred thread (*pūnūl*) which they usually don on *Upākarma* day, (Āvani-Avittam, August) when all the twice-born renew their threads; but some of them observe a regular investiture ceremony (*Upanayana*) on the Brahman model. Their marriage ceremonies, too, closely resemble those of Brahmans, but a bride-price is paid. Most of them claim to be vegetarians. Saivite Artizans dispose of their dead by burial in a sitting posture, Vaishnavites by cremation.[1] Widows are allowed to retain such of their jewels as adorn the head and neck. Women of the Saivite section, unlike those of other castes, throw the end of their body-cloth over the right shoulder; Vishnavites adhere to the usual custom.

Kammālars.

Kammālars, Kamsalas and Pānchālas may not intermarry,[2] but all three linguistic sections are divided into five occupational classes, (1) Goldsmiths (*tattān*), (2) Brass-workers (*kannān*), (3) Carpenters (*tachan*), (4) Stone-masons (*kal-tachan*) and (5) Blacksmiths (*kollan*). These five sub-divisions, descendants respectively of the five sons of Visvakarma, are permitted to intermarry, but the

[1] See the article in *Castes and Tribes*, Vol. III, p. 106 sq., from which much of the above is extracted.

[2] Each linguistic section contains several sub-castes; for example, the Kammālars are divided into Chōla, Pāndya and Kongu, the Kamsalas into Muriki-Nād, Pāki-Nād, etc. (*Castes and Tribes*, Vol. III, sub voc.)

Kammālars.

goldsmiths, not unnaturally, claim social precedence over the rest. There is also a tendency for the families in which the priesthood is hereditary to form a separate exclusive sub-caste. They are also divided into exogamous clans. Their caste administration is elaborately organised. Each of the five occupational sub-divisions has its elective *Nāttānmaikkāran* assisted by a *Kāriyastan*. These sectional *Nāttānmaikkārans* are subject to the jurisdiction of an *Ainthu-vītu-Nāttānmaikkāran* [1] (head of the "five houses") who is elected by representatives of all five sections.[2] There is tendency for these offices to become hereditary. The *Ainthu vītu-Nāttānmaikkāran* is assisted by four other *Panchāyatdars*, of whom one is usually appointed *Kāriyastan*. An appeal from this *panchāyat* lies to a *Guru* known as Jaya Venkatāchārlu, who presides over a *Matam* (*Vipuri Matam*) at Kāvēri-patnam, and this *Matam* in turn appears to be subordinate to Brahmayyagāri *Matam* at Pottalūr in Cuddapah District. Kammālars are mostly Saivites, and some of them have adopted the Vīra-Saiva faith. Their patron deity is Kāmākshi. The Grāma-Dēvatās are also worshipped, but not, it is said, with blood sacrifice. They are on amicable terms with Bēri Chettis, Muhammadans and Pallars, a relationship probably connected with the political conditions which gave rise to the feud between the Right and Left Hand Factions.[3] The Pallars are known as *Jāti-pillais* or "servants of the caste."

(7) Labourers.

The **Oddars** or Navvies number 46,531, and are evenly distributed throughout the District. The Pallans or agricultural serfs number 20,483, and occur mostly in the Taluks of Tiruchengōdu and Salem.

Oddars.

The **Oddars** (Telugu—Odde, Kanarese—Vadda) speak an uncouth dialect of Telugu, and trace their name to the country of their traditional origin, Orissa. They are divided into four groups: (1) Kallu (stone), (2) Mannu (earth), (3) Maram (wood) and (4) Uppu (salt). Those of the Kallu (Telugu-Rāti) section are workers in stone. They claim superiority over the other sections. They are more settled in their habits than the Man-Oddars, and are therefore sometimes known as Ūr (village) Oddars as distinct from Bidāru (wanderers). They are also called Bandi Oddars, on account of the quaint clumsy buffalo-carts in which they carry

---

[1] Also called *Ainthu Vītu Periya-Tanakkāran*, *Aidhiya Yejamān Dharmakartar*, etc.

[2] The procedure is complex and the final choice is by lot; it is described in detail in *Castes and Tribes*, Vol. III, pp. 108–9, and in *Madura District Gazetteer*, p. 99.

[3] See p. 125, footnote.

CHAP. III. SURVEY OF CASTES.

Oddars.

stone.[1] Till recently they have enjoyed a virtual monopoly of the quarrying and well-sinking arts in which they are well skilled, and they are able to command a rate of wages double that of the ordinary labourer. Most of their earnings, however, they spend on drink, and their standard of living is extremely low. The Man-Oddars [2] are in great demand for tank-digging, road-making and other operations requiring earth-work. They are migratory in their habits, shifting their settlements according to the demand for their labour, and forming temporary encampments on the outskirts of towns and villages, or in the vicinity of the work on which they are, for the time being, engaged. They live in one-roomed huts made of mats of split bamboo, fixed on a frame-work rounded like the covering of a country cart. The Mara-Oddars are comparatively rare ; they earn their living by cutting timber and carving wood.[3] Uppu Oddars serve as sweepers in Union towns and villages, and are regarded as out-castes by the other sections. The significance of the term Uppu is not clear. The groups above enumerated are ordinarily endogamous, but it is said that if a Man-Oddar turns his hand to stone-work, he is permitted to marry a Kal-Oddar girl. They will admit into their caste a Kuruba or Golla, or any one of higher caste than themselves. The usual title adopted by Oddars is Bōyi. Caste *Panchāyats* are presided over by a *Yajamān* or Pedda Bōyadu, and more serious disputes were formerly referred to a *Dēsāyi Chetti* of Balija caste. They belong to the Right Hand Faction. They may eat sheep, goats, pigs, squirrels, wild cats, lizards and mice, but not beef. Ellamma is their patron deity, and, the victims sacrificed are slain with the thrust of a spear or crow-bar. Custom formerly prohibited a male Oddar from shaving his head or beard, but this rule is growing obsolete. Their women wear glass bangles on the left arm only, on the right arm they wear brass bangles, or none at all.[4] They never wear the *ravikkai*. It is considered improper for a woman to take much pride in her personal appearance. Music, flowers, and *bhāshinga* are not permitted at marriages. Divorce and widow-marriage are freely allowed, but it is not considered respectable for a woman to change her partner more than eighteen times. When a partition takes place, a pregnant woman may claim a share for her unborn

---

[1] For a description of these carts and the method of quarrying see below, p. 278.

[2] In Telugu "Manti-Oddo." They are also called Bailu ("Maidan") or "Dēsada" (Country).

[3] A new Temple Car at Gangavalli was made recently by Mara-Oddar, but the workmanship is poor.

[4] For the origin of this custom see *Castes and Tribes*, Vol. V, p. 429.

child[1]. An unmarried girl or childless mother is buried without any ceremonies at all. Though Oddars represent a low type of civilization, they may draw water from the common village well, and their proximity does not convey pollution. They are assimilating their wedding and funeral ceremonies to those of the Balijas.

Oddars.

The **Pallans**, an agricultural serf caste of Tamils, numbered in 1901 as many as 32,516. They are mostly found in the Talaghāt Taluks, and their organization and customs follow to a great extent the practice of Konga Vellālars. Their name is fancifully derived from *pallam* (a hollow or low-lying ground) as they are specially skilful in wet cultivation. They are perennially at feud with the Pariahs, and they number among the Left Hand Castes. They respect Muhammadans as well as the higher Hindu castes, and look down upon Pariahs and Chucklers.[2]

Pallans.

The Pallans of the Kongu Country are organised in no less than 24 Nāds, scattered over Salem, Coimbatore and Trichinopoly, of which (1) Pūvāni, (2) Parutti-palli, (3) Elūr, (4) Salem, (5) Vada-karai (Sankaridrug) and (6) Rāsipuram are in Salem District. In the first four the title Palakār is in vogue, in the fifth Pannādi, and in the last Mūppan. It will be observed that these Nāds are almost identical with those of the Nāttāns (see p. 144), and they are probably of similar historic interest.

(8) Menials.

Barbers and Washermen (Dhobies) are of paramount importance in every village. The Tamil Barbers or Ambattans number 14,414, the Telugu Mangalas 1,495; the latter are confined to Hosūr Taluk. Kanarese Kelasis, or Nāyindas [3] as they are also called, do not appear in the Census lists, and have probably been included under Ambattans. In 1901 they numbered 342. The Tamil Washermen or Vannāns number 19,959, and are very evenly distributed throughout the District; the Telugu Tsākalas number 1,839, and are confined to Hosūr Taluk. The Kanarese Agasas are not shown at all.

Barbers.

Almost all castes except Panchamas are dependent on Barbers for the periodic or ceremonial shaving prescribed by custom. Most Brahmanic temples employ Barbers for the *Periya-mēlam*, or temple band[4]. Barber women serve as midwives to the majority

---

[1] Cf. *Castes and Tribes*, Vol. V, p. 425, where a story is related of a pregnant woman claiming wages on behalf of her expected infant.

[2] For their customs see *Trichinopoly Gazetteer*, pp. 128 to 130. Cf. *Castes and Tribes*—Vol. V, p. 472 sq.

[3] For Nāyindas see *E.S.M.*, No. XII.

[4] Their distinctive instruments are (1) the *nāgasuram*, (2) the *tutti* and (3) the *tālam*.

of Hindu castes, and in some castes (e.g.[1] Konga Vellālars, Nāttārs, etc.), a barber has important ceremonial duties at weddings and funerals.

Dhobies.

The Dhoby, too, has many important ceremonial duties to perform on the occasion of births, marriages, deaths, etc., among caste Hindus. In towns he is paid for his ordinary services in cash, but in villages he is rewarded in kind, cooked food being a common form of remuneration. At festivals, marriages, deaths, etc., he is entitled to gifts, and he can also claim a perquisite of grain at the time of harvest.

The customs of Barbers and Dhobies resemble closely those of other Hindus.[2]

(9) Military Castes.

Salem District, and especially the Bāramahāl, is littered with relics of the armies of bygone days. Though 2,267 persons have returned themselves as "Kshatriyas," it is doubtful whether their claims to the title would stand criticism. The military traditions of the Pallis and Vettuvans have already been referred to (pp. 142 and 150). The great wave of Vijayanagar conquest is represented by the settlements of Balijas, Kāpus, Kammas, Telagas and Rāzus. The Bāgalūr Pālaiyam was a military fief of Telugu origin. Fortified villages, such as Pennāgaram, Kōdi-halli, Perumbālai, still retain the descendants of Golla and Balija garrisons, who have substituted ploughshares and pruning hooks for swords, while Umbilikai Inams, which are fiefs granted for military service, are still enjoyed by Gollas, Bestas and Balijas, especially in the surviving Pālaiyams. The warlike propensities of the Kanarese people are testified to by the Māsti Poligārs (Bērikai and Sūlagiri), and by the Umbilikai Inams of Bēdas and Kurubas. Lastly the sanguinary history of the eighteenth century has left its legacy of Muhammadan, Marātha, and Rājput settlements.

Marāthas.

The **Marāthas** number 4,244 and are most numerous in the Taluks of Hosūr and Krishnagiri, where their settlements are rather large.[3] Many of them are military pensioners, and, they still take pride in their connection with the Indian Army. They call themselves Kshatriyas, and look down upon the indigenous Hindus. Like the Rāzus, they don the sacred thread on the eve of marriage. They employ Brahman *purōhits*, and observe

---

[1] See page 146.

[2] Much interesting information is embodied in *E.S.M.*, No. IV, Agasa and No. XII, Nāyinda.

[3] Particularly in Krishnagiri Town and at Nāchi-kuppam (near Vēppana-palli) and Sāmanta-malai (near Krishnagiri) and Virupa-sandiram. There are similar settlements near the Javādis of Tiruppattūr Taluk at Āndi-appanūr and Nāyakkanūr.

the *nāmakaranam*, ear-boring, tonsure, and *sīmantam* ceremonies. They are divided into a large number of exogamous clans, each of which has a family surname, analogous to the *inti-pērlu* of the Telugus. As is natural in a caste which is jealous of the purity of its blood in a foreign country, intermarriage is usually allowed only between such clans as have been previously connected by the marriage tie. The ceremonies preliminary to a wedding are performed separately for bride and bridegroom in their respective houses, and each party should erect a pandal.[1] Their customs follow the Telugu-Kanarese type. They prefer to burn the dead, though sepulture is permissible. They observe the anniversary of the dead by a few gifts to needy Brahmans. They worship Pārvati under the name of Bhavāni, and observe the Sakti cults.[2]

Marāthas.

Rajputs.

Rājputs number only 683, most of whom are to be found in Salem and Hosūr Taluks.[3] The majority of these families migrated from North India not more than half a dozen generations ago. They go by the title Singh, observe *gōsha*, wear the sacred thread, and hold themselves aloof from their Dravidian neighbours. Some of them serve Government as Village Munsifs.[4]

The Rāzus.

Rāzus, who number only 332, occur in Hosūr and Ūttankarai Taluks. They speak Telugu, and are supposed to be descendants of Kāpus who discarded their ancestral vocation for soldiering. They claim to be Kshatriyas, and are invested with a sacred thread of cotton and wool on the eve of marriage, but they eat the flesh of fowls, a diet which a true Kshatriya should avoid. They make excellent peons, and sometimes rise to higher grades in the service of Government.[5]

(10) Sectarian Lingāyats.

The great Sectarian Caste is that of the Vīra-Saivas or **Lingāyats,** who sprang into political importance during the

---

[1] *Baramahal Records,* Section III, p. 170, where a detailed description is given of their customs. An excellent account of the Marāthas by Major (now Col.) R.M. Betham of the 101st Grenadiers will be found in the Indian Army Handbook on *Marathas and Dekhani Musalmans* 1908.

[2] The fighting Marāthas must not be confused with the Marātha tailors (Nāmdēv) and dyers (Rangāris) commonly met with in South India. There are a few Rangāris in Hosūr Taluk. In Tali there is a small settlement of Marātha Bondilis.

[3] The Mittadar of Aikondam-Kotti-palli is a Rājput, and there are small settlements in the head-quarters of that Mitta, and also in Sandūr and Nāgōjana-halli (all in Krishnagiri Taluk).

[4] An elaborate sketch of the customs of the "Rachawaru" is given in *Baramahal Records,* Section III, p. 18, but it is not quite clear to what caste the description refers.

[5] For further details see *Castes and Tribes,* Vol. VI, 247 sq.

CHAP. III. SURVEY OF CASTES. Lingāyats.

brief regime of the Kalachūryas (Bījjala and his sons, 1157-88 A.D.). The essence of their history is a repudiation of orthodox Brahmanism, and their fortunes have been intimately associated with the fortunes of the Kanarese people, though their tenets are also widely spread among the Telugus. Theoretically all castes can be admitted to their fold; internally, however, the community has reverted to the type of orthodox Hinduism, and it is divided into innumerable endogamous groups, the *jus connubii* being defined, sometimes by language, sometimes by occupation, and sometimes by caste distinctions inherited from their unconverted ancestors. Hence it is that many Lingāyats still describe themselves as Kāpus, Balijas, Vakkiligas, etc. In the present District 7,578 persons are returned as Lingāyats, most of them residing in Hosūr Taluk. It is probable, however, that some, if not all, of the Jangams (14,360), Kannadiyans [1] (817), and Sadars [2] (370) are true Lingāyats. The Jangams are numerous in the four Talaghāt taluks, the other two sections are met with in Salem and Āttūr.

Though the Lingāyats as a sect trace their origin to Bījjala's minister Basava in the twelfth century A.D., the Vīra-Saiva faith is said to be of primeval origin, and its tenets are based on the Vēdas. It was founded by a number of Āchāryas, of whom the five most famous are known as the "Gōtrakartas of the Lingāyat Dwijas," having received "their mandate direct from Siva to establish his true religion on earth, or rather to restore it to its purity." [3]

The essence of Lingāyat faith is an unquestioning belief in the efficacy of the *lingam*, the symbol of Siva. The *lingam* is regarded as the "universal leveller," rendering all its wearers equal in the eyes of God. Unlike other Hindus, every Lingāyat always wears a *lingam* on some conspicuous part of his person. These Jangama *lingams*, or moveable *lingams*, are made of soapstone brought from Srīsaila in Kurnool District by a class of Lingāyats called Kambi Jangams. The *lingam* itself is not more than three-fourths of an inch in height; to keep it from harm it is "plastered with a black mixture of clay, cowdung ashes and marking-nut juice, forming a slight truncated cone, not unlike a dark betel nut, about three-quarters of an inch high, and

---

[1] Kannadiyan means literally a Kannada (or Kanarese) man. For further information, see *Madras Census Report*, 1891, paragraph 383, *North Arcot Manual*, p. 225, and *Castes and Tribes*, Vol. III, p. 200.

[2] For Sadar, see Mysore *Census Report*, 1891, p. 226, Buchanan's *Mysore*, I. p. 292, and *Castes and Tribes*, Vol. VI, p. 260.

[3] Mysore Census Report, 1901.

CHAP. III. SURVEY OF CASTES. Lingayats.

narrowing from three-quarters of an inch at the base to half an inch across the top.[1] " It is usually kept in a little silver box suspended by a cord, or tied in a silk cloth, round the neck, arm or forehead. Every child is invested with the *lingam* on the 7th or 11th day after birth, when the naming ceremony is performed, and his *lingam* must never leave his possession till he dies, and it is placed in his left hand when his body is committed to the grave.

The strength of the Lingāyats lies in their ecclesiastical organisation. Each of the five Gōtrakartas founded a ***Matam*** called *Simhāsana*, and these five ***Matams***, each under its own Āchārya, have divided the Lingāyats between them into five territorial dioceses. The five *Simhāsanas* are (1) Ujjani, in Kudligi Taluk, Bellary District, founded by Marulāchārya, (2) Balehonnūr, in Koppa Taluk, Kadūr District (Mysore State), founded by Rēnukāchārya, (3) Benares (Kāsi), founded by Visvāchārya, (4) Himavat-Kedara, in the Himalayas of Garhwal District (U.P.), founded by Ekoramāchārya, and (5) Srīsaila, otherwise called Parvata, in Kurnool District, founded by Panditāchārya. Each of these ***Matams*** has under it, wherever the community is numerous, a number of Sub-*Matams*, each under a Pattadaswāmi and each Sub-***Matam*** has a number of Branch-*Matams* called *Guru-stala-Matams*. The rights and duties of the *Swāmis* of these *Matams* are " to preside at all religious functions, to receive their dues, to impart religious instruction, to settle all religious and caste disputes, and to exercise a general control over all matters affecting the religious interests of the community at large.[2] " The descendants of the five Gōtrakartas form a separate sub-caste called Ārādhya Brahmans, who claim superiority over all other Lingāyats, and only marry among themselves, bury their dead in a sitting posture and observe death pollution for ten days like other Brahmans.[3] In addition to the above executive arrangements, the Vīra-Saivas possess another order of priests called Vīraktas or Shat-stala Nirabhāris, who hold the highest position in the ecclesiastical order, and therefore command the highest respect, from laymen as well as from the above-mentioned *Matams*. There are three chief Vīrakta ***Matams***, of which the Muragi *Matam* of

---

[1] Bombay Gazetteer of Bijāpur quoted in *Castes and Tribes*, Vol. IV, p. 256.

[2] So writes Mr. K. P. Puttanna Chettiyar, late Senior Councillor of Mysore, by whom most of the information regarding the hierarchical system has been supplied.

[3] See *Castes and Tribes*, Vol. I, p. 53, for further details.

CHAP. III. SURVEY OF CASTES. — Lingāyats.

Chitaldrug (Mysore State),[1] exercises authority in Salem District. These Vīrakta *Matams* have their respective Sub-*Matams* and Branch-*Matams* scattered throughout India. "Every Lingāyat centre has a Vīrakta-*Matam* built outside the town, in which the Swāmi leads a simple and spiritual life. Unlike other priests, the Vīrakta-Swāmi is prohibited from pr siding on ceremonial occasions, and from receiving unnecessary alms. He should devote his life partly to spiritual meditation, and partly to the spreading of spiritual knowledge among his disciples, so that he would be the fountain-head to whom all laymen and all priests must resort for spiritual enlightenment, in short his position is that of a pure Sanyāsi or Yati."

Caste disputes in Salem District are decided in the first instance by a *panchāyat*, presided over by a *Mahat-Padam* or *Mata-Mudirai*, the local representative of the *Matam* in whose jurisdiction the contending parties reside, assisted by the local headman (*Chetti*) who holds office by hereditary right, a *Yajamān*, and not less than two other caste-men. From this *panchāyat* an appeal lies to the nearest local Branch or Sub-*Matam*, in the case of Salem District to the *Matams* at Ballapalli, or Gummalāpuram in Hosūr Taluk, or Rājāpuram near Ānekal, all of which are branches of the Balehonnūr Head-*Matam*.

Lingāyats abstain strictly from animal food and from alcohol. They are unique, however, in refusing to observe any pollution period after childbirth, menstruation or death, it being held that, so long as the *lingam* is worn on the person, there can be no pollution. After attaining puberty the girl is purified with holy water, and so also on the tenth day after childbirth, but segregation is not resorted to, and no taboo appears to be observed. A pregnant woman is said to partake of a diet of clay and ashes, and she must not see an eclipse for fear her offspring may be a monster.

(11) Mendicants.

The Mendicant Castes are varied, but not numerous. The strongest numerically are the Āndis (7,128), the Pandārams (1,526) and the Jōgis (1,422), but all these terms are loosely used, and it cannot be said that any one of them refers to a true sub-caste. The word Pandāram is used for a class of priests who serve Vellālars, and whose social position is highly respected. A similar vagueness of meaning characterises the term *Dāsari* or Tāthan, Mondi, Bairāgi and Banda, a few of whom appear in the Census returns. The Vīramushtis and Mailāris beg only from Kōmatis and

[1] The other two Vīrakta Matams are (1) the Dombal Matam at Gadag and (2) the Murusa-Virada Matam at Hubli, both in Dharwar District.

other Vaisya Chettis, while the Pichigundlu (608) beg only from Kāpus and Gollas. The existence of these parasitic mendicants, who depend entirely on the charity of one or two specified castes, is an interesting characteristic of the social life of South India.[1]

(12) Miscellaneous.

A few remarks are necessary on the Kanakkans, Sātānis, Koravas, Dombaras, Lambādis and Irulas, who cannot be grouped under any of the above classes.

Kanakkans.

The **Kanakkans** (a caste of hereditary village accountants) according to the Census of 1911, numbered 3,354, most of whom occur in the taluks of Salem, Ōmalūr, Tiruchengōdu and Krishnagiri. It is possible, however, that many *karnams* were returned as Kanakkans, who do not belong to the Kanakkan caste at all[2]. The post of village accountant in Salem District is virtually a Brahman monopoly, except in the Taluks of Salem, Ōmalūr and Tiruchengōdu, where about 40 Government *karnams* are of Kanakkan caste.

Sātānis.

The **Sātānis**, a caste of temple servants, numbered only 2,479[3] and they are evenly distributed throughout the District. They reside mostly in towns, and are in no sense a rural community. Their traditional occupation is the performance of "menial services in Vishnu temples, but they supplement their earnings by begging, tending flower-gardens, selling flower-garlands, making fans, grinding sandal-wood into powder, and selling perfumes.[4]" They act as *purōhits* to many castes, notably to the Balijas and Kōmatis. They object to the term Sātāni, by which they are generally known, and prefer to be called Sāttāda-Vaishnavas[5]. In their customs they approximate closely to Tengalai-Vaishnava Brahmans. They call themselves "Ayya," shave their head completely, and tie their *vēshti* like a Brahman bachelor. They do not, however, wear the sacred thread, and some of them bury their dead. Their women-folk dress like Vaishnava Brahman ladies. They are divided into four sections; (1) Ēkāksharis, who win salvation by the *one* mystic monosyllable *Ōm*, and who are said

---

[1] An excellent account of the Mendicant castes is given by Mr. Francis in the *Census Report* for 1901 under the head of Āndi (p. 141). An exhaustive list of references is there given.

[2] The extraordinary variations in the proportion of males to females in the several taluks seems to indicate that the Census statistics of Kanakkans are not quite reliable.

[3] In no district of the Madras Presidency are the Sātānis a numerous community, though there are several hundreds of them in every district, except on the West Coast and in the Nilgiris. In 1901 in only two districts (Coimbatore and Ganjam) did their numbers exceed 3,000.

[4] *North Arcot District Manual*, Vol. I, p. 200.

[5] Or Prapanna Vaishnava, Nambi, Venkatapura Vaishnava, etc., see *Castes and Tribes*, Vol. VI, p. 300.

CHAP. III. SURVEY OF CASTES.

Sātānis.

to take precedence of the remaining sections; (2) Chaturākshari whose sacred utterance is the quadrisyllabic Rā-mā-nu-ja; (3) Ashtākksharis whose shibboleth is the octosyllabic Ōm-na-mō-nā-rā-ya-nā-ya (Ōm, salutation to Nārāyana) and (4) Kulasēkharas, who claim descent from the Vaishnava saint Kulasēkhara Ālvār, a king of Kērala. These groups were at one time endogamous, but it is said the first three are now permitted to intermarry.

Koravas.

[1] The **Koravas**, who numbered 14,688, are commonly spoken of as a gipsy tribe, but in some parts of Salem District they have organised a regular *Kāval* system, similar to that of the Kallans in Trichinopoly and Tanjore. They are commonest in Āttūr (5,754) and Ūttankarai (2,486), and they are to be found in every taluk of the District. Their language is a medley of Tamil, Telugu and Kanarese, the Tamil element usually preponderating, and they use their own peculiar thieves' slang. Difference in language is not, apparently, a bar to intermarriage. The exact relationship that their numerous sub-divisions bear to one another is by no means clear. The best known sections are: (1) Dhabbai (basket), (2) Uppu (salt), (3) Karuvēppilai (*Murraya Koenigii*) and (4) Kāvalkāran (guard) Koravas, all of which are probably true sub-castes. The Dhabbai Koravas (also called Ūru-Koravas) make baskets and other articles of bamboo and palm-leaves. The Uppu Koravas, who are also known as Ghattada or Ettina Koravas, are itinerant traders in salt. It is doubtful whether the Kunjam (fan), Nari (jackal) and Pūnai-kutti (cat-killing) Koravas are distinct sub-castes, or whether any of these terms are synonymous with other sections. The Pachai-kutti Koravas enjoy almost a monopoly in the art of tattooing. The Ina Koravas (called also Mudichi-avukki or Mudichumāri) are pickpockets. All Koravas appear to recognise four quasi-exogamous subdivisions, viz. (1) Kāvadi, (2) Mēnpādi, (3) Mēndra-kutti and (4) Sāttupadi. These names are said to be connected with worship; Kāvadis carry the *kāvadi* so frequently associated with the worship of Subrahmanya, who is the patron deity of the whole caste; Mēnpādis sing praises, and Mēndra-kuttis offer shoes to the idol, while Sāttupadis adorn their god with flowers and jewels.[2] The Kāvadis and Sāttupadis rank higher than the other sections, and are alone regarded as true Koravas. Two other clans are reported, the Uyyālu (from *ūnjal*,

---

[1] In the Census Returns they are called Kuruvans; they are also called Korama and Koracha, and appear to be identical with the Yerukalas of the northern districts of the Madras Presidency; see *Castes and Tribes*, Vol. III, p. 439 sq.

[2] The etymology seems fanciful, and has not been tested by observance of actual custom.

a swing) and the Bandi (cart). According to one account the Kāvadi and Sāttupadi sections may not intermarry, and must choose their brides from the Mēnpādis or Mēndra-kuttis, who also are prohibited from intermarrying with each other; according to another account the Kāvadis and Uyyālus form one *dāyādi vaguppu* and the Bandis, Mēnpādi, Mēndra-kuttis and Sāttupadis another, marriage only being allowed between the two *vaguppus*. Kāvalkāra Koravas are also called Morasu, Monda and Kādu-kutti (ear-boring); but the significance of these terms is not clear. The Kāvalkāra Koravas of the Talaghāt are divided into three groups, which are endogamous, viz. (1) Mēl-Nād, residing south of Salem, (2) Āttūr-Nād, east of Āttūr, and (3) Salem-Nād, west of Āttūr and east of Salem. Of these, the Salem-Nād Koravas claim superiority,[1] and are said to employ Brahman *purōhits*, and their customs approximate more closely than those of the other Nāds to the orthodox customs of Hinduism; they also abstain from eating squirrels, cats or tortoises, which are eaten by Koravas of the other Nāds. Korava *panchāyats* in the Talaghāt are presided over by a *Pattanam-Chetti*, a Balija by caste, who resides in Āttūr. The price of adultery is five Pagodas (Rs. 17½), and of assault Rs. 5. In addition to the ordeals of hot iron and boiling ghee, a suspected Korava is sometimes made to drink water mingled with ashes from a burning-ground, and, if he vomits, his guilt is established. Another test, as between two litigants, is for each party to boil simultaneously a pot of rice and water, the party whose pot boils first being acquitted.

Koravas are hard drinkers, and their morals are loose. Polygamy is freely practised, widows and *divorcées* may re-marry. Marriage is usually adult, and the wife may be older than the husband. Among the Uppu and Karuvēppilai Koravas the bride-price is said to be as much as Rs. 70, but this is paid in instalments, and the payment of these instalments is a fruitful source of quarrels, the full amount being but rarely paid up. The *tāli* consists of a string of black beads. At a wedding of Kāvalkāra Koravas a pandal is erected, and covered with leaves of Nāga-maram (*Eugenia jambolana*), and the bride and bridegroom take their seats on a rice-pounding pestle, covered with a yellow cloth. The *tāli* is of gold, and is tied with a yellow thread.

The proper dress for a Korachi is a coarse black cloth, but they also wear stolen cloths of any kind. They affect necklaces of cowries and green beads, bangles of brass from the elbow to the wrist, and cheap rings of brass, lead and silver on all except the

---

[1] The Salem-Nād Koravas use a *Kankanam* of cotton-thread smeared with saffron at marriages, the Mēl-Nād Koravas use a *kankanam* of wool.

CHAP. III. SURVEY OF CASTES.

Koravas.

middle finger. Their criminal methods are described on Vol. II, p. 94. Their *Kāval* fees (*mērai*) consists of 12 Madras measures of grain and a sheep per annum from each household, and Rs. 6 for every tope of coco-nut or areca. The salutary custom of recovering, or giving compensation for, all property stolen in villages protected by the *kāval* is unfortunately dying out. When a burglary is committed, those who enter the houses looted claim two-thirds of the loot, and those who " keep *cave* " outside are entitled to one-third. It is said that two shares are also allotted to the headman, half shares to wives whose husbands are in jail, a fourth share each to old men, and to those who stay at home to guard the huts and personate those who have gone out to commit crime, and an eighth share to their *Swāmi*. To evade identification every Korava has a bewildering string of *aliases*, both for his own, and for his father's name.

Koravas bury their dead. Among the Uppu Koravas, if the deceased be unmarried, the body is wrapped in a yellow sheet and decked with flowers, and if married in a white sheet, while the corpse of a widow is honoured with neither sheet nor flowers.

Dombaras.

The clever acrobats known as **Dombaras**,[1] Dommaras or Domars, are found in every taluk of the District, though they number only 741. Their original habit is nomadic, but in the Bāramahāl some members of the caste have settled. They recount a story that their original ancestor, one Krishna Reddi, being childless, vowed to the god Chenna-Kēsvara that if issue were granted him, the first-born, if a boy, should follow his father's profession, and if a girl, should become a public prostitute. His prayer was granted, and a daughter was born to him, and from her all Dombaras are descended.[2] They are said to recognise four sub-castes[3]: (1) Reddi, (2) Pōkanāti, (3) Ara[4], (4) Marāthi. The first two speak Telugu in a corrupted form,[5] the last two speak Marāthi and Hindustani. The Pōkanātis abandoned their life of wandering and settled round Kuppam. All four groups profess to be Vaishnavites.

---

[1] The name is said to be derived from *dombam*, the vertical pole on which most of their feats are performed. A favourite trick is for one of their company to swarm up this pole, and lying flat in his belly, to turn rapidly round and round (see *Castes and Tribes*, Vol. II, p. 190). On the word Dombar, see also *E.S.M.*, No. XIII, p. 1.

[2] Two interesting legends of their origin are given in *E.S.M.*, No. XIII, p. 2.

[3] In *E.S.M.*, loc. cit. only two sub-castes are recognised, viz., Ūru and Kādu Dombaras.

[4] The word Ara is said by some to mean nothing more than Marāthi. The Ara Dombaras, however, declare it to be a corruption of Arabi, and trace their origin to an Arabian lover of Krishna Reddi's daughter.

[5] See the Vocabulary published in *E.S.M.*, pp. 24–30.

They are divided into numerous exogamous clans,[1] of which the following are reported from Salem District: (1) Matlivāllu, "the people of Matli", the name of their Guru, and, it is said, of the village of Chitvēl in Cuddapah District, which is still their head-quarters, and in which their chief Guru still resides; (2) Dalavāyālu, the clan from which their Dalavāy, or "war minister" is selected; (3) Kāserupu-vāllu, so called from a village in Cuddapah District where a certain Dombara won the prize in a competition of acrobatic feats; (4) Sondūru-vāllu, a clan of Dombaras who lived in a *vanam* (desert) in Cuddapah; (5) Nadu-mulēni-vāllu, "men without waists;" (6) Nātakarāyani-vāllu, "dramatists"; (7) Murāri-vāllu, "the servant people", originally attendants of the Matli-vāllu. Once in five years a great gathering of Dombaras assembles at Bērikai under the presidency of a hereditary *Yejamān* (or *Dorai*), assisted by a hereditary *Dalavāy* or *Mandiri*, and a council of 10 or 15, selected by these officers from their own relatives. The meeting opens on the Telugu New Year's Day, and its time is devoted to deciding caste disputes, arranging marriages, and punishing evil doers. Delinquents are branded on the tongue, or flogged with tamarind twigs till the blood flows. An excommunicate may be readmitted to caste on undergoing the punishments orderedby the Yejamān, who sprinkles him with *tīrtam* and gives him some to drink. A wife suspected of misconduct is made to stand during her trial in a bending posture, onions and radishes are suspended from her ears, and two grindstones are hung by a rope round her neck.

Dombaras of migratory habits live in portable huts of bamboo and the leaves of palmyra or coco-nut, which they carry from place to place on asses; settled Dombaras earn a living by breeding pigs and asses, and selling needles, bhads, combs, etc.[2] Their marriage ceremonies are curious and elaborate, as also are those connected with the attainment of puberty, but unfortunately space does not permit any detailed description.[3] The bride-price is Rs. 54, a figure unusually high. Sometimes a Brahman is called in to officiate on the day the *tāli* is tied, but otherwise Brahmans are not employed. Among the settled Dombaras widow remarriage is forbidden, but a widow is at liberty to live in concubinage, provided she feasts some of her relatives on the

---

[1] See the list on p. 31 of *E.S.M.*, No. XIII, where the subdivisions are, however, described as "neither endogamous nor exogamous."

[2] See *E.S.M.*, No. XIII, p. 21, for the story which accounts for their special industry, the manufacture of wooden combs.

[3] An excellent account of both is given in *E.S.M.*, No. XIII, pp. 5 to 9.

CHAP. III. SURVEY OF CASTES. Dombaras.

night she enters her new house. The wandering Dombaras, however, freely tolerate remarriage. To avert the Evil Eye when performing their feats of skill, they wear a black woollen thread on the leg or arm. They bury their dead, and their funerals are celebrated with much hard drinking. Their patron goddess is Ellamma.

Lambādis.

The itinerant gipsy tribe of **Lambādis**, otherwise known as Sukālis or Brinjāris,[1] numbers only 1,386, and is mostly confined to the taluks of Hosūr, Dharmapuri, and Ūttankarai. In the wars of the eighteenth century they played an important part as carriers for both the British and the Mysorean troops, and the pages of Buchanan and other contemporary writers present a vivid picture of the depredations they committed in the villages along their line of march. Lambādis contributed materially to the depopulation of the Kāvēri-side villages of Hosūr and Dharmapuri.[2] "Even in the time of peace" writes Buchanan,[3] they "cannot entirely abstain from plunder. In the small villages near the forest they occasionally rob and commit murder. Nor is it safe for one or two persons to pass unarmed through places in which they are. On account of their services during the two last wars, they have hitherto been treated with great indulgence. This has added audaciousness to the natural barbarity of their disposition, and in order to repress their insolence it was lately necessary to have recourse to a regular military force." Buchanan mentions a company of them that employed 12,000 cattle, and obtained from Tipu a "monopoly of every article of commerce except cloth, tobacco, and boiled butter, which continued open".

Their criminal propensities have not abated. "In February 1905, a boy who was tending cattle on the banks of the Kāvēri near Pennāgaram was missed by his father, who on search came to know that he has been sold by a shepherd for Rs. 22. Sometime afterwards the boy was recovered near Tumkūr, in Mysore State, from the house of a Lambādi, who had bought the boy from a woman of his own caste for Rs. 32. Both these Lambādis admitted the transaction in the Sessions Court, and pleaded justification, on the ground that it was usual among Lambādis to buy and sell orphans. They admitted, too, that the boy had often

[1] A distinction appears to exist between the terms Sukāli and Brinjāri (or Banjāri), but the nature of the distinction is not clear—vide *Castes and Tribes*, Vol. IV, p. 210. For detailed description of the caste see *E.S.M.* No. XXV, cf. *Bellary District Gazetteer*, p. 74.

[2] See below Vol. II, p. 110.

[3] Buchanan Vol. II, p. 438.

requested them to send him to his parents. The boy said that he had been treated kindly." [1]

Irulas.

The jungle tribe of **Irulas** numbers 4,161, and is practically confined to the Bāramahāl and Bālāghāt. "They are very wild and suspicious in their habits, distrusting their more civilised neighbours, who in return fear them as possessed of mysterious powers derived from witchcraft. The Irulas are supposed to hold some valuable secrets as to the medicinal and other properties of herbs and drugs obtainable in the jungles. It is probable that they do; but they are so reticent on the subject that nothing of value can be extracted from them. Their chief source of livelihood consists in collecting the various kinds of jungle produce, dyes, wax, nuts, etc., for sale."[2] On account of their occult powers they are popularly called *Kāttu Pūjāris*, or "Priests of the Jungle."

(13) Panchamas.

The Panchamas, (the "fifth caste", as the name implies), include (1) the Tamil Pariahs, or, more correctly, Paraiyans, (2) the Telugu Mālas, (3) the Kanarese Holeyas, (4) the Valluvans or Pariah Priests,(5) the Chucklers, or, more correctly, Sakkiliyans, and (6) the Mādigas, both Telugu and Kanarese. The Mālas and Holeyas hold the same position in the social scale of the Telugu and Kanarese castes respectively as the Pariahs do among the Tamils. The Mādigas, or Telugu leather-workers, correspond in the Telugu country to the Chucklers in the Tamil country, though the Chucklers also usually speak Telugu. The Pariahs number nearly 150,000, and are evenly distributed throughout the District, being specially strong in Salem, Āttūr and Ūttankarai Taluks. The Mālas are returned as 16,347. The Census Returns show no Holeyas, but it is certain they have been included in the Pariahs and Mālas. The Valluvans muster nearly 4,000, and are evenly distributed. The Chucklers number nearly 60,000, the Mādigas a little less than 3,000.

Paraiyans.

Unfortunately little is known regarding the various sub-castes of **Paraiyans**.[3] The best known sub-caste is that of the Tangalāns, from whom most of the servants of Europeans are drawn. They are identified by some with the Vadakkatti Paraiyans. These two classes occur throughout the Talaghāt, and are also common in Ūttankarai and Dharmapuri Taluks. Konga Paraiyans are common in Hosūr Taluk, and also in Salem, Ōmalūr and Tiruchengōdu. They comprise two sub-castes (1) Otta-valaiyal, and

[1] *Madras Mail* of 16th April 1907.

[2] S.D.M., Vol. II, p. 166. For further details see *Castes and Tribes*, Vol. II, p. 372 sq. and *South Arcot District Gazetteer*, p. 210.

[3] In the Census of 1891, as many as 348 sub-divisions were recorded, but the list is of little scientific value.

Paraiyans.

(2) Retta-valaiyal; the women-folk of the former wear bangles of the chank[1] shell on the left arm only, the latter wear ordinary bangles on both arms. The females of the Konga Paraiyans are distinguished from others by wearing their upper cloth on the right hip. The Otta-valaiyal Paraiyans, who are found at Rāsipuram and Nāmagiripet, are said to prohibit the re-marriage of widows and the eating of frogs, the Retta-valaiyal Paraiyans permit both practices. The Kīzhakkatti Paraiyans[2] are also described as frog-eating (*Tavalai-tinni*). Sōliya (Chōla) Pariahs are found in Salem and Ōmalūr, and are by some identified with the Kīzhakkattis. Katti Paraiyans are so called on account of their hereditary occupation of iron-smelting (Katti = pig-iron); they are common in Dharmapuri, Ōmalūr, Salem and Āttūr. The Paraiyans are served by Pariah washermen, who do not intermarry with other Paraiyans, and form a true sub-caste, and the same appears to hold good of their barbers also. In Hosūr Taluk, there are several settlements of Tamil-speaking Tigala Paraiyans, who also seem to be a distinct sub-caste, immigrants from the Tamil country, who have settled[3] among the Telugus and Kanarese. The so-called Koleya, Morasu, Magga, and Kannadiya Paraiyans would more correctly be described as Holeyas, and the Manna, Vaduga, and Tonda Paraiyans as Mālas.

Pariahs look down upon Mālas, Holeyas, Mādigas and Chucklers, and will not dine with them. Being of the Right Hand Faction, they appear to bear a special antipathy against Kammālars Vāniyars and Nagarattu Chettis, and will not receive food from their hands. For *purōhits* they usually employ Valluvans.

Valluvans.

The **Valluvans** are Pandārams (priests) to the Paraiyans, and officiate as *purōhits* at their marriages and at most auspicious ceremonies, but do not intermarry with them. They are celebrated as fortune-tellers (*jōsiyam*) and exorcists, and as such are respected even by Brahmans. They occur in all the taluks, but are rare in Hosūr, and most numerous in Salem and Āttūr. The term Valluvar appears to include several sub-castes, such as Tiru-Valluvar, Kai-pidi, Pū-katti, Moram-katti.[4] The Tiru-Valluvars do not interdine with other Paraiyans, and some of them have adopted the sacred thread; they sometimes call themselves "Nāyanār." The other three sub-castes eat with Paraiyans, provided the meal is prepared in a new vessel. Valluvars are reported

---

[1] Perhaps therefore to be identified with the Sanku Paraiyans or Sankū-katti.

[2] Esp. Talaivāsal, Oduvan-kurichi and Rāsipuram.

[3] Cf. Tigala Pallis, p. 143, note 5.

[4] They are divided into two factions, the Arupathu-Katchi and the Nārpathu-Katchi (the "sixty" and the "forty"); *Castes and Tribes*, s.v., p. 305.

to abstain from eating beef; they are both Vaishnavites and Saivites, the latter being buried in a sitting posture; the two sects intermarry, and are common in the Talaghāt and in Dharmapuri Taluk.

Mālas. The sub-castes of the **Mālas** of Salem District are yet to be defined. Though the Census statistics confine the Mālas to Hosūr Taluk, the Vaduga Paraiyans of Ūttankarai Taluk and the Manna (or Mannai) Paraiyans of Dharmapuri, Salem and Ōmalūr Taluks, all of whom speak Telugu, should probably be classed among them.[1] There is a fairly large settlement of Manna Paraiyans in Kichi-pālaiyam in Salem City, who are said to hold themselves aloof from other Paraiyans and abstain from the eating of beef. In Dharmapuri, however, they appear to be looked down upon by both the Tamil Paraiyans and the Holeyas. Generally speaking, Holeyas and Mālas may "interdine", but may not intermarry.

Holeyas. In Salem District **Holeyas** are known as Morasu, Magga, or Koleya Paraiyans. They are common in Hosūr and Krishnagiri, and in the west of Dharmapuri, and a few settlements occur in Ūttankarai, Salem, Ōmalūr and Tiruchengōdu. "Morasu" is a general term for the people of the Morasu Nād, and "Magge" (loom) indicates one of their distinctive occupations, the weaving of coarse cotton cloths, a vocation they follow even in the Talaghāt. It is not clear whether more than one true sub-caste is represented in the District, as the Morasus appear to include the Maggas.

Chucklers. Of the 60,000 **Chucklers** in the District, over 20,000 occur in Tiruchengōdu Taluk, nearly as many in Salem, and about 5,000 in Ōmalūr; they are well represented in all the other taluks, though it is probable that a good number of Mādigas have been classed under this head in Hosūr Taluk and the adjoining tracts. They are usually classed as a Telugu caste, though in some parts they speak Tamil and also Kanarese. Their hereditary vocation is the tanning and working of leather, and they are accounted the lowest of all in the social scale, even the Pariahs despising them. The factious feeling that subsists between the Right Hand and Left Hand castes is concentrated in the primeval feud between Pariahs and Chucklers, and the brawls that still occasionally give vent to this feeling are generally precipitated by a collision between these two castes. The Chucklers beat tom-toms for Kammālans,

---

[1] Half a dozen divisions of "Telugu Holeyas" are given by Mr. H. V. Nunjundayya in *E.S.M.* II, Holeya, p. 5, and another ten in *Castes and Tribes*, Vol. IV, p. 345. These two lists have only one item in common (Pākanāti) and hence generalisation is impossible. An interesting account of the customs of the Mālas by the Rev. S. Nicholson is given in the last-named Volume, pp. 345—384.

CHAP. III. SURVEY OF CASTES.

Chucklers.

Kaikōlans and other Left Hand castes. The habits of their men are intemperate and insanitary, but their women are exceptionally beautiful, and are reputed virtuous. They are said to have no endogamous divisions within themselves, but they are divided into exogamous clans (*kilais*). As might be expected, they reverence the *āvāram* shrub (*Cassia auriculata*), the most valuable source of tanning bark, and at their marriages the *tāli* is tied to a branch of this plant. They worship Madura-Vīran, Māri-amma, and Draupadi, but their special deity is Gangamma, who, in the form of three pots of water, is honoured annually with a ten days' festival. Their name is associated with the worship of Ellamma,[1] but they do not observe the cult of Mātangi, the goddess of their Mādiga cousins, and do not, like them, dedicate their daughters as Basavis.

Mādigas.

The **Mādigas**, or leather-workers of the Telugu-Kanarese country, according to the Census Returns, are confined to Hosūr Taluk, but, as already stated, it is not unlikely that many of them have been included among the Chucklers. The Telugu and Kanarese sections may not intermarry, and each section is divided into three sub-castes, according as they use an eating dish, a basket or a winnow to hold the food consumed at the common meal (*buvva*) at marriage.[2] Their *purōhits*, known as Jāmbavas, are permitted to take to wife the daughters of the other sub-castes, but may not give their daughters in marriage to any but Jāmbavas, an interesting custom, as instances of hypergamy are rare in South India, except on the Malabar Coast. Mādigas have their own mendicant sub-castes, Dakkulus, Māstigas, Māchālas, etc. Their religion is characterised by the cult of the goddess Mātangi (see p. 119), and by the consecration of an unmarried girl as an incarnation of that goddess. Māri-amman is also venerated by the Mādigas, and her worship is accompanied with an elaborate buffalo sacrifice. There is a traditional connection between the Mādigas and the Gollas, Mutrāchas and Kōmatis.[3]

---

[1] Vide p. 119 *supra*.

[2] They are called respectively (1) Tale-Buvvamu-vāllu (Tel.), Taniga-Buvvada-vāru (Kan.) (dish); (2) Gampa-Buvvamu-vāllu (Tel.), Hedige-Buvvada-vāru (Kan.) (basket), and (3) Chātla-Buvvamu-vāllu (Tel.), Mōra-Buvvada-vāru (Kan.) (winnow) (vide *E.S.M.*, XVII, p. 5). In *Castes and Tribes*, Vol. IV, p. 318, six endogamous sub-castes are given.

[3] Excellent notices of the Mādigas are given in *Castes and Tribes*, Vol. IV and in *E.S.M.*, No. XVII.

CHAPTER IV.

AGRICULTURE AND IRRIGATION.

AGRICULTURE.—Staple Crops—Dry and Wet—Seasons—Mixed Crops—Rotation—Implements—Manures—Protection—Threshing—Storage—Hill Cultivation. CHIEF CROPS.—I. IRRIGATED CROPS.—Paddy—Wheat—Sugar-cane—Coco-nut—Areca-nut—Betel-vine—Plantains. II. UNIRRIGATED CROPS.—(a) CEREALS.—Rāgi—Kambu—Chōlam—Minor Cereals. (b) PULSES.—Horse-gram—Dhall—Avarai—Other Pulses. (c) OIL-SEEDS.—Gingelly—Castor—Ground-nut—(d) CONDIMENTS, ETC.—Chillies—Coriander—Other Condiments—Vegetables. (e) SPECIAL PRODUCTS.—Tobacco—Cotton—Indigo—Coffee—Tea—Rubber—Aloe—Hemp. (f) FRUIT CULTURE.—Mangoes—Inarching. IRRIGATION.—Major Works—Minor Works—Turns—Baling—*Kuttais*—Bārūr Project—Penukondapuram—SCHEMES—Kāvēri Project—Gōdumalai—Krishnagiri—Mārūnda-halli—Pula-halli—Badē Talāv—Minor Schemes. AGRICULTURAL ECONOMY.—Census Returns—Rent-Roll—Rents—Sale-values—Land Transfers—Waste—Wages—Credit.

AGRICULTURE.

Staple Crops.

THE chief food grains in the District are rāgi and kambu. Rāgi is by far the most important crop in Hosūr Taluk. In Tali Firkā it covers 85 per cent. of the total area cropped. It also takes precedence of kambu in Dharmapuri and in the southern half of Ūttankarai. In Krishnagiri, however, in the northern half of Ūttankarai, and in Salem, it yields the first place to kambu. In Āttūr rāgi is slightly ahead of kambu, but in Tiruchengōdu kambu covers over half the area cropped. Chōlam (*Sorghum vulgare*) is of importance in the Talaghāt taluks. "Other cereals" are largely grown on the poorer soils, chief among them being sāmai and tenai. Pulses, conspicuous among them being horse-gram, cover about one-fifth of the cropped area in the Bāramahāl and Bālāghāt taluks and in Ōmalūr. They are rather less important elsewhere, falling to a little under 10 per cent. in Salem and Āttūr. Lastly, in Dharmapuri Taluk, gingelly is extensively grown. The subjoined statement[1] shows at a glance the relative importance of these crops as compared with the area under paddy.

[1] Percentage of the total cropped area (including wet lands) in Fasli 1320 (1910–11) in the Taluks of

Grain.	Salem.	Ōmalūr.	Tiruchengōdu.	Āttūr.	Krishnagiri.	Dharmapuri.	Ūttankarai.	Hosūr.
Paddy	19	5	7	18	11	10	7	8
Rāgi	10	21	6	12	17	23	20	50
Kambu	18	21	51	12	25	12	15	6
Chōlam	12	4	6	11	1	3	6	2
Other Cereals ...	15	19	5	25	14	18	22	2
Pulses	9	23	15	10	19	19	22	21
Gingelly	...	2	1	...	6	11	2	6

CHAP. IV. AGRICULTURE.

Dry and Wet.

Salem District, as at present constituted, is essentially a "dry" District. Exact accounts for Mitta villages are not forthcoming, but the statistics of Government villages afford a fair index of the relative proportions of dry and wet. The percentages of wet and dry land under occupation in ryotwari villages are given in the margin. Āttūr is the best watered Taluk and Ūttankarai the driest.

	Wet.	Dry.
Salem ...	6	94
Tiruchengōdu	5	95
Āttūr ...	12	88
Ūttankarai	4	96
Dharmapuri	7	93
Krishnagiri	9	91
Hosūr ...	7	93

The distinction, however, between "Dry" and "Wet" crops is not inflexible. "Dry paddy" is cultivated on a small scale all over the District where suitable conditions prevail, and in Mēchēri Firka plantains are cultivated without irrigation. On the other hand, rāgi, kambu, chōlam, gingelly and castor are cultivated on lands irrigable by wells, tanks and channels, and tobacco may be either rain-fed or irrigated. Though a much larger return is realised under irrigation, rain-fed paddy, plantains and tobacco are usually considered superior in quality.

Seasons.

Roughly speaking, the agricultural year may be divided into three seasons, (1) the dry season from January to mid April, (2) the early rains (inclusive of the mango showers and the south-west monsoon) from April to September, and (3) the later rains, (north-east monsoon) from September to December. The break between the two monsoons is variable in its duration and in the time of its occurrence. In the Talaghāt and Bāramahāl each monsoon has its appropriate cultural operations. In the Bālāghāt, however, there is a tendency to merge the two seasons into one; the early showers are utilised for the preparation of the soil; sowing is deferred till the end of July or August; and the crops are matured by the north-east monsoon. Hence Hosūr Taluk is more dependent on the south-west than on the north-east monsoon, and if the latter is protracted the crops are spoiled.

Mixed Crops.

An interesting feature in the agriculture of the District is the practice of mixing the crops grown on unirrigated lands. Two systems of mixed cultivation are in vogue; one is to scatter mixed seed broadcast, the other to plant it in parallel furrows (*sāl*) about 4 feet apart, the intervening space being occupied by one or other of the staple food grains. By sowing a short crop and a long crop together, both space and labour are economised without exhausting the soil. The short crop matures in three or four months without being cramped by the slower growing long crop, and after the short crop is reaped, the long crop has time and space to mature.

(*a*) The broadcast system is seen to perfection on the Kollimalais, where, on the richest fields, in a good season, six or seven kinds of grain, (among them rāgi, castor, dhall, sāmai, tenai, avarai and mustard), can be seen growing together in one rank tangle, aptly described as a "riot of contending crops." Elsewhere the mixture is not so varied. In Hosūr a favourite mixture [1] is rāgi and mustard in the proportion of 99 : 1, or rāgi, mustard and tenai in the proportion of 200 : 1 : ½. In Tiruchengōdu Taluk kambu is sometimes mixed with gingelly, and sometimes with cotton.

(*b*) Under the furrow system the mixed seeds are either dibbled or sown with the subsidiary or single seed-drill, (p. 209). The chief bye-crops so grown are avarai in Hosūr, dhall in the Bāramahāl, and castor in the Talaghāt; but all three are grown throughout the District, not infrequently together in the same furrow. In Hosūr the usual practice is to sow *sāls* of avarai, wild-gingelly and kāki-chōlam in fields in which rāgi and mustard have been sown, either broadcast or with the multiple seed-drill, the crops being harvested in the following order:—(1) kāki-chōlam, (2) mustard, (3) rāgi, (4) wild-gingelly, (5) avarai. The main crop is most often rāgi, but dhall is grown in rows in fields of kambu or of sāmai, and in Hosūr dhall and makka-chōlam (maize) are grown in rows with black-paddy between them, dhall and castor in rows with ordinary gingelly between them, and wild-gingelly in rows in fields of black-gram. Usually all the seeds are sown simultaneously, but sometimes the *sāls* are sown a month in advance of the main crop. If the season be favourable, horse-gram can be sown between the *sāls* as a second crop after the rāgi is reaped, and iti s ready for harvest about the same time as slowly maturing castor or dhall.

Rotation. Except in Āttūr Taluk, the ryots have not developed the principles of rotation very far. In good seasons the best dry lands bear a double crop, the favourite second crops being horse-gram, sāmai or ground-nut. Horse-gram follows kambu, rāgi, gingelly or sāmai. Ground-nut does well after kambu, and sāmai after rāgi, gingelly or kambu. Gingelly is also followed by green-gram or varagu. In Ōmalūr Taluk rāgi or kambu is sown, in fields irrigable by baling, in June or July, and reaped in November, and is followed in December by irrigated chōlam.

In Āttūr Taluk the wet lands under the Swēta-nadi ordinarily bear five crops in two years, and the rotation is judiciously

[1] These mixed seeds are, however, usually sown in Hosūr Taluk by the ordinary seet-drill (p. 208), and broadcast hand-sowing is only used on about 10 per cent of the area cropped.

CHAP. IV. AGRICULTURE.

selected. For instance, in the first season the ryots raise, in turn, paddy, irrigated gingelly, and kambu, the gingelly being sown late in Tai (early February), and harvested late in Chittrai, or early in Vaiyāsi (May); the kambu follows later in Vaiyāsi (early June) and is reaped in Ādi (late July). The second year's paddy crop is sown late in Ādi (early August) and, after it is harvested, the cultivation of rāgi begins in Vaiyāsi (May-June) to be cropped in Āvani (August-September). The third year's paddy is sown in Kārtigai (November-December) and harvested in Panguni or Chittrai (April), and this is followed early in Vaiyāsi (late May) by a mixed crop of kambu and indigo, the former harvested in Ādi (July-August), and the latter in Āvani or early Purattāsi (late August to end of September). This is followed by a fourth paddy crop, and then a crop of kambu, and so on with endless variety.

Implements.

In the Talaghāt the implements of husbandry are of the type common to most Tamil districts, and include the ordinary wooden plough (Tamil = *kalappai*, Telugu = *madaka*, Kanarese = *nēgilu*), the hand-weeder (Tamil = *kalai-kotti* or *pillu-vetti*, Telugu = *chakrapāra*), the common hoe (Tamil = *manvetti* or *mammatti*, Telugu = *sanika*), the crow-bar (Tamil = *kadappārai*, Telugu = *gadāri*), the pick-axe (the English word is adopted with the vernacular *pikkāsu*, Telugu *guddali*), the heavy bill-hook (Tamil = *koduvāl*, Telugu = *matsu*) for lopping branches, the *akkaruvāl* for hacking at thorns and prickly-pear, the saw-edged sickle (Tamil = *karukkaruvāl*, Telugu = *kodavali*) for reaping, the ordinary agricultural knife (*aruvāl*) and the hooked knife (*kokki*), attached to a long bamboo, for snicking leaves and twigs from trees to feed the flock. For levelling wet lands after ploughing and before sowing or transplanting, the ordinary plank (Tamil = *parambu*, Telugu = *asanu-tōlē-māsu*) is used throughout the District.

The ryots of the Bālāghāt use several implements which are unknown to those of the Talaghāt. The *palaki* is a kind of harrow, used for levelling the ground after ploughing. It consists of a beam about 4′ or 5′ long, set with ten or twelve wooden teeth, like a large rake. To it is attached a long bamboo, to which a pair of bullocks are yoked. The *gorru* (Kan. = *kūrige*, Tamil = *sadaik-kuzhal*), is a seed-drill or drill-plough. It consists of a transverse beam, pierced at equal intervals by 10 or 12 hollow bamboos, which unite at the top in a wooden bowl or hopper. The lower ends of these bamboo tubes are jointed into other tubes, which project 3″ or more below the beam. The ends of these projecting tubes are cut diagonally, so that when the beam is drawn along the ground by a pair of bullocks, they serve at once to make the furrow, and introduce the seeds with which the bowl or hopper is fed. Sometimes a subsidiary tube and hopper are affixed to the extreme end of the beam, or dragged behind the seed-drill by means of a cord, 3′ or 4′ long, attached to the centre of the beam, for the purpose of sowing a *sāl* or row of pulses. Occasionally the *sāls* are sown by a plough with a single tube and hopper attached. The *guntaka*, or weeding-plough [1], consists of a beam, fitted with from 4 to 6 iron teeth, each tooth about 2″ wide, with about 1″ between them. The beam is drawn like a plough by bullocks over the ground, the teeth pointing somewhat forwards, and not straight down like a rake. This operation leaves the ground perfectly clean, except where the drills have deposited the seed. For hand-weeding the Hosūr ryots use, not the *kalai-kottu* of the Talaghāt, but an instrument called *dōkadu-pāra* (Kan. = *orevāre*, or Hind. = *kurpa*), something like a narrow shoe-last in shape, shod with a broad flat piece of iron at the toe, and pierced with a slit at the instep to admit the fingers into a sort of hilt. The instrument thus grasped is exactly at the proper angle to the ground, and the weeders, holding this in the right hand, work down between the drills, loosening the roots with the *dōkadu-pāra*, and pulling up the weeds with the left hand. Bālāghāt farmers also use mallets (Tam. *kottāppuli*, Tel. *kodatalu*) for breaking sods by hand, and to make the ground even ; a hurdle (*etta*), with its underside covered with thorns and twigs, is sometimes drawn over the fields.

In the Bāramahāl the implements used are mostly of the Talaghāt type, but the *palaki*, *gorru*, *guntaka* and *dōkadu-pāra* are by no means unknown.

Manures. In the Talaghāt and Bāramahāl the favourite mode of manuring land, both wet and dry, is to pen cattle or sheep on it. Green manures, of several kinds (see p. 256), are used for wet lands. One of the most valuable of green manures is indigo, but its use is confined to Āttūr Taluk. In the Bālāghāt the penning of cattle and sheep is comparatively rare, the ryots preferring to use their cowdung in the form of *brattis* as fuel. Their household and farmyard refuse, street sweepings, ashes, etc., they store in pits just outside the village. These pits are about 8′ or 10′ square and 6′ deep, and there are generally a couple of rows of them. Each household has its own pit, and no ryot dare pilfer from another's pit. The pit system has its own advantages, for the manure is protected from sun and wind, and its fertilising properties are improved by the retention of moisture. Tank-bed silt is used

[1] Also called *guntika* or *guntuva*, and in Kanarese, *kunte*.

CHAP. IV. AGRICULTURE.

throughout the District to improve the soil of both dry and wet fields, and in some localities pig-dung, purchased from Oddas, is highly valued.

Protection of Crops.

The ryot has to protect his crops against the depredations of beasts and birds, and also against the Evil Eye. On the hills, and in the neighbourhood of forest reserves, fields are frequently fenced with therns and cut scrub, but fencing is usually dispensed with elsewhere. Wild pigs are most destructive of rāgi, kambu, and sāmai, but it is said they will not touch horse-gram or gingelly; hence, for fields subject to their inroads, the latter crops are preferred. Birds are scared by clappers, and on the hills it is the practice to suspend to a long pole a bell or inverted kerosine oil tin, with a slip of wood inside it attached to a winnow in such a way that it rattles with every puff of wind. A similar purpose is served by tying to a tall pole a dead crow, a strip of blanket or cloth, or a dried plantain leaf, which flaps in the breeze. Throughout the District large priapic figures of straw or rags, with outstretched arms, and an inverted chatty for a head, are to be seen in the fields, their function being apparently, partly to scare birds, partly to avert the Evil Eye, and partly, as in ancient Greece and Rome, to induce productivity. The Evil Eye is also averted from the crop by decorating all conspicuous rocks and boulders with white discs, or grotesque white figures, or whitewashing them altogether. Whitewashed chatties, with or without black spots, or palmyra leaves stuck in the ground points uppermost, are equally efficient, and occasionally the skull of an ox on top of a post serves the same purpose. In short, judging from the precautions taken, the Evil Eye is the worst danger the ryot has to contend with.

Threshing.

The processes of threshing are similar to those of adjoining districts. Paddy, and other grain which is readily detached from the stalk, is first of all tied into small bundles and beaten by hand (*kai-adi*) on the threshing floor. It is then thrown loosely into heaps and beaten with sticks (*kōl-adi*). This process is often applied to pulses, gingelly and other pod-seeds. The most thorough mode of threshing, however, is to tread it out with oxen, and this method is applied to almost all grains, especially to those which, like rāgi and kambu, are difficult to extract.

Storage.

The Talaghāt ryots store their grain in little cylindrical granaries with a conical roof. These are built on stones, across which beams are laid. Above the beams are thorns, then kambu stalks, then mud plaster. The roof is thatched with kambu stalks, or sometimes with palmyra leaves. The walls are of dhall stalks, plastered inside with mud. The granaries are sometimes divided inside into four compartments by mud partitions, which cross at right angles. Access to the interior is obtained by an opening in the conical roof. Similar structures are used in the Bāramahāl. In the Bālāghāt grain is often stored in gigantic jars of earthenware (*tombai*). A distinctive feature of the Bālāghāt and the Northern and Western Bāramahāl are the rāgi pits (*pāttirams*), which are excavated in the rubbly subsoil, seemingly impervious to damp; they usually have a small manhole on top, are some 8′ or 10′ deep, and at the bottom average 18′ wide, the bottom being flat and the walls and top forming a dome. Rāgi so stored will remain for many years without spoiling, but it is dangerous to enter a pit till it has been properly ventilated on account of the carbon dioxide which is apt to accumulate within. These pits are less used than formerly, partly owing to so many villages being depopulated, and partly owing to the facilities created by railways and roads for disposing of the surplus produce of a good harvest.

Hill Cultivation. (1) Dry.

Cultivation on the hills differs but little from that of the plains, so far as dry crops are concerned. The Malaiyālis of the Shevaroys are extremely slovenly in their methods; they are in fact demoralised by the good wages offered in coffee estates, and they often leave their own fields fallow, and work on the estates instead. Elsewhere, and especially on the Kolli-malais, cultivation is scrupulously clean, and on the best lands finer crops are grown than can be seen anywhere on the plains. The fields have to be carefully terraced, and the cost of terracing is expressed in terms of grain. A sharp distinction is recognised between *ulavu-kādu*, or land which can be ploughed, and *kottu-kādu*, or land which can only be cultivated with a hoe.

(2) Wet.

Wet cultivation is to be found only on the Kolli-malais, where some 500 odd acres are classed as wet. Some of this *nanjai* is situated at a very high level, and depends for its moisture on the water which oozes from the hillside; some lies in the hollows of the valleys, where the drainage from the higher levels forms a water-logged morass; and occasionally, at still lower levels, where the drainage water emerges from the quagmire and cuts its way through firmer soil, the streamlets are dammed, and little channels are dug to conduct the water to strips of stream-side paddy-flats. The high-level *nanjai* is fairly firm, and most of it can be ploughed. The swampy low-level paddy-flats are often full of boggy pits in which the cultivator sinks up to his armpits or even to his neck; ploughing is impossible, and, in order to transplant seedlings, the labourer must sit on a plank. Two crops are sometimes grown on lands that can be ploughed, but the low-level *nanjai* is more retentive of moisture, and single crop in those fields yields more than a double crop at higher levels.

CHAP. IV. CHIEF CROPS. — I. IRRIGATED. Paddy.

The area under paddy cultivation in Fasli 1320 was a little over 180,000 acres, of which about 102,000 lay in the Talaghāt, and nearly 63,000 in the Bāramahāl. Salem had the largest area, with over 43,000 acres. Āttūr came next with nearly 30,000. Then followed in order, Dharmapuri (26,000), Krishnagiri (23,000), Tiruchengōdu (21,000), Hosūr (15,500), Ūttankarai (13,400), and Ōmalūr (8,000 odd).

The methods of paddy cultivation in Salem District do not differ materially from those of the districts[1] adjoining. There is a similar bewildering list of different varieties, a similar general classification into long-crop and short-crop paddies, and similar puzzling diversities of method and of seed-time and harvest in different localities. Theoretically[2] there are three seasons for cultivation.—(1) Right Season, also called *kālāvadi* :—Vaiyāsi, Āni and half of Ādi (from the middle of May to the end of July); (2) Middle Season : the latter half of Ādi with Āvani and Purattāsi, (from the beginning of August to the end of the first half of October); (3) "Hot Weather" : Kārtigai, Mārgali and Tai, (from the middle of November to the middle of February), the harvest being in the dry season. The month of Arpisi (October-November) is expressly excluded, and paddy cultivation in that month is proverbially unlucky. Again, paddy may be raised (1) entirely by irrigation ("wet" method or *sēttu-kāl*), (2) partly by irrigation and partly without it ("mixed" method or *puzhudi-kāl*), and (3) entirely as a dry crop. Again, paddy is sometimes sown broadcast, and sometimes transplanted; sometimes the seeds are sown "dry", and sometimes they are wetted first.

Long-crop paddy is ordinarily called *sambā*, and matures in from 5 to 8 months; short-crop paddies are classed as *kār* (four months) and *kuruvai* or *kūru* (three months). Usually the *kār* or *kuruvai* crop is the earlier crop, being cultivated in Chittrai or Vaiyāsi (April to June); and the *sambā* crop is planted from Āni to Āvani (June to September)[3]. In the Talaghāt, hot-weather *kār*

---

[1] See *Trichinopoly District Gazetteer* (1907), pp. 132–6, *South Arcot District Gazetteer* (1906), pp. 115–7, *Mysore Gazetteer* (1897), Vol. I, pp. 131–144, *North Arcot District Manual* (1895), Vol. I, pp. 260–2, *Coimbatore District Manual* (1887), pp. 214–6.

[2] Much of what follows is taken from a treatise on Paddy Cultivation in the District by Mr. C. Venkatāchāriār of Kadattūr.

[3] In Salem and Ōmalūr a *kār* crop is sown in Chittrai or Vaiyāsi (April to June), and harvested in Āvani (August-September), the second crop (*sambā*) is sown in Āvani or Purattāsi (September-October) and harvested in Mārgali or Tai (December-February). In Āttūr the seasons are different, a first crop, either *kār* or *sada-samba* is sown in Ādi (July-August), and harvested in Mārgali (December-January), and a second (*kār* or *kuruvai*) is sown in Tai (January-February), and harvested in Vaiyāsi (May-June), this of course being possible only in cases where irrigation is supplemented by wells.

is known as *Māsi-kār*, and in the northern Bāramahāl the *kār* crops are distinguished as *mukkār* and *pikkār* (fore-*kār* and after-*kār*), the latter being, like the *Māsi-kār*, sown in Mārgali. *Kuruvai* crops are sown about a month earlier than *kār* crops, and mature rather more rapidly.[1] Only under exceptionally favourable conditions, such as exist under some of the best irrigation sources of Āttūr, Tiruchengōdu and Salem, and under the Pennaiyar, can two crops of paddy be raised in one season.[2]

Various kinds of "dry" paddy, under the general name of *puzhudi-nel*, are grown to a limited extent in all the taluks. On the Shevaroys it is sown in Chittrai and matures in 4 months, in Āttūr it is sown (usually in saline soils) in Ādi (July-August), and requires 8 months; in the Bāramahāl it is sown in Vaiyāsi or Āni (May-July), and harvested in Mārgali or Tai (December-February). In Hosūr there are two varieties. (1) *Pedda-bairu-vadlu*, a 6 or 7 months' crop, is sown on black sandy soil so situated that it retains moisture for some months after the rains have ceased. It is also sown in wet lands in June, when there is no water in the tanks, and is irrigated when the crop is 3 months old. (2) *Nalla-vadlu*, or "black paddy," is purely rain-fed and does not depend on subsoil moisture. It is also a 6 months' crop, and is sown like *Bairu-vadlu* in April or May. Both varieties are sown broadcast, and are weeded 2 months after sowing, the weeding being repeated once or twice, at intervals of a month. The rice of both kinds, when cooked, is of a reddish colour, and is much esteemed by Brahmans; and both kinds are much in demand for the manufacture of *avul* (pounded rice) in Dharmapuri and Krishnagiri.

Wheat. Wheat (*Triticum sativum = gōdumai*) was cultivated in the time of Read in small quantities on the "Tingrecotta Hills" (Chittēris), and the exclusive privilege of buying up and selling the crop was farmed out by Government. At present it is a crop of very little importance, only about 300 acres, mostly in Salem Taluk, being cultivated, as a dry crop on the Shevaroys, and under well-irrigation on the plains.

Sugar-cane. Sugar-cane (*Saccharum officinarum*) is a crop of small importance, the area totalling about 2,300 acres, scattered throughout the District. It favours black clays and black loams, and, as it

---

[1] *Aruvathām* (Sixtieth) *kuruvai*, so called because it matures within 60 days of transplanting.

[2] Also round Pennāgaram, where two, and sometimes three, crops of *pilan sambā* are sometimes raised in a season, each crop being four months on the ground. The first crop is sown in Vaiyāsi or Āni and the second in Kārtigai or Mārgali.

CHAP. IV. CHIEF CROPS. exhausts the soil, two crops should not be raised on the same ground in consecutive years.

Coco-nuts. Coco-nut Palms (*Cocos nucifera*) are estimated to cover nearly 9,000 acres, of which about 3,700 are in the Bāramahāl, and about the same area in the Talaghāt. Krishnagiri Taluk stands first with over 2,500 acres, Ōmalūr next with 1,700 acres, and Hosūr third with 1,400 acres. Local varieties reported are *senna-pāttiram*, *sevvennīr*, *sevvalanīr*, *kēvuli-pāttiram*,[1] but the kind almost universally cultivated is the common green variety.

Areca-nut. Areca-nut, (*Areca catechu* = Tamil *pākku* or *kamugu*, Telugu, *vakka* or *pōkā*), covers about 2,200 acres, of which about 1,000 are in Hosūr Taluk, (chiefly in Denkani-kōta and Tali Firkas), and nearly 900 in Āttūr. Though the area under cultivation is insignificant, the crop is most lucrative. Areca-nut requires a perennial water-supply, and is not usually manured, but in Āttūr Taluk castor-oil *pūnāk* and pig-dung are sometimes applied, the quantity being one measure[2] per tree in the 4th and 5th years, and one or two *vallams*[3] after the fifth year. Sometimes the seeds are sown in nurseries, (located in a betel-garden, for preference), and planted out after three, or, in Āttūr, six, months. Sometimes transplanting is dispensed with, and the seeds are sown on the site selected for the garden. In the north the plants should be about 6 feet apart, or about 1,000 per acre; in Āttūr 8 feet apart or from 600 to 650 plants per acre. In Āttūr sowing takes place in Arpisi or Kārtigai (October-December), in the north during or after the Makha rains (August). It is customary to grow areca-nut on land previously cultivated with betel-vine or paddy, but it may also be grown on virgin soil, provided that plantains are planted a year beforehand to ensure shade. When a betel-garden is selected as a site for an areca-nut tope, the latter is sown about 2 years before the betel-vine is expected to die out, and the vines are afterwards replaced by plantains. A few fruit trees (orange, lime, guava, jack, etc.,) are often planted in the garden, which is protected from the wind by a fringe of coco-nut palms. Before sowing areca-nut, the ground is loosened to a depth of 18″, and the clods are broken with a short club. If the soil is very heavy, (and areca-nut prefers clayey soils), the land is subjected to a preliminary ploughing. It is then flooded, and the seeds are sown in the damp earth. In Hosūr Taluk it is believed that the Goddess Gauramma takes up her abode in areca-topes, and she

---

[1] A small variety used specially for *pūjā*. It is grown in the Sweta-nadi valley.

[2] One measure = 132 tolas.

[3] One vallam = 264 tolas.

must be propitiated by the sacrifice of a sheep or goat before the crop is harvested.

Betel-vine.

The area under betel-vine (*Piper betle*) is a little over 1,100 acres, of which nearly 400 acres lie in Hosūr Taluk, and most of the rest in Dharmapuri, Krishnagiri and Salem. In the early days of British rule the right to cultivate betel was licensed and farmed out by Government.

The two chief varieties of betel are distinguished as (1) white (*vellai-kodi*) and (2) black (*karun-kodi*). The former is commonest in the Bāramahāl, the latter in the Bālāghāt. Other varieties are (3) *kalpūra* or *kalpūra-kodi*, (said to be a variety of *vellai-kodi*), (4) *joligai* (an inferior variety), and (5) *pavala-kodi*. *Vellai-kodi* is also known in Dharmapuri as *sakkarai-kodi*.

Betel is grown on clayey soil on which paddy has been previously raised; land previously cultivated with sugar-cane or plantains should be avoided. The presence of lime in the soil is considered favourable to growth.

Plantains.

The area covered by plantains totals about 1,800 acres, of which more than half lie in Hosūr (540) and Ōmalūr (437). The varieties most commonly grown in the Talaghāt are (1) *rastāli*, a rather insipid fruit, some 4″ to 4½″ in length; (2) *navaram*, sometimes described as a variety of *rastāli*; (3) *monthan*, a big thick fruit as much as 7″ long and 3″ thick, and (4) *sāmba-vālai*, said to be a variety of *monthan*, but sweeter and more wholesome. Less common are (5) *pachai-nādam*, in size intermediate between *rastāli* and *monthan* and green when ripe; (6) *utiram*, similar in size to *pachai-nādam*, but red when ripe; (7) *mada-vālai*, also called *pēyan*, about the same size as *pachai-nādam*; (8) *pū-vālai* or *suganthamn*, a cheap variety, about the same length as *rastāli*, but more slender; (9) *nandu-kalai*, a smaller fruit about 3½″ in length; (10) *nandan* (rare); (11) *nīlangam* (rare).

The following varieties are reported from Hosūr Taluk:—(1) *yālaki* (Kan.), *sugantham* (Tel.), but apparently not the same as the *sugantham* of the Talaghāt: it is described as a small slender fruit, light coloured and of good flavour, with from 80 to 120 plantains to a bunch; (2) *puttu*, a short thick fruit, light coloured or yellow according to soil; valued for flavour, and also for medicinal purposes, especially for internal fever; bearing about 80 to 130 plantains to the bunch; (3) *pabba* (Tel.), *yēlai* (Kan.), *kāy* (Tam.), a large green fruit of good flavour, with about 40 to 80 plantains to a bunch; (4) *chandra*, the *sevvālai* of the Tamils, a large red fruit of delicate flavour yielding once in 3 years; it bears from 60 to 120 plantains to the bunch; rare; (5) *rājā*, a large yellow fruit of excellent flavour; 50 to 100 plantains to the

CHAP. IV. CHIEF CROPS.

bunch; rare; (6) *rasa*, similar to *suganthom* and valued as medicine; very rare; (7) *nallarati* (Tel.), the *karu-vālai* of the Tamils, a very small fruit, slightly acid in taste and of dark colour; bears from 200 to 400 plantains to the bunch; called also *thoranti* from the thickness of its stem; (8) *būdu* (Kan.), *būdadhi-arati* (Tel.), an insipid fruit, grown chiefly for its leaves; bears 20 to 50 plantains to the bunch; (9) *madhurangi*, (said to be the same as the Tamil *monthan*), a large fruit of indifferent flavour, used as a vegetable; bears from 50 to 100 plantains to a bunch; (10) *yēnuga* (Tel.), *gubbarati* (Kan.), *yānai* (Tam.), Anglice "elephant", so-called from a fancied resemblance which its bunches bear to an elephant's trunk; grows to a height of about 3′ only, the bunches, which carry from 100 to 200 plantains each, touching the ground; fruit small and of indifferent flavour.

Plantains are usually planted in Tai, Ādi, or Chittrai, and the crop is gathered from 12 to 18 months after planting. The plants are allowed to continue for three years, after which a change to another crop is desirable.

Mēchēri Firka is noted for its rain-fed plantain cultivation. The varieties so cultivated are *monthan*, *navaram*, *nandam* and *nīlangam*. The site selected is usually the gently sloping flank of some low plateau; the slope is crossed by strong artificial ridges of stone and mud, which temporarily obstruct such rain-water as may run off the higher ground. There is no particular month for beginning this cultivation. The land is ploughed 8 or 10 times after a shower, and pits are dug 6′ to 8′ apart, and 1′ or 1½′ deep, so that the entire root may be embedded flush with the surface. A heavy rain is then awaited, and after it the roots are planted and covered up with earth and manure. About 400 plants are set in an acre. The first crop is harvested after the lapse of a year, and the plants are allowed to continue for three years, sometimes for more. Side shoots are lopped every three or four months.

The rocky slopes west of Pail-Nād on the Kolli-malais are full of moisture from natural springs, and advantage is taken of the fact to cultivate plantains, mostly the common *rastāli*, on the cliff side; the Kolli-malais are also noted for choicer varieties, in particular the *karu-vālai*, or black plantain, which realises as much as Rs. 2 per bunch, and the big red *pattu-vālai*.

Plantains are an important item in Indian economy; the fruit, when ripe, is a wholesome item of diet; unripe plantains are boiled and eaten as vegetables. The succulent stem is also boiled and eaten by Brahmans, who consider it as a potent digestive[1]; the

[1] So potent that it will digest stone, and is therefore a valuable prophylactic against stone in the bladder and kindred troubles.

leaf and "bark" are used by the higher castes as food-plates; it is only the fibre that has not yet been exploited in Salem District.

II. UNIRRIGATED. A. CEREALS. Ragi.

Rāgi, (*Eleusine coracana* = Tamil *kēvar* or *āriyam*), covers an area of nearly 334,000 acres, of which 136,700 are in the Bāramahāl, 99,700 in Hosūr, and 97,600 in the Talaghāt Taluks.

The principal varieties recognised in Hosūr Taluk, where rāgi cultivation is a fine art, are (1) *gidda-rāgi* and (2) *dodda* (*pedda* or *periya*) *rāgi*, the former a dwarf plant characterised by short thick spikes, the latter a taller variety with long thick spikes; *gidda-rāgi* takes about 4 months to mature, *dodda-rāgi* from 4½ to 5 months. Each of these classes is divided into numerous sub-varieties, e.g., *tella* or *bili-gidda-rāgi*, a short "white" variety; *hasuru*-(Telugu *pasaru*) *gidda-rāgi* or *hasaru-kambi* (yellow or green stalked); *nalla-gidda-rāgi*, a short black variety; *tella-dodda-rāgi*, a tall white kind, etc. *Jen-muttu-rāgi* is a sub-variety of *dodda-rāgi* with rather elongated and compact spikes. *Majjige-rāgi* is a yellowish variety of the *gidda-rāgi* type. *Kaddi-rāgi* is distinct from either *dodda-rāgi* or *gidda-rāgi*, the spikes being long, but thinner than those of *dodda-rāgi*. It has two sub-varieties, (*a*) *kappu-kaddi-rāgi* (black), and (*b*) *bili-kaddi-rāgi* (white). Measure for measure, *kaddi-rāgi*[1] is heavier than that of any other variety of rāgi except *jen-muttu*, the grain being small and dense, while the grain of ordinary rāgi is large and less compact. *Chemma-rāgi* is a term used for grain which has been moistened by the percolation of water into storage pits. In the Talaghāt rāgi is roughly classed as *kāttu-āriyam* and *tūval-āyriam*, the former a dry crop and the latter grown under irrigation. "Dry" rāgi in the south is usually of the short or *gidda-rāgi* type, though *periya-rāgi* is also grown.

In Hosūr the rāgi fields are ploughed three or four times during the rains of May and June. The first ploughing is usually done with a new plough, and *pūjā* is made over the bulls and the implements of husbandry to be employed. After the third or fourth ploughing the land is well manured, and the manure is then ploughed in. The manure used is sheep or cattle-dung, farmyard and household refuse, and the silt from tank-beds. Fifty cartloads of manure are sometimes applied to one acre of land. Then the soil is thoroughly pulverised with a harrow (*palaki*). Sowing usually takes place from the middle of July to the end of August. Seed is sown broadcast, or by the drill-plough (*gorru*), it germinates in three days, and in fifteen days the field is green. Fifteen days after sowing the fields are hoed over with the weeding-plough

[1] The word *kaddi* means a small stick.

CHAP. IV. CHIEF CROPS.

(*guntaka*), and hoeing is repeated a week or so later. One month after the second hoeing the fields are thoroughly weeded by hand with the *dōkadu-pāra.* A shower one month after sowing, two or three showers in the second month, when the stem and leaves are forming, and a good rain in the third month to assist the formation of the seed spikes, suffice to secure a good crop. In the southern taluks the procedure is very similar, but the *palaki, gorru, guntaka* and *dōkadu-pāra* are not used, and the fields are manured by penning cattle and sheep on them, and shifting the pens from place to place, till the whole field is saturated, a process that sometimes continues for six months, from Tai to Vaiyāsi (January to June). In Salem and Ōmalūr Taluks rāgi is usually transplanted, an expedient exceedingly rare in dry cultivation; the seedlings are taken from the seed-bed 3 or 4 weeks after sowing, and are planted 9″ apart. The ground is hoed about one month after transplanting, (or after sowing, if transplanting is not resorted to), and weeded once or twice in the second month. Throughout the District Ādi (July-August) is the chief month for sowing, and transplanting takes place after the Makha rains of Āvani.

The crop is cut in November and December, or even later, from four to five months after sowing. It is usual, before harvest, to sacrifice a fowl or goat, to mingle its blood with boiled rice, and scatter the mixture over the fields. Sometimes the first handful reaped is sprinkled with milk or ghee. In Hosūr the stalks are cut close to the ground, and left *in situ* for four or five days to dry in the sun. They are then tied into small bundles, stacked for a month or two, and then spread over the threshing-floor, and when the stalks are thoroughly dried, the whole is trodden by cattle. The straw is then removed, and the grain is thoroughly winnowed. In the Talaghāt it is often the practice to cut the heads only, to dry them two or three days in the sun, and then store them in heaps or in a closed room. The interval between reaping and threshing is rather shorter than in Hosūr (from 15 to 30 days). The stalks are cut a week or ten days after the heads. On the Kolli-malais the stalks are not cut at all, but are burnt as they stand. Rāgi straw is a very important cattle fodder.

In Hosūr a kind of flour known as *vada-rāgi* is prepared by first soaking the grain in water for a night, and then spreading it out to dry; by this process the grain, when ground, can be easily freed from husk, and is whiter in colour than ordinary rāgi flour.

Tūval-rāgi[1] is the name given throughout the District for those varieties of rāgi which are grown under well-irrigation. *Tūval-rāgi* is sown in seed-beds, and transplanted about 20 or 30 days after

[1] Also called *natta-rāgi*, and, in Āttūr, *puvādam-kēvaru.*

sowing, the seedlings being set from 4″ to 9″ apart. It is irrigated once or twice a week, according to soil and season, and is reaped within two or three months after transplanting. Being independent of rain, *Tūval-rāgi* can be cultivated at all seasons of the year.

Kambu.

Kambu (*Pennisetum typhoideum*, Hind. *bājra*) exceeds even rāgi in importance as a food-grain, being cultivated to the extent of nearly 384,000 acres, of which over 257,000 are in the Talaghāt and about 115,000 in the Bāramahāl; the area in Tiruchengōdu Taluk is over 162,000 acres. It is particularly a favourite grain with Kaikōlar weavers, who use it not only as a food, but also for making *kanji* as size for weaving. On dry lands kambu is grown as a first crop, being sown with the rains of Vaiyāsi (May-June), and harvested in about four months in Purattāsi (September-October). Some varieties, however, have different seasons. Irrigated kambu is a speciality of the Talaghāt, where, on good soil and in a favourable season, it can be harvested in ninety days. In Āttūr Taluk kambu is harvested on wet lands any time between August and February.

The chief varieties are :—

(1) *Perun-kambu*; sown in Chittrai or Vaiyāsi (April-June) and harvested from Ādi-Purattāsi (July-October). In Ōmalūr *perun-kambu* is sometimes sown in Purattāsi or Arpisi (September-November), and harvested in Mārgali or Tai (December-February);

(2) *Kullan-kambu*, or *arisi-kambu*, which matures more rapidly than other varieties, (3 to 3½ months), sown in Chittrai (April-May) and harvested in Ādi (July-August);

(3) *Kāsi-kambu* or *perun-kāsi-kambu* (Āni to Purattāsi);

(4) *Kommai* or *karu-kattan-kambu*, sown in Purattāsi (September-October) and harvested in Margali (December-January). Sown sometimes in a seed-bed and transplanted after thirty days or so.

Other less common varieties are *kottu-kambu*, *pumudi-kambu*, and *sōnāchalam-kambu*.

Kambu flourishes on red loams and sands. The ground is ploughed three or four times before sowing. The manure used is the dung of cattle and sheep, and on better soils animals are penned before ploughing begins. The fields are usually ploughed a month or so after sowing, to prevent the grain from growing too thickly. Kambu is supposed to exhaust the soil, and should not be grown more frequently than in alternate years on the same field. It is often sown on land previously cultivated with rāgi; horse-gram and black-gram succeed it. It is sown mixed with nari-payir, or between rows of dhall, avarai or castor. In Ōmalūr Taluk, when irrigated, it is followed by chōlam. In Āttūr Taluk kambu and indigo are put down as a mixed crop on wet lands in May

CHAP. IV. CHIEF CROPS.

or June, the kambu being harvested in August or September, and the indigo in October and November. When harvested, the heads only are cut off, the stalks being left standing. In Salem and Tiruchengōdu kambu is reaped twice; after the heads which first mature have been removed, secondary heads mature, and are cut 15, 20 or 30 days later. After harvest the stalks are carefully tied into stacks, to prevent rotting in the rains. Kambu stalks are the most valued thatching material in use in the District. Superstition forbids that the heads, when cut, should be allowed to lie pointing towards the north. The heads are thrashed by driving bullocks over them as soon after reaping as the weather permits; if the weather is dry enough the heads may be thrashed on the very day of harvest. The grain is soaked with water before it is husked. The flour is prepared either as a thin gruel with butter-milk or water, or as a thick porridge with dhall, avarai or brinjal.

Chōlam.

Chōlam (*Sorghum vulgare* = Telugu *Jonnalu* and Hindustānī *Juār*) is cultivated on over 96,000 acres, of which more than 73,000 are in the Talaghāt (Salem 28,600, Tiruchengōdu 20,000, Āttūr 17,400), and only 20,000 in the Bāramahāl (Ūttankarai, 11,200). It is both a "dry" and a "wet" crop, and its seed-time and harvest and the methods of its cultivation vary so greatly, that a synoptic treatment of the subject is hardly possible. Roughly speaking, chōlam in one form or another is being sown and harvested all the year round in various parts of the District. The chief varieties grown as food-grains are popularly distinguished as red chōlam and white chōlam. In Ōmalūr and Āttūr these are sown as a second crop on irrigable land in Mārgali (December-January), on fields previously cultivated with kambu, rāgi, pani-varagu, etc., and reaped four months later in Chittrai (April-May). It should be irrigated once in from 4 to 7 days. In Tiruchengōdu, Panguni (March-April), Vaiyāsi (May-June) and Arpisi (October-November) are said to be the months for sowing, in Salem, Purattāsi (September-October). Black chōlam (*karun-chōlam*) and *kākkāy* or *talai-virichān-chōlam* are invariably rain-fed, and are grown for fodder rather than for grain.

The *kāki-chōlam* (also called black or *kari-chōlam*) of Hosūr Taluk is likewise grown for fodder; it is usually planted along with mustard, wild gingelly, avarai, etc., in rows in rāgi fields; it is said to differ from the *kākkāy chōlam* of the Talaghāt. *Makka-chōlam* is not chōlam at all, but maize (*Zea mays*), a crop of small importance in the District, covering less than 400 acres. When ripe for harvest, chōlam is cut close to the ground, and the grain is trodden out by bullocks from 3 to 8 days after cutting; it is then dried in the sun for 2 or 3 days and stored in granaries.

When required for use, the grain is moistened by sprinkling water over it, and then pounded in a pestle and mortar. The stalks and husks are used for fodder.

Minor cereals.

Minor cereals, of which the chief are (1) sāmai, (2) varagu, (3) tenai, are items of no mean importance in the agricultural economy of the District. Though the yield per acre is small, and the grain is not nutritious, the cost of cultivation is trivial, the growth rapid and the crop hardy. Hence a large area of poor soils can be cultivated with sāmai and varagu, which otherwise would be left waste; the ryot stands to lose very little in cost of seed and labour, and he may, if the season is favourable, realise a crop of grain and straw that will suffice for a year's domestic requirements, and enable him to dispose of his more valuable products for ready cash.

B. PULSES. Horse-gram.

The most important pulse is horse-gram (=Tamil *kollu*= Hindustani *kulti*; *Dolichos biflorus*). In the Talaghāt it covers over 96,000 acres, in the Bāramahāl 106,000, in the Bālāghāt a little over 20,000. "Rather desert your wife," runs the proverb, "than fail to sow gram on waste land." Its power of maturing with very little rain, and, after it has got a fair start, of subsisting almost solely on the dews of January, render it invaluable as a second crop. It flourishes on relatively poor soils; on richer soils, or under heavy rains, it runs to leaf and the flowers are few. It is usually put down in September or October, as soon as kambu, sāmai, or gingelly is harvested, the ground being ploughed and the seed sown broadcast; manure is not necessary. A light shower is enough to cause the seed to germinate, and a few more showers are required when the leaves are forming; dew does the rest. The harvest is in January or February, or even March, about four months after sowing. The plants, when mature, are pulled up by the roots, and dried for ten days or so, and are then trodden by cattle. The leaves and pods are valued as fodder. Horse-gram is eaten by the poorer ryots of the Bāramahāl, especially when there is a shortage in the ordinary food grains.

Dhall.

Dhall or red-gram (*Cajanus indicus* =Tamil *tuvarai*) comes next to horse-gram in importance. It covers an area of nearly 19,000 acres, of which nearly 10,000 are in the Talaghāt, over 8,000 in the Bāramahāl, and about 1,000 in the Bālāghāt. Krishnagiri is the chief dhall-growing taluk, with a total of nearly 6,000 acres. Dhall is usually grown in rows 4′ apart in the rāgi fields of the Bāramahāl and Talaghāt; in the Bālāghāt it is sometimes associated with gingelly (p. 207). It is a seven-month crop, sown in Āni (June-July), and harvested in Tai (January-February). It is a kist-paying product; after reaping it is stored in the pod, and broken and sold in instalments as the

CHAP. IV. CHIEF CROPS.

market suits. The stalks are used in Salem Taluk for the construction of small rat-proof granaries.

Avarai.

Mochai or avarai (*Dolichos lablab*) is one of the most valued catch crops of the Hosūr rāgi fields, and is sown in rows, sometimes with castor and mustard; its leaves are said to fertilise the soil. It also thrives on the Shevaroys and Kolli-malais. It is sown in July or August along with rāgi, the seeds being dibbled in; one month after the sowing, the soil is hoed over, and one month after hoeing it is weeded. Avarai is a six months' crop; its growth does not interfere with the growth of the rāgi, but after the rāgi is harvested, it begins to spread like a jungle creeper. The blossoms and pods mature with the heavy dews of December and January, but the pods are not harvested while green; when the pods are thoroughly dried, i.e., by the end of January or early February, the creepers are cut and stored for a few days, after which the stalks are beaten to separate the pods; the pods are then dried separately, and trodden by bullocks to extract the beans, which are then mixed with ash, fried, split in a stone mill, again dried and separated from the husk. The split beans are then ready for consumption. Three varieties are grown (1) *Pedda-* or *Erra-Anumulu*, (2) *Saniga-* or *Chinna-Anumulu*, (3) *Ganda-Sanigalu* or *Tella-Anumulu.*

Other Pulses.

Among the pulses of minor importance may be mentioned black-gram (a little under 10,000 acres), green-gram (about 9,000 acres) and Bengal-gram (about 5,000 acres). The cultivation of these crops fluctuates, and they appear to be declining in popularity. The chief taluks for black-gram (*Phaseolus radiatus* = Tamil *ulundu*) are Ūttankarai and Ōmalūr; for green-gram (*Phaseolus mungo* = Tamil *pachai-payiru*) Krishnagiri and Dharmapuri; and for Bengal-gram (*Cicer arietinum* = Tamil *kadalai*) Ōmalūr and Krishnagiri. The last named is often sown as a catch crop on black paddy soils, when the water-supply is insufficient for a second crop. It is sometimes mixed with onions and coriander. Black-gram and green-gram are often sown in rows (*sāls*) between other crops, but Bengal-gram never.

Gingelly, (*ellu* = *Sesamum indicum*), is a most important crop in Dharmapuri Taluk, where it covers about 30,000 acres; in Krishnagiri it covers over 13,000 acres; in Ūttankarai a little over 4,000, while in the whole of the Talaghāt taluks the area does not reach 9,000, out of a district total of over 40,000 acres.

Two varieties of gingelly are grown (1) *Pēr-ellu* (or *periya-ellu*) and (2) *Kūr-ellu.*

(1) *Pēr-ellu*, the less common and inferior variety, is grown chiefly in the southern taluks, and is always a dry crop. In Omalūr Taluk it is sown in Panguni (March-April) and harvested

CHAP. IV. CHIEF CROPS.

in Ādi (July-August).[1] In Āttur, Salem and Ūttankarai it is sown in Purattāsi (September-October), and cut in Mārgali or Tai (December to February), 90 days after sowing.

(2) *Kūr-ellu* is grown on both dry and irrigated lands. In Dharmapuri and Ūttankarai the seed is usually sown as a dry crop in black loam in Panguni or Chittrai (March to May), as soon as the soil is moist enough to allow germination. The plants attain a fair size within twenty days. The crop is most precarious, and if the weather does not suit it, the failure is complete. A good shower is absolutely necessary as soon as the crop begins to flower, but excessive damp is injurious, and any stagnation of water is ruinous. The harvest is in Ādi or Āvani (July to September), 90 days after sowing.

Irrigated *kūr-ellu* is sown in wet lands in January or February, after the paddy harvest, and matures in April, May or June. It is a favourite catch crop in Āttūr, Salem and Krishnagiri. It requires watering within twenty days of sowing, and again when the plants are in flower. Watering should be done in the morning only, and not in the evening. Gingelly is sown broadcast and never transplanted.

In Dharmapuri and Krishnagiri, at harvest, the gingelly plants are pulled up by the roots, but elsewhere they are cut close to the ground. After drying in the sun for a week or so, the seeds are extracted by beating the plants with sticks, or, in the drier Talaghāt taluks, the plants are stirred occasionally, and the seed pods burst of themselves. If before threshing a snake is found in the heap, the whole stack is burnt, for Hindus believe such an omen portends some fatal disaster. Muhammadans are less sensitive, and do not hesitate to defy fate by buying or selling the crop thus accursed. Pious Hindus sometimes devote the sale-proceeds of snake-stricken gingelly to their gods, and renounce gingelly cultivation for two or three years. The sacrifice of a pig is supposed to avert the evil influence. To avoid risks the ryots usually stack their gingelly in small separate heaps, and put the leaves of *erukku* (*Calotropis gigantea*) with it as a prophylactic against snakes.

Wild Gingelly.

Very little gingelly is grown in Hosūr, its place being taken by the yellow-flowered *Pēy-ellu* or *Huch-ellu* ("Niger" = *Guizotia abyssinica*). *Pēy-ellu* is grown as a catch crop with rāgi, castor or dhall and is invariably sown in furrows. It is hardy, and

---

[1] In Ōmalūr Taluk *Pēr-ellu*, which is the variety usually cultivated, is sometimes, but rarely, sown in Purattāsi (September-October). *Kūr-ellu*, on the other hand, is ordinarily sown in Purattāsi, and rarely in Panguni (March-April). Very little *Kūr-ellu* is, however, sown in the Taluk.

CHAP. IV. CHIEF CROPS.

thrives on poorer soils, red sands, and loams. It is a three months' crop, sown in May or June, and reaped in August or September. It is cultivated mostly in the Hosūr and Kela-mangalam Firkas.

Castor.

The castor-oil plant (*Ricinus communis* = Tamil *āmanakku*, also called *muttu-kottai* or "pearl seed") is grown all over the District, usually as a bye-crop in fields of rāgi or kambu. It is especially important in the Talaghāt, where it takes precedence of dhall and mochai as a kist-bearing crop. The estimated area under castor in Fasli 1320 was over 26,000 acres, of which 14,000 lay in the Talaghāt, 9,000 in the Bāramahāl and 3,000 in the Bālāghāt. Tiruchengōdu is the chief castor-growing taluk, with an area of 8,500 acres. Ordinarily it is an eight months' crop, being sown from Āni to Āvani (June to September), and harvested from Tai to Panguni (January to April), but the period of growth varies with locality and season.[1] In the rich soils of Pancha-palli, Anchetti, and Andēvana-palli, of Denkani-kōta Division, it grows to a man's height in a couple of months, and when mature, it forms a small tree 12′ to 15′ high: the crop does not require constant rainfall, but a few showers are necessary at the time of flowering. The crop is harvested in instalments.

After picking, the seeds are dried for 15 days, and are then beaten, sometimes with brickbats. The stalks, which are valued for fuel, are often left standing till the following cultivation season begins. Two varieties are grown indiscriminately, the "bald" and the "hairy". In Āttūr Taluk, and elsewhere occasionally,[2] it is an irrigated crop.

Ground-nut.

* Fasli.	Acres.[3]
1310	1,465
1311	2,030
1312	3,815
1313	5,576
1314	5,540
1315	6,182
1316	12,756
1317	30,468
1318	39,093
1319	40,879
1320	42,774

The cultivation of ground-nut, (*Arachis hypogæa* = *nela-kadalai*), has shown remarkable progress during the decade ending Fasli 1320 (1910–11), as the marginal figures indicate.* Of the total area, over 36,000 acres lie in the Talaghāt, and not quite 6,000 in the Bāramahāl. Salem Taluk stands first, with over 17,000 acres; Āttūr next, with nearly 8,000 acres, and Tiruchengōdu third, with not quite 7,000 acres. Sowing takes place in July or August, and the harvest is in December.

---

[1] E.g., Salem and Rāsipuram, 300 days, April or May to February; Kāripatti 240 days (May to January); Ōmalūr 180 days (July to December); Mēchēri 90 days; Hosūr four months.

[2] E.g., in Pennāgaram Division, where it is called *tōttatt-āmanakku*, and is planted in Ādi round betel-gardens.

[3] The figures exclude those of Nāmakkal and Tiruppattūr Taluks. Those from Fasli 1310 to 1316 are for Government villages, minor inams and villages under the Court of Wards. Those for Fasli 1317 onwards are for the whole District.

D. CONDIMENTS, ETC.

Chillies.

Chillies (*Capsicum* spp.) form a valuable item of garden produce, and they are grown throughout the District, the estimated area being well over 7,600 acres, of which about 1,700 lie in Āttūr. Chillies are sometimes grown as a dry crop, but more usually they are watered by wells. They prefer rather sandy, ferruginous soils.

Coriander.

Coriander (*Coriandrum sativum* = Tam. *kottamalli*) is a useful bye-crop, covering between 2,000 and 3,000 acres, scattered chiefly over the taluks of Ūttankarai, Dharmapuri and Āttūr. Coriander prefers black soils, and is often associated with gingelly. It is sown as a late crop, in Arpisi (October-November), and harvested in Māsi (February-March).

Other Condiments.

Mustard (*Brassica juncea* = Tamil *kadugu*), cumin (*Cuminum cyminum* = Tamil *siragam*) and fenugreek (*Trigonella fœnum-græcum* =Tamil *vendayam*) are often mingled with the mixed crops that characterise the *punjai* cultivation of the District. Mustard is perhaps the most important of the three, though its cultivation is almost confined to the Hills and to Hosur Taluk. Ordinarily it is a three months' crop, and is therefore among the first of the mixed crops to be harvested. The climate of the Kolli-malais seems peculiarly congenial to the plant, and it is said that the mustard grown on the rāgi fields there is sufficient to defray the whole of the kist.

Other Garden Crops.

The remaining garden crops are of little importance. Onions and garlic cover about 1,000 acres, of which nearly half are in Salem Taluk. "Vegetables," including brinjals, sweet potatoes, yams and innumerable varieties of pumpkins, cover about 2,000 acres in all.

E. SPECIAL PRODUCTS.

Tobacco.

The total area under tobacco is nearly 7,400 acres, of which Āttūr Taluk contributes about 1,700, Tiruchengōdu about 1,500, Salem about 1,000; very little is cultivated in the Bāramahāl, except for some 1,400 acres in Ūttankarai Taluk. Like betel, the right to cultivate tobacco was in Read's time licensed and farmed out by Government.

The chief centre of tobacco cultivation in the District is the Tammampatti Firka of Āttūr Taluk. There the usual variety is that known as "black" tobacco, and it is almost invariably cultivated in dry lands under well-irrigation. Tobacco is said to thrive only when irrigated with brackish water, and hence well-water is preferable to the water of tanks or streams. It is usually grown as a second crop, after irrigated kambu or tūval-rāgi. The soil chosen should be light, but not sandy; the sites of deserted villages or land cleared of prickly-pear are specially suited for rearing tobacco, probably owing to the salts that they contain; the presence of lime in the soil is also beneficial. A light

CHAP. IV. CHIEF CROPS.

ferruginous loam yields the best quality, though the leaves are smaller, and the cultivation requires greater care, than is the case with crops grown on other soils. Tobacco should not be grown for more than two years consecutively on the same plot of ground. Black-cotton soil is unsuited, and in alluvium the plants grow to excessive size and suffer in quality.

Rain-fed tobacco is considered greatly superior in quality to that grown under irrigation, though the outturn is less and the labour involved greater.

When the plants are about 1′ 6″ high, blossoms begin to form : at this stage the top of each plant is nipped off ; no flowers are permitted to mature, except such as are required for next season's supply of seed. The removal of flower-buds is followed by the appearance of lateral shoots or "suckers," and these also must be regularly removed. Not more than 10, or at most 12, leaves should be left on each plant. Light showers are favourable ; heavy showers are injurious ; but the worst enemy of the tobacco grower is a hail-storm, which means the annihilation of the crop.

The Taluks of Tiruchengōdu and Ūttankarai, and Rāsipuram Division, are the chief centres for snuff tobacco in the Presidency.[1] Tobacco grown for snuff is almost invariably rain-fed. When tobacco is cultivated for chewing, watering is withheld for 4 or 5 days before the crop is cut. A special kind of tobacco called "white" tobacco is grown in Āttūr Firka for snuff. In Salem and Tiruchengōdu Taluks, where the leaves are removed from the stalks before pressing, the stalks are sold by the ryots to middlemen. At Edappādi in particular a big trade has developed recently in tobacco stalks, which are exported to Bangalore, whence they are distributed in Mysore State, Dharwar and Coorg, where the Kanarese people chew it with betel. It is sometimes converted into snuff. The stalks are also valued locally as manure.

Cotton.

The area under cotton (*Gossypium* spp.) in the whole District in Fasli 1320 was nearly 12,700 acres, of which 10,100 acres were located in Tiruchengōdu Taluk, 1,200 in Salem and 900 in Āttūr.

The variety of cotton usually grown is known as (1) *nādam-parutti*. Less common are (2) *ukkam-* (or *uppam-*) *parutti*, (3) *sem-parutti*, (4) *adukku-* or *sada-parutti*. *Nādam* is grown on red loams, and is sown after the Chittrai (April-May) rains, or later, the Ādi Festival[2] being a specially auspicious time. Kambu is often sown broadcast with it. *Nādam* plants usually bear for three years, and they bear twice a year, in January and July or a little later.

---

[1] Watt, *Commercial Products*, 1908, p. 802.

[2] See Vol. II, p. 206.

CHAP. IV. CHIEF CROPS.

Ukkam and *sem-parutti* favour black loams ; *adukku-parutti*, like *nādam*, prefers red loam. *Ukkam* is a one year crop. It is from *adukku-parutti* and *sem-parutti* that the sacred thread is spun.

Cotton used to be of much greater importance in the agricultural economy of Salem District than it is now ; the ryot used formerly to gin and spin the produce, and hand the yarn over to the village Pariahs to be woven into clothes. Salem cotton was exploited by Mr. Heath, and after him by Mr. Fischer, and "Salems" were well known in the commercial world.[1]

Indigo.

Indigo (*Indigofera tinctoria* = Tam. *aviri*) is a special product of Āttūr Taluk, where some 2,000 odd acres are cultivated with it. The area under cultivation is steadily decreasing from year to year. It is a three months' crop, and is usually sown with kambu in June and harvested in September. It is chiefly grown as a manure for paddy lands, its value as a dye being subsidiary ; the leaf, as soon as harvested, is carted off to the factory, and is returned a day or two after to the ryot, who receives a rupee on each cartload. An acre of indigo is sufficient to manure three acres of wet land.

Coffee.

The pioneer of coffee cultivation on the Shevaroys was Mr. G. Fischer, who obtained land for that purpose during Mr. M. D. Cockburn's Collectorate (1820–29). The new industry met with the sympathy of Government, and land was granted on favourable terms.[2]

During the past twenty-five years the coffee planter has had to face calamities that threatened him with extinction, and the period of depression has not yet passed.[3]

The chief factors in the decline in prosperity of coffee cultivation are three :—(1) fall in the price of coffee, (2) increase in the cost of cultivation, (3) pests.

Prices.

The marginal statement * shows at a glance the fluctuations in price of coffee from 1874 to 1907, the price obtained in the former year being taken as 100. The actual price realised in 1901–02 was just over Rs. 49 ; in 1906–07 it fell to Rs. 43–11–0 per cwt. The area under coffee in the whole District in 1884 was 10,769 acres ; in 1894, it fell to 8,680 acres, in 1900 to 6,224 acres ; since 1900 there has been a slight revival, the area in 1910 being 7,883 acres, with a yield of about 1,000 tons of parchment and native coffee.

* Year.	Variation.
1877	120
1882	93
1884	83
1890	115
1897	103
1898	85
1899	71
1900	51
1902	65
1907	58

[1] See p. 603, *Commercial Products of India*. [2] See Chapter XI. p. 47.

[3] Most of the matter that follows has been kindly supplied by the late Mr. H. W. Leeming and Mr. C. K. Short.

CHAP. IV. CHIEF CROPS. Cost of Cultivation.

The increase in the price of labour, and the growing necessity for concentrated manure on account of exhaustion of the soil, would have reduced the planter to bankruptcy, if he had not materially modified his methods of cultivation.

When coffee cultivation was first taken up on the Shevaroys, the plants were grown under more or less natural conditions. It was in the seventies that methods of close planting and rigorous handling were imported from Ceylon. Under this system the trees were planted at a distance varying from 4′ to 8′ apart.[1] Coffee pruning comprised three operations, "topping," "handling," and "pruning" properly so called. "Topping" was usually resorted to when the plants were three years old; the top shoot being cut at a height of about 5′ from the ground. The purpose of topping was to check vertical growth and encourage horizontal growth only, producing "a crown or umbrella of primary branches." By "handling" all undesirable suckers and "gormandisers" were systematically removed, and every effort made to restrain the bush severely on fixed lines of growth supposed to favour fruiting, and the most convenient to the pluckers.[2] Pruning proper was carried out after the crop was collected; all shoots that had borne fruits were as a rule removed, and those destined for next year's crop were selected and protected.

A revolution in cultural methods has taken place during the past ten years, in consequence of the success attending certain innovations made by the late Mr. H. W. Leeming of Scotforth, near Muluvi. "Mr. Leeming . . . . ." writes Sir George Watt "was induced some few years ago to believe that a larger plant and more space would give equal, if not better returns, at a much lower cost than the prevalent system of many small plants. He accordingly removed each alternate bush and reduced his estate to 600 plants to the acre. The result was so very promising that he went still further, and reduced it to 300 or 325 plants to the acre. . . . . The yield had been greatly increased, the cost of cultivation lessened, the plants rendered better able to throw off disease, and the produce recorded as fetching a higher price than had been the case under former conditions.[3]" In short, wider spacing has counteracted the increase in cost of labour and manure. Few planters now spend as much as Rs. 100 per acre, and some of the best estates are worked at from Rs. 25 to Rs. 30 per acre, exclusive of picking, curing and supervision. A yield

---

[1] Intervals of 6′ × 7′ give 1,037 plants to the acre; 5′ × 5′, not uncommon spacing, would give 1,740 plants per acre.

[2] *Commercial Products of India*, p. 381.

[3] *Commercial Products of India*, p. 375.

of from $1\frac{1}{2}$ to $2\frac{1}{2}$ cwt. per acre would be a fair average estimate, a well worked estate favourably situated would produce $3\frac{1}{2}$ to 4 cwt. or even 5 cwt.

Drainage. The object of "trenching" is partly to protect the surface soil from erosion, but its chief function is to supply the soil with oxygen, especially with the oxygen conveyed by rain showers. The ferruginous nature of the soil on the Shevaroys makes trenching of special importance, as the ferrous oxide has to be converted to ferric oxide, to render it soluble. A series of drains 3′ deep, arranged herring-bone-wise, is one of the most recent methods adopted. Bunding and terracing is unusual, but parallel contour catch drains are freely used. Pitting is resorted to in some estates, and some planters dig over the whole of their estates once in two years.

Shade. In the early days of coffee culture, coffee was grown without shade. The advent of leaf blight made shade imperative. The dearth of large indigenous forest trees has necessitated the planting out of large areas with the Silver Oak (*Grevillea robusta*), *Erythrina lithosperma, Artocarpus integrifolia* and *Albizzia moluccana*, the surest and quickest method of protecting clearings. Though not deciduous, *Grevillea* is constantly shedding leaves, and its hardiness and rapidity of growth render it popular. The best indigenous trees are Blackwood (*Dalbergia latifolia*) and Selvanji (*Albizzia odoratissima*), but unfortunately most of the Blackwood on the Shevaroys has been cut down. Other indigenous trees of value are *Terminalia chebula* (Gall-nut), *T. belerica, T. catappa* (Indian Almond), *T. tomentosa, Albizzia lebbek, Pterocarpus marsupium* and *Cedrela toona*. Daria (*Sponia wightii*), Nāga (*Eugenia jambolana*), and the figs are to be avoided, as they are very susceptible to bug, and their root growth injures the coffee.

Mulch. A mulch, or litter of dead leaves and dead weeds, is a useful protection against surface erosion and surface caking, and it also checks the evaporation of water in the soil. The best natural mulch is created by deciduous trees. This is supplemented by cutting the weeds before they seed, and leaving them *in situ*. The following leguminous plants have been cultivated for the prevention of wash, and they act as cover plants; *Cassia mimosoides, Crotalaria striata, Tephrosia purpurea*. These should be cut down and spread over the surface of the ground during the hot weather. In a few months it will be found they have rotted, and formed a good mulch, the nitrogen of which is washed into the soil at the first burst of the rains.

Manure. By wider spacing and deeper trenching the cost of manure per acre has been greatly reduced. With 1,200 plants per acre,

CHAP. IV. CHIEF CROPS.

1,200 lb. of manure would be required at 1 lb. per tree, whereas, with 300 trees per acre, 1½ lb. can be given to each tree, and the total expenditure will be only 450 lb. Saltpetre, bone-manure and various kinds of *pūnāk* are the usual manures, but every planter has his own ideas as to what is best.

Varieties.

Almost all the coffee grown on the Shevaroys is *Coffea arabica*. *C. liberica* has been tried, but it does not pay well, the berries being large, with an excess of pulp. *Maragogipe* is cultivated on a small scale, but it is sensitive to leaf disease, and the yield is unsatisfactory, a heavy crop being realised only once in three years. "Pointed Bourbon" has also been tried. More recently experiments have been made with *C. robusta*, an African species imported from Java; it is supposed to be resistant to *Hemileia vastatrix*, but the species has not yet had long enough trial, and nothing can be said of the quality of the bean. The same remarks apply to *C. congensis*, var. *chalotti* and *C. canephora*.

Pests.

The diseases which have devastated the coffee plantations on the Shevaroys are, in order of destructiveness, Blight, Borer and Bug.

(*a*) The fungoid disease known as Leaf Blight (*Hemileia vastatrix*) was imported into South India from Ceylon in 1871. It made its first appearance on the Shevaroys in 1875. Its host is supposed to be *Canthium* of various species which are abundant on the Shevaroys.

(*b*) Borer (the grub of the beetle *Xylotrechus quadripes*) began its ravages in 1897–98, and the damage it has done is enormous.

(*c*) Brown Bug, the scale insect known to science as *Lecanium hemisphœricum*, made its debut in 1870. It first attacked the shade-trees, then the fig, jack, charcoal-tree (Daria = *Sponia wightii*, also called *Trema orientalis*), loquat, guava, oranges and limes, and it shows a special liking for Spanish Needle (*Bidens pilosa*). No certain method of dealing with this pest has been discovered. Spraying and fumigating are impracticable; the importation of lady-birds has failed; a fungus that appears during the north-east monsoon is fatal to it, but unfortunately the fungus attacks the bug usually after the bug has done all the damage it possibly can.

Green Bug (*Lecanium viride*), which dealt the death-blow to the coffee industry in Ceylon, and made its appearance on the Nilgiris in 1904, was introduced into the Shevaroys from the Palni Hills in about 1905. The Green Mealy Scale (*Pulvinaria psidii*) has also found its way to the Shevaroy estates.

In addition to the above pests, much damage is being done by stump-rot or root rot, caused by the fungus *Hymenochæte noxia* which spreads from certain forest and shade trees when they die. The trees which are supposed to propagate this disease are the White Cedar, all Figs, the Silver Oak and the Jack.

Curing.

Shevaroy coffee is sent to the mills of Malabar or Coimbatore, "in parchment."[1] Hence the manufacturing processes necessary before the bean is ready for export from the hills are of a very simple description. The coffee blossoms in March and April, the fruit begins to ripen in October and continues till January. The fruit is hand-picked as soon as it shows a dark reddish tinge. The next process is pulping. The pulper is usually of the disc pattern, and is worked by hand. Pulping should be done as soon as possible after picking, to prevent fermentation and discoloration of the silver-skin. After the pulp is removed, the sticky mucilaginous stuff with which the parchment is coated is removed by first fermenting and then washing the parchment. Fermentation requires from 12 to 24 hours, according to the state of the weather; the higher the elevation, the longer will be the process. The parchment, after thorough washing, is put to dry on specially prepared platforms called "barbecues." On arriving at the mills, the parchment coffee is usually dried a second time. Coffee grown by natives is usually dried without removing the pulp attached.

Tea.

Tea was introduced on the Shevaroys in the fifties by Mr. Fischer, but its cultivation never got beyond the experimental stage, and has since been altogether abandoned. Dr. Cornish, writing in 1870, remarked that the plants attained a height of 20′ and flowered and seeded freely.[2]

Rubber.

In 1881 a few Ceara[3] trees were introduced on the Shevaroys, but rubber cultivation was not seriously thought of till 1898, when Mr. A. G. Nicholson planted several hundred Para and Castilloa plants among the coffee of the Hawthorne Estate, up to an elevation of about 3,500′. He continued interplanting annually, and in 1903 imported Castilloa seed from Mexico direct. About the same time other planters turned their attention to rubber, and interspersed their coffee with Para and Castilloa, and in some instances with Ceara. By 1906 about 1,200 acres were so planted up, most of the rubber being Para. Tapping was

---

[1] For the uninitiated it is as well to note that the ripe coffee fruit is called the "cherry," the succulent outer coat of the fruit is the "pulp," and the inner adhesive layer is known as the "parchment." The seed coat within the parchment, which adheres closely to the seed, is called the "silver-skin." *Commercial Products of India*, p. 388.

[2] Dr. Shortt's *Hill Ranges*, II, p. 21.

[3] For the information on Rubber I am indebted to Messrs. B. Cayley and Morgan.

tried on a small scale by Mr. Nicholson in 1906, and as much as ¼ lb. of dry rubber per tree could be obtained in a month from his best seven-year-old Para trees, results very favourable considering the relatively high elevation and scanty rainfall of the Shevaroys, as compared with other rubber-growing countries. Moreover, in addition to yielding a heavy crop of good seed, (valued in 1906 at from Rs. 5 to Rs. 7 per thousand), Para makes an excellent shade-tree for coffee; it requires no topping, the shade is not too heavy, and the roots do not in any way interfere with the growth of the coffee. Mr. Nicholson was awarded a gold medal for the best rubber grown in India, and a card for "High Elevation Rubber." His success gave an impetus to rubber planting, and it is estimated that in January 1911, the area under Para amounted to 1,829 acres with some 484,000 trees, and of Ceara to 1,987 acres with some 570,000 trees.

Ceara, it will be observed, has overtaken Para in popularity. The climate of the Shevaroys suits it well, good trees, 3 or 4 years of age, attaining a girth of as much as 26″ at a height of 3′ from the ground. The exact outturn is uncertain, but it is said that Ceara trees, 3 or 4 years of age, will yield 4 ounces of dry rubber in a year, rising eventually to 1 lb. As the rains are not continuous during the monsoon months, Ceara is not injured by tapping; the cuts heal up rapidly, and there is a noticeable increase of yield from renewed bark. Hitherto (1912) rubber on the Shevaroys has mostly been planted in coffee, but now that the possibilities of Ceara are gaining recognition, it is not unlikely that in the near future large areas will be devoted to rubber alone.

In addition to Para and Ceara there are small areas under *Castilloa elastica*, *Funtumia elastica*, *Manihot dichotoma*, *M. piauhyensis* and *M. heptaphylla*.

Many systems of tapping have been tried. The "spiral system" was first tried on Mr. Nicholson's Para, and worked well. The system, however, which is considered to work the best is the "half" or "full herring-bone," which can be employed on all trees with a girth of 18″ measured at a height of 3′ from the ground. From a height of 5′ down to within 6″ of the ground level the tree is stripped of its outer bark. A broad shallow vertical incision is then made from top to bottom of the stripped portion, and a tin spout is inserted at the bottom to receive the latex. The original oblique cuts are then made about 1′ apart, at an angle of 45° to the vertical incision. Every other day shallow oblique cuts are made below the originals, until the space between the originals is filled up. Under this system paring is avoided, and when one side of the tree is finished, the other side can be tapped, and the side first tapped will be thus allowed time to heal before it is again interfered with.

Aloe. A start was made in aloe cultivation in the Priaux Verts Estate (Shevaroys) in 1899, when about 40 acres were planted out with Agave (*Fourcroya gigantea*), and in 1904 the Government sanctioned the remission of assessment for five years on all lands newly cultivated with Agave on the Shevaroys. The venture was not a success. Meanwhile, in 1904, about 965 acres of land near Morappūr Railway Station were assigned on a five years' cowle to the Indian Fibre Company of Yercaud. The land was planted with aloes, but the drought of the two succeeding years, and the ravages of cattle and wild pigs, entirely destroyed the plantation. The venture was abandoned, and the lands relinquished in 1907.

Hemp. About 400 acres, mostly in Salem Taluk, are cultivated with San-Hemp (*Crotalaria juncea* = Tamil *sanal*, Telugu *janumu*) and rather under 100 acres with Deccan Hemp (*Hibiscus cannabinus* = Tamil *pulichai*). Both are grown as bye-products on the *sāl* system, in fields cultivated with unirrigated cereals, and neither crop is of much economic value, the produce sufficing only for local consumption.

F. FRUIT CULTURE. Except in the case of graft mangoes, no systematic attempt has been made to develop fruit culture on a large scale. But, judging from the success of experiments carried out by Mr. C. K. Short and other planters on the Shevaroys, there is no reason why a large orchard should not prove a profitable investment. On the Shevaroys no irrigation is required, as at Bangalore, and the soil is all that could be desired. Oranges thrive amazingly, and so does the common cooking pear, and during the season cartloads of these fruits are sent away to the plains. Mr. C. K. Short summarises the present state of fruit culture on the Shevaroys as follows :—

Oranges.—The variety most commonly grown is the tight-skinned St. Michael, which stands transport well, and bears good crops with little cultivation. The tree takes about 8 years to come into full bearing. Excellent as the fruit is, there is room for improvement by grafting and high cultivation. The loose-skinned Coorg Orange (*Cintra*) until very recently was a rarity on these hills, but now its cultivation is being rapidly extended, as there is a greater demand for them. The other varieties grown on a small scale are the Bitter or Seville Orange, and the Kumquat (*Citrus japonica*) ; the former is used for marmalade and the latter for preserve. Amongst those which are being experimentally grown are the Washington, Navel, Nagpore, Sylhet, China, Mozambique, Satghur and the Malta Blood.

Lemons.—The Sour Lime is common on most estates; the Malta Lemon and the Citron do well at elevations of over 4,500′.

CHAP. IV. CHIEF CROPS.

Pomeloes (*Citrus decumana*, or shaddock).—Both the red and the white varieties flourish; the former make good candied peel.

Apples grow to special perfection on Mr. Thurston Short's estate, "Riverdale," a fact due, no doubt, to some peculiarity in the soil and situation.

Pears (*Pyrus communis*), thrive on the higher elevations, 4,500′ and over. They are propagated by cuttings, which take 10 years or more to bear. The La Conte and Keiffer, which bear fruit at Bangalore, are being tried at Nāgalūr at an elevation of 3,800′. Other graft varieties, such as Bergamot, Jargonelle, Marie Louise, and Beurre Hardy, should do well on the Green Hill plateau.

Plums bear abundant crops; some trees carry a bushel each. It would be interesting to see if the variety from which prunes are made would flourish on the hills.

Peaches do well, but the fruit has a tendency to grow elongated instead of round.

The Loquat (*Eriobotrya japonica* or Japanese Medlar) is common. The fruit ripens in September or October. Some years ago a very fine champagne was made from its juice.

Chirimoya (*Anona cherimolia*) indigenous in Peru, was introduced by the late Major Hunter from Madeira, and fruited for the first time in 1884. The fruit resembles the bullock-heart in appearance, and the custard-apple in flavour. The hybrid Chirimoya (a cross between the true Chirimoya and the Custard Apple), produces a very large luscious fruit of exquisite flavour.

Pine-apples.—The common variety flourishes; the fruit, though small, is of very good flavour.

Strawberries were successfully grown by Mr. J. C. Large under irrigation, but they do not thrive if grown on the same ground for two consecutive years.

Other fruits that do well on the Hills are the Papaw (*Carica papaya*), which also thrives on the plains, the Butter-fruit (*Persea vulgaris, P. oblonga, P. macrophylla, P. drimyfolia,* etc.), the Fig, the Guava (*Psidium guayava*), Jack-fruit (*Artocarpus integrifolia*), Rose-apple (*Eugenia jambos*), Custard-apple (*Anona squamosa*), Pomegranate (*Punica granatum*), Plantains and Mulberry (*Morus indica*).[1] Viticulture has not been attempted on the Hills, but the town of Krishnagiri is noted for its grapes, which are trained over pergolas in the backyards of Muhammadan houses.

Mangoes.

Thanks to the enterprise of a few local Muhammadans, Salem Town is famous for its graft mangoes. More than twenty varieties are grown, the most popular being *Gundu*, *Nadu-sālai*, *Kudādād* and *Malgova*. Graft mangoes are also grown extensively

[1] The Mulberry is also grown extensively round Bērikai for the rearing of silk-worms—See Vol. II, p. 124.

at Kāvēri-patnam, but grafting is not done locally, grafts being imported from Salem, Chittoor and Bangalore (*Gundu*, *Malgova*, *Kādir*, *Pīthar*, *Dil-pasand*, *Gathēmar*, *Nīlam*, *Chittura*, and *Bengalura*). On the Shevaroys graft mangoes flourish up to 2,500′, but the fruit-fly destroys the fruit produced at elevations of over 3,500′, by burrowing in the soft tissues and rendering it valueless. Common country mangoes grow everywhere, but the fruit is of very little value.[1] Mangoes flower in Tai (January-February), and are harvested in Chittrai (April-May), and the trees are usually leased to contractors in Māsi (February-March).

Inarching.

In Salem City mangoes are grafted by "inarching." For the stock, ordinary mango shrubs of two years' growth are used. The top of the stock is cut off, the stem pared to half its thickness to a distance of 3″ or 4″ from the top. An incision of similar size and shape is then made in the stem of any suitable shoot in the parent tree, and the two are bound tightly together with a strip of waxed cloth, which is afterwards covered with a mixture of cowdung and earth.

A slightly different method is adopted for inarching Guava, Orange, Lime, Pomegranate, and other fruit-trees, the stock being pared on both sides and spliced into a longitudinal upward incision (technically known as a "cleft") in the parent shoots.

IRRIGATION.

The subjoined statement shows in acres the *āyakat* under the several classes of irrigation for each Taluk in Fasli 1321:—

Taluk.	River channels under Public Works Department.	Other river channels.	Major tanks under Public Works Department.	Minor tanks under Revenue Department.	Wells.	Total, Government.	Mittas.
	ACS.	ACS.	ACS.	ACS.	ACS.	ACS.	ACS.
Salem ...	394	2,186	3,476	5,920	20	11,996	1,327
Āttūr ...	3,153	4,543	6,322	4,554	15,056	33,628	...
Tiruchengōdu	1,059	1,028	3,090	736	11,391	17,304	4,538
Ōmalūr ...	215	1,395	1,142	4,395	2,663	9,810	356
Dharmapuri ...	290	1,243	2,515	9,127	30	13,205	3,686
Ūttankarai ...	979	1,086	1,227	4,962	...	8,254	2,391
Hosūr ...	250	510	837	10,008	...	11,605	4,648
Krishnagiri ...	2,178	1,473	2,163	7,045	...	12,859	8,385
Total ...	8,518	13,464	20,772	46,747	29,160	118,661	25,331

[1] For instance the Puttira-Kavundan-Pālaiyam tope, planted by Mr. Pochin, which measures about 6 furlongs long and 1 furlong broad, only realises an annual bid of about Rs. 18, and a similar tope at Abinavam, planted by the same officer, fetches about the same, whereas one good graft mango tree in Salem realises from Rs. 30 to 50 annually.

CHAP. IV. IRRIGATION.

The operations of the Tank Restoration Scheme Parties have been confined to the Basin of the Pennaiyār, and to the Tirumani-muttār Minor Basin of the Kāvēri. The Pennaiyār Basin has been divided into the Minor Basins of (1) Hosūr, (2) Mārkanda-nadi, (3) Kāvēri-patnam, (4) Pāmbār, (5) Kambaya-nallūr and (6) Vāniyār. Much of the area included in the Pāmbār, Mārkanda-nadi and Tirumani-muttār Basins lies beyond the limits of the District. The results of the investigations are summarised in the subjoined statement :—

Basin.	Area in square miles.	Number of irrigation works.	Number of square miles to a work.	Number of Government works.	Ayakat of Government works as per Tank Restoration Scheme.	Average Ayakat per work.	Number of Government works of over 100 acres Ayakat.
					ACS.	ACS.	
Hosūr	555	538	1·03	147	4,575	31·12	8
Mārkanda-nadi...	276	224	1·23	55	2,530	46·00	4
Kāvēri-patnam.	49	57	0·86	31	1,113	35·90	4
Pāmbār	832	628	1·32	415	13,890	33·47	7
Kambaya-nallūr.	419	575	0·73	326	11,357	34·84	21
Vāniyār	612	192	3·19	155	4,254	27·45	7
Tirumani-muttār.	717	290	2·47	175	15,712	89·78	55

Major Works.

The Public Works Department is in charge of all tanks and anaikats which irrigate upwards of 200 acres, all "railway affecting" tanks, and all tanks, irrespective of size, which are fed by Imperial anaikats. Details of these works are given in the Taluk notices in Chapter XV.

Minor Works.

The number of Minor Irrigation works in the District in charge of the Revenue Department is 2,409, distributed as shown in the margin. Their *āyakat* is a little less than 47,000 acres, and the annual cost of maintenance a little under Rs. 20,000. It will be noted that petty works are far more numerous in the Bāramahāl than in the Talaghāt.

Taluk.	Number of works.
Hosūr	394
Krishnagiri ...	481
Dharmapuri ...	422
Uttankarai ...	446
Salem	219
Ōmalūr... ...	120
Tiruchengōdu...	159
Āttūr	168

"Turns."

Under some of the larger irrigation sources a simple business-like device is adopted for regulating the distribution of water to the several holdings. The *nīrganti*, as the village servant is called whose duty it is to distribute the water, is provided with a small copper cup, in the bottom of which a tiny hole is bored.

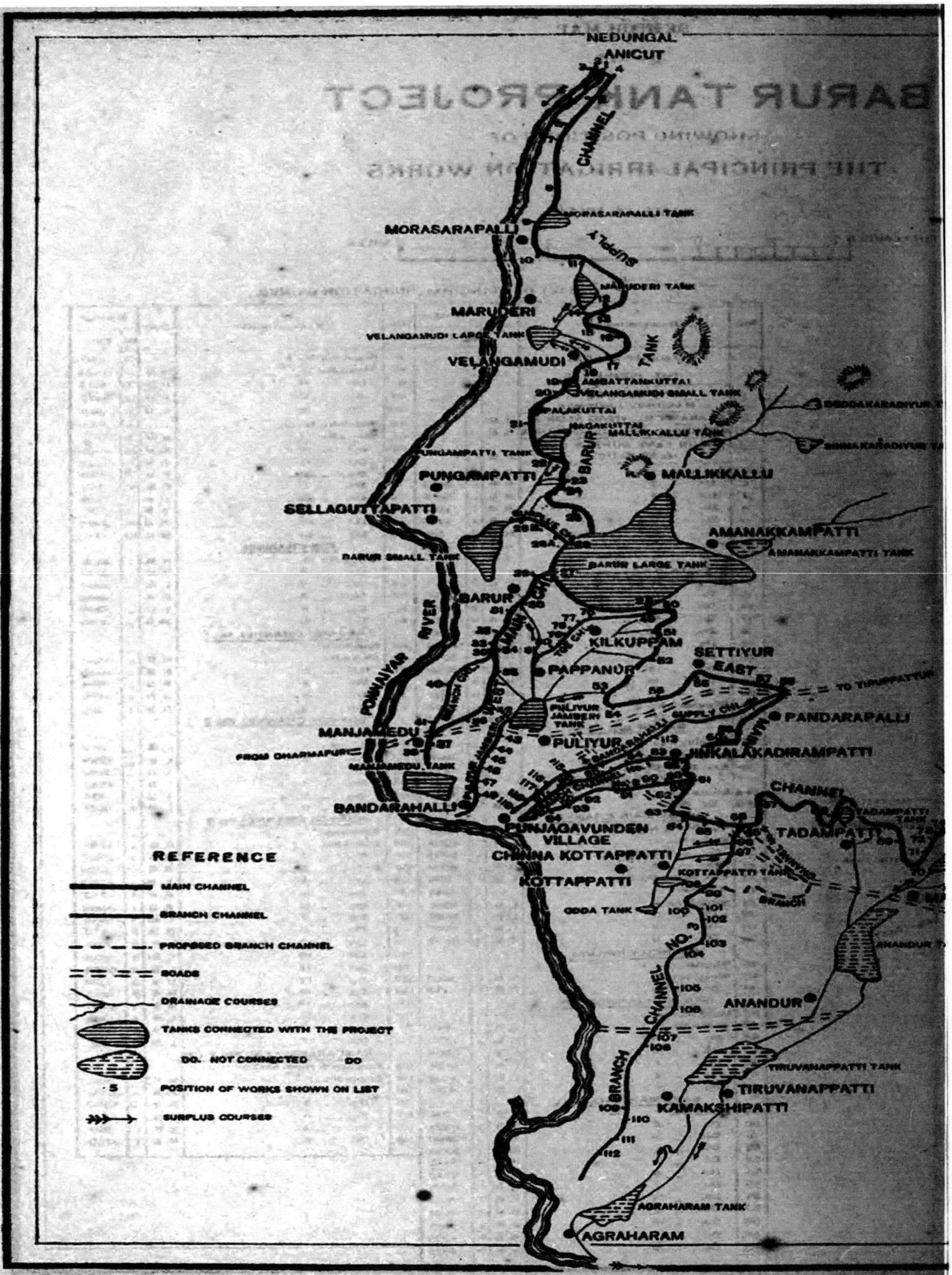

Reg. No. 546
Copies 620

SKETCH MAP

OF THE

BARUR TANK PROJECT

SHOWING POSITIONS OF

THE PRINCIPAL IRRIGATION WORKS

SCALE OF MILES

FURLONGS 8 4 0 1 2 MILES

LIST OF PRINCIPAL IRRIGATION WORKS.

Nos.	Name of works	Side	Mileage Ms.	Mileage Feet
	ANICUT ACROSS THE PONNAIYAR			
1	SAND SLUICES & MASONRY GROYNES			
2	AGARAM CHL. HEAD SLUICE	R. B.		
3	NEDUNGAL CHL. HEAD SLUICE	R. B.		
4	BARUR TANK SUPPLY CHL. HEAD SLUICE	L. B.		
5	Sluice No. 1	R. B.	„	951
6	Do. .. 2	R. B.	„	2879
7	Do. .. 3	R. B.	„	5014
8	Do. .. 4	R. B.	1	1743
9	Do. .. 5	R. B.	1	3740
10	Do. .. 6	R. B.	2	516
11	Do. .. 7	R. B.	2	2210
12	Do .. 8	R. B.	3	215
13	Regulator No. 1		3	472
14	Sluice No. 9	R. B	3	1207
15	Do. .. 10	R. B.	3	2457
16	Do. .. 10 A	R. B.	3	4559
17	Do. .. 11	R. B.	4	1728
18	Do. .. 12	R. B.	4	3045
19	Do. .. 13	R. B.	4	4896
20	Do. .. 14	R. B.	4	5070
21	Do. .. 15	R. B.	5	2088
22	Do. .. 16	R. B.	5	4620
23	Do. .. 17	R. B.	6	1837
24	Regulator No. 2		6	1960
25	Sluice No. 18	R. B	6	4376
	BARUR BIG TANK			
26	Surplus Weir & Surplus Sluices		„	274
27	West Main Sluice		„	2561
28	East Main Sluice		1	1874
	SURPLUS CHANNEL			
28 A	Sluice No. 1	L. B.	„	690
28 B	Do No. 2	L. B.	„	3020
	WEST MAIN CHANNEL			
29	Pipe Sluice No. 1	L. B.	„	523
30	Sluice No. 2	L. B.	„	2208
31	Do. .. 3	R. B.	„	2794
32	Do. .. 4	R. B.	„	5019
33	Pipe Sluice No. 5	L. B.	1	356
34	Regulator	„	1	993
35	Sluice No. 6	L. B.	1	2514
36	Do. .. 7	L. B.	1	5069
37	Do. .. 8	L. B.	2	2880
38	Do. .. 9	R. B.	2	2932
	BRANCH CHANNEL			
39	Regulator	„	„	„
40	Sluice No. 1	R. B.	„	2493
41	Do .. 2	R. B.	1	173
	PULIYUR JAMBERI CHL.			
42	Head Sluice			
43	Sluice No. 1	L. B.	„	945
44	Do. .. 1 A	L. B.	„	1712
45	Do. 2	L. B.	„	2505
46	Do. .. 3	L. B.	„	3135
47	Do. .. 4	L. B.	„	3698
48	Do. .. 5	L. B.	„	4218
	EAST MAIN CHANNEL			
49	Sluice No. 1	R. B.	„	76
50	Do. .. 2	R. B.	„	1000
51	Do. .. 3	R. B.	„	2880
52	Do. .. 4	R. B.	„	5250
53	Do. .. 5	R. B	1	2840
54	Do. .. 6	R. B.	1	3740
55	Do. .. 7	R. B.	1	5100
56	Do. .. 8	R. B.	2	1208
57	Do. .. 9	R. B.	2	4290
58	Do. .. 10	R. B.	3	925
59	Do. .. 11	R. B.	4	1025
60	Do. .. 12	R. B.	4	3375
61	Regulator No. 1	„	5	660
62	Sluice No. 13	R. B.	5	3435
63	Do. .. 14	R. B.	5	4213
64	Do. .. 15	R. B.	5	4576
65	Do. .. 16	R B.	6	703
66	Regulator No. 2	„	6	2951
67	Sluice No. 17	R. B.	6	3102
68	Do. .. 18	R. B	6	4234
69	Do. .. 19	R. B	7	2568
70	Do. .. 20	R. B.	7	4855
71	Do. .. 21	R. B.	8	345
72	Do. .. 22	R. B.	8	3635
73	Do. .. 23	R. B.	9	1710
74	Do. .. 24	R. B	9	3924
75	Do. .. 25	R. B.	10	770
	TOE CHANNEL			
76	Sluice No. 1	R. B.	„	2206
77	Do. .. 2	R. B.	„	2876
78	Do. .. 3	L. B.	„	3148
79	Do. .. 4	R. B.	„	3596
80	Do. .. 5	L. B.	„	3966
81	Do. .. 6	R. B.	„	4916
	BRANCH CHANNEL No. 1			
82	Regulator	„	„	„
83	Sluice No. 1	R. B.	„	1530
84	Do. .. 2	R. B.	„	2430
85	Do. .. 3	R. B.	„	3696
86	Do. .. 4	R. B.	„	4785
87	Do. .. 5	R. B.	1	810
	BRANCH CHANNEL No. 2			
88	Regulator	„	„	„
89	Sluice No. 1	L. B.	„	1110
90	Do. .. 2	L. B.	„	1890
91	Do. .. 3	L. B.	„	2612
92	Do. .. 4	L. B.	„	4565
93	Do. .. 5	L. B.	1	374
94	Do. .. 6	L. B.	1	1017
	BRANCH CHANNEL No. 3			
95	Regulator	„	„	„
96	Sluice No. 1	R. B.	„	1235
97	Do. .. 2	R. B.	„	2654
98	Do .. 3	R. B	„	4620
99	Do. .. 4	L. B.	„	4700
100	Do. .. 5	R. B.	1	742
101	Do. .. 6	R. B.	1	4265
102	Do. .. 7	L. B.	1	4344
103	Do. .. 8	R. B.	2	578
104	Do. .. 9	L. B.	2	695
105	Do. .. 10	L. B.	2	3815
106	Do. .. 11	L. B.	2	5074
107	Do. .. 12	L. B.	3	1120
108	Do. .. 13	R. B.	3	1955
109	Do. .. 14	R. B.	3	4087
110	Do. .. 15	L. B.	4	468
111	Do. .. 16	L. B.	4	2288
112	Do. .. 17	L. B.	5	142
	BANDARAHALLI SUPPLY CHL.			
113	Kondom & Head Sluice	„	„	„
114	Sluice No. 1	R. B	„	900
115	Do. .. 2	R. B	„	3200
116	Do. .. 3	R. B.	„	4000
117	Do. .. 4	R. B.	„	5100
118	Do. .. 5	R. B.	1	820
119	Do. .. 6	R. B.	1	1720

Helio-Zinco., Survey Office, Madras.
1916

This cup is floated on a chatty of water, and in twenty minutes it fills and sinks. On the inside of the cup are marks to indicate when it is a quarter, half or three-quarters full. The time required to fill a cup $1\frac{1}{2}$ times is sufficient to irrigate about an acre. Allowing for delays, the cup is filled about 33 times between sunrise and sunset, and 33 times during night, and about 40 acres can be irrigated in 24 hours. The *nīrganti* is watched by the ryot whose land is to be irrigated, and he is also supervised by one of the other ryots who hold land under the *āyakat*. The ryots take up this work of supervision in turn, and the supervising ryot is allowed 3 out of 33 turns for his own use as compensation for his loss of time.

Baling.

The marginal statement shows the area of Government lands registered as "Baling wet"[1] at Resettlement, together with the number of wells in each taluk in Fasli 1320.

Taluk.	Baling Wet.	Wells.	
		In Nanjai.	In Punjai.
	ACS.		
Hosūr ...	24	1,350	19
Krishnagiri ...	209	3,753	5,231
Dharmapuri ...	67	4,591	6,263
Ūttankarai ...	236	1,293	3,832
Salem ...	825	2,752	11,065
Ōmalūr ..	...	130	592
Tiruchengōdu.	977	7,500	345
Āttūr ...	294	4,208	8,779

Kuttais.

The physical character of the District lends itself readily to the formation by natural or artificial agencies of small ponds or *kuttais*, supplied with water by springs, surface drainage or jungle streams, and permitting the precarious irrigation of small plots of land. Concurrently with the Resettlement of the northern taluks, an exhaustive enquiry was made into the conditions of irrigation under *kuttais* and small anaikats throughout the District, and a record of rights was prepared. As many as 1,118 sources were recognised as private, and *sanads* were issued accordingly.

Bārūr Project.

The Bārūr Project was first undertaken as a famine relief work in 1877. It was completed in 1888 at a cost of Rs. 4,34,415. Since that date several improvements have from time to time been made. The Pennaiyār is dammed at Nedungal, in Krishnagiri Taluk, at a point where its catchment area is 1,900 square miles. The anaikat is 912 feet across. The Supply Channel to Bārūr Great Tank takes off from the left bank of the river; it is 7 miles 1 furlong in length, and is provided with 17 sluices, all opening in the right bund of the channel. These sluices are used for direct irrigation; some of them supply three tanks formerly fed by river channels from the Pennaiyār, viz., Marudēri, Velangāmudi and Bārūr Small Tank.

[1] See Vol. II. pp. 39, 40.

CHAP. IV. IRRIGATION.

Bārūr Great Tank itself covers 688 acres. It lies at the head of a shallow valley, bounded on the east and west by low ridges. The water of the Great Tank is distributed by two Main Channels, which follow the contours of these two ridges, and irrigate the intervening lands. The West Main Channel is 2 miles 5 furlongs in length, and gives off one Branch Channel. The total length of the East Main Channel is 10½ miles, and it also feeds three Branch Channels. The drainage of its tail-end tanks flows through the Mitta tanks of Ānandūr, Tiruvana-patti and Agrahāram.

The completion of the Bārūr Project was not followed by the rapid extension of wet cultivation that had been expected, and the additional revenue derived from it failed to cover the interest on capital expenditure.

In 1893 the Board ordered that, as the Project was a "work for which capital and revenue accounts are kept" the lands commanded by it should be assessed at "first group" rates. This order was revised in 1898 on the recommendation of the Collector, and first-class rates were continued only for lands under the first six sluices of the Main Channels, the remaining sluices of the West Channel, with its branch, and sluices 7 to 11 of the East Channel were reduced to the second class, and the rest of the *āyakal* was placed in the third class.

At Resettlement the three tanks fed directly by the Supply Channel were raised to the second class, while all sluices below the 6th in the West Channel, and below the 11th in the East Channel with the Branch Channels of the latter were reduced to the fourth class.

The result of Resettlement was to raise the assessment of the occupied *āyakat* from Rs. 10,900 to Rs. 24,750. Of this increase, nearly Rs. 9,000 represents the dry assessment and water-rate previously chargeable on the extent transferred at Resettlement from dry to wet.[1]

[1] Description of Land.	Extent.	Revenue.	
		Revenue Accounts.	Resettlement.
	ACS.	RS.	RS.
Wet at Settlement	1,256	6,900	11,245
Transferred from dry to wet between Settlement and Resettlement ...	663	4,002	4,340
Transferred from dry to wet at Resettlement	1,284	1,143	9,163
Water-rate on dry before Resettlement	...	7,704	...
Total ...	3,203	19,749	24,748

Penukonda-puram.

The Pennkondapuram Tank was built as a famine relief work in the seventies, on the site of a ruined bund which was breached apparently before the District came under British rule. The chief source of supply is the Sandūr River; an additional supply is derived from the Mattūr River by an open-headed channel dug in 1898–99. The whole *āyakat* is less than 500 acres; the soil is sandy, saline and poor. Though the catchment area is 52 square miles, the supply is precarious, the bund leaks, and the whole project is rather a dismal specimen of a famine relief work.

Kāvēri Project.

The Kāvēri Project is a scheme for damming the Kāvēri at a point just above the village of Metur, Bhavāni Taluk, Coimbatore District (opposite Panamarattuppatti, Tiruchengōdu Taluk), where the Pālamalai and the Sītā-malai converge[1] 35 miles above Erode and 24 miles above the confluence of the Bhavāni and Kāvēri rivers. The reservoir so formed will hold 80,000 million cubic feet of water, and the water-spread will reach northward to Hōgenkāl falls beyond the confluence of the Toppūr River with the Kāvēri, submerging the villages round Sōlappādi and Baddira-halli in the Dharmapuri Taluk. The Project is intended for the improvement and extension of irrigation in Tanjore District."

Krishnagiri Project.

The Krishnagiri Project provides for the construction of a dam across the Pennaiyār, at a point where the river valley is narrowed to a width of half a mile by two rocky hills, 25 miles north-west of the spot where the Madras-Calicut Railway crosses that river. The catchment area of the reservoir would be 1,431 square miles. The capacity of the reservoir is estimated at 6,000 million cubic feet, a quantity sufficient for the irrigation of 20,000 acres of paddy and 38,000 acres of dry crops. It is doubtful if it will be possible without infringing existing irrigation rights to permit impounding of such large quantities of water and this matter is the subject of further enquiry. Two main distribution channels are provided for. The south main channel would irrigate that portion of Krishnagiri Taluk which lies on the right bank of the Pennaiyār, and stretches as far as the Kambaya-nallūr Mitta. The east main channel is to serve the left bank of the Pennaiyār, bending round the hill to the east of the reservoir and passing near the bund of the Ghouse Saib Tank of Avadāna-palli. Thence it is to cross the road, and curve round the hill near Timmāpuram Tank, irrigating the country just above the Nedungal Anaikat.

---

[1] See p. 21 supra, and Vol. II, p. 276.

CHAP. IV. IRRIGATION.

Mārānda-halli Project.

The Mārānda-halli Project is intended to utilise the surplus water of the Sanat-kumāra-nadi, which at present passes over the Mārānda-halli Anaikat in Dharmapuri Taluk, at which point the river has a catchment area of 340 square miles. The scheme provides for increasing the capacity of Sangam-basavan, Māvēri and Jer-talav Tanks by raising their bunds.

Pulahalli Project.

A further extension of the Mārānda-halli Project is the construction of a reservoir near Pālakōdu, to be filled by the surplus water of the Jer-talāv. This reservoir would irrigate the valley of the Pula-halli river, which crosses the Dharmapuri-Krishnagiri road south of Kāri-mangalam.

Badē-talāv.

Proposals have been formulated for improving the precarious supply of the Badē-talāv Tank, near Krishnagiri, by connecting it, by a channel 12 miles long, with the Mārkanda-nadi near Nidusāl,[1] where an anaikat was to be built. The Krishnagiri Project would, however, be incomparably more useful, and would benefit the same tract.

Minor Schemes.

Suggestions have been made for exploiting the Sanat-kumāra-nadi by the erection of a gigantic reservoir near Pancha-palli, but the Pula-halli Project would serve the same end far more effectively. Two reservoirs have been proposed near Anchetti in Hosūr Taluk. The adjoining tract, however, is sparsely populated, feverish, and mostly covered by reserved forests. Proposals have also been considered for utilising the Vāniyār and the Toppūr River by the construction of dams, and for enlarging the capacity of the tanks fed by the Sarabhanga-nadi and Swēta-nadi.

AGRICULTURAL ECONOMY.

Volumes might be written on the economic condition of agriculture in the District, on the poverty under which the ryot suffers, on his indebtedness, on the increase in the cost of cultivation, the restrictions of Forest Laws, and the weight of land assessment. Unfortunately it is not humanly possible to summarise accurately the little-understood complex of forces that act and react on the ryot's status, and vague generalities are best left alone. Suffice it to say that the ryot shows no sign of being "taxed out of existence," that he is as truly the backbone of the nation to-day as he was a century, or a millenium, ago, and that the soil of Salem District under the British Raj can support nearly four times the population that it supported under Tipu's

[1] A village belonging to Neriyana-kuppam Mitta of Krishnagiri Taluk on the opposite side of Mārkanda-nadi to Māra-samudram.

rule. Indebted the ryot undoubtedly is, was, and always will be, but he is none the less sturdy and virile for that. Munro's impartial summary of the ryot's condition is by no means an anachronism in the twentieth century. CHAP. IV. AGRICULTURAL ECONOMY.

"Though the ryots have little money, I imagine that they suffer less real distress than the peasantry of Europe. The inclemency of the weather is what they hardly ever feel: firewood costs them nothing, and dress very little. Their own labour, for two or three days, is the price of their house, which is built of mud and covered with straw or leaves, and, in a warm climate, such materials answer the purpose just as well as stone or marble. All of them are married, and their families, so far from being a burden, are a great support to them, because their labour produces more than the expense of their maintenance:—this is so generally understood, that nothing is more common than to grant a man a remission of rent on the death of his wife or his son. Learned men who write of India, begin by talking of the sun, and then tell us that its vertical rays make the natives indolent; but notwithstanding all this, the farmers are, at least, as industrious as those of Europe, and their women more so.[1]"

Census Returns.

The Census Returns for 1911 show that nearly 1,300,000 souls, or 73 per cent. of the total population, are dependent on agriculture for livelihood. Out of every thousand so dependent, 35 are classed as non-cultivators (land-owners 24 and tenants 11 per mille), and 965 as cultivators (landowners 709, tenants 76 and labourers 180 per mille).[2] Thus, excluding non-cultivating owners and tenants, the number of souls *directly* dependent on the soil totals just over $1\frac{1}{4}$ millions, or 70 per cent. of the total population. Out of this huge total, 58 per cent. are classed as "actual workers" and 42 as "dependents", against 50 per cent. "actual workers" and 50 per cent. "dependents" for the remaining half million of the population. The percentage of "actual workers" among the cultivating landowners is 56, among the cultivating tenants 54, and among the agricultural labourers 70; and of those "actual workers" the percentage of females is 42 among cultivating landowners, 37 among cultivating tenants, and 56 among field-labourers. The analysis is interesting, as it shows that the peasant proprietor is still the most important person in the District, and that he and his family work hard. No doubt the

[1] Letter dated Ōmalūr, May 10, 1796, Gleig, Vol. I, p. 186.

[2] The actual figures are—

Non-cultivating owners	31,068
Non-cultivating tenants	13,835
Cultivating owners	918,708
Cultivating tenants	99,058
Labourers	232,703

CHAP. IV. AGRICULTURAL ECONOMY.

comparative dearth of capitalists is a check on the rapid development of new methods of agriculture, but the rapid growth of ground-nut and cotton cultivation during the past decade prove that the Salem ryot is by no means buried in conservatism. *Latifundia* are not an unmixed blessing, and Salem District affords a useful object lesson in the vitality of "small holdings."

Rent-roll.

Though "rent-roll" statistics are apt to be vitiated by the fact that a ryot may not only hold several pattas in his own name,[1] but may also have an interest in several "joint-pattas", yet, so far as they go, they corroborate in an interesting way the inferences to be drawn from the census returns. The subjoined figures show the proportion of single and joint pattas in each taluk after the introduction of Resettlement, together with the percentage of pattas paying over and under Rs. 30 :—

Taluk.	Single.	Joint.	Rs. 10 and less.	Between Rs. 10 and Rs. 30.	Total under Rs. 30.	Over Rs. 30.
Salem[2]	60	40	61	34	95	5
Tiruchengōdu ...	41	59	45	48	93	7
Āttūr	66	34	83	14	97	3
Ūttankarai ...	69	31	75	22	97	3
Dharmapuri ...	56	44	74	23	97	3
Krishnagiri ...	55	45	64	28	92	8
Hosūr	55	45	75	20	95	5

Rents.

Such lands as are leased, are usually leased for a share in the produce (*vāram* tenure). The respective shares of contracting parties are, as a rule, determined by local custom. The commonest arrangement is for owner and tenant to take a moiety of the produce each, the owner paying the whole assessment, and the tenant bearing all the cost of cultivation. Sometimes the owner gets only two-fifths, and in the case of lands irrigated by baling, the owner's share is often reduced to one-fifth. The poorer the soil, the lower is the owner's share, and one-sixth is sometimes agreed to. In the Bāramahāl, and also in the Denkani-kōta Division, the so-called *kandāchāram* system is in vogue, by which the owners receive one-fourth of the produce, the tenants three-fourths, each party paying half the kist. Leases for a fixed rent in kind (*guttagai*) are confined to wet and garden lands irrigated by unfailing sources, such as the Pennaiyār channels or "major" tanks; the owner pays the kist and receives 5 or 6 *kandagams*[3]

[1] "Duplicate puttas" as they are called in Settlement jargon.

[2] Inclusive of Ōmalūr.

[3] One *kandagam* = 213$\frac{1}{3}$ Madras measures in the Krishnagiri Taluk and 110 Madras measures in the Dharmapuri Taluk.

of grain. Money rents are paid mostly on betel-gardens, and on paddy land in the few favoured localities where the sowcars find the purchase of land to be a profitable investment for capital.

CHAP. IV AGRICULTURAL ECONOMY.

Sale Values.

The sale value of land since 1871 has fluctuated in rather a curious manner. In preparing the Scheme Reports for Resettlement, the registered sale deeds of nearly 300 typical villages were examined, and it was found that the average sale value of "dry" land in most of the District stood markedly lower in the period 1881–85 than it was in 1871–75. The fall is due partly, no doubt, to the fact that in the earlier period the transactions registered were few in number, and at the later period registration was more in fashion, even for petty transactions; it is probable at the same time that depreciation was due in part to the Great Famine. Since 1885, however, there has been a steady rise in land values, except under ordinary "dry" lands; the value of "wet" lands in the southern taluks rose from Rs. 99 in 1871–75 to Rs. 140 in 1895–1900; the value of "dry" lands with wells rose from Rs. 53 to Rs. 64½; in the northern taluks the value of "wet" lands with wells rose from Rs. 120 in 1871–75 to Rs. 204 in 1891–95, that of "wet" lands without wells from Rs. 131 to Rs. 166; while "dry" lands with wells rose from Rs. 23 to over Rs. 43 in the same period. Ordinary "dry" lands, however, in the southern taluks fell from Rs. 29½ to Rs. 22½, and in the northern taluks the figure for both periods was just under Rs. 23.[1] The decrease is probably due to the fact that the poorer lands, which in the earlier period could command no price at all, in the later period acquired a saleable value.

More recent registration figures for the whole District indicate a further rise; the average value of "dry" land in Government villages for the whole District in 1897 was Rs. 31, in 1904 it was Rs. 45; that of "wet" was Rs. 179 in 1897, and Rs. 221 in 1904; the rise in Mitta lands was less sharp.

Land Transfers.

The stability of the ryots seems to be improving, and the proportion of immoveable property transferred from ryots to non-agricultural capitalists appears to be decreasing. For instance the District Registrar's returns show that in 1897, of the total extent of land purchased, only 74 per cent. was bought by agriculturists, while in 1904 the percentage was 83; in 1897 ryots sold 4,130 acres more than they purchased; in 1904 the difference was reduced to 411 acres. If these figures are any index of the drift of things, there is no serious reason to fear that the ownership of land is passing out of the hands of the agricultural classes.

---

[1] See G.O. 1029, Rev., of 7th October 1903, p. 23; and Board's Proceedings 212 of 15th July 1905, p. 28.

CHAP. IV. AGRICULTURAL ECONOMY.

Waste.

The area of "dry" land classed as assessed waste (*pōdugāl*) in Government villages at Resettlement amounted to about 350,000 acres, assessed at Rs. 2,11,000 odd, and the area under "wet waste" was about 4,600 acres, assessed at a little over Rs. 22,000. [1] In the resettled villages the percentage of "dry waste" to the whole "dry" *āyakat* was as shown in the margin. The figures at first sight are rather startling, especially in Āttūr,[2] Ūttankarai and Hosūr, and the existence of such enormous areas of waste land demands an explanation. The cause can hardly be over-assessment, for a glance at the soil-war abstracts [3] of assessed waste reveals the fact that most of the waste land in the District is very lightly assessed. The average assessment on "dry waste" at Resettlement was a little less than 10 annas per acre, and that on "wet waste" about Rs. 4¾.[4] In the southern taluks nearly 60 per cent. of the waste was assessed at less than one rupee per acre, and in the northern taluks nearly 90 per cent. of the waste comes under the same category, nearly 40 per cent. being placed in the lowest *taram* of 4 annas per acre. The fact is that a very large proportion of the soil in Salem District is extremely poor in quality and barely repays the most meagre culture. Moreover the large tracts that adjoin Forest Reserves are often not only malarial, but also peculiarly liable to be devastated by wild animals. The result is that the ryot tends to concentrate his efforts on the intensive cultivation of the lands which yield the richest produce or lie closest to his home. Especially is this the case in Āttūr Taluk, where the ryot's chief interest lies in his wells and channels. The poorer and remoter soils are not unnaturally neglected. If a few good showers fall at an opportune moment, it may be worth a ryot's while to plough a patch of waste land and sow it with a hardy crop, without asking for its formal assignment. It would not pay him to expend much time or labour on manuring and weeding such fields, and so superficial is the cultivation, that the land must be frequently left fallow to enable the soil to recoup

Taluk.	
Salem ...	13
Tiruchengōdu	9
Āttūr ..	46
Krishnagiri	14
Dharmapuri	17
Ūttankarai	31
Hosūr. ..	26

---

[1] Exclusive of Nāmakkal and Tiruppattūr, but inclusive of the newly-settled villages of Āttūr, Salem, Dharmapuri and Hosūr.

[2] For the peculiar condition of Āttur Taluk, see G.O. 1029, Rev. of 7th October 1903, pp. 14 and 15.

[3] See Appendix XIV-A and XIV-H at pp. 62 and 63 and 74 of B.P. 387 of 19th October, 1906, and Appendices VII-A and VII-B at pp. 55 and 56 of B.P. 9 of 8th March, 1908.

[4]

	Wet			Dry.		
	RS.	A.	P.	RS.	A.	P.
South	5	6	9	0	11	0
North	3	6	11	0	8	4

its exhausted energies. Thus very large areas of waste land are cultivated on *sivāyjama*, and are never assigned, and in many localities, notably in Āttūr and Hosūr, the farmer's etiquette prescribes that, if a ryot has once cultivated a waste field, he has a sort of claim to it, and no other ryot may take it up without his consent.[1] Again, in Hosūr Taluk, custom requires the reservation, by mutual consent of the villagers, of large tracts of waste land for purposes of grazing, and even recognises the preferential rights of individual ryots to graze their stock on particular fields. Lastly, the cost of paying the value of trees on waste land, which is a condition precedent to its assignment, often acts as a deterrent to its being brought under permanent occupation. In view of the above facts, the extent of land remaining unoccupied in Salem District is not so serious a symptom as it might appear, and there is little prospect that the total area permanently under "holdings" will ever be greatly extended.

Wages.

It is by no means easy to express the remuneration of the agricultural labourer in terms of annas and pies. The day labourer is sometimes paid in cash, sometimes in kind, sometimes in both. His remuneration varies with the work he has to perform, and the different rates for ploughing, weeding, reaping, thrashing, etc. When he is paid in kind, he may receive one meal a day *plus* cash or grain, or two meals a day, or so many measures of grain per diem, and the measures in which *kūli* is paid vary widely in different localities, and sometimes special measures are employed for the purpose.[2] The position of farm-servants (*pannaiyāls* = *adscripti glebæ*) is different; they engage themselves to their master (*yajamānan*) for periods varying from a year to a life-time; the terms of the contract are infinitely various; the master usually provides food and clothing, with perhaps a small sum of money annually, and a few customary presents, such as a cloth at Dīpāvali, a *tāli* at marriage, a few rupees at the birth of a child, etc. It must not be forgotten that in the days of Tipu the position of the agricultural labourer was virtually one of hopeless slavery. Among the forms of agreement officially sanctioned by Read is a "Form (No. 38) of Promissory Note to a Servant who engages to serve him for life"; its terms are terse and to the point; they run :—

> "If you serve me while you are able to work, I will maintain you while you live."

---

[1] *Pōdugāl-bāddiyam* or "right to waste land" is the phrase current in Āttūr Taluk.

[2] For the *Kūli-padi* and *Kūli-vallam* see page 287.

CHAP. IV. AGRICULTURAL ECONOMY.

Another Form of Promissory Note (No. 36) of equal interest, and rather more respectful to human liberties, runs as if written by Laban to Jacob :—

"If you will serve me five years from this date to the best of your ability, I will supply you with food and apparel, and at the expiration of that period will give you my daughter in marriage."

Unfortunately documents similar in purport to the former of these promissory notes are occasionally presented, even in the twentieth century, at the offices of the Sub-Registrars. For instance :—

"We are your Pariah servants, and as such we serve you in all good and bad occasions, in all the works you command us to do in our lifetime ; and for our service you have to give us five measures for each *kandagam* of your produce in each year" or

"I have received Rs. 37, and in lieu of interest I have employed my three sons under you for 15 years, on pay of Rs. 1–8–0 per annum and 12 *vallams* of rāgi per mensem. If my sons fail to work, I render myself liable to damages and punishment under the Acts of Government."

But though poverty survives, the position of the labouring classes is undoubtedly improving. In Hosūr, in particular, the supply of labour is unequal to the demand, and the day-labourer can dictate his terms. The counter-attraction of the Kōlār Gold Fields and the Mattigiri Remount Depot, and the high wages offered by estate owners on the Shevaroys and Nīlgiris, and in Ceylon, Mauritius, Penang, etc., partly account for this. Good wages, too, can be obtained on road repairs, irrigation works, new railways, or in gathering forest and avenue produce. Even plague, by restricting the supply of labour, has helped to place the coolie classes in an advantageous position.

Perhaps, however, the ideal of agricultural economy is to be found among the Malaiyālis of the Kolli-malais. There the land-owner may make his own arrangements for ploughing and weeding, but at harvest time every villager may claim the right to join in the reaping, and earn his 3 or 4 measures of grain per diem, whether the owner wants his services or not. The effect of this is that, in years of scanty yield, the poor man, though his whole crop may go to pay those who reap it, can at least save himself from starvation by earning his share of his richer neighbour's produce. Wages are always paid in kind, and very little money is in circulation, the result being that the purchasing power of a rupee on the Kolli-malais is much higher than it is in the plains.

Credit.

The problem of agricultural indebtedness received as earnest attention from Read and Munro as it does from the Government of to-day. Read's very first proclamation provided for the grant of loans (*takkāvi*) by Government to needy ryots and new settlers, as well as for the repairs of tanks, provisions which anticipated the Loans Acts of 1883 and 1884. But Government Loans have not met with the success they deserve, and they have only touched the fringe of the problem. Possibly the abolition of the December kist in Fasli 1316 (1906–07)[1] will do something to improve the ryots' credit, for the December kist undoubtedly placed the ryot under the heel of the sowcar. But brighter prospects are perhaps opening with the rapid growth of the co-operative credit system. The movement began with the registering of an Urban Bank and a Rural Society in Nāmakkal Taluk in 1905. At the close of 1907–08 the number of societies was only 8, but in 1908–09 the number rose to 43, and in the following year to 82. This extraordinary progress was due to the formation of the Salem District Urban Bank in January 1909, which, thanks to the energy of the Secretary Mr. Ādinārāyana Chettiyār, in five months collected "Rs. 10,000 of share capital, obtained over Rs. 20,000 of local deposits, borrowed nearly two lakhs, realised a net profit of Rs. 1,200, and carrying over Rs. 500 to a dividend equalisation fund, and Rs. 300 to the reserve fund, declared a dividend of 9 per cent."[2] In 1910–11, owing to the transfer of Nāmakkal with one Urban and six Rural Societies to Trichinopoly, the number of societies remaining was only 75, but even then their working capital was Rs. 4,15,423, and the credit given Rs. 4,00,691.

---

[1] See Vol. II, p. 57.

[2] Address of Mr. B. V. Narasimha Ayyar at the Salem District Co-operative Conference of 19th March 1910.

CHAPTER V.

FORESTS.

History—Reservation—Distribution—Working Plans—Timber and Fuel—Fire protection—Cultural Operations—Bamboos—Sandal—Grazing—Manure Leaves—Minor Produce—Roads—Revenue—Crime.

History.

FOREST conservancy in Salem District may be said to begin with the advent of the Madras Railway, towards the end of the sixth decade of the nineteenth century. Attempts had already been made by the local authorities to restrict the wholesale clearances of forest growth on the hills by Malaiyālis for purposes of cultivation and the profits to be made by the exploitation of forest products had attracted the notice of Government. With the construction of the railway came a frantic demand for sleepers; an attempt was made to control the supply, and by the year 1860–61 a complete establishment was organised and a set of rules was sanctioned. But the establishment, which consisted of an Assistant Conservator, an Overseer and twelve peons, was too small and too late to prevent a devastation from which the District has not even yet recovered.

For the construction of the Madras Railway the Salem forests were recklessly denuded. In the year 1859–60 seigniorage fees amounting to nearly Rs. 23,500 were realised on sleepers alone, the number of sleepers supplied within the year being 245,743; so great was the demand that trees could not be marked fast enough, and felling was uncontrolled. These sleepers were not sawn but *adzed*, a process involving immense waste of material, for a log, however large, would only suffice for one sleeper. According to a report of 1863, "old stumps show that there used to be good sized teak on the hill forests, but now ryots fell saplings at night, and there is not much left." Nor were the greedy contractors content with destroying all the teak. Fine satin-wood forests round Kōttai-patti were entirely wiped out by them, and, before the new Forest Department could make itself felt, irreparable mischief was done.

The next twenty years were years of experiment, and much bitter experience was gained. Experiments were made in nurseries and plantations in the merits and demerits of the license and voucher system, in departmental felling and in the exploitation of railway fuel, in exploration and in the settlement of boundary disputes, in the construction of forest roads, in the formation of reserves and in the shortcomings of the Law. In 1861–62 there was wholesale theft of timber along the Kāvēri banks; the stolen wood was floated down-stream to Srīrangam on bamboo rafts. In 1865 railway contractors took to robbing the Government forests of timber under cover of Mitta leases. In 1865 the seigniorage of twelve annas for 48 large bamboos and six pies per bundle of small bamboos, imposed in 1861, was removed, and such enormous quantities were exported into Mysore in consequence, that seigniorage had to be reintroduced in the following year. In 1866–67, hundreds of thousands of trees were illicitly felled by cattle drivers, and Government were helpless because the magistracy refused to convict for theft. In 1870 the Conservator writes, "Government have only to look at the amount of timber taken free out of the Salem jungles alone, to see that no forests could possibly stand a drain of this nature"; a rather dispiriting comment on ten years' work. In the following year it was decided to place the Forest Department under the direct control of the Collector, who hitherto had managed the Jungle Conservancy Department with the aid of local cesses independently. This change was brought into force on 1st October 1872 and continued for a decade with rather more encouraging results. By 1880 no less than 222 isolated[1] topes had been set apart as jungle conservancy topes, and twelve reserves had been surveyed and demarcated for the supply of fuel to the Madras Railway, and walled or fenced at some cost.

Until the year 1902 the forests of the District were under the charge of a single District Forest Officer; since then, there have been various changes, the Tiruppattūr and Nāmakkal Taluks having been transferred to the North Arcot and Trichinopoly Districts, respectively, and two District Forest Charges (North and South) being formed; these are divided roughly by a line starting on the Kāvēri near Pūlāmpatti and running to Salem, thence following the road to the foot of the Shevaroys and the bridle-path to Yercaud, the road from Yercaud to Nāgalūr and thence down to near Bommidi along the western side of the Yērimalai reserved forest and then along the northern boundary of the Ūttankarai Taluk to the North Arcot border. The North Salem Forest District now consists of the following Ranges—Anchetti, Denkani-kōta, Krishnagiri, Dharmapuri, Kāvēri and Salem West; those in the South Salem District are Chittēri, Harūr, Pāpireddi-patti, East Salem and Āttūr.

Reservation.

Scientific conservancy begins with the passing of the Madras Forest Act V of 1882. In the first few years subsequent to the

[1] Salem Taluk 38, Āttūr 15, Nāmakkal 18, Tiruchengōdu 16, Hosūr 38, Dharmapuri 29, Krishnagiri 22, Ūttankarai 31, and Tiruppattūr 15.

CHAP. V. FORESTS.

passing of this Act, the policy of the Government towards reservation changed several times, as knowledge of the working of the Act improved; thus, at first, it was intended to set aside certain areas outside the reserved forests, as village forests; it was soon found that the village officers could not be trusted to manage these areas for the benefit of the village community in general, and the idea of village forests was abandoned, the Government reserves being extended so as to include the areas originally left out for village forests. The result was that in some places the reserves were brought so close to cultivated lands that there was insufficient ground left available for extension of cultivation, and the sudden absorption of all the land fit for pasturing the village herds into reserved forests, in which free pasture was not allowed, caused so much ill feeling, that orders were issued to put back reserve boundaries, so as to leave outside them sufficient waste land for the extension of cultivation, and the exercise of ordinary communal privileges. The result of these changes of policy was to delay the final selection and settlement of Government reserves, and to create, at each change of policy, a fresh set of boundary lines. From 1890 till 1898 a special party from the Survey of India was engaged in surveying the reserved forests, and many of the maps bear evidence of the changes then taking place, as they show boundary lines and reserves which have since been abandoned.

The first notifications of reservation were published in 1886, the included area being 550,614 acres. Since then the work of reservation has proceeded actively, as the subjoined figures show:—

Year.	Total reserved in acres.	Total reserved in sq. miles.
1890-91	437,843	643
1895-96	783,749	1,224
1900-01	846,499	1,323
1905-06	1,014,421	1,585
1910-11 [1]	878,929	1,373
1913-14	879,136	1,374

Forest settlement is now practically completed, and it is not likely under existing conditions that the area under Reservation will be materially increased. The area of the unreserved Government Forest in the District is roughly estimated at 1,000

[1] The figures from 1890 to 1906 include the reserves of Nāmakkal and Tiruppattūr Taluks, those for 1910-11 exclude them.

square miles, but this includes several hills almost devoid of vegetation.[1]

Distribution of Reserves.

The principal groups of forests are the following :—

The Kolli-malais in Āttūr Taluk, occupying the northern slopes of the Kolli-malai Hills from the cultivated plateau to the base of the hills, with an area of a little over 16 square miles.

The Pachai-malais on the south border of Āttūr Taluk ; the reserves cover a comparatively small portion of the hills, their extent being over 30 square miles.

The Kalrāyan and Jadaya-Kavundan slopes in the north of Āttūr Taluk, the former of which were decided to be Government property after considerable litigation ; this chain of reserves forms an unbroken line from the east of Tumbal to the South Arcot District boundary, and covers over 60 square miles.

The Chittēris, extending north and east of the above, partly in Salem and partly in Ūttankarai Taluks, where they extend north as far as Tīrta-malai, and cover 250 square miles, of which only 36 lie in Salem Taluk.

The Shevaroys, comprising the outer slopes on all sides of the well-known Shevaroy Hills, and one or two of the interior valleys. This group, which, with the exception of one small isolated reserve in the interior, forms one block of forest, is typical of the manner in which the reserves have been gradually built up, for it consists of no less than 26 separate reserves, with a total area of 113 square miles.

Finally, the large mass of forest lying between Pennāgaram and Denkani-kōta, extending along the Kāvēri from its junction with the Sanat-kumāra-nadi to the frontier of Mysore, and covering an area of 400 square miles.

There are minor chains of reserves, one connecting the last mentioned block with the Shevaroys, across the south of Dharmapuri Taluk, another in the northern portion of Krishnagiri Taluk, and a third along the Kāvēri in Salem and Tiruchengōdu Taluks. The area under reservation in each of the eight taluks is shown in the margin. Lists of Reserves are given in Chapter XV.

Taluk.	Area of Reserved Forest in square miles.
Āttūr	106
Salem	196
Ōmalūr	82
Tiruchengōdu ...	13
Ūttankarai	291
Dharmapuri ...	293
Krishnagiri	54
Hosūr	338

[1] In Salem South 11,620 acres have been notified under section 4 of the Forest Act as proposed reserved forest. The settlement of 29,280 acres of the Hudedurgam proposed reserve in the Hosūr Taluk is almost completed.

CHAP. V. FORESTS.

Working Plans.

So long as the full time of the district staff was devoted to the preliminary formation of reserves, systematic forestry could not be attended to. The first regular working plan was sanctioned in 1900. Since then rapid progress has been made, and up to date working plans have been prepared for all the ranges in Salem South, except six reserves in Ūttankarai Taluk; in Salem North, working plans have been sanctioned for the Krishnagiri and parts of the Kāvēri and Salem West Ranges and are under preparation for Dharmapuri Range and for sandal-wood in Hosūr Taluk.

The aim of the Forest Department is to improve and protect existing growth so that a sustained yield may be assured.

The chief items of produce are (1) Timber, (2) Fuel, (3) Charcoal, (4) Bamboos, (5) Sandal, (6) Grazing, (7) Manure Leaves, and (8) Minor Produce.

In 1893 what are termed "located fellings" were introduced; under this system the area to be exploited was demarcated and the purchasers of permits had to go and cut in this locality—this was a great improvement on the previous system under which the holder of a permit was at liberty to go wherever he wished and take what he wanted, as it rendered supervision so much easier; this system was started, and gradually elaborated by Mr. Brasier, who had done similar work in Tinnevelly before his transfer to Salem, into a regular series of coupes under which the area felled was, as far as possible, in inverse proportion to the volume of timber and fuel which might be obtained from the area; in other words, the poorer the growth, the larger was the area proposed to be cut annually.

As already stated, the first working plans were sanctioned in 1900; they were prepared under Mr. Brasier's auspices; the system followed has been that of "Coppice with Standards", the number of standards varying between 15 and 25 and the rotation varying from between 20 and 30 years to 32 in the Lōkūr and 36 in the Krishnagiri Working Circles. The area of the coupes varies between a minimum of 44 acres and a maximum of 836 acres, principally due to the probable demand and to the area in any one locality which was available for exploitation. The larger coupes are situated near the railway, and within a distance of 20 miles of Salem town, and were at first worked departmentally with a view to supplying the Madras Railway (now South Indian Railway) with the fuel needed for running. The departmental supply began in 1892 with a contract for 200 tons a month, and was raised in 1894 to 500 tons, in 1896 to 1,200 and in 1899 to 2,200 tons per mensem. During the next three years the supply gradually fell to 1,150 tons a month and after 1906 only small quantities of lighting fuel were taken, as the Railway took to the use of coal: thenceforward the principal demand has been from Salem town.

Coupes are now sold to contractors who carry out the felling and removal of the produce, fix their own rates of sale, and maintain their own depots.

The growth in the plains and up to a height of about 3,000 feet is for the most part deciduous; the evergreen forest gradually spreads, from a narrow fringe of trees along the streams to what must at one time have been large masses of dense virgin forest especially on the Shevaroys and Kolli-malais: these have, however, largely disappeared owing to the exigencies of the coffee industry and the demands of the Malaiyāli population for further lands for cultivation.

Timber.

Timber is seldom available of any large size; the commoner species are—

Chloroxylon swietenia which is nearly universal, *Anogeissus latifolia*, the *Albizzias*, *Hardwickia binata*, *Azadirachta indica*, *Cedrela toona*, and various *Acacias*, *Eugenia jambolana*, *Holoptelea integrifolia*, *Gmelina arborea* and in places *Terminalia Arjuna*: Teak, *Pterocarpus marsupium*, *Bridelia retusa*, *Bischofia javanica*, *Elaeocarpus species* also occur on the higher slopes; existing stumps show that the teak used to grow to a fair size on the Shevaroys. There are, of course, numerous other species used for timber.

Fuel.

Albizzia amara is almost universally preferred for fuel, and in the more accessible forests this species probably forms about 50 per cent. of the growth; the other commoner species are—

Wrightia tinctoria, *Premna tomentosa*, *Canthium didymum* and *Erythroxylon monogynum*.

Fire-protection.

The growth of grass and bamboo renders many of the forests especially subject to damage by fires; consequently coupes under felling and those which have been felled within the last five years are specially protected by clearing the lines round them and employing a number of fire patrols who are supposed to keep the lines clear of inflammable materials, and to be always ready to proceed at once to any fires which may occur and to extinguish them. The same procedure is in force for some other areas in the Hosūr Hills with a view to improving the growth which, especially along the Kāvēri, consists of nearly pure *Hardwickia* forest. Fires principally occur during February and March, thunder storms in April and May, as a rule, putting an end to the fire season.

Cultural Operations.

Under the Jungle Conservancy, a considerable amount of work was undertaken in planting Tamarind and Mango near villages; this was later on superseded by the sowing of seed in patches, or broad-cast, in blanks in the coupes when regular

CHAP. V. FORESTS.

working was instituted, the principal tree species put out being Tamarind, *Albizzia Lebbek*, *Albizzia amara*, *Chloroxylon swietenia*, *Azadirachta indica*, *Acacia sundra*, and *Acacia ferruginea*; with these were mixed seeds of various shrubs, e.g., *Cassia auriculata*, *Cassia fistula*, useful for tanning bark and manure leaves, and such other species as *Dodonœa viscosa*, *Randia dumetorum*, *Canthium parviflorum* and others, which would protect any tree seed which germinated; a certain amount of seed of *Tephrosia purpurea*, which is largely used for leaf manure, was also put out. In Sanniyāsi-malai on the Shevaroys a sum of nearly Rs. 9,000 has been spent up to date in fire-protection and in planting out *Grevillea robusta*, *Frenella rhomboidea* and *Acacia dealbata* in the north and east, in the hope of covering the soil and so improving the water-supply in the streams below. In 1913 sandal seed was dibbled in in patches over an extent of about 50 acres of scrub in the Nagara-malai reserve at a small expense, and so far (1915) the results seem promising.

Bamboos.

The small bamboo (*Dendrocalamus strictus*) is one of the most valuable assets of the Salem Forests; it flourishes at any elevation between 1,000′ and 4,000′. The finest Bamboo area in the District is the forest tract on the west of Hosūr and Dharmapuri Taluks. Bamboo is also extensively exploited on the Shevaroys, Chittēris, Kalrāyans, Pachai-malais, Kolli-malais, Aranūttu-malais and on the east of the Bōda-malais. The large bamboo (*Bambusa arundinacea*) is not so ubiquitous, but it is found in fairly large quantities in valleys and near the banks of streams. It occurs in great abundance between Kempakarai and the Āne-bidda-halla, and is common between Pennāgaram and Javulagiri and also on the Shevaroys.

Bamboo coupes are sold to contractors when a reasonable price can be got; in other cases permits are issued to meet the local demand; the rotation varies between three and five years. The chief markets for bamboos outside the District are Erode, Trichinopoly, Karūr and Madras.

Sandal.

The best quality of sandal-wood is found in the forests of Denkani-kōta. It is not uncommon in the Chittēris, Shevaroys, Pachai-malais and Kolli-malais, but the quality is not so good as that from Denkani-kōta and the quantity is far less. The value of the sandal-wood in the District was appreciated as soon as the Company came into possession. Buchanan, speaking of what was then the Ālambādi District (i.e., Taluk), says, "Captain Graham sold a renter all the trees that were fit for cutting and received for them 300 pagodas. The condition of the sale was that only the old full-grown trees should be cut, but the fellow has taken every stick of any size, and there will be no more fit for cutting in less than ten years."

Sandal-wood is always collected departmentally. A Ranger or Forester selects [1] the trees to be felled, marks, numbers and measures them, submitting a copy of his measurement list for approval. On receipt of this the trees are dug up, roots and all, cut into sections, roughly dressed so as to remove bark and sap-wood, and then removed to depot. Each piece of each tree is marked with the number given originally to the standing tree, so that it is possible to reconstruct each tree in depot, and thus to check any tendency to theft; after check in depot, the wood is carefully cleaned of all sap-wood, sawn into convenient lengths, and classified into first, second, third class billets, first and second class roots, etc., down to class VIII, which is sawdust. Auctions used to be held periodically, when good billets realized nearly seven annas a pound. In future the fellings are to be transferred to a central depot, probably at Tiruppattūr, for sale. The marginal statement shows the quantity of sandal felled at different periods.

Year.	Tons.
1862–63	72
1866–67	58
1871–72	166
1880–81	30
1890–91	14½
1900–01	4
1910–11	52
1911–12	15
1912–13	22
1913–14	26¼
1914–15	18½

Grazing.

As a general rule coupes worked on the "Coppice with Standard" system are closed to grazing one year before, and five years after felling. In Harūr Working Circle, owing to poverty of growth, the period of closure is ten years (two years before and eight years after felling). Some specially protected blocks are closed against grazing throughout the whole period of rotation. On the Kalrāyans grazing is combined with manure-leaf cutting under the "pastoral method" (p. 256).

The grazing fees authorised under section 26 of Act V of 1882 were not brought into force in the District till 1888. The license system, worked by a contractor for commission, was introduced in 1889, the rate being two annas per buffalo, one anna per head of cattle, and six pies per sheep. In 1893 this was superseded by the system of half-rates for privileged and other cattle, worked through karnams. Then in 1896 came the issue of permits by Range Officers and travelling "Permit Issuing Officers," at 6 annas per buffalo, 3 annas per head of cattle and 1½ annas per sheep. Goats were altogether forbidden the reserves. In 1899, however,

[1] The original rule was to mark for felling all dead and dying trees and only such green trees as were over 30" in girth at breast height. After 1904 the minimum girth for exploitable trees was raised to 36". Removals are now (1915) restricted to dead and dying trees pending the introduction of a working plan which is under preparation.

CHAP. V. FORESTS.

certain areas were set aside for browsing, the rate being 1½ annas per goat, but in South Salem these were again closed in 1905–06. In 1902 the fees for goat browsing in North Salem was raised to 8 annas a head, and in 1914 goat browsing was altogether prohibited. After the introduction of Working Plans, the Reserves were divided into grazing blocks, some of which extend to more than one reserve. A permit holds good from July to the end of the following June, and gives access to one grazing block only.

Fodder.

To compensate for the closing of coupes to grazing, and to educate the villagers to fire-protection, ryots are encouraged to remove grass for fodder from closed areas. Even in specially protected blocks, grass-cutting is permitted in seasons of scarcity. The grass most commonly cut for fodder is *Andropogon contortus*.

Manure Leaves.

The local demand for manure leaves is almost confined to Salem and Āttūr Taluks, and thousands of tons are exported annually to the adjoining taluks of Trichinopoly and South Arcot. In the Northern Division it is held that the Reserves are insufficient to supply the population with all its requirements in fuel, timber, grazing, etc., and that the supply of manure leaves is incompatible with the persistence of the forests. It is estimated that between 2 and 3 tons of leaves are required to manure one acre of wet land. Manure leaves may be removed from unreserved lands without charge by the inhabitants of adjoining villages. As to Reserves, till 1890 the permit system was in force, and from 1895 the right to remove the leaves of Turinji, *Nux-vomica* and all unclassified trees was leased out annually. But with the gradual introduction of Working Plans came the system of "limited manure-leaf coupes" in the Salem East and Āttūr Ranges, and the closure altogether of manure-leaf cutting areas in Salem West and the two Harūr Ranges. In Salem South no removals of manure-leaf have been allowed from reserves since 1912.

On the "Upper Slopes" of the Kalrāyan Hills in Āttūr Range the method adopted for exploiting manure-leaf and grazing is that known as the "pastoral method." The area to be treated is divided into four coupes, and each coupe in turn serves as an annual cutting area for five years, during each of which all scrub and young trees of the third class (except minor produce trees) and inferior species may be pollarded. After the close of the manure-leaf season in the fifth year, the trees are coppiced, and then given a rest for 15 years. After a coupe is coppiced it is closed to grazing for five years, during which, however, the removal of grass for fodder and thatching is permitted on payment. After the period of closure expires, the coupe is open to grazing for 15 years.

Minor Produce.

In the early days of forestry the minor produce was not under the control of the Forest Department, but its collection was either free or it was leased by the Collector. The right to collect minor produce was first leased out by the Forest Department in 1883, when one contract covered the whole District. In 1896 a separate lease was granted for each Revenue Division, and from 1901 a new system was introduced under which the produce of reserves was leased by reserves, that of unreserved lands by Revenue Inspectors' firkas. More recently the lots have been still further reduced by selling the produce of unreserved lands by villages, or groups of villages, in the hope of realising more revenue.

Roads.

Roads are maintained by the Forest Department in Salem North Division: (1) from Kādaiyāmpatti to Kurumba-patti (8 miles), (2) from Kumbara-patti to the foot of the Shevaroys (5 miles), (3) from Pālakōdu to Kesarguli (16 miles), (4) from Pennāgaram to Anchetti, via Āne-bidda-halla (27 miles), (5) from Denkani-kōta to Ayyūr (8 miles), and (6) from Kundu-kōta to Anchetti (8 miles). In Salem South Division the principal roads maintained by the Forest Department are (1) Mallāpuram Ghāt Road (9 miles), (2) Harūr to Kambalai (9 miles), (3) Kombuthūkki to Papireddipatti bridle path (8½ miles), (4) Chittēri to Vellimadurai bridle path (8 miles), (5) Periyakōmbai to Pūsinikuli bridle path (6 miles).

Revenue

The gross revenue derived from Forests shows a steady increase during the past 30 years, though from year to year the net revenue fluctuates with the expenditure on conservation and exploitation.

The subjoined figures are of interest.

Year.	Gross Revenue.	Expenditure.	Net Revenue.
	RS.	RS.	RS.
1880–81	55,171	19,094	36,077
1890–91	1,54,900	58,347	96,553
1900–01	2,93,012	1,58,218	1,34,794
1910–11 [1]	2,54,890	1,80,813	74,077
1913–14	2,57,347	1,69,417	87,930

[1] The figures for 1910–11 exclude Nāmakkal and Tiruppattūr, the statistics for the previous decades include those tracts.

CHAP. V.
FORESTS.

The chief heads of revenue in 1910-11 were as follows :—

—	Salem South.	Salem North.	Total.
	RS.	RS.	RS.
Timber	11,206	13,716	24,922
Firewood and charcoal	35,504	39,669	75,173
Bamboos	14,057	23,832	37,890
Sandalwood	2,348	20,072	22,420
Gazing	23,323	38,816	62,139
Minor produce and manure leaf ...	28,234	22,614	50,848

Crime.

"Forest Offences" usually take the form of illicit removal of produce, or illicit grazing. The amount of crime fluctuates, but there is no reason to believe that Forest Offences are on the increase. The annexed statement shows the number of cases which the Department has to cope with. More than half the crimes are compounded :—

Year.	Illicit removal.	Illicit grazing.	Fire.	Other offences.	Total.
1890-91	499	199	10	39	747
1900-01	1,409	1,144	11	28	2,592
1910-11	901	325	109	51	1,386
1913-14	1,786	399	95	87	2,367

CHAPTER VI.

OCCUPATIONS AND TRADE.

CONTENTS.

OCCUPATIONS.

IN 1911, of the total population, 73 per cent depended on agriculture for livelihood and 13 per cent. on industries. Those dependent on commerce, including transport, numbered only 5 per cent.[1] The economic status of agriculture has been dealt with on pp. 240–7, and no remarks are needed here.

Pasture.

According to the Census Returns of 1911, some 15,000 persons were dependent on pasture for their living. This represents professional graziers and breeders, but, as a very large number of ryots have stock of their own, the Census figures do not adequately represent the importance of pasture in the economy of the District.

Cattle-breeding.

The forest included in the Pennāgaram Division, the southern portion of Denkani-kōta Division and the Kollegāl Taluk of Coimbatore, a fairly compact block, many hundred square miles in area, stretching on either side of the Kāvēri, is one of the most famous cattle-breeding grounds in South India. In Hosūr Taluk calves are not uncommonly entrusted by their owners to ryots or agricultural labourers to be reared on a *vāram* system : if the animal be a female, the person who rears it is entitled to the first calf or

[1] The actual figures are—

Agriculture	1,295,372.	Commerce	89,961.
Pasture	14,481.	Professions, etc.	18,062.
Industry	237,858.	Others.	110,946.

CHAP. VI. INDUSTRIES.

first two calves dropped by it; if it be a bull, he receives half its estimated value at the time he returns it to its owner.

(1) Textiles. A. Under Read.

By far the most important industry in the District is that of weaving. It is not easy to conjecture why large colonies of the weaving castes should have settled in a tract, the history of which is characterised by so many centuries of political inquietude. The fact remains, however, that, within a few months after the Treaty of 1792 was ratified, Salem was selected by the Board as a suitable field for establishing an "Investment", and in July 1792 [1] Read was informed that Mr. Mitchell, Export Warehouse Keeper at Madras, would be deputed to exploit the textile industries of the "Salem Country". In October of the same year Mr. Robert Dashwood took up his residence at Salem as Commercial Resident, and Read was called upon to provide him with money.[2]

At the very outset friction seems to have arisen over the supply of labour, one of the chief difficulties being the taxes that weavers had to pay. In the Northern Division, for instance, not only were the weavers saddled with loom-tax and house-tax [3], they were also liable to pay *Sāyar* dues,[4] and *chuppa*, or stamp duty, exacted by the *Sāyar* farmer. In Krishnagiri special taxes were levied on Pariah weavers in addition to the loom-tax, and in Kambaya-nallūr special fees were due by weavers to the village accountants. Even before the arrival of Mr. Dashwood, Read had notified [5] the abolition of the loom-tax on every loom employed by the Company, and house-tax was levied on all weavers in proportion to the number of looms they had which were not in the Company's employ. The irksome dues payable to the *Sāyar* farmers, however, remained matter for acrid comment for two years longer.

The methods of recruiting labour appear somewhat drastic. Read, writing on 19th October 1792,[6] informed Mr. Dashwood that he had sent stringent orders "directing weavers of every denomination to obey your summons without least delay or hesitation, on pain of being very severely punished". Not unnaturally this procedure evoked protests, and Munro, in a letter dated 23rd November 1792,[7] expresses a fear that "anything like constraint being used would prevent many who were still in Tipu's country from returning to their old habitation". It was alleged by the weavers of Malla-samudram that their engagements with the Company "were not voluntary, but forced upon them by native

---

[1] *Press list of Ancient Records in Salem District* (1906) No. 65.

[2] *Ancient Records*, No. 75.

[3] See Vol. II, p. 12, Motarpha.

[4] See Vol. II, p. 67.

[5] *Anc. Rec.* No. 76.

[6] *Anc. Rec.* No. 76.

[7] *Anc. Rec.* No. 91.

agents, by threats of punishments. and in some instances by actual confinement,". while the weavers of Tiruchengōdu were "likewise obliged to pay Mr. Dashwood's Dubash ten rupees for every thousand advanced . . . . and were they to refuse to comply with this demand, he would register cloth of the first sort among that of the second, and by this means incur a much heavier loss." It was admitted that the terms offered by the Company's agents would have been profitable before the War, but, since the War, the price of thread had risen so sharply, that they could only carry out their contracts at a loss. In conclusion Munro recommends that the Company should pay a higher price for their cloth and so place their employees on an equal footing with those who worked for themselves. Above all, the contracts should be "voluntary, and for a specific term, at the end of which they should be at liberty to renew them or not as they chose, for at present, they are alarmed at the idea of working for the Company, conceiving it to be a kind of bondage from which they must never hope to escape".

A statement dated 31st January 1793,[1] gives the number of looms in the Southern Division as 1790, of which 488 were worked by the Company. The number of looms for the Northern Division was 631, of which 117 were exempted from taxes. An estimate for the Centre Division, based on accounts of 1789–90, gives the total number of looms at 1,627. The District total would therefore be about 4,048. Read appears on his own authority to have exempted weavers employed in the Company's "Investment" from duties on cotton thread, and in March 1793, the Board suggested to the Government that a general remission of these duties should be granted; but Government ordered (16th March 1893) that "as the weavers in the Ceded Districts were not exempted from the duties on cotton thread, they must continue to pay it in common with others." In May 1793, however, Government freed the Company's weavers, not only from all taxes on their houses and back-yards, but also from all imposts on the raw materials required for their manufacture, including the import duties on yarn, and in September 1794, the general abolition of the loom-tax was authorised.[2]

Meanwhile matters did not improve, and on 11th October 1793, Munro penned a strongly worded letter to Read which deserves quoting[3] :—

"You have given all your attention to the ryots and abandoned the weavers to a set of rascally dubashes. I wrote you a good deal

---

[1] *Anc. Rec.* No. 100. [2] *Anc. Rec.* No. 160. [3] *Anc. Rec.* No. 131.

Textiles.

about them last year, and they are no better off this. All of them have been forced to work for the Company, and whenever they do anything for themselves it is by stealth. It is well for us that Tipu's distresses and his nature makes him tyrannical, for were the oppression not very great on the other side, I am convinced we should have soon lost most of our weavers."

Again, in March 1794,[1] Munro had occasion to complain to Read of *zulum* on the part of the Commercial Resident's agents, this time in connection with the transport of yarn.

In November of the same year Read strongly recommended[2] "the total abolition of road duties on all exports, the productions of these districts," but this the Board (26th November 1894) would not consent to,[3] insisting on the levy of such duties on manufactured cloth.

Some time prior to August 1795, Mr. Charles Carpenter[4] had superseded Mr. Dashwood as Commercial Resident, and under him things seem to have gone more smoothly. In November 1795,[5] Carpenter informed Read of the proposal of the Board of Trade to establish a bleaching green at Salem, and asked him how many dhobies could be procured in the Bāramahāl for the Company. The cloths to be bleached were (1) Long cloth and (2) Salempores,[6] each of three qualities, ordinary, middling, and superfine, (3) Moorees of three qualities, ordinary, fine and superfine, and (4) Ginghams, of two kinds, one red-striped and the other blue. Read replied[7] to the effect that he summoned all the washermen in three "districts," and "they all said that bleaching was a business they did not understand, that they thought they could not do it to his (the Resident's) satisfaction, and that if they were to leave their villages they would lose their situation, which afforded them a permanent provision for life, which their families had enjoyed from time immemorial."

It is hardly necessary to follow the further history of the Company's "Investment." Carpenter died in 1818, and his place was taken by Mr. J. M. Heath,[8] who retired from the Company's service, sold his property to Mr. G. F. Fischer, and sank his

---

[1] *Anc. Rec.* No. 146; Cf. No. 156 of 15th July 1794.

[2] *Anc. Rec.* No. 176.

[3] *Anc Rec.* No. 180.

[4] Brother-in-law of Sir Walter Scott, See Vol. II, p. 243.

[5] *Anc. Rec.* No. 243.

[6] Also spelt "Sallampores" or "Salempoorys"; a coarse dungree cloth usually dyed blue with indigo

[7] *Anc. Rec.* No. 246.

[8] See p. 273.

fortune in the Porto Novo Iron Company. It is not exactly known when the Salem "Investment" ceased to exist.

Textiles—B. Present[1] Condition.

From the Census Returns for 1911 it appears that 88,727 people returned themselves as belonging to one or other of the following four weaving castes:—Sāle, Dēvānga, Patnūlkāran and Kaikōlan, but only 83,005 were returned as supported by this occupation. There are a large number of men of other castes also who have taken to weaving for a living, among them being Muhammadans, Kavarais, Pallis and Sembadavans. Many of the weavers possess looms of their own, and they take their finished goods every evening to the bazaar and offer them for sale. There are also a large number of weavers, somewhat lower in the social scale, who work for hire, being employed by richer men who own three or four looms each. There is yet another class of weavers, comparatively small in number, who take orders from cloth merchants, and receive advances to carry out the same. They represent the highest development of the weaving community.

Chief Centres.

The chief centres of the industry are:—Salem Town, Rāsipuram, Āttayāmpatti and Gurusāmi-pālaiyam[2] in Salem Taluk; Ōmalūr, Tāra-mangalam and Jalakantāpuram in Ōmalūr Taluk; Tiruchengōdu, Edappādi and Kumāra-pālaiyam in Tiruchengōdu Taluk; Āttūr, Āragalūr, Vēppampūndi and Kāmākshi-pālaiyam in Āttūr Taluk; Dharmapuri and Matam in Dharmapuri Taluk; Ūttankarai, Singārapet, Irula-patti, Menisi, Kambaya-nallūr and Kallāvi in Ūttankarai Taluk; Krishnagiri and Hosūr.

All classes of goods are manufactured in the District—woollen rugs and *kamblis*, cotton *vēshtis* and *pudavais*, and silk *vastrams* and *sāris*.

Woollen Weaving.

Wool is used for making coarse rugs and blankets commonly called *kamblis*.

(*a*) Rugs.—For the rugs which are made in Salem Town, wool is obtained from the Mysore plateau through Bangalore, and is delivered to the weavers spun into a coarse yarn ready to be dyed. The rugs are of an inferior quality, and sell at prices ranging from R.1 to Rs. 2½.

(*b*) *Kamblis* are very extensively woven all over the District by Kurubas. The Kurubas purchase wool from flock owners, and their women spin it, using a distaff and spindle. The process of making *kamblis* is an extremely primitive one. A kambli is made in two pieces, each measuring 8′ × 3′ which, when complete, are stitched together. This joint is a source of weakness, and might

[1] The account of weaving that follows has been kindly supplied by Mr. Alfred Chatterton.

[2] In Pillānallūr Taraf, Rāsipuram Division.

CHAP. VI. INDUSTRIES. Textiles.

be readily avoided by using a wider loom. The spun wool is warped on pegs and stretched on a country pit-loom with no treadles. It is heavily sized with tamarind *kanji*. Only one warp is put on the loom at a time, as the wool is so lightly spun that it will not stand any considerable amount of handling. At Bērikai a small industry exists in the manufacture of felt *namdās*.

Cotton Ginning and Spinning.

The hand-ginning and hand-spinning of cotton as industries are extinct. The *charka* has succumbed to the power-driven gin, even as the distaff and spindle or spinning-wheel have given place to the modern spinning-mill. On a very limited scale hand-ginning and spinning are still said to be carried on in a few places, but it is a purely subsidiary business. The hand-gin or *charka* consists of two wooden rollers mounted on a frame, and connected by crudely made wooden spur-wheels so that, when turned by a handle, the rollers revolve in opposite directions. The *kappas* are presented to the rollers, and the lint passes through, whilst the seeds remain behind. The lint is then carded into small sausage-shaped rolls (*tiranai*) handy for the spinner. For spinning, the distaff is not employed, but only a spindle made in the form of a disc of pot-stone. More frequently the cotton is spun on to a bobbin of chōlam stalk, which is fixed to the spindle of a hand-spinning wheel. The flyer, well-known in Europe in the eighteenth century, is never used.

Cotton Weaving.

The coarsest of cotton goods are termed *duppattis*, and they are largely made in and about Āttayāmpatti and Tāttaiyanagārpatti by Kaikōlars, and in a few villages of the Bāgalūr Pālaiyam by Pariahs. *Duppattis* are very coarse cloths made of cotton of counts below 20's, which is obtained from the spinning mills at Coimbatore, Calicut, Madura and Tinnevelly. They are largely used in the cold weather, and the demand for them is extremely steady. The price varies with size, and ranges from Rs. 1½ to Rs. 2½ a piece. Men's cloths of pure cotton and without any admixture of silk are not largely used, imported piece goods having taken their place, but amongst women there is a distinct preference for hand-woven cloths, and the industry is still an important one. They are made all over the District, but the chief centre is Gugai, a division of Salem. The weavers are Kanarese-speaking Dēvāngas. The cloths are of several qualities, and vary in price from Rs. 3 to Rs. 10 each. They are either black or red, and may be quite plain, or furnished with ornamental borders. Usually the cloths have a continuous weft running from edge to edge, but in some cases the borders, which are of a different colour to the rest of the cloth, are what is termed "solid"; that is to say, the weft is not run continuously from edge to edge, but each border has

Textiles.

its own weft ingeniously linked to the weft forming the body of the cloth. For weaving such cloths three shuttles are necessary, and the weaver is generally assisted by a boy who plies one of the border shuttles. Such cloths cannot be made in power-looms, and the labour of making them is considerable, so that they are fairly expensive, and only worn by well-to-do people. In plain cotton cloths, even in those with solid borders, the ornamentation is of an extremely simple character, and does not necessitate the use of the elaborate harness to be found in looms where cloths are made with solid silk borders.

Miscellaneous Goods.

The Dēvāngas of Gugai manufacture what is known as *Kāngu pudavais*, which are very popular among the women of the middle class. A favourite colour is purple, obtained by dyeing red yarn in indigo. A very large number of these *pudavais* is exported to Ceylon and the Straits Settlements. Most of the Gugai weavers carry on their trade independently of the middlemen, and a number of them have settled in Colombo and Singapore, where they carry on business. Unlike other weavers in Salem District, the Dēvāngas of Gugai are a flourishing class, and the number of looms they employ is said to be steadily on the increase. The cloths are cheap, and are always in great demand, irrespective of Pongal and Dīpāvali or marriage seasons. The only other manufactures of pure cotton are "durries" or cotton carpets. They are chiefly made in Salem in the divisions of Gugai and Shevapet, and the weavers are mainly Patnūlkārans. Bright shades of various colours are usually employed, and the patterns are obtained by arranging these colours in stripes of different widths. The commonest colours are blue and red, as these are the only fast colours which the Dēvāngas of Gugai can produce with indigo and alizarine. Other colours are employed, but they fade quickly. Coarse yarn is used for these "durries". Three threads of 20's twisted are usually employed in the warp, whilst the weft is of single threads of from 6 to 10's. Very high class "durries" are made of English yarn of 40's, which is imported dyed of suitable colours.

Men's cloths.—What are popularly called Salem *vēshtis* may be divided into two classes—those that have plain borders, and those that have solid borders. The plain borders are commonly of silk alone, but gold threads are sometimes used to form lines on the edge of the borders. The width of the borders varies from $\frac{1}{8}''$ to $1''$ on the sides, and from $\frac{1}{2}''$ to $2\frac{1}{2}''$ at the ends of the cloth. The yarn used is of counts varying from 40's to 100's, and is imported. The cloths are from 3 to 5 yards long each, and from $50''$ to $54''$ wide. They are sold in pairs, and their values range from Rs. 2 to Rs. 12 a pair.

CHAP. VI.
INDUSTRIES.
Textiles.

Arisi-pālaiyam and Shevapet divisions of the town of Salem, and Rāsipuram and Gurusāmi-pālaiyam in the Salem Taluk are the chief centres where these cloths are made. Weavers engaged in this work are Telugu-speaking Dēvāngas and Sāliyas in Salem, Patnūlkārans chiefly in Rāsipuram, and Kaikōlars exclusively in Gurusāmi-pālaiyam and Tāra-mangalam.

"Solid bordered" cloths are usually wider than plain borders, and not infrequently, with the silk threads of the warp, gold-lace is used. The patterns are somewhat elaborate, and necessitate the use of special harness of a very complicated character. The cloths are always made of fine cotton, and are sold in pairs, the prices varying from Rs. 12 to Rs. 40 a pair. Solid bordered *vēshtis* are made in Shevapet and Ponnammāpet by silk weavers, and by Kaikōlars in Pāvadi Street. Salem is the chief centre in the District for this branch of the industry, and the only other place where it is carried on is Rāsipuram, where Patnūlkārans and other castes have taken it up.

The Salem cloths have long enjoyed a reputation for their close texture and their consequent durability. In recent years, however, this reputation has suffered, as the weavers and merchants have both resorted to devices which, whilst reducing the cost of production, have done so by sacrificing the quality. One trick is to use a more open spacing of the warp threads towards the centre of the cloth, whilst recently mercerised cotton or spun silk is employed in the borders instead of the indigenous reeled silk. It has not been recognised that spun silk requires different dye-stuffs from those which are used for reeled silk, with the result that the colours produced are unsatisfactory and highly fugitive.

At Shevapet turbans called *pēttās* are manufactured by Dēvāngas, most of whom are immigrants from Coimbatore. They are from 4 to 6 yards long, and from 24″ to 27″ broad. The warp is generally composed of cotton, and the weft of silk. Some of the turbans are plain, whilst others have borders of gold thread about half an inch wide. The turbans are usually made of dyed yarn, the most popular colour being an indigo sky-blue, and another shade of blue obtained by the use of coal-tar dyes. Women's cloths are also made of mixed cotton and silk by silk weavers in Shevapet, and by Kaikōlars in Ammapet. These cloths are distinct from those which are ornamented with silk borders. A large number of cloths of the latter kind are made to the order of merchants from South Kanara, some of whom are permanently settled in Salem. There is also a certain amount of business in the manufacture of cloths for rich Muhammadans on the West Coast.

CHAP. VI. INDUSTRIES. Textiles.

The weaving of silk cloths is carried on only in Salem Town, and the products are *sāris*, *urumālais* (handkerchiefs) and *pēttās*. *Urumālais* have a scarlet ground, divided at regular intervals by white stripes into squares. The size of the handkerchief is 2½ yards × 1 yard. For these *urumālais* spun silk is used, either both ways, or for warp or for weft only; similarly with *pēttās*, which are from 4 to 6 yards long, and from 24″ to 27″ wide. For *sāris*, on the other hand, only indigenous silk is used, obtained in a raw condition from Kollegāl or Mysore. It is cleaned and reeled by Patnūl women, and afterwards dyed to the colours required. *Pudavais* of pure silk are very costly, the price ranging from Rs. 100 to Rs. 200. They are generally made with silk borders in which a large amount of gold lace is used in the warp. Figures of animals, birds and flowers are the usual form of decoration, whilst, in the body of the cloth, simple designs of flowers, or simple geometrical patterns appear.

Methods. (a) Warping and Sizing.

The process of setting up the warp is one of the most familiar and picturesque sights of an Indian village. The village *pāvadi* is a level stretch of ground set apart near the weavers' quarters, and is often well shaded with tamarind trees. The warp is stretched on stone posts or stout bamboos, firmly fixed in the ground, by women who walk up and down the row of posts, each holding in the left hand a light swift on which the thread is wound, and in the right hand a short bamboo stick carrying a hook at the end, by which they guide the thread in and out between the posts. The process is a very tedious one and involves on the part of the women many miles of walking to prepare a warp. When the warp is completed, it is handed over to the men, who take it off the posts, inserting split bamboos called lease-rods between the two layers of thread to preserve the arrangement. The next operation is to stretch the warp between two trestles firmly fixed on the ground, to arrange all the threads in regular parallel lines, and then to size it with *kanji* made of rice or kambu flour. This is laid on with brushes and well brushed, so that all the fibres of the cotton thread are drawn parallel to one another and well glued together. This adds greatly to the strength of the warp, and as soon as it is dried, it is rolled up into a bundle, the lease-rods being carefully retained in position, and it is now ready to be put in the loom. This process has been briefly described because, in Salem Town at any rate, it has been almost entirely superseded by the hand warping-mill, of which several patterns are in use. In this respect Salem is in advance of all other weaving centres in the Presidency, as there are a large number of what may be termed warping factories solely engaged in the preparation of warps for

CHAP. VI. INDUSTRIES.

the weavers. These are chiefly in the hands of Kaikōlars and Sāliyas, and their clients are mainly Patnūlkārans.

Textiles.

The commonest type of warping-mill consists of a drum about 15′ in diameter and 5′ wide. It is very lightly constructed of wood and bamboos, and on its circumference carries a number of rows of pegs. The yarn to be warped is wound on bobbins, which are arranged in a frame which may contain from 10 to 20 bobbins. The threads are guided on to the warping drum by hooks fixed in a flat metal bar which stretches the whole width of the drum. By a simple piece of mechanism, driven from the axis of the wheel, this bar is given a reciprocating motion, which causes the threads to pass on to the drum sinuously between the pegs, in one direction during the forward motion of the drum, and in the opposite direction when the motion is reversed, and thus enables the leases to be inserted to prevent the warp from getting hopelessly entangled when it is removed from the pegs. The mill is turned by hand, and as soon as it has made one revolution, it is turned back again, so that the length of the warp is practically twice the circumference of the mill. After the warp is removed from the mill, it is stretched on an open piece of ground, and sized in the usual way. The Salem sizers are very expert in their work, and warps made in Salem are considered almost equal to those produced in Kumbakōnam. These mills are of local construction, and are apparently of local design, as they do not appear to be used elsewhere, and are probably an ingenious adaptation of the old fashioned horizontal warping-mill used in Europe. For short warps they are very efficient, but the method is not adapted for long warps, and the mill is not of a type which can be recommended for general adoption throughout the country.

(b) Looms.

There is nothing special about the looms employed for weaving in Salem District. They are all country looms, fitted with reeds and healds of local manufacture. For pattern-weaving elaborate harness worked on the "draw-boy" principle, similar to that which prevailed in Europe before the Jacquard attachment was invented, is employed; but occasionally, for simple patterns in the borders, a dobby is attached to the loom.

Salem Weaving Factory

An experimental factory was opened in Salem at the end of 1905, and continued in existence till 1910, when, owing to a severe outbreak of plague, it was temporarily closed. At about the same time orders were received from the Secretary of State to discontinue the working of experimental factories, and accordingly it was decided not to reopen the Salem factory. During the five years it was located at Salem, from 40 to 60 looms of various improved types were kept at work, and a great variety of weaving

Textiles.

experiments were made on what may be termed a commercial scale. The factory did not meet with that measure of success which was originally anticipated, owing entirely to the difficulty of dealing with the weavers. Nevertheless the factory did much useful work, for although it did not succeed in actually working at a profit, the cost of running it was small, and there is no doubt that it materially contributed to the success of the movement in favour of the use of the fly-shuttle slay, which within the last few years has been adopted by many thousands of weavers.

(2) Dyeing.

Salem was formerly celebrated for the excellence of the work produced by its dyers, but since they have substituted imported coal-tar dyes for the natural vegetable products they formerly employed, the quality of their work has greatly deteriorated. Vegetable dyeing is now carried on to but a very limited extent, and it is almost certain that, when arrangements are made to provide proper instruction for dyers, it will disappear completely. At the present time a good deal of yarn of such colours as yellow and green is imported already dyed.

Raw silk is first cleaned by boiling it with fuller's earth. To produce a scarlet colour the silk is then soaked for a day in water containing one seer of alum and one seer of turmeric for every two visses of silk. Jungle lac, in the proportion of one maund to every three visses of silk, is powdered, boiling water is poured over it, and the mixture is well churned with a wooden pestle. The mixture is allowed to settle, and the surface liquid is poured off into a separate vessel, and this process is repeated till the lac loses its colour. Tamarind water is then added and the solution boiled. The silk is then dipped in it, and when the requisite shade has been obtained, it is washed in clean water and dried.

The following remarks are taken from a report on the dyeing industry in the Madras Presidency which has recently been prepared by Dr. F. Marsden. They are strictly applicable to the dyers in Salem District:—

"The dyers do not as a class appear well-to-do, the general type of dye-house being small and badly lighted (very often it is part of the dwelling house), and the plant and apparatus employed in the majority of cases is exceedingly simple. In the small dye-houses for cotton, there is usually one round vessel (copper) of about 25 gallons capacity, set over a grate in which leaves, brushwood or wood may be burnt as a source of heat. The hanks of yarn are suspended upon sticks which rest upon the edges of the vessel, and from time to time the yarn is turned during dyeing by inserting a thin stick in the bight of the hanks, and altering the position on the supporting stick, so that the yarn which was previously outside the liquor now

CHAP. VI. INDUSTRIES.

becomes immersed. The preparation of the yarn before dyeing is usually very simple, and consists in steeping in cold water until thoroughly impregnated, the process often being accelerated by "beating", after which the excess of water is removed by wringing. Such a preliminary treatment is quite insufficient to remove the natural impurities of cotton, and this is recognised in some of the better class dye-houses, where the yarn is boiled out in a solution of carbonate of soda, which is far more efficacious than water alone in removing the natural wax, colour and dirt. This preliminary boiling is of importance, as, the more efficiently it is carried out, the clearer and more even are the shades subsequently dyed upon the yarn. A type of dye-vessel which is well suited to the dyeing of small lots of yarn is in fairly general use and consists of a rectangular vessel, some 45″ long, 24″ wide and 20″ deep, set over a grate in brickwork and encased in cement. It is economical in space, and permits, when not overloaded, of the yarn being efficiently worked in the dye liquor".

(3) Cloth Printing.

Wax printing is carried on to a limited extent in Salem Town by Kavarais. The shades generally met with are few in number, and are mainly obtained with indigenous materials, but for red, chay root, munjit, etc., are being to some extent displaced by alizarine. The designs may be stencilled on when very elaborate, but are mainly drawn in by hand, or printed on by means of blocks. The cloth to be treated is first immersed in a solution of cow-dung or goat-dung for about 12 hours, and then taken out and well beaten on a stone slab. This process serves to remove the starch in the cloth, and facilitates the absorption of the colours in the subsequent processes.

The dried cloth is first thoroughly soaked in a decoction of myrabolams and dried, and the design outlined by drawing or printing with a solution of proto-sulphate of iron, thickened with jaggery or gum. The iron solution is sometimes obtained by placing nails or rusty iron in sour rice-water or jaggery solution, and leaving them therein until the acidity, which develops, results in sufficient iron for the purpose being dissolved. Wherever this iron solution is painted on the tannin-impregnated cloth there is a production of "ink", and although the black thus produced has certain drawbacks in dyeing, in this connection it serves its purpose quite well. The next operation is to cover those parts of the cloth which are required to be red-coloured with a thickened solution of alum, and set aside to age for a day, after which the cloth is rinsed to remove unfixed tannin. Upon boiling in a decoction of munjit, chay root or alizarine, the dye-stuff combines with the metallic mordants, deepening the black shade of the iron compound and giving a dull red with the alizarine.

When portions of the design are required to be blue in shade, the other parts of the cloth are impregnated with wax and the cloth immersed in an indigo vat. The wax coating is done by hand, the workman having a metal pen, around the handle of which, and about 1½ inches from the point, is a ball of cotton thread. The pen is dipped (up to the ball) into the melted bees' wax, and drawn over the cloth until all the parts of this which are to be protected from the indigo vat are covered; the penetration of the indigo solution is thus prevented, except into the parts which it is desired shall be dyed blue. When the required shade has been obtained, the cloth is worked in boiling water until the wax has been removed, and having been immersed in buffalo milk (presumably to render the colours faster to rubbing) is dried.

The only other shades met with in the ordinary printed cloths are green and yellow, the latter being produced upon portions of the design which have been unmordanted or reserved during the previous operations, whilst green is produced by dyeing yellow upon the parts required, which have been dyed to the necessary blue shade in the indigo vat. The yellow colour is obtained by painting on a decoction of "pista" (myrabolam flowers ?) or myrabolam extract, drying, and then immersing the cloth in a solution of alum, rinsing and drying. The combination of alum with the tannin matter is of a dull yellow colour, and the shades harmonise well with those of the other dye-wares used upon the cloth.

(4) Oils.

Gingelly-oil is the most important of the vegetable oils[1]. It is prepared all over the District, the chief centre being Dharmapuri Taluk and Kāvēri-patnam, whence there is a large export trade. Oil manufactured from *kūr-ellu* is superior to that made from *pēr-ellu*. In Hosūr Taluk most of the gingelly-oil is made from wild gingelly (*Guizotia abyssinica*, or *pēy-ellu*), the oil of which is very inferior.

Coco-nut-oil is nowhere prepared on a large scale, for want of an abundant supply of coco-nuts. Ground-nut oil is pressed in Āttūr and Dharmapuri Taluks, and to a limited extent elsewhere. The seeds of margosa and iluppai are pressed for oil in parts of the Bāramahāl, but the supply is meagre, the demand small, and in the case of the former, its offensive odour renders it unpopular. Pungam is the staple source of oil in Hosūr Taluk.

Castor-oil is not prepared in the ordinary oil-mill. It is manufactured (often at home) all over the District for local consumption. It is used for lighting purposes, but is being ousted by kerosine. In Edappādi it has attained the dignity of an

[1] For the oil-pressing castes, Vāniyars, Gāndlas and Gāṇigas see p. 182.

CHAP. VI. INDUSTRIES.

important manufacture, and the oil-cake derived therefrom is a greater source of profit than the oil itself.

Lemon-grass oil is distilled by Labbais in some of the hills of Salem and other Taluks, and is used as a basal oil for the manufacture of scent.

(5) Tanning.

Three grades of hides are produced in Salem District, (1) village-tanned, (2) town-tanned, and (3) "finished" hides.

Village-tanned hides are the crudest. The work is usually done by Chucklers, and the leather is known in the market as "Chucklers' leather." Ordinary town-tanned hides are known as "godown leather." It is only in Salem Town that finished hides are produced. They are known locally as *pathan-itta-tōl.*

The Salem tanneries, 14 in number, are located near Kichipālaiyam, and are owned by Muhammadans. The skins are purchased in shandies all over the District. The tannery owners send carts from one shandy to another in regular succession to collect them.

The wool taken from the hides of sheep and goats is cleaned in water, colour-sorted by hand, and sold in Madras or Adoni, where it is in demand for the manufacture of carpets. The *āvāram* bark refuse and the inner scrapings of sheep and goat hides are valued as manure. The inner scrapings from the hides of bulls and buffaloes are exported in large quantities for the manufacture of glue.

(6) Iron.

Iron-smelting in Salem District is an art of extreme antiquity. The remains of slag mounds and furnaces in numerous villages, not only in Āttūr, Salem, Ōmalūr and Tiruchengōdu [1], but also on the border line of Hosūr and Krishnagiri Taluks, and even in the heart of the Anchetti jungles, testify to the wide extent and importance of the industry. Owing, however, partly to the rise in the cost of fuel, and partly to the cheapness of imported iron, the industry has of late years rapidly decayed.

The ore is smelted in a mud furnace about 4′ high, the shape of which, when viewed from the front, is like a bottle, about 2′ in

---

[1] The following were centres of iron-smelting in the Talaghāt Taluks :—

Salem Taluk ; Nāmagiripet Tirumanūr, (south of Vellālagundam), Perumālpālaiyam (near Gōdu-malai), Vēdakuttampatti, Dalavāy-patti, Andi-patti and Ariyānūr.

Tiruchengōdu Taluk ; Padavēdu, Konganāpuram, Valayasetti-pālaiyam (a hamlet of Edanga-sālai), Irukālūr Mitta, Tēvūr, Mattampatti.

Ōmalūr Taluk ; Vānavāsi and Sōragai.

Āttūr Taluk ; Āttūr, Tāndavarāyapuram, Matturutti, Tammampatti, Sendāra-patti, Kōnēri-patti, Tukkiyāmpālaiyam, Kīri-patti, Nāgaiyampatti, Kadambūr, Nāraikkinar.

Ūttankarai Taluk ; Tīrta-malai, Māmbādi, Poyya-patti, Vīrappa-Nāyakkanpatti, Pālaiyam, Kattavirichchāmpatti, Mondukuli (all near Tīrtamalai), Pungani, Attippādi (near Nāyakkanūr), Pallattūr.

CHAP. VI. INDUSTRIES.

diameter at the base and about 9" at the top. The floor of the furnace is sunk about 6" below the level of the ground. At the base is an opening some 10" square. The furnace is partly filled with charcoal, on which the ore is placed. A blast is obtained with a pair of goat-skin bellows, worked by hand alternately, so that the draught may be continuous. The nozzles of the bellows are inserted into the orifice at the base of the furnace, and the rest of the opening is sealed with wet clay. The blast is kept up for about 3½ hours, at the end of which a mass of red-hot metal, weighing about 12 lbs., is withdrawn, and worked on an anvil, and, when sufficiently hammered, a cut is made nearly the whole way through, and the mass is then ready for sale.

Porto Novo Company.

An attempt to exploit Salem iron on a large scale was made by Mr. J. M. Heath, Commercial Resident at Salem, who in 1825 resigned the Company's service, and proceeded to England to study ways and means. In 1830, Mr. Heath returned to India, and established works at Porto Novo.[1]

In 1853, a new Company was formed called the "East Indian Iron Company." The chief beds worked were those of the Kanja-malai. New works were set up at Pūlāmpatti, on the banks of the Kāvēri, whither the ore was taken by road from Kanja-malai (23 miles) to be smelted. The iron produced was of excellent quality, and it was used in the construction of the tubular and suspension bridges over the Menai Straits. The works at Pūlāmpatti[2] were supplied with charcoal from Sōlappādi, 18 miles up the Kāvēri. There the charcoal was made in large furnaces, and it was conveyed to Pūlāmpatti in boats. It was delivered at the works at a cost of Rs. 6 per ton, but the supply was irregular on account of the charcoal burners, who were unable to work continuously owing to the unhealthy state of the jungles at certain times of the year.

Future Prospects.

Elaborate inquiries were made in the last decade of the nineteenth century[3] as to whether the iron ores of Salem District could be exploited on a commercial scale. It has been suggested that blast furnaces might be erected at Kādaiyāmpatti and Hanuma-tīrtam, the former to serve the Kanja-malai deposits,

---

[1] A history of the Porto Novo Iron Company is given in the *South Arcot Gazetteer*, pp. 283 to 290.

[2] According to Mr. Le Fanu, Vol. I, p. 99, the Kanja-malai bed was worked as late as 1861. Mr. Maylor, at that time Manager of the Porto Novo Iron Company's works, estimated that the yield from Kanja-malai ore was about 55 per cent of pig iron, and the quantity of charcoal required was 3½ tons to every ton of iron produced.

[3] See Sir Thomas Holland's paper on the *Iron Ore and Iron Industries of the Salem District* and *Imperial Institute Handbook* on Iron, No. 8 (1892).

CHAP. VI. INDUSTRIES.

and the latter those of Tīrta-malai. Calculating on the basis of one acre of forest to half a ton of wood annually, one ton of wood to 4 cwt. of charcoal, 17 cwt. of charcoal to one ton of pig-iron, and $3\frac{1}{2}$ tons of charcoal to one ton of wrought-iron, it would require $8\frac{1}{2}$ acres of forest to produce one ton of pig-iron and 35 acres to produce a ton of wrought-iron[1]. The estimated outturn arrived at, taking into account (1) the produce of all the forests within 10 miles of the blast furnace, or (2) the produce within a radius of 16 miles, is as follows:—

	Wrought-iron.	Pig-iron.
Ten miles radius.		
Kādaiyāmpatti	1,617	6,659
Hanuma-tīrtam	1,403	5,776
Total ..	3,020	12,435
Sixteen miles radius.		
Kādaiyāmpatti	2,843	11,706
Hanuma-tīrtam	2,363	9,729
Total ..	5,206	21,435

Experts declare that no blast furnace on modern lines can pay, unless the annual output reaches 10,000 tons of pig. It is only Kādaiyāmpatti that could supply the fuel for this. But if operations were conducted on a scale of sufficient magnitude to supply a blast furnace, the cost of labour would be indefinitely enhanced; for Kādaiyāmpatti and Hanuma-tīrtam are two of the most feverish spots in the District, and coolies would never settle in either locality, unless induced to do so by very ample wages. Moreover, to work the forests properly, feeder roads should be opened at heavy cost. Again, the cost of transit of ore to furnace, and pig to rail must be faced, a cost which crushed the Porto Novo Company. In fine, little prospect exists of a blast furnace stoked with charcoal ever paying in Salem District. The adoption of large numbers of small furnaces of an improved type might be attended with success, as it has in parts of America and in Styria where similar problems present themselves. Possibly further advances in electric metallurgy may eventually solve the fuel difficulty.

[1] These figures are taken from a memorandum of the Collector of Salem No. 2784, dated 24th September 1894. The estimates adopted by Sir Thomas Holland in his pamphlet, which worked out at 23 acres for a ton of pig-iron, were warmly disputed by Mr. C. W. MacMinn (See *Indian Agriculturalist* of 8th April 1893, page 196), who estimated that 10 acres would suffice.

Salem iron-ores contain practically no phosphorus or sulphur and are therefore well suited for manufacturing the better quality of wrought-iron or steel.

(7) Steel.

Indian steel was famous from the days of Alexander to the days of Marco Polo, and it is probable that steel has been manufactured in Salem District from a very remote period. In the first half of the nineteenth century steel was brought to England, sometimes in the form of conical ingots, and sometimes [1] in flat round cakes. The conical ingots were evidently wootz, made, as is still done in Trichinopoly, by carburising wrought-iron in crucibles, a principle which was not applied in England till 1800[2]. The flat cakes of steel which are still made in Salem District are produced by quite a different process, namely, by the partial removal by oxidization of the carbon in cast-iron, as in the open hearth finery of Styria and Carinthia and in the ordinary puddling of pig-iron. The process as now carried on is thus described.

In the manufacture of wrought-iron, certain easily fusible beads of iron are produced, and melt off as shot. These are in reality highly carburised particles of cast-iron, and it is from these that the steel is made. The shot are first pounded in a stone mortar with a pestle of the kind ordinarily used for pounding rice. By this process the small particles of slag adhering to the shot are removed, and the cast-iron receives an imperfect polish. The powdered slag-material is separated by sifting in the ordinary manner in a winnow. A hole is dug in the ground about 1′ deep and about 1′ in diameter. At one side a semi-circular groove is excavated from the surface to the bottom of the pit. A large cake of soft clay serves to divide this small excavation from the other part of the pit, and the smaller chamber serves as the finery in which the steel is made. The bottom of this is first covered with a layer of dirty quartz, obtained from sifting the crushed ore when dressing the magnetite for the furnace. On this hearth of quartz an ignited coal is placed, and the small chamber is filled with charcoal. A *tuyère*, previously built in with the clay-partition, points downwards at an angle of about 45 degrees, and receives the nozzles of two goat-skin bellows, by which a continuous blast is maintained. The shot are first wetted and thrown upon the charcoal, the amount used being governed by pure guess-work, as in the wrought-iron smelting. The blast is continued for about half an hour, when the process of decarburisation is complete, and the *tuyère* and clay-partition are broken down for the removal of the

[1] The account which follows is taken from Sir Thomas Holland's Report of 1892 on the manufacture of steel in Salem District.

[2] The same principle governed the later patent of Mackintosh, and has since been modified to the modern cementation process for the conversion of bar-iron into "blister steel" and in "case hardening."

CHAP. VI. INDUSTRIES.

steel-cake, which is first slightly cooled by a dash of water, and then hammered to remove the casing of slag which has formed around it. The workers are quite aware of the fact that if they continued the process too long, the resulting product would be of no more use than ordinary wrought-iron. It seems curious that Pariahs should adopt this interesting process for the manufacture of steel, whilst the typical wootz is made in such an entirely different manner.

In the second half of the nineteenth century the enterprise of the late Arunachala Asari made Salem famous throughout India, and his hunting-knives and pig-sticking lances were in great demand. The manufacture of silver-and gold-mounted "cheetah-tooth" pen-knives still continues a characteristic local industry.

(8) Brass-work.

It would seem that the advent of the Railway has killed the indigenous arts of metallurgy, for even in Edappādi, where brass work is the hereditary occupation of about 30 families, the casting of brass has largely given place to the beating out of sheet-brass. The same remark holds good of Muttu-Nāyakkan-patti, near Omalur, another local centre of brass-casting. In Salem itself no brass is cast, but the manufacture of pots and pans by the local Asaris from beaten sheet-brass is an industry of importance.

(9) Charcoal.

Charcoal burning is carried on on a commercial scale not only in the Reserved Forests, but also in the Pālaiyams of Bērikai and Sūlagiri. There is a large export to Bangalore and the Kōlār Gold Field, as well as to Erode.

(10) Baskets and Mats.

Baskets are usually made of bamboo, and the industry is chiefly carried on by Mēdaras or Vēdakkārars.

Perhaps the most important product of the Vēdakkārars' art is the familiar bamboo-matting, used for flooring and for the construction of temporary sheds and pandals. Their usual size is five cubits square, but they are made of any size to order, and in flooring the house the mat-makers prefer to weave the mat in one piece *in situ*. The best quality of bamboo-matting is the so-called "green-mat," made solely of the smooth exterior shavings of the bamboo. Another item of importance is the manufacture of baskets for coffee seedlings, about 3″ in diameter and 9″ long, sold at Rs. 5 per thousand. Strong baskets are made in large quantities for the transport of mangoes and oranges; bread-baskets, fish-baskets, baskets for carrying fowls, baskets for hand-baling irrigation, winnows, fans, bird-cages, hen-coops, are among the useful articles that these simple workmen will turn out. Unfortunately most of them are indebted to contractors, who enjoy a big share of the profits of their industry.

Grass mats (mostly of *kōrai* grass, *Cyperus rotundus*), are made in many villages, the workers being usually Labbai women. The *kōrai* grass used in Salem is imported from Trichinopoly, that used in Dharmapuri Taluk is cut on the banks of the Sanat-kumāra-nadi. The mat-makers dye the grass themselves, the favourite colours being white, red, black and green. The patterns produced are not very elegant. A mat is worth about 10 annas. Mats of date-leaf are made at Mārända-halli.

(11) Fibres.

The chief fibres of economical importance in the District are those of (1) palmyra, (2) coco-nut, (3) aloe, and (4) janappu (= san-hemp, *Crotalaria juncea*). None of these are manufactured on a large scale.

(12) Indigo.

The manufacture of indigo has been carried on in Āttūr Taluk from time immemorial. The industry was worked up by Mr. Heath, who, in 1833, sold the business, virtually a monopoly, to Mr. G. F. Fischer. At that time there were works at Salem, Kādaiyāmpatti, Vellālagundam, Narasingapuram, Sarvāy, Malli-karai, Singapuram, Siruvāchār, Vīraganūr and other places. The indigenous method of manufacture was to steep the leaves of *aviri* (*Indigofera tinctoria*), or *veppālai* (*Wrightia tinctoria*) in water in large earthen pots, embedded in the ground. The leaves were allowed to ferment, and were then beaten with paddles; the mixture was then boiled till it became viscid like boiling jaggery. It was next allowed to cool in a shady place, and when cooled, the residue was cut into cakes, and sent to market.

The system now in vogue of precipitating the colouring matter with lime-water in a vat or cistern was introduced, it is said, by Mr. James Fischer. The process is as follows:—*Aviri*[1] leaves are cut and tied into bundles. From 10 to 15 *bārams* of them (1 *bāram* = 20 maunds), are placed overnight in the steeping vat, a brick chamber lined with cement. The leaves are battened down by means of beams attached to pegs in the sides of the vat, and water is run in till all the leaves are submerged. The leaves soak all night, and at 6 A.M. the fermenting liquid is let out into the beating-vat, situated at a lower level, and coolies work it about with paddles till 10 or 11 A.M. Lime-water is then added, and within an hour the fluid clears, and the precipitated indigo settles. The clear water is then run off, and the sediment is strained through a thin cloth, and passed into a copper vessel; clean water being added, lime-water is then sprinkled over it, and the mixture is again worked with a paddle; after about 15 minutes the solid matter is deposited, and the water is drawn off through a syphon. The precipitate is then boiled, and when it attains

[1] *Veppālai* leaves are no longer used for the manufacture of indigo.

CHAP. VI. INDUSTRIES.

the proper consistency, it is poured into a thick canvas sheet, supported on a bamboo frame. The sheet acts as a filter, allowing the clear water to drain off, and retaining the indigo as a thick paste. This paste is covered for the night, and on the following morning superfluous moisture is expelled by means of a screw-press; the residue is cut into cakes and dried in the sun.

Mr. Fischer's first factory was set up in about 1860 in Ponnammāpet, a suburb of Salem. Factories at Kādaiyāmpatti, Puttira-Kavundan-pālaiyam, Singāpuram, Āttūr, Talaivāsal and other places followed. Rival factories on the lines adopted by Mr. Fischer were soon started at Ēttāppūr, Āragalūr and other places. The industry flourished till about 1894, when the competition of synthetic indigo began to be felt. Mr. Fischer then closed down his factories and sold them. In 1911 there were 31 factories in Āttūr Taluk, and a few more in Salem, all in the hands of Indian capitalists. The factory owners obtain the seeds from Nellore and other northern districts, and distribute them to the ryots on the condition that the whole of the produce is made over to the manufacturer who advances the seed. The manufacturer pays the ryot about 12 annas per *bāram* for the leaves, and the refuse is the perquisite of the ryot, who uses it for manure (p. 227).

(13) Stone.

There is abundance of good building-stone which has never been commercially exploited. Gneiss lends itself readily to manipulation, for flat slabs of any portable size and of uniform thickness can be obtained by applying fire evenly over the surface of the living rock. To give the slabs the required shape, shallow holes are drilled along the surface.

Pot-stone.

Large quantities of steatite vessels, pots, bowls, plates, dishes, etc., are manufactured in Āttūr and Ōmalūr Taluks, and exported to the Districts of Tanjore and Trichinopoly, where they are in great demand among Brahmans. (See p. 33.)

Miscellaneous.

Other industries of local importance are the manufacture of palmyra-jaggery (especially in the Firkas of Mēchēri and Edappādi), tobacco (an important industry in Āttūr Taluk), cane-jaggery, saltpetre (at Edappādi, see Vol. II, pp. 273 and 79) and pottery.

TRADE.

The trade of the District may be described as centrifugal. That of Hosūr gravitates towards Bangalore; that of Krishnagiri to Tiruppattūr and the Railway: Uttankarai trade hovers between Tiruppattūr and South Arcot, that of Dharmapuri between Salem and the Railway: Āttūr trade is divided between South Arcot and Trichinopoly; that of Tiruchengōdu between Coimbatore and the Railway. Salem is the only important centre; it attracts a certain amount of trade from all the adjacent taluks (Dharmapuri,

Tiruchongōdu, Ūttankarai, and Āttūr), and has an extensive export and import trade.

Weekly Markets.

The economic centres of distribution and exchange are the weekly markets held all over the District. It is in these fairs, or "shandies," that the ryot disposes of his produce, and purchases salt, chillies, cloths and other necessities of life. Wholesale merchants attend the larger markets, and buy in stock on advantageous terms. Petty traders visit a series of shandies, 4 or 5 in a week, in regular rotation, buying in one and selling in another, eking out a profit of 3 or 4 annas a day. Shandies are known by the day of the week on which they occur, and not, as a rule, by the name of the place in which they are held. There are in the District 129 shandies, of which 44 are controlled by the Taluk Boards and produce a revenue of some Rs. 12,480.

Chief Trades.

The chief trade in the District is in agricultural produce, cloth, cattle, salt and oils. There is also a large export by rail of raw hides and forest produce.

(1) Trade in Grain.

The trade in agricultural produce is mainly in the hands of Kōmatis. It is also shared in by Muhammadans, and in the Bālāghāt by Lingāyats, in the Bāramahāl by Vāniyars, Janappars, Balijas and Gollas, in the Talaghāt by Sembadavans and Nagarattu Chettis.

The business which combines grain trade with money-lending is perhaps the most lucrative in the District. In the days when the ryots' first kist fell due in December, full advantage was taken by capitalists of the fact that the crops could not be placed on the market till January. Advances were freely made on the security of the presumptive crops. At harvest-time the loan was paid back in its equivalent of grain at the current market price, and a stipulated quantity per rupee of the loan was added by way of interest. As the big grain merchants are well in touch with each other all over the District, it is easy for them to reduce the market-price of grain at harvest-time, so that they can recover their loans on the most favourable terms. The ryot must realise his produce as soon as harvested, for he has his kist to pay. The merchants, having called in all their dues, can afford to wait for the inevitable rise of prices before they sell. In this way the money-lenders tend to "corner" the food supply of the District annually, and their profits by way of interest are far larger than they appear to be from the terms of the contract. The lender generally makes a clean profit of not less than 25 per cent on his outlay. It is said that since the abolition of the December kist in 1906, this practice is on the wane. The middlemen usually buy up their grain at shandies, and some send their agents to the villages at harvest-time to buy grain cash down.

CHAP. VI. TRADE.

Krishnagiri merchants invest largely in Hosūr rāgi, which they stock, and sell on commission. The larger grain exporters sell to Madras dealers on a commission of one anna in the rupee.

(2) Cloth Trade.

Trade in European textile fabrics is mainly in the hands of Muhammadans. Kōmatis are the chief dealers in country-made cloths, though in some cases the weaving communities themselves, Patnūlkārans, Kaikōlars, Dēvāngas and Sāles trade in their own products. In the Bāramahal and Bālāghāt the local manufactures do not exceed the local demand, but from Salem Taluk there is an extensive export trade. The middlemen in Salem receive from the manufacturer one anna in the rupee on the total value of the cloths sent, and they are also said to get six pies per cloth from the retail dealer.

In out-of-the-way tracts, enterprising Labbais from Palli-patti, in Karūr Taluk of Trichinopoly District, hawk cloths on a system of six months' credit, on account of which they are called *Ārumāsa-kadan-kārars.* They first visit the villages during the cultivation season, and they return to claim their dues at harvest-time. Their prices are fixed high enough to cover the losses inevitable to unsecured credit, but to an ignorant ryot a stiff price is a trifle compared with the advantages of having the goods brought to his door, and postponing payment for six months.

(3) Cattle Trade.

The cattle trade of the District is almost entirely in the hands of Janappars, except for petty transactions between villagers. The centre of this trade is in the Pennāgaram Division. All male calves bred in the Kāvēri-side forests are sold before they complete their first year, for a calf which is allowed to mature in the forests can never be domesticated.

Before the outbreak of plague, most of the saleable calves were disposed of during the festivals at Māthēsvaran-malai (Kollegāl Taluk, thrice a year), Mēchēri (February), Adaman-kōttai (March), and Natta-halli (April)[1]. Attendance at these festivals is now restricted by Plague Regulations, and the cattle trade has gravitated to the weekly market at Pāppāra-patti. The trade is in the hands of petty brokers, resident at Pennāgaram, Halaipuram, Matam and other places in Pennāgaram Division. These brokers own but little capital, and usually 4 or 5 of them work in partnership. They start in person for the forest pens on Fridays, effect their purchases on the Saturday, Sunday, or Monday, return with their calves to their villages by Wednesday, and dispose of them at Pāppāra-patti on the next day. The price is usually fixed not at so much per calf, but at so many calves per Rs. 100.

[1] Or Nattada-halli, a village 7 miles from Dharmapuri near the Pennāgaram road, and adjoining Indūr.

The purchasers at Pāppāra-patti are usually Janappars, resident in the Bāramahāl taluks. These Janappars, in their turn, sell the calves to ryots resident in Mysore State. The Mysore ryots rear and train the cattle till they are full grown; then sell them back once more to Janappars, who dispose of them in the districts of the East Coast, the chief markets being Tiruvannāmalai, Srīrangam, Madura, and Negapatam. From the latter place large numbers are exported on credit, at the risk of the Bāramahāl Janappars, to agents in Singapore and Penang, and it is said that the outstandings on this account with the Janappars of the three villages of Kannānda-halli, Perungōpana-halli and Mādra halli, in Krishnagiri Taluk, amount to nearly half a lakh of rupees. Exact figures are not available to show how many cattle are exported from the District annually, but statistics gathered at the temporary Traffic Registering Office, established at Rāya-kōta in 1901 with a view to ascertaining the merits of a railway project from Hosūr to the plains, show that for the six months, November 1901 to March 1902, a monthly average of nearly 4,600 head of cattle passed down the ghats, against an average of about 1,060 travelling up. Of the 4,600, over 4,100 went via Dharmapuri, the rest via Krishnagiri, and about three out of every four came from Kela-mangalam, where, during the busy season, between 1,000 and 1,500 head of cattle change hands every Sunday shandy.

Cattle dealers have a curious way of clinching a bargain. As soon as a price is agreed upon, the vendor places small pieces of cow-dung in the hands of the purchaser, after which formality neither party dare recede from the contract. When the beast is sold, the rope by which it was led, and the brass ornaments on its horns, are removed and retained by the seller.

(4) Salt Trade.

Most of the salt for the Talaghāt taluks, as well as Ūttankarai, is imported from the Madras Depot. In Hosūr, and parts of Krishnagiri and Dharmapuri, Bombay salt is preferred. Bombay salt is imported through Bangalore and Calicut. As salt is usually bought wholesale by weight, and retailed by measure, the lighter the salt and the larger the crystals, the greater the merchants' profits. For these qualities Bombay salt is preferred to Madras salt. Blackish dirty salt is in favour with the people, as it is said to be more saline.

The wholesale salt trade, like that in grain and cloth, is mainly in the hands of Kōmatis and Muhammadans. Shevapet is the central emporium, the Shevapet merchants supplying dealers in the adjoining taluks, and allowing $1\frac{1}{2}$ per cent commission on the value of salt purchased. The salt is disposed of in shandies, where it is either sold or bartered in small quantities for

CHAP. VI. TRADE.

agricultural produce. Some grain traders in Hosūr Taluk take salt with them to the villages, and exchange it for mustard-seed.

(5) Oil Trade.

The bulk of the oil trade is in the hands of the enterprising Vāniyar community, though the Kōmatis and Balijas have a share in it, and in Tiruchengōdu the Sembadavans take the lead in the manufacture and export of castor-oil. From the Bāramahāl the gingelly-oil of Kāvēri-patnam and Dharmapuri finds its way all over South India.

Rail-borne Trade.

Most of the exports by rail are raw products, the only manufactured articles of importance being cotton-cloths from Salem and the stations in Tiruchengōdu Taluk; dressed skins from Dharmapuri, Krishnagiri and Salem; and gunny-bags, brass and iron work, and indigo from Salem; bamboo mats from the stations at the foot of the Shevaroys; unrefined sugar from Dharmapuri, and jaggery from Salem and from the Taluk of Tiruchengōdu.

Cereals and pulses travel freely all over the District, and large quantities are exported. The chief centres for rice and paddy export are Krishnagiri, Dharmapuri, Salem, Sankaridrug and the southern stations of Ūttankarai Taluk. Fruit and vegetables are sent from stations both in the Bāramahāl and Talaghāt, custard-apples are a speciality of Bargūr, betel-leaves of Sankaridrug, and ground-nuts, areca-nuts, chillies and onions of Salem. Tobacco finds an outlet at Salem, Sāmalpatti, Dāsampatti and Morappūr, and raw cotton at Sankaridrug and Ānangūr; Salem and the stations in Tiruchengōdu Taluk export ghee; oil-seeds, both castor and gingelly, are railed from Krishnagiri and Dharmapuri, and most of the stations between Sāmalpatti and Salem; gingelly-oil is sent from Krishnagiri, Sāmalpatti and Morappūr, and castor-oil from Sankaridrug; oil-cake is an important item at Krishnagiri, Kādaiyāmpatti, Salem, and Sankaridrug, while coffee is sent from Salem, Kādaiyāmpatti, and Bommidi.

The chief items of forest produce are tamarind[1] and tanning barks, which are exported from most of the stations in Ūttankarai Taluk, and also from Krishnagiri and Dharmapuri. The stations round the foot of the Shevaroys provide gall-nuts, timber, bamboos and fuel. Gall-nuts are also railed from Sāmalpatti, and firewood from Sankaridrug. Krishnagiri exports charcoal, and there is a trade in palmyra fibres[2] from Tiruchengōdu Taluk, while Dāsampatti and Sāmalpatti export quantities of dried leaves

[1] Tamarind produce is usually gathered in March.

[2] "A loose fibre which surrounds the base of the leaf-stalk" (Watt, page 170). The export is confined to the months of July, August and September; the Tahsildar writes that about 30 bales, valued at Rs. 500, are purchased per week by Erode merchants, who send them to Tuticorin.

(chiefly of Banyan, *Ficus indica*) to be stitched into food-plates for the higher caste Hindus.

Lastly there is a large export of raw skins from all the Talaghāt stations, as well as from Krishnagiri, Dharmapuri, Dāsampatti and Morappūr, and horns are exported from Salem.

Rail-borne imports are less varied, English piece-goods and yarns, alizarine, kerosine oil, salt, foreign liquors, copper, brass, and iron are freely imported from Madras. Cotton cloths and twist of Indian manufacture from the southern districts of the Madras Presidency, and timber, pepper, spices, betel, and salt-fish from Malabar. Curiously enough, there is a considerable import of cereals and pulses, especially of rice, from adjoining districts, and Salem City stands easily first in the extent and variety of its demands.

WEIGHT AND MEASURES.

Weights.

The weights in vogue are common to the Presidency.

16 pies = 1 *palam* of 3 tolas.
8 *palams* = 1 seer (*sēr*) of 24 tolas.
5 seers = 1 viss.
8 viss = 1 maund.
20 maunds = 1 *kandogam* (Anglice "candy").

In some parts of the District the *pothi* of 10 maunds of 960 tolas, is more generally used than the candy. The *bāram* (load), *mūttai* (bundle), and *sattai* are also used for weights of 10 maunds and upwards. A *bāram* of jaggery in Rāsipuram Division equals 20 maunds. A *pēttai-padi* = 1,000 tolas. Merchants in the northern Bāramahāl are said to allow an excess of 2 *palams* for every viss bought or sold on almost all articles.

In Hosūr and Krishnagiri Taluks the seer is the chief unit. A half *palam* is called *chattāk* (Hindustani for "one-sixteenth"). A *palam* = *ara-pāvu* ($\frac{1}{2} \times \frac{1}{4}$, i.e., of a seer), two *palams* = *pāvu* (i.e., $\frac{1}{4}$ seer), four *pāvulu* = 1 seer. Similarly a quarter viss = *savā-sēr*, a half viss = *adai sēr*, and a viss = *pānch-sēr* (corrupted into *panchēr*), from Hindustani words denoting $1\frac{1}{4}$, $2\frac{1}{2}$ and 5 respectively. These taluks also use the *dadiyam* of 2 viss.

Goldsmiths employ the following scale: 4 paddy-seeds = 1 *kundumani* (the familiar scarlet seed of *Abrus precatorius*), 32 *kundumanis* = 1 *varāhan-edai* (pagoda), $3\frac{3}{16}$ pagodas = 1 rupee.

The weight of a sovereign is variously estimated at $2\frac{3}{16}$, $2\frac{1}{4}$ and $2\frac{5}{16}$ pagodas, discrepancies which suggest that their methods are not very exact. In Salem goldsmiths keep a series of weights representing 1, 2, 3, 5, 10, and sometimes 20 and 30 pagodas, and the sub-multiples of the same, $\frac{1}{2}$, $\frac{1}{4}$, and $\frac{1}{8}$. Read speaks of a grain of rāgi as a goldsmith's weight.

CHAP. VI. WEIGHTS AND MEASURES.

Telugu weights are used by goldsmiths in Hosūr in the following scale:—

4 *guriginjas*, *kundumanis* or *pātikas* = 1 *rūka*.
9 *rūkas* = 1 *varaha* (pagoda).
30 *rūkas* or $3\frac{1}{3}$ *varaha* = 1 tola.

Brass and bell-metal are sold by the *padi* of $12\frac{1}{2}$ seers in Rāsipuram Division.

The *rāttal* is used in weighing hides, and also sheet-brass. It is said to approximate to one pound. Its equivalent is variously estimated at $38\frac{2}{5}$, 39 and 40 tolas. There are 24 or 25 *rāttals* to a maund of 960 to 1,000 tolas' weight. Hides, however, are more commonly sold by number. In Āttūr Taluk indigo is sold by the *rāttal*, 500 of which make a *bāram*, and 25 a maund.

Scales.

There are four kinds of scale:—

(1) The "needle-balance", ordinary metal scales with indicator.

(2) The "rod-balance", a simple wooden cross-beam, suspended in the middle by a string. It is sometimes called "*nāmam* balance" from its resemblance to an inverted *Tengalai nāmam*. In Hosūr it is called *chintāl* or *takkadi*.

(3) The spring-balance, sometimes called "*rāttal*-scale", used chiefly in weighing hides, wool, palmyra-fibre, yarn, jaggery, and tamarind.

(4) The *muttattu-kōl*, *velli-kōl*, *sēda-kōl* or *tūkku-kōl*, a balance on the principle of a steel-yard. It consists of a rod marked at regular intervals to indicate different weights. A single scale is attached at the first notch (called *nāttāngi-vāy*) either to a hook or by simple tying. The rod is then suspended by a looped string, which is moved backwards or forwards till the rod becomes horizontal. The notch at which the loop rests indicates the weight. The notches are called the *vāy*, and there may be 10 or 20 of them. Vegetables, cotton-seeds and tamarind are sold at so many *vāy* per *panam* (two annas). In a 20 notch balance, the 2nd *vāy* = about $3\frac{3}{8}$ viss, the 3rd = $2\frac{1}{2}$ viss, the 7th = 1 viss, the 15th = 10 *palams*, the 18th = 4 *palams*, and so on.[1] Spun cotton is weighed on a similar balance with slightly different intervals.

Measures of capacity.

Till 1873 local grain measures were in vogue. The existence of two or three standards in one taluk was comparatively a small evil, for even in a single village a duplicate system sometimes prevailed, and it is still commonly said that grain merchants, who

[1] A scale in use in Salem Taluk, but not very commonly, is 1st notch = $\frac{1}{2}$ viss, 2nd = 1 viss, 3rd = $1\frac{1}{2}$ viss, 4th = 2 viss, and so on.

deal with Malayālis, measure the grain they receive in measures of larger capacity than those they use in selling, and so add handsomely to their profits.

In the early seventies, however, it was realised that official returns of current prices were valueless so long as the standards of no two recording stations agreed. In 1873, accordingly, an attempt was made to express the various local measures in terms of imperial seers.[1] The basis of comparison was the weight of rice, in tolas, that each local measure would hold, and it was found that in Salem District two measures prevailed; (1) a *padi* which contained from 118 to 150 tolas, and (2) a *mānam* which held from 63 to 86 tolas of rice "heaped moderately."

The object of these calculations was to standardise the price returns, and not the local measures. Between 1876 and 1879, however, the practice of officially stamping approved measures was introduced. Local officers were left to themselves to decide the standard that should be officially recognised in each recording station. Not unnaturally, the Board's list of tolas per local measure was adopted as a basis for the stamping operations. But the Board's estimates themselves were based on uncertain data, because the local measures were all of different diameter, a circumstance which vitiated the estimated allowance for "heaping." Moreover, most of the measures on which the calculations were based were of bamboo, and of all shapes and sizes. But these inaccuracies were a trifle compared with the vagaries of local officers in applying the Board's standards. The universal practice in the District was to estimate capacity by tola-weight of gram, and not of rice. The test by volume of water was nowhere adopted. Now ordinary gram is 3 or 4 per cent heavier than rice, and the difference in weight between old and new gram is 16 or 17 per cent; old, new, or mixed gram was adopted as a test by the stamping maistries, to suit their own interest, or please the merchant who brought the measure. "The Assistant Collector ordered the introduction of the Salem measure (136 tolas gram) into Āttūr, where the true standard was 154 gram; a stamping maistry transferred from Salem to Nāmakkal introduced without orders the Salem measure, altering the standard from 150 tolas gram (double measure) to 136[2]; the Vāniyambādi Sub-Magistrate altered, without any authority, the town standard from 86 tolas rice to 90 tolas gram, and the Sub-Collector took it into his head that it would be a good thing to introduce the *pakka* seer of 80

---

[1] B P. 51 of 15-1-73.

[2] The Board's tables showed 132 tolas. This represented the weight of rice in a Salem measure "struck"; 136 tolas was the locally recognised "heaped" content. See B.P. 1223 of 9-5-79.

CHAP. VI. WEIGHTS AND MEASURES.

tolas into the Sub-Division, and ordered accordingly, but he made a mess of it, for, instead of a seer of 80 tolas rice, he introduced one of about 77 tolas, as the 80 tolas was weighed in gram."[1] At Rasipuram people complained that the new measure, though supposed to be 136 tolas, was really one-eighth measure larger than the old *māmūl* measure, which was 144 tolas. This was due to the use of fresh gram as a test by the stamping maistry, and a similar complaint was received from Dharmapuri.

To clear the confusion it was decided to fix two standards for the District, approximating them as closely as possible to local usage. In the four Talaghāt taluks a standard of 150 tolas rice was sanctioned, Ūttankarai taking as its standard the half measure of 75 tolas. The second standard of 86 tolas was adopted in the three taluks of the Sub-Division. The test was made by volume of water. These two standards continued up to 1st July 1902, when the Madras Measure of 62½ fluid ounces, 4½ inches in diameter, containing 132 tolas weight of rice heaped, with its submultiples, was adopted throughout the District.[2] The Madras Measure has not yet been thoroughly popularised, and the old measures of 1880 are generally preferred.

The favourite scale is

4 ollocks = 1 *mānam* (½ Madras measure).
4 *mānams* = 1 *vallam* (2 Madras measures).
40 *vallams* = 1 *kandagam* or *putti* (80 Madras Measures).

The *mānam* is half a Madras Measure, and the word *padi* or 'measure' is generally applied to the *mānam*, which is in more general use than the full Madras Measure. The *kandagam* is not a constant quantity for, in the southern taluks, the old measure containing 150 tolas of rice is frequently used as the unit, four to a *vallam*. Instead of the *kandagam*, in some parts of the District a *modā* of 16 *vallams* (32 Madras Measures) and a *pothi* of 6 *modās* or 96 *vallams* (192 Madras Measures) is preferred. The *kalam* of 12 *marakkāls* is only used in the east of Āttūr Taluk, bordering on South Arcot.

The Telugu system in vogue at Hosūr is as follows:—

2 *giddalu* = 1 *sōla*.
14 *sōlas* = 1 *mānika*.
2 *mānikas* = 1 *balla*.
2 *ballas* = 1 *ibbaliga*.
2 *ibbaligas* = 1 *tūmu* (Kanarese *kolaga*).
10 *tūmus* = 1 *pandhumu*.
2 *pandhumus* or 20 *tūmus* = 1 *putti* (Kanarese *kandaga*).

[1] B.P. 930 of 9-7-80.
[2] B.P. 205 of 16-9-01.

Separate measures are kept for 2, 3, 4 and 5 *tūmus*. Two *tūmus* make one *nidhumu*.

In Krishnagiri the "seer" is used as a measure of capacity. It contains 86 tolas' weight of heaped rice, and is the same as the old standard grain measure. Eight of these seers make a *sēr-vallam*, and 40 *sēr-vallams* = 1 *sēr-kandagam*. A Madras Measure is equivalent to about $1\frac{1}{19}$ of these seers, and roughly $6\frac{1}{2}$ seers = 1 standard *vallam*. The standard measures are called *kumpani* ("Company") *vallam* and *kumpani kandagam*, to distinguish them from the *sēr-vallam* and *sēr-kandagam*. Krishnagiri people also use a *sōla*, 4 of which go to *mānam*. When paying field-labourers in kind, special measures are used known as *kūli* (coolie) *padi* and *kūli-vallam*, which are equal to three-fourths of the standard *mānam* and *vallam* respectively. The latter are distinguished as *muddirai* or "stamped."

Measures of Length.

The measures of length in common use are an object lesson in anthropometry. Two fingers' breadth (*vira-kadai*) = 1 *angulam* (the length of the first joint of the thumb). Four fingers' breadth = 1 palm. Three palms = 1 span (*jān*). Three spans (or 12 *angulams*) = 1 cubit (*mulam*). Four cubits = 1 *mār* (fathom), the distance between the tips of the middle fingers when the arms are outstretched. The yard of 2 cubits (*gajam*, a Hindustani word) and the foot (*adi*) are also used.

The ordinary word for mile is *kal* (= "stone," i.e., mile-stone). A mile is also called *mukkāl-nāligai-vali*, the distance one travels in $\frac{3}{4}$ *nāligai* (the Indian hour of 24 minutes). The *kādam* of $7\frac{1}{2}$ *nāligais* (= 10 miles) is also in use.[1] Meal-times are sometimes used to describe the length of a journey; a "breakfast-time journey" = 8 miles, "a tiffin-time journey" = 20 miles, "a supper-time journey" = 32 miles. In Hosūr Taluk *kommina kūgu*, the distance that the bugle known in Kanarese as *kommu* can be heard, is used for a distance of about 2 miles. *Madakku-dūram*, or *anaippu-dūram*, signifies the distance that the furrow is driven before the plough is turned (about 50 yards). The word *kādu*, "field," is also used to describe distance. "Calling distance" is of course a familiar expression. Similar terms are used in Telugu and Kanarese.

In selling cloth, Kaikōlars use the word *madi* to indicate a long piece consisting of 8 pairs of men's cloths or 4 female cloths.

Land Measure

In measuring land, the square of any long measure was, in the time of Read's Survey, called *gunta* in Telugu or Kanarese, and *kuli* in Tamil. In the Bāramahāl for both Wet and Dry lands

[1] The *kādam* corresponds to the well-known "coss" of Hindustani (= Sanskrit *krōsam*, Kan. *hardāri*, Tel. *āmada*). The *āmada* is made up of 4 *parugus* (colloquial *paruvu*) and each *parugu* contains 2,000 *niluvus*.

CHAP. VI. WEIGHTS AND MEASURES.

a chain, 33 English feet in length, was usually adopted, exactly half the length of the chain now used in Survey, which, when squared, is equal to $\frac{1}{10}$ acre. The Bāramahāl *gunta* or *kuli* therefore = $\frac{1}{40}$ acre. It was subdivided into 16 *annas*.

In the Talaghāt taluks a variety of *guntas* existed, and the measurements used for Wet and Dry lands were different.[1]

In Rāsipuram and Chennagiri, three different standards were adopted for Dry lands, viz., (1) a "double *gunta*," twice that of Āttūr; (2) a "single *gunta*" of the Salem standard; (3) the Coimbatore *ballah*, 96 fathoms square = 8·6 acres. In parts of Pennāgaram, Dharmapuri and Tenkarai-kōttai, the Ōmalūr standards were adopted. The *kuli* in Hosūr Taluk was 36 feet square.

The *Paimāsh* terminology survives in Mittas. In Rāsipuram Division the "*ballah*" is still called "*vallam*," and 100 "little *kulis*" make one "big *kuli*" or "*sey*." In the south of the District the *sey* varies from 1·75 acres to 2·50, and a big and little *sey* are recognised. The "*vallams*" vary from 5 to 8 acres. In Āttūr there survives a *kāni* (Anglice "cawney"), which is 1·12 acres near Gangavalli, and 1 acre elsewhere. In Ūttankarai an *anna* ($\frac{1}{16}$ *kuli*) is defined as a space sufficient to grow a plantain. In out-of-the-way places the old system of estimating area by the quantity of seed required to raise a crop on it still survives. In Krishnagiri Taluk a *kandagam viraippadu* = 5 acres. So in the southern taluks a "five *pothi* field," an "eight *vallam* field" are spoken of. A *madakku* or "turn" (apparently of ploughing-cattle) = ½ acre. *Anaippu* is explained as the area that can be ploughed by 2 pairs of cattle in a day, and varies from half to one acre. *Ēr-ulavu* (a "plough's-ploughing") is a similar term. The *pangu* ("share") still exists in Inam villages, and is said to equal 16 acres in Dry land, and 2 to 2½ in Wet. The term is vague, however, for it signifies merely the shares into which a common holding is divided among coparceners.[2]

[1] Locality.	Wet or Dry.	Size of *gunta* or *kuli*.	Acres.
Salem	Dry	64 × 64 fathoms of 8 ft.	3·82
Bōlūr	Wet	29 × 29 ft.	·019
Taluks now included in Tiruchengōdu and Ōmalūr.	Dry	24 × 24 fathoms of 6 ft. 4½ in. ...	·846
	Wet	32 × 32 ft.	·023
Āttūr	Dry	36 × 36 fathoms of 6 ft. 4½ in. ...	1·209
Vīraganūr	Wet	9 × 9 fathoms of 6 ft. 4⅓½ in. ...	·0756
Rāsipuram ... ... / Chennagiri	Wet	32·072 ft. square	·024

[2] The *karai* is a larger division of coparcenary land, and is supposed to contain Dry, Wet and Garden fields. The *karai* is divided into *pangus*.

CHAP. VI. WEIGHTS AND MEASURES.

Time.

The ryot's division of time is an epitome of his daily life. About two hours before day-break is "the time when Venus rises" (if Venus happens to be a morning star). Shortly after this comes "first cock-crow." If he has a garden to be irrigated, it is now (4-30 A.M.) "baling time." Half an hour later comes "second cock-crow."[1] Then there is light in the east, "the earth becomes visible," "the sky grows red" and day breaks. These expressions convey as definite a meaning to his mind as hours and minutes do to those who are used to them. When the sun is "one *mār* (fathom) high" it is "time to yoke the morning plough." Breakfast-time varies in different localities, according to the habits of the people of the place. It ranges between 7 and 10 A.M. and is variously described as "early *kanji* time," "morning porridge time" (Tamil *kali* = rāgi pudding), "the time for eating last night's rice" (literally "old-rice-time"). Between 8 and 9 A.M. the sun is "one palmyra-tree high." Between 10 and 11 A.M. is the "time when cattle are let out for grazing." With noon comes "*uchi-kālam*" (literally "crown-time"), "the hour when the sun is over the crown of the head." Some time between 11 A.M. and 2 P.M. the mid-day meal is eaten, at "hot rice time" or "full-meal time." Between 1 and 2 P.M. is the hour when the sun begins to decline (*adi sāya*). In the heat of the day cattle are allowed to rest, but towards 3 P.M. is "the time when the cattle are driven out." The "hour for yoking the evening plough" follows immediately, while at home it is the "time when in a big household they pound kambu" or "begin to prepare the evening meal." The downward course of the sun is measured again in terms of a "palmyra tree" or "fathom." Then comes "the time when the evening grows dim" (Tamil = *mālai masanga*) "the hour when lamps are lit," "when writing cannot be read," "Hirannya's hour," the hour when that Demon met his death at the hand of Vishnu, the Man-Lion, (*Asura-sandhyā-vēlai*). 7 P.M. is "the hour when the field labourer comes home." "Pudding-time" follows, and shortly after one of the household takes food to the watchers in the pens; "sheep-fold meal-time." Last comes the "hour when the village becomes quiet" (Tamil = *ūr-adangum-nēram*), and the night watchers leave for the cattle-pens and sheep-folds (Tamil = *patti-āl-nēram*, literally the "pen-man-hour," a terseness of expression not easy to improve upon). The word *jāmam*, which properly means a watch of 3 hours' duration at any time of the day or night, is applied in Salem District to the hour of mid-night. The old vernacular divisions of time are almost obsolete. Even the

[1] Cf. S. Mark's Gospel, XIV, 30.

CHAP. VI. WEIGHTS AND MEASURES.

nāligai of 24 minutes is not commonly spoken of. A ryot, when asked at what hour of the day an event took place, will usually point to the position the sun then occupied. The rising and setting of the moon are useful aids to memory, and people who live near railways fix time by the passing trains. Ryots who come to Court sometimes show a familiarity with hours and minutes which their status hardly warrants, a familiarity which is not seldom due to "tutoring." Very few people can tell the time by the stars. In distributing water from irrigation channels, two systems are in vogue to time the "turns." One is by the *kinni*, a small brass bowl with a minute hole in the bottom of it, which is floated on a chatty of water and sinks in about 20 minutes.[1] The other method is for the Nīrganti (as the person who distributes the water is called) to calculate the time by measuring his shadow.

Money.

On taking charge of the "Ceded Districts" in 1792, Read and his Assistants were hampered in their administration with a "various and perplexing currency," which Read did his best to "annihilate." Both the Hindu system of pagodas and fanams, and the Mughal system of mohurs and rupees were in vogue, and most puzzling varieties existed of each denomination of coin. Read, writing in 1794, gives a list of 29 different gold coins, 15 silver coins and 8 copper coins in which revenue dues were tendered. In the northern part of the District rents were at the time expressed in Kantirāya ("Kanteroy") fanams, and in the south in "Gōpāli"[2] fanams. The former represents the famous mintage of Kantīrava Narasa Rājā of Mysore (1638-59), the origin of the latter is uncertain. The pagoda (*varāhan*) existed as far back as the Chālukya period, and derives its vernacular name from the fact that it was impressed with the symbol of a boar, one of the incarnations of Vishnu, and the crest of Chālukya as well as Vijayanagar kings. No pagodas were actually minted by Kantīrava Narasa Rājā, but accounts were kept in terms of an imaginary

---

[1] See p. 236.

[2] Regarding the "Gōpāli" fanam Mr. T. Desikachariar, Diwan Bahadur, writes:—

A "Gōpāli" fanam weighing more than 5 grains is recorded as having been received in the Madras Government Central Museum in 1874 from the Salem District. Neither Captain Tufnell nor Dr. Gerson da Cunha, both of whom have published their fanams, nor Sir Walter Elliott, has alluded to the "Gōpāli." In the Rangachari-Desikachari collection is a fanam with the figure of "Krishna with the flute"—"Vēnugōpāla" in Sanskrit—on the obverse, and the Nāgari legend म्व "Mva," standing for "Samvat," on the reverse. The fanam with such an obverse was probably known in common parlance as the "Gōpāli." Chālukya fanams occur now and then in the Salem, Bellary and Bangalore Districts along with "Kanteroys." The fanam with the figure of Gōpāla above referred to was probably of the times of one of the later Chālukyas."

The *Madhura-Gōpāla-chakra* is referred to in the Ēttāppūr *Sāsanam* of 1714 (Vol. II, p. 298).

CHAP. VI. WEIGHTS AND MEASURES.

coin valued at 10 of his fanams. At the time of Haidar's usurpation, the coins in general circulation were those minted by the Ikkēri Poligārs of Nagar (=Bednūr in Shimoga District, Mysore). On the capture of Bednūr in 1763 Haidar decided to issue his own coins, adopting the Bednūr pagodas as a model. Haidar's pagodas were known to Read as Bahadūri pagodas. Tipu in turn issued his own pagodas, which became known as Sultāni pagodas, and he also minted mōhurs and rupees, known respectively as Sultāni Ashrafi and Sultāni or Imāmi rupees. The coins of Haidar and Tipu did not, it appears, obtain general recognition, for Munro, writing in 1796, surmises that all revenue accounts in the Bāramahāl were kept in "Naggarie fanams" (probably the same as the Ikkēri coinage of Bednūr), till Tipu substituted "Kanteroy" fanams in their stead. The rapid development of Pondicherry under Dupleix and his successors led to a large development of trade between Pondicherry and Mysore, and a heavy influx of Pondicherry rupees into the Bāramahāl in payment of goods exported, and to this is probably due the fact, alluded to by Munro, that, among the mercantile classes, rupees were preferred to pagodas. When the Company's "Investment" was established in Salem, Read was called upon to provide the Commercial Resident with Pondicherry rupees. By 1796, however, the coinage of silver at Pondicherry was discontinued,[1] and the Commercial Resident was asked to take Surat rupees in their stead. Meanwhile the pagoda system was adhered to in the land revenue administration, and revenue accounts were kept in terms of pagodas, fanams and cash. An attempt was made to establish the star pagoda as a standard, and on 29th June 1793, orders were issued to Mr. Benjamin Roebuck, Assay Master, to start a mint at Krishnagiri, and another at Salem, for the coinage of pagodas, fanams, Arcot rupees and duddus, the idea being to convert all specie tendered into Company's coin.[2] The star pagoda was divided into 45 maili fanams,[3] and the maili fanam into 80 cash. For the convenience of the ryots and Tahsildars, an elaborate Table of Exchange was drawn up, subject apparently to frequent revision, declaring at what rates, in terms of star pagodas, the many coins in circulation would be accepted at Government treasuries. Any attempt to reduce the list of coins that could be accepted in payment of Government dues was fraught with difficulty. As Read pointed out, the various coins were articles of trade, and their face value meant nothing. The value of any particular denomination

[1] *Anc. Rec.* No. 259, cf. Nos. 246, 247, 259 and 261.

[2] Both mints appear to have been working by August 1793.

[3] Even in February 1796 the number of fanams to the star pagoda was not definitely fixed, and Munro protests against Read's action in calculating 44 fanams to the pagoda.

of coin as a medium of exchange depended on what people would give for them, and this "market value" fluctuated from time to time and varied from place to place. If Government were to insist on the revenue being paid in one particular kind of currency, the shroffs would be sure to buy up the available coins of that currency, and, by creating a "corner," they would inflict great hardship on the public. The establishment of mints was a failure; not only was it expensive, it made matters worse, for the Company's coin itself became subject to fluctuations in market value. In Fasli 1204–05 (1794–6) there was a very considerable rise in the value of silver with respect to gold, a rise attributed by Read to the discontinuance of the coining of rupees at Pondicherry. Hence in 1796 the rupee was in far greater demand among all classes than the star pagoda. The preference for silver was accentuated by the fact that there was a large proportion of filed and counterfeit star pagodas in circulation, and ryots ran a greater risk of being duped if they accepted pagodas instead of rupees in exchange for their produce. Throughout the southern taluks the rupee had, by 1796, attained such general vogue that the Revenue officers settled Revenue demands with the ryots in terms of rupees, though for account purposes the amount was expressed in pagodas. Almost the whole of the gold coins tendered at the Government treasuries were received from merchants, and not from ryots. When a ryot borrowed from a merchant, he was paid in pagodas, but bound himself to repay the loan in rupees, and it was a common practice for Patels and Tahsildars to substitute pagodas for rupees received in the collection of revenue. The Kantarāya and Gōpāli fanams had by this time almost passed out of circulation; in the early years of Read's administration those that were received in collections were re-issued to the troops, a proceeding which created so much dissatisfaction that it was in 1794 decided to stop the receipt of them. The coins issued from the local mints never attained popularity. Krishnagiri pagodas had actually been rejected both by the Revenue Treasury at Madras and by the Paymaster in Salem District. The mint at Salem appears to have been closed by 1795. Early in 1796 Munro recommended that all the Krishnagiri pagodas should be called in and received at their actual value, and re-coined at Madras, and by March in the same year the mint at Krishnagiri was discontinued.[1]

---

[1] Letter from Government to Board of Revenue No. 182, dated 20th March 1796. There were three coinages of pagodas at Krishnagiri. The first issue numbered only 6,788, the second (which contained an excess of pure gold of the weight of 2 rāgi grains) numbered 17,173, and the third (which had an excess of 1½ paddy grains' weight above the Madras standard) numbered 14,875. (See *Anc. Records*.)

In February a notification of Read's had reduced the number of coins in which revenue payments would be accepted to 17, namely, star pagodas, Bahadūri pagodas, Sultāni pagodas, Ikkēri pagodas, Old and New Porto Novo rupees, Old and New Arcot rupees, Old and New Pondicherry rupees, Company's rupees, Imāmi rupees, Kantarāya and Raja Gōpāli chakrams, maili fanams, elephant pice [1] and Krishna pice.

The revenue accounts of the Salem District were written up in terms of star pagodas, fanams and cash, till well on into the nineteenth century, but meanwhile the Company's rupees were steadily gaining ground, and in 1835 the controversy was settled once for all by the adoption for all India of the Madras rupee of 180 grains.

The memory of the old notation still lingers. Old people still reckon in the "pagoda" (*varáhan*) of 3½ rupees, and poorer classes in the *duddu* of 4 pies, six of which make one *panam*, the general name for a two-anna piece. Thus a half-anna piece is popularly called 1½ *duddu* or ¼ *panam*. The pie is known as *dambidi* throughout the Bāramahāl; less generally so in the southern taluks, where *kāsu* is the usual term, and *paisā* is also used. In Āttūr, however, *kāsu* = 2 pies. *Jalli* is another name for a pie. In Ūttankarai a three-pie piece is called *chinna duddu*. In Hosūr and the Bāramahāl two pies are called *duggāni*. A two-anna piece is called *bēda* in Hosūr, and "big anna" (Telugu *pedda ana*) in parts of Krishnagiri. In Ūttankarai this same coin is called *chinna panam* to distinguish it from *periya panam*, a term applied to the four-anna piece. This last coin is known in Hosūr as *pāvala*. The popular term for a sound coin as distinguished from a counterfeit is *kumpani panam* (Company's money).

[1] The Elephant Pice (Āne-Kásu) was first coined by Krishna Rāja of Mysore. (1713-1731).

CHAPTER VII.

COMMUNICATIONS.

ROADS—History of maintenance—Mr. Orr—Road Cess—Mileage—Trunk Roads Shevaroy Hills—Avenues—Bridges—Ferries. RAILWAYS—Famine Feeder Lines—Railway Projects. POST OFFICE. TELEGRAPHS.

CHAP. VII.
ROADS.

THE British were not the first road-makers in India. Tipu's road-engineering was of no mean order. The best known road associated with his name ran through the wild broken country on the left bank of the Kāvēri to the west of Hosūr and Dharmapuri Taluks. The route lay from Denkani-kōta via Anchetti and Geratti to Pennāgaram, thence via Morasara-halli and Donnakutta-halli to the Toppūr River.[1] Wherever this road passed over rock or undulating ground, all vestiges have been washed away by over a century of rain. There are level stretches, however, still well preserved, and marked by fine avenues. A portion south of Pennāgaram would even now be fit for a carriage road, and the road can be traced for some distance near Anchetti, and again at Morasara-halli. Another important road of Tipu's time was that connecting Krishnagiri with Būdi-kōta, a once important fort in Mysore State, seven miles from Bowringpet railway station. It is still called *Dandu Ōni* or the "Army Road."[2] The favourite Ghât used by Haidar and Tipu for access to the plains was that via Rāya-kōta, Pālakōdu and Toppūr. The route via Singārapet was also used by them.

History of maintenance.

The importance of road maintenance did not escape Col. Read, and by 1802 as many as 156 miles of road had been laid down round Salem, and planted with avenues throughout. Little further was done, however, till Mr. Orr assumed charge of the District in 1829.

Mr. Orr.

To Mr. Orr the District is indebted for its chief roads, grandest avenues, and a number of well-built rest-houses known as "Orr's Choultries." By 1836 Mr. Orr had made 316 miles of high-road at an average cost of Rs. 134 per mile, besides 375 miles of cross roads; 20 bridges were built, and 196 stone dams were made, at an

---

[1] Se Vol. II, p. 109.

[2] See Vol. II, p. 108.

aggregate cost of Rs. 14,026. The initial expenditure was made almost wholly on his own responsibility, and "no better proof could be given of his success than the estimation in which his work was held by the natives, who voluntarily agreed to tax themselves for the maintenance of these roads." This voluntary tax of one rupee per cart was first imposed in 1836, and continued till April 1860. But this was not all. Mr. Orr induced the ryots to plant avenues and topes. Under the system introduced by him, the number of avenue trees planted up to 1842 amounted to 129,414, the number previously existing in the District being only 32,960, and the number of palmyra trees planted amounted to 1,819,161.[1] The ryots were permitted to enjoy the usufruct of the avenues and topes they had thus planted on the understanding that they should keep the roads in repair. "In those days it was a far cry to Madras, and as a rule what 'master pleased' was done. Old ryots still tell the tale of the 'zulum' made by the irascible Collector, whose horsewhip occasionally made Ramaswami wince; but generations of grateful travellers and the sufferers themselves in the end testified to the profit and comfort derived from these *travaux forcés*."[2]

Road Cess.

After Mr. Orr left the District in 1838, the villagers did not act up to their obligations, Government contributions proved inadequate, and the roads soon fell into disrepair, their upkeep had before long to be taken over by Government. To meet the increasing cost, Government in 1859 imposed a cess of 2 per cent. of the land revenue on all lands which enjoyed the benefit of Mr. Brett's *Taram Kammi*, the fund so formed to be expended by the Collector and the District Engineer on "District Roads," the trunk roads still being kept up at the cost of Provincial Funds. In 1865 an Act was passed legalising the cess at six pies in the rupee on all lands in occupation, under whatever tenure held. This Act was superseded by the Local Fund Act IV of 1871. Meanwhile the roads had for years been a bone of contention between the Revenue officers and the Public Works Department, the former affirming that they did the work cheaper and better than the professional department. For some time the work of maintenance was divided between the two departments, the tendency being gradually to transfer roads from the Department of Public Works to the Collector. Finally in 1880 the Local Fund Department assumed entire responsibility.

The mileage of roads in the whole District rose from 1,189 in 1871–2 to over 1,828 in 1912–13. The figures for the

---

[1] S.D.M., Vol. I, p. 390.

[2] S.D.M., Vol. I, p. 195.

CHAP. VII. ROADS.

Mileage.

District as at present constituted, are shown in the subjoined statement.

Taluk.	Mileage, 31st March 1911.								Number of miles and furlongs per 10 square miles of area.	
	Village.		Taluk.		District.		Total.			
	M.	F.	M.	F.	M.	F.	M.	F.	M.	F.
Salem	47	7	40	5	129	2	217	6	2	2
Ōmalūr	21	4	74	6	59	3	155	5	4	0
Tiruchengōdu ...	31	1	86	1	76	3	193	5	3	6
Āttūr	22	1	71	3	63	3	156	7	1	7
Dharmapuri	18	2	23	0	136	3	177	5	1	7
Krishnagiri	29	3	57	2	131	6	218	3	3	1
Ūttankarai ...	26	3	110	1	88	0	224	4	2	4
Hosūr...	10	7	71	3	75	2	157	4	1	3
Total ...	207	4	534	5	759	6	1,501	7	2	4

In addition to this, some 92 miles of road are maintained by the Forest Department.[1]

Trunk

Before the construction of railways, the Bāramahāl was the tri-junction of three of the most important thoroughfares in the Presidency.

1. The Madras-Calicut road enters the District near Mattūr at mile 150½ and passes through Mattūr, Irumattūr, Dharmapuri, Toppūr, Ōmalūr, Tāra-mangalam and Sankaridrug, quitting the District by the Kumāra-pālaiyam bridge, opposite Bhavāni, at mile 246¼.

2. The Madras-Bangalore road branches off from the Calicut trunk road at Vāniyambādi, and passes through Bargūr, Krishnagiri, Sūlagiri and Hosūr, leaving British territory at the 193rd mile, in the limits of *Jūjūvādi* village.

3. The easiest, though not the shortest, route from Bangalore to Malabar, passes through Hosūr, Rāya-kōta and Pālakōdu, joining the Madras trunk road at Adaman-kōttai at mile 182¼.

In addition to these three routes the branch route from Ōmalūr to Salem affords communication via Āttūr with Cuddalore, and via Nāmakkal with Trichinopoly. Another useful route is

[1] Vide page 257.

from Krishnagiri through Mattūr and Singārapet to Cuddalore, though in the early days of British rule it was much infested with robbers. Later on, a more direct route with Madras was opened by the road from Tiruppattūr to Salem via Ūttankarai, Harūr and the Manjavādi Ghāt.

Shevaroy Hills.

The Shevaroy Hills are well supplied with roads. From Salem access is easily obtained, either by the New Ghāt road, practicable for carts or even motor-cars, or the Old Ghāt, still used by pedestrians, horsemen, chair-coolies and pack-animals. Bridle-paths ascend from Kādaiyāmpatti and from the Manjavādi Ghāt. A road, suitable for wheeled traffic, runs from Yercaud, via Craigmore and Vellālakadai, to Cauvery Peak, and another from Yercaud, via Hopeville, to Mangalam, the circuit being completed by a road from Mangalam to Cauvery Peak, constructed by Mr. S. M. Hight at his own cost. The New Vāniyār Road, from Yercaud to the Manjavādi Ghāt, was finished in 1908.

When the Madras-Calicut railway was under construction, it was hoped that Mallāpuram would be the centre of Shevaroy Hill traffic, and a railway station of unusually large dimensions was begun. In 1858[1] a ghāt road was constructed by the Forest Department, which it was intended to develop into a regular cart-road for the conveyance of railway fuel, timber and bamboos. Its course ran from Mallāpuram up the Vēppādi valley, from the head of which it rose by zigzags to Muluvi. The total distance from Mallāpuram to Yercaud was 19 miles (Mallāpuram to the foot 8 miles, ascent to Muluvi 3 miles and from Muluvi to Yercaud 8 miles). The project was eventually abandoned, the zigzag portion of the track is now thickly overgrown with jungle, and much of the revetment is washed away.

The New Ghāt road was begun in April 1900. The road was opened for traffic in December 1902, though the work was not completed till March 1903. The new road branches off from the road from Salem to the foot of the Old Ghāt at the sixth furlong of the fifth mile. For nearly six miles it ascends steadily without a turn. It then begins to zigzag sharply up the face of the great rock mass on which Mundagambādi is situated, and after twenty-two turns it reaches the bund of the Yercaud lake. The total length is 12 m. 6 f. 180 ft., the ruling gradient one in 16. There is one girder bridge of 40′ span, another of 66′. The actual cost was Rs. 3,71,000. To secure an unfailing supply of water for

[1] The construction of the Mallāpuram Ghāt road was first recommended by Assistant Surgeon England, who died of fever contracted in the survey of the Shevaroys in 1824. The road is said to have been sanctioned between 1840 and 1850, and 3 miles were constructed, when owing to the outbreak of the Mutiny, the scheme was dropped.

CHAP. VII. ROADS.

road repairs in dry weather, there is an elaborate arrangement of pipes, filled partly by gravitation from the Yercaud lake, partly by an aeromotor pump. The construction of feeder roads was undertaken by the Public Works Department. The cost for 31 miles 4 furlongs 600 feet of road was Rs. 88,179.

Avenues.

No less than 1,068⅛ miles of road, over three-fifths of the total mileage, are provided with avenues. The finest avenues are in the Bāramahāl, and are composed of tamarind, relieved now and again by banyan. The tamarind is more satisfactory for hardiness, shade and produce, as the banyan is apt to fall in high winds. Tamarind does not thrive well in Hosūr and pungam is a poor substitute. Perhaps the grandest stretches of avenue in the District are on the road from Mahēndra-mangalam past Pālakōdu to within a short distance of Dharmapuri. There are some fine trees on the trunk road near Pōdār, in Ūttankarai Taluk, and south of Toppūr in Ōmalūr Taluk, and close to Salem itself, the station road between Hastampatti and "Charing Cross" being remarkably picturesque.

The produce of the avenues is a most valuable asset to the Local Funds, though it fluctuates in a startling manner. At the beginning of 1910–1911 it was estimated that the avenues contained 186,705 trees. The avenues in the Sub-Collectorate were first rented out in 1865 by Mr. Thomas, then Sub-Collector, on his own authority, and in the following year the Board authorised the renting out of all the avenues in the District. This resumption by Government of the usufruct of trees which Mr. Orr had guaranteed to the villagers caused much heart-burning, and the question of the right of the ryots to the avenues was mooted in 1872 and decided against them, but in ignorance of the real reason, which was that the duty of maintaining the roads was no longer exacted from the villagers.[1]

Bridges.

A traveller passing through the District along the trunk roads from Bangalore to Madras via Sūlagiri, to Calicut via Toppūr, or to Cuddalore via Salem, will find the route within District limits completely bridged, the bridges near Pāranda-palli,[2] near Kurubara-palli,[3] at Bargūr, Toppūr, Kumāra-pālaiyam, Ōmalūr, Salem, Krishnāpuram, Āttūr and Talaivāsal being substantial enough for all ordinary traffic. The Pennaiyār is also spanned by a good bridge

[1] When Mr. Dalyell visited Nāttram-palli on Abkári duty in 1876, an old ryot, Dho had planted the avenue in Mr. Orr's time, advanced his claim, but when Mr. Dalyell asked him if it was not true that in former times those who enjoyed the usufruct of the avenues repaired the roads at their own cost, the aged cultivator put his hand on his mouth and said "Appah." S.D.M., I., 195

[2] Four miles east of Hosūr.

[3] Seven miles north-west of Krishnagiri.

at Bāgalūr, and the minor streams which cross the triangle Hosūr-Tali-Denkani-kōta are provided with suitable culverts. Other routes, however, have been neglected, the lesser streams are crossed by the causeways known as "road dams" or "Irish bridges," and the larger rivers present rather difficult fords, the most troublesome being those across the Pennaiyār at Vadakku-patti,[1] Kāvēri-patnam,[2] Irumattūr, and Hanuma-tīrtam, that over the Pāmbār at Singārapet, that over the Kambayanallūr river at the village of that name, and those over the Swēta-nadi at Kōnēri-patti and Vīraganūr.

Ferries.

The only rivers requiring regular ferries are the Kāvēri and the Pennaiyār. Freshes in the Āttūr rivers soon subside, and traffic waits until the ford is practicable. The management of ferries was assigned to the Taluk Boards in 1897.[3] There are 26 Taluk Board ferries across the Kāvēri, of which 11 are in Tiruchengōdu, 4 in Ōmalūr, 8 in Dharmapuri, and 3 in Hosūr Taluk. Across the Pennaiyār there are two ferries in Krishnagiri and four in Ūttankarai.[4] The right of collecting tolls on ferries for the Fasli year is auctioned by the Tahsildar in the month of June. The bids are insignificant. The lease for ferries over the Kāvēri conveys the right to collect tolls on the traffic passing from the left to the right bank only; the proceeds of traffic from the right to the left bank is the perquisite of Coimbatore Local Funds. The ferries are crossed by means of coracles (*parisus*).

RAILWAYS.

The Broad Gauge West Coast Branch of the South Indian Railway runs through Salem District from north-east to south-west. It enters the District (Ūttankarai Taluk) at the 145th mile 32nd chain from Madras, and quits it at the 241st mile 32nd chain, covering a distance of 96 miles. There are 14 stations within the District limits, the first is Sāmalpatti, the last Kāvēri. From Sāmalpatti (1,261·46 ft. above sea-level) the gradient descends to the Pennaiyār and re-ascends to Morappūr (1,305·03 ft.) and Mallāpuram (1,386·59 ft.). The highest point is reached, on a gradient of 1 in 300, at mile 187½ (just beyond Lōkūr station) where it is 1,508·38 ft. above sea-level. The line then descends sharply (the gradient is 1 in 74)[5] to Kādaiyam-patti (1,243·48 ft.), Salem (919·67 ft.) and MacDonald's Choultry (783·59 ft.), rises to 876·38 ft. at Sankaridrug, and descends again to 539·47 ft. at

---

[1] Five miles west of Krishnagiri on the Rāya-kōta road.

[2] A girder bridge of 12 spans of 42½ feet each has since been built by the District Board over the Pennaiyār at Kāvēripatnam.

[3] G.O. No. 376, Revenue, dated 29th July 1896.

[4] For details see the Taluk Notices, Chapter XV.

[5] The steepest gradient is 1 in 70.

CHAP. VII. RAILWAYS.

Erode. The only bridges of note are those over the Pennaiyār and Kāvēri. The latter is a girder bridge, with two clear spans of 62′ and 20 clear spans of 63′ 8′. The former consists of 18 semicircular brick arches, each of 30′ span.

The railway was open for traffic as far as Tiruppattūr on May 23, 1860. The section from Tiruppattūr to Salem was opened on February 1, 1861, and that from Salem to Sankaridrug on December 1 of the same year. The next section opened was from Sankaridrug to Pōdanūr (May 12, 1862).

The Taluks of Krishnagiri and Hosūr are served to some extent by the Bangalore Branch of the Madras and Southern Mahratta Railway (opened in 1864), the stations of Patchūr, Kuppam and Mālūr being chiefly utilised.

Famine Feeder Lines.

Two famine protective lines have recently been opened in the District, the first from Tiruppattūr to Krishnagiri (25½ miles), the second from Morappūr to Dharmapuri (18½ miles) with an extension to Hosūr (54½ miles). On the former line, there are three stations within the District limits; on the latter line, there are ten stations. The Krishnagiri line was opened for traffic on September 18, 1905, the Dharmapuri line on January 18, 1906. They were not constructed as paying investments, but to supply food to the Taluks of Krishnagiri and Dharmapuri in times of famine. The gauge is 2′ 6″, the highest gradient 1 in 66·67, and the sharpest curve has a radius of 955′. In constructing the Dharmapuri line sleepers of jarrah timber were tried. The Krishnagiri Railway was laid with teak sleepers.

The Krishnagiri Railway diverges at a sharp angle from the parent line till it reaches the Tiruppattūr-Krishnagiri road near Periyagaram. Thence it runs parallel to the road, except where gradients and bends do not permit of its doing so.

The Dharmapuri line, on leaving Morappūr, skirts the high ground to the west, rising steadily, so that at 3½ miles out it is 188′ above Morappūr. At mile 7 it approaches close to the Dharmapuri road, and road and railway cross the same saddle between the 7th and 10th miles at 260′ above Morappūr. Between miles 10 and 15 a tortuous alignment was found necessary at the foot of the hills. From mile 15 the line falls by easy grades to Dharmapuri.

Railway Projects.

A proposal to connect Hosūr with Bangalore is under the consideration of the Mysore Durbar. A loop line has been proposed to connect Dharmapuri with Krishnagiri via Pālakōdu and Kāvēri-patnam.

The District Board has levied a railway cess at three pies in the rupee on the annual rent value of all occupied lands since July

1st, 1903, and the balance of this on March 31st, 1913, amounted to Rs. 43,223 in cash, and Rs. 5,31,100 in Government securities. The District Board is constructing a broad gauge line from Sūra-mangalam Railway Station to Salem Town and proposes to extend the line from Salem Town to Āttūr on the metre gauge. This line is eventually to be connected with the line which the District Board of South Arcot propose to construct from Ulundūr-pet to Chinna Salem. Such a line will bring Salem many miles nearer the sea-board, link the District with the deltas of the Vellār and Kāvēri, and provide an outlet for the surplus grain of Āttūr Taluk. The cost of the whole line from Sūra-mangalam to Āttūr is estimated at Rs. 14,21,545.

Another project is under consideration, namely, to connect Salem with Karūr *via* Rāsipuram, Tāttayyangārpatti, Nāmakkal and Nanjai-Mohanūr with an alternative alignment from Nāmakkal to Samayapuram on the proposed Panrūti-Trichinopoly chord.

POST OFFICE.

Till 1854 the Collector of the District was in charge of all postal arrangements.[1] Dykes writes "The over-worked Col-lector-Magistrate is the post-master, and the first step must be to give so troublesome an office a separate and distinct supervision. The postal arrangements for 8,000 square miles may fairly demand an undivided attention. The mails, for instance, are carried on men's heads, each man running from 5 to 7 miles; and to be freed only from this single branch of those duties, from the responsibility and the trouble of overlooking so numerous an establishment as this, would itself be no small gain."[2] The first general issue of postage stamps in India dates from Septem-ber, 1854, and in the same year the Postal Department was taken off the Collector's hands.[3] In March 1875 the executive control of the Salem Collectorate over its District Post was transferred to the Postmaster-General, Madras.[4]

For administrative purposes the whole District lies within the jurisdiction of the Postmaster of Salem Head Office, who in turn is under the Superintendent of Post Offices, Vellore Division.

---

[1] No detailed information is available as to the postal arrangements in the District in pre-post-office days. A letter shown me by Mr. Muhammad Habibulla Sahib, Khan Bahadur, of Krishnagiri, addressed to that town from Pondicherry via Rāyakōta, bears a post-mark "Pondicherry 26th May 1842, paid 3 annas," and another, dated Kumbakōnam, June 26th, 1846, shows on the Kumbakōnam post-mark a pre-payment of 2 annas, and it also bears the Salem post-mark, with date June 30th. This is fairly cheap and quick.

[2] Dykes, p. 377.

[3] For Post Office legislation, see Acts XVII of 1837, XVII of 1854, XIV of 1866, and VI of 1898.

[4] G.O. No. 452, Revenue, dated 20th March 1875.

CHAP. VII. POST OFFICE.

The subjoined statement illustrates the increase in the work of the Post Office since 1861–62.

Year.	Letters and post cards.	Packets.	Newspapers.
1861-62.	275,235	5,220	26,419
1910–11.	4,460,092	355,836	184,574

In the latter year the value of money orders issued was Rs. 15,66,264, and the total amount of Savings Bank deposits Rs. 2,60,838.

TELEGRAPHS.

Telegraph stations were opened at Salem and Hosūr in 1884, at Yercaud in 1889, at Krishnagiri in 1893, at Mattigiri in 1894, at Dharmapuri in 1895, at Tiruchengōdu in 1898, and at Sūramangalam in 1908.

Stations.	Messages.		
	Sent.	Received.	Receipts.
			RS.
Hosūr	736	818	440
Mattigiri ...	719	730	554
Dharmapuri ..	1,986	1,858	1,252
Krishnagiri ..	1,518	1,814	840
Salem ...	13,407	13,619	5,694
Sūramangalam.	904	1,042	1,062
Yercaud ...	1,361	1,422	862
Tiruchengōdu ..	1,059	1,005	648
Railway Stations.	1,650	...	843

The offices at Hosūr and Mattigiri belong to the Bangalore Division, that at Tiruchengōdu to the Calicut Division, and the rest of the District to the Madras Division. The relative importance of the several stations in 1910 is shown in the marginal statement.

CHAPTER VIII.

SEASONS.

SEASONS. FAMINES—Famine of 1833—Famine of 1866—Famine of 1877-78—(1) Till the end of 1876; (2) January to September 1877; (3) September 1877 to end of 1878—Increase of crime—Effect on Revenue—Famine of 1891-92. FLOODS.

CHAP. VIII. SEASONS.

THE capricious nature of the rainfall has already been referred to on pp. 22, 23. Dry cultivation, on which alone the bulk of the population depends for food, begins with the showers of April and May, and the first crop matures with the rains of July and August. The second crop is sown as soon as the first crop is harvested, and drought in October or November will ruin it.

Hosūr and the Bāramahāl are more susceptible to drought than the Talaghāt taluks, and of the latter, Tiruchengōdu and Ōmalūr are the first to suffer. Āttūr and the Rāsipuram Divisions are considered safe from famine; the former is protected by the Vasishta-nadi and Swēta-nadi, and the latter by innumerable wells with good sub-soil water. At settlement, a deduction of 20 per cent of the gross outturn in the northern taluks and of 15 per cent in the Talaghāt was allowed on account of vicissitudes of season.

The danger of drought made itself felt as soon as the District came under the Company's rule, for famine threatened in 1792, and Captain Read established two poor-houses for a short period—one at Tiruppattūr and the other at Pennāgaram.

FAMINES.

Four times during the nineteenth century scarcity deepened into famine with all its terrible concomitants, namely, in 1833, in 1866, 1877-78 and 1891-92. There was acute distress also in 1845 and 1857, dates which suggest a cyclic recurrence of famine once in eleven years.

Famine of 1833.

The cultivation season for Fasli 1242 (1832-33) opened favourably, and the ryots engaged actively in field operations. Then the rains failed entirely, and utterly ruined the crops. In a short time "the price of grain rose 71 per cent., for there was famine in the neighbouring districts also, and the people robbed that they might live. They eagerly sought for the wild fruits of the jungle and of the trees that lined the wayside; they turned up the earth for such roots as possessed nourishment; there was nowhere to fly

CHAP. VIII. FAMINES.

to, and the country was covered with the bodies of those who died of starvation. Fourteen thousand deaths were reported from cholera alone, which probably was not a tithe of the number that so fell; and the sickness extended to the brute creation, for the cattle also were exterminated by herds."[1]

The actual mortality in this famine is not known. It is estimated that over 28 per cent. of the population perished.[2]

Famine of 1866.

The famine of 1866 was by comparison "a mere flash in the pan, but, while it lasted, it was sharp enough." In 1864 and 1865 rains were neither general nor timely, and the year 1866 opened with the District on the verge of famine. The early rains of 1866 almost entirely failed. The public health suffered, and cattle disease became prevalent. By the end of June the Collector reported that "thousands of cattle had perished from want of water and pasture, and thousands of cattle were in a dying state for want of food, and unable to walk." Prices were almost beyond the reach of the poorer classes. In Tiruppattūr, Ūttankarai, Krishnagiri and Salem, the poor were using for food roasted tamarind seeds, jungle roots, aloes, and the fruit of prickly-pear. All the tanks and wells were dry. The dry crops, cultivated in a few places where slight rain had fallen, were withering, and, almost everywhere, both wet and dry lands were left waste. Private subscriptions were raised by the people of Salem for the relief of sufferers within the town, and by July this took practical effect in the opening of a "Kanji-house" where 200 to 3,000 paupers were fed daily. The example of Salem was imitated by several other towns in the District, and further funds were provided by the Relief Committee in Madras. The prices of grain continued to rise, till in September ragi stood at 9¾ seers per rupee. Work for the able-bodied was provided, as far as possible. Fortunately in

---

[1] Dykes, pp. 302-304.

[2] An interesting incident of this famine is the stand made by the then Sub-Collector, Mr. Cathcart, against the practice of subsidising indigenous religious institutions. Writing on 25th August 1832, he says "Among the first official letters I received on coming to Salem was one sanctioning Rs. 50 to be expended in each of the three taluks or districts under me, for the invocation of rain. Rain is indeed much required; the first crops have been almost lost in consequence of the deficiency. I called the taluk servants to give a report of what was done; some Brahmans were to engage in prayer to one of their gods for ten or twelve days, standing up to their necks in water, that their devotions might, I suppose, be instant. Others were to be employed to avert the anger of certain planets; and some to propitiate other gods, the whole to be fed at the expense of Government, to be superintended by Government servants, and to be, in every respect on the part of Government, seeking for the attainment of its revenue by these means." Mr. Cathcart declined to issue the orders, and the Collector issued them on his behalf.

October good rain fell, and cultivation started in good earnest. By November ragi had fallen to 12⅜ seers per rupee, and the crisis was over. The harvest was good, but though the human mortality was not high, it is estimated that 150,000 head of cattle perished from sheer starvation.

Famine of 1877–78. (1) Till the end of 1876. The famine of 1877–78 was the worst the District has ever experienced. "The tail end of the north-east monsoon failed both in 1873 and 1874.[1] In 1875 the north-east monsoon was almost a total failure, especially the latter part of it, and in 1876 the south-west and north-east monsoons, on both of which the District depends for its water-supply, failed almost completely. The pinch began to be felt in October 1876, but people still hoped. In November the failure of the monsoon became an established fact, grain dealers took alarm, and prices rose at a bound. On the average, for five years ending 1874, the price of ragi in Salem was, from January to July, from 37 to 38 lb. per rupee, and from August to December it ranged from 35 to 40 lb. From January to June 1875 the staple was sold at 31 or 32 lb. per rupee. From July to November prices rose to 23 lb., and between January and June 1876 the price was from 20 to 24 lb. From July a steady rise set in, reaching 14 lb. in October, 10 lb. in November, and 9 lb. in December, when the famine was fairly recognised and starvation stared us in the face on every side.

(2) January to September 1877. "The price list is not quite an index of the scarcity, as quotations for dry grains were often a mere form, there being none in the market. The bulk of the population was fed on imported rice, the price of which rose up in August 1877 to one rupee for 11 lb. and for a short period to one rupee for 5 lb. On one date, at the market on the Shevaroy Hills, the price actually rose to one rupee for 2 lb. For the first nine months the district staff was battling almost unaided with the famine. With the exception of one Bengal Civilian, whose services were chiefly utilised in trying magisterial cases, a Staff Corps Officer, a Medical Officer on inspection duty, and a Special Deputy Collector or two made up the sum of the assistance from outside. Meanwhile the duty of providing and superintending camps, hospitals, works, kitchens and payments, the inspection and organisation of gratuitous relief, and, in fact, the whole burden and heat of the day, was thrown on the ordinary district staff.

(3) September 1877 to end of 1878. "It was not until September 1877, when 136,941 deaths had been registered, when 307,776 of the population were being gratuitously fed, and the south-west monsoon had failed, that the Viceroy's visit bore fruit. Then the Public Works Department,

[1] The description which follows is Mr. LeFanu's.

CHAP. VIII.
FAMINES.
Famine of 1877–78.

whose share in famine relief works had previously been somewhat restricted, was more largely employed in providing work for the poor, and a flood of famine officers from all parts of India was poured over the District. The heavy rains were then setting in, and the burden and heat of the day were past; but distress still prevailed, and the *sequelæ* of the great crisis were still strongly marked. It would be hard to exaggerate the horrors of that trying time, when cholera, starvation, small-pox, famine, diarrhœa, dysentery, dropsy and fever were claiming their victims by thousands; the dead and dying lay so close in the camp hospitals, that it was difficult to move without treading on them, and hard to distinguish the one from the other, and up to the pitiless sky floated the black or yellow-green smoke from the pyres on which as many as 24 bodies were sometimes burnt together in a single camp; when the cattle lay gasping for breath, licking the dust for food, and when for miles not a drop of water was to be found.[1] The fruits of the avenue trees, the very leaves and grasses, the roots and berries of the jungles, failed to meet the demand; the ties of maternal affection failed, and even respectable women sold their honour for food. But the sufferings of the people were not yet over. The survivors were to a great extent smitten, a shower of rain or a breath of cold wind smote them down by hundreds, guinea-worm prevailed to an extent never witnessed before, and such was the depraved blood and vitality of the poorer classes, that the slightest scratch or abrasion turned into a spreading and sluggish ulcer.

"The excessive north-west monsoon of 1877 drowned the crops; blights, smut, and insects, in quantities before unheard of, spoiled or devoured the residue. Then came the locusts, almost shutting out the sky and covering square miles in their flight. The south-west monsoon of 1878 was also excessive, and the kambu crop suffered heavily, the tender flowers being washed off, so that the seeds could not form. Then, again, from their fastnesses in the jungles and on rocky hill sides came the young locusts, in uniform of black and gold, marching in armies to the cultivated fields. The Government officers of all kinds did their best to cope with this last stroke of misfortune, but the ryots mostly looked on in helpless inaction, and would not struggle against their fate. Even this, however, passed away, and with the north-east monsoon of 1878 came the finest crop ever seen in the District; stocks were replenished, prices fell, numbers on works and relief fell off, and the weary officials were at last released from their heavy tasks."

---

[1] To save their cattle, ryots stripped their huts of thatch for fodder.

Increase of crime.

As the famine progressed, the jail population increased. In 1877 there were 6,688 admissions into the Central Jail and 18,913 into subsidiary jails. "The jails and their compounds were often full to overflowing. There was little need to guard the prisoners, who fared better in jail than outside. Special buildings, often of the flimsiest character, had to be erected to house the enhanced numbers, but there was little or no mortality which could be traced to overcrowding."[1]

The subjoined statement[2] gives an idea of the rise and fall of the Great Famine :—

—	1877.				1878.			
	Numbers on relief works and in camps.	Numbers on gratuitous relief.	Number of seers of ragi per rupee.	Rainfall in inches.	Numbers on relief works and in camps.	Numbers on gratuitous relief.	Number of seers of ragi per rupee.	Rainfall in inches.
January ...	32,058	6,836	9·0	...	22,495	25,196	11·2	0·01
February ...	32,825	4,309	9·0	...	31,562	25,239	11·7	...
March ...	44,512	6,331	8·6	1·73	32,383	25,536	10·5	0·15
April ...	50,937	27,940	9·0	0·41	31,421	25,787	12·0	2·14
May ...	55,700	54,707	8·2	3·37	31,873	25,344	10·7	3·76
June ...	49,775	82,891	8·2	2·59	27,898	22,886	8·8	3·67
July ..	40,527	105,852	6·1	1·01	30,702	26,007	9·0	4·79
August ...	52,375	165,737	6·1	0·94	23,515	22,446	10·6	5·66
September ...	43,857	325,280	6·1	10·50	15,607	18,498	13·1	5·16
October ...	57,710	221,261	9·7	11·06	10,379	13,634	15·7	4·60
November ..	61,070	64,159	9·7	3·64	4,592	8,093	15·7	3·72
December ...	41,133	27,754	9·7	1·87	1,958	444	15·7	0·60

[1] The following figures, which show the number of persons convicted for various offences under the Indian Penal Code between 1875 and 1878, are very significant :—

Nature of offence.	1875.	1876.	1877.	1878.
Murder	20	16	25	14
Culpable homicide	5	6	13	8
Robbery	27	40	230	82
Dacoity	19	231	480	129
House-breaking	127	219	1,706	733
Theft	733	1,372	9,501	4,015
Other offences	2,366	2,593	2,102	1,973
Total ...	3,297	4,477	14,057	6,954

[2] The number on relief at the end of December 1876 was 12,311, and the number on gratuitous relief 1,952. The figures in the statement are those for the close of each month, and are taken from the Report of the Famine Commission of 1879, Vol. II, Chap. III.

CHAP. VIII. FAMINES.

Effect on Revenue.

In the three years, Faslis 1287–9, the number of processes issued for default of revenue was 765,000, and in 63,000 cases property was actually sold.[1] Rs. 8,50,000[2] of the land revenue had to be remitted. In Fasli 1289, the amount of property transferred by documents registered had risen from Rs. 19,35,733 to Rs. 24,88,568, owing, as the Registrar-General observed, to "pressure of the famine inducing well-to-do classes to pledge or sell their lands." Close on three-quarters of a million sterling were spent on famine relief in the District, and £50,000 from the Mansion House Fund were scattered broadcast among the people. It was found necessary to remit as irrecoverable Rs. 7,00,000, arrears of land revenue, in addition to the 8½ lakhs already remitted. Nor was this all, for the net ryotwari revenue, which was Rs. 16,70,000 in 1874, had fallen in 1879 to Rs. 13,33,500, a decrease of Rs. 3,36,500.

Famine of 1891-92.

The famine of 1891–92 was a small thing compared with the famine just described. The rainfall from 1888 to 1890 was below the average in the Taluks of Salem,[3] Tiruchengōdu, Ūttankarai, and Dharmapuri. The south-west monsoon of 1891 failed, and by the end of September it was thought advisable to open test works in the four taluks. Work was started on four roads: (1) Sankaridrug to Edappādi, (2) Ōmalūr to Chinnappam-patti, (3) Dharmapuri to Hogēna-kal, (4) Mallāpuram to Pāpi-Reddi-patti. Three-fourths of the full task was exacted. A few weeks' trial showed that no great demand for work existed, except in Tiruchengōdu Taluk, and by November 15 all the test works were closed, except that from Sankaridrug to Edappādi. The early rains of the north-east monsoon of 1891 promised favourably, cultivation was

1

Fasli.	Processes issued.		Property attached.		Property sold.		
	Number of defaulters.	Amount of arrears.	Number of defaulters.	Amount of arrears.	Number of defaulters.	Amount of arrears.	Realised.
		RS.		RS.		RS.	RS.
1287 ...	205,153	28,00,933	6,403	1,85,648	1,498	58,035	28,254
1288 ...	288,486	28,46,065	60,402	8,04,985	18,071	3,53,635	39,518
1289 ...	272,291	21,72,739	83,694	10,75,192	44,055	6,28,143	1,20,804

2 Remission—

		RS.			RS.
Fasli 1286	...	4,13,083	Fasli 1288	...	16,024
„ 1287	...	3,78,180	„ 1289	...	42,664

3 That portion which now constitutes Ōmalūr Taluk.

resumed, and prices fell. In the middle of November, however, the rains ceased, grain merchants held up their stock, and prices rose rapidly. Kitchens were opened at Salem and Tiruchengōdu, and relief works were started all over Tiruchengōdu Taluk. The Collector permitted Tiruchengōdu ryots to cultivate dry crops on wet lands at dry rates of assessment, provided no water for irrigation was used. The situation remained unchanged in December, January and February. In March and April some showers fell, from May the season steadily improved, and by July all anxiety was at an end. No gratuitous relief was given except in the form of cooked food. The Salem kitchen was closed on June 25, 1892, and that at Tiruchengōdu on August 20. The Salem weavers were at first seriously affected by a fall in the price of cloths. A grant of Rs. 20,000 was sanctioned to purchase cloths for their relief, but this proved unnecessary. Before it could be disbursed, a Nāttukōttai Chetti, the proprietor of a Salem bank, entered into an agreement with certain weavers of Gugai to pay them the cost of twist and silk used, as well as the usual money wages, on the condition that the weavers sold to the bank all cloths manufactured by them for a period of two years. Following this example, the leading weavers of Shevapet made a similar arrangement with their local caste men, and the price of cloth again became normal.

FLOODS.

Floods on a large scale are fortunately unknown. In May 1872, and again in May 1874, the District suffered from cyclones, which, though they did not, owing to absence of cultivation in those months, do much damage to the crops, caused terrible mortality among cattle, and breached numerous tanks. In 1878 a "plump" of rain fell east of the Mūkkanūr hill and washed away the railway embankment. Such excessive and concentrated rainfall does not appear to have been calculated for when the railway was built, as may be inferred from the enlarged outlet provided when the bridges were rebuilt. In November 1880, a cyclone played havoc in Āttūr Taluk. Thirteen anaikats on the Vasishta-nadi, five on the Swēta-nadi, and two important anaikats on other streams were washed away, and some twenty tanks were breached. The bridge across the Vasishta-nadi near Talaivāsal was destroyed, and many houses perished. The chief anaikat on the Swēta-nadi, however, at Vīraganūr escaped. Prompt measures were taken to repair the damage. Temporary dams were constructed to replace the breached anaikats, and these worked so well that not a single rupee of remission was required. Rebuilding of the anaikats began in February 1881, and by July 15 they were completed and the damaged tanks too were in working order.

In the heavy rains of November 1903, the Pennaiyār rose and swept away a portion of the Hosūr-Sūlagiri road; the water stood 12 ft. over the Nedungal anaikat, the coping stones were loosened and the apron undermined; the Agrahāram channel was seriously disturbed, and the Public Works Department rest-house was flooded to a depth of 2 ft. The rising of the river at Kāvēri-patnam destroyed several houses, and injured the irrigation channels which take their rise near by.

CHAPTER IX.

PUBLIC HEALTH.

GENERAL HEALTH—Prevalent diseases—Sore-eyes—Skin diseases—Dysentery—Fevers—Guinea-worm—Other diseases—Cholera—Small-pox—Plague—MEDICAL INSTITUTIONS—SANITATION—Water-supply.

CHAP. IX. GENERAL HEALTH.

IN the open country the air is dry, the soil well drained, the climate healthy. Forest and hill tracts are feverish. In order of frequency, the diseases most prevalent in the District are those affecting the eyes, the skin, and the digestive system, and malarial fevers. Apart from malaria, the prevailing ailments are due to a want of personal cleanliness among the poorer classes, to scarcity of good water, to a low standard of comfort, to indifferent food and bad housing.

Diseases of the eyes.

From May to July there is usually an epidemic of "sore-eyes," sometimes lasting till September. Eye-flies are plentiful during this season, and are the chief carriers of contagion from one individual to another. Popularly the disease is attributed to the prevalence of high winds in the months when it is at its worst, some ascribe its origin to the pollen of flowers, others associate it with the mango season. Eye disease is the heaviest item in the hospitals of Krishnagiri, Dharmapuri and Hosūr Taluks. In the southern taluks it is less severe. "Sore-eyes" are supposed to be one of the main causes of blindness.

Skin diseases and ulcers are very common among the poorer classes. Skin diseases are worst in the dry and the cold seasons, and are not so bad during the rains. Ulcers are the heaviest item in the hospital returns of the southern taluks; in the Bāramahāl they yield precedence to "sore-eyes."

Dysentery, etc.

Dysentery prevails throughout the District, both in the amœbic and the bacillary form. July to October furnish the greatest number of cases. Deaths from dysentery averaged over 2,000 per annum in the 9 years ending 1906. Chronic dysentery is common among the poor, particularly in times of stress. It is popularly believed that the arrival of the new grain in the market is a primary cause of digestive disorders. Intestinal worms give trouble throughout the year, especially in May.

Fevers.

Of the recorded deaths in the District, 34 per cent. are attributed to "fevers." For the years ending 1906 the average annual number of deaths from "fever" was over 16,500. The figures do

CHAP. IX. GENERAL HEALTH.

not fluctuate much from year to year, the total of 25,000 for 1904 being quite abnormal. These fevers are mostly of malarial origin, and are most prevalent in villages situated near forests, and on the slopes or at the foot of hills. The common form in the plains is a mild type of intermittent fever, rarely attended by splenic enlargements, and amenable to treatment, but in the jungles the tertian and quartan forms of intermittent fever, and bilious remittent fevers, attended by enlargements of the spleen and liver, with anæmia, are very common, and are much more severe in type and injurious to health and life. On the hills the feverish season begins with the hot weather in March, and continues till the rains have fairly set in. Thanks to generations of natural selection, the Malaiyālis themselves are comparatively fever-proof, but to visitors from the plains the climate is deadly. Yercaud and the Green Hills are fairly immune, but the rest of the Shevaroys is as bad as any part of the District, as planters who chose to live on their estates know to their cost. Popularly, malaria on the Shevaroys is attributed to the coffee bloom. The light showers of April and May certainly give a stimulus to the breeding of *Anopheles*. On other hills the increase of malaria in the hot months is ascribed to the drying up of ponds and streams, and the contamination of drinking water by rotting leaves, for it is in February that deciduous trees begin to cast their verdure. In the eastern portion of Hosūr Taluk fever is at its worst from March to July, and abates with the south-west monsoon. The western half of the Taluk is feverish all the year round, but worst from October to December. In lowland tracts the rains bring fever, the dry season being fairly safe. Ūttankarai is the most feverish taluk in the District.

Guinea-worm.

Guinea-worm is common in the southern taluks, especially near Tiruchengōdu and Edappādi. The northern taluks are comparatively free. Scarcity of water in the hot months necessitates the use, for bathing and drinking purposes, of dirty, stagnant pools, which have remained undisturbed for the greater part of the year. Intermediate hosts of the worm (a species of *Cyclops*) abound in these pools.

Other diseases.

Leprosy is less common in Salem than in most districts, the total number of lepers in 1901 being 401, or 1 in every 5,147 persons, against a Presidency average of 1 in every 2,848. It is rather frequently met with among the Malaiyālis of the Kalrāyan and Shevaroy Hills. Elephantiasis is unknown. Cases of yaws occur in the neighbourhood of Edappādi. Syphilis is as common as elsewhere, but Malaiyālis (except on the Shevaroys, where they have degenerated), thanks to rigorous caste restrictions, are exempt

The proportion of deaf-mutes is a little above, that of idiots a little below, the Presidency average.

Cholera.

The District is subject to epidemics of cholera, chiefly in the latter part of the year. Of the deaths recorded in the District over a period of 5 years ending 1902, 10 per cent. were due to cholera, the average per mille of the population being 2. Towns suffered most, Salem itself recording nearly 5 deaths from cholera per mille of its population, a yearly average of 350.

Cholera is irregular in its visitations. For instance, in 1901, over 18,000 attacks and 11,300 deaths were recorded; in 1905 only 21 attacks and 10 deaths. In the former year 1,061 villages were affected, in the latter only 7. Rainfall does not seem to account for the difference, for though the fall in 1905 was 14 inches below normal, the cholera attacks in 1899, when the fall was about the same, numbered nearly 9,000. The worst months undoubtedly are December and January, and next to them come November and February. It is not safe, however, to generalise; for instance April, usually a comparatively safe month, was the heaviest of all in the year 1898, with 1,125 attacks, and *in the same year* December showed only 47 attacks, and November none.

Villages along river banks suffer most, owing to the practice of burying dead bodies in or near the river-beds, and the general use of rivers as latrines. For example, in Āttūr the disease usually breaks out in the neighbourhood of Bēlūr in September, and follows the course of the Vasishta-nadi, attacking village after village in regular succession. Salem Taluk contributes the largest number of attacks to the District total, Āttūr stands next. Yet the local distribution of the disease varies capriciously from year to year. Thus, in 1898, for every attack in Dharmapuri there were 24 in Āttūr, in 1901 for every attack in Āttūr there were 10 attacks in Dharmapuri. Hosūr is comparatively immune from cholera, and the disease never assumes an epidemic form on the Shevaroys. Coolies sometimes contract cholera in the plains, and die of it at Yercaud, but the disease never spreads. On the Kolli-malais cholera is rare; it is occasionally imported, and being unfamiliar to the Malaiyālis, it creates a great panic when it does occur, hamlets are deserted, and corpses thrown by the wayside unburied.

An epidemic may be short and sharp,[1] or it may linger for many months. For instance, in Salem City in November 1900, there

[1] As many as 10 per cent. of the inhabitants of a fair-sized village have been stricken in a single night.

CHAP. IX. GENERAL HEALTH.

were 255 attacks, though for the previous 8 months the town was free. The disease subsided before the end of the following February, the attacks for the 4 months numbering 890. After 3 months' immunity, a second epidemic began, which lasted for 10 months, but the attacks numbered only 660 for this period. One of the severest epidemics on record was that of 1875. The first seizure was on August 16th, there was one attack on the 17th, 2 on the 18th, 12 on the 19th. From the 21st the epidemic developed rapidly, and by the 28th a climax was reached, with 130 attacks and 58 deaths in the 24 hours. Till September 4th the disease was confined to the Fort, Gugai and Shevapet; on September 5th it spread to Salem proper, beginning close to the bridge, and travelling from west to east. The epidemic continued severe throughout September, but by October 7th the number of attacks fell to a single figure, and the worst was over. Between August 16th and September 28th, there were 2,039 seizures and 840 deaths.

Small-pox.

Small-pox may be said to be endemic and the District is never entirely free from the disease. Its ravages vary much from year to year. For instance the average number of deaths per annum for the nine years ending 1905 was 858. The figures show a steady rise from 205 in 1898 to 2,043 in 1901, and then a steady fall. Hosūr Taluk usually suffered most, and the Bāramahāl is worse than the Talaghāt. In 6 out of the 9 years, Salem City showed a clean sheet.

It is commonly supposed that the Malaiyālis of the Kolli-malais are immune from small-pox. This is not correct, though among them small-pox does not assume a virulent form. Any one attacked with small-pox is rigorously segregated for three months, one person only is allowed to attend on the patient, and this nurse is usually one who has either had small-pox himself, or has been vaccinated. While the patient continues sick, Māri-amman is daily worshipped, bathed, and garlanded with margosa leaves. The water poured over the goddess is used for bathing the patient, who is also smeared with the margosa leaves. Should the patient die, he is buried on the spot by his attendant, and no one else takes part in the funeral ceremonies. If he lives, he takes a bath at the end of three months, and is then allowed to rejoin his fellows.

Plague.

Salem District is more exposed to the ravages of plague than any other district in the Presidency except Bellary, the number of seizures up to 30th June 1911 being 21,498 and the death-roll 16,164. The cost of preventive measures between its first appearance in 1898 and the end of the financial year 1910–11 was over

15½ lakhs.[1] The loss to trade and industry is incalculable. Fairs and festivals have withered to extinction, and local and municipal progress is crippled. The amount of clerical labour alone involved may be guessed from the fact that between 1898 and 1903 some 700,000 plague passports were issued. The source of infection is Mysore State. Salem is endangered in two ways. First, Hosūr Taluk is topographically and ethnically part of Mysore, and its peoples freely traffic and intermarry with those of that State; secondly, the Bāramahāl is the recruiting ground for labour in the Kōlār Gold Fields, and there is a constant ebb and flow of coolies and their relatives between the two. Infection usually begins to spread from Mysore with the rains, and makes headway in Hosūr Taluk in September or October. It grows more acute in November, and is at its worst in the cold months, from December to February. After March, infection is almost eradicated, and with the next rains the disease is imported afresh from Mysore.[2]

The first case was imported into the District on August 28, 1898, within a fortnight of the outbreak in Bangalore, by a weaver from that City, whose brother had died there ten days previously. This was followed by scattered imported cases in the taluks of Hosūr and Krishnagiri, which rose in October to 25 and in November to 35. At first most of the villagers exercised a wise quarantine against arrivals from the infected State, but the people of Mattigiri carried on a stealthy trade with Bangalore, and at the end of November the disease became indigenous in that village. The spread was rapid.

The usual methods of evacuation and disinfection were resorted to, to combat the spread of the disease, frontier inspection stations were established on the principal routes from Mysore, and nearly 3,000 persons were inoculated.

		RS.
[1] Provincial funds	... ...	6,05,299
Local funds	... ...	7,07,730
Municipal funds	... ...	2,55,285

The figures relating to charges met from Local funds do not include contributions from and to other District Boards.

[2] The annual ravages of plague from its first advent are illustrated in the subjoined statement.

Period.	Seizures.	Deaths.	Period.	Seizures.	Deaths.
1898–99 ...	591	436	1905–06 ...	150	55
1899–00 ...	919	687	1906–07 ...	307	221
1900–01 ...	1,502	1,112	1907–08 ..	1,298	975
1901–02 ...	1,905	1,291	1908–09 ...	530	381
1902–03 ...	5,702	4,267	1909–10 ...	153	116
1903–04 ...	1,283	912	1910–11 ...	5,185	4,228
1904–05 ...	2,234	1,690	1911–12 ...	1,492	1,124

CHAP. IX. GENERAL HEALTH.

Salem City experienced its first visitation in April 1910. The climax was reached in November, in which month 748 attacks and 594 deaths were recorded, though some 43,000 inhabitants had quitted the town. From December onwards the disease declined steadily, in February 1911 there were only 11 cases, and in March only 2. The total number of attacks was 2,127 and of deaths 1,721. An inoculation campaign began in September 1910, and a good start was made with the inoculation of some 40 Government officials. Inoculation was at first carried on at selected centres, the localities chosen being notified to the public by hand-bills and posters. Private inoculations were occasionally arranged for at the residences of some of the leading citizens. As the epidemic advanced from one quarter to another, all who were not inoculated were compelled to evacuate, and they were not allowed to return to their houses unless they could produce certificates of inoculation. Special arrangements were made for weavers, and Rs. 2,000 was distributed among the more indigent members of the community, at the rate of 6 annas per adult and 3 annas per child of over 12 years of age, as batta to compensate them for being temporarily incapacitated for work by the effects of inoculation. In all 11,800 weavers were inoculated, of whom rather more than half received batta. The total number of operations performed in Salem between September 1910 and April 1911 was 52,440.[1]

MEDICAL INSTITUTIONS.

Between the year 1875-76 and the year 1909-10 the number of medical institutions in the District rose from 5 to 26, the number of in-patients treated from a little under 500 to more than 2,000, and the number of out-patients from just under 31,000 to

[1] The subjoined statement shows the rise and fall of the epidemic, together with the progress of inoculation. The figures speak for themselves :—

Month.	Estimated population at end of each month.	Number inoculated—progressive total.	(A). Attacks and (D) Deaths among Inoculated. A.	Inoculated. D.	Uninoculated. A.	Uninoculated. D.	Total. A.	Total. D.
August 1910 ...	73,000	...	...	...	77	64	77	64
September „ ...	63,000	1,252	...	...	299	250	299	250
October „ ...	48,000	10,720	14	11	270	255	284	266
November „ ...	30,000	20,304	163	86	585	508	748	594
December „ ...	34,000	27,874	156	65	379	338	535	403
January 1911 ...	44,000	39,103	93	59	78	75	171	134
February „ ...	56,000	48,514	7	4	4	4	11	8
March „ ...	60,000	52,440	1	1	1	1	2	2
Total ...	...	...	434	226	1,693	1,495	2,127	1,721

The mortality among inoculates was 52 per cent. against over 88 per cent among the unprotected.

MEDICAL INSTITUTIONS.

nearly 250,000 [1]. In the District as reorganised the number of medical institutions, Local Fund and Municipal, rose from 5 in 1875-76 to 26 in 1908-09. The number of out-patients was just under 31,000 at the beginning of the period, and 227,527 at the end. In the District as reorganised, medical institutions of all kinds number 26, or one to about 73,000 inhabitants. Hospitals are maintained by Local Funds at Yercaud (established in 1872), Āttūr (1874), Tiruchengōdu (1886), Harūr (1876), Hosūr (1874), Dharmapuri (1874) and Krishnagiri (1874), with accommodation for 33 male and 26 female in-patients. The Salem Municipal Hospital can hold 19 male and 12 female in-patients. Police hospitals are maintained by Government at Salem (12 in-patients) and Hosūr (2 patients). There is also a hospital in the Salem Central Jail. Dispensaries are maintained by Local Funds at Rāsipuram (1888), Ōmalūr (1888), Tammampatti (1889), Sankaridrug (1876), Ūttankarai (1881), Pennāgaram (1887), Pālakōdu (1889), Tali (1889), Denkani-kōta (1887), Rāya-kōta (1890). One dispensary is kept up by the Salem Municipality. The Women and Children's Dispensary at Salem was converted into the Alexandra Hospital for Women in January 1910, with accommodation for 12 in-patients, besides 2 beds in the maternity ward. The busiest dispensary outside the municipality is that at Rāsipuram, the slackest that at Ūttankarai [2].

SANITATION.

Indirectly the advent of plague has been beneficial, as it has led to the employment of a preventive staff of sanitary inspectors, which has done much to improve the general sanitary condition of the District when not actually engaged with a plague epidemic. In 1911 as many as 380 sweepers, 69 scavengers and 45 maistries were maintained from Local Funds. Of this staff, 312 sweepers and 61 scavengers served under Unions. It is not easy to obtain the services of scavengers, especially in the northern taluks.

The conservancy establishment of Salem Municipality is a large one. For general conservancy, 135 scavengers and 74 sweepers were employed in 1910, their work being supervised by 4 sanitary inspectors, attended by 15 peons. The private scavenging system was introduced in April 1893, and by 1910 some 2,814 houses were being served. This involved the employment of one sanitary inspector and 69 toties.

WATER-SUPPLY.

In 1876 the water-supply of Salem Town was reported to be "as bad as it well can be as regards the quality, but not the quantity,

[1] Inclusive of Tiruppattūr and Nāmakkal.

[2] Further particulars of these institutions are given in Chapter XV.

CHAP. IX. WATER-SUPPLY. Salem Town.

of water. It is to the water that we must in a great measure look for the reasons of the prevalence of cholera in the town. In addition to the numerous private wells, . . . there are 72 municipal wells, which are sunk in gravelly or rocky soil to an average depth of 20 to 30 feet; these all contain good water, and are kept in repair by the Municipality. They contain a sufficient supply of water, if properly utilised for the requirements of the town; but unhappily the river is the main source of all drinking water, and, in spite of all warning, and in spite of the evident defilement of the water by the filth from the drains, the filth from the dirty clothes, and the filth from the men's bodies, the poorer natives continue to drink river water." In one point this report is inaccurate. Water is as deficient in quantity as in quality. For instance, in 1866 the Collector reported that in Salem the public wells were so low that "people were obliged to scrape the water up in coco-nut shells, and it took 15 or 20 minutes before a single potful of water could be collected." Water famine recurred almost annually, and often began in February. Wells, both private and public, soon became useless, and drinking-water was hawked from door to door.

The first practical improvement in the municipal water-supply was the establishment of an oil-engine pump in Arisi-pālaiyam. During the water scarcity of 1906, when almost all other wells in Shevapet, Gugai and Fort were exhausted, the Arisi-pālaiyam tank was the main supply for thirty thousand people, and a census showed that about 13,000 brass potfuls, amounting to some fifty thousand gallons, were removed daily from this single well. The tank is surrounded by a substantial wall, and water is pumped into a roofed masonry reservoir at the roadside, whence it is directly drawn by taps. Strong springs were struck in deepening the well, and in an ordinary season some 3,000 pots were filled daily. No attempt is made to filter the water, but the quarters that derive drinking-water from the new installation were cholera-free. The whole plant cost only Rs. 5,600 to set up.

The scheme finally adopted was formulated by Mr. Target, the Executive Engineer, in 1884. It received the sanction of Government in the year 1907–08. The Panamarattu-patti tank is an imperial irrigation source with an *āyakat* of 327 acres, situated 9 miles south-east of the town of Salem, at the entrance to the valley between the Bōda-malais and the Jerugu-malais. This tank is supplied, partly by its own free catchment of 8½ square miles, and partly by a channel which takes off just above an old anaikat across the Panamarattu-patti river, otherwise called the Varattār. The scheme provided for raising the full tank level of this tank by 21 feet, and for connecting it with the town of Salem by a

Salem Town.

steel main, 9 miles in length; for the construction of a new anaikat across the Varattār river about half a mile above the site of the old anaikat, for the excavation of a new supply channel to the reservoir, three-quarters of a mile in length, and for the construction of a regulating sluice at the head of the new supply channel; also for the construction of a surplus weir, a valve tower, and an irrigation sluice in the bund of the new reservoir. The filter beds, of which there are three, are situated a short distance below the bund of the reservoir. The water from the reservoir passes through the valve tower into the filter beds, and thence by gravitation through the steel main to the town. At the end of the steel main is situated a service reservoir, which holds sufficient water to supply the present population of Salem with water for half a day, i.e., 420,775 gallons. The capacity of the new reservoir, when full, is 220 millions cubic feet. This quantity of water, after allowing for loss by evaporation and absorption and for the water required for the irrigation of 327 acres of wet cultivation, is sufficient to supply a population of 80,000 for 383 days at the rate of 15 gallons per head per diem. The catchment area of the Varattār above the new anaikat is 16 square miles, and it can be extended by another 3½ square miles, if necessary. The filtering material in the filter beds is partly broken stone and partly well-washed sand. The water is distributed over the town through cast-iron branch pipe lines, and is made available to the public by means of 105 different fountains. The total cost of the scheme was Rs. 8,40,300 [1], towards which Government contributed Rs. 4,65,150, the remainder being met by a municipal loan of Rs. 3,75,150, repayable in 80 years. Work began in 1908–09, and the opening ceremony took place on December 12, 1911. Unfortunately, owing to some defect in the pipes and to the failure of the north-east monsoon, a proper supply was not received during the first year.

---

[1] Including Rs. 30,300 for improving the tank-bund, which had sunk during the progress of the work, and for extending the tunnel to the irrigation sluice.

CHAPTER X.

EDUCATION.

LITERACY—By Communities—By Taluks—By Languages. HISTORY OF EDUCATION.—EDUCATIONAL AGENCIES—Local and Municipal—Aided Schools—London Mission—Industrial School—Missouri Lutheran Mission—Catholic Missions. INSTITUTIONS—(*A*) for Boys—Salem College—Secondary Schools—Primary Schools—Technical Education—Muhammadan Education—Muhammadan Educational Association—Panchama Schools; (*B*) Education of Girls—FINANCE.

N.B.—The Census of 1911 was taken after Nāmakkal Tāluk was transferred to Trichinopoly, and before Tiruppattūr Taluk was lopped off. Hence in sketching the growth of Education comparative statistics for the whole District have been given.

CHAP. X.
LITERACY.

OF all the districts of the Presidency in point of literacy Salem usually stands last. The figures speak for themselves.

Year.	Number of literate persons per 1,000 of the population.		Total.
	Males.	Females.	
1871	56	3	28
1881	65	4	34
1891	75	3	38
1901	74	4	38
1911	81	4	43

In the Census of 1911 out of a population of 1,766,680 as many as 1,691,107 were illiterate. The difficulty of educating a polyglot population partly accounts for this backwardness, and the stagnation shown by the figures of 1901 is due to the advent of plague, and the consequent repeated closure of schools.

By Communities.

The Muhammadans, in both 1901 and 1911, were the least illiterate community, being well in advance of their co-religionists in the rest of the Presidency. The Christians fell a long way behind the Muhammadans in the literacy of their males, and were not up to the Presidency average. The attention paid by Christians, however, to the education of their girls raises the average for the

LITERACY.

whole community almost to the level of that of the Muhammadans. The Hindus were hopelessly in the rear. The figures are subjoined :—

Number of literate persons per thousand.

Community.	Whole community, 1911.	Males.				Females.			
		Salem District, 1911.	Salem District, 1901.	Presidency average, 1901.	Literate in English, 1911.	Salem District, 1911.	Salem District, 1901.	Presidency average, 1901.	Literate in English, 1911.
Muhammadans ...	128	233	229	141	8	19	19	9	...
Christians	127	171	158	198	66	86	90	91	42
Hindus	40	77	68	116	5	4	3	9	...

By Taluks.

The marginal statement shows the number of literate males per mille in each taluk in 1911, and exhibits the improvement effected since 1901. Female literacy is highest in Salem Taluk (9 per mille), Krishnagiri comes next with 6 per mille, Āttūr third with 4, Hosūr and Tiruchengōdu stand between 3 and 4, while Ōmalūr, Dharmapuri and Ūttankarai stand between 2 and 3.

Taluk.	1901.	1911.
Salem ...	86	116
Āttūr ...	68	96
Hosūr ...	71	80
Krishnagiri ...	69	75
Dharmapuri ...	60	68
Ūttankarai ...	53	65
Tiruchengōdu ..	48	63
Ōmalūr ...	...	61

In 1901 Salem Town stood tenth among the 11 largest cities of the Presidency, with an average of 136 literate persons per mille. Though, owing to plague, the figures for 1911 are hardly an accurate test, the average rose to 155 per mille, the figure for males being 286 and for females 27.

By Languages.

In 1901, for the whole District, 71,712 persons were literate in Tamil, against 8,380 in Telugu, and 988 in Kanarese. As many as 2,517 were literate in "other languages," among them being 2,187 Muhammadans. Of the Telugu literates, more than half (4,133) lived in Hosūr Taluk, and in that Taluk only 1,369 were literate in Tamil. Two-thirds of the Kanarese were in Hosūr (674). In Krishnagiri the figures were Tamil 4,445, and Telugu 1,285. In Salem Tāluk there were 1,080 literate in Telugu, of whom 788 were in Salem Town itself.

Under Mysore rule the art of writing seems to have been a Brahman monopoly. Haidar and Tipu relied mainly on Brahman

CHAP. X. HISTORY OF EDUCATION.

accountants, and the Muhammadan Tahsildars appointed by Tipu were often quite illiterate.

The first educational effort under British rule was made by Sir Thomas Munro, who in 1822 called for reports on the educational status of each district. The report for Salem, dated 8th June, 1823, shows 386 schools in existence, with a strength of 4,650 pupils, in an estimated population of 1,076,000. The financial resources available for educational purposes were hardly encouraging. The one existing endowment for Muhammadan education yielded Rs. 20 per annum. For Hindus there was no endowment. Inam lands, yielding Rs. 1,109 per annum, provided for 20 teachers of theology, law and astronomy; other lands, yielding Rs. 384 per annum, had formerly been devoted to the same object, but the land was sequestered before the cession to the British, and the proceeds were included in Government revenue. Sir Thomas Munro's scheme, March 3, 1826, did not contemplate "any interference whatever in the native schools. The people should be left to manage their schools in their own way." A Hindu and Muhammadan school was to be established in each collectorate, and inferior schools in each taluk. A Committee of Public Instruction was organised to carry out Munro's proposals. But official enthusiasm was evanescent, at least in Salem District, for, in 1827, Mr. M. D. Cockburn handed over five "schools under the patronage of the Magistrate" to the Rev. Henry Crisp, of the London Mission, who settled in Salem in October of that year. The total strength of these five schools was only 127 pupils. In each school, it appears, a different language was taught, for they are described as "English, Tamil, Telugu, Mahratta and Persian." Official responsibilities did not, however, cease with this transfer, for a report of 1834 on "Tahsildari schools" mentions three, viz., a Tamil school at Salem, another at Tiruppattūr, and a Telugu school at Hosūr.[1]

The next move on the part of Government was in 1854, when Lord Ellenborough's Despatch was written, and it resulted in the establishment of a school in Salem in 1856, under the auspices of

[1] The actual figures at this early date may be of interest.

—	Brahmans.	Vaisyas.	Sudras.	Other.	Total Hindus.	Muhammadans.	District Total.
Boys ...	783	324	1,671	1,382	4,160	432	4,592
Girls ...	...	...	3	28	31	27	53

CHAP. X. HISTORY OF EDUCATION.

Sir A. J. Arbuthnot[1] which was raised to the status of a Zilla School on April 14, 1857. In the following year, 1858, Taluk Schools were opened at Hosūr (May 1), Dharmapuri (November 18) and Krishnagiri (December 31), with a strength of 62, 41 and 70, respectively. This was a good start, but for the next 12 years the advance of education was by no means general, and depended mainly on the enthusiasm of a few individuals. The Grant-in-Aid system was introduced in 1863-4.

Fresh impetus was given to education by the passing of the Local Fund Act IV, 1871, and from that date the burden of education devolved mainly on Local Funds.[2] An attempt was made in 1873 to impose upon the District the "Union System" and the Town Improvement Act (III of 1871), but the scheme was strongly opposed by Lord Hobart, the then Governor, and fell through. Under the system, "Rate Schools" were to be established in rural tracts, and their cost defrayed by a house tax on all houses within a radius of 2½ miles of each school.

The progress of educational work since 1871-2 is shown in the subjoined statement.[3] The ravages of plague are seen in the drop from 1896-7 to 1901-2 :—

Year.	Institutions.	Boys.	Girls.
1871-2	190	4,609	240
1881-2	600	12,384	838
1891-2	845	20,330	3,020
1896-7	1,239	29,030	4,058
1901-2	1,030	26,765	4,921
1906-7	1,037	30,940	4,973

EDUCATIONAL AGENCIES.

In 1907 the work of education was distributed as follows :—

—	Boys' Schools.		Girls' Schools.	
	Institutions.	Scholars.	Institutions.	Scholars.
Government ...	1	41	9	963
Municipal	26	3,000	2	151
Local Fund	259	12,477	...	...
Aided	334	9,729	24	1,721
Unaided	283	5,954	1	30
Private	94	1,751	1	35
Total	997	32,952	37	2,900

Local and Municipal.

Thus Local and Municipal Funds were responsible for not quite half the scholars in boys' schools, while rather less than

[1] The first Director of Public Instruction.

[2] Vide Report on Public Instruction in the Madras Presidency for 1871-2, page 68 sq.

[3] The figures for 1871-2 and 1881-2 include only scholars "connected with the Department." The latter figures include "indigenous scholars." The figures given for boys include the pupils in Normal Schools.

CHAP. X, EDUCATIONAL AGENCIES.

Local and Municipal.

one-third were in Aided Schools. One-third of the scholars in girls' schools read in Government institutions, and most of the remaining two-thirds in Aided Schools. The only Government boys' school is the Normal School at Salem.

The Local Boards were, in 1907, responsible for 9 Secondary Schools with 1,353 scholars, inclusive of their Primary Departments, and Municipalities for two with 287 scholars, in addition to Salem College. With the excision of Nāmakkal and Tiruppattūr, however, the number is reduced to 3, namely, the High School classes of Salem College, and the Incomplete Secondary Schools at Krishnagiri, and Dharmapuri. In the District as at present constituted the Salem Tāluk Board maintains 66 Elementary Schools, that of Sankaridrūg 42, that of Hosūr 65, that of Dharmapuri 68, and the Salem Municipality 13.

Aided Schools—London Mission.

Since 1827, when the Collector handed over to Mr. Crisp the five schools above referred to, the London Mission has rendered great educational service to the District. By 1833 the number of schools had risen to 7. In 1841 schools were opened at Rāsipuram and Dharmapuri, and the number of scholars was 467. In the next decade there was falling off, the number in 1851 being only 194, of whom 48 were girls. In 1861 a great blow was dealt to the educational institutions of the Mission by the death of Mr. Lechler. By 1872 there were 321 boys and 216 girls. Since 1881 the figures are as shown in the margin.

Year.	Boys' Schools.	Pupils.	Girls' Schools.	Pupils.
1881 ...	6	669	3	180
1891 ...	11	680	6	390
1901 ...	11	711	7	880
1907 ...	13	856	8	972

The most important institution under the Mission is the High School, Salem. Founded in 1863 as a primary school by the Rev. G. Mabbs, it was raised to the status of a high school by Mr. Phillips in 1877. The Mission led the way in female education with the Shevapet Girls' School, which was founded in 1835 by Mrs. Walton. A boarding school was opened by Miss Lodge in Hastampatti in 1891. Several elementary schools, for girls as well as boys, are maintained in Salem Town and in the Talaghāt taluks, the most important being that at Āttūr, founded by Mr. Mabbs.

Industrial School.

The London Mission was also the pioneer of industrial education in Salem District. As far back as 1840 the Rev. J. M. Lechler opened a small school in Salem, and admitted 6 pupils, three of whom were taught carpentry and three tailoring. Later on he brought two artisans from Germany, one of whom, Mr. C. Rahm, after working in the school for ten years, left and

Industrial School.

settled as a planter on the Shevaroys. The school was well equipped with tools, and did good work for some 21 years. The crafts taught included carpentry, turning, cabinet-making, blacksmith and locksmith work and brick-laying. Unfortunately, on the death of Mr. Lechler in 1861, the whole of the valuable property and plant was sold by his successors, who objected to industrial education as tending to secularise Mission work.

In 1896 Mr. Dignum decided to make a fresh start, and issued an appeal for subscriptions to enable him to build a small school and provide the necessary plant. For two years the school was maintained by the subscriptions of friends in Salem. It was then recognised by the London Mission Society, and subsidised by a grant of Rs. 30 per mensem from Mission funds. It was also recognised by the Director of Public Instruction, who made a grant of Rs. 100 per annum, which he afterwards raised to Rs. 150. At the beginning of 1900 he recognised the school as an Advanced Technical School. The proceeds of the sales of work done in the school amounted to Rs. 5,000, and no difficulty has so far been experienced in obtaining orders for work.

Missouri Lutheran Mission. Catholic Missions.

The Missouri Lutheran Mission supported a number of elementary schools in Krishnagiri Tāluk. The Leipzig Evangelical Lutheran Mission maintained a small school at Yercaud. The Roman Catholic Missions are not ambitious in their educational work in the District; elementary schools are kept up at their chief settlements, and at Yercaud there is a flourishing boarding school for European children, and another for native girls, conducted respectively by the European and Native nuns of St. Joseph of Cluny.

INSTITUTIONS. A. FOR BOYS. Salem College.

The Municipal College traces its origin to the first elementary school already referred to, established in the District by Sir A. J. Arbuthnot in 1856, with Mr. C. J. Macarthy as headmaster.[1] The school was formally opened on May 1st of that year by the Collector, Mr. H. A. Brett. In the year following (April 14, 1857) the school was raised to the rank of a "Zilla School", with a strength of 195 pupils. Next year more than one-third of the pupils deserted, because a boy of low caste was admitted on the rolls. It was many years before the school recovered its original strength. Up to 1863 the school was held in a rented building. In that year the present school house was erected at a cost of Rs. 6,850, partly by public subscriptions, partly by Government contributions. The President of the school committee was Mr. George Fischer. Candidates were first sent up for Matriculation in 1866. Thirteen years later (1879), College classes

[1] For the account which follows I am indebted to Mr. S. A. Shutie, Principal of the College.

CHAP. X. INSTITUTIONS.

were opened with six students in the junior F.A. class. On January 1st, 1884, the management of the Middle School department was transferred to the Salem Municipal Council, which took over the College and High School department also on October 1st of the following year.

Mr. C. J. Macarthy was succeeded as Head Master of the Zillah School by Mr. T. M. Scott. The first Head Master of the College was Mr. J. Small.[1] He was followed by Mr. E. E. Perrett in January 1883, and he in turn by Mr. S. A. Shutie in August 1892. The marginal statement* shows the number of students on the rolls of the College department for each quinquennium from 1881–1882 up to date.

* Average number on roll.		
1881–1885	...	17·2
1886–1890	...	29·5
1891–1896	...	17·2
1897–1901	...	28·2
1902–1906	...	44·8
1907–1910	...	42·5

Secondary Schools.

Secondary education in the District has so far made slow progress.† The progress of the schools at Salem, Krishnagiri and Dharmapuri has been continuous from the date of their foundation, but the school at Hosūr was reduced to elementary status in 1908.[2] Āttūr School has suffered the same fate. Spasmodic attempts have been made from time to time to extend the scope of the schools at Tiruchengōdu, Rāsipuram, Sankaridrūg and Denkani-kōta, above the fourth standard.

† Year.		Boys.	Girls.
1892	...	699	?
1902	...	1,235	75
1907	...	1,683	119

Primary Education.

The progress of primary education has not been rapid ‡. In 1907, out of every 100 boys in primary classes, 47 were in schools run by Local Boards and Municipalities, 32 in aided schools, and 21 in unaided schools. Of the several classes of the community that avail themselves of elementary education, the sons of landowners are most numerous, merchants stand second and artizans third. Board schools attract the middle classes, officials, Brahmans, Muhammadans, merchants, and, in the north, artizans. Unaided schools depend on the poorer and "coolie" classes; their mainstay is the agricultural classes, and, in the south, the artizans.

‡ Year.		Boys.	Girls.
1892	...	17,716	2,952
1897	...	24,538	3,904
1902	...	23,466	3,734
1907	...	27,398	4,808

[1] Appointed Head Master of the Zillah School in July 1864 and of the College in January 1879.

[2] The schools at Hosūr and Denkani-kōta are now "High Grade Elementary Schools," the former reading up to the Seventh Standard, the latter up to the Fifth.

Another point worth noting is the contrast between the northern and the southern taluks. In the first place the schools in the northern taluks are smaller than those in the south. Again the northern taluks depend more on board schools, than the south, where the proportion of boys in aided and unaided schools is relatively large. Thirdly, poor and backward classes, artizans and coolies, attend school more freely in the south, while the northern schools contain a larger proportion of merchants, officials, Muhammadans and Brahmans.

Muhammadan Education.

In 1896–1897 it was estimated that 86 per cent. of the Muhammadan boys of school-going age, and nearly 20 per cent. of the girls, were under instruction, as against 20 per cent. of the boys and 2½ per cent. of the girls of the District as a whole. In the next ten years there was a slight falling off, owing to the plague epidemics. The Taluk Boards maintain about 20 Hindustani schools, and the Salem Municipality 5.

Muhammadan Educational Association.

The Salem Muhammadan Educational Association was founded in 1895 by Khan Bahadur Muhammad Aziz-ud-din Husain Sahib Bahadur under the presidentship of Mr. (now Sir Gabriel) Stokes. For the use of its members, the Sir Gabriel Stokes Hall was erected in Salem by public subscription, and was opened by the founder of the Association on February 17, 1912.

Panchama Schools.

The education of Panchamas is a formidable problem in a District in which the Pariahs, Chucklers, Valluvars and Pallars alone number over 300,000. In 1903–1904 the number of Local Fund Panchama schools was only 19, and their attendance 571. These schools were situated mostly in small villages where the Panchama quarters are large. A feature of Panchama education is that a school rarely thrives for many years consecutively in any one place, and hence little continuity of policy is possible. It is difficult to secure regular attendance, because among the poorest classes children begin at a very early age to assist their parents in earning their daily bread.

B. EDUCATION OF GIRLS.

A peculiar feature of "Female Education" is that a large proportion of girl scholars read in boys' schools, as the subjoined statement shows :—

—	Institutions for girls.	Scholars in institutions for girls.	Total girl pupils.
1871–1872	5	218	240
1881–1882	23	806	838
1891–1892	38	1,681	3,020
1901–1902	45	2,447	4,021
1906–1907	37	2,891	4,973

CHAP. X.
INSTITUTIONS.

Girls' schools are maintained by Government at Salem, Shevāpet, Āttūr, Tiruchengōdu, Dharmapuri, Hosūr and Krishnagiri. That at Shevāpet is for Muhammadans only. Of aided institutions, Nabi Sahib's School at Āttūr deserves mention. The secondary education of girls has made very little progress.

Finance.

In 1862–63 the cost per pupil in the Zilla School was Rs. 40. Government granted Rs. 5,660, and fees (at Re. 1 and 8 annas per head) realised Rs. 1,445. The net expenditure from public funds from 1881 as compared with the gross total expenditure on Education for the whole District is as follows:—

Year.	Provincial.	Local Fund.	Municipal.	Total.[1]
	RS.	RS.	RS.	RS.
1880–1	13,873	16,359	2,673	63,087
1890–1	16,870	27,169	5,814	1,17,801
1900–1	23,566	32,128	9,554	1,52,482
1906–7	17,632	55,472	15,176	1,99,536
1910–1	47,277	63,470	19,694	2,42,253

[1] Inclusive of fees and of expenditure met by endowments, subscriptions and Mission and other private funds.